The French and Indian War
and the Conquest of
New France

The French and Indian War and the Conquest of New France

William R. Nester

UNIVERSITY OF OKLAHOMA PRESS | NORMAN

ALSO BY WILLIAM R. NESTER

"Haughty Conquerors": Amherst and the Great Indian Uprising of 1763 (Westport, Conn., 2000)

The Frontier War for American Independence (Mechanicsburg, Penn., 2004)

The Epic Battles for Ticonderoga, 1758 (Albany, 2008)

Globalization, War, and Peace in the Twenty-First Century (New York, 2010)

Napoleon and the Art of Diplomacy: How War and Hubris Determined the Rise and Fall of the French Empire (El Dorado Hills, Calif., 2012)

George Rogers Clark: "I Glory in War" (Norman, Okla., 2012)

Publication of this book is made possible through the generosity of Edith Kinney Gaylord.

Library of Congress Cataloging-in-Publication Data

Nester, William R., 1956–
   The French and Indian War and the conquest of New France / William R. Nester.
      pages cm
   Includes bibliographical references and index.
   ISBN 978-0-8061-4435-1 (hardcover : alk. paper) 1. United States—History—French and Indian War, 1754–1763. 2. France—Colonies—America—History—18th century. 3. Louis XV, King of France, 1710–1774. 4. Seven Years' War, 1756–1763. I. Title.
   E199.N475 2014
   940.2'534—dc23
                                  2013044687
The paper in this book meets the guidelines for permanence and durability of the Committee on Production Guidelines for Book Longevity of the Council on Library Resources, Inc. ∞

1 2 3 4 5 6 7 8 9 10

Interior layout and composition: Alcorn Publication Design

Contents

PART 4. THE LONG DENOUEMENT

Illustrations

FIGURES

MAPS

Acknowledgments

To varying degrees, I am indebted to the secondary works cited in the notes of this volume (see especially those of the introduction). Of course, they are only the most important of the hundreds of books and articles directly or indirectly related to the subject, scores of which have also aided this book. As for primary sources, I spent eight enchanting months living in Paris and traveling around France, during which I tapped into the incredible array of archival material in various institutions, especially the National Archives, National Library, and Foreign Affairs Library. This book also depended on crucial sources explored during periods of research at the Clement Library in Ann Arbor, Michigan, and the Huntington Library in San Marino, California.

It is a great pleasure to work with an editorial team whose members are as nice as they are professional at the University of Oklahoma Press. I am especially grateful to Kelly Parker for her incredibly meticulous editing and to Jason Petho for his latest set of excellent maps. I also greatly appreciate Managing Editor Steven Baker and Manuscript Editor Emily Jerman for their wonderful oversight, and Editor-in-Chief Chuck Rankin for wanting to publish my book. I cannot thank you all enough!

Most importantly, I want to thank Edith Kinney Gaylord for her generosity in making the publication of this book possible.

MAPS

European Settlements and Indian Tribes, 1750.
Map by Jason Petho.

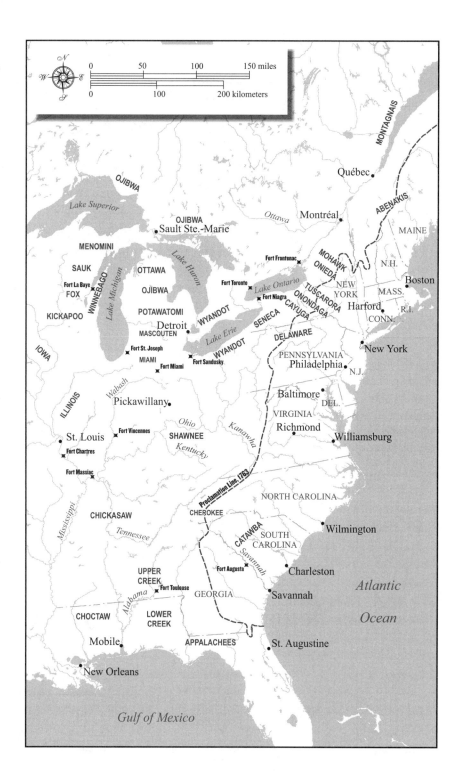

British
Mainland
Colonies and
New France,
1754–1763.
Map by Jason
Petho.

Lake Superior

Sault Ste.-Marie

Lake Huron

Fort La Baye

Lake Michigan

Fort Toronto

Lake C

Fo

La Belle Famille

Detroit

Lake Erie

Fort Presqu

Fort St. Joseph

Fort Le Boeu

Fort Sandusky

Fort Mac

Fort Miami

Kuskuski

Logstown

Kitt

Fort Duquesne

Fort Lig

Fort N

Illinois

Wabash

Fort Vincennes

Ohio

VIRG

Kanawha

Mountains

Louis

Fort Massiac

Chiswell's Fort

Blue Ridg

Cumberland

Allegheny

NC

Ft. Loudoun

Tennessee

Ft. Prince George

Mississippi

Ninety Six

SOUTH CAROLIN

Savannah

Orangeburg

Santee

Ft. Augusta

Charleston

GEORGIA

Savanna

O

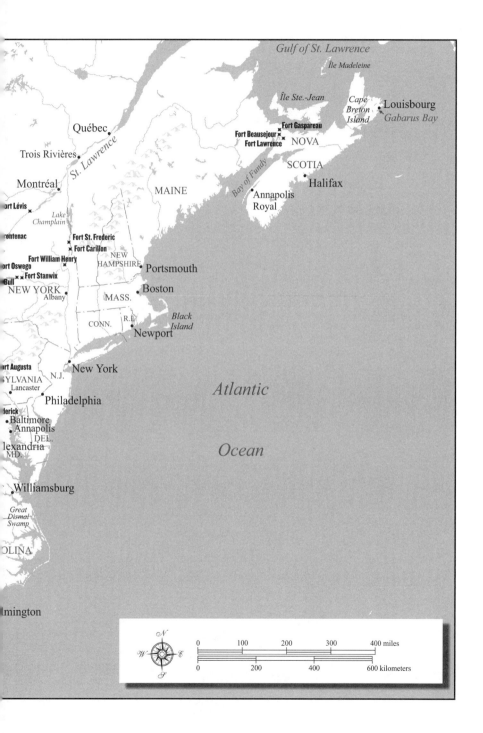

Gulf of St. Lawrence

Île Madeleine

Île Ste.-Jean

Cape
Breton
Island

•Louisbourg
Gabarus Bay

Québec•

Fort Gaspareau

Fort Beausejour ✕
Fort Lawrence ✕

NOVA

Trois Rivières•

St. Lawrence

SCOTIA

Montréal•

MAINE

Bay of Fundy

•Halifax

•Annapolis
Royal

ort Lévis ✕

*Lake
Champlain*

ontenac

Fort St. Frederic
✕ Fort Carillon

Fort William Henry
ort Oswego ✕

NEW
HAMPSHIRE

✕ ✕ Fort Stanwix

•Portsmouth

Bull

NEW YORK•
Albany•

MASS.

•Boston

CONN.

R.I.

*Black
Island*

•Newport

ort Augusta

•New York

YLVANIA
Lancaster

N.J.

Atlantic

lerick

•Philadelphia

•Baltimore
•Annapolis
DEL.

lexandria
MD.

Ocean

•Williamsburg

*Great
Dismal
Swamp*

OLINA

mington

N

W — E

S

| 0 | 100 | 200 | 300 | 400 miles |

| 0 | 200 | 400 | 600 kilometers |

Northeast Colonies and New France, 1759.
Map by Jason Petho.

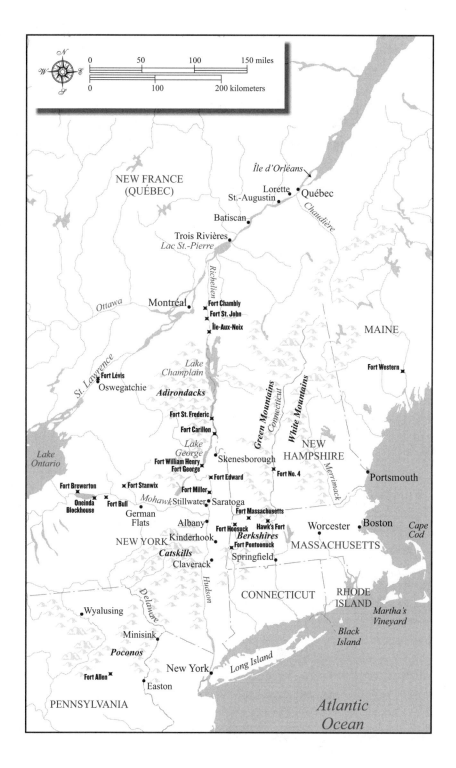

Saint Lawrence
River Valley
and Quebec,
June–September
1759.
Map by
Jason Petho.

NEW FRANCE
(QUÉBEC)

Jacques-Cartier River

Point-aux-Trembles

Deschambault

St. Lawrence River

St.-Antoine

Rapids of
Richelieu

0   5   10   15   20 miles

0   10   20   30 kilometers

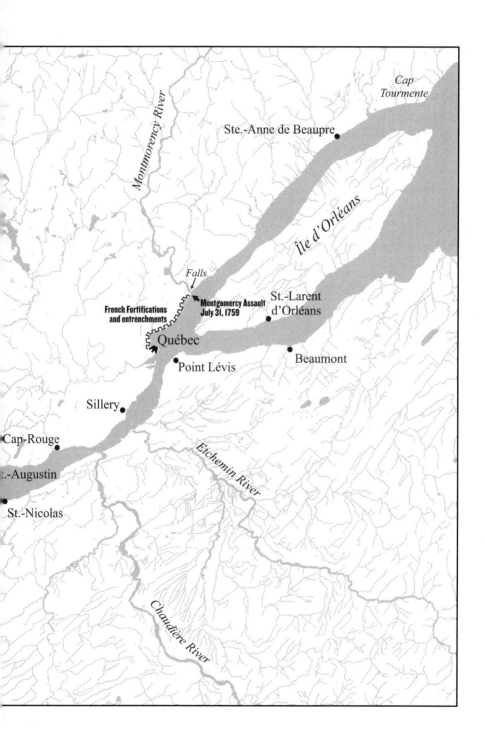

Cap
Tourmente

Monmorency River

Ste.-Anne de Beaupre

Île d'Orléans

Falls

French Fortifications
and entrenchments

Montgomercy Assault
July 31, 1759

St.-Larent
d'Orléans

Québec

Point Lévis

Beaumont

Sillery

Cap-Rouge

Etchemin River

..-Augustin

St.-Nicolas

Chaudière River

Introduction

The perfection of history is when it displeases all sects and nations, this being a proof that the author neither flatters nor spares any of them, and tells the truth to all parties.

Pierre Bayle

I am forced to admit that we ourselves are the authors of almost all of our woes and grieves, of which we so unreasonably complain. If I could live my life over again, should I be any wiser? Perhaps; but then I would not be myself.

Giacomo Casanova

In his brilliant satire *Candide,* Voltaire dismissed New France as "a few acres of snow" for which Britain and France warred at a cost "much more than all of Canada is worth."[1] Voltaire was not alone in condemning France's imperial exertions in North America. Even during its rare interludes of peace, New France remained an enormous financial drain on Versailles. In the century and a half from New France's founding until its demise, the French poured much more money into the colony than they extracted in furs and fish, its only two significant sources of wealth. Ever more prominent people at court and in finance recognized that conundrum and wondered why it persisted.

The answer was always the same—the logic of empire rather than economy dictated Versailles's policy toward North America. Ideally, an empire paid for itself by providing products and markets that at once enriched the imperial regime while denying those to rivals. But throughout history, every imperial state and every foreign land that it conquered and exploited was different; some conquerors were better administrators, entrepreneurs, and settlers, and some lands were riper for exploitation than others.

France proved to be as inadequate an imperial power as Canada, and Louisiana proved to be stubborn in yielding wealth. New France was locked into a vicious cycle of underdevelopment whereby few people with too few skills, opportunities, and ambitions tried to survive in too harsh an environment. To worsen matters, by the Seven Years' War, New France was ruled not by professional administrators but by an organized crime syndicate known as the "Great Society" that milked the colony of any wealth that it produced. When the king's ministers were confronted with these realities, they could at best reply that at least they had denied New France to England.

Armed with that "logic," France fought five wars to defend its North American empire—the Huguenot War (1627–29), the League of Augsburg or King William's War (1689–97), the Spanish Succession or Queen Anne's War (1701–13), the Austrian Succession or King George's War (1744–48), and the Seven Years' or French and Indian War (1754–63). Each war either followed or preceded the outbreak of war in Europe in which France and England by design or fate found themselves on opposite sides.[2]

The first four of these conflicts were wars of retaliation rather than conquest. They were fought mostly by Canadian and American colonial troops, bolstered by American Indian allies, and consisted of frontier raids interrupted on those few occasions when the British mounted major expeditions against Montreal, Quebec, or Louisbourg. Except for the capture of Quebec in 1629 and Louisbourg in 1745, which were both later returned, the French trounced the British tactically and strategically. Despite all the disadvantages plaguing New France, including eventually being outnumbered by twenty British to every one French colonist, the Canadians had mastered the art of North

American wilderness warfare. To survive with so few amidst such a vast wilderness filled with so many potential or real native enemies, the French had to adapt to Indian ways, including their way of war. Indian alliances for trade and raid were central to New France's existence, and the French were masters at forging and sustaining them.

The final war began as a typical frontier struggle between the two expanding North American empires. When word spread that on May 28, 1754, Virginian troops under Lieutenant Colonel George Washington had ambushed Canadian troops under Ensign Joseph Coulon de Villiers, Sieur de Jumonville, in disputed territory, most expected that if a war did follow it would simply repeat previous patterns. None could have imagined that the war would spread to engulf not only Europe but parts of the West Indies, West Africa, India, South America, the East Indies, and the Philippines, along with the seas linking these far-flung regions. The Seven Years' War was the world's first truly global war.

Furthermore, the war resulted in France's loss of its entire North American empire. In the 1763 Treaty of Paris, Versailles yielded all of New France except New Orleans east of the Mississippi to Britain, and New Orleans and all of New France west of the Mississippi to Spain. Of his once vast holdings across half the continent, King Louis XV retained merely the Gulf of Saint Lawrence island scraps of Saint Pierre and Miquelon upon which French fishermen could dry their catch.

When the war erupted, the British government's intention was not to destroy New France. King George II and his ministers wished merely to roll back its borders from the Appalachian watershed to the Wabash River, lower Great Lakes, and Saint Lawrence River, thus granting elbow room to the footloose adventurers and entrepreneurs of its American colonies. The British had made that demand repeatedly during sporadic negotiations with the French in the years preceding the war. The justification for their demand was an ambiguous tenet of the 1713 Treaty of Utrecht that granted Britain sovereignty over the Iroquois, who themselves made unrealized claims of sovereignty over the Ohio valley tribes. The French rejected the Iroquois gambit as nonsense and instead insisted that the disputed region was theirs by right of discovering it and, by extension, all waters that flowed into it.

Thus New France's frontier would remain on the Appalachian watershed. A similar semantic and imperial dispute embroiled the French and English over Acadia's boundaries.

Versailles would not have bowed to Britain's demands even if they had been legally well rooted. The Ohio valley was a wedge between Canada and Louisiana. The French saw British traders invading this region in the decade preceding the war not just as adventurers greedy for riches but as agents of a deliberate effort by Whitehall to split New France asunder before devouring each half. There was ample truth in that perception, but it involved British hopes rather than plots.

Though unplanned, Washington's attack became the perfect British excuse to take by war what the French would not yield peacefully. In 1755, Whitehall launched four offensives against New France's frontier. The expedition against Acadia succeeded in capturing it, that against Fort Duquesne ended disastrously, a third against Fort Niagara never left Oswego, and the last against Fort Saint Frederic got no farther than Lake George's southern end, where American provincials repulsed a French attack.

As in previous wars, the French fought the British to a bloody standoff that persisted for the next three years. What differed was that both France and Britain committed ever more regular infantry regiments to the struggle until the scale of this war's number of soldiers, ships, munitions, provisions, expenses, campaigns, and carnage dwarfed all those that had preceded it.

It was the British navy that let the British army eventually conquer the French empire in North America and elsewhere around the world. British warships captured increasing numbers of French vessels packed with supplies and troops sailing the Atlantic gauntlet. This same sea power let the British safely send more regiments to North America until their troops outnumbered French forces by ten to one.

The year 1758 was the war's turning point. Although repulsed in an assault on Fort Carillon, the British captured Louisbourg and Fort Duquesne and destroyed Fort Frontenac. It was not until early 1760, however, following a succession of British victories the previous year in Germany, the Caribbean, West Africa, India, and on the high seas, capped by word of Quebec's capture, that the cabinet's leader, William

Pitt, committed Britain to the outright conquest of France's entire overseas empire. Canada's surrender in September 1760 merely sealed Pitt's determination.

Versailles lost the war as much as Whitehall won it. The Seven Years' War was truly one that France "entered . . . without enthusiasm, fought without distinction, and emerged from . . . without victory."[3] France needed a Colbert to organize, a Necker to finance, a Talleyrand to negotiate, a Nelson to lead its fleets, and a Bonaparte to command its armies to win the Seven Years' War. It had to make do with much less.

Although France ultimately lost New France through land and sea battles, the strategic and diplomatic decisions emanating from Versailles were just as crucial. Like those of any government at any time, French policies during the Seven Years' War were shaped by a tug-of-war among rival personalities and institutions that in turn were constrained and warped by broader national and international military, economic, technological, social, and cultural forces. That matrix's core was Louis XV; behind him was his beguiling mistress, Jeanne Antoinette Poisson, marquise de Pompadour. With Pompadour's constant nudging, Louis tried and failed to become his own prime minister. He was incapable of fulfilling the role himself and would not let anyone else fill that role. When a French minister or general suffered defeat, Louis, usually at Pompadour's insistence, merely shuffled him off to his château and replaced him with yet another mediocrity or worse. Throughout most of the war, the result was the most rickety of governments, wobbly spokes leading to a wobbly hub.

Men of ability like Machault, Argenson, Bernis, Belle Isle, and Choiseul at times did head ministries if not armies or fleets during the war. Yet except for Choiseul, their performances were lackluster. And, aside from Bernis, nearly all the able or bumbling ministers alike were unenthusiastic or outright opposed to the war. While each had his own reasons, most were united in disgust at Louis XV's secret decision, guided by Pompadour and Bernis, to reverse the alliance from Prussia, whose King Frederick II was greatly admired by France's philosophes and more progressive aristocrats, to the ancient enemy Hapsburg Austria. Thus was Versailles defeatist even in the early years when it presided over one victory after another. But even if patriotism had animated them, these ministers would still have faced the Sisyphean dilemma of trying to implement their decisions through the bewildering labyrinth of French bureaucracy and finance. As if all that were not debilitating enough, each minister devoted far more time to intriguing against his rivals and enriching himself than in fulfilling the duties with which Louis XV had entrusted him. Jealousy, greed, pomposity, pettiness, and lust poisoned the king's council and its policies.

Although rightly accused of personifying all those sins, Choiseul was the only French minister who displayed any strategic vision and skill. Alas for France, he became foreign minister in 1758 when the war was essentially lost, at least in North America. By then all he could do was try to win the least humiliating peace for France. It took him four years to do so. During this time the king heaped upon his foreign ministry duties the portfolios of war and marine. More than Choiseul's brilliance let him amass such power—he was Pompadour's latest favorite.

But French policy was made by more than the king, his mistress, and ministers. Rival personalities and factions at court mirrored those in the king's council as they jostled to head armies and ministries, or simply snatch more perks of title, status, and wealth, thus complicating and impeding policies. Louis XV often found himself torn between yielding to the pressure of Pompadour or other powerful courtiers to retain an inept minister or fire a competent one, while the sheer extravagance of Versailles's spectacular and frivolous rituals drained French finances and energies. The king wrestled ceaselessly with defiant *parlements* in Paris and twelve other regions, which used their powers to register laws to thwart his attempts to raise taxes to pay for the war and impose a settlement on a religious dispute that had dragged on for more than a century.

As if the array of political factions was not enough to thwart the king's will, there were financial constraints. Although France's economy expanded throughout the eighteenth century, Versailles could not mobilize more than fragments of it for war. Wretched roads and seas haunted by British fleets and privateers isolated the economy's more dynamic agrarian regions, industries, and ports. While the realm's bourgeoisie and peasants alike ceded as little coin as possible to tax collectors, the burden typically fell mostly on those least able to pay.

Nonetheless, with Europe's largest population in France, Versailles mustered the largest armies, at least on paper. But getting soldiers to distant campaigns and getting them to prevail once they got there was a daunting challenge on every front. France's generals, a lethargic lot at best, struggled to survive the military brilliance of Frederick the Great and Prince Ferdinand of Brunswick in Germany. Nor could France's sea captains impede Britain's Royal Navy, with three times more warships when the war began, to transport a stream of regiments across the Atlantic to North America.

Yet another vital force distorting Versailles's policy toward New France was what happened in the colony itself. Plagued by all the corruption, greed, intrigues, snobbery, ineptness, and rivalries among the Canadians and French charged with its defense, Quebec was a miniature version of Versailles. Still, New France's bitterly split leadership merely contributed to rather than caused the colony's conquest. As will be seen, though Governor Vaudreuil and General Montcalm warred constantly, New France's fate was determined on the battlefield rather than in their council chamber. Had different strategies and tactics been pursued by its land and naval commanders, New France might have been saved rather than lost.

The French and Indian War and the Conquest of New France turns history inside out. Every English version from Francis Parkman through the most recent tells the tale largely through British and American eyes.[4] This book counterweighs and complements those accounts. It is the first book to explore the fascinating personalities and epic events that shaped French diplomacy, strategy, and tactics during the global war that determined North America's destiny.

PART 1

Powers

CHAPTER 1

The "Absolute" Monarchy

I often started wars on whims and prolonged them out of vanity.
Do not imitate me. Be a peaceful ruler, and let your first duty be
to look after your subjects.

Louis XIV to Louis XV

In my person alone resides the sovereign power. . . . To me alone
belongs the legislative power, unconditional and undivided. All
public order emanates from me. My people and I are one.

Louis XV

Two fascinating personalities dominated French policy throughout the Seven Years' War, Louis XV and Madame de Pompadour.
The king and his mistress were the only characters who remained at
France's center stage from the war's beginning to its end. French policy, however, was shaped by more than two people. Their power and
glamour can obscure just how decisions were made and carried out.
As in any political system, policies emerged from a perpetual multi-
stranded tug-of-war among shifting personalities, factions, institutions,
and issues. A myriad of suitors jostled for a voice in the king's councils,
while the stultifying bureaucracy charged with implementing policies
and raising revenues to pay for them more often than not distorted
and impeded those very same policies and pocketed the change.

So an exploration of Versailles's policies toward New France during the Seven Years' War only begins with Louis and Pompadour. The matrix of rival formal and informal power holders and seekers struggling against each other within Versailles must be mapped out and then set within the confines of the realm's broader economic and cultural straitjackets. And even that only partly explains what happened to New France. The impact of the international distribution of military, economic, diplomatic, and colonial power will await the next two chapters.

Louis and Pompadour

Louis XV was plopped atop the throne at age five on September 1, 1715, and there he remained for the next fifty-nine years until his death on May 10, 1774.[1] Despite his long reign, he never quite escaped the shadow of his great-grandfather, Louis XIV. The Sun King was a tough act to follow.

Louis XIV had tamed a rebellious nobility by locking it up in the gilded cage of Versailles. To divert his nobility's ambitions, wealth, and power, he constructed a vast, intricate theater of the absurd in which everyone had a role, however frivolous, in serving him. The king deliberately made a spectacle of himself. From his morning *lever*, or official rising, to his nightly *coucher*, or official retirement, the court crowded into his chambers to gaze on his every move. The favored were allowed bit parts in the endless theater, slipping shoes on his royal feet or a robe around his royal body. While Louis XIV reveled in the world he created, his great-grandson thoroughly loathed the legacy. But Louis XV could resign himself to his fate by reflecting that the endless pomp was part of the price of wielding nearly absolute power.

Louis XIV had forged a powerful state through the fire of marriage, war, and his indomitable will. The state was indeed his. He ruled and spent its money as he decreed. When the burdens of rule seemed too onerous, he could always divert himself by beckoning to one or more beauties from his royal harem. The Sun King tangled more than French nobility in his web of etiquette. Great and petty rulers alike across Europe strove to imitate the splendor and silliness of Versailles.

Yet, on his deathbed, Louis XIV realized that his megalomania had nearly ruined France through gluttonous luxury and disastrous wars. He drew his heir to his bed and whispered, "War is the ruin of nations. Do not follow my bad example that I have bequeathed you. I often started wars on whims and prolonged them out of vanity. . . . Be a peaceful ruler and let your first duty be to look after your subjects."[2]

Few kings have had more unhappy a childhood than Louis XV. He was orphaned at age two when doctors bled to death his parents and older brother after they caught the measles. Louis would have suffered the same fate had not his governess, Charlotte Eleonore de la Mothe, duchess de Ventadour, whisked him away from the doctors' razors. Ventadour was the only mother he knew. That relationship ended when she was torn from him on his seventh birthday and replaced by François de Neufville, duc de Villeroy, a distinguished general, whose duty was to tutor Louis in the art of being a monarch. Alas, the aging but still robust warrior and womanizer Villeroy was incapable of educating the lad in anything other than earthy passions and the idea that he was an absolute monarch before whom all must bow.

Louis XIV's other choices to guide his great-grandson were much more capable—his bastard son, Philippe d'Orléans, served as regent while André Hercule de Fleury, Bishop de Frejus, tutored the lad in more pedestrian subjects. As a result, royal France was rarely better administered than during the regency. Though debauched in private, Orléans governed France with skill and vision. The economy expanded. Morals, censorship, and etiquette lightened. Arts flourished. Aside from a short-lived border war with Spain, peace reigned.

Prosperity sprang largely from the Scottish financial wizard John Law, whom Orléans tapped to handle the kingdom's finances in 1716. Law used sophisticated monetary and fiscal policies to cut much of the crushing debt left by Louis XIV, bolster revenues, lower interest rates, balance the books, and invest in industries and infrastructure that diversified and expanded the economy. In 1716, he created a central bank for France, the Banque Générale, renamed the Banque Royale in 1718. To stimulate trade, he organized the Compagnie de l'Occident that developed Louisiana, and Compagnie des Indes, which expanded France's ties to all known continents.

Midas-like, all Law touched seemed to turn to gold. In 1720, Orléans made him comptroller general. Unfortunately, Law's success inspired a speculative wave of pyramid stock purchases that bubbled then burst that same year. Thousands who had gambled all their wealth were ruined. In December 1720, Orléans fired Law and dissolved the Banque Royale. Yet Law's reforms proved more powerful. The financial meltdown burned away much of the economic fat while leaving the muscle. Within a year the economy was booming again. The expansion would last most of the century and allow Louis XV a reign as decadent and luxurious as it was long.

The regency formally ended on February 5, 1723, when Louis came of age at thirteen. The Council of Regency was renamed the King's Council. On October 25, 1723, Louis XV was formally crowned at Reims cathedral. Two months later, on December 23, 1723, a lifetime of debauchery finally claimed Orléans. Louis Henri, duc de Bourbon, quickly stepped into his place. He would not last long. Greed and a novice queen prompted his downfall.

Though teenage Louis was strapping and handsome, he was too shy to toss a handkerchief to any of the swirling parade of women and girls who longed to steal his virginity. Many wondered if the king would not satisfy his carnal hungers until his wedding night. In 1721, he was given a fiancée, Maria Ann Victoria, Spanish King Philip V's daughter. But in 1725 the Spanish princess was sent packing when Bourbon and his wife found another through whom they hoped to manipulate Louis. Bourbon convinced the council to choose as queen Marie Leszczynska, the daughter of Stanislaus, Poland's dethroned king living in exile in Nancy.

Louis was fifteen when he joined hands with Marie on September 5, 1725. The lad was a sexual wallflower no more; it was boasted that he had exercised his royal lust seven times on the wedding night. The honeymoon ended abruptly, however, when Marie tried to sweet-talk Louis into dumping his tutor and surrogate father, Fleury. The suggestion angered Louis. A tearful Marie admitted that Bourbon was behind it. This knowledge enraged Louis into committing his reign's first important decision. He abruptly dismissed Bourbon and named the seventy-three-year-old Fleury his chief minister.

Fleury held this power for the next seventeen years. He proved to be as able a ruler as Orléans, striving and largely succeeding in keeping France peaceful and prosperous by avoiding war and encouraging trade. All along he tried to instill in Louis the skills of monarchy. When Fleury died on January 29, 1743, Louis felt ready to rule alone: "As soon as the death was announced to the King, his Majesty said, 'Messieurs, I am now prime-minister.'"[3]

As for the queen, though Louis remained true to his royal duty to produce an heir, her intrigue had forever cooled his ardor for her. Louis became a father at age seventeen, and the queen would give birth to nine more children, the third of which was the long-awaited dauphin or royal heir. During the queen's pregnancies, the royal doctors forbade Louis from sleeping with her. The highly sexed king compensated with a string of three mistresses, all sisters!

What manner of king was he? Louis XV's first sobriquet was "the beloved," which became popular in 1744 after he accompanied his army to victories against the Austrians and British, followed by his illness at Metz. The sentiments of those who called him "beloved" were well-founded only by comparison to his predecessor, who had bankrupted and bled France. In 1747, René de Voyer, marquis d'Argenson, bluntly stated that "Louis XV is cherished by his people without ever, as yet, having done them any good."[4] The king never really would.

The courtiers and masses alike gradually awakened to this reality. Yet through good and bad times, public opinion was always fickle; moods shifted with the winds of fashion and fate. In such a climate, the king could be lauded one day and pilloried the next. As Louis's popularity faded, Argenson explained that the French, "more attached to persons than to [institutions] . . . attack the king in the first instance with much injustice, and oftener Louis XV, than any other." The king stood fire for the sins of his advisors—"with dull, inhuman ministers such as his, he attracts to himself more and more daily a national hatred." But rumors of his private life also turned people against him. He was hypersensitive to all the criticism, only fragments of which filtered through the layers of court to his royal ears. Louis was often "tortured with remorse; the songs and satires have had this effect upon him. He sees himself hated by his people, he considers that the hand of God is in it."[5]

Louis meant well, but, unable to know and better himself, he could do little for his kingdom. Argenson offered this penetrating portrait: "Our monarch is a kind man at bottom, but small in conception; he understands nothing about elevated things; his mind is indolent in . . . resolution and action. . . . He fears philosophers, without hating them; he follows courtiers of common minds and false hearts, without liking them. . . . He has right-mindedness, but . . . lacks courage."[6]

Why was he like that? His childhood traumas worsened Louis's natural shyness and melancholy. He was miserable during the daily rituals of exposure to a fawning or mocking court from the time they crowded into his royal bed chamber to watch him rise to the moment he turned in at night. He hid his timidity and self-doubts behind a mask of icy reserve. His introversion combined with bouts of melancholy, boredom, and inertia to make him cling to the same routines and faces as if to a social life raft; speaking to strangers terrified him.[7]

Though bright and informed enough, Louis lacked the confidence to challenge his ministers and tended to follow the last opinion foisted upon him. He never quite reconciled the paradox of his supposed absolute, divine rule with the reality that he was the greatest prisoner of Versailles's maze of etiquette, intrigue, and ridicule. Nor, to his dying day, did he ever quite escape being a revered but powerless child manipulated by those around him.

Louis hated confrontation. The supposed absolute monarch could not criticize anyone directly. Instead, Louis displayed his displeasure with a royal snub, a refusal to speak or even look at the miscreant, let alone dine with him. Serious offenses called for more serious penalties. Unable to face those who had betrayed or disappointed him, he remained civil to the very moment when the lettre de cachet was delivered and the miscreant escorted to his country estate or to the Bastille.

Yet the popular belief that the king was lazy was untrue. Between hunts, banquets, and trysts, Louis put in long hours at the office: "The King works at present with his ministers, acquits himself well, and decides with judgment; he has a well-stored memory. . . . He listens to everything, even the smallest details. . . . It is true that he goes but little to the bottom of things . . . never lending himself to a long discussion."[8]

Louis was brave personally but despaired at witnessing the suffering of others, especially if he was partly responsible for it. The illness Louis suffered at Metz in September 1744 was likely as much psychological as physical. The campaign had emotionally drained him. The stress of presiding over the fate of tens of thousands of lives and his kingdom was withering enough, but all along he was harshly criticized for bringing along his mistress, Marie Anne de Nesle, marquise de Châteauroux.

In 1745, Louis and the dauphin rejoined Maurice de Saxe at the front, this time to witness France's narrow victory at Fontenoy on May 11. The sight of blood always nauseated him; carnage on such a vast scale shook him profoundly. He was no warmonger like his great-grandfather, and Fontenoy haunted him until his own dying day. He would do what he could to avert France's slide into the Seven Years' War, but the diplomatic slope became too slippery to avoid the plunge.

From 1745 to 1765, one advisor transcended all others at the king's side. Many believed then and now that France's policies during those two decades were largely shaped in Louis's boudoir rather than in the council chamber. Perhaps no royal mistress has ever wielded as much power as Madame de Pompadour, who served the king as both his unofficial queen and prime minister.[9] The eighteenth century's most famous and powerful mistress was born Jeanne Antoinette Poisson in 1721 to a libertine father and social-climbing mother. Actually, her paternity remains obscure. The most likely suspects are Jean Paris-Marmontel, her mother's lover about the time she was conceived, and Fermier Général Charles François Paul, Le Normant de Tournehem. Both were extremely powerful men who would help her rise to society's pinnacle. She was educated by the Ursuline sisters at Poissy and then, more importantly, at various salons, where she refined her natural gifts for conversation, music, and acting. A convenient marriage in 1741 renamed her Madame d'Étiolles. She and her husband, Charles-Guillaume le Normand d'Étiolles spent little time together, though her beloved child Alexandrine came of their marriage.

How did Pompadour snare the king? An elaborate conspiracy won her the royal heart. She and her confederates contrived a "chance" encounter between her and Louis at the Yew Tree Ball in February 1745.

Dressed as Diana, goddess of the hunt, she shot a miniature arrow at Louis, who turned and smiled. She bowed and dropped her handkerchief as she retired coquettishly. He retrieved it and threw it after her. The smitten king pursued. Their love was consummated a few days later. Within a week of the ball, he was hers.

What did the king see in his mistress? She was renowned for being one of those rare women who radiated such powerful inner and physical beauty that most people melted in her presence. George Leroy, Versailles's head huntsman and an obvious connoisseur, described her as

> a little taller than most, slim, graceful, supple, elegant; her face was well assorted to her height, a perfect oval, beautiful hair, closer to light brown than blonde, rather large eyes with fine eyelashes of the same color, a perfectly shaped nose, a charming mouth, very beautiful teeth and the most delicious smile; the most beautiful skin in the world gave her a dazzling look. Her eyes had a peculiar charm which they may have owed to the uncertainty of their color; they did not have the lively sparkle of black eyes, the tender languor of blue eyes, the subtlety which belongs to grey eyes; their indeterminate color seemed to render them able to seduce in every possible way and to express all the feelings of a rapidly changing mood; thus her face reflected all sorts of looks, but always without any discordance between her features. . . . The ensemble of her person seemed to bridge the fine line between the last degree of elegance and the first of nobility."[10]

More than beauty, Pompadour brought Louis gaiety through plays, concerts, dinner parties, and conversations with that age's greatest wits, artists, and philosophers, all of which animated his dull life. It was well known that she could "divert the melancholy cast of his mind from sinking into a habit of devotion. She perpetually varied his pleasures, and carried him from one palace and hunting seat to another, journeys which cost immense sums, and made the people join in the clamor which the clergy had conjured up."[11] Even more vitally, she brought the king the intimate sanctum from others that he had wanted all his life. He discovered a woman "alluring his nature by the charm of gentleness, she soon won all and obtained the most extreme authority that can be procured by confidence, comfort, secrecy, and all the maneuvers that render courtesans by profession more completely the masters of their lovers."[12]

What did Pompadour get in return? Vast mountains of wealth, status, and power were hers for the asking which she did not hesitate to take—officially she spent 36,327,268 livres in those two decades; the real debt is impossible to say. It did not all go to dressmakers and hairdressers. She amassed a library of 3,500 volumes including 738 on history and 215 on philosophy. Her books were not only for show; she was a voracious reader. As important as the unbelievable luxury were the titles. On March 6, 1745, for her exquisite services the king bestowed upon her the title the marquise de Pompadour, lifting her with a pen stroke from the bourgeoisie to the nobility. On October 17, 1752, he elevated her to the duchesse de Pompadour. Her final honor was to become lady-in-waiting to the queen in 1756.[13]

Nearly all the court was bitterly jealous that an upstart bourgeois courtesan should siphon off so much French wealth, status, and power for so long. Those few who were fiscally responsible at Versailles condemned her for the "great harm in turning the king from all economy at Court, and in promoting unworthy persons to office . . . therefore her good counsels are expensive; mildness and equity are bought by luxury."[14] It was her sway over state policy that rankled many the most. From their first tumble, Pompadour employed her charms to twist the king to her bidding. Sometimes sterner measures were necessary. When Louis was obstinate, she did not shrink from displaying "a good deal of vehemence; she intimidated the king which is the surest way of persuading him."[15] By 1751, it was widely resented that "the mistress is prime minister and is becoming more and more despotic, such as no favorite has ever been in France."[16]

To what ends did Pompadour wield power? Culture rather than geopolitics was her initial concern. It was Pompadour who forced such royal decisions as easing censorship on Diderot's *Encyclopedia* and other works by freethinkers. Voltaire was especially favored with such awards as Royal Historiographer, Gentleman of the Bedchamber, and two thousand livres a year. Conservatives in the court and church later pressured Louis to crack down on the philosophes with their dangerous liberal ideas, and to censor their work and imprison or banish them. Pompadour also swung the royal favor behind the establishment of l'École Militaire in 1751 and the Sevres porcelain factory in 1752.

During the Seven Years' War, Pompadour turned from art to diplomacy. Courtiers and even ministers sought to sway the king through her. Though Louis "thinks he rules her; she rules him, she makes him see merit in those who have no reputation, nor the appearance of any. . . . She determines, she decides, she regards the King's ministers as hers."[17] All along she tried to get Louis "to pronounce in the council an opinion which would appear to be his own. In consequence she had the courage to take a part in business matters and was soon up to them because she had a lively and accurate mind. . . . Louis XV acquired the habit of letting himself be guided by her advice, and she became arbitress of the destinies of the kingdom."[18]

Pompadour was skilled in many arts, but highly sexed she was not. She just could not keep up with Louis's voracious needs. She consumed every known love potion to sharpen her appetite, but they just made her nauseous.[19] Over the years, lovemaking dwindled steadily between them. By 1753, it was loudly whispered that "Pompadour was no longer the king's mistress."[20] Swallowing the venom, Pompadour agreed to Louis's pleas that he satisfy his lusts elsewhere. The Petite Trianon, a short stroll across Versailles's gardens from the palace, and the Parc-aux-Cerfs mansion in town served as the royal love nests. Somewhat sheepishly at first but with increased gusto, Louis enjoyed a succession of "ephemeral loves; he throws the handkerchief to young girls or women whom he sees at mass or when he dines in public. . . . Bachelier, his old head valet, assists him. . . . The marquise bears it as best she can; the king had compelled her to make certain visits she did not wish to make. Influence diminishes always when the attractions of love do not support it, but art can substitute itself for nature."[21]

Abstinence was a tonic to the relationship between Louis and Pompadour. Their friendship deepened as the sexual tension between them faded. She remained his confidante until death.

What role did Queen Marie play in all this? She was no queen bee, the court's center of devotion, let alone of policy. It was said she was "very gracious and polite. . . . She takes no part in government. She likes neither splendor nor ceremony."[22] As for her character, she "has an extremely susceptible heart, though religion manages the rest of her."[23] Marie could be vindictive and heaped it upon those who slighted her, especially her husband's mistresses and Pompadour above all. If she had a skill it was getting others to share her hatred. The wife avenged herself on her errant, indifferent husband, the son and daughters on their aloof father, and all other French on their father figure—at once a demigod and a buffoon. The royal family despised Pompadour and sought her ruin by a hundred petty intrigues, all of which she managed to blunt.

No one's venom toward Pompadour exceeded that of the dauphin, who according to Argenson, "increases in coarseness, in apathy, in hatred to his father's mistress; the moment he sees her his tempers shows itself; the queen fans the flame."[24] A curious but all too common mentality had arisen in a son dominated and shamed by a distant, amoral father: "The dauphin has the characteristic of wanting to do in all things precisely the opposite of the king, his father; he loves women ardently, but contents himself with his wife, whom he does not love; he is bigoted in a way in which the king is not, he likes priests and bishops because the king ill-treats them. With all these practices, he gives no prospect of being the delight of the human race when he reigns. Listen to the bourgeois, and you will hear them dreading his accession to the throne as a calamity; the contrast makes them cherish the father. It is fear of the priesthood that inspires these sentiments of dread in the people."[25] Such a personality could have been a disruptive presence in the king's council, but his father barred him from it.

The king presided over and worsened two severely dysfunctional families, his own and France.

Governance

So who then ruled France? Theoretically, the king was an absolute monarch whose powers and rights derived from God Himself; as such, he decided all important state questions through his councils or by personal decrees, declared war and peace, ratified all treaties, taxed and spent as he wished, and with lettres de cachet censored, banished, or imprisoned undesirables. After Fleury's death in 1743, Louis XV worked very hard to fulfill his duties and act as his own prime minister. He and his realm, however, would have been better served had he instead found another Fleury; the challenges facing France exceeded his talents.

In reality, Louis XV did not rule; he presided over most policy debates and lent his royal signature to the decisions of his advisors and ministers. The king was the hub for half a dozen ministers shuffled among four overlapping advisory groups. The most important was the Council of State, which was charged with foreign, military, and other vital issues, and which also served as a last court of appeals. That body was supposed to coordinate policies among the other councils and ministries, though in practice each went its own way. It met every Sunday and Wednesday. The other three were the Council of Dispatches, which met every Saturday to decide most domestic issues and hear appeals from the parlements; the Council of Finance, which usually met every other Tuesday; and the Council of Administrative Justice, which was France's supreme court and met as needs arose. Decisions were reached by majority rule if a consensus could not be forged, then were signed off by the king. In addition to the councils, he spent several hours daily meeting with various ministers, advisors, and courtiers over policy.[26]

Just who joined these councils? Five ministries formed the administrative pillars of France's central government: war; foreign affairs; marine, which included naval, colonial, and commercial duties; finance, which not only raised taxes and prepared the budget but was responsible for regulating commerce, agriculture, and industry; and the King's Household, which included not just court affairs and finance but also all secular and religious issues within France.

A secretary headed each ministry except for finance, whose minister was called a comptroller general. Often joining these ministers at the king's councils were two other royal advisors, the keeper of the seals, who sealed the king's decrees and pocketed a fortune in fees for the privilege, and the chancellor, who headed the judicial system.

The king's ministers were not a policy team but rivals who employed all means fair and foul to undercut one another. Personalism rather than professionalism governed. Stronger characters tended to manipulate the weak. To avoid being dominated, Louis played off the ministers against each other. And then, of course, there was Pompadour; though she did not attend formal meetings, her views spiced any policy discussion. The result of all this discord, combined with the administrative musical chairs and overlapping jurisdictions, was confused, vacillating, poorly implemented, and, at times, contradictory policies.

Like the king, the ministers had no permanent home but followed the court in its yearly circuit from Versailles to Compiègne to Fontainebleau and back again to Versailles, with visits at half a dozen other châteaux en route. Each ministry's clerks were scattered among rooms at Versailles and other palaces and sometimes the residences of the ministers themselves. Each ministry's bureaus generally pursued their respective tasks with complete autonomy from one another and frequently at cross-purposes. Clerks complained of the fifteen-hour days, miserly stipends, and endless frustrations. Factionalism, red tape, corruption, sycophancy, incompetence, wretched morale, and favoritism characterized each bureaucratic pyramid of France's government from bottom to top. In all, the organizational principles behind French bureaucracy were as chaotic and surreal as anything depicted by Franz Kafka.[27]

Among these administrative problems, the rapid turnover of ministers might have been the easiest to rectify but never was. Of the royal advisors, only the chancellor held his position for life; the others could be dismissed at the king's will. Indeed, Louis often expressed his royal displeasure with a minister or advisor. From 1748 to 1762 alone, twenty-three men served in the key ministries of foreign affairs, treasury, war, and marine, a rather disruptive experience for a nation at war. Why did France's ministries suffer such a revolving door? Personality clashes more than professional failings explain it. Incompetence and corruption were tolerated to a point; offending Pompadour, however, was punished sooner or later with dismissal.[28]

Even if the king had desired the most capable ministers, he would have had trouble finding them. "Careers open to all talents" characterized the rule of Napoleon, not Louis XV, and was possible only after the Revolution. In Versailles's stifling world, one rose through the stratum by skillfully wielding powers of flattery, wit, and etiquette rather than a hardnosed understanding of French interests and the means to obtain them. Although truly talented men like Machault; Jean Frédéric Phélypeaux, comte de Maurepas; Argenson; Conti; Richelieu; Belle Isle; Bernis; and Choiseul served the king, Versailles tended to stifle their abilities.

The king's ministers simply reflected the court's prevailing fashions, fortunes, and follies. Giacomo Casanova offered a scalding view: "All the French ministers were the same. They lavished money which came out of other people's pockets to enrich their creatures, and they were absolute; the downtrodden people counted for nothing, and of this course the indebtedness of the state and confusion of finances were the inevitable results."[29]

The root of these problems was the king himself. Louis XV proved incapable of converting his courtiers into ministers. Though he tried not to be overbearing at council, his advisors tended to tailor their reports and proposals in ways that avoided arousing his royal displeasure rather than providing him realistic assessments of French interests, power, and policy options. The king's personality was perhaps more important than the aura of his position in stifling honest debate over policy. It was well known that "when a minister talks to the King about anything in his department, His Majesty remains silent as a fish, a sort of behavior that upsets them."[30] Such behavior preserved propriety at the cost of hammering out comprehensive policies.

As if all these conflicting personalities, positions, and powers that shaped French policies were not Byzantine enough, Louis pursued a secret set of foreign policies that paralleled and often conflicted with his official ones.[31] Louis François de Bourbon, prince de Conti, was the king's cousin and confidant. Intelligent, sophisticated, a brave though controversial general, a renowned libertine, and, above all, ambitious, Conti longed for his own throne. Louis agreed that it was in French and family interests to find him one. The royal wombs of eastern Europe seemed the most promising for Conti and France. To that end, in 1745 Louis set up *le secret du roi*, a clandestine network of diplomats and agents that at once conspired to advance French and Conti goals in eastern Europe. Louis's most important agents were Jean Pierre Tercier, the foreign ministry's deputy minister, and Charles François, comte de Broglie, ambassador to Poland. Yet, despite all these efforts, Louis and Conti met with nothing but rejection. Over the years, Poland, Saxony, the Duchy of Courland, and Russia spurned their advances.

The secret du roi's only genuine success was remaining secret in that gossip-drenched age. Overall, these clandestine efforts undermined rather than advanced French interests. A succession of foreign ministers unwittingly pursued policies that were as much impeded as aided by that secret network. Currying favor with one prospective bride and her court often meant inadvertently threatening the others that feared French power. During the Seven Years' War, the official and secret policies clashed, most disastrously with Saint Petersburg. While the foreign ministry tried to nurture an alliance with Russia, the secret du roi sought to stem Russian advances in Poland and elsewhere. In the end, Conti never got his throne and French influence in eastern Europe withered.

France's central government was chaotic enough. Then there was the rest of France. The kingdom was an administrative mess, a hodgepodge of overlapping jurisdictions that included thirty-two generalities or provinces, thirteen parlements, thirty-nine military governments, and hundreds of ecclesiastical dioceses. There was nothing "general" about the generalities split between the *pays d'etat*, or provinces that had long been part of France, and the *pays conquis*, or more recent conquests. But the term "pays," or country, was appropriate. Each differed so sharply in power, wealth, institutions, customs, and even language that it was almost its own realm. Some of those provincial states had the power to tax themselves; others did not. The prince de Condé ruled Clermontois, which barred the king's tax collectors. Marseille and Dunkirk were free ports. Having been subjected

more recently, provinces from Languedoc and Brittany enjoyed considerable autonomy. Then there were outright independent enclaves
within France such as the papal state of Avignon or secular states of
Mulhouse, Henrichemont, Dombes, Orange, and Bouillon.

Carrying out the royal will in France's hinterlands were around
thirty intendants vested with varying powers to impose justice; appor-
tion and collect taxes; raise troops and supplies; regulate manufactures, agriculture, and commerce; share military powers with the
local commander; and send reports and recommendations back to
Versailles. Each intendant's power, however, varied with the region he
was supposed to administer. The Council of Dispatches devised policies for the intendants. Though most intendants were responsible to
the comptroller general, the war ministry could dispatch intendants to
regions threatened with invasion or rebellion.[32]

And then there was the church, yet another autonomous and
splintered realm whose factions fought to shape government policies.
The interrelated questions of theological, religious, and secular power
burned through eighteenth-century France. "His Most Christian
Majesty" presided over a kingdom torn by religious gulfs so great that
they impeded his ability to wage war or even govern. Dating back to
Philip the Fair of the fourteenth century, Gallicanism was the concept
that justified the king's autonomy from Rome and his power over the
Catholic Church of France. God Himself delegated his divine right
to rule upon the French king, who appointed the bishops. The pope
then approved the king's choices.

Yet the king's power was limited in doctrine and finance, especially the latter. The church tightly clasped its own purse strings. In
financial crises the king could humbly ask the church for donations,
the permission and amount subject to a national convocation of the
clergy. In 1749, fed up with a miserly church and soaring national
debt, Comptroller general Jean-Baptiste de Machault d'Arnouville
boldly proposed a 5 percent tax on all church income, the annulment
of all new orders since 1626, and the bar of all legacies to the church
without the king's permission. The church erupted in protest. Louis
reluctantly ordered Machault to shelve his proposals and shifted him
to head the marine ministry.

At first glance, the church seemed to be a religious monolith and economic powerhouse. By law Catholicism was France's only religion; all others were condemned. The church owned as much as 20 percent of France's soil and 35 percent of its wealth, all of which escaped taxes. Yet the church was split over doctrine, power, and wealth; its hierarchy and tensions mirrored France's class divisions. In 1763, the church counted 18 archbishops, 109 bishops, 40,000 priests, 50,000 vicars (assistant priests), 27,000 priors or chaplains, 12,000 cannons, and 20,000 clerks, as well as 100,000 monks, friars, and nuns in more than 740 monasteries. Rich and usually well-educated nobles filled the upper echelons; most bishoprics and abbés had become family heirlooms passed down from one generation to the next. The priests formed the church's middle class, with income and prestige varying considerably. In stark contrast, the tens of thousands of parish cures and vicars annually lived off 300- or 200-livre stipends. Most rose from the poor they shepherded.[33]

Jesuits tended to dominate the church's top echelons. Not only in France but across Catholic Europe, Jesuits had become the confessors of kings and princes. They also dominated France's university and secondary education, seconded by the Christian Brothers, Benedictines, and Oratorians. Most parishes had a school that gave children the rudiments of reading, writing, and the catechism. Unenforced edicts of 1694 and 1724 required attendance. Parents could send their children to school free if they could not afford the small fee. With their training in the humanities and etiquette, the Jesuits mixed well with court sophisticates and philosophes alike. They "are usually very learned, studious and civil and agreeable in company. In their whole deportment there is something pleasing. It is no wonder therefore that they captivate the minds of people. They seldom speak of religious matters, and . . . they generally avoid disputes. They are very ready to do one a service. . . . Their conversation is very entertaining and learned."[34]

It was the Jesuits' close ties with the court and its attendant corruption, luxury, and decadence that steadily eroded their prestige. Those French who longed for a church devoted to pure spirituality increasingly turned to Jansenism. The movement started in 1640 with the posthumous publication of Cornelius Jansen's *Augustinus*. In that book, Jansen, a theologian and Bishop of Ypres argued that the papacy should shed a millennium's accumulation of gaudy rituals and dogmas in favor of Saint Augustine's austere teachings. The core of Jansen's assertions was that salvation comes from predestined grace rather than worldly good works.

Jesuits condemned Jansenism as Calvinism in Catholic garb. They countered with the free will doctrine of Luis Molina that, while God does indeed grant grace, humans still had to perform good works to reach salvation. The conflict between Jansenists and Jesuits lasted more than a century. At first the Jesuits enjoyed the upper hand. In 1653 they convinced Pope Innocent X to declare Jansenism a heresy. The declaration muzzled Jansenists for nearly five decades until 1699, when Pasquier Quesnel revived the movement with his *The New Testament with Moral Reflections on Every Verse*. It was not until 1708, however, that Pope Clement XI condemned Quesnel's work, followed by an even more sweeping attack on 101 of his tenets with a papal bull in 1713.

The bull split France's church and state. A coalition of forces (*parti Janseniste*) hostile to the king, Jesuits, and Rome itself, or favoring freedom of religion and thought embraced Jansenism as a cause célèbre; among those Jansenist supporters were the *zeles* in the parlements who burned with Enlightenment ideas. When Louis XIV tried to register the bull with the Paris parlement, he met with a remonstrance. Parlement refused to accept the bull unless France's bishops unanimously declared their support for it. Though 112 bishops did so, 9 were opposed. Parlement continued to resist until a *lit de justice* forced it to submit in 1714. The issue smoldered for the next four decades until it burst forth again in the 1750s, gridlocking French policy on the brink of the Seven Years' War.

As if the conflict within the church were not debilitating enough, animosities still burned between France's Catholics and its Protestants, or Huguenots. Two centuries earlier religious wars spawned by the Reformation had savagely torn France apart. During the 1560s, Catholics and Huguenots murdered each other in pitched battles for domination of the kingdom. The struggle's turning point came with the Saint Bartholomew's Day Massacre of August 24, 1572, when Catholics hacked or burned to death over 3,000 Huguenots in Paris and 8,000 elsewhere. Most survivors went underground; the fighting for France's throne continued. The Protestant Henry of Navarre actually won the crown in 1589, but only after he agreed that Paris was worth a mass and converted to Catholicism. On April 13, 1598, King Henry IV ruled in favor of toleration when he issued the Edict of Nantes granting Protestants the freedom to worship, hold public offices, and print religious tracts.

The truce was brief. The throne crushed Protestant revolts during the 1620s. The Peace of Alés of 1629 allowed Protestants to retain their freedom to worship but snatched away their civil and political rights. Upon taking power in 1661, Louis XIV warred periodically against Protestants at home as vigorously and more successfully than he warred against France's neighbors; hundreds of churches were razed, thousands of Protestants were slaughtered, tens of thousands were forced to convert or flee. Those prosecutions culminated on October 17, 1685, when Louis XIV revoked the Edict of Nantes. Henceforth, Protestants were forbidden to practice their faith. The Huguenot population plunged from its peak of 750,000 in the 1680s to perhaps 590,000 by 1760.[35]

Louis XV was mostly indifferent to the Huguenots. The laws remained but were rarely enforced so long as Protestants did not publicly profess their faith. From 1744 to 1752, over 600 Protestants were imprisoned while 800 others received lesser punishments. Although Pompadour convinced Louis to end the persecution, the fear lingered that Protestants were a traitorous fifth column in league with France's enemies to destroy Versailles. During the Seven Years' War, France's militia and coast guard companies were stiffened with about 80,000 regular troops as much to repress an imagined Huguenot threat as to repel English raids. Those regulars might have tipped the war in France's favor had they been deployed in Germany and America.[36]

Louis XV bore many crosses as His Most Christian Majesty. The most burdensome were the thirteen regional courts or parlements that administered French law. Parlement was first instituted simply to register the king's edicts. However, over the centuries it amassed more power and increasingly challenged royal policies. Parlement could note its disapproval by filing a remonstrance instead of approving the law. The king could then finesse that by summoning the magistrates to a lit de justice or royal audience that required them to register the edict. Even then, parlement could counter with a *lettre de jussion* that protested both the original edict and the king's demand to register it. The only way for the king to break this deadlock was to appear before parlement and repeat his demand that they conform to his will. At this point parlement usually gave in. All along, parlement justified its resistance by arguing that its role was respectfully to enlighten the king. It asserted a "constitutionalist" theory of government whereby the king and parlement were both as venerable as France itself, dating back to the Merovingian Dynasty, and had developed their mutually supportive powers hand in hand ever since.

Louis XIV snapped parlement's power in 1673 with a law requiring it to register an edict before issuing its own remonstrance. The parlements laid low and bided their time. Upon the Sun King's death, they reasserted their power, refusing to accept Orléans as regent unless he allowed them once again to remonstrate and delay registering edicts. Orléans had no choice but to give in. Ever since then, the parlements, especially that of Paris, had been the bane of Louis XV's reign. The tug-of-war infected a range of issues, especially the power of the purse. During the wars of Austrian Succession and Seven Years', parlement repeatedly stymied Louis XV's efforts to raise taxes and thus fouled his power to wage war.

The largest and most powerful parlement sat in Paris with a jurisdiction that sprawled over one-third of France. It was the only parlement that could try a peer. The most important of its seven chambers was the *grand chambre*. A chief magistrate and attorney general appointed by the king presided over the grand chambre and its nine superior magistrates (*presidents a mortiers*) and thirty-three judges (*conseillers*). Over two hundred other noblemen purchased seats in the other chambers. Many of the members were zeles—young, impassioned, and often Jansenist.

During the 1750s, the issues of royal, religious, and parlementary power became thoroughly entangled. The conflict between the Catholic Church and the heretical Jansenist sect that had smoldered for nearly a century meshed with the struggle between the king and parlement that had endured even longer. Jansenism and parlement were natural allies against the absolutism asserted by the king and Gallicist upper-church hierarchy.[37]

The catalyst occurred when Paris archbishop Christophe de Beaumont forbade any priest from performing or receiving the sacraments, including the Eucharist and extreme unction, without a signed oath to the 1713 papal bull. Parlement defended the Jansenist by threatening to refuse to register the king's edicts unless he forced the bishops to allow Jansenist priests to perform and receive the sacraments. In doing so, parlement violated a 1695 edict it had registered that required parlement to acquiesce to any doctrinal judgments reached by France's bishops and archbishops. Parlement countered with claims for ancient rights to judge any royal or church decrees superseded any recent edicts.

At first, Hamlet-like, Louis XV vacillated between the two sides. Finally, on February 22, 1753, he sent an edict to parlement that forced it to withdraw from the sacrament controversy and instead empowered the king's council to decide the issue. Parlement debated the edict for weeks before issuing, on May 4, 1753, a grand remonstrance that, with exquisite politeness, condemned the king for usurping power and violating sacred French laws. Louis XV refused to receive the remonstrance and, on May 9, issued *lettres de cachet* that exiled parlement to Pontoise, hoping the judges' increased longing for the delights of Paris and Versailles would render them pliant. He miscalculated their determination. All new laws, edicts, and taxes ground to a halt as parlement defiantly refused to register them. On the Seven Years' War's eve, parlement had again deprived the king of the power to tax and barely let him and his ministers govern. The standoff lasted eighteen months. On September 4, 1754, Louis finally caved in and reluctantly invited them back to Paris.

But the struggle between king and parlement was far from over. During the 1750s, the Paris parlement alone issued eighteen remonstrances, of which nine involved fiscal matters, two jurisdictional, four support for other parlements, and three religious; the 1760s brought twenty-five representations and six remonstrances from parlement, all along straitjacketing Versailles as it tried to wage war. Parlement

was deaf to patriotic appeals. The king usually retreated before parlement's opposition. Throughout those two decades that engulfed
the Seven Years' War, Louis issued only six lits de justice that forced
parlement to bow to his will. The squabbles drained Louis and his
ministers of time, energy, and attention vital for fighting a world war.
"Absolute monarch" indeed![38]

If France had a public opinion with any impact on policy, it came
mostly from aristocratic voices. The nobility were a tiny and largely
parasitic sliver of mid-eighteenth-century France; only one of 50 people or about 80,000 families with 400,000 members held titles. The
king, of course, peaked the noble pyramid followed by the princes of
the blood or descendants of former kings, seven bishops, fifty dukes,
and then ever-greater numbers of marquises, counts, viscounts, barons, sieurs, and chevaliers. Royal princes topped the pecking order but
had no political power; fearing their ambitions, Louis XIV had banned
them from the ministries and councils.

Two broad orders split the nobility. Noblemen of the sword (*noblesse
de l'épée*) had pedigrees traceable to medieval knighthood and mostly
filled officer ranks in the army and navy. Those of the gown (*noblesse
de la robe*) received their titles either by extraordinary service or outright purchase; they mostly filled the ranks of the bureaucracy or parlements. Only several thousand nobility of the sword or robe actually
served the state. The vast majority of nobles quietly leeched off the
labor of peasants on their rural estates. Thousands of nobles themselves lived in genteel poverty. France's nobility was surprisingly fluid.
Intermarriage gradually erased the distinctions between nobles of the
sword and gown. Bought titles bridged that once vast chasm between
the nobility and the bourgeois; by 1789, nearly 95 percent of nobles
were recently middle class.[39]

Only a sliver of the aristocrats ever made it to Versailles. The court
numbered from 2,000 to 4,000 powdered, silk-cocooned souls, of whom
most happily immersed themselves in the minutiae of court etiquette,
gossip, and intrigues. Not everyone at court adored it unconditionally.
Argenson reckoned that "the greatest vice of monarchial governments
is what is called a court. . . . Flattery is there disguised as wisdom and as
love; poisons are there refined, and virtue is there despised. . . . The two

idols there are fortune and fashion. . . . The first of talents is cleverness; the last, and most dangerous is to be a great man."[40]

The court dictated more than fashion. For Argenson, it was a vast swarming parasite that leeched France's vitality: "The Court prevents all reform in finance and increases disorder. The Court corrupts the military and naval professions by promotions from favoritism; it prevents officers from rising to the generalship by good conduct and emulation. The Court corrupts morals; it preaches to the young men entering their careers, intrigue and venality, instead of emulation by virtue and labour; it breaks the neck of merit, if merit shows itself. The Court impoverishes the nation so that soon the financiers themselves will have no money. The Court prevents the king from reigning, and from developing the virtues that he has."[41] Every livre squandered at court meant a livre less to invest in industry, trade, infrastructure, empire, and, if necessary, war.

Though many tried, no one outdid the king in extravagance. In 1751, the royal household consumed 68 million livres, or one-quarter of the government's budget. Where did all that money go? Louis XV enjoyed access to 10,000 servants, 3,000 horses, 217 carriages, 150 pages, and 30 physicians. The king imposed an extra 100,000 livres on his taxpaying subjects with every "progress" from one château to the next.[42] The monarch set the standard for the court's morals as well as its purchases. Some worried that the king's liaisons were corrupting not only him but his realm. By 1754, Argenson reported that Louis "is more than ever plunged into ephemeral loves; he has several little grisettes at once, and does not follow either reason or nature." Where the king led, his courtiers gaily followed: "The poorer the nobles are becoming in revenue, the more they are increasing in magnificence of luxury on their tables, houses, furniture, snuff-boxes, mistresses." Not all succumbed to the seduction of licentiousness, although Argenson reasoned that exaggerated piety was just as bad: "The dauphin and the rest of the royal family are all equally sunk into subjection to priests, which makes one despair for the kingdom of France."[43] Louis and his court played or prayed while their kingdom burned.

The government, like the royal household and court, lived far beyond its means. As with any system, the government could run and policies could be asserted only so far as money could be scraped up to pay for it all. This was hard enough during peacetime and nearly impossible during war. France's budget did not exist in the modern sense of a central plan that included all projected spending, debts, and income. Versailles had no idea how much its army of officials and tax collectors had respectively spent or gleaned until all the accounts dribbled in. With such a system, the comptroller's budget estimates were often grossly inaccurate. For example, in 1758 the anticipated deficit was 133 million livres; when the accounts were tallied, the real debt was 217 million livres.[44]

The types and amounts of taxes varied among the provinces. For direct income taxes (tailles), France was broadly divided into a *pays de tailles réelle* whose taxpayers declared their revenues and were assessed accordingly, and a *pays de tailles personnelle* where the intendants made that assessment. Tax evasion characterized both systems. As if these income taxes were not burdensome enough, Versailles imposed two other direct taxes. Starting in 1695, the capitation or hearth tax included twenty-two income categories assessed by the tax collector. In 1710, a self-assessed *dixième* income tax was imposed, which was raised to a *vingtième*, or 5 percent income tax, in 1750, with a second imposed in 1756 and a third in 1760. Indirect national taxes included those raked in by the government monopolies on salt and tobacco, along with customs and excises.

Louis XV received only a portion of the taxes annually raised in France.[45] While intendants collected the direct taxes, farmers-general, who bid for the privilege, gathered the indirect taxes. The farmers-general grew rich on the difference between their bids and the amounts they pried from the peasants and other unfortunates. During the 1750 to 1756 lease, the farmers-general annually raised an average 122.2 million livres, of which they paid 101.6 million to the royal treasurer, 3.0 million in related royal expenditures, 3.6 million for the *frai de régie* (public company expense), and 2.0 million in hidden charges for obtaining the lease, while pocketing at least 12.0 million. A typical tax year was 1750 when Versailles received 104.6 million livres in revenue, of which 28.2 million came from *gabelle* (salt tax), 10.8 million from farmers-generals, 36.6 million from mostly excise taxes, 12.6 million from *domaines de France* (non-Royal lands), a measly 1.8 million from *domaines de l'occident* (New France), and 12.6 million from the tobacco monopoly.[46] France was actually lightly taxed—royal tax revenues were only about 15 percent of the nation's economy. But, as in most countries, the tax burden fell heaviest on those least able to pay. The aristocrats, bourgeoisie, and church enjoyed a range of exemptions designed to keep the taxman at bay. In addition to the royal tax burden, the church commandeered annual tithes from professed Catholics, Huguenots, and skeptics alike.[47]

The intendants and farmers-generals could only collect so much money. Unfortunately, even in peacetime revenues were only one-quarter of expenses. To make up that difference, Louis XV increasingly relied on Pompadour's close friends, Joseph Pâris-Duverney and Jean Pâris-Montmartel. The Paris brothers largely financed both the War of Austrian Succession and the Seven Years' War. All along it was clear to most observers that "the Paris [brothers] want only valets in the ministry; at the cost of a little work and a few successes they attain their end, which is to continue the war, make much money out of it, and so master the State."[48]

Being the comptroller general was a thankless task that exhausted, humiliated, and often disgraced each man unfortunate enough to be placed in that position by the king. France's wartime finance ministers included Jean Moreau de Séchelles, who succeeded Machault on July 30, 1754; followed by François Marie Peyrenc de Moras on April 24, 1756; then Jean Nicholas de Boullongne on March 25, 1757; the short-tenured Étienne de Silhouette on March 4, 1759; and finally Henri Bertin on November 21, 1759, through December 1763. None of those comptrollers general acquired fame as a financial wizard. Indeed, each was dismissed as an amateur at best and often condemned as a bumbler, thief, or outright traitor. It was not all their fault. Each was in far over his fiscal head. Then, just when a minister was acquiring some rudimentary understanding of his job, the king would yank him from office and plunk another down in his place.

The core problem was that France was deeply in debt when the Seven Years' War began, and the debt and the government's credit only worsened with each year of war. On the war's eve, Versailles's accumulated debt was 819.6 million livres, upon which was owed 40.98 million livres in interest payments for 1753 alone.[49] The Seven Years' War cost twice as much as the War of Austrian Succession, while taxes increased at only half the rate. From 1756 through 1762, Versailles raised 1,105,616,261 livres and spent three times that much. In 1758, for example, Versailles's budget called for 237 million livres in spending, of which 84 million livres went to the army, 25 million livres to the navy, and 45 million livres for debt service. The real cost for the army and navy combined may have been as high as 160 million livres. No kingdom wasted money more spectacularly than France. Each soldier on campaign cost Versailles three times more than those of Prussia.[50]

Every year a vast treasure flowed from France through spending by armies and navies serving abroad and subsidies to allies. The average of 200,000 French troops and 70,000 mercenaries that served in foreign lands from 1757 to 1763 annually cost around 24.5 million and 12.5 million livres, respectively. Subsidies to French allies annually cost another 55 million livres. By the late 1750s, Versailles was broke; any taxes went to creditors who refused to loan the government any more money. By 1760, Versailles owed officers and soldiers alike as much as three years of wages. The arrears sapped the army's spirit to mutiny's brink.[51]

How then did Versailles pay for its war? In previous struggles such as the Thirty Years' War (1618–48), War of the League of Augsburg (1689–97), War of the Spanish Succession (1701–13), and War of the Austrian Succession (1740–48), the king raised money through forced loans and higher taxes.[52] At each war's end, the king simply repudiated his debts. Financiers approached any war with enormous trepidation knowing they would most likely lose rather than make huge amounts of money.

Versailles would break with its rapacious tradition during the Seven Years' War. Tax hikes were relatively limited during the war, and no debt repudiations accompanied peace. Louis and his ministers dared not do more. Parlement had grown increasingly assertive. Three times during the war—in 1756, 1759, and 1763—Louis raised or prolonged taxes to avert bankruptcy. Each time the Paris parlement resisted and a crisis ensued. Although each time the king eventually used a lit de justice to force parlement to register his taxes, he did so at an enormous political and psychological cost. Parlement retaliated by rejecting more laws and dragging Louis into a perpetual, humiliating tug-of-war that diverted him from the hunt and his mistresses, not to mention presiding over the war.

The comptroller general financed the war more by raising loans than taxes. Charging interest on loans was illegal in France. Financiers skirted the law by describing interest as "rente." Versailles capped its own official interest rate on government borrowing at 5 percent. But while these low interest rates saved Versailles money in the short run, it made borrowing increasingly difficult. As the war dragged on and debts soared, public credit dried up as private financiers either ran out of money or invested it elsewhere for higher returns. Virtually no one wanted to lend Versailles money. Even Spanish King Ferdinand VI refused Louis XV's request for a loan in 1757.

France increasingly lacked even enough gold and silver with which to mint coins. In 1759, the treasury minted 50 million livres of gold and silver coins, mostly from plate and jewelry. It tried to stretch its precious metals by devaluing the livre from 8.22 grams to 4.45 grams an ounce. But the reserves continued to fall. In 1760, a desperate Louis sent most of Versailles's silver to the mint, and politely insisted that his courtiers to do the same. Thus were exquisite treasures lost forever to extend the killing a little longer.[53]

While Versailles's finances may have been a disaster, France's economy was actually humming powerfully as Louis plunged it into yet another war. Europe and France were in the midst of a long cycle of economic expansion that the war would merely ripple. Excellent grain harvests brought down prices during the war; trade and industry flourished.[54] The endless government spending and debt had a bright side as they helped fuel the steady expansion of France's economy throughout the eighteenth century at a lumbering 0.3 percent annual rate that actually swelled slightly to 0.4 percent during the 1750s and 1760s. The money supply exceeded economic growth, rising from 500 million livres in 1683 to as much as 1.5 billion by the 1750s. Prices rose 60 percent from 1716 to 1788. This modest but steady growth rate would tally slightly higher, perhaps by 0.7 percent annually, had the official statistics somehow included the rampant smuggling and income hidden from tax collectors.[55]

Versailles's policy of mercantilism worked—France enjoyed huge trade surpluses throughout most of the eighteenth century. Trade expanded faster than the economy, anywhere from 1.0 to 1.7 percent annually from 1716 to 1788; it rose in value from 215 million livres in 1715 to 600 million in 1759. On the Seven Years' War's eve, 88 percent of French trade was with Europe, 8 percent with its overseas colonies and other regions, and 3 percent with the Levant. During the war, while its overseas trade plummeted, its continental trade rose while domestic industries made up the difference, all to the economy's net gain.[56]

Of course, very little of the wealth France created trickled down to those who created most of it; poverty imprisoned nine of ten people. In 1755, Louis employed the sweat and coin of 25 million subjects in France alone, a number that increased to 26.1 million by 1765. Only 4.4 million, or 18 percent, of France's population swelled the cities. Among the 800,000 people who crowded Paris were 100,000 servants, 40,000 prostitutes, 6,000 wigmakers, and 20,000 beggars.[57]

The vast majority—82 percent—of the king's subjects lived in the countryside. At midcentury more than half of the peasants tilled another man's land; about one million, 5 percent, were serfs tied to a lord who took up to a third of their harvest, demanded several days annual corvée, or unpaid labor, and imposed a range of fees for such privileges as marriage, milling or storing their grain, and so on. Plows were mostly wooden; one of three hectares was left fallow each year rather than rotated as in England.[58]

From the windows of their gilded coaches rumbling across France, the aristocrats could gaze with ennui or shame on the peasants who were "no longer anything but poor slaves, beasts of burden fastened to a yoke, moving where they are whipped to go, caring for nothing, troubled for nothing provided they can eat and sleep in their own homes. . . . The people in the provinces are becoming more barbarous, coarse; vices will become more violent, industry less strong, no emulation, no civility; the arts will die out . . . despotism will strengthen itself, and that is what those wretched ministers at Court are seeking."[59]

In short, France was on the road to revolution with no leader or institutions capable of reversing that course. Argenson predicted "the destruction of the kingdom" as "all things are falling to pieces; and private passions burrow their way beneath the surface to undermine and destroy us."[60] The irrepressible urge to destroy the institutions and people who exploited them had not yet rendered that mass poverty in the cities and countryside combustible. Yet that revolution would come just a quarter century after the 1763 Treaty of Paris ended the Seven Years' War, provoked by the pent-up explosion over ancient abuses and a state bankrupted by a succession of ruinous wars. That revolution would be more violent and destructive than even the gloomiest Cassandras had feared.

Ironically, the ideas that eventually destroyed the regime were being encouraged among circles within the court itself. Eighteenth-century France was the age of the salons presided over by brilliant, charismatic women. Wit, learning, decorum, and ridicule reigned at such gatherings. Philosophes, painters, writers, architects, and all manner of other artists and thinkers received or were denied acclaim and patronage. Denis Diderot explained that those great women "accustom us to discuss with charm and clearness the driest and thorniest subjects. We talk to them unceasingly; we wish them to listen; we are afraid of tiring or boring them. Hence we develop a particular method of explaining ourselves easily, and this method passes from conversation into style."[61] It was not just the aristocracy who enjoyed such intellectual delights. The six hundred cafés of Paris in 1750 served as salons for the petite bourgeois and bohemians.[62]

Two great writers and thinkers personified the Enlightenment burning through mid-eighteenth-century France. Through their respective prolific arrays of novels, plays, essays, poems, histories, and autobiographies, François-Marie Arouet Voltaire appealed more to the depth of man's reason and Jean-Jacques Rousseau more to his feelings. Most of polite society despised Rousseau as thoroughly as they toasted Voltaire. The different receptions had more to do with their manners than their ideas. Voltaire was the epitome of polish, wit, cheer, and wealth; Rousseau was boorish, bohemian, and ill-at-ease. Voltaire was also an unabashed admirer of "enlightened monarch" Frederick II;

that enthusiasm was infectious and complicated French policy after the war in North America spread to Europe.

France's artistic world was as much in turmoil as its leadership and policies, with a profusion of styles, ideas, and personalities all competing for patrons at once. The Baroque of Louis XIV was giving way to the ornate swirls and arabesques of Rococo under Louis XV, an apt metaphor for the effete confusion of his policy making. This style and spirit inspired all French arts and crafts.

Painters did not want for patronage. State and church, nobles and bourgeois, tapestry and porcelain factories commissioned either paintings or designs. Then there were the rival Académie Royale des Beaux-Arts and Académie de Saint Luc to award prizes. Most large cities in the provinces hosted their own academies. The court's frivolity, decadence, and artifice was best captured by Antoine Watteau, François Boucher, Jean Marc Nattier, Maurice Quentin de La Tour, and Jean-Honoré Fragonard. Boucher, Nattier, and La Tour all left us portraits of Pompadour herself. In contrast, Jean-Baptiste Greuze and Jean Baptiste Siméon Chardin preserved the bourgeois lives of hard work, piety, and family. Other painters immersed themselves into different genres—such as Hubert Robert's depictions of ruins, François-Hubert Drouais's portraits of beautiful ladies and children, and Claude-Joseph Vernet's famous paintings of seaports depicting daily life at that time.

French sculpture of that era owes much to Pompadour. Among the celebrated works that appeared amidst the war were Jean-Baptiste Pigalle's *Deese de l'Amitie* (1753), for which Pompadour herself modeled, and Étienne-Maurice Falconet's *Baigneuse* (1757). From 1749, Pompadour patronized porcelain at Vincennes; in 1752, she moved the works to Sevres. Leading French painters created scenes and designs for French faience or porcelain. Pompadour's extravagances sparked buying frenzies in all the arts. Juste Aurèle Meissonnier created masterpieces in interior decoration, architecture, furniture, silverware, watches, and other fine crafts. He had many imitators. Cities specialized in materials and styles of dress, such as velvet from Amiens and silk from Lyon, Nimes, and Tours, or tapestries such as Les Gobelins from Paris.

Amidst the Seven Years' War, wealthy Parisians fought a different struggle over whether French or Italian music was superior. The court split over the issue. Pompadour favored the French; the queen allied with the Italians. Jean-Philippe Rameau was France's champion in the music war; he not only wrote operas and concertos but also developed musical theory. Italian music's champion was none other than Jean-Jacques Rousseau. In addition to pamphlets expounding his music ideas, Rousseau wrote an opera, *Les Muses Galantes*, which is not performed today.

Voltaire was that age's leading French playwright, above rivals like Prosper Jolyot de Crébillon, Pierre Carlet de Chamblain de Marivaux, and Jean-François Marmontel. Such works and a profusion of operas and lighter works appeared at the Théâtre-Francais, Comédie-Francaise, Théâtre des Italiens, and Opéra Comique, or at châteaux including, of course, Versailles.

Of all the arts, architecture was the most avant-garde as it underwent a stylistic revolution from the glittering rococo arabesques of Louis XV to the classic austerity of his grandson Louis XVI. Excavations at Herculaneum (1748) and Pompeii (1748–63) had sparked a classical revival that would eventually engulf all the arts. Nothing did more for the new style than the teachings of Jacques-François Blondel at the Royal Academy of Architecture, Julien-David Le Roy's *Le plus beaux monuments de la Grèce* (1754), and Anne-Claude de Tubières, comte de Caylus's *Recueil d'antiquities egyptiennes, etrusques, grecques, romaines, et gauloises* (1752–67). The Church of Saint Genevieve, later renamed the Panthéon, was the first great building erected on classical principles; Jacques-Germain Soufflot began it in 1757. The greatest classic architect was Ange Jacques Gabriel, who remodeled Compiègne and built the opera house and right wing of Versailles and the École Militaire.

The French language dominated Europe's world of court, diplomacy, love, and belles lettres. Literate French devoured their nation's literature. Paris alone had 360 bookshops and dozens of publishers. French literature's most important impact was in ideas rather than stories, characters, or styles. The eighteenth century was the golden age of French political philosophy. Among the philosophes' illustrious ranks were Voltaire; Rousseau; Charles Louis de Secondat, baron de la Brède et de Montesquieu; Denis Diderot; Jean-Claude-Adrien Helvétius; and Paul Heinrich Dietrich von Holbach, among many others. The worlds the philosophes explored were real (empiricism) rather than ideal (metaphysics). They powerfully criticized society and proposed alternatives. They dared to blast the church and court for their corruption, decadence, oppression, and exploitation, though most tiptoed around the king. As for God, some philosophes like Voltaire, Rousseau, Diderot, and Helvétius did believe in some sort of divine, universal spirit; others like Holbach and Julien de La Mettrie were outright atheists. And for government, the philosophes largely agreed that some sort of constitutional monarchy best suited France and most societies. As with most thinkers, the philosophes' perspectives tended to develop over time. Overall, their arguments intellectually strengthened parlement's hand in its struggle with the king and adored the nation's then enemy Frederick II, all to the detriment of France's war effort.

Some philosophes urged economic rather than political reforms. Unchain the economy from its straitjacket of guilds, taxes, tolls, and regulations, and free its peasants from landlords, debts, and ignorance, then entrepreneurs and farmers would lead France into unimagined heights of prosperity. So argued physiocrats like Jean-Claude Vincent de Gournay, François Quesnay, Victor Riqueti, marquis de Mirabeau, Holbach, Anne-Robert-Jacque, baron de l'Aulne Turgot, and Pierre du Pont de Nemours.

The physiocrats influenced, of all people, the king himself. In a celebrated exchange, Louis XV asked Quesnay what he would do if he were king. "Nothing," the physiocrat replied. The king asked, "Who then would govern?" "The laws," Quesnay asserted, meaning those of supply, demand, and human nature. Impressed with Quesnay's argument, Louis issued a decree on September 17, 1754, that abolished all restrictions and tolls on the grain trade. Prices did indeed drop, along with profits. The grain merchants howled in protest. Louis dared not free the economy any further. France has spurned the physiocrats' advice ever since.[63]

A few called not for reform but revolution. Communists like Jean Meslier, Rousseau (in his early work), and André Morellet sought to abolish all private property and create a just society based on Morellet's ringing phrase "from each according to his abilities to each according to his needs." Rousseau later muted his youthful enthusiasm and celebrated reform instead. That did not halt the radicals from using those communist ideas during the revolution.

In addition to politics, religion, and economics, the Enlightenment illuminated new frontiers in mathematics, physics, chemistry, astronomy, geology, botany, zoology, geography, psychology, medicine, and evolution. The French pantheon of scientists included Joseph Louis Lagrange, Antoine Lavoisier, Pierre Simon Laplace, Étienne Bonnot de Condillac, George Louis de Buffon, René Antoine de Réaumur, Victor Riqueti, marquis de Mirabeau, and Louis Antoine de Bougainville. The expanding volumes of editor Diderot's *Encyclopédia* exemplified the philosophes' ambition to know all knowable subjects and speculate over the rest. The first volume appeared in 1751; by 1756, six volumes were out thanks to Pompadour but subject to censorship. In 1758, church and state conservatives agreed to outlaw the *Encyclopédia*. Diderot finessed the suppression by getting it published in Holland. Twenty-eight volumes eventually appeared. It is said that the eighteenth century was the last in which the learned could learn all known knowledge. That insatiable hunger to know all with its accompanying questioning, skepticism, and criticism defied and undermined the power of France's church, state, and king, Louis XV.

Consequences

The "absolute" monarch was anything but absolute. Indeed, Louis XV was a prisoner, not only of Pompadour's ambitions and prejudices; the overbearing but mostly mediocre rivals in his council; a stifling bureaucracy; parlements that jousted with him for power; a church that interfered much in politics and gave little in return; the court's intrigues, extravagances, and ridicule; a financial system in which revenues fell further behind spending despite an expanding economy; and an "Enlightenment" that celebrated parlement and Frederick II to Louis's detriment, but also of his own vacillating personality. Policies did, of course, emerge from that system. But they tended to be insipid compromises that would stave off defeat a little longer rather than the decisive military and diplomatic efforts that might have brought victory.

New France would be lost as much by inept leadership at Versailles as by inept leadership on the far-flung battlefields of land and sea. As will be seen, had Versailles pursued different policies, the war might have ended quite differently. But given the array of political, economic, social, religious, and cultural forces hemming him in on all sides, Louis XV could only agree to do what he did.

CHAPTER 2

War, Wealth, and the Great Powers

I think the French are living in Europe on credit like some rich man who is growing unconsciously poor.

Voltaire to Frederick II

Everywhere the weak loathe the powerful before whom they crawl, and the powerful treat them like flocks whose wool and flesh are for sale.

Martin in Voltaire, *Candide*

The rivalry between France and Britain in North America cannot be understood apart from the ever shifting alliances, threats, and interests among Europe's great powers. The wars in North America and Europe reflected and shaped one another. Mercantilism was a strategy that recognized the vital relationship between wealth and power.[1] Under mercantilism, government and business worked as partners to develop the realm's wealth and power. The government promoted industries with subsidies and protection from competitive imports; invested in economic infrastructure like roads, ports, and canals; encouraged trade; granted monopolies as incentives for investors to tackle risky ventures; patronized scientists and inventors;

imposed navigation laws that required trade to be carried in that kingdom's ships; and built a larger army and navy to seize colonies for
markets, commodities, and position. The strategy's success was mea-
sured by the trade and payments accounts. If more money flowed
in than out of the kingdom, and more products were exported than
imported, and ever more revenues flowed into state coffers from tariffs and taxes, then mercantilism was working. The government then
reinvested some of that money into a stronger navy and army to protect and enlarge the empire, and most of the rest into industries, infrastructure, and inventions, which in turn reaped yet more wealth for
the nation and revenues for the government.

Mercantilism made explicit what had been intuitively understood
and practiced by governments all along: there was no ideological alternative to mercantilism. By the mid-eighteenth century, free markets
did not exist in practice and they only vaguely existed in physiocratic
theory. Mercantilism could only be practiced systematically or not, well
or poorly; it could not be avoided.

By most measures, French mercantilism was an enormous success. No one mastered and implemented mercantilism more skillfully than Louis XIV's principal minister, Jean-Baptiste Colbert. Few
French statesmen have shaped and advanced their nation's power
in Europe and the world as much as Colbert. He recognized that
trading companies could advance French interests at all times,
while armies and navies should be unleashed only as a last resort.
He blunted Dutch and English power by imposing tariffs to protect domestic industries from voracious foreign rivals and by form-
ing the East India Company, West India Company, Company of the
North, Levant Company, and Senegal Company to square off with
foreign trading companies. All would have been well had Louis XIV
not been a megalomaniac. Alas, Louis XIV milked the profits of the
mercantilism strategy' to finance his wars, which became increasingly
disastrous after 1689. Despite these shortcomings, Colbert had his
imitators not only among his successors at Versailles but to varying
degrees in every council of state across Europe. Yet no French minister who followed, except perhaps Fleury, practiced mercantilism as
well as Colbert.

If Colbert led in the art of creating wealth, another Frenchman helped revolutionize power's lesser half, the art of waging war.[2] More than anyone, François Michel le Tellier, marquis de Louvois—Louis XIV's war minister of twenty-three years until his death in 1691—was responsible for stamping the pattern of early modern warfare whereby professional ministries raised and directed professional armies and navies. Louvois was an administrative genius who recruited, trained, fed, clothed, armed, and sent into the field 400,000 French troops a year, up from 175,000 when he entered the ministry, nearly twice the number France fielded in the Seven Years' War. In addition, Louvois was responsible for founding a medical corps that accompanied the armies and the Hôtel des Invalides where cripples could recover in Paris. He standardized artillery batteries and engineer companies. He abolished remaining feudal military customs and institutions and established a nascent chief-of-staff system headed by a marshal.

To survive, the other capitals across Europe eventually emulated Louvois's innovations. That professionalism, however, only went so far. Governments lacked the power to mobilize their entire realm for war. Supplies were hard to gather and to send to the front on the wretched roads. Armies were firmly tied to their supply depots or magazines. Each campaign was preceded by the buildup of supplies at magazines just behind the army. As armies slowly advanced, huge new magazines sprouted in a lengthening chain behind them. As a rule, generals ranged their armies no more than two days from their bread ovens, which were no more than a three-day wagon haul from a magazine where the grain stores and other supplies were stockpiled; magazines in turn were ideally no more than ten days beyond the last navigable river. Campaigns were waged mostly during the summer when forage was most abundant. Road conditions and dead grass made supply and thus campaigning in winter nearly impossible, though Frederick II occasionally tried. Communications were tenuous. The relays of post horses took a week to carry a message and reply between Versailles and Potsdam. Further slowing warfare's march were the vast fortresses that ringed many cities, which could only be taken after long, elaborate sieges. Even when armies and navies met in open combat, kings and their officers were reluctant to risk all for a decisive battle because of the expense of raising and maintaining the forces.

As a result, war was probably never fought more like a chess game than during the eighteenth century. Lacking the power or will to annihilate their enemy, leaders waged war not for conquest but for position. Weeks and sometimes months of maneuver were punctuated by one or two pitched battles or sieges. Usually with the first frost, armies withdrew into winter quarters. This pattern of warfare varied little in North America despite the impact of wilderness and Indians.

The ends of war were as limited as the means. Dynasty rather than ideology sparked most eighteenth century wars as royal families feuded over vacant thrones. Three of that century's greatest wars were fought for the crowns of Spain (1701–13), Poland (1732–35), and Austria (1740–48). In that era of divine monarchs, the major powers might war to conquer provinces or minor principalities, but it would have been bad form indeed to destroy and subject one another.

Like the organization and strategy for war, tactics changed significantly. Tactics adapt to technologies. The checkerboard formations of pikemen alternating with musketeers armed with heavy, slow-firing, inaccurate matchlocks of the sixteenth and seventeenth centuries gave way to ranks of troops armed with lighter-weight, bayoneted muskets during the eighteenth century. All along the accuracy, fire rate, and durability of cannon gradually improved.

Yet once the armies massed onto a battlefield, their commanders were limited to a handful of means to resolve the issue. Battlefield formations consisted of battalions lined end to end, each with its troops in three ranks, batteries studding the long front, cavalry squadrons anchoring each flank, and a reserve of grenadiers, hussars, and dragoons behind the center to exploit any breakthrough. Artillery opened fire along the line, with concentrated batteries firing on those enemy battalions at the focus of attack. When a general deemed that his artillery had done enough damage, he might order a cavalry attack followed by an advance of his entire line with more troops massed against the place he hoped to punch through. Ideally, the attack drove the enemy from the field. Often a commander watched as the enemy repelled his army with the battalion ranks depleted and disordered. Frederick the Great innovated the era's warfare by employing his troops in an oblique rather than linear formation. He won most of his battles by sending forward against the enemy's weakest flank his own reinforced flank first, followed by his center and, finally, his other flank.

The Age of Reason governed both the construction of fortresses and their capture, which were developed into high art by yet another French genius, Sébastien Le Prestre, de Vauban. A standard siege involved the digging of the first "parallel" trench studded with batteries about six hundred yards from the enemy. From there, several trenches would be zigzagged forward to within four hundred yards of the enemy, where a second parallel of batteries would be dug. Depending on how resistant a fortification's walls were to artillery, trenches might be snaked forward to a third parallel two hundred yards from the enemy position. Few walls, no matter how thick and low, could long withstand such point-blank pounding. The defenders usually tried to disrupt the siege with sorties against the enemy trenches.

Each siege, of course, depended on the relative numbers of troops, cannon, and supplies, and relative amounts of skill, will, and time split between the defender and attacker. The longer a defender held out, the more he weakened the besieger and raised the chance for rescue. Honor demanded that a defender fight at least until the enemy artillery had breached his wall; only then could he honorably capitulate. When a besieged commander wished to negotiate, he had his drummers mount the walls and beat the chamade. Officers, often blindfolded, were then exchanged to discuss terms. If the defending commander remained defiant, the besieger ordered an assault on the breach. Troops that had successfully attacked a town were usually rewarded by being allowed to sack it, a custom involving mass looting, rape, and mayhem.

Naval wars were also limited in strategy and tactics. Squadron commanders could only choose the direction and time of attack; the tactics were predestined. Each navy bound its commanders with some version of England's Permanent Fighting Instructions—the first version dates to 1691, and a second, which all navies emulated, emerged in 1703—which stifled initiative. Sea battles were fought by neat lines of ships that approached one another, exchanged broadsides, then sailed away. Technology largely determined these tactics. The limited

ability to communicate among ships made rigid battle orders necessary. There was a financial rationale as well; like armies, navies were
too expensive to risk in a decisive battle. The cost of this caution, of
course, was the inability to adapt to changing opportunities or threats.
Thus, instead of wiping out the enemy's warships and then its merchant ships, the primary duty of one's own fleet was to protect trade
and, if engaged, fire back before sailing to the horizon.

Like armies, navies holed up their ships in port during winter. This
practice was complicated in the western hemisphere. When the Saint
Lawrence froze over, the fleets had to sail back to a French port or
a Caribbean colony. The Caribbean, however, also could not succor
ships all year; its westward winds from May to October, capped from
August to October by the hurricane season, influenced the pattern of
warfare there. The English and French squadrons would sail north to
their respective American and Canadian ports during the dangerous
summer months and then sail south to the Caribbean for the winter.

That twist in naval strategy was not the only North American anom-
aly. Indeed, the art of making money and fighting on land in North
America would prove even more unfamiliar and challenging to European patterns, a reality that Versailles's ministers never fully grasped.

The French Art and Science of War

During the Seven Years' War, Versailles was barely capable of waging
war in Europe, let alone in North America.[3] France's greatest want
was the political and military leadership vital for victory. Most ministers were mediocrities. Yet even those few skilled leaders who took the
helm of a ministry found themselves mired in a bureaucratic, psychological, and political morass. Experience, continuity, and vision in a
minister was no panacea for the problems plaguing the kingdom.

Ideally, states wage war with their diplomatic and military strategies
working in harness. France's first two foreign ministers during the war
failed, to varying degrees, to conceive and wield diplomatic offensives
that could have exploited the initial military successes. Antoine-Louis
Rouillé was foreign minister until June 1757, when Louis replaced him

with François-Joachim de Pierre, abbé de Bernis. Bernis lost favor with Pompadour and was retired in December 1758 in favor of Étienne-François, duc de Choiseul. Had Choiseul's gifted hand been at the tiller of state from the war's beginning, its course might well have turned out quite differently. But Louis named him foreign minister when France had largely lost the war. All that remained was for Choiseul to limit the defeat. In October 1761, Choiseul stepped aside for his cousin, César-Gabriel de Choiseul-Chevigny, duc de Praslin, but continued to rule through him.[4]

France's war minister during the war's first four years was another capable leader stifled by the system. Marc Pierre de Voyer de Paulmy, comte d'Argenson, was named to the position in 1743 and held it until he offended Pompadour and was sent packing in February 1757. Though clearly competent, he was simply overwhelmed by the myriad of problems afflicting France; how much his pro-Frederick sentiments impeded his policies cannot be known. Argenson was replaced by his nephew and understudy, Marc-René de Voyer, marquis de Paulmy d'Argenson—an unfortunate choice. His inept tenure lasted little more than a year. Louis named Charles Fouquet, duc de Belle Isle, war minister in March 1758. Though a skilled general, Belle Isle was no more able than his predecessors at managing that unwieldy bureaucracy. Choiseul took over the war ministry when Belle Isle died in January 1761.

The marine ministry suffered the worst turnover and leadership. Jean-Baptiste de Machault d'Arnouville served until February 1757, when he lost the same fight with Pompadour that had toppled Argenson. He was replaced by François Marie Peyrenc de Moras, who was succeeded in May 1758 by Claude Louis d'Espinchal, marquis de Massiac. In October of that year, Massiac was replaced by Nicholas René Berryer, who clung to power until October 1761, when Choiseul took that position as well. For six crucial months, from June to October 1758, a political quirk prevented Massiac from being officially named a minister, and thus he was barred from the Council of State—not that his presence there would have really mattered.

As with any government, the war minister was in charge of land warfare and issued the general campaign plan; the generals filled in the details in the field. Belle Isle nicely captured the relationship: "One cannot command an army from Versailles. All that the minister can and should do is to make known to the general the political and military objectives and the King's manner of thinking."[5] The value of these plans depended on accurate information about the intentions and capabilities of enemies and allies alike. French intelligence was actually quite adept at extracting military and political information via a network of diplomats and spies in each capital and foreign army. The information's accuracy, however, varied wildly. In the field, deserters were the most common source of information; they tended to exaggerate numbers up and conditions down. Even when Versailles or the field commanders got their hands on reliable information, they rarely seemed to make the best of it.

Complicating France's ability to wage war on land was the fact that no permanent French army existed, only infantry regiments, cavalry squadrons, and artillery batteries. As if the need to create a new army for each campaign were not challenging enough, this army would have not one but two commanders, a general who planned the grand strategy and tactics, and an intendant who served as the chief of staff and quartermaster. Wielding royal powers to requisition supplies, it was the intendant's duty to organize, mobilize, and supply the army. Once this task was complete, the commander joined the army and led it on campaign. At times this dual command worked well; more often than not different strategies, jealousy, intrigue, and ambitions caused the commander and intendant to war with each other as much as with the foreign enemy.

Yet another burden was that the French army was top-heavy with officers. The ratio of officers to troops was one to eleven in the French army compared to Prussia's much more efficient one to twenty-nine. France's bloated officer corps weakened its fighting ability. Pay for that largely parasitic body drained the army budget of money to buy food, munitions, and uniforms for the soldiers. In 1758, there were 3 princes of royal blood, 5 other princes, 11 dukes, 44 counts, 38 marquis, 14 chevaliers, and 6 barons among the 181 top officers. That year, the French army included 16 marshals, 172 lieutenant générales, 176 maréchaux-de-camp, and 389 brigadiers.[6]

The war ministry approved all ranks of captain and above. The officers' ranks were not confined to the nobility. All commoners needed was lots of money and connections. An infantry colonelcy could cost as much as 75,000 livres while an even more desirable cavalry colonelcy might reach 100,000 livres. The bourgeoisie accounted for between one-third to one-half of the officers. Up to twenty-two officers of an infantry regiment and seven of a cavalry squadron could be promoted from the ranks. Foreigners squeezed into the officer corps beside native-born Frenchmen.[7]

Regardless of their backgrounds, all those officers drained France's army of money, efficiency, spirit, and supplies, especially the latter. Officers could draw rations according to their respective ranks. A lieutenant general, for instance, received eighty men's rations. Officers pocketed huge profits as they sold that food back to malnourished soldiers and civilians alike. As if this practice were not corrupt enough, most officers drew the additional rations of nonexistent soldiers on the muster rolls. These practices simply mirrored what the aristocracy did to the entire kingdom.[8] One officer described the army as "like the court: it is the seat of intrigues, jealousies, and bad faith."[9] Many officers tended to treat a campaign like an extended, extravagant picnic and debauch attended by thousands of servants rather than a means to destroy the enemy and advance their nation's interest. One participant recalled,

> There was no discipline, no subordination, no order on the march, in the camp, or even on the battlefield. The very subalterns had their mistresses with them, and the officers often left their men to accompany them on the march in their carriages. Everything that could contribute to the luxury of the officers was found in the French camp. . . . At one time there were twelve thousand wagons accompanying Soubise's army which belonged to sutlers and shopkeepers, though the army was not fifty thousand strong. . . . Balls were given in camp, and officers often left their posts to dance a minuet. They laughed at the orders of their leaders and only obeyed them when it suited them.[10]

Officers learned the art of war from personal experience and study. They could read a wide range of books by such masters as Maurice de Saxe, Frederick the Great, and Vauban.[11] Ironically, France's commanders in North America's wilderness better applied those lessons than its generals campaigning across Europe's familiar fields.

Toward the war's last years, officers began graduating from France's military academy, l'École Militaire. Pompadour deserves credit for its founding. For years, she had urged Louis to create an officer-training school. While France's war needs were probably paramount for her campaign, perhaps she also hoped to emulate the success of an earlier royal mistress, Madame de Maintenon, who had sweet-talked Louis XIV into creating the Saint Cyr school for girls of the nobility. Regardless of her motives, Pompadour succeeded in 1751 to get Louis not only to establish l'École Militaire but to decree that those officers of common blood could receive patents of nobility if they won a Cross of Saint Louis from valor on the battlefield. The era's greatest architect, Ange Jacques Gabriel, received the royal commission to design l'École Militaire. But the academy did not open until 1757, too late to affect France's military fortunes in the ongoing war.

France's military at once reflected and shaped French society. Its officers were cemented to tradition, etiquette, honor, and personal enrichment, and lorded their status contemptuously over the masses of common soldiers. The army numbered 157,000 when the war began, nearly five times more than Britain's 35,000 troops. During the war, the army peaked at 612,000 troops, which included 200,000 French and 70,000 foreign troops in the field, supplemented by 100,000 militiamen and 242,000 coast guards at home. That number may seem large but actually drained only 2 percent of France's population, 2.5 percent if the navy is included. About 1 million French, or 4 percent of the population, served during the war. Disease, battle, and desertion cost the army one of five men each year. This meant somehow scrounging up 38,000 new recruits to keep the total force of 270,000 regulars intact. This number was actually below the 650,000 regulars with 50,000 new annual recruits during the War of Spanish Succession or the 345,000 regulars with 49,000 new annual recruits during the War of the Austrian Succession.[12]

Each regiment was responsible for filling its own ranks. During the winter, officers scoured taverns and markets trying to drum up recruits for six-year enlistments. Versailles helped underwrite recruiting by giving 125 livres to arm and clothe each man dragged in. A regiment's colonel and often the other officers would chip in to pay each recruit an enlistment bonus, usually 75 livres. Each soldier then received a daily wage of 5 sous and 8 deniers, with deductions made for expenses like clothing and food.

The army did not take just anyone—exemptions were granted for physical or mental infirmities, age, and height, or for men from professions like trade or manufacturing. To be a soldier, one merely had to be between sixteen and forty years old and five feet one inch or taller. As the war ground on, the quality of recruits decayed noticeably and the price of enlistment bonuses soared. Each regiment could incorporate up to five enemy deserters in its ranks. Much of the army hailed from northeastern France, given that region's convenience to recruiting officers serving in Germany's killing fields. About two of three soldiers were peasants while the third came from a large town or city. Swiss, German, Irish, and other nationalities formed independent regiments within the French army.[13]

Regiments had from one to four battalions, each ideally numbering 31 officers and 525 men. Each battalion had one grenadier and one light infantry company, along with a gun crew for a four-pounder cannon, and two supply wagons. A company included a captain, a lieutenant, two sergeants, a drummer, and forty-seven men. The army's elite were the grenadiers and carabiniers, of which the very best entered the royal regiments. Until 1758, the artillery and engineers were combined under the Royal Corps of Artillery and Engineers, when war minister Belle Isle split the two into separate administrations.

Ideally, the army maintained a supply of sixty rounds per musket and two hundred rounds per cannon. Soldiers were issued either a 1728, 1746, or 1754 model musket produced at Charleville, Saint Étienne, or Tulle. The musket weighed about eleven pounds and fired a .69 caliber lead ball. Twelve commands forced troops to load and fire in unison. With proper training, a soldier could fire four rounds a minute. Cannon were forged at various ironworks throughout France. French guns were far more unwieldy than those of other nations. A French three-pounder cannon, for example, weighed 1,000 pounds while the Prussian and Austrian versions respectively weighed only 450 and 430 pounds. The heavier the gun, the worse its maneuverability on the battlefield and the more horses and forage it took to drag the gun there.

Feeding, clothing, sheltering, and arming several hundred thousand soldiers and sailors in France and elsewhere was a Sisyphean challenge. Versailles contracted those endless and intricate tasks out to private firms that bilked the government for all they could. It took at least one civilian worker to maintain every two soldiers in the field. Just to haul supplies to the 270,000 French troops on campaign took 23,000 horses and thousands of teamsters. It was as vital to feed draft animals and teamsters as it was soldiers. An army of 100,000 troops consumed 200,000 pounds of flour daily. The winter months were the toughest. Draft animals and cavalry horses emptied warehouses of hay and oats cut the previous summer. It was easier to lead the horses to grain than the opposite; to relieve the stress on supplies in Germany, each winter the army sent 20,000 horses back to France to live off local stores.[14]

Men could suffer death or maiming several ways, all gruesome. A 1762 survey at the Hôtel des Invalides found that musket fire accounted for 80 percent of all wounds; cannon fire, 11 percent; and bayonets, only 9 percent. Those men who were trampled by horses or whose heads were split like melons with sabers went unrecorded. Three times more soldiers, however, died from disease. The era's medicine was usually incapable of treating even minor ailments and often hastened the victim's death. Hospitals were vile cesspools of germs and viruses that killed forty of every one hundred dragged there.[15]

Discipline was harsh, with the death penalty threatened for desertion, marauding, and other crimes. It was rarely invoked. Soldiers were too valuable to shoot or hang as often as they legally deserved it. Instead, the accused might have to run a gauntlet of soldiers armed with iron ramrods or have his naked back whipped with a cat-o'-nine-tails. Yet despite, or perhaps because of, these severe penalties, thousands of men tried to desert each year. Many a deserter tried to make it to neutral Holland to sit out the war; by 1760 an estimated 12,000 deserters found refuge there.[16] Those in North America had to dodge

Indian war parties as they blundered through the wilderness to the British lines. Relatively few made it.

The Seven Years' War has been called "the most disastrous maritime war in French history," which "ended with the destruction of the navy as a fighting force."[17] That was no exaggeration. From 1754 to 1763, the French lost ninety-three warships, which collectively mounted 3,880 cannon. Of those ships, about one-third were ships of the line with fifty or more guns. Eighteen ships of the line and thirty-seven frigates were destroyed or captured in battle while nineteen ships of the line and nineteen frigates were wrecked or burned at anchor. In 1755, the French fleet lost in battle only a seventy-four and two sixty-fours, and lost none in 1756 or 1757. Then, during 1758 and 1759, the French lost seventeen seventy-fours and sixty-fours, half of its ships of the line.[18]

Many interrelated weaknesses contributed to that debacle.[19] The navy was the neglected stepson of French power. Versailles wanted all the prestige of an overseas empire but was not willing to create a navy powerful enough to supply and defend it. The French empire, however, did have a bureaucracy that was supposed to provide all it needed to flourish and expand. The marine ministry was responsible for administering colonial, naval, and trade affairs. These three duties were symbiotically linked; the navy protected commerce and colonies, which in turn produced revenues that could be reinvested in the fleet. The first navy secretary was named in 1547. More than a century would pass before a department was created by Colbert in 1669. The Naval Ordinance of 1689 outlined the marine ministry's duties. During the war, the marine ministry had eight bureaus—colonial, commerce, police, funds, classes, officers, archives, and accounts—each of which combined, to varying degrees, duties for the colonies and navy. In 1761, Choiseul consolidated the funds, accounts, and archives bureaus of the war and marine ministries and shifted the commerce bureau to the foreign ministry.

The marine ministry was split between two classes of officers, commanders (nobles of the sword) and administrators (nobles of the robe) whose duties overlapped and egos and interests clashed. The number of administrators peaked at 409 on November 1, 1758. About two-thirds of the administrators served in the three main arsenals of Brest, Rochefort, and Toulon; a fifth were divided between the central bureaus and the colonies; and the final fifth were dispersed among smaller arsenals, ports, and factories across France. Naval intendants served at Toulon, Marseille, Rochefort, Brest, and Le Havre. Colonial intendants were posted to Canada, Martinique, and Saint Domingue. Unlike the army, the navy was anything but top-heavy with officers; the number of naval officers rose from 715 in 1751 to peak at 1,005 in 1759 then dropped to 829 in 1763. About one-third of the corps served as marine officers, many of those in Canada.[20]

Spending for the navy fluctuated during the war. The navy's budget rose from 14,603,542 livres in 1753 to 15,424,262 livres in 1754; 24,897,472 livres in 1755; 42,959,888 livres in 1756; and 49,712,985 livres in 1757. Spending dropped to 40,949,164 livres in 1758; rose again to 51,800,243 livres in 1759; then plummeted to 17,289,289 in livres 1760 and 16,722,415 livres in 1761. It nearly doubled to 30,529,650 livres in 1762 when Spain entered the war.[21]

The building and repairing of ships devoured most of that budget.[22] Ships that escaped combat did not last long; a wooden ship's average life was a dozen years. After each long voyage, a ship's hull had to be scrapped and caulked, and its rotten timbers replaced. Neither the cannon forges nor the press-gangs ever provided all that was needed. Many a warship rotted at anchor for want of enough crew or guns to sail.

To build and repair its navy, Versailles had three large arsenals at Brest, Toulon, and Rochefort, and smaller ones at Le Havre, Dunkirk, Port Louis, Nantes, Bordeaux, Saint Malo, Marseille, and Port Mahon. Each arsenal was an industrial complex filled with dry docks, ropewalks, blacksmiths, woodworks, supply warehouses, sailmakers, caulkers, drillers, carpenters, hospitals, barracks, and offices. Workforces combined small numbers of skilled craftsmen with day laborers and convicts chained by twos. Work hours varied with the season but always lasted from sunrise to sunset.

Each arsenal suffered both unique and common limitations to fulfilling its mission. Located at Brittany's western tip, Brest had a deep harbor and immediate access to the Atlantic. Ships sailing from Brest to Canada had a jump on British warships based at Plymouth or Portsmouth. Yet Brest's isolation was as much a curse as a blessing. The immediate region was poor while the wretched roads connecting Brest with the rest of France could not handle the port's needs. Thus, virtually all its supplies arrived by ship, an advantage during peacetime. But Britain's ever-tighter blockade made the shipments increasingly subject to capture. Fires in December 1742 and January 1744 devastated most of the warehouses and workshops. Despite the infusion of millions of livres to rebuild the complex, Brest had not recovered its productivity. Still, Brest's shipyards built nearly two-thirds of the French fleet.

Toulon enjoyed a spacious harbor ringed by fortified hills. Its shipyards were productive and supplied most of the Mediterranean fleet's needs. Supplies were easily transported down the Rhone River from the hinterland. Of the three arsenals, Toulon's was the best managed and most easily supplied. Yet France's empire lay on the far shores of the Atlantic and Indian Oceans, not in the Mediterranean. However, the Toulon fleet did threaten British shipping in that sea and its bases at Gibraltar and Minorca.

Rochefort was a half dozen miles up the narrow Charente River, which flowed into a wide, shallow bay, and was easily supplied by ship from Nantes and Bordeaux, France's greatest merchant ports. The climate, alas, was unhealthy. Swarms of malarial mosquitoes descended on Rochefort from the surrounding marshes. Versailles failed to invest enough to arrest Rochefort's crumbling wharfs, warehouses, and machinery or to dredge its silted harbor.

Ideally, it took only eight months to construct a ship from laying its keel to hanging its sails. The average building time stretched to five years toward the war's end. Dismal and worsening management at all levels explains this plunge in productivity. Versailles failed to provide adequate wages, supplies, and equipment. Intendants and lesser officials pocketed vast fortunes meant for building ships and paying workers. Safety and health conditions were abysmal, accidents maimed hundreds, diseases killed thousands, and fires destroyed workshops and even ships. Strikes became more frequent as pay dwindled or stopped altogether. Theft was rampant, carrying away vital stores of wood, rope, tools, food, and other supplies. Hundreds of workers slipped away to distant inland provinces.[23]

French cannon forges were scattered across the country at a half dozen spots where iron ore could be mined and forest cut and burned for charcoal. The forges could not keep up with the soaring demand, and the quality of guns ranged from poor to dismal. French gunners stood a greater chance of being gruesomely killed or maimed from their own guns bursting than from enemy fire. Although Jean Maritz, a Swiss gun forger employed by France, had mastered cannon boring as early as 1742, Versailles did not force its forges to adopt the method until 1755, and the method did not become universal until near the war's end. By then, another problem arose—a lack of wood for charcoal as adjacent forests were clear-cut.[24]

Despite these problems, French ships were the world's best designed. With their square-rigged sails, streamlined hulls, and carefully spaced cannon, any French ship could theoretically outsail and outfight its British counterpart. The British tried to concentrate firepower in three-decked ships packed with eighty or more cannons. Such ships, however, were slow, maneuvered poorly, and in rough seas could not open their lower gunports. While the French had their own "first-rate" three-deckers, they recognized the flaws in such ships. During the 1740s and 1750s, the marine ministry concentrated on building double-decker twenty-four-pounder eighties and seventy-fours, designated "second-rate" but superior fighting and sailing vessels. In addition to these modern warships, the French still maintained a fleet of sixteen galleys in the Mediterranean, mostly to fulfill their traditional role of escorting ambassadors on their diplomatic missions.

But the French never matched in seamanship their mastery of design. Here, the British excelled. King George II's captains, officers, and crews were generally first-rate, able to maneuver their lumbering ships and hammer shot into enemy vessels. Abysmal morale ate away at the French navy's officers. A gerontocracy officered the navy; in 1749, the average age of its admirals was sixty-nine, hardly the age for the élan and imagination vital to winning battles. Worse, connections and seniority rather than naval victories secured promotion. Not only were officers miserly paid, but the marine ministry's worsening financial problems often meant that they received nothing for months. It was not unknown for officers to mix duty and private gain. A captain and his officers might typically buy a load of salt in France, use it for ballast, then amply profit from its sale in Canada.[25]

How did the navy fill its ships? Few volunteered for the service. Sailors found privateering and working for the India Company or other commercial ventures far more profitable and less deadly. The marine ministry had to rely on the draft and, as a last resort, press-gangs. The Naval Ordinance of 1689 required all able-bodied sailors between eighteen and sixty years of age to register with the marine ministry. Sailors in each coastal province were divided into three, four, or five classes, depending on its population. The number of classes called up to man the fleet depended on France's needs. Those registered were exempt from taxation, the billeting of troops in their homes, night watch, and civil proceedings against them for debt. Sailors not called into the navy received half pay and could sail with the merchant fleet.

During the Seven Years' War, the navy's manpower declined even faster than British guns, storms, and rot destroyed one French warship after another. It was an extremely serious problem. Without enough hands, a ship could not sail. Thus did supplies vital for Canada's survival sit for months in ships anchored in French ports. If a captain did manage to find enough hands to sail, he often lacked enough to fight when British warships appeared before him.

Capture was the most common cause of the loss of French seamen. From October 14, 1755, to November 11, 1762, the British took 64,373 French sailors, of which 8,499, or 13 percent, died in captivity. Though thousands who survived were exchanged, 25,793 remained prisoners when the Treaty of Paris was signed in 1763. Disease killed anywhere from one-quarter to one-third of those who served. The worst epidemic raged through Admiral Toussaint Guillaume La Motte-Picquet's fleet en route from Louisbourg back to Brest in the autumn of 1757. By the time it reached Brest on November 22, 4,000 sailors were sick, of which 1,600 would die. A further 12,000 died that winter as the disease spread through Brest and other ports. The navy never recovered its manpower during the war. Desertion depleted the ranks almost as severely as capture or death. Needless to say, a seaman's life was one of chronic drudgery, malnourishment, brutality, and misery, punctuated by moments of terror.[26]

The French navy was innocent of decisive battle tactics. With more daring captains, skilled gun crews, and able sailors, along with a fleet that eventually numbered three times that of the French, the British naturally sought battles of attrition. The French just as naturally followed tactics of fleeing engagements to survive and evade yet another day. The gunnery tactics complemented the different strategies. When a British ship or squadron closed in, its gun crews aimed at the enemy's waterlines to sink those ships. French gunners shot chain, dumbbell, and solid shot at the enemy's masts and rigging to slow the ship. As a result, the French lost every naval battle during the war except the battle of Minorca in May 1756 when Roland Michel Barrin La Galissonière's squadron defeated Admiral John Byng's. New France would be lost as much on the sea as in North America.

Finally, Versailles lacked a rational grand strategy that integrated its navy and empire. As historian James Pritchard put it, "Maritime commercial and colonial growth appeared to develop independently of foreign policy and without the development of a comprehensive naval strategy; it was not at all clear that any relations existed between naval and foreign policy. As a result, naval policy lagged behind new realities, remaining subject to the traditional continental orientations of French statesmen. The navy largely reacted to events that it did not influence."[27]

France's strategy, such as it was, centered on convoying supply fleets to Canada, Louisiana, the Caribbean islands, and other distant colonies. The warships accompanying the supply fleet often sailed *en flute*, with the main batteries stowed below as ballast and the deck packed with provisions or troops. This was not as risky as it may sound—the top deck's guns remained mounted for action, and the French ships could still usually outsail a British pursuer. The lower guns could be remounted for the return to France. Still, the convoy strategy was one of survival rather than victory.

The Imbalance of Power: Thwarting Enemies and Wooing Allies

When the word of the battle of Fort Necessity reached Versailles in late summer 1754, France's ministers asked several basic related questions. How could France contain England's latest threat to its North

American empire? In the likely event that war in North America spread to Europe and elsewhere, just which states would be France's likely enemies and which potential allies could be enticed? What military and diplomatic strategies could best serve French interests?[28]

For guidance, French policy makers recalled the century's shifting alliances, powers, reasons for war, strategies, and results. The distribution of power and ambitions among European states had changed little following the War of the Spanish Succession (1701–13). The Peace of Utrecht, which ended that war, included eleven treaties signed among the belligerents. These treaties mostly papered over rather than resolved outstanding conflicts; most subsequent wars of that century broke out over issues left unsettled by Utrecht.

International relations were never as fluid as they were from 1714 to 1756 as alliances formed, dissolved, and reformed. Yet there were some constants. France and England competed for markets and colonies in North America, the Caribbean, West Africa, and India. French ambitions in the Low Countries collided with those of England and Austria, making those two countries natural allies. Austria and Prussia battled for Germany. Spain struggled to fend off rapacious English merchants and privateers in the Caribbean. The Bourbons, Hapsburgs, and other ambitious royal families continued to jockey for heirless thrones.

The most recent war, that of the Austrian Succession, broke out in 1740 and was fought inconclusively by most European states for eight years until the Treaty of Aix-la-Chapelle ended it on October 18, 1748. That treaty was no more successful than previous treaties in resolving deep-rooted conflicts. In the end, most of blood and treasure was shed for nothing. The treaty required most belligerents to accept the status quo ante bellum in Europe, North America, and elsewhere. Thus did France surrender the chunk of the Austrian Netherlands it had bought at such an exorbitant price in blood. Versailles also agreed to accept the Hanoverians as England's legitimate royal dynasty and expel the Jacobite claimants to that throne from France. Though its concrete gains were limited, France enhanced its already daunting position as Europe's core power. French influence expanded by diplomacy in Poland, Saxony, and Sweden. Bourbons ruled the kingdoms of Spain, the Two Sicilies, and Savoy. England returned Cape Breton to France in exchange for Madras, India. Still, France's enduring legacy from the war was mostly mass graves and debt.

Some states and individuals did advance their interests. The biggest winner was Prussia which retained Silesia and Glatz, in return for which Frederick II agreed to accept Maria Theresa as Austria's empress and her husband Francis of Lorraine as Holy Roman Emperor Francis I. Ironically, Spain played a peripheral role in the war but won the most at the negotiation table—the Italian duchies of Parma, Gustalla, and Piacenza went to Don Philip, the husband of Louis XV's eldest daughter, Louise Elizabeth.

As with most treaties, Aix-la-Chapelle at once ended one war and sowed the seeds for the next. In the years leading up to the Seven Years' War, statesmen trapped themselves in a security dilemma's vicious cycle. Anticipating war, each kingdom sought allies and raised military budgets. The scramble for allies and greater military spending worsened tensions and made war all the more likely. The secret diplomacy and treaties contributed to the frenzied cycle of fear and alliance building. Reports of enemies colluding trickled back to state councils via rumors and spies. Those not privy acted on the worst possible threat. History allowed policy makers no other choice. No government could be trusted. Although some were more untrustworthy than others, all had at times violated agreements or switched sides for raison d'état. The closer states marched toward war's brink, the less power diplomats had to avert the plunge. Hoping to gain as much as possible by splitting the difference, governments demanded more than the other side could possibly yield honorably. Then, not wanting to appear weak, governments refused to split the differences they had created. By 1754, with varying degrees of unenthusiasm, each European state was bracing itself for the latest round of European warfare. As they prepared for war, they made war more likely.

Of all the great powers, none posed a worse threat to France than Britain. In peace and war alike, Whitehall, the palace complex that housed Britain's government, strove to fulfill the interrelated goals of containing French power and maintaining England's naval superiority.

English diplomats busied themselves at Europe's courts, swaying rulers and courtiers alike with bribes, arguments, and thinly disguised threats to turn them against France. In all, Britain's government, economy, navy, and empire were more efficient and powerful than those of France. These attributes, however, did not make England's victory in the Seven Years' War inevitable, only more likely. Indeed, Versailles might well have won the war in its early years had it more skillfully wielded its own enormous military and diplomatic power.

Britain's advantage over France was most obvious at sea. When the war began, Britain had three times as many warships. That gap widened each year as Britain produced more of its own ships and sank, captured, or bottled up in port more French ships. Unable to send enough troops and supplies to North America to hold it, Versailles eventually gave up trying to do so.

In contrast, Britain's army was only one-sixth the size of France's in 1754. That year's troops numbered 30,000 in forty-nine regiments, with two-thirds deployed in the British Isles and the rest scattered among the colonies. However, during the war, Britain closed the gap with France, quadrupling the army's size by 1760. Taking advantage of its superior sea power, Whitehall dispatched more regiments to North America until it eventually outnumbered the French army there by ten troops to one. Though France's North American commanders competently staved off the enemy's advance for seven years, inflicting numerous bloody defeats during that time, they were eventually crushed by the sheer number of British soldiers arrayed against them.

The asymmetry between French and British military power reflected the nations' vastly different geographies, economies, empires, threats, and traditions. For England, the army was the sword in the navy's hand. Naval superiority allowed Whitehall to project power around the world in amphibious raids and outright invasions of Canada, the Caribbean, West Africa, India, the Philippines, and the French coast itself. It enabled Britain to win the Seven Years' War by simultaneously destroying France's empire and aggrandizing its own.[29]

England outgunned France in more than naval power. Military power, of course, is rooted in economic power. The British Isles and empire far exceeded that of France in economic dynamism—the ability to find ever better ways to produce food; invent, manufacture, transport, and sell goods; and make and invest money. During the eighteenth century, England's economy was transformed by interrelated technological, agrarian, manufacturing, and financial revolutions.

Changes in the countryside helped promote changes in the factories and counting houses. Crops were rotated, steel ploughs increasingly used, marshes drained, livestock selectively bred, more productive seeds planted, and lands enclosed, all of which provided the extra food, workers, technologies, and money that helped fuel the start of the Industrial Revolution. The enclosure movement among the gentry consolidated land for livestock and crops, forcing subsistence tenants to move away. Many of those expelled provided extra hands for factories, ships, or regiments. For those allowed to stay on the land, though many remained tenants, serfdom was no more.

In industry, the guilds, which had protected the crafts and craftsmen but stifled innovation, had disappeared. Scores of inventions applied to manufacturing allowed Britain to produce ever more. Machines spun and wove fibers, forged iron, steam-powered mills, pumped water from coal mines, and stamped out or molded parts for yet more machines. Operating the machines demanded not skill so much as diligence. Britain had an overabundance of human fodder for the factories; owners were free to exploit laborers with minimum wages and maximum hours. And, of course, entrepreneurs needed money with which to realize their manufacturing dreams. By 1750, they could ask for loans from any of twenty banks in London and another dozen scattered among other British cities. Britain's industrial production expanded about 1.2 percent from 1700 to 1790, a much higher rate than that of France.[30]

Production, of course, depended on consumption. Here too Britain had an enormous advantage even though France's 25 million people outnumbered Britain's 6 million by four to one. Unlike the mosaic of tolls and taxes that afflicted France, the British Isles had a unified market. Merchants were hindered from selling elsewhere in the realm only by transportation costs, which dropped as ports, roads, and canals improved. Uniform tariffs protected English industries from foreign rivals, allowing them to enjoy vast sales and profits in large and increasingly affluent home and colonial markets.

Competition among English manufacturers kept prices low and quality high. Thus could English goods beat out European versions to capture foreign markets around the world that had so far escaped colonization. Between 1720 and 1763, British trade nearly doubled from £8 million to £15 million.[31]

A positive attitude toward dirtying one's hands to make money was yet another British advantage. Unlike their equivalents across the channel, British aristocrats did not turn up their noses at the notion of investing money, tinkering with machines, running a factory, or organizing a trading company. Men, ideas, inventions, and money were more fluid; they could rise higher and fall faster in Britain than elsewhere. The marriage of capital, ideas, enterprise, and families between the noble and common rich was far more frequent in England than in France. The Royal Society, scores of business clubs, and three thousand London coffee houses were to England's Industrial Revolution what salons and art academies were to France's Enlightenment. British science was more applied and less theoretical than French science; "How can we use it?" was a more important question than "What does it mean?" During his two-year sojourn there, Voltaire was smitten with England's economy, government, society, and intellectuals, exclaiming, "How I love these people who say what they think!"[32]

All of Britain's military and economic power was of little use without firm, skilled, and visionary leadership. That leadership could not come from the king. The British empire was ruled by a constitutional rather than absolute, divine monarchy. The British Parliament checked royal powers to an extent unthinkable in France. But Parliament's primary business was business, as members passed laws that served first agrarian, then mercantile, and finally industrial interests. To varying degrees, each of the 558 elected members of the House of Commons and roughly 250 hereditary or life peers in the House of Lords spent considerable time debating how to enhance British economic, colonial, and military power. In France, that essential debate over national wealth, power, and strategy was no more than a periodic and shallow discussion, largely confined to the king's council.

Yet Britain's Parliament merely debated and ratified decisions made elsewhere. Real power lay in a subcommittee of the king's Privy Council known as the cabinet council whose members came from Parliament and were accepted by the king. The cabinet decided most policies, then submitted them first to the king in Privy Council and then to Parliament for formal acceptance. As in France, there was no official prime minister; decisions were reached by debate among the rival personalities filling the key formal and informal positions. The cabinet's most important posts were the two secretaries of state, the first lord of the treasury, first lord of the admiralty, lord president, and lord chancellor.[33]

Britain had not one but two foreign ministries. The Northern Department's duties embraced northern Europe, and the Southern Department's encompassed the Mediterranean basin and the rest of the world, including the American colonies. A secretary's duties included gathering information, assessing problems, leading cabinet debates, helping organize expeditions and financial aid, and conveying the decisions to those in the field who implemented them.

On the war's eve, Whitehall was just as divided as Versailles, with some calling for compromise and others unyielding with France. Those willing to negotiate held the most important posts. In 1754, Thomas Pelham-Holles, Duke of Newcastle, had become first lord of the treasury after his brother's death. Robert Darcy, Earl of Holderness, was secretary of the Southern Department from June 1751 to March 1754, whereupon he served as secretary for the Northern Department until 1757, and then as Southern secretary again until March 1761. Sir Thomas Robinson served as secretary for the Southern Department from March 1754 to November 1755.

Until William Pitt took over in 1757 and exceeded them in vehemence, four fire-breathers blasted any notion of compromise with the French. John Carteret, Earl of Granville; Richard Grenville, Earl of Temple; George Montagu-Dunk, Earl of Halifax; and William Augustus, the Duke of Cumberland, the king's second son, shuffled among various formal or informal cabinet positions during the war. At the council meetings, they shouldered aside less aggressive ministers like Newcastle, Robinson, and Philip Yorke, Earl of Hardwicke, with the force of their rhetoric and personality.

George II exceeded his ministers in advocating a hard line against France. Though his formal powers were constrained by law, the king did sharply influence policies. George II wore two crowns, one as Britain's king and another as Hanover's elector. In all, the king had an English home and a German heart, which he did not hesitate to reveal: "The Devil take your ministers, and the Devil take your Parliament, and the Devil take the whole island, provided I can get out of it and get to Hanover."[34] Horace Walpole listed George II's passions as "Germany, the army, and women."[35] The imperative to defend Hanover grossly complicated British policy. As the realm most vulnerable to French armies, it served as Britain's Achilles' heel. Yet Hanover's defense rested on more than George's sentimental ties as the land of his birth and legal duties as its elector—that German realm annually garnered £100,000 of revenue for England.[36]

Though it committed both, Whitehall preferred pouring gold rather than troops into the continent. The strategy of at once encouraging and avoiding Europe's killing fields made perfect sense. England's interest lay not over the channel but on far more distant horizons in North America, the West Indies, and India. By subsidizing Versailles's enemies in Europe, Whitehall diverted French armies, finance, and energies from threatening Britain's blossoming empire. Yet intentions and actions were often at odds. While most English ministers recognized that committing troops to the continent damaged rather than enhanced their nation's interests, almost invariably they were sucked into the whirlpool of European rivalries and war. That would surely happen in the Seven Years' War. The Prussian king and German princes first demanded money, then a commander, and finally an army. Whitehall grudgingly but eventually met each demand.[37]

A vital element in Britain's ultimate victory was its war leader from 1756 until 1761. William Pitt was the Winston Churchill of the Seven Years' War. He combined a fiery, inspirational rhetoric that lifted or browbeat others to his will, a single-minded determination to conquer the entire French empire, and the grand strategy to do so. That strategy involved holding the line in Germany while committing enough regiments to North America and elsewhere until the Union Jack fluttered over every French colony. Yet diplomacy and politics frequently forced him to compromise that strategy. He ended up agreeing to send far more regiments to Germany than he had originally intended and launching pinprick raids on the French coast that did little but divert an enormous amount of troops, supplies, ships, and money that could have been much better deployed elsewhere. He also annually ordered the colonial governors to raise far more provincial troops than were needed for those campaigns, thus expending badly needed supplies and money for no military gain. Nonetheless, he was essential in shifting Britain's strategy from merely defeating France to conquering New France.[38]

The most important change in eighteenth-century diplomacy was the rise of Prussia.[39] In 1701, Frederick I transformed his realm from the electorate of Brandenburg into the kingdom of Prussia. Upon taking over from his father in 1713, Frederick William I built on that legacy. He was progressive in a statist sense. He not only decreed that primary education was compulsory but used state funds to build more than 1,700 schools. He created a bureaucracy that was a model of austere efficiency in maintaining order and collecting taxes. Most importantly, he forged an 80,000-man army that observers believed was the best trained in Europe.

When Frederick II inherited the throne on May 31, 1740, few would have imagined him soon launching his realm to war, let alone that he would be reckoned among history's military geniuses.[40] Frederick was a philosopher, poet, musician, historian, amateur scientist, and intimate of the age's greatest minds. He swiftly decreed that henceforth his subjects would enjoy religious freedom, the abolition of torture, the distribution of surplus grain to the poor, the lifting of censorship, and the revival of the Berlin Academy of Sciences. He would later revoke almost all of his liberal measures. For now, however, Europe's philosophes celebrated him as an enlightened monarch, a model for a just state.

Then, on December 23, 1740, Frederick led his 100,000-man army into Silesia. It seemed like an easy picking. Maria Theresa had just taken over Austria's contested throne, and many questioned her rule's legitimacy. Prussia had an obtuse legal claim to the region. Frederick used Maria Theresa's rejection of this claim as the excuse to invade that wealthy province in hopes of scoring a rapid victory that all would grudgingly acknowledge. This goal would take eight years of blood and treasure to realize. Prussia and Austria would again war for Silesia between 1756 and 1763, with the same results.

All along, Frederick barely clung not only to Silesia but to power itself. No state was geographically more scattered and difficult to defend than Prussia, a dismembered series of clustered territories. The official Prussian capital was at Berlin in the region of Brandenburg; Frederick's palace of Sans Souci was actually outside Berlin in Potsdam. Brandenburg was the central realm to which such far-flung possessions as East Frisia on the North Sea, Lower Pomerania, the Rhenish provinces of Wesel and Rheinberg, Mark County and Ravensburg in Westphalia, and East Prussia sent tribute and soldiers. Distributed among those provinces were a mere 4.5 million subjects.

Prussia was organized for war. With the smallest population of the great powers, Frederick faced the worst challenge of mobilizing enough troops to stave off, let alone vanquish, his enemies. For that, each canton was required to supply a regiment to the army and levy of taxes to the state. Ninety percent of government revenues were poured into the Prussian army. By 1761, the Prussian army had recruited 4.5 percent of the realm's population, a greater proportion than any other government.

For both strategic and popular reasons, Versailles favored Frederick. Prussia was the underdog that offset Austria and threatened neighboring Hanover. Under a 1741 treaty, France was required to pay the upkeep of 20,000 German troops under Frederick's command. Only Louis and Pompadour questioned whether Frederick was reliable enough to serve French interests. Though the countries were allies during the War of the Austrian Succession, Frederick had frequently weaseled out of commitments to France. Even worse, he openly denigrated Pompadour. Louis XV might well have echoed the sentiments of George II, who described his nephew Frederick II as "a mischievous rascal, a bad friend, a bad ally, a bad relation, and a bad neighbor . . . the most dangerous and evil disposed prince in Europe."[41] In all, Frederick II was Europe's military and diplomatic wild card who could send his army in any direction.

Charles VI wore two crowns, those of Austrian king and Holy Roman emperor. Yet all the pomp and power that attended his life was soured by a terrible dilemma—he could not produce a legitimate male heir.

From the day he took the throne in 1711 until his death on October 20, 1740, Charles VI's foreign policy focused on getting other countries to accept a "pragmatic sanction" to allow his eldest daughter, Maria Theresa, to take his place. Through diplomacy and war, one by one the great powers agreed. Then, when he died, most promptly rallied behind either Charles Albert of Bavaria or Frederick Augustus II of Saxony, who both claimed the throne. Amidst this uncertainty, two months after Charles VI died, Prussia invaded Silesia. The result was the War of Austrian Succession.

Maria Theresa was only twenty-three years old when she became Austria's queen.[42] Her husband, Francis of Lorraine, served as the Holy Roman emperor and duke of Tuscany. Francis was much more skilled at affairs of the flesh than of state, both with Maria Theresa and a host of others. With him she bore sixteen children, among whom was her capable co-ruler and eventual successor, Joseph II, and France's future queen, Marie Antoinette. Maria Theresa admirably performed her duties during the War of Austrian Succession but could do nothing to prevent the bitter defeat. To her dying day, she remained obsessed with reconquering Silesia and destroying Frederick. From 1748 until 1763, virtually all Austrian foreign policy questions demanded the means to that end.

The obvious answer was once again to ally with Britain and Holland against Frederick and, probably, France. Austria, Britain, and Holland had long shared a common interest in containing France, especially from overrunning the Low Countries, where Austria owned a slice of territory in what is today mostly Belgium. Under the Third Barrier Treaty of 1715, Austria was obliged to kept 30,000 troops in Netherland fortresses bordering France in return for British subsidies and Dutch troops. Though no mutual antagonisms troubled relations between Austria and Britain, no mutual affection bound them either. However, Maria Theresa did blame Britain's separate peace with Prussia in 1745 for her loss of Silesia.

In March 1749, Wenzel Anton von Kaunitz-Rietberg, the queen's advisor, offered an intriguing answer to the question of how to regain Silesia. Why not forge Austria's ancient Bourbon enemy, France, to an anti-Prussian alliance that also embraced Russia, Sweden, and Saxony, and perhaps even England and Holland?[43] It was an outrageous idea. After all, the Hapsburgs and Bourbons had feuded for over two centuries to place their respective progeny on Europe's vacant thrones. During that time, much of Europe's diplomacy, wars, and shifting constellations of alignments had revolved around that struggle. Now Kaunitz was asking Maria Theresa to join with that old enemy to destroy a more recent enemy.

The empress enthusiastically agreed and dispatched Kaunitz to Versailles as Austria's ambassador in 1750. For the next three years, Kaunitz tried hard and failed miserably to interest first foreign minister Louis-Philogène Brulart, de Puysieulx, then his successor, François-Dominique Barberie, de Saint Contest, in a Franco-Austrian alliance. Most courtiers deified Frederick as an enlightened monarch and demonized Austria as France's worst enemy, even worse than England as the Hapsburgs threatened to impose their brood on as many European thrones as possible. The endless frustration prompted Kaunitz to complain that the French "are employing against us a thousand wretched chicaneries."[44] He was not impressed with the French ministers or their court. He moaned that their "multiplicity of affairs does not allow the ministers, what with the time that they need for acting as courtiers, to have enough time to inform themselves of their business."[45] In 1753, Kaunitz was recalled to serve as Maria Theresa's state chancellor. Their hope for an alliance with France was abandoned but not forgotten.

Vienna's interests extended far beyond Silesia. Its polyglot empire included Austria; Stygia; Carinthia; Bohemia; Moravia; Hungary; Carniola; Tirol; the archbishoprics of Mainz, Trier, and Cologne; Tuscany and Milan in Italy; and the Austrian Netherlands. It was a nightmare to defend all those far-flung states. Yet that realm supplied its own soldiers and money. In 1754, greater Austria had about 6.1 million souls from which to draw troops and taxes; Hungarians numbered another 5 million, and various other Hapsburg lands totaled collectively another million. Vienna could have ruled over an even greater population had it not over the previous century hounded into exile hundreds of thousands of Protestants, many of whom settled in Prussian territory.[46]

Yet Maria Theresa made the best of what she had. With such skilled advisors as Kaunitz, Ludwig Haugwitz, and Rudolf Chotek, she revamped Austria's administration, law, industries, finances, and army. She founded a war college that trained Austria's officers in strategy, tactics, engineering, history, diplomacy, geography, and mathematics. Austria's peacetime army numbered 108,000, which nearly doubled in size during the war.

Just where would those soldiers march? Starstruck with Frederick and mired in France's traditional enmity toward Austria, most at Versailles had assumed that they would fight against rather than with Maria Theresa. France's foreign ministers had snubbed Kaunitz's broad hints that their two kingdoms rethink the power balance and their own interests. Eventually, Versailles would gingerly embrace Vienna in a military alliance that did France little good and much harm. But in 1754 Austria was still Britain's de facto ally and had to be treated accordingly.

Elizabeth Petrovna was Peter the Great's daughter by his second wife Catherine I. The woman who would join Russian armies in the War of the Austrian Succession and the Seven Years' War delighted in Orthodox piety, on the one hand, and in vodka-soaked banquets, virile men, 15,000 dresses, and 2,500 pairs of shoes on the other hand. She was as ruthless as she was sensual. She stole the throne in 1741 after a midnight coup exiled the infant Ivan VI and his regent and mother, Anne of Brunswick. During her twenty-one years of rule, excessive living steadily thickened and diseased a face and body once renowned for its beauty. She would linger throughout the Seven Years' War until near its end when she died in time to save her archenemy, Frederick II, from being crushed.[47]

Waiting impatiently for Elizabeth's death was her nephew Peter and his wife, Catherine. Both were thoroughly German in birth and loyalty; the grand duke was from Holstein and the grand duchess from Anhalt-Zerbst. Dictates of state rather than love had made their marriage. Each deeply admired Frederick the Great as much as they detested each other. Peter was an alcoholic, foul-tempered, uneducated profligate, characteristics that certainly would not disqualify him for any European throne, let alone Russia's. But the heir to the Russian throne had the unfortunate habit of sneering at all things Russian. The court sneered back. In contrast, Catherine was intelligent, sophisticated, and iron-willed, and every bit as voracious a lover as her husband's aunt. French philosophes and culture entranced her. Britain did too, not so much for any strategic interests that it might have shared with Russia nor for its own luminous high culture, but by the glitter of English gold that helped underwrite her extravagant lifestyle and gambling debts.

Like any court, Elizabeth's was split among factions vying for power, wealth, and policy. Alexander Petrovich Bestuzhev-Ryumin, the grand chancellor, dominated Russian foreign policy for the first fifteen years of Elizabeth's rule. Bestuzhev feared and hated France and Prussia. He bent his efforts at eliminating French influence in Poland, Sweden, and Turkey, and outright destroying the upstart Frederick II of Prussia. To these ends, he allied Russia with Austria and England. His Russian nemesis was Mikhail Vorontsov who, upon becoming vice chancellor in 1744, struggled continually to assert a pro-French policy. Elizabeth tilted toward France more for reasons of fashion than state. Yet she did little to advance that cause.

Russians were united in a dream of expanding their empire in all directions—the Baltic basin, central Europe, the Balkans, the Black Sea, and eastward across Siberia. With nearly 20 million serfs by midcentury under its thumb, Saint Petersburg had more than enough manpower to pursue these ambitions. What it lacked was an economy vigorous enough to pay for it. It was this weakness that foreigners were happy to exploit.

Russia's leaders had a well-deserved reputation for being despotic, crude, sexually voracious, and easily bought. Enriching Bestuzhev in his policies and pocket was Sir Charles Hanbury Williams, Britain's ambassador to Saint Petersburg. British gold paid for Russian blood during the War of the Austrian Succession's last year in 1748. Vorontsov's attraction to French power and culture was sweetened by generous gifts of French gold. Saint Petersburg's embrace of Whitehall and animosity toward Versailles before 1756 did not only result from Britain's deeper pockets and Bestuzhev's higher rank.

Russia and Britain shared an interest in containing Prussia in Germany and France in eastern Europe.

Indeed, Versailles outright provoked Russian antagonism; French support for Poland, Sweden, and Turkey at once contained and infuriated an ambitious, expansionist Russia. At Aix-la-Chapelle, Versailles vetoed any place for Russia. This incensed and humiliated Elizabeth and her court, who had hoped that Russia would finally come of diplomatic age by being invited to a European peace congress. To add injury to insult, a French man-of-war captured a Russian merchant ship after the war's end; Versailles pointedly ignored Saint Petersburg's protests that it be released.

Economics reinforced these geopolitical leanings. Little direct trade bound France to Russia. The Russians' insistence that they be allowed to drag out payments for imports over a year or more rather than all at once also stymied French interests. Finally, Russia discouraged foreign traders with heavy tariffs, greedy corruption among officials, and unreliable transshippers, warehouses, money changers, and the like. Yet Russia's aristocracy highly valued and demanded French luxury goods such as porcelain, tapestries, chocolate, wine, indigo, furniture, textiles, and so on. In return, France imported Russian furs, timber, sailcloth, copper, potash, and flax. Though France was Russia's biggest trade partner, most of those goods were carried and profits reaped by English, Dutch, and German ships. In 1754, the direct trade of England and Holland with Russia was ten and three times, respectively, more valuable than France's. A smaller stream of trade ran through the Black Sea; that too was controlled by foreigners, mostly Greeks and Armenians.[48]

In 1754, an alliance with Russia was as unthinkable as one with Austria. Louis XV's secret de roi sought simultaneously to strengthen French ties with Poland, Saxony, Sweden, and Turkey in order to contain Russian power behind its present boundaries and to provide potential second fronts against Austria and Prussia. An alliance with Russia would cost France that influence and thus was strictly avoided. Two years later, Versailles would abandon its traditional policy toward eastern Europe as it gingerly embraced Russia.

France's closest friend in the east was also Russia's most tempting conquest. Poland was not so much a state as a confederation of several hundred nobles who ruled 6.5 million serfs. Nine of ten Polish subjects were Polish Catholics; the remainder spoke German, Ukrainian, Yiddish, Lithuanian, or Russian, and bowed before an Orthodox, Protestant, or Jewish God. The nobles elected a diet, which in turn elected a king and every half year appointed seven councilors to keep him in line. To further raise their own income and weaken their king's power, the Polish lords dangled their throne before every ambitious court in Europe. A bidding war ensued as each court tried to bribe a majority of electors behind its candidate. Not surprisingly, a Polish election often sparked civil and occasionally international wars.

Versailles believed that Poland was the key to French interests in eastern Europe. It was thought that with a pro-French candidate on Poland's throne, France could at once divert and crimp Austrian, Russian, and Prussian expansion. That strategy would repeatedly backfire. In September 1733, French gold got Louis XV's father-in-law, Stanislaus Leszczynski, elected Poland's king. Within a year, Austrian and Russian armies had chased the hapless Stanislaus from his throne. France joined the War of the Polish Succession. Under the 1738 Treaty of Vienna, Stanislaus renounced his claim to the Polish throne for the duchies of Lorraine and Bar, to be inherited by his daughter Marie, the French queen. Though criticized at the time, that actually was a much better future gain for France than the immediate but distant Polish throne. During the 1740s and 1750s, Louis XV's secret du roi agent at Warsaw, Charles François, comte de Broglie, intrigued incessantly to swing Poland's electors behind the king's cousin, Louis François de Bourbon, prince de Conti. With Conti on Poland's throne, France could at once check the expansion of its various neighbors in the region and strengthen ties with Sweden and Turkey. That strategy would divert a horde of French gold and energies with no concrete gain.

Poland's current king, Augustus III, was called Frederick Augustus II as Saxony's elector, and resided at Dresden rather than Warsaw. Like Maria Theresa, he hated Frederick II and conspired with her against him. He also had de facto allies with England and Holland, which, under the 1751 Treaty of Dresden, paid Saxony £48,000 in return for 6,000 troops and its vote in the imperial election. Finally, the king hoped that eight of the Holy Roman Empire's nine electors, which included Prussia, Austria, Saxony, Bavaria, Hanover, Mainz, Trier, Cologne, and Frankfort, would support him in a showdown with Frederick II.

Still, for Frederick Augustus II and his mere 17,000 troops to join the containment of Prussia was a potentially disastrous policy given Frederick's military gifts, proximity, and huge army. As will be seen, the king lost his gamble and his Saxon kingdom. France's support was small comfort to Frederick Augustus II as he wore his Polish crown in exile at his Warsaw palace.

During the eighteenth century, Sweden declined from a great into a secondary power. While the War of the Spanish Succession raged across the rest of Europe, Charles XII's Sweden battled against Peter the Great's Russia, Augustus II's Poland-Saxony, and Frederick II's Denmark for control of lands surrounding the Baltic Sea. Charles XII lost. Sweden emerged from the Great Northern War (1700–1721) stripped of most of its German and Baltic possessions. Under the Treaties of Stockholm (1719–20), it surrendered its duchies of Verden and Bremen to Hanover; under the 1721 Peace of Nystad, it handed over Livonia, Estonia, Ingermanland, and eastern Karelia to Russia. In hopes of regaining its lost lands, Sweden again warred against Russia in 1741. That gamble cost Sweden Finland at the Peace of Albo in 1743. By midcentury, Sweden held only the toehold of Swedish Pomerania on the Baltic's south shore.

Charles XII's defeat discredited the monarchy. His sister and successor, Ulrika Eleanora, succumbed to a 1720 constitution that gave most power to a Riksdag composed of four estates—nobles, priests, burghers, and peasants. Thereafter, as in Poland, Sweden's kings were elected, and the winner usually was the candidate who most generously bribed the most electors. In 1751, Adolphus Frederick, a cousin of Russian empress Elizabeth, became king and would reign throughout the Seven Years' War. His queen was Louisa Ulrika, one of Frederick the Great's sisters. Not surprisingly, Sweden's court was just as split over which side to join or whether to remain neutral.

As Swedish power diminished, its potential use to France lessened accordingly. Nonetheless, the French and Swedes continued to share an interest in containing the ambitions of the central European powers. In 1754, Sweden did not top Versailles's list of possible allies. Yet within two years the two kingdoms would indeed share a common enemy, Prussia, and Versailles would continually pressure Stockholm to join its war against England.

After a long Hapsburg decline in military power, wealth, and population during the seventeenth century, Spain experienced an eighteenth-century revival. When an heirless Charles II died in 1700, Spain's treasury was empty and the empire mustered no more than 20,000 troops and twenty warships. By the 1750s, Madrid commanded nearly twice as many soldiers and ships.[49] A vigorous new Bourbon dynasty explains the reversal of fortune. It was certainly not the kings themselves who were responsible—depression and lethargy bordering on madness afflicted both Philip V (1700–1746) and Ferdinand VI (1746–59). Instead, a series of vigorous, farsighted, hard-nosed advisors stimulated the economy by promoting trade, manufactures, and agriculture; revamped the bureaucracy so that debt fell and revenues rose; shored up Spain's sagging empire; rebuilt its army and fleet; and expanded its power in the Mediterranean.

The most important of those advisors was Elizabeth Farnese who, for thirty-two years between wedding Philip V in 1714 until his death, ruled Spain as its unofficial regent. Under her ruthless, skilled diplomacy, Spain regained ground in its tug-of-war with Austria over Italy. Her greatest coups were to place one son, Charles, as king of the Two Sicilies at Naples and another, Philip, as duke of Parma and Piacenza. The 1748 Treaty of Aix-la-Chapelle confirmed the legitimacy of their thrones.

Appearances, of course, could be deceiving. Spain proved to be a paper bull when it jumped imprudently into the ring near the end of the Seven Years' War. But perceptions tend to rule policy. The belief in Europe's capitals that Spain would be a powerful ally or enemy bent diplomacy during the Seven Years' War as rival diplomats jostled each other to win Madrid to their respective sides. They should have known better. Spanish power remained stunted despite its advances.

Spain's nemesis remained Britain, which, through brutality and guile, had wheedled its way into the Spanish empire. Under a 1667 trade treaty, Madrid had granted London the right to the asiento, or slave trade, and an annual trade ship to Portobello, Panama; these concessions were not as rapacious as they have sometimes been depicted. Only eight of the annual ships actually reached Portobello while, more often than not, the slavers claimed to have lost money.

Other losses stung Spain much worse. Under the 1713 Utrecht treaty, Spain gained international acceptance of its Bourbon king at the loss of Naples, Sardinia, and Flanders to Austria; Minorca and Gibraltar to Britain; and Sicily to Savoy. Madrid spent much of the century trying to win back those losses. It took the Quadruple Alliance of Austria, France, England, and Holland to blunt a Spanish attempt to conquer Sicily from 1718 to 1720. The struggle for trade rather than dynasty sparked a war between Spain and England from 1739 to 1744.

Trade losses hurt Spain much more than the loss of territory. Under the 1713 Treaty of Madrid and 1750 Commercial Treaty, English merchants were granted the same tariffs in Spain as the Spanish themselves. Whitehall did not reciprocate; Spanish merchants trying to sell in the British Isles faced the same huge tariffs that shut the door to other foreigners. With low tariffs on manufactured imports and high tariffs on raw materials, Spain's trade policies seemed designed to mire the kingdom in economic stagnation. The result was that Spain suffered huge annual trade deficits with Britain. These were not the only means by which the British exploited Spain. British loggers had planted fortified settlements in Honduras and Yucatan, which Whitehall refused to remove despite persistent Spanish protests. Such were the manifold ways by which Britain prospered at Spain's expense. With the 1748 Aix-la-Chapelle peace, Madrid did win back the exclusive right over its own slave and colonial trade, but at a cost of £100,000 to Britain.[50]

In the 1750s, all those British crimps on Spanish power and pride would seem to push Madrid into the arms of a beckoning France. Yet, as with any royal council, differences in outlook, ambition, and personality split Spain's government. On the war's eve, though Spain's king, court, and geopolitical interest would seem to lean toward France, its policy tilted toward England.

Having won all its concessions by force, the British maintained them by bribes to and mutually profitable trade with powerful Spaniards, especially its foreign minister, Don Joseph de Carvajal y Lancáster, until his death in 1754. Yet Carvajal was overshadowed by Zenón de Somodevilla y Bengochea, marquis de Ensenada, who served as minister of war, finance, marine, and the Indies and led the court's pro-French faction. Ensenada was a great reformer, abolishing internal tolls; building roads and ports; subsidizing manufacturing, mining, and trading firms; rebuilding the fleet; and strengthening the king's power over the church. Ensenada's ambitions would eventually trip him and any prospect of an alliance between Spain and France for the foreseeable future.

During the seventeenth century, the Dutch had skillfully wielded mercantilism to assert a stranglehold over much international trade. They mastered not just the carrying trade but, more vitally, such industries as insurance and finance. Ironically, Dutch mercantile power rose as its naval power declined through a midcentury series of disastrous wars with England for mastery of the seas. During the eighteenth century, Britain and France competed both with each other and with the Dutch for global trade supremacy.

While Britain was the greater economic threat, France was the greater military threat. Separating the Dutch Netherlands or seven United Provinces from France was the Austrian Netherlands. To defend themselves from France, the Dutch naturally looked to Austrian troops and English sailors. During the War of the Austrian Succession, those three countries joined in a Triple Alliance. That war drained Holland of treasure and blood to no gain but survival.

In 1754, French diplomats once again had to calculate Holland as a potential enemy or ally in the looming war with Britain. Throughout the Seven Years' War, French and English diplomats, along with those of other belligerents, would vie with each other for a Dutch alliance. The Dutch would wisely chose to trade rather than fight. Britain had the best legal claim to a Dutch alliance while its policies almost provoked Holland to declare war upon it. Whitehall tried to convince The Hague that the 1674 Anglo-Dutch treaty required the Dutch to ally with Britain. The Dutch just as persistently insisted that the alliance would be triggered only if Holland were the victim of an unprovoked attack. The Dutch then claimed that the treaty required England to respect Holland's neutral trade. In response, the British countered that the treaty did not apply to war supplies; British ships would continue to stop, board, and, if justified, seize Dutch ships carrying war supplies bound to or from France.

Fighting would break out between England and Holland in, of all places, India and the Dutch East Indies. But it did not escalate into a general war despite all the French encouragement.[51]

Portugal should have escaped the Seven Years' War but was dragged into the fighting at the last moment. With three million inhabitants, it was a minor power on Europe's fringe. Like Spain, Portugal was experiencing a revival of power under its brilliant and ruthless foreign minister Sébastien-Joseph de Carvalho e Mello, later marquis de Pombal, who held power from 1750 to 1777. Using as a pretext a failed assassination of King Joseph I in 1758, Pombal assumed dictatorial powers first by expelling the Jesuits and then by suppressing the nobility.

Trade and treaty bound Britain and Portugal. British merchants dominated the trade at Lisbon, Oporto, and various Brazilian ports, buying wine and selling duty-free textiles. England was committed to Portugal's defense by treaties of 1654, 1661, and 1703. If Portugal were invaded, Britain was required to send 20 warships, 10,000 infantry, and 2,500 cavalry to its rescue. That commitment should have deterred a Spanish attack on Portugal; instead, it acted as a magnet for Spanish fears and ambitions.

In 1754, given those ties between Britain and Portugal, Versailles would not think twice of the latter as a potential ally but did all it could to ensure that Lisbon remained neutral during the war.

Unlike Portugal, Italy would escape the fighting if not the diplomacy and strategic calculations among the belligerents. As ever, Italy was little more than a geographical expression, splintered among a dozen political territories. Only a few of the more prominent realms were actually ruled by Italians—the kingdom of Sardinia-Piedmont and republics of Genoa and Venice. Rome ruled the Papal States across a swath of central Italy. The Spanish Bourbons and Austrian Hapsburgs continued their struggle over the peninsula as if it were a wishbone; each had succeeded in tearing off a chunk. Spain controlled Naples and Parma; Austria controlled Tuscany and Lombardy. Had Austria and Spain gone to war, their armies and fleets would have met on Italian earth and seas.

Bogged down in an ever-bloodier stalemate against Prussia, Maria Theresa put her Italian ambitions on hold during the war. But the stirrings of those two Bourbon brothers perched atop Italian thrones forced her periodically to glance over the Alps. Charles IV, Spanish King Philip V's son, was the king of Naples and Sicily, and Philip was the duke of Parma. Yet neither took advantage of Austria's travails in central Europe to grab its Italian possessions. Given how deeply involved Spain and Austria were in Italy, Versailles stayed clear during the war for fear of alienating either power.

The Ottoman Empire had steadily receded from its height in 1683 when it besieged Vienna for the second time, although it lingered as a military and diplomatic power. During the eighteenth century's first half, Constantinople lost wars against Venice, Austria, Russia, and Persia. The 1718 Treaty of Passarowitz required the Turks to surrender Hungary, Belgrade, and part of Wallachia to Austria, and parts of Albania and Dalmatia to Venice. By a series of wars early that century, Russia pushed back the Turks from the Ukraine and nibbled away at their Balkan vassal states. The Ottomans scored some victories. By midcentury, they had conquered all of Greece and Crete, and had retaken Belgrade from Austria and Kilburun and Ochakov from Russia. In the 1750s, an unstable truce reigned between the Turks and their enemies, the former too exhausted and the latter too preoccupied elsewhere to resume the wars for now.

France had both economic and military interests in forging closer ties with Constantinople. In 1740, Versailles succeeded in getting the sultan to grant French imports virtually equal access to the

Ottoman Empire as native goods. French trade with the Levant soared. During the War of the Austrian Succession, Versailles pursued a classic "the enemy of my enemy is my friend" strategy through intrigues at Constantinople to enlist the Turks against the Austrians and Russians. In 1754, Versailles was ready to resume that policy.

Two years later, Versailles would reverse this strategy after allying with Austria and Russia. Now its policy was to thwart intrigues by Prussia and England to enlist the Turks against Russia and Austria. Here the French won by default. Constantinople would have been hard pressed to fight a war even if it were attacked—state coffers were empty, and the army and navy were badly trained, armed, and fed. Osman III, the sultan from 1754 to 1757, was a fundamentalist Muslim who disdained any significant relations with infidels. His successor, Mustapha III, hated Russia and was prevented from immediately declaring war by his advisors, who understood the frailty of Ottoman military and finances. He would sign a treaty of trade and friendship with Prussia on April 3, 1761, that stopped just short of committing the Ottomans to an attack on Austria.

Regardless of the issue, diplomacy with the Turks was never easy. For fear of alienating the other Christian powers, Versailles refused to accord full diplomatic relations with Constantinople. This and Ottoman court etiquette required the French ambassador to negotiate with the Sultan via dragomans, go-betweens who demanded huge bribes for their services and even then usually failed to convey the proper messages.[52]

Consequences

Colbert and Louvois may have mastered the arts of making money and waging war, respectively, during the late seventeenth century, but their successors at Versailles proved to be poor pupils. French administrative and military leaders during the Seven Years' War were at best mediocre and sometimes criminally inept. On the whole, France's rivals succeeded in waging war, asserting mercantilism, and conducting diplomacy better than Versailles.

A grossly corrupt bloated bureaucracy and officer corps partly accounted for France's sluggish leadership. Many of the political and military leaders admired Frederick II and could not understand why France warred against him. Thus, they dragged their feet on implementing policies or campaigns. France's armies were poorly trained, supplied, and motivated compared to those of many of its enemies, especially Prussia. Even at the best of times, the troops more nearly resembled semi-mutinous pillagers than professional soldiers. And who can blame them given their leaders' ineptness and decadence?

Although Louis XV and his ministers recognized France's weaknesses, they did little to alleviate them. For this reason, as word arrived in late 1754 of the fighting between Virginians and Canadians, Versailles dreaded the probability of once again locking horns with Britain in its century-and-a-half contest for supremacy in North America. Like its predecessors, the looming war would most likely spread to Europe. Versailles had to calculate what other French interests were vulnerable and who were its potential allies and enemies.

Three years after the Aix-la-Chapelle treaty, Versailles feared that Britain was again trying to enlist Austria in an alliance. That was a natural alliance since France was the only great power that stymied British and Austrian ambitions to assert hegemony over the sea and land, respectively.

How could this threat be defeated? Only Spain stood as a potential French ally. These two kingdoms shared not only a ruling Bourbon family but a common threat to their American empires. A 1753 Council of State memorandum concluded that Versailles must "lead Madrid to adopt measures in concert to avoid the danger. There remain no defenders for Europe except the King of France and the King of Spain, and on their combined foresight rests the safety of their Empire and that of the entire of Europe."[53] The memorandum mentions Prussia merely as the target of Russian aggression, not as a potential ally. This thoroughly reasonable assessment would become irrelevant within two years.

France's military strategy in Europe depended on its enemies. In 1754, aside from probably Austria, no other threats were then clear. There was little likelihood that foreign armies posed any immediate threat to invade France. The most important military and diplomatic problem was how France could defend its colonies in North America and elsewhere. It was a problem that Versailles never resolved.

Versailles faced a hard choice over how to use France's outnumbered navy if a war broke out. Not only was France's navy one-third the size of Britain's, but its two largest fleets, at Brest and Toulon, were at France's far ends; Toulon's could join that at Brest only by sailing around the Iberian Peninsula through a gauntlet of British squadrons based at Minorca, Gibraltar, and Lisbon.

What could Versailles do? It could disperse the navy in convoys that supplied France's far-flung colonies in North America, the Caribbean, West Africa, and India, at the risk of being destroyed piecemeal. It could mass its ships to sail against British fleets at the risk of losing more ships at once. Or it could guard a fleet of transports packed with troops to invade England itself at a risk of losing an army along with its fleet. Unable to agree on one strategy, Versailles each year employed versions of all three, which, to varying degrees, failed miserably. Throughout the war, the navy proved largely incapable of guarding convoys, winning sea battles, invading the British Isles, or even defending France's coast.

By 1759, most French leaders would probably have agreed with foreign minister Choiseul if they weighed the relative importance of land and sea power: "The superiority of land forces is without doubt a great source of power, but since commerce has become the object of all the kingdoms, it is clear that the relative weight of power leans toward a maritime empire."[54] By this time, of course, it was too late to act on that understanding. The British navy had swept the seas of French war and merchant ships alike and bottled up the rest in port to rot at anchor. In all, it is difficult to assess which of Versailles's interrelated policies it bungled worse, that toward North America or that toward Europe.

CHAPTER 3

The French Empire

The sea of this new world is already better than our European
seas; it is calmer, the winds more regular. It is certainly the New
World that is the best of all possible worlds.

Candide in Candide

When we work at the sugar cane, and the mill snatches hold of a
finger, they cut off the hand; when we attempt to run away, they
cut off the leg; both cases have happened to me. This is price at
which you eat sugar in Europe.

slave in Candide

I admire with what persistence and what industry they use all
means here to squander the King's money.

Bougainville

Man is by nature good and only our institutions have made him
bad.

Rousseau

Only after Versailles lost New France did it get around to estimating
just what it was worth. In a 1761 report analyzing New France's
liabilities and assets, foreign minister Choiseul observed that the "two
colonies include vast territories full of fertile lands, with healthful

climates, though with temperatures varying widely. . . . Canada supplies grain, vegetables, hemp, attle, leather, peltry, especially beaver, lumber and planking, moldings, ginseng, iron, fish-oil. There are lead mines. Louisiana furnishes cotton, oil, wheat, vegetables, indigo, vegetable wax, rice, tobacco, fats, wine, lumber, peltry, leather, salt meat, moldings, etc. The mountains contain mines of copper and other metals."[1]

Despite this Eden-like cornucopia, New France steadily lost money during its century-and-a-half existence. Year after year Versailles and French trading companies invested enormous sums into New France but usually reaped debt rather than profit. Any money skimmed from Canada mostly found its way into the coffers of merchants at Bordeaux, Rouen, La Rochelle, and other ports, as well as into the pockets of greedy officials. By 1753, New France was in hock to Versailles for 3,495,675 livres.[2]

What explains Versailles's failure to convert such natural bounty into a financially enriching rather than draining colony?[3] Canada and Louisiana were trapped in a vicious cycle of economic stagnation that included a want of mass markets, enterprise, and skills, and a surfeit of corruption and incompetence. Versailles was aware of the dilemma but never devised a way of breaking it.

Governor Michel Barrin La Galissonière complained that New France "is a country very susceptible of useful husbandry and lacking only settlers."[4] In 1763, New France's 83,600 people included 63,100 Canadians and 20,500 Louisianans, of which 10,900 were whites and 9,600 mostly enslaved blacks. Before the war in 1754, 8,000 people lived in Quebec, 4,000 in Montreal, and 800 in Trois Rivières, while 42,300 lived in rural districts, totaling no more than 55,000 French in all of Canada. The influx of thousands of soldiers and sailors combined with the birth rate to prompt this dramatic jump in population from 1754 to 1763. Yet New France's population was dwarfed by the 1,593,600 Americans, of which 1,267,800 were white and 325,800 black, crowding the thirteen colonies next door. In all, there was only one French subject for every twenty British subjects, a glaring disadvantage in commerce and war alike.[5]

Paradoxically, New France had at once too few and too many people. Far too few skilled hands and ambitious minds were available to clear enough land and manufacture enough goods to transform New France from a subsistence economy into a dynamic competitive economy like those of the American colonies. Yet that very scarcity of skilled labor tended to make people more self-sufficient and thus stifled the division of labor upon which a modern economy depends. That dilemma was explained by Swedish naturalist Peter Kalm, who traveled through Canada on the war's eve: "The scarcity of laboring people occasions the wages to be so high; for almost everyone finds it easy to be a farmer in this uncultivated country where he can live well, and at so small an expense that he does not care to work for others."[6]

In both Canada and Louisiana, nine of ten colonists were peasants who were trapped in a vicious economic cycle. With no means or incentive to do more, they produced just enough to feed, clothe, and shelter themselves. In those years when their wooden plows and primitive seed combined with fine weather to reap a small surplus, they rushed to sell it in village markets that were usually already glutted. Annual supply fleets dumped French grain in Canada and Louisiana to rescue those colonies from any possible crop failures of the previous year. New France suffered a perennial shortage of coin, which, when it appeared in the colony, was whisked away to France to pay for imported goods. Money was not saved; it was spent as soon as it was made. Thus there was never enough money in New France for entrepreneurs to invest in even the most modest of ventures. With nearly all its population trapped in a subsistence economy, New France was too.

Short growing seasons combined with primitive farming methods to render Canada's food supply precarious during peacetime. During the French and Indian War, with Canada's population swollen by several thousand more unproductive mouths to feed, starvation stalked the colony if the supply fleet did not arrive by late spring. For the war's last three years, stomach-pinched Canadians spent months vainly scanning the Saint Lawrence before a few ships finally appeared that managed to evade the British blockade.

New France and the American colonies shared the same continent but exploited and developed it differently. Over time to varying degrees, the American colonies diversified economically as artisans mastered the manufacture of sophisticated products like clocks, guns, furniture, ships, and glass. This never happened in Canada or Louisiana. Manufactured goods imported from France or smuggled from America destroyed any incentive and profit for local artisans even when they could find the spare parts to build that product.

Colonies were there to be milked by the metropole. Like other colonial powers, Versailles enacted laws forbidding certain industries in the colony so that those of France would not suffer. Thus did Versailles value subjugation and exploitation over dynamism and wealth. As for those goods made in Canada "such as architecture, cabinet work, turning, and brick making," Kalm found that they "are not yet so advanced here as they ought to be, and the English in particular outdo the French. The chief cause is that scarcely any other people than dismissed soldiers come to settle here."[7] Versailles tried further to develop Canada by subsidizing the founding of the royal shipyard at Quebec and the Saint Maurice ironworks near Trois Rivières. Though both industries were perennial money losers and produced poor quality goods, they provided most of Canada's needs.

Canada's most abundant products were furs and fish. Yet the fisheries mostly made and the fur trade mostly lost money. What explains the difference? The thousands of fishermen casting nets off Canada's shores came from Rouen, Saint Malo, Dieppe, Havre, and a dozen other small ports. Thus did both the wages and product return to France. The cost of fishing was largely confined to the boats, which were threatened only by storm or war. Another contribution the fisheries brought France was a training ground for the navy. Given all that, Versailles was quite willing to cede all of Canada when negotiating the 1763 peace trade, but fought hard to retain fishing rights in Saint Lawrence Bay and the tiny islands of Pierre and Saint Miquelon as shelters for its fishermen.[8]

In contrast, the fur trade eventually stretched from Paris and other French cities as far west as the Saskatchewan River, running a gauntlet of grasping hands and hazards along the way as goods were dispatched and, ideally, furs returned. Choiseul's 1761 report explained the vast extent of that trade in Canada alone:

The peltry, and especially the beaver, is exhausted in the vicinity of Quebec, and that for a hundred leagues around that city none has been obtained for a long time. The peltry . . . come . . . from very far off to the west and north . . . two ways: from the Ottawa and other Indians of the western shores of Lake Superior who come down the lakes to Montreal, and from the . . . colonists who carry on the fur trade in the forests. These last ascend the lakes and trade in the country of the Indians just mentioned or . . . to the southern end of Lake Michigan from which, by . . . a very short portage, they descend the Illinois River to the Mississippi. They then ascend that last river and sometimes the Missouri and trade with the Pawnee, the Sioux, and other numerous tribes . . . in search of the furs they bring back.[9]

The value of the furs that eventually reached France was usually more than offset by other costs. Lost or looted goods or furs, of course, could devastate any hope of profits that year. Yet the worst obstacle to profit was the glut of furs in French markets. Paradoxically, the deeper into North America the trade penetrated and extracted ever more furs, the more profits eroded and seeming gains became losses. Heavy taxes on the fur trade, widespread mismanagement, and corruption further sapped the bottom line. Then, to add insult to injury, the Indians diverted an increasing amount of their furs to the English, who provided them with less expensive, better made, and more abundant trade goods. All that combined with the expenses of salaries, insurance, transportation, and trade goods withered potential profits. These challenges were compounded during the years France warred against Britain.[10]

Versailles repeatedly reorganized the fur trade, but nothing worked. It handed the trade monopoly, like a baton, to a series of companies. When one failed to make a profit or fulfill its duty to settle and administer the land, the king revoked its charter and granted the privilege to another company. Though these private entrepreneurs were naturally more interested in profit than settlement, they failed to realize either goal. In 1663, Louis XIV eased that burden when he decreed that henceforth he would directly rule New France, while the West India Company, which then enjoyed the royal monopoly, could concentrate on reaping profits. Yet even that advantage was not enough to offset soaring expenses and losses. In 1674, the West India Company bankrupted itself. The king then chartered the West Company, which lasted until 1718. In 1696, Versailles tried to pare costs by shutting all but one of the trading posts and forbidding unlicensed Canadians from traveling west of Montreal. These harsh measures backfired. Distant tribes dependent on easily accessible French goods despaired at their loss as they became prey for musket-less tribes they had formerly bullied. In 1716, Versailles returned to its old system of licensing traders and opening more trading posts.

Louisiana also lost money for Versailles despite its vast potential wealth. It was estimated that Louisiana's "commerce is not worth 1,200,000 livres a year. Indigo is the greater part of it. The crops of that article before the war amounted to more than 800,000 francs. The other exports are chiefly deerskins and lumber for the islands."[11]

Yet, whether they were peasants, merchants, soldiers, or officials, Canadians lived better than those they had left behind in France. The peasants were poor but not stricken by poverty. When the harvests were bountiful and the nation was at peace, most of New France's subjects actually ate quite well. Aside from enjoying generally larger plots of land and usually more abundant food, Canadians escaped paying the income (taille) and salt (gabelle) taxes.

Smuggling also contributed to the higher living standards. Laws forbade any trade between the French and British empires. Smuggling occurred because France failed to supply all the high-quality, inexpensive goods that Canadians demanded or to buy all the furs that Canada produced at high prices. With their myopia assisted by generous "gifts," most officials turned a blind eye to it. It was most rampant between Montreal and Albany but also ran between the Great Lakes and Oswego, Louisbourg and New England, and New England and the French West Indies. Smuggling at once alleviated and provoked shortages. It relieved some of Canada's fur glut and pent-up demand for badly needed products while repressing the enterprise that might have allowed Canadians to manufacture more of their own goods.

On paper, New France's administration seemed a sensible structure for governing such a vast empire; in practice, its officials emulated those of France in venality, inefficiency, and sloth. The marine ministry administered New France along with other overseas colonies and the navy; annually, it submitted instructions and budgets, reviewed and approved or rejected the governor's plans, and organized and dispatched the supply fleet. Communications between Versailles and Quebec were routine. Instructions arrived at Quebec with the fleet in late spring; reports left on the ships packed with that year's annual haul of furs that trickled down from the Great Lakes and elsewhere by late summer. Though nominally under Quebec's rule, Louisiana and even Île Royale (Cape Breton) were separate colonies whose governors and intendants received orders and filed reports directly with Versailles, while maintaining only a cursory relationship with Quebec. The division between Canada and Louisiana was always hazy but was generally marked along the watershed between the Great Lakes and Mississippi valley. Just where to draw that line would become a contentious issue during the peace negotiations.

Whether he was residing at his Quebec palace during the summer or his Montreal palace during the winter, Canada's governor general presided over a miniature court, with every public act filled with pomp and ritual. The governor was assisted by an intendant with enormous powers of his own. Ideally, the two men worked together. The governor general was in charge of all military, diplomatic, and ceremonial affairs. From his own Quebec palace, the intendant immersed himself in the details of administration—finance, lower courts, public works, and trade. Assisting him were deputies at Montreal, Trois Rivières, and Detroit, along with a bureaucracy split into the Bureau de la Marine, which administered the royal storehouse filled with trade goods, munitions, and provisions, the Domaine d'Occident, which collected and distributed tariffs, and the "grand voyer" in charge of public works. In 1755, 218 officials served under the intendant.[12] The Superior Council served as New France's supreme court, and included the governor general, the intendant, the bishop, twelve councilors, and the attorney general, assisted by a clerk and a half dozen scribes.

There was some local autonomy. Quebec, Montreal, and Trois Rivières each had its own governor general appointed by Versailles and subordinate to New France's governor. Likewise, each of those towns had its own court that dispensed civil and criminal justice. A lieutenant general led each court and was assisted by a lieutenant particulier, a king's attorney, a clerk, and a half dozen scribes. Crime was not a problem in Canada; most cases involved debt collection, and three-quarters of those were filed in Quebec.

Canada was further divided into 124 parishes, each headed by a *capitaine de milice* (militia captain) appointed by the governor general and supervised by the intendant, who oversaw not only the militia but also welfare, public works, and law enforcement. Some populous parishes had more than one captain and militia company. All able-bodied men between sixteen and sixty years of age were required to attend militia musters. In 1750, there were 11,687 militiamen in 165 companies; by 1758, 15,000 militiamen were on the rolls. Canadian militiamen were more effective fighters than militiamen anywhere else.

The Catholic Church dominated the lives of Canadians as much as it did the French. The king appointed a bishop of New France and gave him annual subsidies to underwrite the parishes and missions. Each parish could levy a tithe of one twenty-sixth of a peasant's wheat harvest. Since the harvests varied considerably from one parish to the next, so too did a parish's relative income. Only forty-four parishes were self-supporting; the rest received state subsidies. The Jesuit, Sulpician, Recollect, and Ursuline orders practiced their vows, nurtured converts, schooled the young, and succored the poor and dying. In 1756, of Canada's 163 priests, 84 were secular, 30 Sulpician, 25 Jesuit, and 24 Recollects; 81 were born in Canada and the remainder were from France.[13] The Canadians were religious, spending "more time in prayer and external worship than the English or Dutch. . . . The French here have prayers every morning and night. . . . They regularly say grace both before and after their meals and cross themselves."[14] Protestantism was as illegal in New France as it was in the mother country.

Overlapping the parishes were 238 seigneuries, or landed estates, which averaged 55 square miles or 35,000 acres. Versailles had granted most of the seigneuries to those who promised to settle them with immigrants and develop them into productive fields and pastures; most seigneurs were of common rather than noble blood. The church owned one in four seigneuries, most of which were narrow strips fronting the Saint Lawrence and extending several miles inland. By law, the seigneurs had the right to collect 10 percent of each peasant family's income as rent; in practice, most lived off their own large family earnings.

The most important reason for New France's failure to turn a profit for the king was that its administration was corrupt in varying degrees and ways, from the governor general to the lowest militia captain or trading post commandant. Everyone pocketed fees or the king's goods. It was not until François Bigot arrived to become intendant in 1748 that New France's corruption was transformed from a petty into a grand scale.[15] Bigot organized a criminal hierarchy that straddled the Atlantic and cooked the books to skim enormous amounts of goods and profits from the king. A universal scam was to pocket salaries for fictional people on a muster or administrative roll. The number of Indians who arrived at councils was exaggerated to allow those officials involved to sell the excess trade goods. Louis Bougainville estimated that officials stole and sold as much as two-thirds of the king's supplies sent to New France, and most of the rest were sold by post commanders who were supposed to give the goods to the Indians.[16]

As in most societies, in New France a tiny political, economic, and social elite of 400 families amassed most of the wealth, whether it was taken by means fair or foul. That handful of families eagerly awaited the annual supply fleet as much for the latest Parisian fashions as anything else packed aboard. New France's elite "dress very finely, are extravagant in their repasts, and their ladies are every day in full dress and . . . dress and powder their hair every day, and put their locks in paper every night. . . . The gentlemen generally wear their own hair, but some have wigs. People of rank are accustomed to wear lace-trimmed clothes and all . . . crown officers carry swords. . . . Acquaintances of either sex, who have not seen each other for some time, on meeting again salute with mutual kisses."[17]

Civility extended to the poorer classes. Kalm was "quite amazed at the . . . people who treat one another with such politeness both in word and deed [even] in the homes of the peasants. I frequently happened to take up my abode for several days at the homes of peasants . . . who . . . showed me a devotion paid ordinarily only to a native or a relative. Often when I offered them money they would not accept it."[18]

Relations between Canadian men and women impressed many visiting Frenchmen as a more affectionate version of Versailles's dangerous liaisons: "There exists no country in the world where the women lead a happier life than Canada. The men have a great deal of consideration for them & spare them all the hard work that they can. It can be said that they deserve it, as they are well-mannered, attractive, spirited, & inclined to intrigue. It is only through them that their husbands obtained their posts which put them in easy circumstances & above the common run of people."[19]

Many an unmarried young lady stood impatiently at the quay scanning those disembarking for any potential bachelors. One French officer fondly recalled, "The inclination for marriage is dominant; very pretty persons engage you; we have already five officers married there."[20] Most men must have delighted in the coquetry of Canadian women: "One of the first questions they put to a stranger is whether he is married; the next, how he likes the ladies in the country, and whether he thinks them handsomer than those of his own country; and the third, whether he will take one home with him. . . . When a young fellow comes in, whether they are acquainted with him or not, they immediately set aside their work, sit down beside him, and begin to chat, laugh, joke, and invent double entendres and make their tongues go like lark's wings."[21]

Such liaisons actually became a controversial issue during the war. General Louis Joseph, marquis de Montcalm, thought them dangerous, at least for his officers, who "I have found . . . inclined to contract bad marriages . . . for the political interest of the Colony [and] for that of the King." While opposed to any breeding of his noble officers with common colonial stock, the general delighted in such couplings among his soldiers: "I believed I could do nothing better for the interest of the Colony and Kingdom than to encourage those of the soldiers. Accordingly in the winter of 1755–56, there had been only seven marriages of soldiers, and this year eighty."[22]

Canada needed settlers. The more people there were, the more farmers, fishermen, and fur traders there would be to reap wealth from these vast lands and the more soldiers there would be to defend it. Montcalm suggested that before withdrawing "his troops from Canada, his Majesty ought to give a small gratuity to all his soldiers who would then desire to settle and die there. We would leave the greater part of them. They would make excellent colonists, brave defenders of New France."[23]

The Defense of New France

If only most Frenchmen got along with Canadian men as well as they did with the women. Throughout the war, Versailles committed twelve battalions or about 5,000 troops to defend its North American empire—four battalions reached Quebec and two arrived at Louisbourg in 1755, two more reached Quebec in 1756, two more in 1757, and the final two in 1758. There was a natural tension between the men from opposite sides of the Atlantic, with the French openly disdainful of their colonial inferiors and the Canadians resentful of the others' wealth, privileges, and appeal to their women. Many a Frenchmen echoed Captain Pierre Pouchot's remarks about Canadian character: "The Canadians are well built, very robust & active, with an admirable capacity to endure hard work & fatigue, to which they are accustomed through long & arduous journeys connected with their trading activities, in which a great deal of skill & patience are required. As a result of their travels, they are habitually rather idle because of the type of life they lead during them. They are brave, fond of war and very patriotic. They have an extraordinary affection for their mother country. Their lack of knowledge of the world normally makes them liars & rather boastful as they are ignorant of almost everything."[24]

The Canadians in turn may have wondered whether the French soldiers had come as protectors or conquerors. Over time, "nothing equaled the devastation committed by the troops throughout the rural districts where the army was encamped; complaints were made; [Montcalm] answered that everything belonged to the soldier. . . . A woman . . . reproached M. de Montcalm with the profligacy with which he allowed his soldiers to pillage cattle, fowls, gardens, tobacco plantations, and even wheat."[25]

Montcalm blamed Canada for his soldiers' excesses. The country corrupted his soldiers, whose "discipline is becoming relaxed despite my care and severity. The recruits that arrived last year are a collection of bad boys. The soldier to be subsisted . . . must . . . be dispersed among the farmers. There he lives . . . out of sight of officer or sergeant. . . . I have had sixteen soldiers . . . tried this winter either by the ordinary tribunals or court martial. Three of them have been shot for desertion, two condemned to the galleys for mutiny against their sergeants; the rest for theft."[26]

Montcalm did not exaggerate the soldiers' easy life when not on campaign. Their rations included "a pound and a half of wheat bread, which is almost more than they can eat . . . plenty of peas, bacon, and salt or dried meat. Sometimes they kill oxen. . . . In time of peace the soldiers have very little guard duty. . . . Each soldier got a new coat every two years; but annually a waistcoat, cap, hat, breeches, cravat, two pair of stockings, two pair of shoes, and . . . five sols . . . every day, which is augmented to thirty sols when they have any particular labor for the king. When this is considered it is not surprising to find the men are very healthy, well fed, strong, and lively here."[27]

This abundance was not to last. As the war progressed, soldiers rarely got a fraction of their promised rations, and what they received was often wretched. Bougainville noted, "From all our posts great complaints of the bad quality of the food. . . . The Canadians and soldiers are almost all sick . . . low in spirits, [and] ready to desert at the first chance."[28]

Compounding tensions between the French and Canadians was the interservice rivalry between the marines, who were mostly recruited in New France to defend their colony, and the army soldiers, who reinforced them during the war. The first marine companies reached New France in 1683. Each company ideally included fifty troops and four officers, who wore light grey coats and leggings with blue facings, linings, cuffs, and trousers. Over time, Canadians filled both the soldier and officer ranks. By 1754, ninety marine companies were deployed across New France, including thirty in Canada, twenty-four in Île Royale, and thirty-six in Louisiana. A royal decree of March 14, 1756, raised the number of men in each company to 65, which on paper meant that New France's marines now numbered 1,950. Recruitment, however, could not keep up with the rampant losses from desertion, disease, and battle deaths. Versailles dispatched ten more marine companies to Quebec in 1757.[29]

Marine and army officers were ranked according to seniority, which favored the marines since they enjoyed more rapid promotions. Thus did marine officers rise "from the rank of captain to make up the general staff. Those who had been awarded the Cross of St. Louis were as highly esteemed as lieutenant generals & cordon bleus in France. Those who had commanded armies, of which the largest were 300 men, were respected in the colony like field marshals in France."[30]

French officers both lauded and condemned the marine companies and their officers raised in Canada. The marines were experts at wilderness warfare, something all French observers admired. But Montcalm despaired that the marines knew "neither discipline nor subordination."[31] Even more rankling was that "Canadian officers, although courageous, knew hardly anything of their profession."[32] Captain Pierre-André Gohin, comte de Montreuil, contemptuously dismissed Canadian soldiers as "independent, wicked, lying, braggart, well adapted for skirmishing, very brave behind a tree and very timid when not covered."[33] One reason for the discipline problem was that each company was autonomous. That independence and initiative was essential for winning wilderness skirmishes but could be fatal in a European-style battle. It was not until July 1757 that eight companies were formed into the first marine battalion to address the weakness of the independent companies not cooperating with one another on the battlefield.

French officers underestimated Canadian fighting skills. Actually, Canadians had mastered the art of warfare in North America as it had been wielded to that time. For a century and a half, warfare had consisted of large-scale raids on the enemy's forts and settlements followed by carefully laid ambushes of pursuing forces.

North America's geography dictated the strategy and tactics, largely to France's advantage. A vast wilderness separated the settlements of the two empires. River and lake valleys provided the only possible land routes to reach the enemy, and these paths were tough enough to traverse for raiding parties, let alone armies. In this realm, the much-maligned Canadians had matched their Indian allies in mastering the art of war and survival.

During a war, the only alternative to wilderness campaigns was for the British to sail an expedition directly to Louisbourg or Quebec. Indeed, in previous wars the British had launched three attacks on Quebec, of which the first succeeded as had the siege of Louisbourg. Lacking adequate sea power, the French lacked the option of assaults on, say, Boston or New York.

But geography did not always favor the French. Climate sided with Britain. While most American ports remained ice-free year round, the Saint Lawrence and its tributaries annually froze over for several long months, thus effectively severing Canada from France. The milder climate in the American colonies allowed the British to begin their war season several weeks before and end it several weeks after the French did theirs.

Despite this severe disadvantage, the French always reached the field before the lumbering British forces did. In fact, the French raided the American settlements all year, even through blizzards. During the war, only one British commander, American-born Major Robert Rogers, matched the skills of the Canadians and Indians in wilderness and even winter warfare.[34]

Year after war year the French had to run their supply ships across the Atlantic through a gauntlet of prowling British warships and then 400 miles up the Gulf of Saint Lawrence before reaching Quebec. Supplies were usually transferred to smaller boats for the 160-mile passage to Montreal, where they were transferred again to canoe fleets to be conveyed to distant frontier forts.

To worsen matters for the Canadians in the field, Versailles tended to supply them with second-rate equipment. Captain Pouchot noted that the marines "were extremely ill armed, because they sent to the country all the rejects from the King's magazines. The same was true of the artillery, the guns were all rust-worn."[35] The quality and quantity of supplies improved after French regular forces took the field.

The Indian Way of Diplomacy and War

If the French had trouble fully appreciating their Canadian counterparts, they were utterly baffled when it came to Indians.[36] Though Generals Jean Armand, baron de Dieskau, and Montcalm understood that Indian allies were essential to French success in North America, they often blundered in wielding them. It took an enormous and continuous effort just keeping Indian lands open to Canadian traders, let alone rallying warriors to raid the British. Every spring the governor general hosted a grand council with the Indians at Montreal where he tried to strengthen ties with eloquent speeches, effusive promises, heaps of gifts, and abundant food and drink. The same protocol accompanied any trade or war council at the most remote fort, trading post, or forest glade.

Councils meshed diplomacy, psychology, and spirituality. Pouchot recalled a typical session:

> The orator was carrying strings of wampum & a fine wampum belt of about five thousand beads. By the first string he said: "Brothers, I thank the Master of Life who has given us a fine day to see you in good health, as I am myself." By the 2nd string: "I am unblocking your ears, so that you may hear what we have to say." By the 3rd string: "This one is to empty your stomach of all that evil bile which puts one in a black mood, so that you may listen to me calmly & with pleasure." By the 4th: "I bury the death of all your warriors, since we live in times when all our mats are together and so that, once you have come out of mourning, you may listen with gaiety & contentment." By the belt, he said: "Brothers, we have listened carefully to your words. We are delighted that you have not lent your ears to evil

birds. . . . That is to show intelligence, as did our ancestors who are no longer on the earth & who thought only of good feelings. We have great pleasure in seeing what your feelings are, but we beg you to speak from the heart and not from the lips."[37]

The French and Indians each maintained their own illusions about the relationship between them. The French officially considered the Indians royal subjects, which the Indians went along with as long as the gifts kept coming; indeed, for Indians the protocol of gift giving had as much to do with the practical business of expecting an outsider to pay for access to transit, trade, and residence on their land as it did the ethic whereby those with more naturally gave to those with less. Indians regarded the French as guests in their land when both sides knew that they were there permanently and ever more powerfully. These respective fictions helped keep the relationship together.

Some Canadians and French recognized the injustice laden in their relationship with the Indians. In his memoir's opening paragraph, Pierre Pouchot ironically promised not to "speak of the rights of the natural owners of the country, which these great powers entirely discount, even though the natives find it very strange that others should fight for a country where the author of life has, in their view, created them, where they have always lived & of which the bones of their ancestors have had possession from the beginning of time. They are unwilling to recognize any foreigner as their master, just as they have none amongst themselves."[38]

This very sensitivity had enabled the French to survive and expand in North America for a century and a half. The French had no choice but to understand and adapt to Indian ways. To have failed to do so would have long ago lost them New France. With their superior numbers and with fewer Indians east of the Appalachians with which to contend, the British could afford to be insensitive, arrogant, and voracious in their demands.

Though war was an integral part of Indian culture, most tribes were not eager to get involved in European wars unless they had suffered directly from one side or the other. An Iroquois chief eloquently rebuffed a French attempt to enlist him and his followers against the Americans in 1745 with these words: "Father . . . we pray you not to carry the war into our country. No war is declared between your [Indian] children; it is only between you and the English, and we are ignorant of the cause of it; we leave you to fight, and we pray you to let the Nations belonging to our cantons alone, so as to leave our hunting grounds undisturbed. We make the same request of the English by a similar belt."[39]

Thus were European ambitions continually frustrated by Indian realities. By the mid–eighteenth century, European powers had claimed practically every known inch of the Western Hemisphere, despite having set foot on but a fraction of it, as their own. By right of the international law then prevailing, any peoples living in those lands were subject to the state that claimed them since sovereignty, following the 1648 Treaty of Westphalia, lay in each state's ruler.

The Indians had their own subtle notions of sovereignty and suzerainty. If sovereignty lay anywhere among Indians, it resided within the individual. The ties that bound an individual were relaxed enough within one's family and loosened further with clan, religion, and government. Indians accepted "only voluntary subordination. Each person is free to do as he pleases. The village chiefs and the war chiefs can have influence, but they do not have authority."[40] Individuals owed gratitude and various duties to all the interrelated human and nonhuman forces that had conceived and raised them. Much more so than individuals in European societies, an Indian was quite free to choose his or her path in life. Ultimately, of course, one's fate and choices depended on the Master of Life itself.

Kinship ruled relations among nations. If nations were not brothers or fathers and sons, they were enemies. While chiefs in council may have uttered quite sincere homilies to the "Great Father," they insisted that the "'master of life' caused them to be born in the territory they inhabit and that no one has the right to interfere with what they possess. Since they do not recognize land ownership, they consider that the whole country is common property & that any territory they inhabit where the bones & spirits of their ancestors reside is sacred & inviolable. . . . Since the French only occupied the banks of the St. Lawrence, they have not worried the Indians up to now, as the latter have retained all the interior."[41]

Indians varied in their willingness to follow the French. As happens so often, familiarity did tend to breed contempt among the Indians for the French. Bougainville found that the "nations of the Far West are, in general, easier to lead than our domesticated Indians. They have greater respect for the French whom they see less often, moreover their great distance from home is a reason why they do not relax every time they have made a strike."[42] Some of the converted Indians could be readily mobilized for war, especially in the missions led by the warrior-priests Abbé Jean-Louis Le Loutre among the Micmacs and Sulpician abbé François Picquet at the predominately Iroquois La Présentation on the upper Saint Lawrence.

Despite the Indians' reluctance to entangle themselves in most European wars, the French and British alike retained a trump card in negotiations. Most Europeans noted with glee, a few with regret, the "misfortune of these Indians [that] we arrived in their land & taught them to use our materials for their garments. They could not now dispense with gunpowder & brandy without the majority of them perishing."[43] The French and British did not hesitate to threaten subtly or openly that if warriors did not join their side, supplies would not appear in the villages.

The Indians could be at once ferocious and infuriating allies. Tribes were warrior societies. A man was valued according to how bravely and skillfully he hunted humans and other animals. Once a council had agreed either reluctantly or enthusiastically for war, the bravest men immediately began rallying followers to take the warriors' path.

On the warpath, the "Indians determine the route, the halts, the scouts, and the speed to make, and in this sort of warfare it is necessary to adjust to their ways."[44] Indian wilderness skills never ceased to astonish the French and British. Bougainville marveled at "this talent they have of finding tracks in the woods and of following them without losing them. . . . They see in the tracks the number that have passed, whether they are Indians or Europeans, if the tracks are old or fresh, if they are of healthy or sick people. . . . It is rarely that they are deceived or mistaken."[45]

The Indians were masters of war psychology. They struck when and where least expected. They covered their bodies and faces with garish war paint and tattoos, shaved their heads except for a defiant scalp lock, and "utter the most frightful yells they can manage, in order to give themselves courage & to intimidate the enemy. . . . Although they find these atrocities repugnant, they nonetheless commit them in order to steel themselves to the slaughter & induce in themselves a kind of rage. This makes them appear insensitive to danger & more courageous to their fellows."[46]

Ambush was the favored tactic. The war party would disappear into the forest around a path, fire a fusillade on any enemy that blundered into it, then sprint with earsplitting war cries and brandished hatchets against the survivors. Only the most hardened frontiersmen could stand firm against such a charging horde of screaming, devilishly painted "savages."

Capture was often a fate worse than immediate death. An Indian family who had lost loved ones at war might insist on either torturing the prisoner to a hellish death or joyfully adopting him as a son to replace who was lost. Most Indians occasionally engaged in cannibalism to sustain themselves spiritually and nutritionally. Bougainville wrote of a Delaware and Shawnee war party that had "eaten an English officer whose pallor and plumpness tempted them."[47]

The viciousness of Indian warfare troubled nearly all French officers who had recently arrived in Canada; some, of course, worried more than others over the morality of employing Indians. It was an especially haunting dilemma for an intellectual like Bougainville: "The cruelties and the insolence of these barbarians is horrible. . . . It is an abominable way to make way . . . and the air one breathes here is contagious of making one accustomed to callousness."[48] Yet the only thing worse than having Indians for allies was having them for enemies. Bougainville vividly expressed that moral dilemma: "We can unleash nearly three thousand Indians on the English colonies. What a scourge! Humanity shudders at being obliged to make use of such monsters. But without them the match would be too much against us."[49]

Sugar and Slaves

In the last years of the war, a debate raged in both Versailles and Whitehall over whether the British should take "Canada or Guadeloupe" as a war prize. The uninitiated might wonder why either side would question the relative worth of half a continent versus a tiny Caribbean island. But Guadeloupe and France's other Caribbean islands produced more wealth in sugar, cotton, coffee, cocoa, hardwood, dyewoods, tobacco, and indigo than the vast half continent of New France for a tiny fraction of the latter's administrative and military costs.

The value of France's "sugar islands" expanded in the eighteenth century, partly thanks to the British. By passing the Molasses Act of 1733, which raised taxes on molasses from its own colonial islands, Whitehall inadvertently boosted profits for French West Indian planters. New England smugglers loaded their ships with French molasses and took it home where it was distilled into rum.

Unlike in North America, power was distributed relatively equally in the Caribbean. Over the previous century, France had amassed a considerable empire in the Caribbean, including Hispaniola's western half called Saint Domingue (Haiti), Guadeloupe, Marie-Galante, and Martinique; the navy's most important ports of call were Cap François on Saint Domingue's north coast and Fort de France or Port Royal on Martinique. The British, meanwhile, had acquired Jamaica; Barbados; the Leeward Islands group of Antigua, Saint Kitts or Saint Christopher, Nevis, and Montserrat; Providence in the Bahamas; and some of the Virgin Islands in the Lesser Antilles. To defend its scattered holdings, Whitehall had maintained squadrons at Jamaica and the Leeward Islands since 1745. Spain held Cuba, Hispaniola's eastern half, called Santo Domingo, Puerto Rico, the Bahamas Islands, and Trinidad, all way stations to the vast empire sprawling over North and South America. The Dutch were a secondary power with Curaçao off Venezuela's north coast, and Saint Eustatius, Saint Martin, and several of the Virgin Islands. Privateers and pirates foraged throughout the Caribbean. To defend themselves from the myriad of threats, each power used convoys to carry supplies to and wealth from the Caribbean.

Under the Aix-la-Chapelle Treaty, a string of four disputed islands, Dominica, Saint Lucia, Saint Vincent, and Tobago, were designated the Neutral Islands, which no nation could control. For decades France, England, and Spain had asserted claims to all or part of those islands. With settlers on all four islands, the French had the strongest footholds but had agreed not to convert their holdings into formal colonies. The English had no permanent settlements but frequently sent expeditions there to cut dyewood. The Spanish claim was abstract legally and economically. The Neutral Islands were among the handful left where the Carib Indians survived and the only ones that they formally governed. The European powers paid the Caribs for permission to exploit their lands. Of the four islands, Saint Lucia was the most productive, but for France these islands garnered a mere fraction of the wealth created by Martinique, Guadeloupe, and Saint Domingue. Lying upwind of England's Barbados and astride Martinique's sea-lane with Grenada and Guadeloupe, the Neutral Islands were far more important strategically than economically.

Nearly all that West Indian wealth was extracted from the sweat, blood, and bones of slaves. Thus did a triangular trade link French manufactured goods, Caribbean commodities, and West Africans. The demand for more slaves was insatiable. Procreation could not keep up with the number of slaves killed by overwork and disease. The annual net attrition rate was 5 percent; 1,200 new slaves were needed to fill Martinique's ranks emptied by exhaustion and disease, while another 1,800 were needed to work the plantations on the other French islands. French planters made up this loss by buying directly from French slave ports at Gorée and Senegal or from the English colony of Barbados. Though Jean Baptiste Colbert, Jean Talon, and others tried to promote a quadrangular trade among France, Canada, the West Indies, and West Africa, its development was crimped by the great distances, dearth of Canadians to buy or sell, and smuggling by the British and others. Bordeaux, Nantes, and La Rochelle carried the bulk of trade with the West Indies and West Africa.[50]

To the Ends of the Earth

India was yet another arena of European imperial rivalry and war. Starting with the Portuguese in the 1490s, European companies had wrangled leases for trading posts from local rulers along India's coasts and up rivers into its interior. To survive, let alone prosper, the Europeans competed for the patronage of native rulers, employed native (sepoy) troops, mastered the Byzantine maze of local politics and customs, bought ever more concessions with liberal gifts of gold and guns, and took sides in succession struggles. The trading firms even fought wars against resentful native princes. Superior weapons, discipline, and tactics allowed European troops and sepoy auxiliaries to rout native forces many times larger. Over two and a half centuries, the rival firms had occasionally skirmished against each other but lacked the resources, proximity, or confidence to risk an all-out war. This was no longer true in the 1740s. By then, the English and French had amassed enough power to match their ambitions in destroying one another.

When word of the War of the Austrian Succession finally reached India, the rival merchant leaders jumped at the excuse to destroy or engulf rival posts. The war in India started in 1744, was interrupted briefly by news of the Aix-la-Chapelle Treaty, sputtered on until 1754, and ended with a formal truce signed between the French and English governors in January 1755. Ironically, the colonial war in India ended just as the latest began in North America. When the smoke had cleared in India, thanks largely to the vision, enterprise, and ruthlessness of its president, Joseph François Dupleix, assisted by Bertrand de la Bourbonnais, the French East India Company had bested its English rival in India. English losses would have been greater were it not for Robert Clive, a chief clerk of the British company, who displayed his military genius. After the war, Dupleix returned to France; Clive remained in India.

By the mid-1750s, India's elaborate political mosaic was dominated by three large empires, the Mogul, the Maratha, and the Deccan, which sprawled across swaths of the subcontinent. Those in turn were divided by scores of principalities or nabobs. And, finally, tiny European trading posts dotted the coast and nearby interior. Those of the French and English were the most numerous. The French and English East India Companies could each muster several thousand European and native troops. By 1756, the leaders of those rival firms were itching for an excuse to resume warring against the other. The side that struck first and most decisively might well conquer the other. The French East India Company had posts at Surat, Masulipatam, Pondicherry, Chandernagore, Balasore, Kasimbazar, Calicut, and Mahe. The French had also planted a colony on Madagascar, a vital stepping stone on the trade routes to and from India. The English East India Company had trading posts on India's west coast at Bombay, with satellites at Surat, Amdavad, Agra, Swally, Broach, and Lucknow. Three clusters of English forts or factories dotted India's eastern coast: Karwar, Tellicherry, and Anjengo in Malabar; Chinghee, Orixa, and Fort Saint George guarding Madras, and Fort Saint David in Coromandel; and Dacca and Fort William at Calcutta in Bengal. The Dutch were the third-ranking European power overall, except in Bengal with its constellation of trading posts surrounding its headquarters at Chinsura. There Dutch power actually overshadowed that of England until Robert Clive captured those Dutch posts in 1759. Elsewhere in India the Portuguese had posts at Goa, Diu, and Daman, while Danish and Swedish firms traded in the region. Besides their Indian holdings, the Dutch had trading posts at Batavia and Ceylon. Spain had the Philippines; a vigorous trade linked Manila and Acapulco, Mexico.

Consequences

So just how could Versailles defend its empire, not only in North America, but in the West Indies, West Africa, and India as well? All it could do was keep sending enough troops, munitions, and provisions to each colony to thwart any British march or landing, and, if that failed and the French had to retreat to a fort or city, survive a prolonged siege. The French did not need to match the number of British troops; they only needed enough to blunt any offensive against them. Given British naval supremacy, Versailles had to steel itself against the likelihood that a portion of any supply ships it dispatched overseas would be captured.

Meanwhile, Versailles had to act on the reality that it could best defend its empire by winning victories in Germany—conquering Hanover and defeating Prussia. British Hanover along with Minorca, which the French captured in 1756, would be vital bargaining chips to trade for British acceptance of the Appalachian border between their North American empires or to get back Canada and any other colonies that fell.

The rest depended on its commanders in Canada and the other colonies. To hold Canada, Governor Pierre Rigaud, marquis de Vaudreuil de Cavagnial and first General Dieskau (1755), then General Montcalm (1756–59), and finally General François Gaston Lévis (1759–60) had to pursue two interrelated policies. The first was diplomatic—every Indian tribe east of the Mississippi River had to be courted for an alliance that supplied warriors against the British. Neutrality could be grudgingly accepted, but resistance had to be crushed as swiftly as possible. Winning over the Indians demanded continual generosity, sensitivity, and firmness from the governor on down to the lowest post commander. Gaining Indian loyalties demanded yet one more requirement—victories. Ideally, the French would capture a virtuous cycle of war whereby Indian allies helped bring French victories, which in turn would rally more warriors to the fleur-de-lis.

How could the increasingly outnumbered French defeat the British armies launched against them? The field commanders had to pursue an active defense in which they continually dispatched raiding parties to harass the enemy's communication lines and wipe out small forces, forts, and settlements. Key positions in any corridor leading toward Canada had to be fortified to withstand a prolonged siege, with an escape route if British cannon and mortars breached the walls. The French could then retreat to another fortress a few days' march or row away. By skillfully using a defense in depth against the invaders, the French could slowly grind down a British army into pulp, then counterattack.

The French had just enough troops and supplies to embark on one large-scale offensive a year, ideally against the key and most vulnerable

British position along the frontier—Albany. If the French annually threatened to attack, and certainly if they managed to take, that strategic town, the British would divert their troops arrayed elsewhere such as Louisbourg for Albany's defense or recapture. As will be seen, a portion of that scenario actually occurred in 1757.

The Seven Years' War in North America was a hybrid of European and American methods. By 1759, General Montcalm noted that the "nature of war in this colony has totally changed. Formerly the Canadians thought they were making war when they went on raids resembling hunting-parties—now we have formal operations; formerly the Indians were the basis of things, now they are only auxiliaries. We now need other views, other principles. I say this; but the old principles remain."[51] Bougainville also noticed the change: "Now war is established here on the European basis. Projects for the campaign, for armies, for artillery, for sieges, for battles. It is no longer a matter of making a raid, but of conquering or being conquered. What a revolution!"[52] Indeed, the war was filled with European-style sieges, assaults, and field battles, interspersed with raids deep behind the enemy lines to strike at their supply lines or simply terrorize. As Montcalm pointed out, this war was won by regular troops and navies, with first provincials and then Indians playing supporting roles.

Still there were some significant differences from European warfare. Most battles were staged in forest clearings rather than on farmland. Cavalry squadrons were not present to charge or scout; infantry did the charging while fleet-footed Indians or rangers reconnoitered. Artillery played a secondary role in field battles but was, of course, decisive for sieges. The number of troops massed on a battlefield usually numbered in the hundreds or thousands rather than the tens of thousands as in Europe.

New France might have survived the shift from limited to total war had Versailles committed more resources and had Montcalm been bolder. Divided war councils, corruption, incompetence, and indecisiveness at both Versailles and Quebec ultimately straightjacketed its field commanders and made New France's fall all but inevitable.

Successive kings and their minions had never committed enough resources to make New France a viable colony. Indeed, the expense of administering and defending New France far exceeded any wealth brought back across the Atlantic. So why then did Versailles annually pour enough treasure into New France to keep it alive but not enough skilled, ambitious settlers who could transform it into a dynamic, wealthy colony?

Foreign minister Choiseul succinctly explained the rationale: New France was important "not for the products themselves but for preventing the English from profiting by them."[53] England's empire made money; France's did not. Yet for a century and a half Versailles annually poured a fortune into an empire it could not profitably exploit or would not properly defend just to deny that vast land to the British.

PART 2

The Years of Victories

CHAPTER 4

The Clash of Empires through 1754

A little more or less territory in North America should not cause a war; each nation possesses more than she can use for a long time to come.

Rouillé

We have hitherto been sheltered from the rapaciousness of European nations, who have an inconceivable passion for pebbles and dirt of our land, for the sake of which they would murder us to the last man.

old Indian in *Candide*

Our war is just; theirs is like that of Algiers or the wolf and the lamb.

Argenson

Competition among the European powers for the Western Hemisphere began to rage not long after Columbus first "encountered" it in 1492. The papal bull of 1493 granted any new discoveries only to Spain and Portugal. Under the Treaty of Tordesillas of 1494, those two Iberian kingdoms agreed to split the entire New World between them, with a line drawn from the north to south poles about three hundred miles west of Portugal's Azores islands. Spain made good on the deal; within a half century, its conquistadors had rampaged over Central and South America. Portugal, meanwhile, planted colonies in Brazil. A succession of sixteenth-century Spanish attempts to explore and conquer North America, however, met mostly with disaster. Aside from Spanish outposts in northern Florida and New Mexico, that continent remained free of European conquest.

During the sixteenth century, England, Portugal, and France launched several probes into North America. With Henry VII's support, John Cabot embarked on a voyage in 1497 during which he discovered the Gulf of Saint Lawrence. England, however, failed to capitalize on it. Portugal's Corte-Real brothers sailed along the Northeastern American coast in 1500 and 1501. Their reports encouraged Basque fishermen to drag nets in those distant seas and actually maintain a small port on Cape Breton from 1520 to 1525. About the time the Basques abandoned that post, the French arrived.

Learning that Ferdinand Magellan's expedition had sailed around the world via South America's southern tip, a group of Italian financiers at Lyon decided to find a shortcut. They commissioned Giovanni da Verrazano to explore the unknown world north of Florida. In 1524 Verrazano did so, claiming and mapping for France America's East Coast as far north as Newfoundland, which he called "New France" ("Nouvelle-France"). Though interested, Francis I was too bogged down in his Italian wars to exploit that claim, leaving other powers to dispute it. Within a few years after Verrazano's voyage, Spain's Esteban Gomez and England's John Rut had sailed and mapped that same coast, respectively putting Spanish and English place-names on the features.

It was not until 1534 that someone loyal to France again reached America. In his first voyage, Jacques Cartier explored the Gulf of Saint Lawrence before sailing home. When he returned the next year, he journeyed as far up the Saint Lawrence as where the river turned to rapids at Hochelaga (Montreal), before wintering downstream at Stadacona (Quebec). The Iroquois peoples then living along the Saint Lawrence valley largely welcomed him. In 1541, Cartier reached a site called "Canada" after the Iroquoian word for "village" and tried to plant a trading post there. After a harsh winter and spoiled food killed off many of his men, Cartier abandoned the site and sailed back to France in 1543.

Though Breton and Basque fishermen annually fished the Newfoundland and Saint Lawrence banks, it would be another six decades before France reasserted its claim to Canada. Two other French expeditions, however, did try to settle elsewhere in the New World. In 1555, Admiral Gaspard de Coligny and Nicolas Durand de Villegaignon stepped ashore at Guanabara Bay (Rio de Janeiro), Brazil, but the Portuguese drove them off. Francis I tried to insert a legal claim to France's discoveries while negotiating the Treaty of Cateau-Cambrésis of 1559 with Spain; Madrid denied France any right to those lands. Two years after Jean Ribault and René Goulaine Laudonnière erected Charlesfort (near Beaufort, South Carolina) in 1562, a Spanish expedition destroyed it. In 1564, Laudonnière recklessly founded Fort Caroline on the Saint John's River in northern Florida. Pedro Menéndez de Avilés wiped out that colony as well.

The dream of New France did not die but seemed impossible to realize. Though named by Henri III as New France's viceroy in 1577, Trolius de La Roche de Mesgouez did not weigh anchor until 1597. A settlement on Sable Island lasted until the starving survivors were rescued in 1603. Henri IV granted Pierre de Chauvin de Tonnetuit a monopoly to Canada's interior. Tonnetuit's post at Tadoussac where the Saguenay joins the Saint Lawrence lasted a year from 1600. The king then handed the monopoly to Aymar de Chaste and François Gravé Du Pont, who first set up a trading post on Saint Croix Island in 1603 then transferred it to Habitation near Port Royal (Annapolis Royal). Pierre Du Gua de Monts replaced de Chaste in 1604 and dispatched two intrepid subordinates, Jean Biencourt de Poutrincourt et de Saint Just and Samuel de Champlain, to explore the Atlantic and Saint Lawrence shores. In 1608, Champlain founded Quebec. While all previous French settlements had withered and died, Quebec clung to life and would eventually flourish.[1]

Ironically, Quebec's founding coincided with the first successful English settlement in North America, that at Jamestown in 1607; an English post at Kennebec that same year died. Raiding between the French and English in North America began shortly thereafter.

The first recorded fighting occurred in 1613 when Captain Samuel Argall destroyed a French settlement on Mount Desert Island, then in 1614 burned Habitation in Nova Scotia. The next round of fighting, however, did not break out for another two decades.

While the English attacked Canada only two more times during the seventeenth century, the Iroquois threat was nearly permanent. Not long after arriving, the French found that befriending some tribes meant enraging others. The Iroquois who had greeted Cartier had abandoned the Saint Lawrence valley for the Mohawk valley and Finger Lakes region to the south. Champlain allied with the tribes that had settled in their wake, the Montagnaises, Naskapis, Nipissings, and Algonquins, and eventually sent traders to the Huron, Petun, and Neutral tribes north of Lakes Ontario and Erie. In the Acadia region, the French brought peace to the previously warring Malecites, Micmacs, and Abenakis and forged an alliance with those three tribes, which would later terrorize New England.

But in reaping these diplomatic and trade triumphs, Champlain joined his allies in wars against the Iroquois in 1609 and 1615. This provoked an enmity between the French and Iroquois that lasted nearly the entire century. The Iroquois strengthened steadily after the Dutch founded Fort Nassau (Albany) at their eastern doorstep in 1624 and began trading them muskets for furs. During the mid-seventeenth century, the Iroquois launched a series of Beaver Wars in all directions to destroy their rivals and capture the fur trade; many of their raids devastated French settlements. The Iroquois wars did help the French in one important way—the Indian tribes ravished by the Iroquois became all the more dependent on the French.

Despite the perennial Iroquois threat, the French slowly solidified their settlements in the Saint Lawrence valley and dispatched traders and missionaries up the Great Lakes. Champlain acted upon a Huron invitation to visit the tribe in 1615. Recollect friars began proselytizing at this time, too. The Jesuits landed their own missionaries in New France in 1626. The Company of One Hundred Associates in 1627 received a fifteen-year tax holiday and perpetual monopoly over Canada's fur trade in return for settling four thousand Catholics there by 1643 and underwriting their clergy. The company nominated and the king approved a governor general with supreme power over Canada's military, civil, and legal affairs.

That effort was no sooner begun than an English expedition under David Kirke captured first the French supply fleet in 1628, then a starving Quebec from Champlain in 1629. Sir William Alexander meanwhile planted a colony at Annapolis Royal in Acadia. The French and English ended their short war with the 1629 Treaty of Susa based on the status quo ante bellum. Kirke refused to surrender Quebec until London forced him out after signing the Treaty of Saint Germain-en-Laye with Paris, whereby each recognized the other's North American colonies. Had England decided to keep rather than return New France, it could have saved itself another 130 years of rivalry and war for the continent.

Ironically, that second round of fighting between the French and English in Canada was paralleled by an alliance between them in the Caribbean.[2] The West Indian islands that arc across the Caribbean Sea are split into two groups, the four large islands of the Greater Antilles of Cuba, Jamaica, Hispaniola (Haiti and Santo Domingo), and Puerto Rico on the sea's north side, and the tiny islands of the Lesser Antilles on the sea's eastern side. Not long after the Spanish first began settling the Caribbean basin, privateers from France, England, Holland, and other nations began raiding its treasure ships. It was not until the early seventeenth century, however, that those rivals began seizing small islands in the Lesser Antilles, which the Spanish had neglected to conquer. The first invasion occurred in 1624 when the French and English agreed to jointly settle Saint Christopher (Saint Kitts). The French took Martinique and Guadeloupe as early as 1635. Sugar plantations soon made those tiny islands more valuable than any furs or fish hauled out of Canada. They were also excellent bases from which to attack Spain's treasure ships and fight with the English, Dutch, and even Danes for control of other islands.

With their Caribbean conquests, the French and English established overlapping rectangular trade routes around the northern Atlantic basin whereby manufactured goods from the home countries, West African slaves, West Indian sugar and other tropical products, and American or Canadian grains, dried fish, or livestock were exchanged. England's North American colonies enjoyed several vast advantages over France's Canada and later Louisiana. The more numerous, prosperous, and productive Americans could buy and sell more, their voyages were shorter, their growing seasons were longer, and their products were more diversified with New England rum, fish, and lumber, mid-Atlantic grains, and southern rice.

While France's efforts in the Caribbean showed considerable promise of profit, Canada's economy was all but dead. The Company of One Hundred Associates failed to wring earnings from or bring settlers into Canada. In 1643, fed up with that monopoly's failings, Louis XIII hived off the government functions to the Community of Inhabitants. This time the king appointed a council, which included the governor general, governor of Montreal, and Jesuit superior to rule Canada; councils were formed in Montreal, Quebec, and Trois Rivières with their members elected by the leading citizens of those towns. Meanwhile, the Company of One Hundred continued to enjoy its fur trade monopoly. But this arrangement too withered as the government failed to defend Canada from the Iroquois or increase immigration, while the fur trade failed to make money. In March 1663, the Company of One Hundred Associates returned its charter to the king.

The great division in French imperial policy occurred in 1664. In that year, Louis XIV's principal minister, Jean-Baptiste Colbert, transformed French imperialism from the king's practice of simply issuing monopoly charters to a succession of private ventures that failed to profit from the New World to the monarchy's direct control of New France, underwritten by royal finance, supplies, soldiers, and ships. With Colbert's advice, Louis XIV appointed a royal governor general, Augustin de Saffray de Mésy, who, along with Bishop François de Laval, set foot in Quebec in September 1663. In 1664, a fur trade monopoly was granted to yet another group of entrepreneurs, the West India Company. That same year four French regular infantry companies were sent to New France. In 1665, the king dispatched Jean Talon to serve as Canada's first intendant. Accompanying Talon were the 1,200 troops of the Carignan-Salières Regiment. New France's population was now 3,035, of which nearly half were soldiers. Colbert and Talon worked together to develop New France by setting up shipyards and ironworks, and settling more immigrants. By 1685, the population had risen to 10,977 and Canada actually exported wheat to France.

The French were now established firmly enough in the Saint Lawrence valley to allow them to expand elsewhere. The infusion of troops shifted the power balance with the Iroquois. A successful expedition against the Iroquois in 1666 led to a peace treaty the following year that allowed French missionaries access to that tribe. During the late seventeenth century, French explorers and missionaries spread up the Great Lakes and down the Mississippi valley and erected trade posts and missions throughout those regions. In 1670, Jacques Marquette established Fort Michilimackinac. In 1672, Marquette and Louis Jolliet reached the Mississippi River and descended it as far as the mouth of the Arkansas River. Receiving a five-year monopoly over the western Great Lakes fur trade, Robert Cavelier de la Salle founded Saint Joseph in 1679, Fort Crevecoeur in 1680, Fort Prudhomme in 1682, and Fort Saint Louis in 1682. In 1682, he led an expedition that descended the Mississippi River to its mouth, thus showing the way for Louisiana's founding two decades later. La Salle's attempt to found a settlement on the Gulf of Mexico in 1684 ended in disaster. The settlers endured disease, malnutrition, and Indian attacks until the men murdered La Salle and fled back to France. A French expedition led by Chevalier de Troyes not only trekked all the way to Hudson Bay in 1685 but also captured three British trading posts along its shores. It was the golden age for French exploration of North America.

Meanwhile, the power balance elsewhere in North America shifted as well. In three naval wars (1652–54, 1665–67, and 1672–74), the English defeated the Dutch and conquered New Netherlands. Now England's American colonies stretched from Maine to South Carolina, and England replaced the Dutch as the Iroquois ally against the French. By 1676, the English had further consolidated their power by crushing the Narragansetts and their allies in New England and the Susquehannas and their allies in Virginia.

Versailles managed to quell this invigorated English threat with diplomacy. The English renounced claims to Acadia under the 1655 Treaty of Westminster and the 1667 Treaty of Breda. With the 1668 Treaty of Whitehall and 1670 Treaty of Boston, they agreed to delineate part of the boundary between their two North American empires, with the English conceding to France all territory from the Penobscot River to Cape Breton. Versailles built upon these diplomatic victories with the 1684 Truce of Ratisbon, whereby Spain finally agreed to recognize France's North American empire. Finally, under the 1686 Treaty of Whitehall, the English and French sought jointly to exploit Hudson Bay and Acadia, though neither side rewrote its trade laws to allow it.

Then, in 1689, France and England fought once more as they were drawn into the War of the Augsburg League, which engulfed Europe. The Iroquois struck the first blow. Learning of the war, they launched a devastating attack on Lachine. This prompted the French, for the first time, to join Indians in raids on the northern tier of the American colonies. In 1690, in retaliation for Lachine, the French led their allies against Schenectady, Salmon Falls, and Fort Loyal. That same year Sir William Phips succeeded in capturing Port Royal, Acadia. In 1691, Phips devised a grandiose plan to capture Canada with a two-pronged offensive via Lake Champlain and the Saint Lawrence. Phips's sea expedition anchored before Quebec but failed to take it, while Pieter Schuyler's raid reached Montreal's outskirts before turning back. New France had barely escaped conquest. The French struck back. In 1693, over six hundred Canadians and Indians invaded the Iroquois lands; though they inflicted no significant defeat, they did quell any counterattacks for a while. In 1695, the French erected Fort Frontenac on Lake Ontario's northern shore. A 1696 expedition against the Iroquois ravaged many Onondaga villages.

Despite these victories in North America, the French lost elsewhere, most notably at the sea battle of La Hogue in 1692. The 1697 Treaty of Ryswick that ended the War of the League of Augsburg resulted in the first rollback of France's North American empire. France conceded to England its claims to Newfoundland, Hudson Bay, Acadia, and the West Indian island of Saint Christopher. Once again Paris and London promised to form a commission to settle their boundary. The commission met in 1699 but failed to reach an agreement. That failure was offset by a diplomatic triumph two years later.

The near century of war with the Iroquois ended in 1701 when that tribe, exhausted and diminished, signed treaties with both the French

and the English. Henceforth, the Iroquois promised to remain neutral in any war between the European rivals. The French were now too
numerous for the Iroquois to dream of exterminating. It made much
more sense to play off the French and English against each other and
thus gain far more from trade than from war.

That same year, Antoine de la Mothe Cadillac founded Detroit,
which would serve as the western country's key trading post, and
encouraged the region's tribes to immigrate there. Within a decade,
Ottawa, Ojibwa, Fox, and Mascouten villages sprawled near Detroit.
Elsewhere in the region, officers supplanted missionaries as the most
important French envoys at the trading posts. Though the Detroit system made it easier to supply Indians and convey furs back to Montreal,
it worsened existing animosities among the tribes. The Fox especially
could not get along with their neighbors. In 1716, war broke out and
the French joined the others in trying to crush that tribe. The war
lasted sporadically until 1737 when the Fox finally found refuge with
the Sacs beyond the Mississippi.

During this time, the French also expanded north from the Gulf
of Mexico. To diversify New France's economy and strengthen it strategically, Versailles decided to create yet another colony, Louisiana.[3] In
1699, Pierre Le Moyne d'Iberville founded Biloxi, where he presided
as Louisiana's first governor. In 1702, his brother, Jean-Baptiste Le
Moyne de Bienville, replaced him as governor and erected a fort above
Mobile; in 1711, Bienville settled Mobile itself and named it the new
capital. Natchez was founded in 1716. In 1717, the Illinois country was
joined to Louisiana. That same year Bienville erected Fort Toulouse
on the lower Coosa River in the Creek heartland, and the following
year established Fort Natchitoches high up the Red River among the
Caddos. Bienville founded New Orleans in 1718 and transferred the
capital there in 1722.

Despite that promising beginning, Louisiana's Mississippi Company went bankrupt when the speculative bubble in Paris burst in 1720.
The king imposed direct royal rule. Within a generation of its founding, Louisiana rivaled Canada in its expanse of territory and its inability to make a profit; Louisiana, like Canada, was a perennial drain on
French finances. New France now stretched from Fort Toulouse to

Lake Winnipeg and from Cape Breton to Natchitoches. Few empires have boasted more land or suffered from fewer settlers.

Perhaps New France might have been less unsuccessful had Louis XIV not again plunged France into his most financially and militarily disastrous war of all, that of the Spanish Succession in 1701. In North America, the French resumed their strategy of raids and the British continued that of invasion. Of a half dozen large-scale French and Indian raids along the northern frontier, the most devastating struck Deerfield in 1704. The English repeatedly attacked Acadian settlements and, in 1710, succeeded in capturing them. As in King William's War, this was the first step in an attempt to take all of Canada. In 1711, Sir Hovenden Walker sailed a fleet of 32 ships packed with 6,500 troops toward Quebec. Foul weather rather than French arms defeated Walker as fog and storm wrecked nine of his ships on rocky shores.

The 1713 Peace of Utrecht was a package of eleven overlapping treaties that attempted to settle the War of the Spanish Succession's outstanding issues. By one of those treaties, France accepted Britain's claim to Newfoundland, Acadia, Rupert's Land, and Hudson Bay. A boundary commission would delineate the frontiers. As usual, negotiating and signing a treaty was much easier than fulfilling it. For the next fifty years, France and Britain squabbled over just how to interpret the Utrecht treaty. At first glance, the agreement seemed clear enough, including Article 10 whereby France surrendered "Nova Scotia, otherwise called Arcadia, in its entirety, conformable to its former limits, and generally all the dependencies of the said lands."[4] Alas, no one knew just what Acadia's "former limits" were, while the word "generally" contradicted "all" its "dependencies." Those who negotiated the treaty believed that "Arcadia" and "Nova Scotia" were synonymous. For various reasons, later diplomats distinguished between them. In 1719, a commission actually met in Paris but failed to agree on the boundaries.

Another ambiguous clause caused endless debate. Article 15 described the Iroquois as English subjects. Whitehall would later use that clause to claim not just Iroquois lands but any territories that those Indians had previously conquered, tried to conquer, or merely claimed. This led to the biggest obstacle to negotiations in the early

1750s, the conflicting French and English assertions to the Ohio country. Unable to finesse the dispute, the French and English would choose to go to war instead.

Likewise, a seeming solution to a conflict between England and Spain would haunt them a half century later. The two kingdoms tried to settle their North American rivalries by the 1707 Treaty of Barcelona, the 1713 Treaty of Utrecht, and the 1721 Treaty of Madrid. In the last two treaties, Spain acquired a vague right to participate in the Newfoundland fisheries. Though Spanish fishermen rarely ventured there, Madrid's attempts to uphold its legality would foul peace negotiations during the Seven Years' War and would eventually become a casus belli.

Utrecht's peace did keep France and Britain from each other's throats for a quarter century. Each used that breathing space to expand its empire. As early as 1676, the French built Fort Niagara where the Niagara River flows north into Lake Ontario's southwestern corner, but soon abandoned it after Iroquois protests and raids spooked traders. Within two generations, the power balance shifted from the Iroquois to the French. When the French reoccupied and rebuilt Fort Niagara in 1720, the Iroquois were too politically split and depopulated to do more than protest. The French anchored another corner of their empire that year when they founded fortress Louisbourg on Île Royale's eastern coast to guard against English Nova Scotia and to serve as a protected drying ground for fishermen.

The founding of Fort Niagara and Louisbourg provoked English fears and countermeasures. In 1721, the British Board of Trade recommended erecting forts at key passes along the Appalachian mountain chain and on Lakes Ontario and Erie to keep the French at bay. The board declared that "although these Mountains may serve at present for a very good frontier, we should not propose them for the boundary of your Majesty's empire in America. On the contrary, it were to be wished that the British settlements be extended beyond them, and some small forts erected on the great lakes, in proper places, by permission of the Indian proprietors."[5] Five years later the British acted on that strategy. In 1726, New York governor William Burnet negotiated the Treaty of Albany with the Iroquois, which gave the British the right to build a fortified trading post at Oswego on Lake Ontario's southern shore. Burnet promptly ordered the post built. Over the next quarter century, more Indian canoe caravans paddling down from Lakes Erie and Ontario ground ashore at Fort Oswego, attracted by the better prices and quality goods they could receive there for their furs. Albany's gain was Montreal's loss.

Versailles protested the founding of Oswego as an invasion of French territory but chose not to fight over it. Instead, the French advanced their own frontier deeper into the Indian lands between the two empires when, in 1731, they built Fort Saint Frederic on Lake Champlain's southwest shore. Although Whitehall protested that the fort was illegally erected on English lands granted by the Iroquois, the time was not deemed right to war with more than words.

The biggest conflict during these interwar decades arose over a region that neither the French nor English had previously exploited, the upper Ohio River valley.[6] In 1739, the French made their first recorded visit to the region when Governor Jean-Baptiste Le Moyne de Bienville led 123 French troops and 319 Indians through it en route to attack the Chickasaws on the lower Mississippi River. It would be another decade before the French again ventured there. Meanwhile, British traders increasingly ranged west into the Ohio valley and by 1743 reached the Illinois country. With their better-made and cheaper goods, the British ate away at France's market share.

In the Southeast, three rather than two empires overlapped.[7] France, Britain, and Spain struggled for the trade and loyalty of that region's tribes. Throughout most of the region, the primary conflict was between the French and English. Each tribe split along pro-French, pro-English, and neutral factions; the Choctaws and Creeks generally leaned toward France while the Natchez and Chickasaws tended toward the British. The French tried to advance their interests primarily through trade and diplomacy, but sometimes by war. Like Montreal, New Orleans was the site for an annual spring council between the governor general and delegations of Indian tribes from the region. But when negotiations broke down and Indian raids began, the French did not hesitate to fight. The French warred against the Natchez in 1727 and extirpated them. They fought against the Chickasaws from 1732 to 1739 and subjected them.

While French and British traders ranged across much of the region, Spain's ventured little beyond their few settlements in northern Florida facing the Gulf of Mexico or Atlantic. For decades, the French and Spanish debated just where to draw the line between Louisiana and Florida, but never came to blows over the dispute. Territorial and trade conflicts between Spain and Britain, however, would lead to war. When the British founded Fort King George at the mouth of the Altamaha River in 1721, Madrid vainly protested. With the 1729 Treaty of Seville, Britain and Spain tried to settle their boundary dispute but never actually got around to marking the frontier. Instead, the British exacerbated the conflict in 1733 by founding Georgia with its Atlantic-to-Pacific claim that would have cut across both French Louisiana and Spanish Texas, New Mexico, and California. Despite this affront, none of the states were yet willing to go to war. Britain and Spain tried to demarcate the border again with the 1739 Convention of Pardo. A commission actually met but resolved nothing. For that and failures to resolve other disputes, the War of Jenkins' Ear between Spain and Britain erupted later that year.

The Anglo-Spanish War bled into the War of the Austrian Succession, known as King George's War to Britons. Though the war began in 1740, Versailles and London did not officially declare war on one another until 1744. The pattern of previous North American wars was repeated. French and Indians bloodied the frontier at Canso, Annapolis Royal, Saratoga, Fort Massachusetts, and Grand Pré, to name the more notorious raids. One decisive victory overshadowed the numerous skirmishes; in 1745, three thousand New England troops led by William Pepperrell sailed aboard a fifty-two-ship fleet commanded by Peter Warren to Louisbourg and managed to capture it, though the British failed to follow it up with another try at Quebec.

As disturbing to Quebec and New Orleans were rumors that wampum belts were circulating among the Miamis, Wyandots, Iroquois, Shawnees, Creeks, and Choctaws to forge an alliance to drive the French from their lands. Though the alliance fizzled, in 1747 Wyandot chief Nicolas actually wiped out Fort Sandusky on Lake Erie and then fled with his people to the upper Ohio valley, while Miami chief Memeskia (also known as La Demoiselle or Old Briton) hoisted the British flag over his village and led an unsuccessful attack on Fort Maumee.

In investigating the conspiracy, Lieutenant Charles Deschamps de Boishébert et de Raffetot found its source in "the English, who, by force of presents and lies, excite the Indians against us, insinuating in their minds that we are not in condition to furnish them with any supplies; that we have no goods, as they take all our ships, and that Quebec has been already captured."[8] The French empire was fraying, and its leaders seemed incapable of doing anything to prevent it.

The war ended not a moment too soon for the French in North America, though their armies were victorious in Europe. Under the 1748 Treaty of Aix-la-Chapelle, the belligerents agreed to turn back the imperial clock to when before the war erupted. All conquests were to be returned. The French handed Madras in India back to Britain and once more raised their flag over Louisbourg. Finally, the treaty called for a commission to resolve all outstanding territorial disputes. Despite this seemingly favorable settlement, only six years separated this latest "peace" from the final war.[9]

To Fort Necessity

Aside from Louisbourg's loss, the French had once again clung to most of their empire while inflicting punishing raids on the American frontier. Yet King George's War exposed French weaknesses. Not only did the French have trouble rallying warriors for raids against the American settlements, but some Indians actually killed French traders in their midst. For several decades now, more Indians had become more contemptuous of the shoddy, expensive French goods and actively sought superior British goods. A Wea chief patiently explained to Captain Charles de Raymond, Fort Miami's commander, that profit rather than sentiment led the Indians to British goods: "We are no longer able to keep them from going to the English, who give them everything very cheap. You see yourself, my father, that the traders are hard on us. A man must hunt a year to clothe himself. With the English our young men for a buckskin have a yard and a half of cloth: and all things in proportion."[10]

The drain of fur wealth from Canada's hinterlands to the American colonies worsened after the war. Four smuggling corridors linked the empires—the Great Lakes and Oswego, Montreal and Albany, Louisbourg and New England, and the Ohio valley and mid-Atlantic colonies. The smuggling and bolder forays of British traders into Canada and Louisiana threatened eventually to destroy those French colonies. The flag followed trade; if not stopped, France's economic loss would become a political loss as well as one tribe after another switched allegiances, followed by the establishment of British trading posts, and finally colonies.

The French faced hard choices for their empire. They could insist on stamping out smuggling, which would fatten the profits of French producers at the cost of higher administrative and consumer prices and lower living standards in New France, along with ever more disgruntled Indians. Or they could buy trade goods from the lowest-priced source, Britain, and compete on an equal footing with American traders, to the benefit of Indian and Canadian living standards, but at the cost of French producers. Finally, they could continue the policy that forced Canadians to rely on French producers for most trade goods while turning a blind eye to the smuggling that relieved shortages and inflation in New France.

Governor La Galissonière served from 1747 to 1749 while its official governor, Jacques-Pierre de Taffanel, marquis de la Jonquière, was a British war prisoner. He recognized the dilemma facing New France and explained to Versailles that "to secure the Beaver trade to the Colony and to prevent the English from becoming masters of it . . . [we desire] to procure lighter, more merchantable and cheaper hollow-ware [kettles] than usual."[11] French industry, however, was incapable of matching the English goods in quality or price.

Nowhere was French power more tenuous than on Lake Ontario. Fort Oswego had been a painful thorn in New France's side since the British established it in 1726. Located astride the canoe route between lower and upper Canada along Lake Ontario's southern shore, the post's cheap, well-made goods became a magnet that drew Indians from as far away as the upper Great Lakes. To the fury of the French, the Indians bypassed their posts at Niagara and Frontenac to reach

Oswego. The British traders garnered not just furs but vital information and allegiances from their customers.

In 1748, Abbé François Picquet tried to soften some of Oswego's power when he founded La Présentation mission on the Saint Lawrence River's south shore midway between Lake Ontario and Montreal. The strategy provoked rather than subdued the Indians. That October "a party of Indians, supposed to be Mohawks . . . attacked Picquet's mission. . . . The loss by this fire was considerable. . . . The Indians were instigated to this attack by the English."[12]

Stronger measures were essential to recapturing the region, and only Versailles could supply the necessary authority and resources to act. In 1749, Governor La Galissonière and Intendant François Bigot submitted to Versailles plans to reassert French power over the empire's crumbling frontier. Bigot proposed building Fort Toronto to entice fur-laden traders heading by canoe across Lake Ontario to Oswego, but conceded that his plan would only work if goods were sold there as cheaply as at Oswego.[13] To match English prices, Fort Toronto's goods would have to be sold at a loss. Bigot did not explain why the same could not be done at existing forts Niagara or Frontenac at Lake Ontario's southwest and northeast ends respectively, thus avoiding the construction of an expensive new fort. Bigot's proposal, of course, was designed to enrich himself and his cronies rather than the king. A new post was a new source of patronage that Bigot could ladle out to his sycophants in return for a cut of the profits. Versailles granted Bigot the authority to build Fort Toronto, which became yet another drain on France and source of wealth for a privileged few.

Another crisis loomed elsewhere along New France's long frontier. Under the 1713 Utrecht Treaty, France had ceded Acadia, or Nova Scotia, to England. Thereafter, the two rivals quarreled over just where Acadia's boundary lay. Versailles insisted that it ended at the Chignecto Isthmus while Whitehall countered that Acadia included modern New Brunswick as well as Nova Scotia.

With few of its own settlers there amidst perhaps as many as 12,000 Acadians, the British hold on Nova Scotia seemed tenuous. The British took formal possession in 1717 and immediately began imposing loyalty oaths on the Acadians. The hearts of most Acadians remained with

France. During King George's War, many Acadians assisted Abbé Jean Louis Le Loutre, a Spiritian missionary, who led raids on the British. After the war, Whitehall was determined to solidify its rule over Nova Scotia. To do so, however, it needed English settlers. In 1749, Whitehall dispatched Colonel Edward Cornwallis with 2,500 immigrants packed aboard fourteen ships to found Halifax, Nova Scotia, a settlement that not only would offset the Acadians but also would fortress Louisbourg just a couple of hundred sea miles up the coast.

Halifax's founding alarmed the French. In an August 29, 1749 dispatch to the governors of New France and Île Royale, Versailles admitted that the English

> are within their rights in making in Acadia such settlements as they see fit, as long as they do not pass its boundaries, there remains for us only to bring against them as many indirect obstacles as can be done without compromising ourselves. . . . The only method we can employ to bring into existence these obstacles is to make the savages of Acadia and its borders feel how much it is to their advantage to prevent the English fortifying themselves, to bind them to oppose it openly, and to excite the Acadians to support the Indians in their opposition in so far as they can do without discovery. The missionaries of both have instructions and are agreeable to act in accordance with these views.[14]

Governor La Galissonière acted on Versailles's instructions with measures designed to contain the British east of the Missaguash River and south of the Kennebec River. In 1749, he dispatched Captain Claude de la Martinière with 2,500 troops to build Fort Beauséjour on the Missaguash River's west bank on the Chignecto Isthmus and Fort Gaspereau nearby; in 1750, he sent Lieutenant Deschamps de Boishébert to build Fort Saint Jean at the mouth of the Saint John River. The governor also encouraged warrior priest Jean Louis Le Loutre to renew his efforts to infiltrate the Acadians and undermine English rule. The British countered; in April 1750, Major Charles Lawrence disembarked his troops at the isthmus's east end, marched them a few miles inland, and erected Fort Lawrence on a ridge overlooking the Missaguash. This was the only spot along the frontier between the two empires where French and British forts stood defiantly within sight of one another.

Seemingly no region of New France was immune from the aggression of British traders. The marine ministry received a 1750 report from Louisiana governor Vaudreuil that "the English are more active than ever, not only in spreading themselves over the Continent, both in the direction of Louisiana and in the interior of the Canadian territory which unites the two Colonies, but moreover in exciting the different Nations of Indians against us . . . so as to be able to interrupt the communication between the two Colonies."[15] As elsewhere, British gains were French losses.

The worst threat to the French empire, however, was in the upper Ohio valley, which American traders had reinvaded with heavily laden pack animals after Aix-la-Chapelle. All along, the French had neglected that region, expecting the Indians there to journey to Fort Niagara on Lake Ontario, Fort Miami on the Maumee River, or Fort Ouiatenon on the Wabash River to trade their furs for goods. As for communications between Quebec and New Orleans, the Wabash River rather than the upper Ohio served as the conduit.

The American traders spreading throughout the region were supported by the governors of their respective colonies. Each governor competed with the others to convene Indian councils where they distributed gifts, made conciliatory speeches, and talked the chiefs into signing treaties that conceded land and trade. Under the Lancaster Treaty of 1748, a delegation of Iroquois, Delaware, Shawnee, and Miami Indians surrendered all their lands between the Allegheny Mountains and the Ohio River to Pennsylvania, Virginia, and Maryland. These colonies then squabbled over how to divvy the spoils. As if this cession were not contentious enough, France also claimed that region along with all other lands west of the Appalachian divide.

That same year the Ohio Company of Virginia formed to petition Whitehall for a 500,000-acre land grant in the upper Ohio valley. Whitehall approved a modified version of the petition; the Ohio Company would receive an initial grant of 200,000 acres from the

Ohio forks to the mouth of the Kanawha River, and take 300,000 more acres if it settled 100 families and built a fort in the region. That grant directly challenged French claims to the region. Getting wind of Whitehall's policy, Governor La Galissonière responded by organizing and dispatching into the Ohio valley an expedition of 20 soldiers, 180 Canadians, and a score of Indians under Captain Pierre Joseph Céleron de Bienville. His mission was to intimidate the tribes into subservience, drive out British traders, and impose French power in the Ohio valley.

Throughout the summer of 1749, Céleron convened Indian councils and nailed lead plates to trees at river mouths that asserted French sovereignty over the land. All the Indians bristled at this French invasion of their home. Céleron expelled a British trader with a letter to Pennsylvania governor James Hamilton that read: "I have been much surprised to find traders belonging to your government in a country to which England never had any pretension. . . . Those whom I have just encountered . . . I have treated with all possible courtesy, though I had a right to regard them as interlopers . . . their undertaking being contrary to . . . the peace treaty signed over fifteen months ago. I hope, Sir, that you will be so good as to prohibit that trade in the future. . . . I know our Governor . . . would be very sorry to be forced to have recourse to any violence, but his orders are very strict not to suffer any foreign traders within his government."[16] Despite Céleron's strenuous efforts, the mission was doomed to failure. Upon returning to Montreal in November, he gloomily admitted, "The nations of these localities are very badly disposed towards the French, and are entirely devoted to the English. I do not know in what way they could be brought back."[17]

By the time Céleron returned to Quebec, New France's official governor had finally arrived. Jacques-Pierre de Taffanel, marquis de la Jonquière, was sixty-one years old in 1747 when he was appointed New France's governor, a post that capped a distinguished naval career. Unfortunately, he was captured en route and did not reach Quebec until September 2, 1749. In his two and a half years as governor before his death on May 17, 1752, Jonquière was harshly criticized for mismanaging the English threat to the Ohio valley while enriching himself through avarice and corruption.[18]

With Céleron's report and a succession of Indian councils, Jonquière soon understood clearly the challenge facing New France. The hostility Céleron encountered in the Ohio country softened when Indian delegations journeyed to Montreal. Yet the Indians' opposition to any French presence in their homeland was unmistakable. At a 1750 council, a Cayuga chief handed Jonquière a wampum belt and said, "Father, it appears that you wish all the Indians who are on the Beautiful river [Ohio] to withdraw. . . . This island belongs to the Indians; it is the Master of Life who has placed them on it, for he hath located those who are White on the other side of the sea. . . . I . . . often know not whom to believe. You tell me to distrust the English; the English say the same to me of you."[19]

With a few eloquent words, that anonymous Cayuga chief captured the essence of the problems between his people and the Europeans. The French and British alike were invaders who had seduced the Indians with goods, demanded obedience, and stirred them to war. Having said all that, to Jonquière's relief, the chief stated, "We see clearly that the English seek only our destruction, and are grasping all the lands we inhabit. . . . Here is a Belt which we present you, whereby we assure you of our fidelity. It is our heart we leave in your hands."[20] Like most tribes trapped between the jaws of two empires, the Cayugas recognized that survival now depended on playing the Europeans off against each other while tilting toward the less powerful French.

Meanwhile, Jonquière's predecessor, La Galissonière, had returned to Versailles to pen two important reports for the king's council. His December 1750 report systematically analyzed the strengths and weaknesses of France's North American empire and offered proposals for revitalizing it. He admitted the mercantilist "utility of Colonies . . . to a great State . . . which contributes essentially to make the balance of wealth incline in favor of France." Colonies, however, varied enormously between those that made or lost money. France's Caribbean sugar islands produced vast revenues for France at minimal administrative costs. La Galissonière then explained why Canada and Louisiana sapped French wealth, citing the impossibility of administering such vast lands; the dependence on supply fleets, which are vulnerable to the storms of enemy warships or weather; the ease with which the British could plug supply to the interior by seizing Quebec and New Orleans; the inability of French manufacturers to match British producers in price, quality, and quantity; and the exorbitant expense of annual gifts to keep the Indians subdued. Yet, despite all these weaknesses, La Galissonière insisted that "motives of honor, glory, and religion forbid the abandonment of an established Colony." Canada, he continued, "has been always a burden to France, and it is probable that such will be the case for a long while; but it constitutes, at the same time, the strongest barrier that can be opposed to the ambition of the English." La Galissonière then noted that the French enjoyed some advantages over the British with the Indians, who "love us . . . a little, and fear us a great deal, more than the English. . . . The second reason of our superiority is, the number of French Canadians who are accustomed to live in the woods like the Indians, and become thereby not only qualified to lead them to fight the English, but to wage war even against these same Indians when necessity obliges."[21] Still, he feared that even this advantage could pass to the English if Versailles failed to maintain the investments necessary to keep the Indians fearful and dependent.

The report failed to provoke the decisive policy from Louis XV's Council of State for which La Galissonière had hoped. So, in 1751, he penned a more vivid report that, Cassandra-like, warned of an inevitable English conquest. That defeat, in turn, would lead to an eighteenth-century version of the domino theory, whereby the British would take Spain's empire as well: "The utility of Canada does not end with preserving the French colonies and making the English fear for their own. That colony is not less essential for the preservation of the Spanish possessions in America, and above all of Mexico." All this would happen unless Versailles decisively committed itself to "omit no means, and . . . spare no expense to assure the preservation of Canada, since English ambition . . . and the progress of their empire in that part of the world is . . . likely to give them the upper hand in Europe."[22]

La Galissonière's dire prediction for New France combined with other reports of British aggression in the Ohio valley, Southeast, Oswego, and Acadia to grab finally the attention of Louis XV and his ministers. After a lengthy debate in September 1751, the council issued a report that echoed La Galissonière's outlook: "The English, always intent on ways of extending their possessions in North America and of violating those of His Majesty, have since the last war undertaken to carry their trade toward the Ohio, which is the heart of the country between Canada and Louisiana, and which is the principal communication of the two colonies; they also seek to seduce the Indian tribes of these districts, and even to make settlements."[23] As for British claims to the territory, the ministry found no "justifiable complaints on the part of the Court of England. The French were the discoverers of the Beautiful [Ohio] river, which has always served as a communication between Canada and Louisiana. We always carried on trade there without interruption, and have sent considerable detachments thither on various occasions."[24] Yet, in the end, Versailles did nothing more than order Governor Jonquière to eject the English traders from the Ohio valley, but failed to bolster his power to do so with additional troops or trade goods.

The governor tried a less expensive and risky method. He sent Lieutenant Daniel Marie Chabert de Joncaire, a half dozen soldiers, and five canoes filled with gifts to the region in the spring of 1752. Joncaire found British traders in nearly every village his expedition reached. The Indians shunned Joncaire's diplomacy and embraced the far more generous gifts from the Virginia and Pennsylvania traders. Under the Treaty of Logstown, signed on June 13, 1752, the local Mingo, Shawnee, and Delaware chiefs ceded 200,000 acres of land in the Ohio valley, including a patch for a trading post at the Ohio River forks, to Virginia. Joncaire returned in despair to report that France had lost the region to Britain.

That same summer, however, the French scored a victory when Captain Charles Langlade led 250 Indians from Detroit against the pro-British village of Pickawillany, burned it, captured 3 British traders, and killed Chief Memeskia. Word of Langlade's attack spread quickly through the region, rallying French supporters and cowing their enemies. British traders streamed back across the Appalachians to safety. Langlade's lesson was clear—to preserve their influence in the Ohio region, the French could only offset the British trade advantage with force.

Jonquière never fulfilled Versailles's demands; he died on March 17, 1752. Charles Le Moyne, baron de Longueil, Montreal's governor, stepped temporarily into his place. Conveniently, Versailles had given up on Jonquière even before learning of his demise. As the governor lay on his deathbed, Louis XV chose his successor.

Like the man he would replace, Ange Duquesne de Menneville, marquis de Duquesne, was a distinguished naval officer. He stepped ashore at Quebec in July 1752 armed with clear instructions. First, he was to reject the English argument that the Utrecht Treaty allowed them to trade with Indians anywhere: "Nothing can oblige us to suffer this trade on our territory. . . . The Ohio River . . . and its tributaries belong indisputably to France, by virtue of its discovery by Sieur de la Salle; of the trading posts the French have had there since, and of possession which is so much the more unquestionable as it constitutes the most frequent communication from Canada to Louisiana. It is only within a few years that the English have undertaken to trade there; and now they pretend to exclude us from it." He was to reject the "pretended sovereignty of the English over" the Iroquois as "a chimera." Conceding to England the Ohio valley would be disastrous to French interests: "Should they succeed there, they would cut off the communications between the two Colonies of Canada and Louisiana, and would be in a position to trouble them, and to ruin both the one and the other, independent of the advantages they would at once experience in their trade to the prejudice of ours." What then should be done? Versailles ruled out any diplomatic protest to King George II as "altogether futile." Instead, Duquesne was to "make every possible effort to drive the English from our territory, and to . . . give the Indians to understand that . . . no harm is intended them, that they will have liberty to go as much as they please to the English to trade, but will not be allowed to receive these on our territory."[25] By this policy, Versailles tried deftly to play a weak hand by at once asserting an exclusive privilege to territories claimed by France and recognizing that it could not provide all that the Indians desired, thus permitting those subjects to journey to the English colonies for their unfulfilled wants. To fulfill this policy, Duquesne began preparing an expedition to the Ohio country powerful enough to expel the British from the region indefinitely.

All along, Whitehall's view of the worsening tensions in North America was the mirror image of Versailles's. The British saw themselves as the besieged victims and the French as the rapacious aggressors. This outlook was shaped by alarmist reports from experts on North America. La Galissonière's counterpart at Whitehall was George Montague Dunk, Lord Halifax, secretary of state for the Southern Department. His report of August 1753 listed all the French forts, intrigues, and expeditions that contained, threatened, or outright violated England's North American empire. England faced worsening French threats along its entire frontier from Nova Scotia to the Carolinas, of which the most menacing emanated from Forts Saint Frederic and Niagara. The French had used the peace since 1748 to prepare for war. If the French succeeded in controlling the Ohio valley, they would "be in possession of nearly two-thirds of the very best unsettled land on this Side of the Mississippi and Saint Lawrence, while Great Britain will not only lose near one-half of the Territory, to which it is indisputably entitled, but in case of a future Rupture, will find it extremely difficult to keep the other half."[26] Within a week, the cabinet adopted Halifax's analysis of the French threat. On August 21, 1753, Whitehall agreed that "General Orders should be sent to the Several Governors in North America, To do their Utmost, To prevent, by Force, These, and any such Attempts, That may be made, by the French, or by the Indians, in The French Interest."[27] With that, Whitehall essentially issued an unofficial declaration of limited frontier war.

Meanwhile, a French expedition of 2,200 men led by Captain Paul Marin de La Malgue reached the region and began constructing three forts—Presque Isle on Lake Erie, Le Boeuf at the head of the Rivière aux Boeufs (French Creek), and Machault (Venango) downstream on the Allegheny River. Marin's first council with the Indians was a disaster. The chiefs, led by Seneca Tanacharison, angrily demanded that the French "cease setting up the establishments you want to make. All the tribes have always called not to allow it. . . . I shall strike at whoever does not listen to us. . . . We ask you only to send us what we need, but not to build any forts there." Marin refused to be intimidated, asserting that he would "continue on my way, and if there are any persons bold enough to set up barriers to hinder my march, I shall knock them over so vigorously that they may crush those who made them."[28] To Marin's relief, a Shawnee delegation arrived to welcome the French and plead with them to rid their country of the British.

The Indians reluctantly bowed to French power. Their delegations to councils at Winchester, Carlisle, and Albany failed to convince the respective colonies of Virginia, Pennsylvania, and New York to drive off the French and then withdraw east over the Appalachians. The governors pleaded lack of money, troops, and will. This professed weakness elicited the chiefs' contempt. Mohawk chief Hendrick issued a stern rebuke to New York governor George Clinton: "Brother when we came here to relate our Grievances about our Lands, we expected to have something done for us. . . . Nothing shall be done for us. . . . [A]s soon as we come home we will send up a belt of Wampum to our Brothers the 5 Nations [Iroquois] to acquaint them the Covenant is broken between you and us. So brother you are not to expect to hear of me any more, and Brother we desire to hear no more of you."[29]

Marin hoped immediately to follow up his council by descending the Allegheny to the Ohio River forks. Low water, however, crucially delayed that expedition. As if that were not irritating enough, Marin faced another problem. If Governor Jonquière had previously sent too few men to the region, Duquesne sent too many. Supplies dwindled quickly; sanitation was appalling. Disease and malnutrition killed hundreds, including Marin himself on October 29, 1753. Captain Claude-Pierre Pécaudy de Contrecoeur eventually took command, sent back most troops to Montreal, and prepared the rest for a long winter in the wilderness. The winter was interrupted by an extraordinary visitor.

On December 4, 1753, Captain Philip Thomas Chabert de Joncaire, Fort Machault's commander, was startled to learn that a young Virginian gentleman, his guide Christopher Gist, Tanacharison, and several others were at the door. Joncaire must have blinked in astonishment at the tall, twenty-one-year-old standing before him. The man introduced himself as George Washington and soon displayed a hot temper behind his grave demeanor. Governor Robert Dinwiddie had chosen Washington, who packed some frontier experience but more importantly came from one of Virginia's most prominent families, to carry a message to Governor Duquesne politely warning him to withdraw from the region.

For three days, Joncaire tried to woo the delegation with charm and to intimidate it with assertions of French power. The delegation then trekked on to Fort Le Boeuf, where on December 11 Washington delivered Dinwiddie's letter to Captain Jacques Legardeur de Saint-Pierre. The governor's letter read, "The lands upon the River Ohio, in the western parts of the Colony of Virginia, are so notoriously known to be the property of the Crown of Great Britain that it is a matter of . . . concern and surprise to me, to hear that a body of French forces are erecting fortresses and making settlements upon that river, within his Majesty's dominions. . . . If these facts be true . . . it becomes my duty to require your peaceable departure."[30]

If that challenge ruffled Saint-Pierre, he did not reveal it. After days of entertainment, he formally replied on December 15 that he would forward Dinwiddie's letter to Governor Duquesne. He then asserted that the French were unshakably determined to defend their empire against British aggression. The Virginian and his men headed back to their settlements. It would not be the last the French saw of George Washington.[31]

These territorial disputes were supposed to be settled by a boundary commission designated by Article 18 of the Aix-la-Chapelle treaty.[32] That commission would soon deadlock like its predecessors. Indeed, even before the Aix-la-Chapelle treaty was signed, a commission of French, English, and Dutch diplomats met at Saint Malo to deal with shipping seizures. This effort accomplished nothing. In April 1749, French foreign minister Louis-Philogène, Brulart de Sillery et de Puysieulx proposed an Anglo-French commission to settle boundaries in Acadia and the Neutral Islands. Whitehall first rejected the idea, then grudgingly accepted it when Versailles agreed that the commission would negotiate all North American and Caribbean disputes.

It was not until 1750, however, that diplomats were finally named to the Paris commission. Representing France were La Galissonière and Étienne de Silhouette. Whitehall appointed Massachusetts governor William Shirley and Walter Mildmay. The commission's first meeting opened on August 31, 1750 at La Galissonière's home. The order of business was to decide what to decide. In that and subsequent meetings, the diplomats failed to reach agreement. By October they had merely agreed to conduct all subsequent negotiations by the exchange of memorials to avoid any misunderstandings.

Mildmay and Shirley submitted on January 11, 1751, a memorial prepared by Britain's Board of Trade. They claimed that Acadia and Nova Scotia were the same and included "ancient limits" from the Penobscot River north to the Saint Lawrence and east to land's end, along with Isle Saint Jean (Prince Edward Island). They argued that the French diplomats at the Treaty of Utrecht understood that Acadia included this territory when they signed it away. The English commissioners did concede that Cape Breton belonged to France according to the Treaty of Aix-la-Chapelle. Inexplicably, it took the French ten months to reply. On October 4, 1751, La Galissonière and Silhouette submitted their own memorial asserting that Acadia was only those lands east of the Chignecto Isthmus. The English also took a long time to respond, mostly because Shirley and Mildmay squabbled incessantly and contemptuously. In 1752, Shirley was replaced by Ruvigny de Cosne. The English submitted their counterargument on January 23, 1753, refuting each French point and elaborating their original points. The French prepared a second reply but were not allowed to deliver it.[33] The reason was that Whitehall, amidst the worsening tensions, suspended the commission in a dispute over, of all things, language. From the first negotiation round, the French had huffily complained about the English lack of proficiency in the French language. The English just as huffily responded by writing their memorials in English, which the French refused to accept. The English then walked out. The deadlock continued as each side refused to budge.

The commission accomplished nothing during its six years of existence from 1750 to 1756. During that time, not only did neither side compromise, but once-vague claims hardened into unassailable positions fortified with their own respective elaborate legalities and logic. In all, the commission worsened rather than alleviated tensions.

By 1751, with the commission clearly stalemated, Whitehall suggested bypassing it with direct negotiations. Versailles rejected the request. But after the commission failed to meet for a year after the language dispute, Versailles finally agreed on direct negotiations. To lead these talks, Louis XV tapped the man who had served as ambassador to the Court of Saint James's since 1749, Gaston-Charles-François de Lévis, duc de Mirepoix. Through the eyes of the French and English alike, Mirepoix seemed a fine choice. Versailles esteemed him as a distinguished diplomat and soldier; Mirepoix had previously served as ambassador to Vienna from 1737 to 1740 and had campaigned in Bohemia, Italy, and Flanders during the War of the Austrian Succession. If anything, he was even more popular among his English counterparts, who saw in him "little of the manners of his country, where he had seldom lived; and except a passion which he retained for dancing and for the gracefulness of his own figure, there was nothing in his character that did not fall in naturally with the seriousness of the English and German courts."[34]

In the year before the war broke out, Mirepoix did his very best to avert it. All along he urged Versailles to make genuine concessions, the only way he saw of breaking the deadlock with Whitehall. Versailles studiously ignored his pleas. He also suggested that each side present a formal claim that could then be negotiated by Ambassador George Keppel, Earl of Albemarle, and foreign minister François-Dominique Barberie de Saint Contest in Paris. This too was rejected. Mirepoix asked that each side withdraw from positions that threatened the other. Versailles vetoed this as well, arguing that Whitehall would equate compromise as weakness.[35]

The French inability to break the deadlock with England was exacerbated by one within their own ranks. Louis XV's council was especially weak that summer as it was split more than ever by conflicting policy proposals and insipid personalities. Pompadour's influence faded briefly when her beloved daughter, Alexandrine, died on June 15, 1754, at age ten, probably of appendicitis. Inspiring little respect were foreign minister Saint Contest, who had served in that post from September 11, 1751, until his death on July 24, 1754, and Antoine-Louis Rouillé, comte de Jouy, the marine minister since April 26, 1749. Critics debated which was more inept.[36] It was commonly believed that both Saint Contest and Rouillé were the respective mouthpieces for tough insiders Jean-Baptiste de Machault d'Arnouville and Marshal Adrien Maurice, duc de Noailles.[37]

Overshadowing both men was war minister Marc Pierre de Voyer de Paulmy, comte d'Argenson, who led that ministry from 1743 until 1757. Of his brother, the marquis wrote that he "has all the air of a prime minister; when he enters the King's apartment, it should be seen what a swath he cuts through the crowd of courtiers."[38] Comte Argenson, he explained, "is not susceptible of hatred, his bile is never stirred, but he dislikes having equals, and is naturally inclined to sarcasm on his superiors. . . . He has never for a moment meditated on the public good; he has always shown an indifference to it."[39] Perhaps most importantly for French diplomacy, Argenson was an unabashed admirer of Frederick II.

After Saint Contest died, Louis XV replaced him with Rouillé. He then named Machault his marine minister, the latest honor following his being named president of the Grand Council in 1738, intendant of Hainaut in 1743, comptroller general in 1745, keeper of the seals in 1750, and comptroller general again in 1754. Until Machault was dismissed in 1757, no minister during the early war was a greater defender of the colonies and Austrian alliance, and enemy of Frederick the Great, than Machault.

Though the king's council did not agree on any new policy or reinforcements for New France, it did reason that with war increasingly likely it was time to cast about for allies. Spain was a logical choice. Versailles ordered the French ambassador, Emmanuel-Félicité, duc de Duras, to talk the Spanish into a Bourbon pact. Duras conveyed Rouillé's appeal to Ferdinand VI's familial sentiments and Spanish interests when he wrote of the "tender friendship which unites us. . . . The English have been for all time, the constant and implacable enemies of our nations and our house; we have never had more dangerous adversaries."[40] Duras pressured Madrid to press Spain's claims against Whitehall on illegal British logging in Honduras, Spanish rights to fish off Newfoundland, and the unwarranted seizures of Spanish merchant ships. He continually argued La Galissonière's case that New France shielded New Spain from British imperialism; England's conquest of New France would inevitably lead to the loss of Spain's American empire. Only if France and Spain stood together would England's ambitions be thwarted.[41] Finally, Louis XV himself joined the diplomacy with a letter to his cousin Ferdinand VI to resist England's insults to the "glory of our house." He repeated the now familiar argument that England threatened to destroy the North American empires of Spain and France, and urged Ferdinand to offer his good offices between France and England.[42]

Ferdinand diplomatically spurned these advances. Though the Spanish court was split between pro-French and pro-English factions, one thing united it—no one then wanted a war. Ferdinand himself was a proud Spaniard who feared France would overshadow his kingdom through a Bourbon family pact. More practically, with its fleet rotting and cannons rusting away, Spain was unprepared for war. War would simply bring humiliating loss.

Aware of Spain's weaknesses, Versailles hesitated to solicit an outright alliance, fearing it would be more a burden than asset. Upon any Spanish war declaration, England would quickly sweep the seas of Madrid's decrepit navy and capture its ill-defended colonies. In the subsequent peace conference, France might well find itself trading any of its own hard-won conquests to England so that Spain could rejoin dismembered trunks to its empire. This is exactly what happened after the Bourbon pact was finally signed in 1761.

Until his death in 1754, foreign minister Don Joseph de Carvajal y Lancáster was Britain's champion at Madrid. To replace him, Ferdinand chose as foreign minister an even more fervent anglophile, Ricardo Wall, who not only probably had his hand deep in Whitehall's pocket but also was Irish by birth and British by sentiment. Wall feared that France would engulf Spain through any sort of family pact joining the Bourbon kings. Thus, he sought England to counterbalance France, and staved off any French initiatives for closer ties. In this task he was aided by British ambassador Benjamin Keene, who had all but immigrated to Spain. He had first arrived as agent for the South Sea Company before being named English consul in 1724 and minister from 1727 to 1739; he then served as envoy to Lisbon from 1746 to 1748 before returning as minister to Spain from 1748 until his death.

Leading the pro-French faction at court was the brilliant Zenón de Somodevilla y Bengochea, marquis de Ensenada, who headed the ministries of war, finance, marine, and the Indies. In April 1754, Ensenada almost sparked a war between Spain and England. Had he succeeded, the Seven Years' War might have had a quite different set of victors. Carvajal's death presented Ensenada a chance to shift Spain's foreign policy. Behind Ferdinand's back, he encouraged the colonial governors to retaliate against the British in Honduras. A Spanish expedition scattered the British loggers at Labouring Creek but did not follow up by attacking other settlements. When Wall got wind of the policy and informed the king, Ferdinand dismissed Ensenada. Wall then sent orders to the Spanish governors canceling any other attacks against the English and promised Whitehall the same. Though the crisis died, the Spanish resentment continued to smolder.

The incident raises an interesting what-if question for the Seven Years' War. Spain's threat to England's illegal logging settlements was a pinprick compared to the conflict enflaming the frontier between the British and French empires in North America. Even had Ensenada won King Ferdinand over to his plan, Whitehall most likely would have resolved the issue through diplomacy rather than war. However, in the unlikely event that the Duke of Newcastle's government took a hard line, Britain might well have found itself embroiled in two colonial wars in 1754. The Bourbon pact could have been sealed then rather than seven years later. With the French and Spanish fleets combined, the war's course would have shifted dramatically.

Over time, Spain's interest in staving off British encroachments slowly asserted itself over the pecuniary and sentimental attachments of leading court members. From 1754 until its Quixote-like entrance into the war in 1762, Madrid shifted from neutrality to alignment with France and finally to outright alliance against Britain.

As Louis XV's reshuffled council debated policy and fished for an alliance with Spain, the French and the Virginians opened 1754 with a race to plant a fort at the Ohio River forks. The Virginians won—initially. On January 26, Governor Dinwiddie ordered Ohio Company field captain William Trent to lead a forty-two-man expedition to seize the forks. Trent reached that strategic slice of land on February 14 and immediately set his men to work erecting Fort Prince George. Leaving Ensign Edward Ward in charge, Trent returned to the Wills

Creek settlement to gather more volunteers and supplies. Meanwhile, Dinwiddie petitioned the other colonial governors and Indian tribes to send him men and supplies. Newly commissioned Lieutenant-Colonel George Washington assembled several hundred militiamen at Wills Creek.

On April 17, Captain Claude-Pierre Pécaudy de Contrecoeur and six hundred troops ground their canoes ashore just beyond musket shot of Fort Prince George. Contrecoeur paraded his troops and eighteen cannons before the fort, then demanded that Ward surrender. Ward prudently did so and was allowed to retire with honors of war. Contrecoeur renamed the fort after Governor Duquesne and sent delegations to nearby Indian villages demanding that they expel any British traders among them and send him warriors.

Ward's arrival at Wills Creek was just the latest and worst setback for George Washington. None of the hoped-for colonial or Indian reinforcements had so far arrived. Supplies of all kinds were limited. Disease and desertion depleted the ranks. Yet Washington chose to march on Fort Duquesne anyway. By late May his force was camped at Great Meadows about halfway to the forks. Learning that a small force commanded by Michel Pepin La Force had seized the home of his guide, Christopher Gist, Washington sent troops to recapture it. La Force withdrew before the Virginians arrived.

Contrecoeur dispatched Ensign Joseph Coulon de Villiers, Sieur de Jumonville, and thirty-three troops to carry a message to Dinwiddie to stay out of French territory. Getting wind of Jumonville's advance and assuming it was hostile, Washington led a small force of troops and Indians to ambush the French on May 28. The attackers killed Jumonville and nine others, and captured twenty-one troops, while suffering only one man killed and two or three wounded; one Frenchmen escaped to carry word of the ambush to Fort Duquesne. Washington's first battle was also the first in which he commanded and the first he won. It would be another twenty-two years before he again commanded victorious troops.

Washington returned to Great Meadows, where reinforcements, including a company of British regulars, swelled his force to over four hundred. But those troops were poorly trained, equipped, and motivated, and were encamped around a tiny stockade in a meadow within musket shot of the surrounding forest. Not surprisingly, most Indians deserted along with many militiamen; scores more sickened.

On June 26, Captain Louis Coulon Ecuyer, Sieur de Villiers, reinforced Contrecoeur with 20 soldiers and 130 Indians. As a veteran frontier raider from the last war and Jumonville's older half brother, Villiers was eager for revenge. He called a council and harangued the Indians with impassioned words: "The English have murdered my children; my heart is sick; tomorrow I shall send my French soldiers to take revenge. And now, men of the Sault St. Louis, men of the Lake of Two Mountains, Hurons, Abenakis, Iroquois of La Présentation, Nipissings, Algonquins, and Ottawas,—I invite you all by this belt of wampum to join your French father and help him to crush the assassins."[43]

The next day, Villiers led seven hundred French and Indians down the trail toward Great Meadows. Upon arriving on July 3, they encircled and opened fire on Washington's troops. The firing lasted all day and into the evening. With as many as thirty of his men dead and seventy wounded, Washington agreed to surrender when Villiers promised honors of war. The Virginian undoubtedly would have protested one tenet had it been properly translated to him—it named Washington as Jumonville's assassin. Washington and his remaining troops marched south the next day which was, ironically, the fourth of July. Indians began plundering and murdering his troops. When Washington sent protest to Villiers, he swiftly stopped the depredations. Villiers later revealed that the large "Number of their Dead and Wounded, moved me to Pity, notwithstanding my Resentment for their having in such a Manner, taken away my Brother's Life. The Indians, who had obeyed my Orders in every Thing, claimed a right to the Plunder; but I opposed it; However, the English being frightened, fled and left their Tents, and one of their Colours."[44]

At the Edge of the Abyss

Other than isolated Indian raids, a tense peace was maintained in North America the rest of 1754. Representatives of six American colonies—New York, Massachusetts, New Hampshire, Connecticut, Rhode Island, and Maryland—met at Albany in June and July to forge an alliance with the Indians and a defense and political union among themselves. Though agreements were signed, neither initiative came to fruition. Massachusetts governor William Shirley sent Colonel John Winslow with eight hundred militiamen up the Kennebec River to establish Forts Western and Halifax to bar a French invasion down that valley. But the colonies were too divided among and within themselves to muster enough financial support for a campaign to drive the French from the Ohio forks that year.

As for the French, they hoped that the border dispute had finally been resolved in their nation's favor as they now commanded the Appalachian watershed. As one officer wrote, they had "good reason to believe that this action will disgust the English with the Beautiful River, and that the defeat will entirely disgust the Indians with taking any . . . part with them."[45] The victory at Fort Necessity boosted the French standing with all the tribes. Hundreds of Indians from nearly all the tribes trickled into French posts for raids against the British. Those that the French could not enlist they cowed.

No tribe was more important than the Iroquois. The renewal of conflict between the French and British had once again split the Iroquois Longhouse, with the western bands leaning toward the former and the eastern bands toward the latter. At a September 23, 1754, council with Cayuga, Tuscarora, and Oneida representatives at Montreal, Governor Duquesne boasted the Fort Necessity victory and promised future French triumphs. He not only reproached them for "their infamous treason" but also threatened to punish them if they joined the British.[46]

Duquesne's tough policy toward the Iroquois worked for now. Indians respected the strong and despised the weak. The Iroquois, like virtually all the tribes, saw the French as the lesser of two evils. At that council, an Oneida chief captured the essential difference between the French and English: "Are you ignorant of the difference between our Father and the English? Go see the forts our Father has erected, and you will see that the land beneath his walls is still hunting ground, having fixed himself in those places we frequent, only to supply our wants;

whilst the English, on the contrary, no sooner get possession of a country than the game is forced to leave it; the trees fall down before them, the earth becomes bare, and we find among them hardly wherewithal to shelter us when the night falls."[47]

Governor Duquesne wrote to marine minister Machault his fears that Whitehall was preparing an all-out war against France in North America: "It is not possible that the King of Great Britain has not consented to and even ordered all the movements which the English are making on this Continent. . . . The Governors of New England, besides being independent one of the other, cannot levy troops without an order of the King of Great Britain, and you will have observed by Mr. Washington's Journal that all the Provinces have furnished a quota to his detachment." He denounced the British for threatening the Acadians with hanging if they took up arms and incited the Indians against the French. Even more worrisome was the possibility that these aggressions were simply the prelude to "attempts to push on to . . . Quebec" itself. In the face of British provocations Duquesne had strained to maintain his own "cautious conduct."[48]

Versailles received Duquesne's reports with relief. The king and his ministers were pleased that the French had blunted the British advance on the Ohio but dismissed Duquesne's assertions about Whitehall. In his reply to Duquesne, Machault wrote, "The views evinced by the King of Great Britain up to the present time, for the maintenance of peace, do not permit even the belief that he has authorized the movements which make so much noise along the beautiful river; and there is still less appearance that he has ordered similar movements on the other frontiers." The council instructed Duquesne "to confine yourself to the adoption of all possible measures to be in a position to repel force by force. If, to assure this defensive policy . . . you consider it necessary to make the Indians act offensively against the English, his Majesty will approve . . . [but] his Majesty wishes you to avoid, as much as it will be possible, the shedding of blood . . . [and] make your operations subordinate to the situation of the finances, as far as the safety of the Colony will permit." However, if war erupted, Duquesne should take all measures "for the good of his [Majesty's] service and the glory of his arms."[49]

Ironically, as Versailles reassured Duquesne of Britain's friendly intentions, Whitehall was mobilizing for all-out war in North America. After a debate that lasted months, the cabinet's hawks, Halifax, Cumberland, and Henry Fox, finally pressured chief minister Newcastle and the others into invading New France rather than simply reinforcing with troops and money the most threatened frontiers. The war plan was Cumberland's and involved four offensives. Colonel Edward Braddock would lead two regiments to Virginia, join with provincial troops, and march to capture Fort Duquesne, then advance north to take the three French forts (Machault, Le Boeuf, and Presque Isle) leading to Lake Erie. Provincial commanders would launch offensives against Fort Niagara on Lake Ontario, Fort Saint Frederic on Lake Champlain, and Fort Beauséjour on the Chignecto Isthmus. With those four victories, the French would undoubtedly sue for a peace on British terms.

Secrets were hard to keep in a relatively open society like Britain's. The French learned of the plan to send Braddock and two regiments to America from English newspapers. On November 27, 1754, foreign minister Rouillé asked if the troop movement was true and, if so, its purpose. Albemarle assured him that that two regiments had a purely defensive mission. Several weeks later, armed with more evidence of British preparations for war in North America, Rouillé again confronted Albemarle and received the same denials.[50]

Versailles sent Mirepoix, then on leave at Paris, to London to "represent to the King of England and his ministers that [Louis XV] has seen with surprise the armament taking place both in England and in the English colonies of North America, and that his steady zeal for the maintenance of the good understanding with the crown of England, and for the general peace, allows him to defer no longer asking that the King of Great Britain have the goodness to enter into an open explanation with him on the objection of preparations so considerable and apparently so little conformed to the principles of the pacification of Aix-la-Chapelle." Mirepoix concluded, "His Majesty awaits a prompt reply from the King of England, and trusts it will be favorable to the maintenance of the accord of the two crowns, to the safety of America, and to the peace of all Europe."[51] This trust would be misplaced.

CHAPTER 5

Escalation, 1755

History knows no example of a country playing for such high stakes with the insouciance of people taking part in a quadrille.

Bernis to Choiseul

I will not pardon the pirates of that insolent nation.

Louis XV

Humanity shudders at being obliged to make use of such monsters.

Bougainville

The French and English were at war's brink in North America. Crucial national interests were at stake. Each nation saw itself as the victim of the other's aggression that endangered its imperial ambitions. Yet war was not inevitable. Astute diplomacy could still have defused that crisis.

Upon returning to London in January 1755, French ambassador Mirepoix did his best to preserve the peace, but to no avail. He and Thomas Robinson, the secretary of state for the Southern Department, got nowhere as each pressed the same accusations against the other's government while cloaking his own with the purest motives for peace. Mirepoix cannot be blamed for the steady slide into war. He was a mere messenger who all along received very mixed messages from Versailles. Official dispatches from foreign minister Rouillé told him to hold firm with the English; secret messages from Louis and Pompadour encouraged him to compromise if need be to avoid a general war. What was a diplomat to do?[1]

This was not Mirepoix's only handicap. Robinson clearly knew more about North America. Mirepoix's ignorance of the conflict's details undercut his mission. To many a specific point raised by Robinson, Mirepoix could only reply, "I had not the necessary instructions to discuss the basis of the question."[2] Instead, he pleaded for both sides to stand down and let negotiations rather than violence resolve the dispute. To underline his argument that Whitehall was the aggressor, he insisted on an explanation for the Crown's dispatch of two regiments and General Braddock to America. In a conciliatory gesture, he softened Rouillé's demand for satisfaction for Jumonville's "assassination." Yet he was unyielding in his stand that the Ohio valley was French by discovery, watershed, and usage. Thus the French were merely defending what was rightfully theirs against the British invaders.[3]

Whitehall's position was the mirror image. Robinson painted Britain as the victim fending off French trespassers. The Ohio valley had been rightfully Britain's since the 1713 Utrecht Treaty, which subjected the Iroquois and all their lands and vassals to the Crown. Canada and Louisiana were not linked by the upper Ohio valley into which the French rarely ventured, but by the Wabash River route far to the west. British troops were vital for defending the American colonies, including the Ohio valley, from French aggression. The dispatch of Braddock, recently appointed to major general, and two regiments was merely a response to French reinforcements being sent to Canada. Versailles could defuse the crisis by abandoning all posts it had built on Iroquois lands since 1715, including Niagara, Toronto, Presque Isle, Le Boeuf, Machault, and Saint Frederic, and open the Ohio valley as far west as the Wabash to British traders. Negotiations should sidestep the stalled commission for a court-to-court settlement.

Mirepoix countered by asserting that the Iroquois were neither the masters of the Ohio valley nor subjects of Britain. The Utrecht Treaty did not mention any river or territory dividing the two North

American empires. International law clearly rewarded the Ohio valley to France by, once again, discovery, watershed, and use. French troops would soon disembark in Canada for purely defensive ends.[4]

Rouillé best exposed the folly of Britain's claim to the Ohio River via their "subjects" the Iroquois: "The enumeration of Indian tribes who are subject to the domination of either of the two crowns is neither exact nor well founded. . . . The American tribes have preserved their liberty. . . . One of these tribes today is friendly to one of the two crowns; tomorrow it will be an enemy of that same crown. . . . The territory of these tribes is as uncertain as their alliance. . . . They often change their dwelling place. . . . It would therefore be impossible to fix a district and boundaries for tribes which have never known them and which do not wish to know them." As for why the diplomats at Utrecht included such a vacuous tenet in the treaty, he attributed it to their "small acquaintance with American affairs."[5]

The same fruitless exchanges animated discussions between Rouillé and acting English ambassador de Cosne in Paris. On February 3, Rouillé explained the king's insistence that the commission must be reactivated while parallel discussions continued via the ambassadors. To that end, Louis XV had sent Mirepoix full negotiating powers.[6] Mirepoix made a bold offer to resolve the crisis on February 19. He called for a neutral zone between the Appalachian Mountains and the Wabash River, within which all forts would be dismantled and the troops sent home. Traders from both nations, however, would be welcome. This was a stunning reversal of French policy. In opening the region to free trade, Versailles would have essentially conceded it to the British with their lower-priced, better-quality, and more abundant goods.[7] Ironically, Mirepoix issued his concession the same day that Rouillé sent him instructions to call for both sides to withdraw from the upper Ohio valley for two years while a comprehensive settlement was negotiated by the commission in Paris.[8] Rouillé initially agreed with Mirepoix's offer when he learned of it, but later rejected it when hard-liners in the king's council erupted in anger.[9]

It might be expected that Whitehall would have leapt upon Mirepoix's offer as a godsend to expand the British empire without war. Instead, after bitter debate, the cabinet demanded an even greater concession, that the French roll back their empire behind the lower Great Lakes, Saint Lawrence River, and Wabash River. American traders could freely ply their goods not only in the extension of Britain's empire to the Wabash but in the upper Great Lakes as well. Though Mirepoix did not formally receive this counteroffer until March 7, he informally learned of it by February 28 and immediately conveyed it to Rouillé.[10]

Britain's demands in response to Mirepoix's compromise provided a seemingly priceless lesson for French leaders—compromise was wrong because it simply signaled a weakness that the other side would exploit by demanding more. This "lesson" would prove to be a chimera. Versailles did not compromise again until 1760, after British arms had captured Canada and other colonies around the world, and had destroyed much of their fleet, while the French were bogged down in an unwinnable war in Germany. Not surprisingly, the British then demanded much more—the entire French empire in North America.

Versailles angrily dismissed the British demand. Almost as shocking to the king and most of his ministers was Mirepoix's willingness to put virtually any French interest on the diplomatic chopping block. Rouillé twice warned him against negotiating away the empire. Rouillé was skeptical of Mirepoix's assurance that the British were committed to the peaceful settlement of the conflict. If true, Rouillé noted, the British had a strange way of showing it with their navies sailing, armies marching, and diplomats making unacceptable demands.[11]

Newcastle received Mirepoix's rejection with a shrug. Whitehall was chiefly concerned with safeguarding British traders in the Ohio valley and dismantling French forts built since 1715; access to the upper Great Lakes was negotiable. Nonetheless, for now Britain's official position remained unchanged. The only fear was that, by demanding too much, Whitehall had bloated public expectations. If those expectations were frustrated, the result might an explosion of pressure on Whitehall to launch a total rather than the planned limited war.[12] In separate meetings with Mirepoix on March 22, Newcastle and Robinson took turns expressing their fears that war was imminent while demanding that France accept Britain's terms for peace; Newcastle's appeals were more velvety, Robinson's steelier. But neither yielded not only on taking the upper Ohio River valley but on pushing the French back to the Saint Lawrence River, Great Lakes, and Wabash River. As instructed, Mirepoix was polite and encouraging but noncommittal.[13]

Two days later, Mirepoix was subjected to another tag team of diplomatic wrestling with Newcastle and Robinson. Once again the Englishmen's manners were as impeccable as their demands were implacable. Curiously, they exposed a weakness that Mirepoix, characteristically, did not exploit. George II was adamant about visiting Hanover that summer despite his cabinet's opposition for fear he could be captured or cut off if the war broke out. Thus, the cabinet was anxious to strike a deal before the king embarked. Mirepoix expressed his sympathy for their plight but nothing more. On March 24, King George II made a bellicose speech before Parliament that verged on the brink of a war declaration. Instead, he asked Parliament for a million extra pounds sterling for the military and offered bounties for navy enlistments.[14]

Mirepoix asked whether the king's speech proved that persistent rumors of British war preparations were true. He accepted the bland assurances that such tales were completely false. He was blind to the possibility that the British were simply dragging out negotiations while they prepared for war. His belief that the British wanted a peaceful settlement was largely wishful thinking reinforced by the conciliatory banter. He concluded that this Gordian knot could only be cut by caving in to the British position, and he was ready to do so.[15]

Indeed, the British were just playing for time and trying to lull Versailles through the gullible Mirepoix into a false sense of security. In all, the British ministers had skillfully snookered Mirepoix. They were interested not in peace but conquest. All they needed was time to get their regiments to America, mobilize the provincial troops, and march against four strongpoints to crush the French defense of Canada. By the summer's end, Whitehall expected to celebrate an overwhelming victory in North America.[16]

As Mirepoix's hopeful dispatches crossed the channel, Whitehall escalated the conflict. On April 10, Whitehall issued secret orders to all naval commanders "for seizing and securing any French ships or War, or ships having Troops or Warlike Stores on board, which He may meet . . . and for Taking and Destroying any such Ships, in case of Opposition to His so Seizing and Securing them."[17] Admiral Edward

Boscawen left with eleven ships of the line on April 27; Captain Charles Holmes followed with six ships of the line on May 11. Those two squadrons would meet Commodore Augustus Keppel's squadron at Halifax. From there the combined fleet would blockade Louisbourg. The British were confident that with naval superiority and the planned four offensives, they would quickly and decisively win on the battlefield what Versailles refused to concede at the diplomatic table.

Thanks to Mirepoix's optimism, Louis XV and his council clung to the belief that the British shared their commitment to peace. On April 13, Rouillé softened the French position. While he still rejected Britain's demands as unacceptable, he agreed to use it as the basis for negotiation. This was a huge concession. On May 9, Mirepoix submitted an analysis that rejected the south shores of the Saint Lawrence and lower Great Lakes as the frontier, but left open where to draw the line below those waters and repeated the claim for the Ohio while allowing that region to be open to French and British traders alike. All forts would be dismantled within the region bound by the Appalachians, lower Great Lakes, Ohio, and Wabash. Among the posts razed would be Britain's trading post at Oswego, on Lake Ontario's southern shore. On April 25, Whitehall responded to Mirepoix's presentation with a diplomatic note that asserted the Saint Lawrence, Great Lakes, and Wabash frontier, and nothing less.[18]

Mirepoix's eyes only began to open on June 7, when Whitehall issued an ultimatum that France surrender to all British demands or else. The demands were harder than ever. Now Whitehall denied any French rights to Lake Erie or Lake Ontario! The boundary would be on the north rather than south shore of the lower Great Lakes. In the same proposal, the British reasserted that the Saint Lawrence divide the two empires and added that the French must evacuate all four Neutral Islands in the Caribbean.[19]

While Whitehall had clearly hoodwinked Mirepoix, Rouillé may have been playing his own game when he seemed to accept his ambassador's reports of a peace-loving Britain. To prepare for war, France needed even more time than Britain. Too firm a stance on British fleet and troop movements might have prompted Whitehall to order them into action all the sooner.[20]

It was there that the negotiations stalled for another half dozen years. The negotiations failed for one simple reason beyond the power of Mirepoix or any French minister to change—Versailles was willing to split the difference with Whitehall; Whitehall was not.

Versailles Prepares for War

While the English were united on war, Louis XV's council was as badly fragmented as ever. Upon returning from Venice, Ambassador François-Joachim de Pierre de Bernis vividly described the chaos infecting France:

The finances of the Kingdom, which were governed by M. de Sechelles, a clever but worn-out mind, only appeared well-managed, for since the Peace of Aix-la-Chapelle the State's expenses had yearly exceeded its income: the people's burdens remained unchanged, and all the Kingdom's money was in the hands of financiers. Our overseas trade flourished but could not count on the protection from the navy; we had many hulks and few vessels. The armed forces, though numerous, were neither well organized nor disciplined, and our frontier forts lacked provisions and repairs. . . . There was no union in the Council, with open war between M. d'Argenson and M. de Machault, rambling debates and no subordination; the Prince de Conti meddled in everything, yet headed no ministry; Madame de Pompadour brawled openly with the prince; the King held the balance amidst these divisions; an outrageous display of luxury; the populace miserable; the Council unenlightened; no one at Court with a trace of patriotism; no worthy generals nor admirals available at war's eve.[21]

It was not an exaggerated picture.

The council could agree only that France was unprepared for war and thus must avoid it at all costs, while New France must be reinforced with troops and a new governor. Until then, marine minister Machault instructed Duquesne to avoid causing any offense with the British. If violence erupts, Machault advised, "repel force by force . . . in such a manner as not to appear the aggressor." Cut loose the Indians against the British settlements, he counseled, only if it is "indispensable to the safety and tranquility of the Colony." Machault specifically authorized Duquesne to destroy Fort Halifax, which a Massachusetts expedition under Colonel John Winslow had erected on the Kennebec River the previous summer.[22] This last instruction was curious. Given Versailles's watershed theory of empire, the Kennebec River clearly fell within the British realm, and thus Fort Kennebec was a thoroughly legal establishment. Yet Versailles here seemed to find it as offensive as the former English fort on the Ohio forks in what it considered French territory.

While Versailles downplayed the possibility of war, some of New France's officials sent Duquesne alarming warnings of pending British attacks. From Louisbourg, Île Royale governor Augustin de Drucour passed on intelligence garnered by spies in New York that the provincial governors were mobilizing troops for spring attacks on Forts Duquesne and Saint Frederic.[23]

As Duquesne mobilized Canada for war, Versailles chose Pierre de Rigaud de Vaudreuil de Cavagnial, marquis de Vaudreuil, as his replacement. New France's last governor general was its first who was born there. Vaudreuil had entered the world in 1698 as the governor's son. He was named governor of Trois Rivières in 1733 then of Louisiana in 1742. He governed Louisiana until 1753, when he was recalled to Versailles, where, on January 1, 1755, Louis XV tapped him to lead New France. His instructions acquainted him with the diplomatic history involving the frontier between France and Britain in North America from the Utrecht Treaty of 1713 to the present, including the stalemated boundary commission. Vaudreuil was to remain on the defensive and give the British no cause for war. However, if war did erupt, he should launch expeditions against Forts Oswego on Lake Ontario, Lawrence in Nova Scotia, and Halifax on the Kennebec River, and even those on Hudson Bay, if possible. Likewise, the governor should do all in his power to sway the Indians toward France and against the British. To that end, he should entice them to settle near French trading posts. Though he would command the colony's military as well as its administration, Vaudreuil knew little of war; his only taste of it was from leading a bloodless campaign against the Fox Indians in 1728. Vaudreuil's inexperience would soon become quite evident, especially to the French officers who would serve in Canada.[24]

In all, Versailles committed three thousand troops to New France's defense, including the second battalion of the Bourgogne, La Reine, Languedoc, Guyenne, Béarn, and Artois Regiments. The first four would sail to Quebec and the last two would reinforce Louisbourg. To command those troops, Versailles chose Jean-Armand, baron de Dieskau, promoting him from lieutenant colonel of the Bentheim Regiment to major general. The marine ministry rather than the war ministry would command Dieskau, with Vaudreuil his immediate superior.[25] Assisting Dieskau would be André Jean-Baptiste Doreil as deputy commissary general for New France and Louis-Hyacinthe Boyer de Crémille as inspector general.

But could those battalions safely reach New France? On paper, France's navy seemed formidable. There were eighteen ships of the line with fifty or more guns, along with three frigates at Brest, and six ships of the line at Rochefort. Yet, after decades of neglect, France's navy was in wretched shape to fight what would become a world war, something no last-minute infusion of gold could swiftly remedy. Argenson explained, "They say our navy is in a very bad state; always an 'affair for show only'; seventy vessels constructed since the peace are rotting in port: no rigging, no guns, no munitions, and no possibility of arming them." The crisis demanded extreme measures, some of which the marine ministry took: "They have just given orders to the Company of the Indies to deliver over to the navy all the iron and bronze guns which it has on its own vessels, ours being almost without any."[26]

By early May, Versailles had readied a fleet to convey the leaders and troops to New France, with Admiral Emmanuel-Auguste de Cahideuc, comte de Dubois de la Motte, commanding fourteen ships of the line and two frigates. That formidable appearance was deceptive. Only three warships were fully armed; most guns were stripped from the rest (*en flûte*) to make room for the troops and supplies, a decision deemed safe by the marine ministry since England and France remained officially at peace. Escorting La Motte's squadron was Lieutenant General Jean-Baptiste de Macnemara in command of six warships.

The fleet set sail from Brest at noon on May 3, 1755. The second day at sea a British frigate appeared and shadowed the fleet for three days. Macnemara finally sent warships in pursuit, but the frigate outsailed them and disappeared. The squadrons separated on May 8, with La Motte's surging on toward Canada and Macnemara's returning to Brest. As if fear that the British might try to intercept them were not worry enough, foul weather bedeviled La Motte's convoy with calms, fog, icebergs, and wind. On June 4, the French saw what they assumed was a British fleet bearing down on them, but they disappeared to safety in a fog bank.

Admiral Boscawen's fleet caught up to Macnemara's fleet on June 8. Once again, most of the French ships sailed into the fog. However, Captain Richard Howe caught up to three stragglers, the *Lys* mounting only twenty-two of its sixty-two guns, the *Dauphin Royal* with twenty-four of seventy-four guns present, and the *Alcide* with all sixty-four guns ready. When Captain Hocquart of the *Alcide* called out to Howe, asking whether their nations were at war or peace, the English gentleman announced that they were at peace then ordered his gunners to open fire when his ship sailed alongside the other. The broadside killed or wounded about one hundred men. Hocquart's surviving gunners managed to fire a few shots that killed seven and wounded twenty-seven of the enemy. But as three other British warships closed, Hocquart wisely struck his colors. The *Lys* also surrendered; the *Dauphin Royal* managed to escape. Aboard the *Lys* and *Alcide* were eight companies of French regulars.[27]

When word of the unprovoked British capture of the *Lys* and *Alcide* reached Versailles in mid-July, Louis XV exclaimed, "I will not pardon the pirates of that insolent nation."[28] The news outraged French passions vividly expressed by Argenson: "These arrogant, ambitious, and usurping Englishmen declare war and attack, unjustly, what they pretend to be usurping claims. Our war is just; theirs is like that of Algiers, or like the wolf and the lamb."[29]

The British attack provided Versailles with a casus belli. Should France declare war on England? As usual, the council split. Argenson, backed by Rouillé, called for conquering the Austrian Netherlands with the assumption that Vienna would soon join London in war against France. Machault protested any retaliation until the army and navy were ready for war. After the passions cooled, the ministers agreed to delay war's formal advent as much as possible. Argenson explained why: "The Council steps back from the decisions it made at first in our violent resentment against England. It fears great losses; such as the intercepting of our rich fleets from the Indies; it fears for our cod-fisheries; it fears for all our maritime wealth, and it is to be observed that the Court people hold a large part of it, which makes them prefer their own interests to the general welfare. The King has sent orders to all ports to notify merchant vessels that they must return as soon as possible, as the country is on the eve of a declaration of war."[30]

These fears would be tragically realized in the years ahead. The British fleet would systematically sweep French naval and merchant ships from the seas and capture its overseas colonies one by one. For now the council hoped that the reinforcements that made it to Canada would be sufficient to defend New France. The council agreed to sever diplomatic relations while accelerating its war preparations. On July 18, Rouillé sent word to Mirepoix at London and Ambassador François de Bussy at Hanover to pack their bags and return home. Formal diplomatic relations were now ended. But it would be nearly another year before war was officially declared by either side despite all the carnage reaped before then.[31]

The first French ships of the convey reached Quebec on June 19. Vaudreuil himself did not step ashore until June 23, when he officially took over from Duquesne. The former governor gave Vaudreuil a full account of New France's defenses. What Vaudreuil learned was not encouraging. Duquesne reported that, during the "first campaigns on the Ohio, a horrible waste and disorder prevailed at the Presque Isle and Niagara carrying places, which cost the King immense sums." Fort Niagara was "undermined by the lake and crumbling in every direction." Fort Saint Frederic "is threatening to fall on all sides, in consequence of the walls being too weak to support the terraces." In all, those forts could not sustain even a brief bombardment from British gunners. The forts' supply situations, surprisingly, were not as bleak—cornfields had been planted near Forts Duquesne and Machault, relieving the need to provision them.[32]

Vaudreuil expressed to Machault his distress at how unprepared New France was for war.[33] He had no military background and had not lived in Canada for twenty years. Yet he was expected to defend that province against reports of pending British offensives against Forts Duquesne, Saint Frederic, Niagara, and Beauséjour, while mounting his own expedition against Oswego! Vaudreuil blamed Duquesne for the problems and complained of his continued presence and duties. This criticism angered Duquesne. In a letter to Machault, he protested Versailles's decision to recall him before he could command the Oswego expedition that he had devoted so much effort to preparing.[34] Duquesne's point was well-taken even if it was petulantly expressed. It made no sense to switch commanders mid-campaign, especially when a novice replaced a veteran.

The troops fresh from France soon suffered a blow to their morale. Shortly after arriving, Pouchot reported that they "were handed over to the Marine [ministry's authority]. This change from land to marine upset the troops. . . . Subsequent events will show that they were much worse off than if they had passed into the service of an absolutely foreign prince, either because of different traditions or the way they were treated."[35] Morale dropped further when the army troops were issued marine clothing to supplement their own. While the coats were similar, the facings were a different color. These troops would be forced to wait until 1758 before the war ministry got around to sending them their own uniforms.[36] To worsen matters, the officers and troops alike soon came to despise Dieskau, their field commander, who "began to treat the troops in the German manner. He was no longer willing to speak to common officers and only received representations from corps commanders whom he never consulted—a very great drawback in a small army."[37]

The British Onslaught

Of Britain's four offensives, two met with partial success, one never took place, and the last ended with a devastating defeat. Ironically, while the much-maligned American provincials provided the bulk of troops for the first three offensives, it was General Edward Braddock and his regular regiments, supplemented by colonists, who suffered a near massacre on the Monongahela.

No friend of Braddock, Horace Walpole characterized him as "a man desperate in his fortune, brutal in his behavior, obstinate in his sentiments, intrepid and capable."[38] In America, Braddock certainly lived up to all those characteristics but the last. Shortly after arriving, his arrogance alienated virtually all of the provincial and Indian leaders who were forced to serve beneath him. He was determined to conduct war by European methods no matter how much the colonists advised him to adapt his tactics to the wilderness. In a letter to Benjamin Franklin, Braddock revealed the depths of his arrogance and delusions by at once denigrating an enemy he had never fought against and an ally he had never fought alongside: "These savages may, indeed, be a formidable enemy to your raw American militia, but upon the King's regulars and disciplined troops, sir, it is impossible they should make any impression."[39]

By mid-June, Braddock had massed at Fort Cumberland 2,200 troops, of whom about 800 were regulars and the rest provincials; only 8 Indians managed to swallow enough pride to stay with him. On May 29, his army began the tedious process of converting the trail to the Ohio forks into a road. They crawled forward only a half dozen or so miles a day. French and Indians picked off stragglers. Reports arrived that 500 French troops would soon arrive at Fort Duquesne. At a war council on June 18, Braddock agreed to George Washington's proposal to split the command and hurry forward with the faster half.

The French commander, Claude-Pierre Pécaudy de Contrecoeur, received daily reports of Braddock's slow progress and numbers. He had at Fort Duquesne only 258 Canadians and several hundred Indians. Just how many of those Indians would fight was, however, as yet an unanswerable question. No matter how many gifts he gave them, most of the Ottawas, Pottawattomis, Abenakis, Caughnawagas, Mohawks, Shawnees, Delawares, Hurons, and Mingos clamored to go home. Contrecoeur himself was frustrated by how Braddock kept his troops "so constantly on guard, always marching in battle formation, that all the efforts that our detachments put forth against them are useless."[40] Fort Duquesne itself was little more than a stockade that would be blasted to splinters if Braddock arrived with his cannons. Contrecoeur mulled burning the fort and retreating up the Allegheny River to join the 104 troops at Fort Le Boeuf. History would read quite differently had he done so.[41]

Then, on July 7, Captain Daniel Hyacinthe-Marie Liénard de Beaujeu arrived to replace Contrecoeur as Fort Duquesne's commander. Beaujeu had come to fight. When scouts reported the next day that Braddock was only nine miles away, Beaujeu gathered the Indians and sang the war song. Even then the Indians split over whether to join him. The next morning on July 9, Beaujeu led out 254 Canadians commanded by Captain Jean-Daniel Dumas and himself commanded the 637 Indians. The two enemy columns collided only seven miles from the fort. A bullet from the first volley killed Beaujeu. The French and Indians hesitated briefly. Some Canadians fled. Dumas managed to rally the men and send them around the British flanks, where they poured a murderous fire into the milling, panicky redcoats. Forbidden by Braddock to break ranks and shoot from shelter, the British troops crowded along the trail, firing blindly into the trees and often into each other. The French and Indians fired continuously, slaughtering hundreds of redcoats and provincials. A bullet mortally wounded Braddock; only then did he give the order to retreat. Of the 1,373 British troops under Braddock that day, 519 were killed and 607 were wounded, compared to only 28 Canadians and 11 Indians killed and about the same number wounded. The British also abandoned four twelve-pounders, four six-pounders, four eight-inch howitzers, several hundred horses and cattle, and tons of supplies. Almost as important were captured documents that revealed that the British were clearly guilty of premeditated aggression, having planned their attacks nine months earlier. Those documents were later published. The British retreated to Fort Cumberland whereupon the new commander, Colonel Thomas Dunbar, eventually took his regulars all the way to New York. The French and Indians followed up their brilliant victory with raids along the Pennsylvania, Maryland, and Virginia frontier.[42]

News of the Monongahela victory eclipsed that of an earlier defeat. Two forts guarded the Chignecto Isthmus. Fort Beauséjour was commanded by Louis Du Pont Duchambon de Vergor and Fort Gaspereau by Benjamin Rouer de Villeray. Vergor got the job largely because his wife was one of Intendant Bigot's mistresses. The intendant had encouraged the cuckold to "profit by your place, my dear Vergor; clip and cut—you are free to do as you please—so that you can come soon to join me in France and buy an estate near me."[43]

Yet even a capable commander could not have withstood the British army sent against those forts. On June 2, Colonel Robert Monckton disembarked at the head of 280 British regulars and 2,000 New England troops commanded by Colonel John Winslow. To worsen matters, Fort Beauséjour's commissary, Thomas Pichon, was a British spy who sent detailed reports to Fort Lawrence across the valley. Monckton knew all the fort's weaknesses.

Vergor sent pleas for help from the warrior-priest Jean Louis Le Loutre in Acadia and from Fortress Louisbourg on Île Royale. Le Loutre quickly gathered 1,200 militiamen and Micmacs and brought them to Fort Beauséjour; no help would come from Louisbourg. On June 4, Monckton marched his army across the Missaguash River, brushed aside 400 Canadian skirmishers, and entrenched his army on the ridge on which Fort Beauséjour was sited. It was not until June 12 that the British began to construct a mortar battery within range of the fort. The British repulsed a sortie by 180 troops against the battery. The mortars opened fire the next day. One shot tore through a casemate and killed an officer, two soldiers, and an English prisoner. Though the French casualties totaled only nine killed and seven wounded, the lucky shot "increased the disorder which reigned in the fort. The settlers went in a body to the Commandant to demand that he should capitulate, saying that, if there were any opposition to the decision . . . they would no longer respect the garrison . . . and would turn their arms against the officers and the soldiers, and deliver the fort to the English."[44] On June 16, Vergor asked for terms. Monckton granted honors of war in return for a six-month parole for the French. Vergor gratefully accepted. Monckton received Fort Gaspereau's surrender from Captain Villeray on June 17 without a fight. On June 21, a

British expedition disembarked and marched into an abandoned and torched Fort Saint Jean. The Chignecto Isthmus and much of Acadia's coastline were now in British hands.

To solidify their hold, the British rounded up and expelled the Acadians. From 1755 through 1762, some 11,000 of the 15,000 Acadians were allowed to take only what they could carry, were crammed aboard British ships, and were sailed away to be dumped on distant, alien shores. The French greeted with outrage news of the Acadians' forced exile. Argenson wrote of the "deplorable news" of the Acadians "carried off and distributed . . . among the various English colonies, where they are destitute, treated like slaves, and naked."[45]

The other two British campaigns took longer to get started. Massachusetts governor William Shirley led the expedition against Fort Niagara, and Indian superintendent Colonel William Johnson led that against Fort Saint Frederic. Inexperience, mismanagement, supply shortages, and a tug-of-war between the two commanders over who got the loyal Iroquois warriors delayed their respective offensives. Shirley's never left its staging area at Fort Oswego. On September 27, having amassed there several thousand troops and tons of supplies, Shirley abruptly canceled the campaign. Not only did Braddock's debacle demand more caution, but Shirley's son was among the dead. Shirley finally judged the season too late and the reported 1,500 French troops at Fort Frontenac and 1,200 at Fort Niagara too numerous. He feared that if he tried to besiege one fort, the other French force would attack his rear at Oswego.

Johnson's troops, meanwhile, built a road and several forts from Albany up the Hudson River valley and over the low divide to Lake George's (Sacrament) south shore. There, Johnson set his men to work building boats for his campaign north down Lake George, and then the portage down to Lake Champlain. At the Lake George camp, he had 2,200 provincial troops and several hundred Iroquois warriors, most of whom were Mohawk. Another 500 troops were camped around Fort Lyman, fourteen miles east where the Hudson River bends south toward Albany.

When Vaudreuil received the documents detailing Braddock's strategy, he changed his own plans. Originally, he had intended to send

Dieskau with the regulars to attack Oswego. Now, Johnson's campaign to Lake George seemed the greater threat to New France. He ordered Dieskau to proceed there "with the entire of his army without ever dividing his forces."[46] As New France's commander, Vaudreuil prepared an extensive campaign plan for Dieskau to implement. Fired with confidence, Dieskau dismissed that plan and embarked on his own.

By August 16, Dieskau had massed 3,573 troops at Fort Saint Frederic.[47] He reported that his troops were "panting only for the attack. All I fear is that the enemy, who imagine all our troops to have gone on the expedition against Chouaguen [Oswego], will beat a retreat on learning that we are on the march."[48] His optimism is understandable. After all, not only had Braddock's expedition been devastated, but his secret plans had been captured so that the French now knew just where each British offensive could be expected. Trying to keep the Indians in line exhausted Dieskau: "They drive us crazy from morning to night. There is no end to their demands. They have already eaten five oxen and as many hogs, without counting the kegs of brandy they have drunk. In short, one needs the patience of an angel to get on with these devils; and yet one must always force himself to be pleased with them."[49]

Dieskau decided on August 24 to establish a fort farther south on Lake Champlain where the La Chute River flows down from Lake George. There, on September 2, his troops began constructing Fort Carillon (later named Ticonderoga by the British after they captured it). This same day, Dieskau interrogated a prisoner who claimed that 2,400 troops had returned to Albany, leaving only 500 remaining to defend a partially constructed Fort Lyman. Whether the prisoner deliberately misinformed the French general is unknown, but this misinformation would have enormously tragic consequences for the French cause.[50]

An emboldened Dieskau chose "to leave the main body of the army where I was [Fort Carillon], and to take with me a picked force, march rapidly, and surprise Fort [Lyman] and capture the 500 men."[51] He took with him 1,500 men including 216 grenadiers from the Languedoc and La Reine battalions, 684 militiamen, and over 600 Indians from various tribes. His forced paddled down Lake Champlain and reached South Bay by September 5. There, he left 200 militiamen to guard the boats while he marched overland with the rest on the path toward Fort Lyman.

Surprise was lost when his advance guard attacked a supply train on the road between the two forts and the survivors fled to give word. The warning confirmed a scouting report Johnson had received earlier that day that a large raiding party had crossed over from South Bay where the raiders had undoubtedly left their canoes. At first, Johnson wanted to send 500 troops to clear the road and 500 troops to attack the canoes. Mohawk chief Hendrick convinced him to keep the entire attacking force together. Johnson reluctantly agreed to send all 1,000 troops up the road the next morning.

Meanwhile, Dieskau learned from prisoners that Johnson's army was on Lake George. He convened a war council of his own officers and chiefs. The officers urged an attack on Fort Lyman, which had only 500 troops. The chiefs warned they would only fight Johnson on Lake George. Dieskau had no choice but to bend to their will. Thus were both the British and French strategies determined by their Indian allies.

On the morning of September 8, scouts discovered the approaching provincials and Mohawks. Dieskau deployed his troops and Indians in an ambush along the road. Once again, the Indians decided the issue. The French Mohawks called out to the British Mohawks to change sides, thus spoiling the surprise attack. Shots broke out, followed by fusillades. The provincials and Mohawks fled back to the Lake George camp. Dieskau urged an immediate pursuit, but the Indians took their time plundering the dead and wounded.

Johnson thus had a breathing space in which to ready his men for an attack. By noon, most of Dieskau's troops and warriors were blasting away at the fortified camp. Dieskau ordered a general charge, led by his grenadiers. American cannonballs tore through the grenadiers' ranks, forcing them to retreat, while musket fire kept the Canadians and Indians at bay. Discouraged, Canadians and Indians began to melt away into the forest. Bullets wounded both Dieskau and Johnson. Dieskau turned over command to Pierre-André Gohin, comte de Montreuil, who promptly ordered a retreat. Just then, a force of 200 troops from Fort Lyman caught the remaining French and Indians in the rear, turning their retreat into a rout. Dieskau was abandoned, probably inadvertently, on the field. In addition to their commander, the French lost 107 dead and 130 wounded; the Americans suffered 120 dead, 80 wounded, and 62 missing. Though Johnson initially called for following up their victory with an advance against the French on Lake Champlain, his officers talked him out of it.[52]

Though Vaudreuil had received the shocking news days before, the September 15 letter from the captive Dieskau himself must have sickened him again: "I am defeated; my detachment is routed; a number of men are killed and thirty or forty are prisoners. . . . I have received for my share, four gunshot wounds, one of which is mortal. I owe this misfortune to the treachery of the Iroquois."[53] Vaudreuil, however, placed the blame squarely on Dieskau. In his extensive report to Machault, the governor concluded that had Dieskau "conformed to his instructions and marched with his entire army, he might have been able not only to force the enemy's entrenchment at Lake St. Sacrament [Lake George], but even to reduce Fort [Lyman]. . . . Had M. Dieskau carried out my views, the English would be much humbled and the Five Nations would have abandoned them."[54]

Vaudreuil's scenario is certainly plausible. If Dieskau had all his troops and cannon on hand and besieged rather than assaulted the Lake George camp, he might well have bagged Johnson's entire army. Then he could have marched on Fort Lyman with its 500 defenders, who mostly likely would have either fled or soon surrendered. The decision then would have been whether or not to march on to lightly defended Albany fifty miles south. Then again, transporting 3,500 men and cannon by water and trail would have taken longer and would have been discovered sooner, allowing Johnson to retreat to Fort Lyman then down the Hudson if necessary. The season was advanced and Dieskau's supplies were too limited for a prolonged campaign that might have taken him to Albany's gates.

Captain Pierre Pouchot spoke for most French and Canadian officers when he noted a silver lining in the Lake George defeat. He declared Dieskau's capture a blessing in disguise. Not only had the French army rid itself of an arrogant martinet, but otherwise

Versailles, "confident in the country's forces, might have neglected it & we would have been utterly incapable of resisting the enemy operations."[55] Vaudreuil despised Dieskau and had not hid his feelings from Versailles. He explained to Machault that war "in this country is very different from wars in Europe. We are obliged to act with great circumspection, so as not to leave anything to chance; we have few men, and however small the number we may lose, we feel its effects. However brave the commander of those troops may be, he could not be acquainted with the country. . . . The Canadians and Indians would not march with the same confidence under the orders of a commander of the troops from France that they would under the officers of this Colony."[56]

Regardless, by late fall the fighting had sputtered to a close on all fronts. On Lake Champlain, Montreuil withdrew all the regulars back to the Saint Lawrence valley, leaving four hundred men at unfinished Fort Carillon under the command of Captain Louis-Philippe Le Dossu d'Hébécourt of La Reine battalion. New France's engineer, Captain Michel Chartier, marquis de Lotbinière, supervised Fort Carillon's construction. At the other frontier forts, the Indians dispersed to their villages for the long winter.

The French had managed to hold the entire frontier except Acadia. They had inflicted a critical defeat on the British on the Monongahela while suffering a much less serious setback on Lake George. Yet most of the French officers were pessimistic for the colony's future.[57] Detailed accounts of the year's startling events in Canada penned by Vaudreuil and other officials sailed on the frigate *La Syrenne* from Quebec on November 8 and arrived at Brest on December 10. Typical was the report of Chief of Staff Doreil to war minister Argenson. After detailing all the weaknesses and setbacks afflicting Canada, Doreil concluded, "The situation of this Colony is critical in all respects; it requires prompt and powerful assistance. I dare even assert that if some one be not sent, it runs the greatest risks next year, for there is no doubt the English will make the greatest efforts to invade the country, and that we shall be attacked next spring."[58]

The biggest and most worrisome question was which side tribes would support in the spring. After news of the Monongahela battle, all of the Iroquois except the Mohawks seemed to tilt toward the French, only to lean the other way after learning of Dieskau's defeat. To regain their confidence, Vaudreuil held councils with the Senecas on October 1 at Montreal and other Iroquois tribes at La Présentation on October 22. Most refused to be swayed to the French despite the governor's presents, promises, and threats, and instead maintained a tense neutrality. Vaudreuil warned them that "should any of the Five Nations be found next spring among the English, I will let loose all our Upper and domiciliated Nations on them; cause their villages to be laid waste and never pardon them."[59] Mass death did indeed come to the Indians this year, but not from battle. Smallpox broke out in mid-summer and slowly burned its way across New France, ravaging one tribe after another.

Meanwhile, the worst threat to New France arose not by land but by sea. On June 29, 1755, Whitehall began an undeclared naval war on all French shipping though it would not begin issuing letters of marque to privateers until August 29. Thereafter, English warships fired shots across the bows of French merchant ships then boarded and seized them. By the year's end, British warships and privateers had captured over three hundred ships and six thousand sailors of France.[60]

War or Peace?

As the fighting exploded along the North American frontier, two vital questions assailed Louis XV's council. Given all the violent British insults to France, should the undeclared war be made official? Regardless, how could France's army and navy blunt the British attacks?

Britain's vicious sea and land war against France deeply rankled Louis and his ministers. Machault spoke of the "pain that his Majesty sees himself forced, by the hostilities of the English, to adopt measures so opposed to his love of peace, and to the efforts he has made to maintain it with that nation. There is not, however, any declaration of war on either side."[61] How much of this "pain" was genuine and how much was contrived to justify past, current, and later offensives? While the king's aversion to war was sincere, practical constraints explain

Versailles's policy. The British had clearly escalated a crisis into an all-out war with their four offensives against New France and naval campaign designed to sweep the seas of French war and merchant ships. Yet France was hardly a passive victim. After all, Versailles had ordered the Ohio forks captured, had sent three thousand troops to Canada, and planned to take Oswego. Yet, without naval superiority, it could do little more. The withdrawal of the French ambassadors from London and Hanover was the final step before a war declaration.

Louis XV and his ministers held a clear-eyed vision of the English threat. They feared that English sea power would sever France from its colonies and strangle the kingdom itself. If so, any French military efforts overseas were tenuous at best. The war on the high seas and North American frontier would inevitably lead to war in Europe. There, France did have some cards of its own to play. It was well known that George II's sentimental attachment to his ancestral home exceeded his appreciation of the American colonies. Versailles and its diplomats made no secret that if war broke out French armies would march on Hanover, followed up ideally by invading Britain itself. Yet those campaigns would have to await the next year. Only La Galissonière urged an immediate war against the British. Though rejected then, his reports became the foundation for French policy.[62]

Until France was ready, Louis and his ministers had to grind their teeth at British outrages while carefully plotting French attacks that stood a chance of succeeding. As it prepared for war, Versailles could merely issue bitter protests to England. Whitehall ignored the protests. Versailles fumed but turned the other diplomatic cheek. The French navy was not yet ready to challenge England on the high seas. It would never truly become ready.

Versailles was not immediately worried about New France falling to British arms. The regular battalions would prevent that for now. The worst fear was over the vulnerability of France's Caribbean sugar islands, whose wealth exceeded that garnered from all of New France. As early as February, marine minister Machault had written France's Windward Islands governor, Maximin de Bompart, ordering him to seize Saint Lucia as soon as he heard that war had broken out between France and England. Learning of the English capture of the *Alcide* and *Lys*, Bompart sent warships and troops to occupy Saint Lucia. In December, Versailles sent a squadron to protect Saint Domingue and the other French islands.[63]

All along, French and British ambassadors engaged in a tug-of-war for the hearts and minds of chancelleries elsewhere, especially in Madrid, Vienna, and Berlin. With its war against France rapidly escalating, England cast about for allies. Defying his advisors, George II sailed to Hanover on April 28, 1755, to spend several months at his ancestral home, where he hoped to negotiate alliances with the German princes and possibly Russia. Of the king's visit, Walpole wrung his hands that given "the French armaments, the defenseless state of the kingdom, the doubtful faith of the King of Prussia, and above all, the age of the King, and the youth of his heir at so critical a conjuncture, everything pleaded against so rash a journey. But as His Majesty was never despotic but in the single point of leaving his kingdom, no arguments or representations had any weight with him."[64] The king proved the naysayers wrong. On June 18, England and Hesse-Cassel signed a treaty whereby Whitehall would hire eight thousand Hessians and join them with George II's Hanoverian army.

While George II was away, England was governed by a regency presided over by William Augustus, the Duke of Cumberland and the king's second and favored son. The regency's efforts to find allies failed. Whitehall's prime hope was to revive England's Triple Alliance with Holland and Austria to contain France. English gold and the common threat of France had cemented the Triple Alliance in the past. While the English still had plenty of gold to offer, the Austrians and Dutch did not currently fear France as they once had. The Dutch spurned the English offer of money to war against France, arguing that the English attack on the French convoy made them the aggressors. To Maria Theresa, Whitehall made an explicit offer to renew its subsidy agreements with Saxony and Bavaria, hire 8,000 Prussians for Holland's defense, and negotiate an alliance with Russia if Vienna placed 30,000 troops in the Austrian Netherlands and promised to help defend Hanover if France attacked it.

Vienna seriously considered the proposal. The Austrians definitely wanted an alliance with England, but against Prussia rather than

France as that new threat had arisen to surpass the old. Maria Theresa hated Frederick for his conquest of Silesia and dreamed not only of retaking that former Austrian province but of destroying the Prussian king and his realm. To that end, she sought her own triple alliance of Austria, Russia, and England. The glitter of English gold could not tempt her from that obsession. In June 1755, foreign minister Wenzel Anton von Kaunitz-Rietberg promised to send 20,000 troops to the Netherlands if England joined Austria against Prussia. Whitehall did not reply.

When Britain turned down his offer of an alliance against Prussia, Kaunitz revived his idea of an alliance with France against Prussia. Once again, Maria Theresa agreed, formally accepting the policy on August 21, 1755. The question was how to get to Louis XV through his pro-Frederick advisors and court. It was ambassador Georg Adam von Starhemberg who talked Maria Theresa into using Pompadour as the conduit for an alliance. Pompadour was clearly the power behind the throne, discreet, utterly devoted to Louis, and the avowed enemy of pro-Prussian Argenson. The suggestion must have taken the empress's breath away. Over the decades, her husband's ill-concealed philandering had deeply hurt Maria Theresa. Now Starhemberg was urging her to treat with that age's most famous mistress. Realism won out over sentiment. Maria Theresa remained obsessed with retaking Silesia, and any means to that end was justified. On August 30, Kaunitz sent a note to Pompadour urging her to carry secretly the enclosed letter from Maria Theresa to Louis XV.

The timing was propitious. By the late summer of 1755, France had suddenly found itself diplomatically isolated. Russia had aligned itself with Britain. Austria would likely follow suit. Spain was aloof to all French entreaties. Officially, France and Prussia remained bound by a 1741 treaty, but it would expire on June 5, 1756, and Frederick held back from renewing it. Rumor had it that while leading on the French, Frederick was secretly trying to entice the British into an alliance. Louis XV was of two minds about Frederick. France needed an ally, and Prussia seemed to be the only possibility. However, though most of his court adored the philosophe Prussian king, Louis XV had come to hate him for his "numerous infidelities which he might well repeat . . .

and the offhand remarks that the King of Prussia had made regarding our government and matters which concerned him closely."[65] These close matters concerned Pompadour, whom Frederick had called, among other things, "la demoiselle poisson" ("Miss Fish") and "cotillon IV" ("Mistress Number 4").[66] To all this, Louis XV and his council knew not what to do.

All along, Versailles overlooked a possible rapprochement with Vienna, something Kaunitz and Starhemberg had hinted at for years. Until 1755, Louis politely spurned those advances, citing loyalty to France's ally, Prussia. Nonetheless, Maria Theresa's letter startled Louis. The empress did not need to urge secrecy; the king knew well that his pro-Prussian ministers would scuttle any talk of an alliance if they caught a whiff of it. Louis needed someone outside his council who was thoroughly trustworthy and knowledgeable and an experienced diplomat. Pompadour argued that only one man fit that description—François-Joachim de Pierre, comte de Bernis. The king promptly summoned him.[67]

Louis had chosen an unlikely go-between for what would be known as the "diplomatic revolution." From his birth in 1715 to his death in 1794, Bernis's life would span eighty years of France's eighteenth century, from Louis XIV to Robespierre. The Jesuits educated him, made him an abbé, and prepared him for the priesthood whose vows he would imperfectly keep. Bernis was a sensualist, poet, gourmet, gossip, wit, and confidant of pretty, powerful women. His cherub's merry face, plump body, and short legs likely stirred most women maternally rather than sexually. His poetry was like Fragonard's paintings, frivolous and playful. That being the age's tenor, his poetry got him elected to the French Academy in 1744. In all, Bernis was "the wit of the Academy, a languid abbé, making pretty verses that escape his laziness, disdainful, nothing of a man, liking to sit up at night in the society of the fair sex, and getting up at midday."[68]

Apparently Bernis counted voyeurism among his sensual pleasures. While ambassador to Venice, he shared a richly imaginative ménage à quatre with Casanova and two young beauties, who happened to be nuns in a convent. Casanova noted with admiration that Bernis was a refined and successful lover in his own right, describing him as "a man whom Fortune has smiled upon, but he captivated her by his merit; he is not less distinguished by his talents than by his birth. . . . The serious character of our first meeting did not prevent the utterance of witty jests, for in that respect M. de Bernis was a true Frenchman. . . . The ambassador owed his great fortune entirely to the fair sex, because he possessed to the highest degree the art of coddling love; and, as his nature was entirely voluptuous, he found his advantage in it because he knew how to call desires into existence and this procured him enjoyments worthy of his delicate taste."[69]

It was these characteristics that won Bernis Pompadour's friendship and patronage. They first met in 1745 shortly after she had seduced Louis, and thereafter they whiled away many an hour in happy gossip. He gave her sound advice on retaining the king's love and keeping rivals at bay, served as liaison in a host of intrigues, and helped her stage her plays. In return, she promoted him. In 1751, she got Louis to appoint him ambassador to Venice, the perfect post for a sybarite like Bernis. He returned to Paris in June 1755 to apply for a more important post at Madrid or Vienna. In August, he received the Madrid post, but he never got there.

The royal summons was surprise enough. Bernis met first with Pompadour, who showed him that astonishing Austrian letter. The abbé trembled that news of an alliance with Austria would provoke a European war. He recalled,

> The King, with whom I had never talked about affairs of state, came in and asked me suddenly what I thought of M. de Starhemberg's letter. I repeated to his Majesty what I had just said to Mme. de Pompadour. The King listened to me with impatience and when I had finished he said, almost angrily, 'You are like the others, the enemy of the Queen of Hungary.' I replied, 'No one admires that Queen more than me. . . . Your Majesty has everything to gain in finding out more about the Austrian Court's intentions, but it is necessary to take care with your response.' The King's face became more serene; he ordered me to listen to M. de Starhemberg in the presence of Mme. de Pompadour, who was to be present only for the first

conference. . . . The King did not conceal from me that all his life he had wanted an alliance with Austria, that he thought it was the only way to establish a lasting peace and maintain the Catholic religion.[70]

Additionally, Louis wished Bernis to negotiate secretly with the Austrians for an alliance. Fearing the consequences, Bernis asked the king for a written order to undertake the mission. Louis complied.

Negotiations were conducted in a romantic setting—beside the Seine River's swirling waters in a pavilion on Pompadour's Bellevue château near Sevres. The first meeting among Bernis, Pompadour, and Starhemberg took place on September 3, 1755. To stymie any spies, each had arrived in a separate coach at a different time. While Pompadour witnessed, Bernis faithfully copied Starhemberg's instructions and conveyed them to the king. Maria Theresa had called on Louis to renounce his alliance with Prussia in return for which Austria would not only refuse to ally with Britain but would allow France to occupy Nieuport and Ostend during the war, and, even more astonishingly, would allow France to actually take over the Austrian Netherlands if Silesia were rejoined with Austria! To worsen French fears, Starhemberg confirmed the rumor that Frederick was secretly negotiating with the English against France.

Maria Theresa had made an extraordinary offer, one that Louis XV could not lightly accept or reject. Louis decided to play for more time, information, and concessions. Bernis and Starhemberg met frequently the rest of that year and into the next. It was not until late October that Louis XV let in foreign minister Rouillé, marine minister Machault, controleur-general Séchelles, and household minister Louis Phélypeaux, comte de Saint-Florentin La Vrillière. These four men, Bernis, and the king formed a secret committee to nurture the Austrian alliance. Bernis conducted the talks, drew up reports, and drafted treaties, all subject to the committee's approval. Only pro-Frederick war minister Argenson was left in the dark. It was feared that if that he heard of the king's diplomacy, he would surely try to disrupt it.

Bernis labored for eighteen months on these negotiations with only a single secretary to assist him. He complained persistently that his duties were driving him to an early grave by ruining his health with endless long days of work and sleepless nights of worry. Adding to the incredible stress were the slights and intrigues of the jealous ministers. Without a portfolio, Bernis was denied access to foreign ministry documents vital for successfully steering the talks with Austria. Bernis implored Louis to remedy the absurdity. The king demurred, fearing to hurt Rouillé's feelings.

To share Pompadour's confidence was to share the hatred of her enemies and the jealousy of her friends. United against the upstart Bernis, the other ministers employed every means to trip up his policies. Reasoning that "the enemy of my enemy is my friend," Bernis encouraged Pompadour to cozy up to Argenson and the prince de Conti; both men spurned her advances. This same axiom soon shaped French foreign policy—with as little success.

All along, Bernis dangled by Pompadour's smile above a fickle, spiteful council and court. A favor bestowed today could be withdrawn tomorrow. The ministers would gloat if Bernis fell into that merciless coliseum to be torn apart with ridicule by the courtiers. Bernis wrote how as ambassador, "I was confident of being a success. But it was not the same at Versailles where I had against me the jealousy of all the ministers and all the courtiers. A single misunderstanding with Madame de Pompadour might ruin me: I know how easy it is, in matters of Court influence, to get embroiled with friends, especially female friends."[71] That pressure slowly suffocated Bernis.

Rumors of negotiations between Whitehall and Potsdam were true, but an agreement was still months away at that point. When talks between Bernis and Starhemberg opened, Whitehall was much closer to concluding an alliance not with but against Prussia. A British nightmare scenario was a joint French and Prussian attack on Hanover. To dilute that chance, Whitehall nurtured ties with Russia. On September 30, 1755, the two countries signed a convention whereby Whitehall would give Saint Petersburg £100,000 a year if Empress Elizabeth kept a 55,000-man army in Livonia. If Hanover were attacked, this Russian army would march or sail to its rescue while Britain dispatched a fleet to the Baltic and gave Saint Petersburg £500,000 for the war's duration. The English and Russians interpreted the treaty's "common enemy" tenet differently. Whitehall declared that it included France; Saint Petersburg insisted it meant only Prussia.

Well aware of the negotiations and not to be undone, Versailles sought to pry Russia away from the English. It was an ambitious policy. France had no diplomatic and few commercial contacts in Russia. In June, Louis got the foreign ministry and secret du roi to dispatch Alexander Mackenzie, chevalier Douglas, to Saint Petersburg to discover the extent of British influence and any opportunities to advance French interests. Douglas seemed a good choice. A Scotsman loyal to Versailles would attract less suspicion than a Frenchman. He had fled to France in 1746 after Bonnie Prince Charles's rebellion and bid for the British crown was finally defeated at Culloden.

Shortly after arriving at Saint Petersburg in October, Douglas reported to Rouillé that Grand Chancellor Alexander Petrovich Bestuzhev-Ryumin and British ambassador Sir Charles Hanbury Williams seemed firmly in control of Russian foreign policy. For the next two years, Douglas would engage Hanbury in a fierce tug-of-war for influence in Elizabeth's council and court. Each had his own advantage. Hanbury had more money with which to fill the pockets of court officials. Douglas played on the common fear of Prussia and upon a snobbish thirst among the court to immerse itself in French culture. He also had an ally in Vice Chancellor Mikhail Vorontsov, who despised Bestuzhev. And the tsarina was also open to French ties. She made it clear that her loyalty could be bought for paintings rather than gold. She pressed Douglas to bring to Saint Petersburg Louis Tocqué, renowned for his portraits of the French court. Douglas hurriedly sent a letter to Versailles, urging them to send Tocqué before Elizabeth found an English painter she liked as well.

Ironically, the kingdom that was most interested in allying with Britain was the one that Whitehall had feared the most after France—Prussia. Using the August Wilhelm, the duke of Brunswick-Bevern, as their initial go-between, talks between Prussia and Britain began in the summer of 1755. Whitehall first requested that Frederick unilaterally declare that he would not invade Hanover. This Frederick at first would not do. News of the Anglo-Russia alliance spurred Frederick to redouble his efforts to split them asunder and hew Britain to Prussia.

Among Frederick's nightmares was the appearance of the combined fleets of Britain and Russia bearing an invasion army off Prussia's Baltic coast, while Austrian armies converged on Berlin from the south. Frederick had his own card to play, the threat to realize Britain's nightmare. In the War of the Austrian Succession, Frederick II had nearly invaded Hanover. Now he promised to protect Hanover in return for English gold to help him fend off Austria and its allies. Whitehall reasoned that Prussia would do as an ally against France if it could not have Austria. Versailles would think twice about attacking Hanover if it faced Prussian grenadiers. Negotiations for a defensive alliance between British and Prussian diplomats began in late 1755, but would not succeed until early the new year.

Consequences

Throughout 1755, the slide into war and an alliance with Austria had exacerbated Louis XV's natural indecisiveness and fickleness, a void ambitious ministers rushed to fill. Argenson noted that the king "dares a thing lightly and with temerity; then he wearies of it and grows timid; never was there a man with less courage of mind than his. Hence it has happened that every minister coming into relations with him feels little by little his own strength, and has merely to dare to exercise it."[72]

Pompadour supplied the backbone that Louis lacked. Her will made and broke ministers and shaped most major decisions, though not always to good effect. Yet even her seemingly indomitable will could falter. When that happened, Pompadour turned to Bernis, whose witty company and soothing, sage advice she had sorely missed while he was in Venice. By late 1755, she was much in need of help. Over the years, a thousand snubs from the jealous had taken their toll. Pompadour was exhausted by the king's constant advances and the threats of rivals. As if to appease God from her earlier excesses and the recent death of her only child, Pompadour became increasingly religious and longed to retire from court.

Bernis convinced her to retain the king's friendship and to steer him to a succession of mistresses obsessed with baubles and prestige rather than affairs of state. She took his advice and managed to cling to power for another decade. By October 1755, Louis and Pompadour agreed to enjoy a purely platonic relationship. Bernis remarked that Louis, "could now give her his friendship, confidence and the ties of habit."[73] Seeking sex without commitment, Louis converted the Parc-aux-Cerfs, a small mansion in the town of Versailles, into his own private bordello though which passed a parade of lovely young women who had caught his royal eye. When he tired of one, he would grant her a generous pension and order his procurer to usher in the next.

Pompadour was by no means all-powerful. Competing with her influence and exceeding that of his other ministers was Louis François de Bourbon, prince de Conti, who gave the king "advice on matters of government. They write to each other every day, and the prince of the blood carries great portfolios to his work with the king. He has made himself minister without any formal right to be one. . . . He holds his place exactly as Mme. de Pompadour holds hers; by habit, friendship, and semi-confidence. They tell me that all the ministers and secretaries of State have fallen in the king's esteem, and that he treats them cavalierly. My brother [war minister Argenson] seems to have lost favor with him; his Majesty scarcely looks at or speaks to him."[74]

The war minister's brother offered a dismal portrait of Versailles politics at war's brink: "Intrigues are redoubling at Court. Mme. de Pompadour seems to be increasing in favor; but [Argenson] . . . still presents a bold front and sustains himself. . . . It is noticed that he follows the King and watches him more assiduously than ever. He studies him, he reads in his eyes, for the king needs to be followed closely; if you leave him to himself he forgets you and will fail you. They say that [Argenson] . . . is advancing in his design, which is nothing less than to get the marquise sent away. His pretext is the wants of the State and the necessity of not wasting money; for Mme. de Pompadour continues to pillage the treasury to glut her sordid greed."[75]

All of these intrigues, personality spats, and ambitions grossly fouled the council's ability to make and implement policies. Add to that the king's fickleness and a nearly empty treasury, and the result was virtually a policy gridlock. It took the council half a year after the British captured the *Lys* and *Alcide*, followed by their undeclared naval war against French shipping, to decide, in October, to issue licenses to privateers to retaliate. Yet any more ambitious minor military moves threatened to bankrupt the treasury.[76]

Amidst the financial crisis, Louis for once set a virtuous example. The war forced him to make "extraordinary retrenchments in journeys, dinners, cooks in his country-houses, horses, etc., in all amounting to more than ten millions a year. It is also certain that all expenditure on buildings is stopped, except for the Louvre. . . . The King has reduced the horses in his stable by fifteen hundred. . . . He has reduced his suppers to few persons and few dishes. He declares that now he shall not sleep away from Versailles from now till next October, neither at Compiègne nor at Marly. It is not impossible that, economy finding favor in France, it might become a characteristic of the nation."[77]

In his last observation, Argenson was overly optimistic. France's financial woes far surpassed the king's extravagances. Impressive as Louis's efforts seemed, these savings would amount to no more than a dollop of what would be needed. It was vital to tap every source of finance: "The Company of the Indies assembled yesterday and resolved upon a loan of twelve millions for which it will give five percent. M. de Montmartel is also raising money at the same interest, whereas the government is trying to establish the rate at four percent. People remark that here is a great deal of money to raise at once, and that it will . . . cause a furious shaking of the Paris money-market, the only market in the kingdom."[78] The speculators eventually saw the ever-swelling financial bubble that would pop behind them as they stampeded away.

France's depressed economy exacerbated the government's money woes. The kingdom was "impoverished; the fields are deserted, agriculture diminished in abundance, luxury increases everywhere, commerce is losing its economics, it turns solely to luxury, it lacks raw material, which is the essence of commerce; we have nothing to sell but the trifling things that are now the fashion. . . . The whole management of commerce and the circulation of money is left to the ministers, that is to say to courtiers who corrupt its methods. . . . The present reign is tyranny and anarchy both."[79]

Desperate to avert war, Louis XV wrote George II on December 21, 1755, an extraordinary letter whereby he proclaimed his devotion to peace and called for negotiations to resolve all outstanding differences between their realms. He protested the four separate British armies that had marched against New France's borders and the British naval attacks on French shipping in 1755. He demanded compensation for all French losses incurred by British depredations on land and sea. He ended his letter with a stark warning: "If, contrary to all hopes, the King of England shall refuse what the King demands, his Majesty will regard this denial of justice as the most authentic declaration of war, and as a formed design in the Court of London to disturb the peace of Europe."[80] The new year would dawn before Louis received a reply.

Rouillé noted the ironies, historical forces, and psychologies pushing the great powers into a war that none wanted: "It would be very sad and vexatious for mankind and for all Europe, if England rekindled a war the extent or results of which no one can foresee, for interests . . . to get our colonies. A little more or less territory in North America should not cause a war; each nation possesses more than she can use for a long time to come . . . [but] the trade of the Ohio River has been made the means of inflaming men's minds."[81]

The Seven Years' War would neither be the first nor the last to erupt because passions and follies triumphed over reason.

CHAPTER 6

World War, 1756

Europe would have been at peace, a million men's lives would
have been spared. . . . But everyone just laughed at me.

Bernis

The English are repenting this war; we are stronger than they—
having more discipline, and all these cruel barbarians for friends.

Argenson

In 1756, the undeclared war between France and Britain in North
America and on the high seas escalated into a struggle that embraced
all the European powers and that was fought in every ocean and on
parts of five continents. The world war began shortly after a realignment of the great powers known as the "diplomatic revolution."[1]

The Spite of Rivals

The French stumbled unwillingly into this war as Louis XV presided
over a council bitterly split over policy and Pompadour. War minister
Marc Pierre de Voyer de Paulmy, comte d'Argenson, spoke for most who
believed that it was the mistress who actually ruled France through its
supposed master: "The party of the marquise de Pompadour influences

more than ever the government, and the King seems to be submissive to this corps of favorites."[2] All resented her influence; some resisted, others submitted. Argenson lost no chance to skewer Pompadour while his own mistress, Madame d'Etrades, rallied support among the Pompadour bashers at court. Yet Argenson had his own enemies, none fiercer than Keeper of the Seals Jeanne-Baptiste de Machault d'Arnouville. Each minister employed virtually every means fair or foul to discredit the other in the king's eyes. Although no love was lost between Pompadour and Machault, she naturally weighed in with him, and in doing so grossly disadvantaged Argenson. The war minister did not lack allies; all who hated, feared, or resented Pompadour tended to side with him whether they liked him or not. Thus did the issue of alliance with Austria turn on this personal conflict. But since the king favored both Austria and Pompadour, Argenson was doomed to fail.

The king's most trusted advisors were not in the council. After Pompadour, no one was closer to him than Louis François de Bourbon, prince de Conti, who, from 1745 through 1756, headed the king's secret du roi, a policy to get Conti elected to the Polish throne. Louis admired Conti's wit, intelligence, bravery in war, and wenching exploits, along with his foreign policy advice. Conti was Louis's younger cousin by seven years and became a surrogate kid brother. Unsurprisingly, Conti and Pompadour despised each other and jousted constantly for Louis's heart and mind.

In the spring of 1756, Conti tried to topple Pompadour by getting Louis enamored with Marie Anne de Mailly de Coslin, a woman renowned for her beauty and skill in bed. She soon lost the king's favor by yielding too quickly and demanding too much—a million livres a year. Conti survived the king's knowledge of his role in that intrigue. By the year's end, however, Conti's ambitions and hatreds would lead him to self-destruction.[3] On April 3, 1756, Adrien Maurice, duc de Noailles, an ally of Argenson and Conti, could take it no longer. He stormed out of the council in protest that Louis only listened to Machault and, especially, to Pompadour. None of these maneuvers or confrontations shook Louis's confidence in his closest confidant. So far all attempts by jealous rivals of Pompadour to discredit her had failed.

The Scramble for Allies

Unfortunately, rival personal interests rather than a systematic, rational effort to define and realize national interests shaped the crucial decisions that decided the fate of New France and hundreds of thousands of lives. The endless squabbles persisted and obscured momentous diplomatic and military actions.

Though Louis XV and his ministers did not want war, George II and most of his cabinet did. George II refused to respond directly to Louis XV's letter pleading with him for peace. Instead, his cabinet penned a reply that turned the French accusations of English perfidy on its head—it was France that was the aggressor and England the victim. The actions of Britain's army in North America and its navy on the high seas were purely defensive responses to French attacks. The English claimed not to understand how his "resolution to defend his American dominions and hinder France from insulting his Kingdoms, can be construed into a denial of justice, and a design formed by the King to disturb the repose of Europe."[4]

Aware that Britain and Prussia were secretly negotiating for an alliance, Louis XV dispatched a special envoy to Potsdam to swing Frederick II back to France's side. Louis Jules Barbon Mancini-Mazarini, duc de Nivernais, seemed a good choice for the mission. Not only was Nivernais a veteran diplomat, but he was notorious for worshiping Frederick the Great and for sharing with him an orientation that went beyond philosophy. If anyone could divert Frederick, Nivernais could. But the envoy arrived too late. Frederick kept him cooling his heels while he put the finishing touches on a secret treaty.[5]

Prussian and British diplomats furtively signed the Treaty of Westminster on January 16, 1756. The treaty's key clause required each to join the other if Hanover or Silesia were attacked. Whitehall and Potsdam hoped the public unveiling of their alliance on January 27, 1756, would deter the other powers from joining in the so-far limited conflicts embroiling Prussia and Britain, and thus would prevent a European-wide war. Instead, the treaty accelerated the diplomatic revolution. The announcement at once frightened France and Russia and heartened Austria. To assuage or perhaps just to taunt the stunned

Nivernais, Frederick offered to sign a similar treaty with France. Nivernais replied that France would only ally with Prussia if Frederick broke his treaty with Britain.

The French desperately cast about for allies. At Madrid, Ambassador Emmanuel-Félicité de Durfort, duc de Duras, again lobbied the court for a Bourbon "family pact." While Duras's overbearing personality undermined his diplomacy, foreign minister Ricardo Wall and English ambassador Benjamin Keene led the effort to kill the proposal. Versailles also hoped to forge an alliance with Sweden. Swedish chancellor baron Anders Johan von Höpken spurned any idea of a military alliance. Throughout the war, Stockholm remained cool to Versailles's various entreaties even though France and Sweden were indirect allies in their overlapping wars against Britain and Prussia, respectively. Sweden's other disappointment to France will be revealed shortly.

In early 1756, Russia appeared to be the most fertile ground for French diplomacy. Rouillé sent envoy Alexander Mackenzie, chevalier Douglas, back to Saint Petersburg to redouble his efforts to strengthen the bilateral relationship by offering generous subsidies in return for Conti's heading both the Russian army and the Duchy of Courland. There was, however, a catch. To avoid alienating Poland, Sweden, and Turkey, Versailles sought not only to avoid openly allying with Russia but even exchanging ambassadors. It was a very delicate diplomatic balancing act, which Douglas badly bungled.[6]

Douglas certainly seemed to enjoy greater prospects to advance French interests in 1756 than in the previous year. Britain's Prussian alliance had simultaneously weakened its alliance with Russia and Chancellor Bestuzhev's power; only liberal disbursements of English gold kept either from being immediately swept away. At a March 25 council meeting presided over by Empress Elizabeth, all but Bestuzhev favored alliance with Austria and neutrality with France. To that end, a deal with Poland would have to be cut that let Russian armies march across it against Prussia. Peace had to be kept with Sweden and Turkey, which might be tempted to strike at Russia's flanks while its armies were fighting deep in Germany. In return for agreeing that Silesia and Glatz would go to Austria, the Duchy of Courland would be headed by Conti, and an adjustment of Ukraine's border would be made to favor

Poland, Saint Petersburg wanted an overt alliance from Vienna, neutrality and subsidies from Paris, and transit rights for its troops from Warsaw, all to the end of taking East Prussia from Berlin.

Vice Chancellor Vorontsov asked Douglas for a 5-million-ruble subsidy and formal diplomatic relations. Douglas turned down a direct subsidy, but did suggest that France could funnel money to Russia indirectly via Austria. Then, exceeding his instructions, he and Vorontsov agreed to name and dispatch ambassadors by September 15, 1756. Finally, Douglas told a disappointed Elizabeth that the painter Tocqué could not be induced to give up his French clients to travel all the way to Russia. The empress convinced him to try harder. Tocqué finally succumbed to a personal appeal and generous gift from Louis XV, and he and his wife set off on the long journey to Saint Petersburg.

To further complicate French diplomacy, thanks to Louis XV's secret de roi, the efforts of one French diplomat in eastern Europe often conflicted with others. While Douglas forged closer ties with Saint Petersburg, in Warsaw, Ambassador Charles François de Broglie worked with the Polish court to resist Russian pressure to allow its armies passage. Broglie would not succeed.

But Russian politics most complicated Douglas's efforts. Though Bestuzhev had been sidelined, others impeded stronger ties between France and Russia. Crown prince Peter and his wife, Catherine, remained the core of anti-French sentiments at court. Ambassador Hanbury Williams generously distributed English largess, especially to Catherine as her gambling addiction deepened her debts. He also serviced Catherine's insatiable libido by offering her his secretary, the dashing Stanislaus Poniatowsky. This last strategy fizzled when Elizabeth found out and sent Poniatowsky back to Poland.

Vienna had much more success in forging closer ties with Saint Petersburg. After learning of the treaty between Prussia and Britain, Vienna intensified its efforts to ally with Russia and France. On March 13, Maria Theresa instructed her ambassador to Saint Petersburg, Prince Nicholas Esterházy, to reveal the secret negotiations between Austria and France, and ask Russia to join their attack on Frederick. In April, through Vorontsov, Elizabeth signaled her desire for Saint Petersburg and Vienna to each provide 80,000 troops for a joint offensive against

Prussia; the reward would be East Prussia for Russia and Silesia and Glatz for Austria. Bestuzhev retained enough influence and British ambassador Hanbury enough gold to stall a treaty until December.

Having upset the European power balance by allying with Britain, Frederick then made a startling offer—he would mediate peace between Britain and France. The offer took Whitehall by surprise but was not completely unwanted. For some cabinet members, the enthusiasm for their hard-line position had cooled since Braddock's debacle and the limited successes elsewhere on the North American frontier the previous year. Only in Acadia and on the high seas were British arms truly victorious. As the war in North America was linked with alliances across Europe, some of the less aggressive ministers debated trying to find a diplomatic resolution. When Frederick volunteered mediating the conflict, they seized the offer.

In February, Robert Darcy, Earl of Holderness, recently appointed secretary of state for the Northern Department, penned a reply to Frederick. After heaping all blame on France for the crisis, he ventured a surprising concession. Britain would grant France a corridor from the Saint Lawrence to a point opposite Isle Saint Jean, but would demand all lands on both sides of the Bay of Fundy and Acadia's entire isthmus and peninsula. He did not mention the other territorial conflicts in North America or the Caribbean. Frederick passed on the proposal.

Louis and his council eagerly accepted Frederick's role. The king had copies of the correspondence between Rouillé and Thomas Robinson sent to Frederick, along with word that France was prepared to reopen negotiations, but only after Britain released the merchant ships it had seized and compensated their owners. On at least one issue Versailles refused to budge. To Whitehall's indignation, the French adamantly rejected any notion of surrendering land around the Bay of Fundy between Beaubassin and the Saint John River. On May 11, 1756, Holderness sent a letter to Frederick informing him that George II had lost all hope of a diplomatic solution and was about to declare war on France.

Why did Versailles toss away this last chance to avert war by refusing to cede a relatively small patch of territory that it did not actually control? Two minor and two major reasons explain the decision. Locked into the mentality that any compromise was a sign of weakness that would be met with more demands, Versailles refused to make any. Besides that, Louis XV and his ministers were still seething from the British reaction to the French king's plea for peace. That Whitehall's response was a litany of accusations against France was bad enough, but that the letter came from the cabinet rather than from George, to whom Louis had written, added insult to injury. But two far more important reasons lay behind the suddenly tough French position—an alliance with Austria and a pending expedition against Minorca.

The Diplomatic Revolution

Maria Theresa sent word to Ambassador Starhemberg on March 6, 1756, to push once more for an alliance. By now, Louis and the secret committee were eager to link arms with Austria. The terms rapidly evolved from the original proposal for a nonaggression pact into an outright defensive alliance. War minister Argenson was not let in on the secret until April 19. By that time, the plans were so advanced that he could do nothing to derail them. All he could do was to step up his attacks on Pompadour as the root of all evils for France.

On May 1, 1756, at Rouillé's château of Jouy, Bernis and Starhemberg signed two documents known collectively as the Treaty of Versailles. France renounced its alliance with Prussia for neutrality, while it supported Austria's retaking of Silesia. Austria likewise agreed to remain sidelined in the fighting between France and Britain, although Versailles could send troops to Ostend and Nieuport in the Austrian Netherlands once its war with Britain officially began. Each promised to send either 18,000 infantry and 6,000 cavalry or a monthly subsidy of 8,000 florins per 1,000 infantry or 24,000 florins per 1,000 cavalry to the other's aid if it were attacked. These tenets were publicly revealed. Secret deals were cut and signed as well. Austria would back the Prince Conti's election to the Polish throne after Augustus III died. The Duke of Parma, Louis's son-in-law, would take the Austrian

Netherlands after Silesia returned to the fold. They also promised to bind their royal houses with future marriages.

Word that Bourbon France and Habsburg Austria had buried their ancient rivalry in a Catholic alliance against Britain and Prussia electrified the courts and public opinion across Europe, including that of France. Typical was the reaction of Casanova, who interrupted his amours to express "the astounding news of the treaty between France and Austria . . . by which the political balance was entirely readjusted and which was received with incredulity by the Powers."[7]

The diplomatic revolution bridged two distinct conflicts, a war for supremacy in North America among France, England, and later Spain, with a war for supremacy in central Europe among Prussia, Austria, Russia, and Sweden. Yet the reversal of alliances in May 1756 made war among the great powers more likely but not inevitable. After all, Louis and Pompadour had agreed to ally with Austria to avoid rather than provoke war. The trouble was that alliances tend to embolden rather than restrain their members. The diplomatic revolution eventually led to the world's first truly global war.

Certain common interests led to each alliance; divergent other interests would strain each alliance for the war's duration. Britain's alliance with Prussia at least helped protect Hanover and divert France's military efforts from North America, but at an enormous financial cost. France's alliance with Austria and, indirectly, Russia and Sweden, was even more burdensome. Unlike Maria Theresa, Versailles did not want to destroy Prussia. A stable power balance in central Europe between Prussia and Austria served French interests. Yet the Anglo-Prussian alliance provoked one between France and Austria. Versailles could use its allies to pin down and impose a limited defeat on Frederick while French armies conquered and held Hanover for ransom. That would indeed have been a realistic aim had Louis XV found better generals to lead his armies. Over the next seven years, each French advance into Hanover was invariably defeated, while the huge annual cost of subsidies to Austria weakened France's ability to pay for its war in North America. Though Versailles could not know it at the time, the alliance with Austria would aid France's defeat rather than victory.

Diversions and Attacks

By early 1756, Whitehall had a rough idea of Versailles's plans. British intelligence scored two remarkable coups. Copies of Swedish ambassador Bunge's letters to his foreign minister of December 23, 1755, and January 6, 1756, ended up on the desk of Thomas Pelham-Holles, the Duke of Newcastle. What struck Newcastle was that the French plans "contain no scheme or hint of any scheme for striking any blow against England by way of invasion or otherwise."[8] The fact that France's position was essentially defensive did not deter George II and his cabinet from pressing their own attacks. They soon received a purloined document with a quite different view of French intentions. Britain's ambassador to The Hague, Colonel Joseph Yorke, got hold of the plan by French council member Charles Louis Auguste Foucquet, duc de Belle Isle, to invade England, preceded by an attack on Minorca.[9]

Just how real was France's invasion plan? It was certainly formidable on paper. In all, Versailles massed ninety-three infantry battalions and twenty-two cavalry squadrons in nine channel ports. The problem was how to unite that scattered army and sail it safely to England. The entire French navy could muster only forty-five ships of the line and thirty frigates, of which only half were then in French waters.[10] Yet that potential invasion threat certainly alarmed Whitehall, which massed all available warships to counter it. Admiral Edward Hawke was sent from Portsmouth with most of the channel fleet to blockade Brest and Rochefort, to be joined from Spithead by Admiral Francis Holburne.

Meanwhile, Admiral John Byng, who commanded ten ships of the line at Gibraltar, was ordered to protect Minorca by joining with Commodore George Edgecombe's squadron of three ships of the line and four frigates at Port Mahon, Minorca. The island's land defenses were ill-prepared for a French attack. General William Blakeney, then a gout-ridden, somnolent eighty-four-year-old, commanded the 2,860 troops from four regiments. Only Port Mahon on Minorca's southeastern tip was strongly fortified.

Two of France's ablest commanders would lead the attack on Minorca. Former Canadian governor La Galissonière commanded the invasion fleet of 173 transports guarded by 12 ships of the line and 3 frigates, and Louis François Armand du Plessis, duc de Richelieu, commanded the 15,000 troops from 25 battalions. One French historian contrasted the two leaders, who "give us the most perfect image of this incomparable age. Richelieu represents its airy grace, its impudent gallantry, its unscrupulous intrigue, all its defects and extravagances, with the two qualities for which our country forgives everything—courage and wit. La Galissonière represents, like the Marquis de Montcalm in Canada, the vigorous uprightness, the moral rectitude, the absolute devotion to duty, all those military virtues of old France, which should be the example of France today."[11]

The fleet weighed anchor at Toulon on April 7 and disembarked the army at undefended Ciudadela on Minorca's western tip on April 18. As Richelieu marched his troops across the island toward Port Mahon, La Galissonière's fleet sailed to intercept Edgecombe's squadron, but it had escaped to Gibraltar. Blakeney concentrated his troops in Fort Saint Philip overlooking Port Mahon. Though Richelieu's troops reached Port Mahon on April 23, it took until May 8 before they could drag up, entrench, and fire their heavy artillery. That same day Byng sailed from Gibraltar for Minorca. The two fleets closed for battle on May 20 off Port Mahon. With his ships battered and having suffered over six hundred casualties, Byng sailed back to Gibraltar. The admiral would be relieved of his command, court-martialed, and found guilty of failing to relieve Minorca. As Voltaire concisely explained it, Byng was shot on March 14, 1757, "to encourage the others."[12]

Over the next month, Richelieu's siege lines crept closer and the bombardment systematically destroyed the fort's walls. In the early morning of June 27, his troops launched a night attack that carried key outworks. Blakeney surrendered after sunrise. Richelieu granted the British honors of war and passage back to Gibraltar. The victory was not cheap—about 2,000 French and 400 British were killed or wounded during the seventy-day siege. Nonetheless, Minorca's capture was cause for pride and riotous celebrations.[13]

Versailles's original plan was for Richelieu to destroy the island's fortifications and retreat to Toulon. Richelieu found them too extensive to destroy easily, so he left eleven battalions to garrison Minorca before sailing away on July 15. With Minorca in French hands, the British could not effectively blockade Toulon whose fleet, in turn, was freed for more distant campaigns, including the Caribbean and India. The British would never attempt to retake Minorca.

More importantly, Minorca's capture gave France a golden opportunity to end the war with minimal losses and maximum gains. Versailles could have dangled Minorca's return as a reward for a North American boundary that contained the British at the Appalachian divide. Yet when foreign minister Bernis, Pompadour's closest ally among the king's advisors, suggested this, the council's members set aside their mutual antipathies for a collective sneer at the foreign minister. Bernis wrote that had Versailles sincerely attempted negotiations, "Europe would have been at peace, a million men's lives would have been spared. . . . But everyone just laughed at me."[14]

The decision to widen the war rather than negotiate its end had its own logic. Minorca capped two years during which the French had inflicted sharp defeats on the British in North America and seemed capable of staving off the enemy there indefinitely. True, the British navy did reign supreme on the sea, but its warships could not be everywhere at once. French supply convoys could slip through to Canada while privateers harassed British shipping. George II's beloved Hanover, meanwhile, was a plum ripe for plucking. Ideally, the French could overrun this realm while Frederick was busy fighting off converging Austrian and Russian armies. If they could do so, Versailles could dangle two valued British possessions—Hanover and Minorca—before the British at the diplomatic table. To get them back, Whitehall would have to grant major concessions to France in North America and possibly elsewhere. Though the council could not know it at the time, Minorca would be France's greatest victory of the war. Soon Versailles found itself impotent as British and Prussian forces scored one crushing victory after another against France in Europe, North America, the Caribbean, West Africa, India, and the high seas.

Shortly after learning of Minorca's invasion, Britain declared war on May 18, 1756. France's formal war declaration followed on June 9, 1756. The two powers were more desperate than ever for more allies.

Whitehall once again demanded that Holland provide England with six thousand troops as required by a 1678 treaty if war broke out.

The Hague countered that because the British had started the war with its naval attack on the French convoy the previous year, Holland was off the legal hook. Still, even if France had been the aggressor, the Dutch would most likely not have joined Britain without Austrian troops shielding them from French armies. On June 14, 1756, when the Dutch formally declared neutrality, the French breathed an enormous sigh of relief. Frederick had also approached the Dutch about an alliance but had been turned down as well.[15]

Versailles had more luck with Holland, but at a terrible price. By 1756, with its own war and merchant ships sunk, captured, or bottled up in port, Versailles finally agreed to hand French trade over to neutral ships, of which most were Dutch. Marine minister Machault distributed passports to intendants or chambers of commerce at French ports at home and in the colonies. Neutral merchants could purchase passports and then trade in the ever-diminishing French empire, something they were formerly forbidden to do. At first, the chambers of commerce were reluctant to issue passports to their rivals but eventually yielded. They had no real choice. Either they surrendered a profitable but increasingly risky trade to neutral merchants willing to pay the soaring insurance costs or watch French trade completely collapse. The British soon became wise to Versailles's Faustian deal and scoured the seas of neutral ships just as mercilessly as they had French ships, prompting Holland to seriously consider a war declaration. During the war's last years, the number of French merchant ships venturing back to sea steadily edged up as more neutral ships were captured.[16]

French entreaties to Spain continued to be rejected. Versailles had Ambassador Duras offer Spain Minorca for an alliance against Britain. For some in the Spanish court, this offer must have been mighty tempting. After all, a core aim of Spain's foreign policy had been to recover Minorca and Gibraltar ever since Britain took them during the War of the Spanish Succession, a possession the 1713 Utrecht Treaty legalized. Yet the pro-English foreign minister Ricardo Wall succeeded in getting the court to reject the offer. Whitehall worried that Wall might fail. On his own initiative, Henry Fox, secretary of state for the Southern Department, actually offered to return Gibraltar to Spain if it allied with Britain against France to retake Minorca. Newcastle, however, repudiated the offer; Gibraltar, which let the British navy cork the Mediterranean, was too valuable ever to give up. Meanwhile, complaints about Duras's arrogance and blundering reached Versailles. Rouillé recalled him in October but did not appoint a successor. At this critical time, France lacked an ambassador in Madrid until April 1757.

Montcalm Takes Command

New France needed a new field general in Canada to replace General Dieskau, captured at the battle of Lake George. It took Versailles until February 1756 before it found one. In a February 29, 1756, letter, after diplomatically alluding to the faults Governor Vaudreuil had found with Dieskau, war minister Argenson expressed his "hope that you will have reason to be satisfied with the prudence of the gentleman whom the King has named as his successor, and that you will find in him all desirable dispositions to concur with you for the good of the King's service and the successful achievement of the operations which you will judge proper to entrust in him."[17] Argenson then explained that, since they did not share the same cipher, he could not reveal just who Dieskau's successor would be. Vaudreuil would find out soon enough. The war minister could communicate in code with André Doreil, his financial commissary in New France, and he sent Doreil word the same day.[18]

The mystery general that Louis XV tapped was Louis Joseph, marquis de Montcalm. The king had "concluded that a better choice could not be made . . . considering the proofs he has given us of his valor, experience, capacity, fidelity, and affection to our service."[19] The flowery praise for Montcalm was all quite true. At age twelve, he received his first commission although his first battle did not come until Philipsburg in 1734 when he was twenty-two. Many battles followed; by 1756, he had fought bravely in eleven campaigns and had suffered five wounds.[20] Accompanying Montcalm were Colonels François Gaston, duc de Lévis, and François Charles de Bourlamaque, the second and third in command, respectively, along with the general's aide, Louis Antoine de Bougainville, and engineers Captain Jean Claude Henri Lombard de Combles and his assistant Jean Nicolas Desandrouins. In addition, around 1,200 troops of the second battalions of the Royal Roussillon and La Sarre Regiments crammed into the ships.

Montcalm and his entourage sailed from Brest on April 3 and reached Quebec on May 13. Relations started out amiably enough between Vaudreuil and Montcalm. In a June 1756 report to the war minister detailing that year's operations, Vaudreuil expressed his "real pleasure . . . with M. de Montcalm. . . . I act in concert with him."[21] This concert would not last long and would be followed by ever more sour and shrill notes. For his part, Montcalm found that the "Governor-General overwhelms me with politeness; I believe him to be satisfied with my conduct towards him, and I think it convinces him that general officers can be found in France who will study the public good under his orders. . . . He is acquainted with the country; possesses in his hands both authority and means. . . . He it is who must prescribe it; it is mine to relieve him of the details relative to our troops, in what regards discipline and the execution of his plans."[22] Yet Montcalm did immediately perceive at least one flaw in the governor's character, noting that Vaudreuil "is well intentioned but very irresolute."[23] At first Montcalm was impressed with Intendant Bigot, who "has essentially aided me in restoring order to matters so necessary to the men's lives. No person could employ more activity and expedition in his labors than this Intendant."[24] Montcalm's view of Bigot soon changed drastically as well.

Montcalm's presence was an enormous relief to Pierre-André Gohin, comte de Montreuil, who had been Dieskau's chief of staff and had taken command after the general was captured. Montreuil proclaimed himself "very well satisfied with Montcalm. I shall accomplish impossibilities to deserve his confidence." Starkly contrasted with Montreuil's description of Montcalm's sterling qualities was his opinion on the venality of New France's government: "It is incredible to what a degree luxury prevails in this country, and to what an extent the King is robbed in consequence of the of the bad administration of affairs. All the French who arrive here are shocked at the waste that is made. The Governor and Intendant are too easy and too remiss in a country where greater strictness is required than in any other."[25]

Montcalm had mixed views of his own subordinates. He did not return Montreuil's adulation: "Montreuil is a brave man without any detail or talent for the position."[26] In contrast, he had the highest respect for Lévis, who, "without possessing much genius . . . has considerable practical knowledge, good sense, is quick-sighted, and . . . has derived profit from his campaigns."[27] Montcalm's view of Bourlamaque was less lofty: "He does not yet possess the tone of command; is too much addicted to minutiae, follows too literally orders issued eighty leagues off, by a General [Vaudreuil] who knows not how to speak of war."[28] This opinion would change. In July 1757, Montcalm wrote that Bourlamaque "is an excellent officer; he has acquired much and gained a great deal within a year."[29]

Most impressive of all to Montcalm was Bougainville, who, as the son of a lawyer rather than an aristocrat, proved that in rare cases merit could take a man to the heights of French society. By the time Montcalm met him at Versailles in February 1756, he had gained fame as a mathematician and scientist. Montcalm was so taken by his intelligence and energy that he insisted on making him his aide. Bougainville was an excellent choice. He was as comfortable singing the war song at Indian councils as he was offering sage perspectives with Montcalm and his officers. And to the glee of historians ever since, he left a fascinating journal of his North American experiences.[30]

North America also received a new British commanding general in 1756. Whitehall grew increasingly disillusioned with William Shirley, who had become acting commander after Braddock's death. His political enemies had gathered evidence that the Massachusetts governor had engaged in widespread corruption, which he expanded with his power as commanding general. Though aware of the storm brewing to his rear, Shirley plunged deeper into his duties. In December 1755, he devised a strategy for 1756 that was every bit as ambitious as that of the preceding year. He called for campaigns against Forts Saint Frederic, Niagara, Toronto, Frontenac, and Duquesne, after which the victorious British forces would take Montreal and Quebec. He never got a chance to implement the plan.

Whitehall appointed John Campbell, Earl of Loudoun, as North America's new commander in chief on March 20, 1756. Before being given the high command, Loudoun had risen to become colonel of the 40th regiment in 1749, then was chosen to raise and command the 60th regiment composed of largely foreign officers and American troops. Why would Whitehall pick such a relatively undistinguished colonel for such a vital position? The choice made political rather than military sense—Loudoun was a good friend of the Duke of Cumberland, the king's son. Loudoun proved to be an inept leader against the French. He did, however, quite effectively war against the American colonists he was supposed to protect by quartering his troops in their homes and embargoing sea-going trade before campaigns. Loudoun and his entourage reached New York in July 1756.

Montcalm and Loudoun found a stalemate along the frontier. While British and French envoys struggled for the loyalties of the tribes, most French and Indian raids had largely petered out during the winter. The most active fronts were the Lake George region and the 217-mile supply line between Albany and Oswego. Around Lake George, the British had found a tireless, intrepid, brilliant ranger leader in Robert Rogers, who harassed the French around Fort Carillon all winter. But Rogers's successful raids were overshadowed by news of a French attack on Fort Bull that took place on March 27.

On that day, 259 regulars and Canadians and 103 Indians commanded by Captain Gaspard Joseph Chaussegros de Léry overran and destroyed the fort, which helped defend the watershed between the Mohawk River and Wood Creek, which eventually led to Lake Ontario. Fort Bull's destruction made Oswego's survival ever more tenuous.[31] With the spring flowers, French and Indian raids blossomed all along the frontier, especially around Oswego. The biggest battle occurred on July 3, when Captain Villiers and 700 French and Indians attacked a column of 350 supply barges and 1,000 men led by Colonel John Bradstreet about nine miles up the Oswego River from the forts. The forest battle lasted most of the day and finally ended when reinforcements from Oswego arrived to drive off the remaining French and Indians.[32] But these actions, however horrifying and bloody to those involved, were indecisive. In midsummer, the soldiers and civilians on both sides anxiously awaited the decisions of the two new commanders.

The Oswego Campaign

Montcalm was an eager student of North American warfare. Eight days after reaching Canada, he wrote Argenson, "I have taken information respecting a country and a war in which everything is different to what obtains in Europe."[33] Although he agreed with Vaudreuil that the first blow should fall on Oswego, Montcalm first visited Fort Carillon to ensure that front was secure. While there in June, he found

> the works of Fort Carillon, begun last year, very little advanced; a number of necessaries wanting in the store; order to be introduced everywhere; reconnaissance of the locality, of the passes through which the enemy can come, and the arrangements for the defense of that frontier. . . . That fort consists of pieces of timber in layers, bound together with traverses, the interstices filled in which earth. Such construction is proof against cannon, and in that respect is as good as masonry, and much better than earthen works; but is not durable. The site of the fort is well adapted as a first line at the head of Lake Champlain. I should have wished it to be somewhat larger, capable of containing five hundred men, whereas it can accommodate, at most, only three hundred.[34]

Despite Fort Carillon's vulnerability, all scouting reports revealed no preparations being made at Forts William Henry or Edward (formerly Fort Lyman) for an immediate offensive.

By July 19, Montcalm was back in Montreal to confer with Vaudreuil and put the finishing touches on his Oswego campaign. Two days later he headed up the Saint Lawrence. On July 29, he reached Fort Frontenac where the La Sarre and Guyenne battalions were based. On August 4, Montcalm and his men embarked for the long row across Lake Ontario to Nioare Bay, where they joined the

Béarn battalion along with Canadians and Indians. Of Montcalm's 3,100 men, 1,350 were regulars, 1,500 were militia, and 250 were Indians; he also had 29 cannon. His army ground ashore a few miles from Oswego on August 11.

With three forts manned by 1,100 provincial troops, Oswego's defenses appeared formidable. None of those forts or the troops, however, were ready for combat. The forts were log stockades. Training among the troops was as abysmal as their morale. Supplies were short and diseases were prevalent. Sickness had killed more than 1,200 men during the previous year. A succession of French and Indian raids had terrified the survivors.

Montcalm spent August 11 and 12 supervising the building of a road from his army's landing place to gun emplacements on the Oswego River's east side aimed at Fort Ontario on the west bank. On the night of August 13 after the French cannon had opened fire, the British abandoned Fort Ontario. Montcalm sent the Canadians and Indians under the governor's brother, François Pierre de Rigaud de Vaudreuil, across the river to harass the other two forts. The French occupied Fort Ontario and trained its cannons on Fort George; the bombardment began on August 14. One of the first shots killed the commander, Colonel James Mercer. Lieutenant Colonel John Littlehales took command and promptly ordered the third fort, Oswego, abandoned and all troops concentrated in Fort George. Although only a dozen men had so far been killed or wounded, Littlehales asked for terms. Montcalm insisted that all soldiers would be interned and all civilians released. Littlehales agreed. The French took 1,658 prisoners. The surrender was marred when Indians swarmed into the fort and butchered about a hundred sick and wounded before Montcalm and the chiefs managed to pull them off.[35]

Montcalm had won a major victory at a minimal cost. Of casualties, he reported that the French lost "only about thirty men killed or wounded . . . the English about 150, including several soldiers, who, wishing to escape across the woods, fell into the hands of the Indians. The number of prisoners was nearly 1,700. . . . We captured, also, 7 vessels of war; one of 18 guns, one of 14, one of 10, one of 8, three mounted with swivels, 200 barges or bateaux, 7 pieces of bronze, 48 of iron, 14 mortars, 5 howitzers, 47 swivels, a quantity of shot, bombs, balls, powder, and a considerable pile of provisions." When those supplies were tallied, the French had taken 28,000 pounds of powder; 8,000 pounds of lead and balls; 2,950 shot of various calibers; 150 shells of 9 inches and 300 of 6; 1,416 grenades; 730 muskets; 340 grapeshot; 704 barrels of biscuits; 1,386 barrels of pork; 712 barrels of flour; 11 barrels of rice; 1 garret full of vegetables; 32 live oxen; 11 hogs; and 3 chests of specie.[36]

More importantly, the French now dominated Lake Ontario. Rather than occupy Oswego, however, Montcalm loaded all the loot aboard his boats, ordered the forts burned, and then rowed back to Montreal. Why he did not construct a powerful fortress at Oswego and another at the Great Carrying Place at the watershed between Wood Creek and the Mohawk River remains a mystery. Had he done so, the French would have slammed shut the only corridor to Lake Ontario open to a British invasion, while threatening Albany with twin French invasions, east from there and south from Lake Champlain.

Disappointments, Delusions, and Deceptions

The Indians had very mixed feelings about Oswego's destruction. Those present at its taking exulted in the glory and plunder. But Bougainville observed that soon "all the Indians of this region sigh over the destruction of Oswego, where they use to find trade goods at low prices, all they needed and more. On the other hand, all the things they use are sold at an excessive price at Frontenac, Niagara, and La Belle Riviere. Moreover, these posts are badly supplied with food and merchandise. The Indians realize this difference only too well."[37]

While Montcalm was campaigning against Oswego, Vaudreuil was holding the annual council with the Indians in Montreal between July 28 and August 20. As usual, the governor employed a subtle mixture of threats and promises to gain the Iroquois allegiance. After presenting the chiefs with a two-thousand-bead wampum belt, he warned them to "pay particular attention that your warriors be not, on any pretences whatsoever, with my enemies. . . . My love for my Children, the Five

Nations, is so great, that I should be sorry that any accident should befall them. . . . I have an infinite number of children who, in these troublesome times . . . might commit a mistake in taking [you] for the other." Curiously, Vaudreuil admitted, "I know the majority of my children of the Five Nations would be delighted, were their brother the English our conqueror, and if you speak otherwise tis contrary to your true sentiments. You pretend to be friends of the French and of the English, in order to obtain what you want from both sides."[38] Vaudreuil dramatically concluded the council by announcing Montcalm's destruction of Oswego and ushering the victorious general before the assembled chiefs. The French would not want for Indian allies that year or the next.

Yet Montcalm's triumph was undercut by increasingly poor relations between the French and Canadians. Even as the French officers paddled back down the Saint Lawrence, they received news from Vaudreuil that deflated their heady victory—Versailles had terminated the food and wine allowance granted the French officers. Montcalm's protests to both Vaudreuil and Versailles went unheeded—the measure trimmed costs. The policy was penny-wise and pound-foolish. Canadian prices were then three times those in France and would rise to ten times that by 1760. The cost swallowed the officers' salaries, forcing them ever deeper into debt. The army officers grumbled more acidly than ever against Canada, Canadians, and Vaudreuil, and, more guardedly, against Versailles.[39]

Still, when Montcalm penned a report to war minister Argenson on November 1, he had reason to be pleased with his half year of war in North America. His capture of Oswego with its 1,650 prisoners and mountain of supplies was the most important victory. War parties stalked, scalped, and terrorized the frontier from Acadia to Virginia, throwing the enemy into confusion and indecision. The general foresaw the French retaining the initiative in 1757 with the British too cowed by two years of bloody defeats to mount an offensive toward Lake Ontario, Fort Carillon, or Fort Duquesne. With those fronts firmly commanded by France, Montcalm would try to retake Acadia "were France willing to send a fleet with some troops; but provisions are needed most of all." Yet his elation over the year's military successes and next year's opportunities was deflated by conditions in the colony. He reported that New France's "situation is critical; provisions are needed; the harvest has failed, and people are compelled to mix oats with wheat. . . . Should supplies not be received early it will be impossible to effect against the enemy" next spring.[40]

Four days later, Vaudreuil penned his own version of the year's events to his boss, marine minister Machault. Although the governor never left the safety of Montreal or Quebec that year, he was somehow magically the hero of all France's victories. He boasted of his

> expedition against the English fort at [Oswego] which was the enemy's principle depot of provisions and ammunitions which I carried by assault. . . . The prompt reunion of my forces at Carillon where I kept General Loudon [*sic*] in check, though he had at his disposal an army of 20,000 men. . . . The two forts I caused to be taken from the enemy in the direction of Virginia and Pennsylvania by small detachments of our Canadians. . . . The district of Acadia, where I have constantly maintained myself, and where the enemy has been constantly harassed by my attention to setting the Acadians and Indians in motion. . . . It appears from all this, my Lord, that I not only kept the English in check, but seriously humbled them.[41]

In a letter of nearly one thousand words, Montcalm is mentioned once, not for his capture of Oswego but for when Vaudreuil "sent the Marquis de Montcalm and Chevalier de Lévis to Carillon in order to make the enemy believe that my principal object was to offer resistance at that point."[42] The governor clearly suffered from severe delusions of grandeur. These delusions would damage relations with Montcalm and the other French officers to the point where cooperation nearly vanished.

The War for Germany

War broke out in Europe on August 29, 1756, when Frederick II marched his army into Saxony. What inspired this invasion? For

over a year, Frederick had watched in anger and fear as the diplomatic noose tightened around him. His diplomats and spies had fer-
reted out the details of the grand coalition that Austria had forged
against him.

Anticipating that Frederick might be tempted to launch a preemp-
tive attack, Whitehall urged caution. At first, not wishing to strain his
new alliance, Frederick heeded the advice. In June, he sent an envoy
to Vienna to ask Maria Theresa for her word that she would not attack
Silesia. She offered two troubling, ambiguous replies. First, she stated,
"In the present crisis I deem it necessary to take measures for the security of myself and my allies," and, she added in a second message,
she "would not bind herself by promise from acting as circumstances
required."[43] Then Frederick learned that his neighbor, King Augustus
III, planned to increase the Saxon army from 17,000 to 40,000 troops.
If this army joined those of Austria and Russia, and perhaps even
France and Sweden, against him, all would be lost.

To Frederick the choice was clear—either crush or be crushed.
His strategy had two stages.[44] First, he would quickly overrun Saxony
and merge its treasury, fortresses, and soldiers with Prussia's. From that
stronghold, he then would destroy any Austrian and slower-moving
Russian armies that marched against him, and finally negotiate a favorable peace after the troops went into winter quarters. At first all went
according to plan. The Saxons withdrew into the fortress of Pirna while
Augustus III fled to his fortress of Konigstein and later to his other capital, Warsaw, where he placed his Polish crown on his head. At the head of
his army, Frederick rode into Dresden on September 9. There, he glee-
fully took 500 cannon, 10,000 muskets, and 5 million thalers of annual
income. More importantly, a thorough investigation of the state archives
revealed that Saxony had indeed been plotting with Austria against him.

Maria Theresa declared war on Prussia. Elizabeth soon followed
but admitted she could not send a Russian army westward until spring
of 1757. Two Austrian armies marched against Frederick, Field Marshal
Maximilian Browne with 32,000 men from Bohemia and General
Prince Octavio Piccolomini's 22,000 from Moravia. Frederick concentrated his 28,500-strong army between them with hopes of defeating
each separately. On October 1, 1756, his army attacked Browne's at

Lobositz. The battle was indecisive. Suffering roughly the same casualties as the Austrians' 700 killed and 1,900 wounded, the Prussians
retained the field. Browne withdrew to Budin. Piccolomini hesitated.
Neither side was strong enough to attack the other. Frederick marched
on Pirna and forced its surrender on October 15. The armies then
went into winter quarters.

Whitehall viewed Frederick's war with very mixed feelings. Of
course, the ministers were relieved that so far the Prussians were victorious. But the war had only just begun. The real bloodbath would
start next spring, and the British would soon be dragged into it.
After Minorca, Hanover was Britain's most vulnerable possession in
Europe. With Frederick's invasion of Saxony, France would undoubtedly join Austria and Russia in attacking him. Frederick pressured his
new ally for help. George II was only too happy to aid his nephew,
and thus himself. In September, Whitehall decided to raise an army
of 40,000 Hanoverian, Brunswick, Hessian, and, ideally, Danish and
Dutch troops, to which it hoped Frederick would add 11,000 Prussians.
English diplomats were dispatched to negotiate subsidy agreements
with those realms. The Germans fell into line but not the Danes or the
Dutch. Copenhagen rejected a £200,000 offer to supply 8,000 troops
and twelve warships to the alliance. One more try to elicit a Dutch alliance also fell on deaf ears.

For now, Denmark and the Netherlands would be neutral, although
they leaned away from Britain and Prussia. Dutch ships carried most
of France's trade and suffered depredations from British warships
and privateers. After Frederick marched into Saxony, Copenhagen
and Stockholm signed a treaty creating a neutral maritime union that
would consider an act of war any passage of foreign warships through
the straits. The union was chiefly designed to deter the British fleet
from sailing to Frederick's aid.

Versailles, meanwhile, pursued two contradictory policies in east-
ern Europe. Foreign minister Rouillé instructed Douglas to join with
Austrian ambassador Esterházy into getting the Russians to ally against
Prussia. At the same time, he urged Douglas in Saint Petersburg and
Broglie in Warsaw to do all they could to prevent the Russians from
marching across Poland. Extracting two such weighty and contradictory

favors from Russia's ministers would be costly. Douglas pleaded with Versailles to send him more money to match the bribes stuffed into Russian pockets by English ambassador Hanbury Williams.[45]

Bestuzhev predictably demanded a high price for the alliance. Not wishing to disrupt the flow of British gold, he insisted that Hanover be spared any fighting. Hanover, of course, was the only European state whose conquest was currently worth any loss of French blood and treasure. He also declared that Versailles must sever its alignment with Constantinople and support Russia if it went to war against the Turks. Finally, he explained that he could only attack Prussia through Poland, France's ally. Even before a treaty was signed, Saint Petersburg darkly warned Warsaw that "notable prejudice would result for Poland if they impeded or opposed that operation."[46]

Upon hearing these demands, Rouillé reasoned that the alliance with Saint Petersburg was of little benefit if the Russians could not assault the enemy, so he sent word to Douglas and Broglie to encourage the Russians to march through Poland as swiftly as possible. But he insisted that Versailles would not pay a livre to support Russia's war against Prussia. Let Vienna pay the Russian piper if need be; after all, the Austrians and Russians both hoped to aggrandize their empires at Prussia's expense. Despite those intentions, some French subsidies to Vienna ended up in Saint Petersburg.[47]

Broglie protested the irony of France's alliance with Russia, remarking, "Our reconciliation with Russia, far from putting us in a position to ensure the tranquility and happiness of Poland, serves only to impede us from working to preserve Poland from the yoke which the Muscovites have sought so long to impose upon her."[48] Broglie's concern was understandable. For five years, he had labored to prevent what he was now ordered to permit. Over the years, his commitment to the old policy had become an obsession that blinded him from the new.

The great fear in Versailles and Vienna was that Empress Elizabeth's unhealthy lifestyle would kill her. Ambassador Paul François de Gallucci, marquis de l'Hôpital, reported that the empress "never slept at regular hours, dined at midnight, arose at four in the morning, ate voraciously at some times and fasted for weeks at others. Recently she fell into such rigorous devotions that it seemed more idolatry than religion."[49] Her nephew, the Frederick-worshiping and French-hating Peter, impatiently waited in the wings for his aunt's death.

Political Tugs-of-War

As France plunged into the cauldron of war on two continents, Louis XV's council remained split by internal animosities and beset by conflicting external demands. The worst immediate problem was the nearly empty treasury. The king needed much more money if he hoped to fight, let alone win, the ever-widening war.

On July 7, 1756, Louis issued an edict extending the existing vingtiéme, or 5 percent income tax, which had been imposed fifteen years earlier, for another ten years, and creating a second vingtième, which would continue until three months after the war's end. Grumbling was universal. The Paris parlement protested; the most zealous members spoke of rejecting the measure. But the king stood firm and convened a lit de justice that forced parlement to register the taxes. Then parlements at Rennes, Besancon, Rouen, and Bordeaux dared to protest, along with the Cour des Aides, which registered certain types of taxes. But in the end, they all bowed to royal authority and registered the new taxes.

Atop this fiscal challenge landed another—the Jansenist crisis erupted again. On December 7, 1756, the Paris parlement rejected Pope Benedict XIV's encyclical "Ex Omnibus," which Louis XV had submitted. The encyclical tried to bridge the opposing sides by allowing priests to give the Eucharist to Jansenists if they first warned those heretics that they would inevitably suffer eternal damnation. Incensed at parlement's obstinacy, Louis invoked, on December 13, 1756, a lit de justice at which he issued two decrees. With one he deftly softened some measures of the bull, while with the other he announced a reform of parlement that eliminated sixty-five offices, mostly from the lower and more Jansenist chambers, and forbade parlement from striking or any member from voting on measures other than judicial cases unless he had served more than ten years.

This measure was an naked attempt to neutralize the more asser-tive younger members. Though forty offices were already vacant and the other twenty-five would be lost by attrition, the king's will struck too close to home for most parlementarians. In protest, all the coun-cilors in the lower chamber and more than half of the Grand Chamber resigned. Only eleven councilors and the ten presidents remained. The situation was explosive. The ever-astute observer Argenson feared "some kind of revolt. . . . All the people have become partisans of the Parlements; they see in them the only remedy for their vexations; they have a hatred for priests. Thus it is feared that at Paris Jesuits and priests will be massacred one of these days."[50] The tense standoff would drag into the next year.

As if parlement's persistence in stirring trouble by refusing to reg-ister fresh tax edicts or the papal bull then stomping out on strike as France slid deeper into war were not bad enough, the royal council erupted in yet another battle over personalities, policies, and power. The war raised many questions that demanded answers from Versailles. One of the more basic that arose in 1756 was, who would command the French army in Germany?

Prince de Conti seemed the logical choice; after Maurice de Saxe, no one had won more French victories during the War of the Austrian Succession or was more admired by officers and troops alike. Besides, Conti was Louis's oldest advisor on foreign affairs and headed the secret du roi. For a decade, he had suffered rejection from one eastern European court after another as an eligible husband for future queens and princesses, capped by Saint Petersburg's refusal to allow him to head the Russian army. Conti needed something to do with his talents and time. Commanding the army seemed just the thing for him.

In November, Louis was leaning toward this appointment when Pompadour intervened. She forbade her rival Conti such a distin-guished position. Louis hesitated. Who would the marquise have? Pompadour championed Charles de Rohan, prince de Soubise. Pompadour's ways with the king proved, as usual, more influential than Conti's. Soubise would be the army commander in Germany. Conti bitterly protested to an unyielding king. Complaining he had been dishonored, Conti resigned his position as head of the secret du roi, stormed out of Versailles to a self-imposed exile at his château, and dismissed all immediate royal pleas to return. He would unexpectedly rejoin the king in January 1757.

Conti would have made a much better general than Soubise. Not only would he have most likely spared France some of its humiliating defeats, but he just might have taken and held Hanover. As Argenson put it, "Pompadour wants to rid herself of the Prince de Conti and thinks it would rebound to the glory of the king, but the injury to France touches her little."[51]

Louis was now more dependent than ever on Pompadour at a time when she was becoming increasingly religious. She had largely given up not only the court but even her public toilette, had been named one of the queen's grande dames, and had struggled to get Jesuit confessors to receive her. Hers was not the best frame of mind with which to contemplate grand strategy and diplomacy.

Consequences

Despite all the intrigues of parlement and council plaguing Louis XV, he could note some successes in 1756. After all, he had wrung that tax hike from parlement to help pay for the war. The news from New France was encouraging, what with Montcalm's splendid victory at Oswego and the valor with which the French, Canadians, and Indians held the frontier elsewhere. Yet the western horizon was not cloudless. Letters from Governor Vaudreuil and General Montcalm strongly hinted at worsening relations between them. The split command whereby Vaudreuil was the commander in chief and Montcalm the field general was becoming more stressful to each. Montcalm and other officers increasingly questioned the governor's competence and lambasted the corruption permeating New France's government. All that, of course, was troubling. But such is human nature to grab and quarrel, Louis reasoned. As long as Montcalm and his officers held off the British, all would be well enough.

Good news also arrived from the West Indies, where French naval captains played a deadly cat-and-mouse game with superior British forces. In May, Admiral George Townsend sailed his three ships of the line and four frigates from Jamaica to blockade Cap François, Saint Domingue. Captain Jean Salvert managed to slip in with four ships of the line and two frigates. Meanwhile, from Fort Royal, Captain Charles Alexander, comte de Aubigny, sailed to capture the fifty-gun HMS *Warwick* then withdraw to port. Learning of the capture, Townsend set sail for Fort Royal. Aubigny sailed north to join Salvert at Cap François. There was no immediate British threat to any of the French islands. Though the British warships in the Caribbean outnumbered those of France, they did not have enough troops to invade successfully any island. If French sea captains kept picking off British warships, they might eventually shift the power imbalance there.

As for Europe, Louis XV still savored Minorca's conquest by General Richelieu and Admiral La Galissonière. Versailles further strengthened its power over the western Mediterranean when it signed a treaty with Genoa on August 4, 1756, allowing French troops to garrison Ajaccio, Calvi, and Saint Florent on Corsica. This agreement gave the French a strategic triangle among the ports of Toulon, Port Mahon, and Saint Florent with which to help keep the British fleet at bay. In Germany, Frederick's hold on Saxony seemed secure, after he defeated Austrian attempts to dislodge him that autumn. But, on December 31, 1756, Russia signed the Franco-Austrian treaty; its armies would march west against Prussia in the spring, in conjunction with those of Austria and the Holy Roman Empire. Ideally, these allied armies would catch Frederick II in a vise and squeeze him to a pulp while French armies conquered Hanover. French victories in North America and Hanover in 1757, atop Minorca's conquest, would give Versailles a brilliant bargaining position in any peace talks. Perhaps the war might not be as long, bloody, and expensive as ever more voices darkly warned.

Those who feared the worst were proven right. By the year's end, Versailles learned of a shake-up in the British cabinet with profound consequences for the war and fate of New France. On November 19, 1756, William Pitt was appointed secretary of state of the Southern Department and leader of a shaky coalition of powerful egos.

Who was this man who would lead Britain until October 1761 when the war was all but won? Connections got him into Parliament and propelled him upward. In 1735, he inherited his father's rotten borough of Sarum with seven voters whose allegiance was generously awarded. He expanded his secure base through a politically inspired marriage that made George Grenville and Richard Grenville, Earl of Temple, his brothers-in-law. His fame rested on a voice that combined gifted oratory with perpetual attacks on Whitehall. An exasperated cabinet head Newcastle finally agreed to muffle him with minor financial posts first as Ireland's vice treasurer and then army paymaster. These stints revealed little of his future policies. When he dominated the cabinet from 1757 to 1761, Pitt continually subordinated fiscal prudence to strategy. More importantly, neither did his loud and eloquent condemnations of British aid to Hanover before November 1756 continue once he was in office. He increased British subsidies and troops to Hanover until, by 1761, he could proclaim that "Canada was conquered in Germany." Just as his views of Hanover's importance to England's strategy changed, so too did his war goals. With increasing British victories on land and sea around the world, Pitt demanded ever more concessions from the French until finally he sought their entire empire. He nearly succeeded.

CHAPTER 7

Killing Fields, 1757

The Indians jumped into the water and speared them like fish. . . .
They put in the pot and ate three prisoners.

Bougainville

Why should anyone want to kill me? I have harmed no one.

Louis XV

Such is the effect of men's passions and women's whims.

Bernis

L ouis XV had reason to feel optimistic as the new year dawned. French victories had filled the previous year, and he had no cause to believe that 1757 would differ. Able advisors surrounded him. On January 2, 1757, he had greeted Pompadour's favorite, François Joachim de Bernis, into the Council of State, despite the grumbling among the other ministers. True, the squabble with the Paris parlement was as troublesome as ever; the resignation of most of its members hindered Louis's ability to govern and, especially, to raise taxes high enough to keep pace with the war's soaring costs. He diverted his mind from all his royal burdens with bouts of hunting, gambling, or wenching.

By late afternoon on January 5, the day had been exceptional only for its numbing cold. The king met with a succession of courtiers and ministers at the appointed times. He attended a feast celebrating the Epiphany. The most gratifying of that day's activities was the visit he had just concluded to cheer his favorite daughter, Victoire, who was in bed with a cold. Then something extraordinary happened.

Emmanuel, duc de Croÿ, has left this vivid account: "Around six in the evening, the sky being rather light but cloudy, there being a full moon and torches which dazzled the eyes, the King decided to return to Trianon, where everybody had remained. As he came down the last step of the small guardroom to step into his carriage, leaning on his Grand and First Equerries, the duc d'Ayen and M. le Duc following him, the Captain of the Swiss Guard walking before him, a sufficient number of troops being lined up."[1] Argenson continued the story: "The king had noticed him in passing, and said, 'There is a drunken man.' Then the traitor, who was fifteen feet behind the king, rushed quickly on his sacred person, and struck him with a dagger between the hip and ribs. . . . The king, feeling himself weak, though he was about to fall, but had the presence of mind to say, 'Arrest that unhappy man, but do him no harm.' They carried his Majesty at once to his chamber, and cared for the wound. . . . As they carried the king upstairs, he said, 'Why should anyone want to kill me? I have harmed no one.'"[2]

Louis XV had escaped death by inches. The knife was three and a half inches long and razor sharp. The assassin was powerfully built and had thrust it against the king's ribs with all his might. Had not Louis worn so many layers of clothing to keep the cold at bay, the knife might have punctured a lung and he would have slowly drowned in his own blood. The surgeon quickly pronounced His Majesty out of danger. The news relieved all but Louis, who feared his wound was mortal. Poison tipped the knife and would kill him, he cried. Always troubled by his life of irresistible sin, he called for his confessor. Meanwhile, he beckoned the dauphin, to whom he said, "My son, I leave you a kingdom in much trouble; may you govern it better than I have."[3]

The days passed with Louis certain that his time had come. To those who reassured him, he replied, "It is deeper than you think, for it reaches the heart."[4] He still believed he was as "beloved" by his subjects in 1757 as he was in 1744 when the sobriquet first arose. The thought that anyone would think otherwise of him profoundly disturbed his royal sense of being. Gradually, Louis roused himself to shuffle about the room. On January 13, he felt strong enough to preside over his council, which the dauphin had chaired in his absence. By January 19, he was immersed again in court rituals. By January 23, he could boast of killing a deer on a royal hunt. Though his body had healed, Louis would never again escape from the deep melancholy into which the attack had plunged him.

Meanwhile, burly guards supervised by marine minister and Keeper of the Seals Jean Baptiste de Machault d'Arnouville, tortured the assassin to reveal all. His name was Robert-François Damiens. He had spent most of his forty-two years as a servant, first for a Jesuit college then for a succession of noble and bourgeois families. Recently, as a footman for several members of parlement, he frequently overheard them denounce the king. It was their despair that had inspired his attack. Who else had conspired with him? Though he named names under torture, he retracted these confessions when the henchmen briefly withdrew their devices. But no matter how excruciating the pain, Damiens refused to admit that he intended regicide. All he wished was to awaken the king to parlement's remonstrances.

Damiens was brought to trial before parlement's grand chamber, on whose behalf he had claimed to act. The ties of Damiens with some of its members made them and many of their colleagues prime suspects. Louis XV hoped to take advantage of parlement's eclipse by trying to transfer its powers to the hitherto moribund grand council of princes and peers. This backfired when the two institutions, parlement and grand council, cooperated. Then Conti, the king's most recent nemesis, reemerged from his self-imposed exile to work closely with Paris police magistrate Nicolas René Berryer to crack the assassination case. After two months of exploring various conspiracy theories, the investigators reached a verdict. No alleged conspiracy proved to be a genuine plot to murder Louis. However, all exposed the worsening animosity against the king, the court, corruption, high taxes, and war. Louis was no longer cheered and was often mocked. To the relief of some and the disappointment of others, the investigators found no evidence that Damiens was the point man for a Jansenist, parlement, or even Jesuit plot—Damiens was the lone assassin. That conclusion was controversial at the time and ever since.[5]

And what of the assassin's fate? Damiens was found guilty of lèse-majesté and parricide. On March 28, he was carted to the Place de Grève before the Hotel de Ville. The executor first hacked off his right hand, then poured boiling lead over his body, When Damiens's screams proved too annoying, the executioner ripped out his tongue to stifle them, perhaps disappointing some in the dense crowd. Damiens was still alive when a horse was strapped to each of his arms and legs. Drovers whipped the horses forward, but they could not rip apart Damiens. The executor chopped the joints of each limb. The horses were spurred. Each of Damiens's limbs tore off from his trunk, leaving his quivering body and head lying on the stone pavement in pools of spreading blood.

Damiens's execution may have brought some relief to French subjects chilled with dread by the attempt on Louis XV's life. The king's brush with death reawakened popular sentiments for him that most of his subjects had not felt since his near fatal illness at Metz in 1744. Looking back a generation to 1757, Casanova recalled that during "this period the Parisians fancied that they loved the King. At the present day they are more enlightened."[6] When the news reached Canada, Montcalm forbade his men "to mention the horrible attempt on his sacred person. It caused us all to shudder with horror, and these barbarians so ferocious, so humane in their lodges, might waver in their esteem for us, seeing us capable of producing such monsters."[7]

Pompadour Supreme

Pompadour used the attack on Louis XV to inspire him to reassert his power. On January 27, the king sent sixteen of those parlementarians who had resigned the previous December into exile. An even more dramatic shake-up occurred on February 1, when Louis dismissed from his council his two best ministers, war minister Argenson and marine minister Machault. Argenson had troubled Louis for some time. That his pro-Frederick sentiments kept Argenson from pursuing the war vigorously was bad enough, but his sniping at Pompadour had become unpardonable. Her tears finally convinced Louis to act. As for Machault, his loathing for Pompadour had become increasingly open. He also incurred the clergy's wrath by trying to impose on them the dixieme tax. The parlementarians hated him for championing the December Declaration of 1756, which reasserted royal powers at their expense. For a decade, Machault and Argenson had poisoned council meetings and other affairs with their searing hatred of each other. Then, after Louis XV was struck down, they briefly united to urge Pompadour to retire. This seems to have been the last affront for the king. Yet, while Louis detested Argenson, he would miss Machault, whom he genuinely liked. As a mark of his affection, the king let Machault keep his 20,000-livre salary and post as keeper of the seals.

Louis did not look far to replace Argenson. René de Voyer, marquis de Paulmy d'Argenson, took his uncle's seat as war minister. Paulmy would fail to win the distinction as war minister that he had achieved in his other endeavors. Only thirty-five years old when he took office, he had studied law, joined the French Academy in 1748, and accumulated one of France's largest libraries. When Louis had appointed his uncle war minister, he had tapped Paulmy to be commissary general. Paulmy had no sooner settled into that post when he was named ambassador to Switzerland, where he served from 1749 to 1751, then was appointed general secretary in the War Department. On February 2, 1757, he replaced his uncle. His tenure as war minister would last little more than a year until he was forced to resign in March 1758, although he would hold a council seat until 1762. At best, it can be said that Paulmy was hardworking and conscientious but ungifted.

Louis handed the marine ministry portfolio to François-Marie Peyrenc de Moras, who retained his post as comptroller general. Those two hats gave one man enormous power to bring coherence, vision, and decisiveness to France's global war. Whether this actually happened, of course, depended on the man. Moras was a poor choice to head either ministry. Then again, given France's chaotic administration, vapid leadership, and slide into bankruptcy, only a few gifted men could have retrieved the realm's fortunes with vigorous policies.

Overwhelmed by the burdens of heading two ministries, Moras begged to be relieved of the treasury so that he could concentrate on marine affairs. The king agreed on August 25, 1757, replacing Moras with Étienne de Silhouette, who had made his name and fortune as a fermier général. Louis hoped he would bring the same vigor to managing the royal finances. In this hope, the king was disappointed. Silhouette floundered in the morass for a few months before he was forced to resign. His name, however, inspired a new word for the French language—"silhouette" has since meant a dark, flat, lifeless profile.

Pompadour was the real winner in this game of council musical chairs. With first Conti then Argenson and Machault—her three fiercest and most capable rivals—gone, Pompadour was more powerful than ever. Argenson observed that most of the court was "convinced that Mme. de Pompadour has become the prime minister of France, and that the king is delivering himself over to the false contradictory counsels of that woman; his subjection through the senses is over, but he remains under that of souls. This favorite has little mind; but Louis XV, by his timidity, by his lack of clear-sightedness and of expedients, has put himself far below her; thus in all discussions and proposals she has over him the superiority of a strong soul over a weak one. She wills firmly."[8]

The challenges facing France amidst the loss of two experienced ministers seemed overwhelming to Bernis: "France's misfortune began at that hour. The King's Council no longer commanded respect. The army and the navy soon realized that the hands controlling them were feeble. Confusion and graft spread in both Departments. Madame de Pompadour, with her childlike conceit, believed that she alone could make all go right, but I thought differently, as did our allies. They regarded the banishment of the two ministers in the existing circumstances as a gross mistake."[9] Perhaps even worse, the public fervently opposed the war in Germany, an opposition that strengthened with each bloody year of stalemate: "The entire nation, which had applauded the Treaty of Versailles with the naïve hope that it would bring us peace, uttered loud cries against the war we were about to undertake in Germany—they accused the ministers of folly."[10] It turns out they were right.

Diplomatic and Military Blunders

At a half dozen capitals, diplomats and ministers prepared for a scale of warfare in 1757 that far surpassed in troops and carnage that of the previous year. In January 1757, Whitehall and Potsdam signed a second treaty by which England granted Prussia a £300,596 subsidy for that year.[11] On January 17, 1757, the imperial electors declared Frederick the bane of the empire and began to gather an army at Erfurt to march against him. On March 21, 1757, the noose around Prussia drew tighter when Sweden signed an alliance treaty with France and Austria. Sweden promised to send 25,000 troops against Prussia if its two allies would pay for them. At scores of depots across central Europe, supplies and regiments were massed or moved toward the front.

In France, it was not just the king's council and public support that unraveled. The sacrifice of Poland to the Russian alliance and Conti's retirement destroyed the rationale for the secret du roi. Yet Louis kept his network intact even if he could not explain why. He appointed his man in Warsaw, Charles François de Broglie, the secret du roi's field commander, and ordered him and Jean Pierre Tercier in Paris to coordinate their activities. Yet the king had no marching orders to give them. Not surprisingly, Broglie kept up his old work of blunting Russian and Austrian intrigues that undermined France's alliance with them.[12]

At the same time, Louis's official diplomacy centered on Russia with which he hoped his envoy, Alexander Mackenzie, chevalier Douglas, would forge stronger ties. What the king and his council got was not what they wanted. On January 11, 1757, Douglas signed an amendment to the Treaty of Versailles that brought Russia into the alliance. When foreign minister Rouillé and the council received the draft, they erupted in anger. Those veterans of intrigue, Russian ministers Bestuzhev and Vorontsov, allied with Austrian ambassador Esterházy, found the diplomatic amateur Douglas an easy mark. Hoping to destroy Versailles's ties with Constantinople, they spread rumors of an impending Turkish attack on Russia. Bestuzhev then insisted he would only sign the treaty if France agreed to help Russia in any war with the Ottoman Empire. Esterházy implored Douglas to accept the

Russian demand. Recalling his orders to follow the Austrian ambassador's lead, Douglas signed a secret clause that committed Versailles to
pay Saint Petersburg either the upkeep of 18,000 infantry troops and
6,000 cavalry troops or 23,000 florins a month for the war's duration.[13]

Austria and Russia then linked arms more tightly with the Treaty
of Saint Petersburg, signed February 2, 1757. The treaty required each
to send 80,000 troops against Prussia, forbade a separate peace, invited
other powers to join, and updated an earlier alliance treaty signed on
May 22, 1746. Secret clauses committed Austria to pay Russia 1 million rubles yearly until the war ended and 2 million rubles after Silesia
was conquered. Vienna also promised to help Russia take the Duchy
of Courland from Poland and favorably adjust its Ukrainian border.[14]

In mid-February, Versailles received the treaty Douglas signed.
Louis and his council wrung their hands in despair that a pen stroke
could unravel decades of careful diplomacy. Rouillé hastily wrote
Douglas a letter blasting him for signing such a treaty at odds with
French policy: "I cannot express our shock and pain at seeing this secret
declaration. . . . I cannot hide from you that His Majesty is extremely
upset at the ease with which you signed. . . . It is up to you to repair
the fault. If you say Esterházy got you in, then let Esterházy get you
out."[15] To undo the damage, Louis XV wrote Empress Elizabeth a letter lauding her virtues and humbly requesting that France be excused
from the treaty that its unskilled envoy had unwisely signed. Elizabeth
graciously excused France from the anti-Turk clause. Bestuzhev, however, took advantage of the French embarrassment to request a loan of
5 million livres. Douglas politely refused. On April 19, 1757, Douglas
signed a revised amendment to the Treaty of Versailles with the clause
about the Turks deleted.[16]

Versailles had accepted the need for Russian armies to march
across Poland to attack Prussia yet feared that Saint Petersburg would
use that as a chance to aggrandize itself at Poland's expense. Now
bound to Russia, France could not in good faith attack its new ally in
defense of its older ally. Yet the king and his ministers felt they had to
do something to deter Russia. Twice in early 1757, Versailles threatened
to unleash its distant subsidized allies, the Turks and Tartars, against
Russia if it took advantage of Poland. It also spread an unfounded

rumor that Britain had sent its own agents to Warsaw to stymie any Russian inroads into Poland.[17]

Saint Petersburg ignored such warnings. Instead, hoping to deepen Versailles's commitment, Elizabeth finally offered Conti the Duchy of Courland and command of the Russian army. For years, the secret du roi had worked for offers like this. Elizabeth's gift was a remarkable coup for French interests that, given Russian general Stepan Fedorovich Apraxin's failure to march on Berlin later in 1757, might well have defeated Frederick that year had it been accepted. Yet Louis XV spurned the offer! The king was still so angry over Conti's abrupt retirement in a huff after not receiving command of the French army that he refused Elizabeth's incredible gift. Louis also rejected any mention of Conti when talks opened among France, Russia, and Austria for Poland's future king. Though he toyed with various candidates, Louis eventually accepted Frederick Christian, Saxon king August III's son and the first choice of Austria and Russia. On such whims rest the fate of nations.[18]

As for Versailles's military strategy, that of defending Canada and conquering Hanover continued. On May 1, 1757, France and Austria signed the second Treaty of Versailles. France's obligations deepened. In addition to the 24,000 troops already in the field, Versailles promised to send a 105,000-strong army and pay for 6,000 German mercenaries in Austria's army. Atop all that, France would pay Austria 12 million florins yearly for the war's duration, and half the Saxon and Swedish subsidies. In return, Maria Theresa was required simply to maintain an army of 80,000 in the field, something she would have happily done anyway. France and Austria pledged not to sheathe their swords until Prussia was defeated. And then what? Prussia would be conquered and partitioned. Austria would take Silesia, Glatz, Crossen, Magdeburg, and Halberstadt; Philip, the Duke of Parma, would take the Austrian Netherlands in return for handing over his Italian duchy to Austria and renouncing claims to all other Italian lands. As for France, its northeast frontier would advance to engulf Ostend, Nieuport, Ypres, Mons, Chimay, and Beaumont. Once again the Austrians had diplomatically snookered the French. What could France's diplomats have been thinking? Versailles's pledge to underwrite Austria as long as it warred against Prussia forbade France from making a separate peace no matter how advantageous it might be.

No sooner was the ink dry on the treaty than Versailles tried to squirm out of it. Rouillé instructed Ambassador Louis Auguste Augustin d'Affry at The Hague to approach English ambassador Joseph Yorke with a suggestion that France and England negotiate a separate peace that would extract them from the German bloodbath. Whitehall rejected the notion. Vienna got wind of the French initiative and castigated its ally for any attempt to betray its commitment. Exhausted by all the work and criticism, Rouillé resigned. Bernis took his place as foreign minister on June 28, 1757.

Despite Versailles's increasingly cold feet, it was dragged deeper into the alliance. In June 1757, France and Russia exchanged ambassadors. Paul François de Gallucci, marquis de l'Hôpital, arrived at Saint Petersburg while the chancellor's brother, Mikhail Bestuzhev, reached Versailles. Neither man would distinguish himself in boosting his country's interests.

Meanwhile Chancellor Bestuzhev, with his hand as deep in Britain's financial pocket as ever, struggled to damage relations with France. Though the trade between France and Russia was considerable, in 1756, 90 percent of the 2 million rubles of French exports and 1.6 million rubles of imports with Russia were packed in English, Dutch, and German rather than French hulls. In April 1757, Bestuzhev threatened even the indirect sales the French enjoyed in Russia when he slapped a 164 percent increase on the tariff for luxury goods, most of which came from France. It was curious treatment for an ally. Of course, in Bestuzhev's mind England, not France, should have been Russia's partner. He justified the tariffs by arguing that Saint Petersburg needed more revenues with which to pay for its war, something Versailles had steadfastly refused to provide.[19]

By April the military situation in Germany looked bleak for Britain and Prussia. Allied armies with a combined strength of 250,000 troops nearly encircled Frederick's various armies numbering 120,000 troops and Hanover's 47,000-man Army of Observation. Two French armies slowly gathered and marched off to war. Victor Marie d'Estrées, marquis de Coeuvres, boasted 105,000 troops in his Army of the Lower Rhine. Charles de Rohan, prince de Soubise, joined his 20,000-man Army of the Upper Rhine with the 33,000-man Imperial army at Erfurt under Marshal Joseph Friedrich von Sachsen-Hildburghausen. In Moravia, Marshal Leopold von Daun commanded 58,000 troops, backed by a reserve army of 90,000. Prince Charles of Lorraine was encamped around Prague. A Russian army of 18,000 troops under General Count Wilhelm von Fermor marched toward Memel on the coast while Marshal Count Stepan Apraxin's 70,000 troops headed straight toward Berlin through central Poland. At any moment, Stockholm could order Gustav, Duke Hamilton, commanding the 16,000 Swedish troops guarding Stralsund in Swedish Pomerania to march on Berlin.

To worsen matters, the Army of Observation needed a commander. As the British army's captain general, William Augustus, Duke Cumberland, seemed a logical choice. Though his record as a general was mixed—he was trounced by Marechal Maurice de Saxe at Fontenoy in 1745 but brutally crushed the Jacobite uprising at Culloden in 1746—the British army had no Marlborough or Wellington waiting in the wings. And, after all, George II's second son was his favorite. Cumberland demanded a price for his appointment. He despised Pitt and swore that he would go to Germany only if "the Great Orator" returned to the House of Commons. A majority in the cabinet concurred.

George II dismissed William Pitt on April 5. For the next fifteen weeks amidst a world war, England wanted a government. None of the ministers the king approached to form a cabinet had the confidence and political support to do so. Finally, on July 29, with both men holding their noses, Pitt and Thomas Pelham-Holles, the Duke of Newcastle, agreed to a political marriage of expediency. Pitt would head the Southern Department; Newcastle, the treasury; Robert Darcy, Earl of Holderness, the Northern Department; Richard Grenville, Earl of Temple, the privy seal, with Philip Yorke, Earl of Hardwicke, serving as his advisor; William Barrington, the war ministry; and George Anson, the admiralty. Henry Fox would serve as the army's paymaster.

Upon taking the government's reins in July 1757, Pitt declared with typical pomposity, "I am sure that I can save this country and that no one else can."[20] Once universally praised, Pitt's strategy has more recently been assailed for its failings and exposed as only partially his. Two certainties do characterize his leadership. First, his ideas were never in doubt even if his power to implement them was. Rhetoric was Pitt's strongest suit. Whether Pitt mesmerized or enraged his listeners, he rarely misled them over where he stood or wanted to go. Second, his strategy changed with time. Before entering the cabinet, Pitt condemned any link to Hanover and the war in Europe. Once in power, he saw British financial and military commitments to Germany as a wonderful means of diverting Versailles's efforts from the decisive battles being fought elsewhere around the globe. When he entered office, Pitt sought merely to defend Britain's far-flung empire; by the time he left, he had vowed that Britain would chew up and swallow the French empire.[21]

The campaign opened in April when the Austrians marched against the Prussians. Frederick was not content to await an attack. He marched his 64,000 troops against 61,000 Austrians under Prince Charles, defeated them before Prague on May 6, and besieged the city. The victory cost Frederick nearly 15,000 casualties; among the 13,500 Austrian casualties was General Browne, who died from his wounds. Charles refused to surrender Prague. With 64,000 troops, Daun marched to Prague's relief, forcing Frederick to break off the siege and intercept him with 32,000 troops. On June 18, their two armies battled at Kolin. The Austrians suffered 8,000 casualties and inflicted 14,000 dead and wounded on Frederick, who retreated into Saxony. On July 14, Daun and Charles followed.

A desperate Frederick implored Whitehall to reinforce the Army of Observation, launch attacks on French ports, and send a fleet into the Baltic, all to divert France and Russia from Prussia. To offer something in return, Frederick withdrew his 10,000 troops from Wesel and attached them to Cumberland's army. This was a strategic mistake. Wesel guarded Hanover's southwest border. The French occupied it on the heels of Prussia's evacuation. Meanwhile, Whitehall debated and rejected sending a fleet into the Baltic, fearing it would provoke Denmark and Sweden into war against England. It also decided that no more troops could be spared for Cumberland's Army of

Observation. Instead, the cabinet approved Pitt's pet scheme of attacking La Rochelle.

Frederick was increasingly desperate to extract himself from the tightening noose by any possible means. On July 7, he asked his beloved sister, Wilhelmine, to offer Pompadour 500,000 crowns if she could convince Louis to accept peace. Pompadour greeted the offer with silence. Wilhelmine then wrote Voltaire to ask the Cardinal de Tencin, who had opposed France's alliance with Austria, to work for peace. Tencin agreed. Pompadour rejected his advance as well.[22]

This was no time for peace when the French appeared to be on the brink of a brilliant victory. Outnumbered two to one, Cumberland had no choice but to retreat toward his supply bases on the North Sea as the armies of Estrées and Soubise marched steadily after him. The French captured Emden on July 2, then Bremen a few days later. Cumberland hurried to Stade at the mouth of the Elbe River, now his last supply source. Estrées caught up and bloodied Cumberland badly at Hastenbeck on July 26.

Nearly everyone cheered that victory except Pompadour, who loathed Estrées for overshadowing her favorite, Soubise. So she pulled every string possible to drag him down. Pompadour's will prevailed as usual. Louis XV reluctantly agreed to recall the victorious Estrées and replace him with Richelieu, an ironic choice given that he hated Pompadour even more. Bernis despaired that "all Europe was astonished that after what was a considerable victory we should have dared to recall the general who won it; but Europe knew nothing of the intrigues at Versailles. . . . One can say that our conduct throughout the war disconcerted the calculations of every man of commonsense. Such is the effect of men's passions and women's whims."[23]

Richelieu's army marched triumphantly into Hanover on August 11. From there, the French armies steadily shoved Cumberland toward Stade and a sea empty of British ships. Now Pitt too was as desperate as Frederick. At Madrid, Ambassador Benjamin Keene dreaded that the day was not far off when "the Empire is no more, the ports of the Netherlands betrayed, the Dutch barrier an empty sound, Minorca, and with it the Mediterranean, lost, and America itself imperiled."[24]

Britain needed another ally to stem the enemy advance. The only remaining neutral great power was Spain. That summer, Pitt made an extraordinary offer to Madrid. With England's fortunes so low, Pitt actually promised to return Gibraltar and Minorca to Spain in return for an alliance against France and the Spanish enclave of Ceuta or Oran in North Africa. Incredibly, Madrid rebuffed that advance. In 1763, Spain's ministers must have kicked themselves when they recalled rejecting the offer that would have given them two long-sought goals and would have prevented Britain's subsequent humiliation of the Spanish navy and capture of Cuba and the Philippines.[25]

In Europe, Britain and Prussia faced seemingly imminent and humiliating defeats. Indeed, Frederick appeared on the verge of extinction. On August 30, Marshal Apraxin's 100,000-man Russian army sharply defeated Marshal Hans von Lehwaldt's 30,000 Prussians at the Battle of Gross-Jagersdorf. Few Prussian forces stood between Apraxin's army and Berlin. With a forced march, the Russian army could have reached Berlin within a week. Learning of the defeat, Stockholm declared war and ordered Hamilton to march on Berlin. Frederick debated whether to swallow an overdose of opium or gather the remnants of his troops and race back to Berlin for a last stand.

Then a seeming miracle occurred. Apraxin ordered his troops to withdraw into Poland. What explains such defeatist and perhaps even treasonous behavior? Versailles attributed Apraxin's foot dragging and retreat to English bribes, Bestuzhev's machinations, the desire to wring more subsidies and territory from Austria, and, especially, Elizabeth's wretched health. The latter reason was probably the most important to Apraxin. The rumor that the empress was dying had spread as far as his army. If the rumor were true, the pro-Frederick Peter would mount the throne and might well demonize anyone who had warred against his hero. To guard his own interests if not those of Russia, Apraxin chose to disperse his troops into winter quarters in Poland. The official explanation was that his army lacked enough forage. If so, Apraxin could have found plenty in the fields surrounding Berlin. On October 20, Elizabeth's council replaced Apraxin with the more vigorous Count Wilhelm von Fermor. But the chance for victory had long since vanished.[26]

Meanwhile, Richelieu skillfully backed Cumberland into a dead end at Stade then waited at his headquarters at Kloster Zeven between Bremen and Harburg for Cumberland to ask for terms. With Britain's naval squadrons fighting elsewhere and his troops outnumbered two to one, nothing could save Cumberland. George II increasingly despaired as his son's plight became more desperate. On August 11, the king sent the duke the authority to negotiate a separate peace on his behalf as Hanover's elector, whereby Britain would withdraw from the war in Germany if Hanover and the Army of Observation were preserved and French troops were withdrawn. On September 5, Pitt finally gave in to pressure to send a squadron with supplies to help Cumberland defend Stade. That help would arrive too late. On September 15, George II wrote Cumberland a letter that canceled his previous authority to negotiate a peace. Cumberland should defend Stade at all costs. That order would arrive too late as well.

Richelieu and Cumberland signed the Convention of Kloster Zeven on September 10. The Hanoverian army would take winter quarters while the Brunswick and Hessian troops had to surrender their arms and dissolve. A supplementary agreement was signed by which Richelieu's troops would withdraw from Bremen if the British squadron blockading it would withdraw. The French army, however, would occupy most of Hanover. The convention would please neither Whitehall nor Versailles.

George II repudiated Kloster Zeven and recalled his "rascally son" in disgrace; for months, his father would barely speak to his off-spring and lamented his "tainted blood."[27] The veteran general John Ligonier was tapped to replace him as captain general of the British army. More importantly, the king convinced Prince Ferdinand, the Duke of Brunswick's brother and a brilliant general, to command the reformed Army of Observation.

Though the convention appeared to be a British defeat, Versailles had its own reasons for criticizing it. Richelieu's victory would have been decisive had it been accepted as a capitulation, which the defeated must follow, rather than a convention, which must be ratified. George II simply tore up the convention. Yet, even then, Richelieu might have ended the war in Germany had he acted decisively. Compounding his diplomatic folly, he squandered his victory by hunkering down in Hanover rather than immediately marching against Frederick. When he did march, he refused to join Soubise but contented himself with besieging Halberstadt then ravishing distant parts of Hanover. All along, he ignored repeated orders from Versailles to join Soubise against Frederick. He signed an armistice with Prince Ferdinand of Brunswick that was supposed to hold until the next spring; it would last only a few weeks.

What explains such a cavalier attitude toward war and diplomacy? Richelieu was not so much a general beholden to France as one beholden to his own passions. He was described as "a man, who had early surprised the world by his adventures, had imposed on it by his affectations, had dictated to it by his wit and insolent agreeableness, had often tried to govern it by his intrigues, and who would be the hero of the age, if histories were novels, or women wrote history."[28]

While Cumberland negotiated his humiliating surrender, a British fleet with a small army aboard that might have rescued him was sailing in the wrong direction. Pitt justified that armada on strategic grounds, but a desire to avenge Cumberland's intrigues against him may have played a role. In July, Frederick had issued the first of several pleas to Whitehall to reinforce Cumberland with 6,000 infantry and 3,000 cavalry. Pitt was glad to rid England of Cumberland when he was dispatched to lead the Army of Observation but refused to commit any British troops to Germany. Instead, he organized a massive British expedition against Rochefort. The attack was originally supposed to divert French troops from Germany and thus relieve pressure on Cumberland, as well as destroy the port of Rochefort and inspire a Huguenot revolt in the region. It would accomplish none of those missions.

By the time the expedition's eighteen ships of the line, six frigates, and forty-four transports packed with eight thousand troops sailed on September 8, Cumberland was two days from surrender. After the British forces bombarded, captured, then abandoned small Fort Aix on the Isle de Ré guarding Rochefort's bay, the army's commander, General John Mordaunt, got cold feet. On September 25, Mordaunt convinced all his leading officers except one, Colonel James Wolfe, that Rochefort was too formidable to take. After all, it was a dozen miles up the Charente River and was guarded by fortresses and thousands of troops with probably many more on the way. Though Admiral Edward Hawke accepted the decision, he wondered why Mordaunt delayed ordering an assault for several weeks after the fleet had appeared, thus giving the French ample time to mass troops, Catholic and Huguenot alike, and strengthen fortifications. On October 1, the fleet ingloriously sailed back to England. Mordaunt would be court-martialed and acquitted of cowardice.[29]

What for Canada?

Though Versailles did not receive word for months, the prospects in North America seemed as promising as those in Europe. Versailles was committed to retaining New France, though at a minimum cost. On January 15, 1757, the council approved the requests from Vaudreuil and Montcalm for more troops and supplies, but not as many as were asked. The ministers noted that the number of regular troops in Canada had risen from 800 in 1750 to 4,820 in 1756 and would reach 6,600 if the planned reinforcements safely arrived there. After considerable debate, however, the council rejected the request that it match the number of troops Britain deployed in North America. Canada's defense was already a vast financial drain. With Britain's command of the sea, any dispatch of troops was a roll of the dice; the more sent, the more that could be lost. Also, it made no sense to Versailles to pour reinforcements into Canada without knowing Whitehall's intentions— what if the British planned to stay on the defensive as they had in 1756? If so, several thousand more French troops would not be enough to win a decisive offensive victory but would further strain Canada's ability to feed and shelter them. Finally, to send more troops would divert strength from French armies fighting in Germany, the main theater; Canada remained a sideshow.

As always, British sea power intimidated Versailles from committing more troops and cash. In 1757, England's fleet numbered 239 in service, of which 98 were ships of the line, 25 were being overhauled, and 49 were being built. With seventy-two warships in service, France had less than one to every three of Britain's. Most of France's navy was bottled up in port.[30]

The fear that more troops would strain already-depleted food supplies was well founded. That winter and into the spring, Bougainville noted, there was "great misery at Quebec. Bread is scarce, and what little there is of the worst quality. The Intendant has been obliged to distribute two thousand bushels of wheat to the inhabitants for seed. This quality is far from sufficient and part of the land will remain unsowed. They will even have to bring from the depots food intended for the troops in order to feed the capital. No news of any ships, and this occasions much alarm. The lack of provisions prevents us from starting the campaign."[31]

Greed rather than nature caused the famine that forced the peasants to slaughter their draft animals and eat their seed corn to survive. The previous October, Intendant François Bigot's chief henchman, Commissary General Joseph Cadet, ordered the peasants to sell to the state all their crops at fixed prices or else have it confiscated with no compensation. After the Canadians' larders emptied, Bigot and his machine then sold the food back to peasants at prices four to five times higher. When a delegation of housewives protested and threw horse-meat at Governor Vaudreuil's feet, he exploded in anger and warned them to disperse or else "he would have them all put in prison, and half of them hanged."[32]

Meanwhile, at Versailles, Belle Isle reopened the debate over the proper war strategy. He tried to convince the king and his ministers that "as America is the principal and true cause of the war, our attention ought to be directed to that quarter of the globe. . . . We should forward to America, independent of the necessary recruits to complete our Colonial troops and French regiments, Sieur Fischer's corps of 4,000 men." Belle Isle's analysis was sound. Circumstances demanded a quick decision, he informed the council, "as we are approaching the time when those transports sail, and those troops have a great many days march to make before they reach their places of embarkation. . . . Not a moment is to be lost in coming to a conclusion."[33]

The council did decide quickly—it rejected Belle Isle's plan. That decision more than any other by Versailles may have sealed

Canada's fate. Some or all of those 4,000 men could have meant the difference between victory or defeat at Gabarus Bay, the Plains of Abraham, or any number of other battlefields. Then again, those troops had to be fed. If not enough supply ships could run the Atlantic gauntlet, those 4,000 extra mouths to feed might have starved New France into an even earlier surrender.

Vaudreuil and Montcalm at War

Though the council was dead set not to commit any more troops to defend New France, one minister did address a related problem. Though a mediocre war minister, Paulmy was a good diplomat and psychologist. In separate letters penned the same day to Vaudreuil and Montcalm, he assured each of the other's high regard, thus briefly checking worsening feelings between them. To the governor, he related that the "King had observed, with pleasure, the harmony that exists between you and the Marquis de Montcalm, and that you have reason to be satisfied with Chevalier de Lévis as well as with the other officers. I must then give, in turn, the justice to assure you that in the letters they have written hither, they are highly pleased with the kindness you show them." Paulmy wrote the general that "his Majesty is highly satisfied with the union which appears to exist between you and the Governor-General, and is persuaded that you will not neglect anything that will possibly maintain it. . . . The Marquis de Vaudreuil . . . bestows the highest accolades on your military talents as well as on your personal qualities."[34]

Paulmy understood well how quickly a relationship between any two men filled with ambition and pride could deteriorate into mutual hatred in which any action by one, no matter how innocuous, was viewed instantly by the other as an affront to be avenged. Thus did Paulmy try to create a climate where Montcalm and Vaudreuil would feel compelled to shelve their growing mistrust and cooperate with one another. To do so meant seizing the first positive impressions that either shared of each other, and ignoring the contempt that had swelled between them and burned through their letters to Versailles.

Montcalm, at least, was willing to try to get along with the governor. He still believed that Vaudreuil was "a kind man, mild with no character of his own, surrounded by men who seek to destroy all confidence he might have in the General of the land forces."[35] Evidently, Montcalm had not yet penetrated Vaudreuil's bland surface that hid an ego of monstrous proportions—Vaudreuil stole credit for all of Montcalm's victories and projected his own failings onto the general. Montcalm did vent the familiar gripes of being overworked, overcriticized, underpaid, underappreciated, and besieged by those who would humiliate him: "My pay is only twenty-five thousand livres; I have none of the perquisites of the Governors or Intendants of Canada, I must support a Staff. . . . I am obliged to give myself importance, singlehanded; no person seeks to give me any here; they would fain try to deprive me of it, but they will not succeed."[36]

The war minister's concern with good feelings extended to the troops. In an April letter, he wrote Montcalm that it was "very important that the officers of the Regular troops in Canada live in close union with those of the Colony. 'Tis to be feared that the former treat the Canadians with hauteur and harshness; above all things, it would be of the greatest consequence were the Indians not pleased with them. . . . You cannot exhibit too much graciousness and affability on all occasions, both to the Canadians and Indians." In that same letter, Paulmy revealed that unofficial ties were as important as official ones in France's government, by asking Montcalm "to keep up, independent of your ordinary relations with the Minister of War, a personal and secret correspondence with me. My uncle has delivered to me an address and little cipher which will serve us in this particular."[37]

Wilderness War without Mercy

During the winter months of early 1757, while Versailles pondered then decided what it was willing to donate to its North American empire, its commanders launched a spoiling attack. On the night of February 18, Captain François Pierre de Rigaud de Vaudreuil, governor of Trois Rivières and Vaudreuil's vigorous younger brother, led

50 grenadiers and 200 regulars from the La Sarre, Royal Roussillon, Languedoc, and Béarn battalions; 250 Marines; 600 Canadian militiamen; and 300 Indians south from Fort Carillon down Lake George's snow-covered ice toward Fort William Henry. They arrived before the fort on February 20. Firing broke out. The French and Indians peppered the fort with musket balls but, without cannon, could not breach its walls. They did succeed in burning "four brigantines of 10 to 14 guns, two long-boats of fifty oars . . . over three hundred and fifty transport bateaux; a considerable quantity of building timber, several campaign carriages, a sawmill, the sheds and magazines which were enclosed by a . . . fort, and finally all their supply of firewood. The fort remains isolated; 'twas saved from the flames only because no wind was blowing during the whole of the conflagration." Rigaud could do no more. He and his frostbitten men began their thirty-five-mile trudge back to Fort Carillon on February 22. Fort William Henry's defenders got a taste of what awaited them that summer.[38]

The rivalry between Canadians and French could at times be healthy. Fear of Canadian ridicule caused Montcalm to take extra precautions for the success of Rigaud's winter campaign. The general noted, "We are not accustomed to such marches in Europe, and as the Canadians who are accustomed to brag, asserted that our troops could not support such fatigues, I paid particular attention carefully to select officers and soldiers qualified in every respect. Therefore were the Canadians forced to admit that we were not inferior to them in any point. To be six weeks on the march and to sleep . . . continually on snow or ice, reduced to bread and pork, and often to drag or carry 15 days' provisions, will give you some idea of fatigue unknown in Europe; it was sustained with great gaiety without the slightest murmur."[39]

What Montcalm neglected to say was that snow blindness afflicted most of those 1,500 men on their way back up Lake George. The gaiety surely ended then, if it ever existed. Those troops must have been miserable throughout the campaign. And, as for the destruction they wrought, they could have safely committed their arson with half as many men. That was certainly the conclusion drawn by Bougainville, who noted that Rigaud's campaign "would have accomplished the same objectives with more glory, have cost less in money and food, and we would have been able to get started as soon as the ice went out. It seems to me that they should not have summoned the commander to surrender until after they had burned all the surrounding structures, but have taken a firmer tone, not speaking of an escalade but of reducing the fort to ashes and putting the garrison to the sword."[40]

As the winter ice began to melt, Governor Vaudreuil convened Indian councils at Montreal and sent word to frontier commanders to try to rally every tribe east of the Mississippi River, including the neutral Cherokees and Creeks, against the Americans. Ideally, Vaudreuil hoped to spread the Indian war down the entire Appalachian frontier to Georgia. Fearful that efforts of British agents with southern and Ohio valley tribes could threaten the slender link between Canada and Louisiana, Vaudreuil proposed erecting a fort at the Falls of the Ohio River (near today's Louisville), which he argued would hold the Cherokees and Creeks. If Vaudreuil's strategy was sound, his geography was shaky. The French would later build Fort Massac on the Ohio River, but near the mouth of the Tennessee River, the actual back door to Cherokee and Creek country; the Falls were far from most tribes.[41]

If virtually any settlement along the American frontier was vulnerable to Quebec-inspired Indian attacks, the French could at best launch only one large army offensive. Any planning had to await the supply ships that managed to slip past the ever-tighter British blockade of the French coast and safely reached Quebec. Those supplies came late that year—not until July did the last of the forty-three ships dock at Quebec; British warships picked off sixteen others en route. Those ships disgorged hundreds of tons of supplies and 1,500 troops, including two battalions of the Régiment de Berry, 400 replacements for the ranks of other regular battalions, and 26 artillerymen from the Corps Royale.[42]

So it was not until July 9, 1757, that Vaudreuil could issue Montcalm his marching orders. Montcalm's primary and secondary objectives would be Forts William Henry and Edward respectively. If Montcalm took the first, he should press on and besiege the other. If Fort Edward surrendered, the general should carry back to Fort Carillon all the provisions, munitions, and guns of both forts, which would then be destroyed. Vaudreuil never considered holding either fort let alone advancing on Albany. Perhaps the most important reason why those options were not entertained was the necessity by late August to return most Canadians for their fall harvest and to release the Upper Great Lakes Indians to the long journey back to their homes before the cold weather and storms appeared.[43]

The British campaign in North America that year also concentrated on taking one strategic spot. On May 1, England's North American commander in chief, John Campbell, Earl of Loudoun, received an order from Pitt to take Louisbourg. To that end, Pitt organized and dispatched the necessary warships, transports, troops, and supplies. Throughout the summer, the British squadrons and regiments slowly assembled at Halifax.

Gaining word of the British plans, Versailles ordered three French squadrons to converge on Louisbourg, Captain Revest from Toulon with four warships, Admiral Dubois de la Motte from Brest with nine ships of the line and two frigates, and Captain Joseph Bauffremont from Cap François, Saint Domingue, with four warships. By July all three squadrons managed to evade British blockades and prowling squadrons, and sail into Louisbourg's harbor. Along with the warships already there, La Motte commanded eighteen ships of the line and five frigates.[44]

With the English and French fleets equal, Loudoun refused to risk his transports. At a council of war among Loudoun's army and navy commanders on August 4, they agreed to send Admiral Francis Holburne's squadron to Louisbourg to draw out La Motte. If he defeated La Motte, Loudoun would join him before Louisbourg; if not, the campaign was over. Holburne set forth and anchored off the mouth of Louisbourg Bay. Though he had twice as many ships, La Motte refused to sail out and fight. After Holburne returned to Halifax, Loudoun canceled the campaign and dispersed the army and fleet to winter quarters. Holburne reappeared before Louisbourg and challenged La Motte. On September 24, a hurricane blew up and battered Holburne's fleet to destruction's brink. The gale demasted six of his ships and would have shoved them all into the rocky shore had it lasted but another hour. Among La Motte's fleet, only the eighty-gun *Tonnant* and thirty-six-gun *Abenaki* suffered damage.[45]

This was La Motte's golden chance. He could have sailed out and taken Holburne's entire squadron, possibly without firing a shot. History would recall him as a great sea captain who dealt a decisive blow to British naval power. Instead, he chose to sit tight. Holburne eventually managed to patch up his battered squadron and sail back to Halifax. Within months, his ships were repaired and back at sea. Then typhoid broke out in the French fleet. Over 1,000 sailors died during and after the voyage to Brest that November, and another 10,000 died that winter as the disease spread on shore. It would take years for the French fleet to recover those losses.

What explains La Motte's timidity if not cowardice? Marine minister Moras was partly to blame for sending La Motte ambiguous orders. La Motte's mission was "to foil the projects which the enemy have made against Louisbourg or Quebec." However, Moras instructed, if he "will find himself able to attack them with advantage . . . his first object must be to assure the safety of the places which the enemy may wish to attack to threaten." This La Motte had done. But then the marine minister insisted that "the best means of securing the failure of their plans will be to destroy the fleet and transports. . . . With such forces he should have superiority over the enemies." Having said that, Moras then cautioned La Motte to act "without too greatly risking the forces committed to his care, the safe keeping of which so vitally affects the navy."[46]

As the standoff between Loudoun and La Motte droned on, Montcalm captured and destroyed yet another frontier fort.[47] But this triumph did not lighten his deepening gloom. The corruption, fierce winters, lack of supplies, and endless wilderness were all burdensome enough. But what especially rankled Montcalm was Indian diplomacy: "I have been obliged here to gratify the Indian Nations, who will not leave without me, and am obliged to pass my time with them in ceremonies as tiresome as they are necessary."[48]

Yet Montcalm proved himself a very capable diplomat to the Indians. His reputation soared among them after he had captured Oswego. He and Vaudreuil held a series of councils to which hundreds of warriors gathered. At a council on June 14, the orator for a delegation of Great Lakes chiefs proclaimed, "We wished to see . . . this famous man who, on putting his foot on the ground, has destroyed the English ramparts. From his reputation and his exploits we thought that his head would be lost in the clouds. But behold, you are a little fellow, Father, and it is in your eyes that we find the grandeur of the loftiest pine and the spirit of the eagle."[49]

The French scored an overwhelming diplomatic triumph. When Montcalm arrived at Fort Carillon on July 18, he found awaiting him the largest and most diverse Indian army in history—820 from Saint Lawrence villages and 979 from Great Lakes basin and Ohio valley villages, or 1,799 from 33 tribes in all. When Montcalm added these Indians to the 2,570 troops of the 6 army battalions, 524 marines, 188 gunners, and 3,470 militiamen, he commanded an army of 8,551 men along with 36 cannon and 4 mortars. It would take 247 bateaux to transport this army down Lake George to Fort William Henry.[50]

Just before they embarked for the front, the French learned that, ironically, the starvation of the previous winter and delayed campaign to await the supply ships were completely unnecessary. Incompetence had triumphed along with corruption. An audit of the royal storehouse revealed

enough to feed an army of 12,800 men for a month. If they had made this study two months earlier, Fort William Henry would now be in our hands, and we would have been in position to thrust our advance still farther, instead of which the projected expedition today is quite uncertain. But this study of the wheat supply was against the interests of the Commissary General and his crew, of which the Marquis de Vaudreuil is himself one. They then waited as long as possible, and the delay in the arrival of ships from France at last forced them to take an action which they had been advised to take as early as April. All preparations for the expedition are being hurried in all departments.[51]

The French won two bloody victories even before Montcalm launched his offensive. To Vaudreuil, Montcalm reported that "Lieutenant Marin, of the Colonial troops, who has exhibited a rare audacity . . . carried out a patrol of ten men, and swept away an

ordinary guard of 50 like a wafer; went up to the enemy's camp under
Fort [Edward, where] he was exposed to a severe fire, and retired like
a warrior. . . . He was unwilling to amuse himself taking prisoners; he
brought in only one and 32 scalps." On July 26, Lieutenant Corbiere
"remained in ambush day and night. . . . At break of day the English
appeared on Lake Sacrament [George] to the number of 22 barges,
under the command of Sieur Parker. . . . The whoops of our Indians
impressed them with such terror that they made but a feeble resistance; two barges only escaped; all the others were captured or sunk.
I have 160 prisoners here. . . . About 160 men have been killed or
drowned. These two affairs cost us—that of M. Marin, a Canadian who
died of his wounds, being unable to run, two slightly wounded; that of
M. de Corbiere, one Indian slightly wounded."[52]

The second battle must have been especially horrifying for the
Americans. Bougainville vividly described how the Indians "jumped
into their canoes, pursued the enemy . . . and brought back nearly 200
prisoners. The rest were drowned. The Indians jumped into the water
and speared them like fish, and also sank the barges by seizing them
from below and capsizing them. . . . The English, terrified by the shoot-
ing, the sight, the cries, and the agility of these monsters, surrendered
almost without firing a shot. The rum which was in the barges and
which the Indians immediately drank caused them to commit great
cruelties. They put in a pot and ate three prisoners."[53]

Montcalm sent Lévis and 2,488 men along the trail on Lake
George's western shore on July 30. The next day Montcalm embarked
the rest of his army on a fleet of bateaux and headed south up the lake
as the Indians paddled alongside in 150 canoes. On August 1, these
forces united at Ganaouske Bay, about two-thirds of the way down the
lake. The next day they approached within three miles of the British.
Fort William Henry stood on the lake's southernmost shore. Only 500
troops could cram into its walls. A fortified camp with 1,800 troops
stood several hundred yards away atop a low hill. About one-third of
the troops were British regulars and the rest American provincials.
Colonel George Monro was in command.[54]

Montcalm's troops and the Indians surrounded the two forts on
August 3. The soldiers then began hacking away at the woods and

digging entrenchments for a succession of batteries. The Indians meanwhile "kept up a sharp fire on the fort, repelled several sorties, killed more than one hundred men, took 4 prisoners, killed a hundred beeves, 150 sheep, took 40 oxen and 20 horses." Montcalm sent into Fort William Henry a message under a truce flag in which he pleaded with Monro to surrender before the Indians became unmanageable: "I owe it to humanity to summon you to surrender. At present I can restrain the savages, and make them observe the terms of a capitulation, as I might not have power to do so under other circumstances; and an obstinate defense on your part could only retard the capture of the place a few days, and endanger an unfortunate garrison which cannot be relieved, in consequence of the dispositions I have made. I demand a decisive answer within an hour."[55] Monro rejected Montcalm's plea.

The laborious siege work continued. Montcalm received good news on August 5 when "the Indians brought a prisoner and the vest of a man they killed, in which was found a letter from General [Daniel] Webb . . . to the Commandant of the fort, to the effect that, considering the position of Fort Edward, it did not appear to him prudent to march to the aid of Fort William Henry, or to send him any reinforcements; that he had learned from a French prisoner that the French army is composed of eleven thousand men, two thousand Indians, and is supplied with a considerable train of artillery; that he communicates this intelligence in order that the Commandant . . . may . . . obtain a favorable capitulation."[56]

Rather than immediately send in Webb's message to Monro with another surrender demand, Montcalm chose to reinforce the psychological impact with a bombardment. His first battery was in place on August 6 and promptly opened fire. Troops dug a parallel to another point where another battery was emplaced. The batteries opened fire on August 7. On that day Montcalm revealed Webb's message. Monro remained defiant. The bombardment continued methodically to demolish both forts. By August 9, nearly all of the British cannons had burst from overheating. After tersely counseling with his officers, Monro finally agreed to surrender.

Montcalm offered Monro generous terms. He chose to send home Monro and his troops under parole not to fight for eighteen months rather than feed them in captivity. Though the British could march out with honors of war, they had to leave all their supplies behind. Monro agreed. Writing in the third person, Montcalm explained "that he could not pledge his word . . . before the Indians had accepted them, for which purpose he called a General Council. There he explained the conditions where the English were offering to surrender. . . . He demanded of the chiefs their consent and whether they could answer for their young men not answering the terms. The chiefs unanimously assured him that they approved all he would do and would prevent their young men committing any disorder."[57] Montcalm and Monro then signed the surrender agreement.

The French general had scored yet another nearly bloodless victory. In all, Montcalm's army had captured "36 pieces of ordinance, 2,500 shot, 545 shell, 36 thousand weight of powder, 350 thousand rations . . . two sloops in the harbor, two on the stocks, 4 flat bateaux, and eight barges. In this expedition we have lost 13 men killed and 40 wounded. The English say they have lost 200."[58] That victory, however, would be marred by two events for which Montcalm was ultimately responsible.

Tarnished Victory

The chiefs did not keep their promise. The warriors swarmed over the forts and prisoners, looting, murdering, and capturing hundreds. When Montcalm learned of the mayhem, he "ran thither with almost all the officers; rescued out of their hands all the English he discovered with them, made all reenter the fort who had escaped their fury, and all those return who could not reach Fort Edward without danger."[59] In a letter to war minister Paulmy, Montcalm was philosophical about the atrocities: "I cannot conceal from you that the capitulation has unfortunately suffered some infraction on the part of the Indians. But what would be an infraction in Europe cannot be so regarded in America, and I have written with firmness to General Webb and to Lord Loudon [sic] on the subject, so as to deprive them of all excuse for not observing the terms on a slight pretence."[60] In his letters to

Webb and Loudoun, Montcalm asked them to imagine "what it is to restrain 3,000 Indians of 33 different Nations. . . . I consider myself lucky that the disorder was not attended by consequences as unfortunate as I had reason to fear."[61] Yet Montcalm could have impeded those atrocities had he posted regulars with fixed bayonets around the British to protect them from the Indians. Loudoun would indeed use the "massacre" as an excuse to tear up the surrender document. That freed the 2,000 troops who made it back to Fort Edward immediately to take up arms again.

Even more disturbing is the question of why Montcalm, having taken Fort William Henry, did not immediately march another fourteen miles and besiege Fort Edward. The campaign plan Vaudreuil submitted to Montcalm on July 7 had designated Fort Edward the ultimate objective. Instead, Montcalm hastily reembarked his troops and plunder for the row back to Fort Carillon. The two excuses he gave for disobeying Vaudreuil's order to march on Fort Edward if he took Fort William Henry were at best flimsy—he claimed that the pressure of the Canadians to return to their harvest and the lack of draft animals with which to drag cannon to Fort Edward forced him to retreat.

The draft animal excuse is weak on several points. Surely, Montcalm must have known that he would need draft animals. Since there were few available to take with him, he would have had to rely on capturing Fort William Henry's draft animals. Yet he stood helpless as the Indians rounded up and butchered those at the fort. Had Montcalm deployed troops to back up his army's needs, he would have most likely secured his animals. But this issue was moot. The draft animals were not essential to dragging the guns to Fort Edward; attaching long ropes to the cannons and ammunition carts and having the troops pull them could have accomplished the task just as well. The road between the forts was relatively flat enough to cover the distance in a couple of days at most. The cowardly Webb would probably have been so spooked by that advancing horde that he would most likely have either run or hoisted the white flag.

In a letter penned on August 7, Vaudreuil hoped "this courier will join you at Fort [Edward]. . . . Should we fail to reduce Fort [Edward] this year, we may as well give it up, as we shall never again have such a fine opportunity. . . . Nothing ought to be an impediment to you in that regard."[62] In this, the governor, who lacked any military experience, proved to be far more sagacious than the general, who was a veteran of nearly three decades of warfare. Vaudreuil dismissed the need of the Canadians to return to their fields since enough food was available to succor the colony until next spring's supply fleet arrived.

The Indian army broke up, with each nation's warriors returning with their scalps, prisoners, and plunder to their distant villages. On August 29, Montcalm set off with most of his regulars and Canadians to Montreal, leaving Lévis in charge of Fort Carillon's token winter garrison. He undoubtedly got an icy reception from a disappointed Vaudreuil.[63]

If Vaudreuil's disapproval shamed Montcalm, he did not show it. In each of his two summers in Canada, Montcalm had besieged and captured an important frontier fort. At the cost of a mere handful of casualties, he had bagged nearly five thousand British troops and mountains of supplies at Oswego in 1756 and William Henry in 1757. In doing so, he had overcome numerous obstacles to thwart British offensives for two successive years.

Dazzling as those victories may have seemed, Montcalm squandered them by failing to follow them up. In 1756, had he fortified rather than destroyed and abandoned Oswego, he would have slammed shut the door to any British advance toward Lake Ontario. In 1757, had he marched on Fort Edward, he most likely would have forced the spineless Webb to surrender. If so, nothing but a few militia companies would have stood between his army and Albany. Montcalm could have triumphantly wintered there on British rations. Then, in the spring of 1758, he might well have repelled a massive British assault on his Albany entrenchments, just as he actually did at Fort Carillon that summer. After all, General James Abercromby, the butcher of his own army in the assault against Fort Carillon in July 1758, would have commanded those British forces.

Vaudreuil made this argument to Versailles. As he had in 1756, the governor stole credit for Montcalm's 1757 victory, while heaping on the general blame for all that had gone wrong. He blasted Montcalm for failing to march on to Fort Edward: "I even wrote to the Marquis de Montcalm, on the seventh of [August], to . . . impress upon him still more the importance of this second expedition. . . . He had only about six leagues of a very fine road before reaching Fort [Edward], and I am confident that the reduction of the first fort would have inevitably drawn down that of the second."[64]

In weighing the conflicting reports of the general and governor, Versailles sided with the latter. Versailles noted with royal disapproval Montcalm's failure

> pursuant to the Marquis de Vaudreuil's orders, to attack Fort . . . Edward, after having reduced Fort . . . William Henry. . . . Montcalm's reasons for having confined himself to the capture of Fort George are, the fear of wanting provisions, the necessity of sending back the Canadians to save their crops, and the difficulties of reducing Fort [Edward], which was defended by a strong garrison. . . . The Marquis de Vaudreuil submits in his letter, which is also annexed, some observations that do not accord with those of the Marquis de Montcalm. He appears much pained that Fort Edward had not been attacked. . . . Could it have been destroyed like Fort George, the enemy would have been obliged to make Albany the entrepôt of their expeditions, where 'twould have been easy even to force them to keep on the defensive, since nothing would have prevented our attacking that place or making other attacks in that quarter.[65]

Here in the tug-of-war between Vaudreuil and Montcalm for the hearts and minds of the king and his ministers, the governor had clearly triumphed and the general had stumbled badly.

Unaware that Vaudreuil was undercutting him, Montcalm fired off his own report to Versailles lauding his latest victory and lamenting worsening shortages of troops, provisions, and money. Two years of frontier campaigns and sheer survival had whittled the army's ranks. So far, the reinforcements that Versailles had sent had failed to keep his battalions at full strength. Montcalm's alarm at this seethed beneath his courtly missive to the war minister: "Since our receipt of

326 recruits, I am able to raise all the companies to 39. You perceive, my Lord, that we are very far from . . . the augmentations authorized to fix all the companies at 50. . . . 'Tis asserted that the English have captured about 600 recruits in divers ships; 'tis much to be feared that no more will arrive."[66] Montcalm explained that it was not enough to send more troops—they along with those soldiers and marines in Canada had to be fed when New France already suffered a severe "want of provisions. The people reduced to a quarter of a pound of bread. It will be probably necessary to reduce still further the solders' ration. Little powder; no shoes."[67]

With these lines, Montcalm captured the essence of the dilemma facing Versailles in New France. Even in those rare times when peace prevailed and harvests escaped early frosts, Canada could barely feed its own people. Now, Canada had nearly five thousand more hungry bellies to fill. Versailles somehow had to find the proper troop level that defended but did not starve New France. British naval superiority grossly fouled that task. Warships flying the Union Jack fired shots across the bows of French ships laden with food, munitions, Indian gifts, and recruits wallowing through the high seas or, ever more frequently, even the Saint Lawrence Gulf. Just how much was Versailles willing to lose to keep New France?[68]

Montcalm got his commissary chief, Captain André Doreil, to write his own letter to Versailles elaborating just how destitute the army had become: "The critical moment is arrived; the funds are exhausted; the battalions . . . no longer receive their pay in French coin since the first of September."[69]

Yet by one glaring measure there was already too much money circulating. Ever greater demand for dwindling supplies sent prices soaring. That demand was exacerbated by the flood of new currency submerging the economy. Bougainville estimated that of the paper money notes used by the French army to pay for expenses, "twelve million have been taken to the treasury . . . [and] at least a million more [are] in private hands, [plus] . . . a million in card money, 500,000 livres in beaver notes, 600,000 livres in species in gold and silver. That makes today more than seventeen million circulating in a country where in 1730 they had barely 800,000 livres. Whence has come this quantity of money, so greatly increased in so short a time? From the enormous sums paid by the King in this colony."[70]

Through his own reports and those of his subordinate, Montcalm paraded his triumphs and tribulations. He then raised the delicate question of promotion. He reminded his war minister to remind the king that he was "entering on my 36th year of service; I date from 1721. I am the only Major-General commanding . . . a corps of troops and small armies 1,500 leagues off, having made two successful campaigns and sieges. But if I be made Lieutenant-General, can I be under the orders of a Captain of a ship; he is Governor-General. . . . Can I be promoted without favors being conferred on the Marquis de Vaudreuil?"[71] Here Montcalm presented the politics entangling protocol and command. In previous letters, he had tossed compliments Vaudreuil's way while hinting that the man knew nothing of military affairs. And yet Montcalm was Vaudreuil's subordinate. Unspoken but perhaps as irritating to the aristocratic general was that Vaudreuil was a colonial born and bred.

Though Versailles failed to alleviate the shortage of men, food, and money, it did agree to do what it did best—dispense honors. As will be seen, the king's confused attempt to elevate the general's status and power in 1759 only worsened the relationship between Montcalm and Vaudreuil. This split and antagonistic command merely reflected that between the ministries of war and marine.

Tragically for New France, bitter differences were not confined to the governor and general. Montcalm made an astonishing claim to war minister Paulmy: "In regard to our troops, I have established the greatest political harmony. There will never be anything else between our officers and theirs."[72] Actually, the animosities between French and Canadian officers and troops alike were worsening and would contribute to, if not cause, the colony's ruin. The general's own attitudes and policies poisoned his hope for harmony. His refusal to permit French officers smitten with Canadian lasses to marry beneath their station epitomized the snobbery of not just himself but France's nobility.

The Global Struggle

The war spread to a third continent in 1757 when the tense truce the French and English had established in India in 1755 broke down. As with most truces, each side had positioned itself for the next war. Sepoy, or native, troop ranks swelled. Reinforcements and munitions arrived from Europe. Bidding wars raged for the loyalty and troops of local princes. Fighting had erupted in 1756 but between the British and the Bengal nabob or ruler, Suraja Dowlah, who was financed and goaded by the French to destroy Britain's presence in the region. Dowlah almost succeeded. He captured most of the British trading posts in Bengal, including their headquarters at Calcutta. Robert Clive led the small army that defeated the nabob and forced him to sign on February 9, 1757, a treaty by which each promised to restore the status quo ante bellum.

By this time, word finally reached India of the war between France and Britain. Charles-Joseph Patissier de Bussy promptly gathered a small army and marched to reinforce Fort Orléans, the French headquarters in Bengal at Chandernagore on the Hugli River. Clive got to the fort first. On March 23, after a two week siege, Clive forced the fort's commander, Captain Renault, to sign an agreement whereby the French gave up all their trading posts in Bengal. Upon hearing of the capitulation, Bussy prudently retreated to the Malabar region.

Clive followed up this triumph by trying to enlist the nabob against the French. When Dowlah rejected the pressure, Clive turned to a rival for the nabob's throne, Meer Jaffier. On June 4, 1757, the two men signed a treaty whereby the British would topple Dowlah and make Jaffier the new nabob if Jaffier conquered the French posts in Bengal and handed them over to Britain. On June 13, Clive set off up the Hugli River against the nabob. The two armies met at Plassey on June 23. About 50 French advisors and gunners accompanied the nabob's army, which may have numbered as many as 34,000 infantry and 15,000 cavalry; Clive had about 1,000 Europeans and 2,000 sepoys. Nonetheless, Clive's small army routed the nabob's and won for Britain the provinces of Bengal, Orissa, and Behar. With this region largely secure, the British could concentrate on defending their vulnerable posts on the Malabar and Coromandel Coasts. There, the French captured several small British trading posts by the year's end. But the decisive battles for that region lay in subsequent years.

While they lost Bengal, the French held their own in the West Indies. There, naval squadrons and privateers from each side tried to cripple the other economically by hunting down its richly laden merchant ships. To counter this threat, both powers assembled huge convoys of vessels together at their key ports before sailing across the Atlantic. With five ships of the line, Admiral Joseph de Bauffremont, prince de Listenois, prowled the Caribbean for British prey. He just missed a British convoy of 170 ships that sailed from the West Indies in June packed with 2 million pounds sterling worth of uninsured goods, though he did pick off many single vessels. On October 21, a 150-ship convoy guarded by Captain Kersaint de Coetnempren with 4 ships of the line sailed from Cap François into the guns of three blockading warships commanded by Captain Arthur Forrest. As the British veered down on the convoy, Kersaint met them. After a series of broadsides, Kersaint retired to Cap François and Forrest's ships straggled off to Port Royal. The convoy escaped to France. Forrest was luckier after he joined Admiral Thomas Cotes in November; they captured a ten-ship convoy shortly after it left Port-au-Prince.[73]

It took months for war news from North America or the West Indies to reach Versailles, and that from India took nearly a year. But only days passed for relays of post riders to convey word from Germany. By late summer, news from that front was promising, though Versailles and its allies would ultimately be disappointed by the failure of their generals to follow up their victories. What one might call the "Montcalm syndrome" characterized the pre-Napoleonic age.

France's limited victories that summer at Fort William Henry, Louisbourg, Kloster Zeven, and Rochefort gave Versailles a chance to reopen negotiations with England from a powerful position. Once again, Versailles threw away that advantage. It did, however, sign a secret treaty with Sweden on September 22, 1757, whereby France promised Stockholm to help protect Swedish Pomerania. In doing so, Louis and his council thought they had secured an enemy to the rear of both Ferdinand and Frederick. But the treaty was meaningless.

France was in no position to send troops to Pomerania while Sweden had already joined the alliance against Prussia.

At first, Russia opposed the alliance between France and Sweden, but grudgingly agreed when Whitehall blundered. Fearing Prussia's encirclement, the British threatened to send a fleet to the Baltic and warned Saint Petersburg not to interfere. The threat aroused Russian pride. Elizabeth ordered the Russian fleet to sea with orders to join with Sweden's fleet against the British. Whitehall eventually backed down, but the diplomatic damage had been done. On November 16, 1757, Elizabeth signed the treaty of alliance with France, Austria, and Sweden.[74]

Despite Russian general Apraxin's fearful withdrawal from a few days' march from undefended Berlin back into Poland, Frederick's position was still perilous. In early October, a small Croat army under Count Andreas Hadik von Futak actually reached the Berlin's outskirts. There, to his dismay, he learned that the Russian and Swedish armies had retired into winter quarters. After taking a 27,000-taler bribe, he also withdrew into Poland. Meanwhile, two massive enemy armies marched ever-closer to Frederick, that of Sachsen-Hildburghausen and Soubise from the west and that of Daun and Charles Alexander, prince of Lorraine from the south.

For Frederick, desperate times called for desperate measures. As the circle of enemy armies crawled toward him that autumn, he secretly opened communications with Louis XV over a possible separate peace. Vienna once again found out and criticized Versailles for even considering the possibility. Louis kept his commitment and urged Soubise to march on with Sachsen-Hildburghausen against Frederick. The French king and his court soon greatly regretted doing so.[75]

When the Austrian advance slowed, Frederick struck at the French and Imperial army. On November 5, Frederick won at Rossbach his first decisive victory of the war; his 21,000 troops inflicted over 7,700 casualties on the 41,000 allied troops at the cost of only 550 Prussians killed and wounded. Soubise did not stop his retreat until he reached Frankfort. Not all the French casualties were in the field. Though the wound was slight, Pompadour was pained that her favorite, Soubise, had been humiliated. She clung to Soubise even after his incompetence was glaringly apparent to nearly all, including the king.

Frederick had little time to savor his victory—as always, new dangers arose. General Ferenc Lipot Nadasdy captured 7,000 Prussian troops, 330,000 thalers, and two months' worth of supplies at Schweidnitz on November 16. Prince Charles routed August Wilhelm, Brunswick-Bevern's army on November 21, captured him in the pursuit, then forced Breslau's surrender. To worsen matters, in Hanover, Richelieu showed signs of movement. Richelieu's threat, however, was easily checked. Prince Ferdinand stood in his way at the head of an army rebuilt with a £1.2 million subsidy voted by Britain's Parliament. On November 28, Ferdinand informed Richelieu that he had repudiated the Convention of Kloster Zeven and immediately marched against him. Richelieu retreated his army beyond the Weser into winter quarters.

Frederick had one throw of the dice left. On December 5, he hurled his 43,000 troops at the combined 72,000-man Austrian army of Charles and Daun at Leuthen. While suffering 6,500 casualties, Prussian troops devoured swaths of the Austrian army, inflicting 3,000 dead and 7,000 wounded, and capturing 12,000 troops and 131 cannons. The Austrian army's remnants retreated to Konigsgratz. Frederick then recaptured Breslau along with 17,000 prisoners on December 18. The Austrians held out only at Schweidnitz. Meanwhile, General Lehwaldt checked another advance by Hamilton's Swedes and drove them back into Stralsund. Only then did Frederick II send his exhausted troops into winter quarters.

Amidst the seesaw carnage in Germany, the diplomatic debacles could be just as startling. Until late 1757, France had avoided seeking an outright alliance with Spain, fearing that it would be a deadweight. In October, Versailles renewed its diplomatic offensive to get Spain in the war, hoping to force the already stretched British fleet beyond the ability to blockade so many enemy ports effectively. France's new ambassador to Spain, Henri Joseph Bouchard d'Esparbès de Lussan, marquis de Aubeterre, was instructed to query Ferdinand VI on joining their Bourbon kingdoms against England. Though the offer initially intrigued Ferdinand, the French debacle at Rossbach scuttled his hope that France would prevail in Germany.[76]

Consequences

All during 1757, Louis XV could not shake off the emotional blow of his near murder. His depression persisted and eventually infected his council. Horace Walpole reported that the king "threw a damp on all operations: melancholic, apprehensive of assassinations, desirous of resigning the crown, averse to the war from principles of humanity, perplexed by factions, and still resigned to the influence of his mistress, every measure was confirmed by him with reluctance or obtained by intrigue."[77] On August 5, 1757, an English spy reported that the king was worse than ever: "Ever since the attempt on the King's life by Damiens, His Majesty has been daily growing more uneasy and melancholy. Lately, He has frequently burst into tears; and, at times, discovered an inclination to resign the Crown. At first, this was only regarded as an Effect of His melancholy; and it was hoped would pass with it. But having lately persisted in so extraordinary a resolution, the whole Court is alarmed. The Queen, the Dauphin, Madame de Pompadour, the Nuncio, the Confessor, and several of the Court, who were honored with his Majesty's Confidence, were employed to prevent the accomplishment of so ill-timed a design."[78]

Damiens's attack cast a pall over more than the king's mind. In April 1757, Pompadour could not prevent Louis from issuing a royal edict that promised death for "all those who shall be convicted of having written or printed any works intended to attack religion, to assail the royal authority, or to disturb the order and tranquility of the realm."[79] This decree cast a dark legal shadow on the French Enlightenment. The philosophes increasingly diverted their work from Paris to publishers in Geneva and The Hague.

One good thing did come of Damiens's attack. The sympathy aroused for Louis and suspicions of a conspiracy briefly humbled parlement. The crisis that had exploded the previous December was resolved on September 5, 1757, when the king let the sixteen exiled members return to Paris in return for parlement's acceptance of the December 10, 1756, declaration. This latest truce between the king and parlement would not last long.

The king's despair infected everyone in the council and court, perhaps no one more than Bernis. By New Year's Eve, France's failures had sunk Bernis into a deep depression. He had much to lament. After Rossbach, the realm's creditors hoarded their money or demanded exorbitant interest rates to keep France solvent. The war and the king became increasingly unpopular. Those who once attacked Louis through his mistress now openly and somewhat contradictorily scorned Bernis as an inane despot and Pompadour's pet. Bernis felt hopeless to arrest France's declining prospects: "What remains for me—the Minister for Foreign Affairs—to do? Nothing but to prophesy and announce defeats, to depress my friends and myself. . . . It is useless for me to scribble and ponder if we cannot wage war effectively. . . . History knows no example of a country playing for such high stakes with the insouciance of people taking part in a quadrille—the idea of a Prime Minister frightens everybody but without one there is no government."[80] Bernis envisioned himself in that role. He was confident that with enough power he could lead France out of its military, economic, and diplomatic morass. It is unlikely that his skills or emotions matched his ambitions.

Bernis feared that "If we win we cannot follow up our victory for lack of supplies and if we lose we shall be driven out of Hanover, Westphalia, Hesse, and the Low Countries. . . . The Russians are the cause of our troubles; they must now move rapidly to relieve us."[81] The foreign minister was half-right. Apraxin failed to follow up his victories with bold advances against the rear of Frederick's army. The same charge, of course, could be levied against Richelieu and Montcalm. Yet ultimately the blame ricochets back against Louis XV and his council. It was they who, by failing to take advantage of diplomatic openings and by appointing bumbling generals, had bogged the nation down into a war that increasingly seemed unwinnable.

View of the Grand Trianon, Seen from the Avenue in 1723, by Pierre Denis Martin.
© RMN-Grand Palais / Art Resource, N.Y.

Louis XV, by Maurice Quentin de la Tour. Alfred Dagli Orti / The Art Archive at Art Resource, N.Y.

Marquis de Pompadour, by François Boucher. © RMN-Grand Palais /
Art Resource, N.Y.

Cardinal de Bernis. © RMN-Grand Palais / Art Resource, N.Y.

Duc de Choiseul-Stainville, by Louis Michael van Loo. © RMN-Grand
Palais / Art Resource, N.Y.

Pierre de Rigaud de Vaudreuil de Cavagnial, Marquis de Vaudreuil, by Donat
Nonnotte. Library and Archives Canada, reproduction copy number C-147536.

Louis Joseph Marquis de Montcalm, by Théophile Hamel. House of Commons Heritage Collection, Ottawa, Canada.

Louis Antoine, comte de Bougainville, by Joseph Ducreux. © RMN-Grand Palais / Art Resource, N.Y.

Montcalm and Languedoc Regiment, Fort Carillon, July 1758, by Eugène Leliepvre.
Beaverbrook Collection of War Art, © Canadian War Museum.

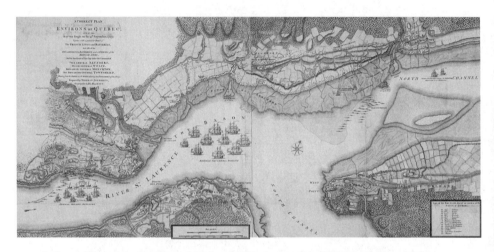

A Correct Plan of the Environs of Quebec, 1759, engraved by Thomas Jefferys. Library and Archives Canada, reproduction copy number e010769953.

Cap Lagos, Victory of Admiral Boscawen, by Richard Perret. Beaverbrook Collection of War Art, © Canadian War Museum.

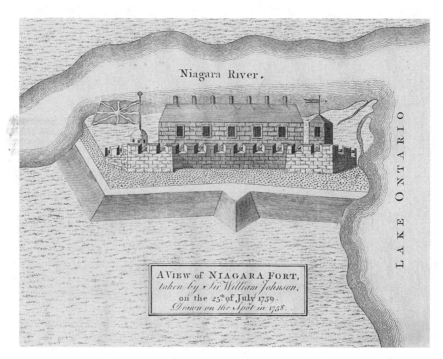

A View of Niagara Fort, anonymous sketch. Beaverbrook Collection of War Art, © Canadian War Museum.

The Plains of Abraham, by William Henry Bartlett. Beaverbrook Collection of War Art, © Canadian War Museum.

A View of the Orphan's or Urseline Nunnery, taken from the Ramparts, by Richard Short. Beaverbrook Collection of War Art, © Canadian War Museum.

The Death of General Wolfe, by Benjamin West. Beaverbrook Collection of War Art, © Canadian War Museum.

The Years of Defeats

CHAPTER 8

Turning Point, 1758

The English have involved us in a war in Germany while we lose our colonies, our commerce, and our life.

Bernis to Hôpital

Great misfortune for this country; it will perish, victim of its prejudices, of its blind confidence, of the stupidity or the roguery of its chiefs.

Bougainville

I found Your Majesty's Army divided into three parts. The first, which is above ground, is composed of thieves and marauders. The second is already under ground, and the third is in the hospitals.

Clermont to Louis XV

Here old men covered with wounds, beheld their wives, hugging their children to their bloody breasts, massacred before their faces; there, their daughters, disemboweled and breathing their last after having satisfied the natural wants of . . . heroes. . . . The Earth was strewed with brains, arms, and legs.

Voltaire, *Candide*

The year 1758 was no different for French strategists than any that had preceded it. A French victory in the war clearly depended on holding New France and taking Hanover. Those goals, of course, depended on a myriad of others. New France's defense did not rely only on Montcalm's ability to capture and destroy Britain's frontier forts. Eventually, the British would find a competent enough general and amass enough regular and provincial troops in North America to steamroll any French force before them. Versailles had to send enough fresh troops and supplies to New France to counter the steady buildup of British troops. So far, Versailles had done that. But Britain's tightening blockade picked off ever more supply ships dispatched to Quebec. All this made it imperative to overrun Hanover as soon as possible. And this depended on the skills and grit of French and allied generals. New France would be won or lost in Germany.

As 1758 opened, Louis XV's council agreed that if Russia were prodded into a more sustained, vigorous offensive, Frederick would be pinned down and possibly crushed. The fear was that the Russians would be just as balky this year as they had been the last. To the French ambassador at Vienna, Étienne-François, comte de Stainville (he became known as duc de Choiseul in August of this year), Bernis wrote that "Russia alone at this moment can restore the balance and give us breathing space." Though he despaired of that coming true, Bernis insisted that the Russian alliance must be preserved "even if she does nothing for us so that she may do nothing against us."[1] To that end, a dispute arose between Bernis and Broglie, ambassador to Poland. Hoping to induce a greater war effort from Saint Petersburg, Bernis ordered Broglie to pressure the Poles into allowing Russians to base troops in Danzig and acquire the Duchy of Courland. Still committed to a strong Poland, Broglie dug in his heels. On February 1, 1758, Bernis sacked him.

Louis XV had lost his man in Warsaw, the field commander of his secret du roi. It was no great loss. The king's secret du roi tended to foul rather than advance French interests. The Poles erupted in impotent fury against the march of Russian troops into Danzig and Kovno, Courland's eastern gate. France had finally given up in its long struggle with Russia over Poland's fate when Versailles conceded Poland to Saint Petersburg's sphere of influence and got nothing of substance in return. It was just the latest French retreat.

Versailles's worst nightmare with Russia involved Empress Elizabeth's death, pro-Prussian Peter's ascension to the throne, and a

Russian alliance with Prussia that let Frederick launch knockout blows first against Austria then against France. In January 1758, Versailles concocted a harebrained scheme to avert that dreaded possibility. Johanna Elisabeth, the princess of Anhalt-Zerbst despised her son-in-law Peter. Empress Elizabeth had expelled Princess Johanna from Saint Petersburg for intriguing on behalf of her daughter Catherine. Though exiled in Anhalt-Zerbst, Johanna was thought to still strongly influence Catherine. Hoping to get to the daughter through the mother, Versailles dispatched Jean Jacques Gilbert, marquis de Fraigne, to swing Johanna to France. Learning of the scheme, Frederick sent troops to invade Anhalt-Zerbst and capture Fraigne at Johanna's palace on January 19. The aborted and well-publicized plot embarrassed Versailles. Peter's suspicion and hatred of France deepened, along with his adoration of Frederick, who now was his savior as well as his hero.

But Peter was isolated from the Russian council. It was Chancellor Bestuzhev who remained the biggest impediment to a vigorous alliance against Frederick. In February, to the enormous relief of Russia's allies, Elizabeth ordered Bestuzhev arrested when he appeared at Apraxin's court-martial. He was eventually found guilty of delaying that general's advance, but Elizabeth commuted his death penalty to Siberian exile. Dramatic as Bestuzhev's arrest, trial, and exile were, not much had changed. English ambassador Hanbury-Williams simply outbid his French counterpart Hôpital in corrupting onetime Francophile ministers Mikhail Vorontsov and Ivan Shuvalov. The Russians again dragged their military feet so thoroughly that Louis gently complained of it in a letter to Elizabeth. The expected but unwanted answer was that the pace of Russia's advance depended on the number of troops and supplies sent to the army, which was, of course, increasingly immensely expensive. Saint Petersburg wanted Versailles to sign the January 1757 treaty between Russia and Austria whereby the latter paid huge subsidies for the former's armies. The Russians maintained that without French subsidies reinforcements could not be sent to armies already in the field.[2]

Versailles desisted from any formal alliance with Russia that included direct subsidies. The alliance with Austria alone drained France of vast amounts of treasure and blood. Versailles certainly did not support Maria Theresa's goal of destroying Frederick and Prussia.

The rivalry between Prussia and Austria diverted money, soldiers, and energies that could otherwise threaten French interests and ambitions. Thus, Versailles's goal was for victory over Prussia to be limited rather than total.

The alliance with Austria remained unpopular with many at Versailles, especially the vociferous and enthusiastic fans of "enlightened" Frederick. As the war dragged on and the death and debt toll rose, more voices were raised against France's ties with its old enemy. Even the man who had negotiated the alliance began to have second thoughts. To Ambassador Choiseul at Vienna, Bernis wrote, "Believe me, without peace we will perish and we will be dishonored. . . . We need peace because all our affairs are in disorder and the treasury is empty."[3]

Bernis had dispatched Choiseul to Vienna to implore Maria Theresa and her council for a peace based on the status quo ante bellum. On April 20, Choiseul reported that she had agreed to the French peace proposal. A thrilled and rejuvenated Bernis got to work. Dejection followed when the official Austrian response reached Versailles on May 9. Under the influence of Kaunitz and other advisors, Maria Theresa had backpedaled to the point of making a mirage of her verbal promise to Choiseul. Now, she and her council merely agreed that Versailles could send peace feelers to England and Prussia.

Bernis continued to press Choiseul to change Maria Theresa's mind. Choiseul refused, explaining that Maria Theresa and her court were dead set to crush Frederick; pressing for peace now would simply cause the Austrians to question France's commitment.[4] Pompadour had had a strong hand in turning Maria Theresa against peace. She and the empress corresponded regularly. Choiseul knew well that pushing peace would jeopardize his own position with Pompadour; refusing to do so would elevate him in her eyes, while exacerbating her quarrels with Bernis. Pompadour would see Choiseul as the new white knight to champion her policies. Whether or not he was fully aware of Choiseul's ambitions, Bernis affably supported them. He asked Choiseul to "reflect seriously on an idea that I have had for a long time. I believe that you would be a fitter man than I at the Ministry of Foreign Affairs, from the point of view of the alliance."[5] Choiseul must have smiled wryly at that suggestion.

On the European chessboard, no piece was too trivial to neglect. Denmark's neutrality was highly valued. If Denmark joined England and Prussia, a British fleet could sail into the Baltic and cut off Swedish and Russian supply ships from their armies in Germany. Denmark had its own ambitions—its neutrality could be bought in return for Holstein. There was a significant obstacle for that acquisition to take place—Russian grand duke Peter was born and bred in Holstein. And Peter had his own ambitions. Between Holstein and Denmark lay Schleswig, which Peter had long openly demanded to join to his own realm. Peter's ambition had been thwarted by Sweden, Denmark, and Prussia, which all asserted claims to Schleswig as well. The result was a standoff between the conflicting ambitions of Denmark and Peter.

France and Denmark signed a treaty on May 4, 1758, whereby Copenhagen promised to remain neutral if Versailles pressured Saint Petersburg to relinquish the Duchy of Holstein in return for other lands. Once again Versailles's diplomacy complicated and undercut rather than advanced French interests. It should have been obvious that Peter would never give up his birth place and that any attempts to convince him otherwise would enflame his hatred of France. That is exactly what happened when Ambassador Hôpital began making the rounds of officials to curry support for Holstein's transfer to Denmark. So Versailles then reversed its policy by sacrificing its newfound influence with Denmark, again to the end of getting the Russians to fight harder against Frederick, and again attaining similar results: the Russians marched no faster.[6]

Until 1758, Versailles had firmly supported Schleswig's independence. Now that support wavered. A showdown erupted in October 1758 when Danish troops marched into Schleswig and massed on the border with Holstein. Peter was incensed and got Elizabeth to demand that the Danes retire. In this dispute, Versailles chose to sit on the fence, thus infuriating both the Danes and the Russians.

Unlike Versailles, Whitehall did not hesitate to fund its own allies, especially Prussia. Not only did Britain's virtuous cycle of naval and trade power give it the wealth to do so, but the cabinet agreed that it was better to send money than troops to Germany. On April 11, 1758, Britain and Prussia signed a subsidy treaty whereby Whitehall would grant Potsdam £670,000 that year, maintain a 55,000-man German army to defend western Germany, coordinate its strategy with Frederick, divert Versailles with raids on the French coast, and establish a base at Emden at the mouth of the Ems River at the North Sea. Neither side could sign a separate peace. Now two treaties bound England to Prussia, the 1758 subsidy treaty atop the 1756 Westminster Treaty. The subsidy treaty had to be renewed annually.[7]

Although the cabinet was divided over just what Britain should win from the war, no one hungered more for conquest than George II. The king demanded that the army and navy take as much from France as possible and return nothing. Pitt eventually became as voracious for expansion as the king, but at this point he was willing to compromise. Just what prizes to demand at any future bargaining table depended, of course, on the fortunes of war.

All of these diplomatic maneuvers had little effect on France's ability to wage war. By 1758, Whitehall had 138 ships of the line—of which 10 were captured from the French—to Versailles's 77 ships of the line. Britain's shipyards would launch 10 more ships of the line that year. With its overwhelming naval power, the British systematically destroyed French shipping. In 1758 alone, the British captured 15 French warships, 49 privateers, and 104 merchant ships, along with 176 Dutch ships carrying French goods. Those naval victories cost the British little—3 warships and 8 privateers. French privateers, however, managed to seize 313 British merchant ships.[8] Most of the French warship losses occurred in two large naval battles.

In January, Versailles ordered Admiral Ange Duquesne-Menneville to sail his squadron from Toulon, join Admiral Jean François Bertet de La Clue-Sabran's fleet at Cartagena, and together sail to Brest. On February 25, Duquesne was off Cartagena and signaled La Clue to join him. The message from a junior admiral upset La Clue's sense of protocol; he petulantly kept his ships at anchor for three precious days as alerted British squadrons converged. On February 28, a gale shoved Duquesne's ships before the guns of an approaching British fleet. The British caught up to and battered into surrender two French ships as the rest scattered to neutral Spanish ports. One was the sixty-four-gun *Orphee*. The other was Duquesne's flagship, the eighty-gun *Foudroyant*.

Such was the humiliating end of the naval career of the same man who had ordered French troops into the Ohio valley, thus sparking the crisis with Britain that later exploded into war.

In April, Admiral Edward Hawke's seven ships of the line flushed a French convoy of forty merchant ships, five ships of the line, and seven frigates that had just emerged from Rochefort bound for Louisbourg. As usual, the French commander chose to run rather than stand and fight. The French ships scattered like a covey of quail. The captains ordered their cannon dumped overboard as they sailed their ships onto the mudflats. Though the ships were saved, those vital supplies would stay in France rather than feed and arm Canada.

The British naval war demolished French trade with its colonies, which plummeted from 30 million livres in 1755, to 8 million in 1758, then 4 million by 1760.[9] Trade was a vital link in the circular chain of French power. With that trade link destroyed, France was all but helpless. Bernis understood this and to Choiseul despaired, "No trade left, consequently no money or circulation. No navy, consequently no strength to resist England. The navy has no more sailors, and having no money, cannot hope to procure them. What must be the result of this state of affairs? The loss of all our colonies for ever; our land forces cannot protect our coasts. . . . I tell you . . . that even if the King of Prussia were crushed, we should be ruined none the less. England carries on all the trade there is, and we shall never reduce her to reasonable conditions unless we can interrupt it."[10]

Versailles hoped to offset its loss of the sea with the weight of its armies in Germany. In 1758, the French army included 395 battalions and 236 squadrons, of which two-thirds were deployed in Germany while only 12 battalions served in New France and 4 in India.[11] The combined armies of France, Austria, Russia, and Sweden outnumbered those of Britain and Prussia by three to one. Yet those allies never coordinated their strategies or matched the tactical brilliance of their enemies. Time and again, Frederick and Ferdinand beat each converging army in turn.

No matter who served as war minister, no one succeeded in forging a common strategy among the allies. War minister Paulmy's amateurish reign ended on May 3, 1758, when Louis replaced him with

Belle Isle, the first professional soldier to hold that position during the war. He would not bring to the administration the same élan and skill he had displayed on a dozen battlefields. Belle Isle was then a frail seventy-three years old, crippled in spirit by the hopelessness of his task and in health by old war wounds, erysipelas, and sciatica.

Nor did the new marine minister prove any more capable. Moras resigned in May. Many gasped when the king replaced him with Claude Louis d'Espinchal, marquis de Massiac, on May 31, 1758. Massiac was the first naval officer tapped for the job, but he had built his career on capturing ever-higher bureaucratic positions rather than enemy warships. How he did it is unclear, but before becoming marine minister he rose to admiral in 1751, commandant of Toulon in 1752, and courtier at Versailles in 1754. He would not last long in his newest post.[12]

Equally divided were the French army commanders who shared nothing but a rich mutual antipathy that caused them to spend more time squabbling and snubbing one another than marching against France's enemies. In February 1758, Louis de Bourbon-Condé, comte de Clermont, was Richelieu's lackluster replacement. If nothing else, the new general was capable of the occasional bon mot. After several days with his army, he wrote Louis that "I found Your Majesty's Army divided into three parts. The first, which is above ground, is composed of thieves and marauders. The second is already under ground, and the third is in the hospitals."[13] But all the world's wit cannot win a battle.

Neither Clermont nor Soubise did much to alleviate the chaos in their ranks. The fighting in Germany began early that year. In March, Ferdinand's troops captured Minden while two British frigates packed with troops sailed up the Weser and took Emden. Clermont retreated before Ferdinand until he crossed over to the Rhine's west bank at Emmerich, thereby surrendering all of last year's conquests. All the while Soubise was deaf to Clermont's pleas to march to his aid. Gambling that his superior generalship could prevail, Ferdinand crossed the Rhine after him. His gamble paid off; his troops sharply defeated the French at Crefeld on June 29.

A British army with Ferdinand might have turned that field victory into something more decisive. Yet, once again, Pitt chose to launch a raid on the French coast rather than commit those troops to Germany. He justified his strategy with the hope that it would draw French forces from Germany. That would prove to be a futile hope. On June 5, over 150 transports packed with 13,000 troops, 22 ships of the line, and 8 frigates commanded by Admiral Richard Howe dropped anchor in Cancalle Bay, eight miles from Saint Malo. The army commander, Charles Spencer, the latest Duke of Marlborough, proved to be a pale successor to his illustrious grandfather.

Leaving a brigade to defend his landing place, Marlborough marched the rest of his troops toward Saint Malo. There the British burned over thirty privateers and one hundred other vessels in the undefended harbor but retreated with word that a superior French army under Brittany's governor, Emmanuel Armand, duc d'Aiguillon, was approaching from the west. Marlborough reembarked his troops and sailed to Granville twenty miles east of Saint Malo. Foul weather prevented the British from landing there or later at Cherbourg, so the fleet returned to Portsmouth.

Meanwhile, as usual, the seesaw German war tilted the other way. In June, upon sending Pompadour's favorite, Soubise, packing as the Upper Rhine army commander, Broglie promptly advanced against Ferdinand's rear and defeated an enemy force at Sandershausen on July 23. Ferdinand withdrew east of the Rhine and, by forced marches, managed to get ahead of Broglie's army. Despite his retreat, Ferdinand's earlier victory at Crefeld emboldened Pitt to send him six thousand British troops commanded by Marlborough. Using Emden as his supply port, Marlborough and his command joined Ferdinand at Coslin on August 21.

Pitt, however, had not yet given up on his obsession with raiding the French coast. Deaf to appeals from Ferdinand and Frederick for more troops, he instead launched not one but two more raids. On August 6, the British fleet, again commanded by Admiral Howe, bombarded Cherbourg. Two days later, General Edward Bligh led the troops ashore and drove off three thousand French troops. Without fortifications facing the land, Cherbourg could not be defended and was surrendered. Bligh's troops looted and burned much of the city and destroyed or sailed back to England thirty-five French ships.[14]

The expedition then sailed to Saint Lunaire Bay, twelve miles east of Saint Malo. Foul weather prevented all of Bligh's force from landing until September 5, when there was a brief lull before the weather worsened. Howe informed Bligh that he must sail or else risk the winds and waves driving his fleet onto the rocky shore. They agreed to rendezvous at Saint Cast nine miles west of Saint Malo. It was an extremely dangerous operation, but they had no choice. Bligh marched his troops west, skirted Saint Malo, brushed aside small French forces, and reached Saint Cast on September 9. Learning of the raid, Governor Aiguillon quickly gathered 7,000 troops and marched to meet Bligh. The French arrived on September 11 just as Bligh was hastily packing his troops in boats, which had been rowed through the raging surf to the transports anchored a half mile away. Aiguillon's troops attacked the rear guard on the beach, killing 1,160 and capturing 400 redcoats while losing only about 160 of their own.[15]

Meanwhile, Frederick maneuvered and fought against the ever-converging allied armies. He marched his army on Olmutz, hoping to draw Daun to its defense. Daun instead sent General Gideon von Laudon against the Prussian supply lines. Laudon's cavalry inflicted over 2,400 casualties and captured 3,000 wagons packed with food and munitions bound for Frederick's army. Even with Frederick's troops starved of supplies, Daun hesitated to attack. He awaited the arrival of Fermor's 80,000 Russian troops slowly marching west. Frederick was determined to meet Fermor first. At Zorndorf on August 25, he threw his 36,000 men against Fermor's 42,000 Russians. After suffering 21,000 casualties to Frederick's 13,500, Fermor withdrew his army's remnants to his supply base at Landsberg. Frederick led his army toward the approaching Austrians. General Karl von Wedell smashed the Swedish advance at Fehrbellin and forced the Swedes back to Stralsund. In mid-October, Frederick caught up to Daun at Hochkirch. Early on the morning of October 14, Daun launched his 90,000 troops in a surprise attack on the 37,000 Prussians, crushed their right wing, and routed them. The Prussians left 9,450 casualties and over 100 cannons on the field to the Austrians' 7,590 casualties. Daun then marched on to besiege Dresden.

This year France would lose its African colonies. Though the slave port of Gorée and Fort Louis on the Senegal River reaped a hefty annual profit, Versailles neglected to reinforce them after the war broke out. In January 1758, Pitt sent Commodore Henry Marsh with 200 marines aboard two warships and two transports to take those colonies. Marsh's command reached the mouth of the Senegal River on April 23 and immediately closed in with seven French warships anchored there. The French set sail upriver. Marsh's little flotilla pursued the French until they reached Fort Louis on April 30 and surrendered the next day. Within weeks, all the other French trading factories in the region had given up as well, except Fort Saint Michaels, guarding Gorée Bay. Leaving garrisons behind, Marsh sailed back to London. Pitt was determined to complete his conquest of French Africa. He sent newly promoted Admiral Keppel with four warships and seven transports crowded with 600 troops. Keppel's force reached Gorée Bay on December 28 and accepted Fort Saint Michaels's surrender of 300 troops and 100 cannon two days later. The Union Jack now flew over every French West African post. The loss of France's West African slave ports further damaged the economy of its Caribbean islands, already suffering from blockade. These islands depended on a steady influx of new slaves to replenish the ranks of those annually killed by disease. Production and wealth dropped with the number of slaves.

In contrast to the bad news Versailles would receive from various parts of the world, France held its own in India in 1758. As elsewhere, command of the sea was essential for command of the land. Off India's coasts, the French matched the English in ships but fell short in daring. Admiral Anne Antoine, comte d'Aché de Marbeuf's squadron of twelve warships, which had sailed from Brest in March 1757, finally arrived off Saint David on April 28, 1758. It did not take a skilled captain thirteen months to sail from France to India. Aché took his time, dawdling at various ports en route, adding a crucial three months to his voyage. A mere month earlier and Aché could have severed all of British India from supply. By the time he reached his destination, a British squadron under Admiral George Pocock awaited him.

The two squadrons closed for battle on April 29. Though no ships on either side were sunk or captured, Aché lost 600 seamen and Pocock only 100. Aché sailed back to the safety of Pondicherry's bay while Pocock returned to Madras. Each would race to refit and reappear before Saint David. The same day of the sea battle, French commissioner general Thomas Arthur Lally de Tollendal led 2,000 French and sepoys just out of cannon-shot of Saint David's walls. Over the next few weeks, reinforcements swelled that force to 5,000 troops, of which about half were French and the other half sepoys. On May 6, Aché's squadron again appeared offshore. By May 15, the first trenches were dug. On June 2, 1758, Fort Saint David capitulated.

Lally's next great object was Madras, Britain's headquarters for southeastern India. At this crucial time, Aché rejected Lally's pleas that he help take Madras, and instead informed Lally that he would sail to Ceylon and back to raid English and Dutch shipping. Thus, Lally marched his army south with his sea flank open and with no means of choking off Madras from all sides. He was forced to turn back when the pillage and rape by his soldiers so infuriated the natives that a rebellion broke out in his rear flank. Lally chose to besiege Tanjore, hoping that the loot would quell his increasingly mutinous ranks. Unexpectedly, Tanjore's rajah ordered his troops to sally out and attack the French. Lally lost five hundred troops in repelling the assault. On August 2, Pocock and Aché fought another battle, which forced the battered French squadron to shelter at Pondicherry, where Lally reluctantly returned to refit his army. By November, he marched out again. Determined to take Madras, Lally foolishly left untaken the British garrison at Chingleput astride his supply line. Lally began his siege of Madras in late December. It would not succeed.

In Bengal, Clive schemed and maneuvered to replace French with English influence in Hyderabad, He sent 500 Europeans, 2,000 sepoys, and 100 lancers under Lieutenant Colonel Francis Forde to assist Rajah Anunderaj, who had revolted against the French. There, Hubert de Brienne, comte de Conflans, commanded 500 European and 6,000 sepoys. The two armies tangled at Chundoor on December 7. At first, Conflans's troops routed the rajah's troops then swarmed across the plain against Forde's. The British troops stood firm, fired a series of volleys that shattered the French advance, then charged. The French retreated, leaving 187 Europeans on the field and hundreds of sepoys, compared to the English loss of only 40 Europeans and around 200 sepoys killed or wounded. Conflans retreated the remnants of his troops to Masulipatam. The rajah aborted Forde's hope to follow up his victory with six weeks of negotiations among various factions. Thus did the year end with a standoff on all fronts in India.

By the late summer of 1758, France was either barely holding on or steadily losing ground in Europe, the Caribbean, West Africa, India, the high seas, and, especially, North America.

The Empire Crumbles

Most of that year's news from New France would be dismal. The French found themselves outgunned and fighting desperately to stave off four separate British offensives. Britain's new commanding general, General James Abercromby, himself led 6,300 regulars from nine regiments and 9,000 provincials against Fort Carillon. General Jeffery Amherst sailed against Louisbourg with 14,000 regulars from thirteen regiments and 600 rangers. General John Forbes marched west across Pennsylvania with 5,000 regulars and provincials against Fort Duquesne. And Colonel John Bradstreet led 2,000 provincial troops against Fort Frontenac. The French would suffer defeat on three of these four fronts.

To survive, New France needed far more troops than Versailles was willing to send. As of April 1758, Doreil reported that 3,781 troops filled the regular battalions, including 465 in La Reine, 499 in La Sarre, 508 in Royal Roussillon, 474 in Languedoc, 508 in Guyenne, 811 in Berry—of which 409 were in the 2nd Battalion and 402 in the 3rd—and 516 in the Béarn. The battalions were understrength: "The complete ought to be 4,230; it consequently lacks 449 men, and 1,250 more would be required to carry the companies of the six battalions . . . to 50 men."[16] As for the recruits Versailles had sent to fill the regular battalions' depleted ranks, Montcalm dismissed them as a "bad class. They require severity and frequent examples. I fear desertion during the campaign."[17]

Not only were the French battalions understrength, but the morale of the officers and enlisted alike was near rock bottom. With their dabblings in various enterprises, colonial officers enjoyed a much richer income than the French officers. With goods scarcer in Canada, prices averaged three times higher than those in France. The haughty French officers boiled at their impoverishment and even more at the mocking Canadians. Montcalm himself felt the pinch of Canadian inflation. As the commanding general, he was expected to entertain on a lavish scale, a demand that financially ruined him. In this letters to Versailles, he frequently called for higher allowances for his officers and himself. With Versailles sucked ever deeper into a broadening world war, pay raises for its officers were a very low priority.

Two bright spots alleviated some of this gloom. Canada was a vigorously healthy climate for the French posted there. Doreil found only "one hundred men in the hospitals of Quebec, Montreal, and Three Rivers. The number will, 'tis to be feared, be increased on the return of the fine weather."[18] Also, Montcalm reported, the "soldiers appear to relish the sojourn in this Colony. Many marriages continue to be contracted; several have taken up lands to clear, without marrying, and without being discharged from military service. I freely facilitated all the arrangements which the political interest of the Colony exacts."[19]

Another trouble weighing heavily on Montcalm's mind was the fighting skills of the Canadian marines and militia. He tried to give a balanced view: "In respect to Canadian valor, no one renders it more justice than I and the French do, but a nation so much accustomed to brag, will glorify itself. . . . I will not employ them except in . . . their sphere . . . the woods."[20] These views were not Montcalm's alone. A January 1758 memorial identified severe inadequacies with Canada's marines and militia alike. While nodding to the Canadian skill in "bush fighting . . . navigating rivers and lakes . . . and summer or winter marches," it lamented their brief musters, shoddy equipment, unhealthy salt pork diet, ill-discipline, and unskilled officers.[21]

What could ameliorate these problems? The memoir recommended inspecting the militia and splitting the men into three classes—effective, middling, and bad. All effective fighters would be marched off each year; those left behind would be responsible for all sowing and reaping. An inspection of the effectives would divide them among the regulars, marines, and militia, according to their relative abilities as soldiers. With fewer numbers of militiamen, it would be easier to find them better officers. The governor would be authorized to grant royal commissions to the bravest militia officers. Equipment, clothing, and training would be uniform for all militia units, both effectives and those who would remain at home.[22]

These proposals seemed reasonable and were enacted. Alas, the infusion of militia into the regulars tended to fray rather than elevate morale, cohesion, and fighting ability. Wearing the same uniform did not lessen the blistering contempt French and Canadians hurled at one another. Even worse, the close-order drill could not alter the ingrained tendency among Canadians to fight from cover. This would be most tragically obvious on the Plains of Abraham. When Montcalm led his battalions against the British, the French marched forward while the Canadians among them crouched, fired, and reloaded at will. Thus did the French battalions dissolve into a mob before Wolfe's redcoats.

Then there was the perennial problem of food shortages. The subsistence rations that winter almost sparked a mutinies in the ranks and riots among the populace. Montcalm lamented, "The reduction of the ration and the change of food have not failed to excite a ferment. . . . Some difficulties have occurred at Montreal where the people are less docile. The spirit was gaining among the colonial troops and even the soldiers of the regiment of Béarn, who are in garrison."[23] Though well aware that Bigot's machine milked profit from the pockets and food from the mouths of Canadians, Montcalm remained circumspect, merely alluding to the "great abuse" among both government and private contractors who are not "clear-sighted or disinterested."[24]

As if starvation and the closing British armies and fleets were not perilous enough, the French faced a potential rebellion in their rear. Bougainville reported in May of the "great unrest among the Indians of the Far West. The Menominee besieged the fort at the bay for three days and destroyed a French family in Wisconsin. The Ottawa have evil designs. The Potawatomi seem indisposed." A litany of insults and tragedies provoked those attacks: "The great loss they have suffered from the smallpox, the bad medicine the French have thrown to them, the great greed of the commanders of the posts and their ignorance of Indian customs? They are merchants that favor and intrigue while charged with a business most important to the safety of the colony.

Besides the English have sent a wampum belt to all the nations, and they make them the finest offers."[25]

No Indian tribe was more important to the power balance between the French and English than the Iroquois. The Iroquois message at every council was the same. They were subjects only to themselves, not to the English or the French. They wished to remain neutral in the war. Any warriors were free to fight for either side if they so desired. Indians, like others, were inclined to fight for the side that offered the highest pay. Without the quantity or quality of trade goods, the French were enormously disadvantaged.[26]

To the relief of all, eight supply ships and a frigate dropped anchor before Quebec on May 19. Aboard were 7,500 barrels of flour and 2,400 barrels of salt pork and beef, enough to relieve the famine until the harvest. Two more ships arrived at Quebec a few days later. The army now had enough rations for two hundred days. Several other heavily laden ships reached Quebec that summer. In early June, the people celebrated the arrival of a frigate and thirteen merchant ships packed with 12,000 barrels of flour. That not only saved the colony from starvation but allowed Vaudreuil to dispatch the battalions to the frontier.[27]

Canada would have received even more had all the ships that sailed from French ports managed to evade the British blockade. Doreil reported, "Of 36 ships that sailed from Bordeaux in 3 divisions, 24 are missing, which were all freighted with provisions and necessary supplies. Not a single vessel has as yet made its appearance from Rochelle, whence many are expected; neither from Bayonne nor Marseille, from which ports several had sailed. The sea swarms with English privateers. . . . These privateers are supported by men-of-war, and there is hardly a frigate to escort twelve of our merchantmen."[28]

Despite these handicaps, the French managed to gain a victory on March 13, 1758, when they nearly wiped out an American raiding party commanded by Robert Rogers near Fort Carillon:

> The English detachment, composed of picked men and 12 officers, under the command of Major Rogers, their best partisan, has been totally defeated. The Indians have brought back 146 scalps; few prisoners. . . . The remainder have perished of

want in the woods. A few . . . voluntarily surrendered themselves prisoners at our fort at Carillon, at the end of five days,
their guide having died the night before. We lost in that actions
8 Indians, and have had 17 wounded; also two Cadets of the
Colony and one Canadian. The dead have been covered with
great ceremony; presents have been made to the families in
the name of the King (the Great Ononthio). The Governor-
General will reward the bravery of our Iroquois by a promotion and presentation of some gorgets and medals to those
who have distinguished themselves; they will be thereby more
encouraged to revenge the loss they have suffered.[29]

The defeat of such a vaunted ranger leader as Rogers shifted
more Iroquois sentiments toward the French. Vaudreuil hoped to follow up that victory by ordering Lévis to take 3,000 troops, including
800 regulars, from Montreal to Oswego's ruins then head east toward
Albany through the heart of Iroquois country while rallying as many
Iroquois as possible to his ranks. This threat to Albany might divert
Abercromby's campaign against Montcalm at Fort Carillon and catch
him between two forces.[30]

It was a bold plan that might have succeeded if it not been
launched two years earlier. Had Montcalm attempted it after taking
Oswego in August 1756, the war's history would have differed greatly.
But Vaudreuil had to abort the plan when word arrived in late June of
the British offensives against Louisbourg and Duquesne, and of the
massive army Abercromby would lead against Fort Carillon. On June
26, 1758, Vaudreuil ordered Lévis to join his troops to Montcalm's
at Fort Carillon. Ironically, Lévis's troops would arrive there after
the decisive battle was over. Had Vaudreuil stuck to his original plan,
Lévis might have taken a sparsely defended Albany in the rear of a
defeated Abercromby. What then would the inept Abercromby have
done? Yet Vaudreuil's decision was prudent given the 25,000 British
troops reportedly arrayed against Fort Carillon alone.[31] That estimate
would be proven to be a gross exaggeration. Nonetheless, Abercromby
eventually led nearly 16,000 troops against Fort Carillon, a formidable
enough number.[32]

The Fort Carillon Campaign

On the Fort Carillon campaign's eve, the suspicions, jealousies, and slights that had smoldered ever more heatedly over the previous two years between Vaudreuil and Montcalm finally erupted into an angry exchange. Vaudreuil issued Montcalm orders on June 23. Montcalm reacted by declaring, "That proposition is so contradictory, that it must be owing to some error of the secretary."[33] Bougainville explained, "Vaudreuil this evening at ten o'clock gave the Marquis de Montcalm two obscure . . . orders. If our general was charged with them, they were so worded that any unfortunate results could be blamed on him, no matter how he acted. He returned them to Vaudreuil with a memoir justifying his action in so doing. . . . It is more than enough that a base jealousy should impede the result of zeal and talent, without suffering still more as a black, senseless intrigue associates one with follies over which one may groan but cannot stop."[34] In the end, Vaudreuil let Montcalm implement his own plan.

With his rear temporarily protected, Montcalm departed with the Bern Battalion for the front, arriving at Fort Carillon on June 30.[35] The fort was so small and poorly built that he initially considered blowing it up and retreating up Lake Champlain. Instead, Montcalm decided on a defense in depth along the trail that began two and a half miles away on Lake George and followed the La Chute River, which arched from there down to Lake Champlain. On July 1, he sent Colonel François Charles de Bourlamaque with the La Reine, Guyenne, and Béarn battalions to fortify the portage over the river, while he marched with the La Sarre, Royal Roussillon, Languedoc, and second battalion of Berry to a sawmill at one of the river's falls. Berry's third battalion garrisoned the fort. On July 2, Montcalm decided to fortify the low plateau a quarter mile from Fort Carillon. He set his troops to work digging trenches and redoubts, erecting log walls and felling trees for abatis in an arc.[36]

Only a handful of Indians loitered about Fort Carillon. Bougainville found them "extremely insolent" as "they wished to kill all the General's hens. They forcefully take away barrels of wine, kill the cattle, and we must put up with it. What a country! What a war!"[37] At a council, the Abenakis, Nipissings, and Ottawas told Montcalm that they would not return to Montreal unless they received blankets, clothing, and other supplies. Montcalm had no choice but to bow to the demand. Resentments between Montcalm and the Indians were rapidly heating to the boiling point.

The flaw in Montcalm's defense in depth was that it did not cover the landing place on Lake George. Instead, on July 4 Montcalm sent Ensign Jean Baptiste Langis-Montegron and 178 troops in bateaux down the lake to scout for Abercromby's approach and on July 6 dispatched Captain Trepezac with 300 troops of the Béarn battalion to Bald Mountain to watch for the British army's approach. Langis returned to report the advance of the British army. Bourlamaque sent Langis to join Trepezac atop Bald Mountain. There, Trepezac, Langis, and their men viewed a terrifying and magnificent sight. On the lake below, rowing north were "6367 regulars, officers, light infantry, and rangers included, and 9024 provincials, including officers and bateau men . . . in about 900 bateaux and 135 whale boats."[38]

Trepezac and his men scrambled down the mountain and through the thick, tangled forest to rejoin the army. To their horror, their Indian guides deserted. Meanwhile, Montcalm ordered Bourlamaque to retreat from the portage to the sawmill line. Trepezac and his troops blundered through the forest in what they hoped was the direction to Fort Carillon. It was. Unfortunately for them, the British army was disembarking on Lake George, and Abercromby had dispatched Rogers's rangers and the 80th Light Infantry to scout ahead. A firefight exploded when the British advance guard and Trepezac's troops collided. The rangers and light infantry devastated the exhausted French regulars, killing about 100 and capturing 148. But among the score of British deaths was Brigadier General George Howe, the inspiring and decisive second-in-command. With Howe's death, the British army suffered a terrible blow to its morale and leadership.

Montcalm withdrew his battalions to the fortified plateau before Fort Carillon. There, Hamlet-like, he debated whether to stand or flee. Pouchot recalled that "M. de Montcalm was rather irresolute all that morning. He did not know whether to resist the enemy or to withdraw to St. Frederic. . . . When he was on the point on sending them off, he had a consultation with his officers." They advised him to stay and fight. Montcalm agreed. It was a crucial decision that may well have saved Montcalm and France from a crushing defeat: "It is certain that if we had been obliged all his army would have been killed or captured, lacking a line of retreat. Moreover, he could not have got all his troops into the fort, nor could they have found any security there, since it was overlooked on all sides and surrounded by water."[39]

Fortunately for the French, they faced one of British history's more criminally inept generals. After spending the rest of July 6 disembarking his troops and supplies at the landing place, Abercromby ordered them to advance the next day until they encountered the enemy. By midday, the advance guard of rangers had reached the plateau and stared across several hundred yards of felled trees to the horseshoe-shaped French entrenchments. Behind those earth and wood barricades were 3,600 troops. The position was strong, but if the British carried it, Montcalm's army had nowhere to retreat; the cramped fort and the lake were a quarter mile to their rear.

Abercromby and his officers debated what to do. French prisoners doubled the size of their army. The prisoners told Abercromby's interrogators that Montcalm had 6,000 men and Lévis would soon arrive with 3,000 more. The nightmare scenario was for the British to get sandwiched between Montcalm's troops to their south and Lévis's approaching troops from the north. Abercromby feared that there was no time for an elaborate siege. Instead, he ordered his troops to attack on July 8 for what he hoped would be the decisive battle. It was, but not in the way he intended.

Throughout the afternoon, Abercromby ordered one mass attack after another on the French, who shattered each charge with concentrated musket fire. By the day's end, the British had suffered 1,948 casualties—554 officers and men killed, 1,357 wounded, and 37 missing—while the French had 12 officers killed and 25 wounded, and 92 soldiers killed and 248 wounded.[40] Abercromby hastily withdrew the remnants of his troops to the landing. The next day he reembarked them and withdrew back down Lake George.

The debacle before Fort Carillon was Britain's worst defeat in the North American war. Bougainville attributed "this victory which, for the moment, has saved Canada . . . to the sagacity of the dispositions, to the good maneuvers of our generals before and during the action and to the unbelievable valor of our troops."[41] All this was certainly true. But Bougainville left out the most important reason of all for the French victory—Abercromby's murderous incompetence.

Despite enjoying a victory each summer for three years, Montcalm despaired for New France's future. On July 28, 1758, just four weeks after routing the British at Fort Carillon and before receiving news of Louisbourg, he wrote that the "situation of the Colony is most critical should not peace interpose." The British had at least 30,000 troops divided among various campaigns against New France, which was defended by no more than 5,000 troops. While Montcalm admitted that victory against such odds was impossible, he promised Versailles that "we are resolved to bury ourselves under the ruins of the colony."[42] After requesting that his officers be rewarded for their bravery, he asked for himself nothing more "than to procure me the King's leave to return. My health suffers, my purse is exhausted."[43]

Unfortunately, controversy darkened Montcalm's greatest victory. In a letter Vaudreuil wrote on July 12, just four days after the bloody repulse of the British army at Fort Carillon, he did not congratulate Montcalm for his victory, but instead urged him to follow up the British defeat.[44] The letter deeply rankled Montcalm, who felt Vaudreuil was setting him up in a trap whereby the general would be blamed if he did not advance against an enemy that outgunned his army four to one, and would be blamed if he did advance and was defeated.[45] While French forces raided the British army camped around Fort Edward, Montcalm did not order a general advance.

Though Montcalm restrained his direct fire at Vaudreuil, he launched a massive attack on the governor through Versailles. To Belle Isle, he condemned Vaudreuil as "desirous of having us strangled, by giving us so small a force to face a real danger." Why would the governor general undermine the general's campaign? Vaudreuil was "jealous no doubt of the glory that the Marquis de Montcalm has acquired" and thus "deprived him of the means of succeeding in making a good defense."[46] These are extraordinarily serious charges. Montcalm essentially accused Vaudreuil of an offense akin to treason.

The governor pleaded his own case to Versailles. He accused the general of stirring hatred against Canada's government, alienating the Indians, taking all credit for the victory, insulting the militia, panicking before the initial British landing, and failing to follow up the victory. Vaudreuil concluded by advising that Montcalm be recalled: "He desires it himself and has requested me to demand it of you. So far from thinking of injuring him, I consider, my Lord, that he deserves to be promoted to the rank of lieutenant-general; he will be able to serve much more usefully in Europe. No person renders more justice than I do to his excellent qualities, but he does not possess those which are required for war in this country."[47]

Although Captain Doreil, the commissary general, weighed in on Montcalm's side in letters to the war and marine ministries, he promoted an even more important issue. Doreil urged Belle Isle to accept "Peace, Peace, my Lord, no matter at what sacrifice as regards boundaries." New France "has been maintained by a miracle up to the present time and with nothing, by the conduct, talents, and virtue of the Marquis de Montcalm, seconded by Mess de Lévis, de Bourlamaque, and the bravery of all the officers individually, by the goodness of the French soldier. . . . In return, we have experienced only unworthy preferences, endless injustices, calumnies, treachery."[48] If Belle Isle was moved by Doreil's eloquent and reasoned arguments, he did not act on it. The war would continue. The Fort Carillon victory, its luster clouded by controversy, would be the last decisive battle won by the French in the war for North America. There, as elsewhere around the world, French forces would suffer one humiliating defeat after another, culminating in the destruction of New France.

Decisive Defeats

Louisbourg was France's worst defeat that year. General Jeffery Amherst led the 13,142 troops crammed aboard 150 transports and guarded by 23 ships of the line and 18 frigates commanded by Admiral Edward Boscawen. That massive fleet dropped anchor off Gabarus Bay a half dozen miles south of Louisbourg on June 2. Facing them was a French garrison of 3,520 regulars and militiamen, commanded by Governor Augustin de Drucour, and a fleet of five ships of the line and seven frigates led by Admiral Jean Antoine Charry, marquis Des Gouttes. Though Louisbourg seemed a formidable fortress from afar, its walls and the morale of its troops were steadily crumbling from neglect. Louisbourg would be won or lost at its outer defenses, those batteries ringing the bay on whose southern horn stood Louisbourg, or, more importantly, those guarding the Gabarus Bay beaches.[49] Once again, a French naval commander squandered a chance to score a decisive victory. A fierce storm on June 5 battered the British fleet. Yet, rather than sail his squadron against the British transports, Des Gouttes pleaded with Drucour to let him sail for France. Permission was denied.[50]

The British army assaulted the three Gabarus Bay beaches on June 8. With Colonel James Wolfe leading the way, the redcoats routed the French and advanced just beyond cannon-shot of Louisbourg. Once the British were rooted ashore, the siege was all but won. It took weeks for the guns and supplies to be landed and dragged to the trenches zigzagging toward the citadel. Wolfe, meanwhile, sent his troops around the bay to capture the other batteries. The first siege guns opened fire on Louisbourg on July 5. French sorties over the next few weeks were repulsed. The British trenches snaked ever closer. More batteries opened fire and systematically destroyed Louisbourg. The French ships in the harbor were sunk or captured. By July 29, the French had suffered 411 dead and 1,790 wounded or sick; the British casualties totaled 195 killed and 363 wounded. That day, after a council of war with his officers, Drucour surrendered. In all, 5,637 French soldiers and sailors—at least those who did not sicken and die—spent the war's duration in captivity.[51] Though Wolfe was all for sailing on to Quebec, Amherst and the others protested that the season was too late. Instead, the British followed up their victory by raiding French settlements up and down the coast.

The next British victory that summer was notable more for the audacity with which it was conducted and the destruction it wrought than for any dangers it encountered. Colonel John Bradstreet got Abercromby's permission to lead 2,761 troops, of which only 181 were regulars, overland to Oswego then across Lake Ontario to attack Fort

Frontenac. On August 22, Bradstreet's army landed near the fort. Commanding Fort Frontenac's garrison of 5 marine officers and 48 soldiers, 24 civilians, and 27 voyageurs was Captain Pierre-Jacques Payen de Noyan et de Chavoy. Outnumbered over twenty-seven to one, Noyan's men endured two days of bombardment before giving up on August 24. Noyan surrendered sixty cannon of various calibers, nine ships, and a vast store of supplies. Bradstreet took away "the bark Marquise & the Brigantine. The remainder of our shipping was burned. It was said that they captured or set fire to nearly two million livres worth of goods. They also seized 2000 quarts of flour & 500 quarts of salt pork."[52]

The nine French vessels, if properly equipped and manned, could have ensured French naval superiority on Lake Ontario. Nothing in Bradstreet's vast flotilla could match the French fleet's firepower. But Bigot's machine had blinded and disarmed the French on Lake Ontario. That fleet could not sail because Captain Jean Michel Hugues Péan "and his company had commandeered all the rigging for the vessels & sold it for profit."[53] Had the French fleet been intact and vigilant, "It is likely that this English expedition would have failed."[54] Frontenac's destruction at once eliminated a mountain of desperately needed supplies and a vital link in the chain of forts from Quebec through the Great Lakes. After destroying the fort and what they could not carry off, Bradstreet and his men began the long haul back to Albany.

The final French defeat that year was the British capture of Fort Duquesne.[55] General John Forbes commanded the 6,000 provincial and regular troops that laboriously hacked a road and built forts westward across Pennsylvania. Awaiting the British at Fort Duquesne was its commander, François-Marie Le Marchand de Lignery, about 1,000 troops and Indians, and ever-dwindling supplies. As Forbes got closer, Lignery and his officers debated blowing up the fort and retreating up the Allegheny River to Fort Machault. On September 15, Lignery and his troops inflicted a bloody defeat on a force of 800 troops led by Major James Grant that hoped to take the fort in a lightning strike; in all, the British lost 273 killed, wounded, and captured while the French and Indians suffered only 8 dead and 8 wounded. It was a minor version of the Monongahela battle. Hoping that one more defeat might force Forbes to retreat for the winter, Lignery dispatched Captain Charles Philippe Aubry with several hundred troops to attack the British advance forces. Aubry's troops skirmished with the British before withdrawing. French prisoners revealed the fort's weaknesses. Forbes ordered his troops to press on. On November 24, Lignery ordered his troops to retreat and had Fort Duquesne blown up. Forbes's army entered the fort's charred ruins the next day.

The string of defeats provoked a crisis for New France. By seizing points along Canada's fringe, the British had positioned themselves for attacking its heartland in 1759. At Vaudreuil's request, Montcalm journeyed to Montreal to meet with him in late October. Each proud man managed to quell his passions and constructively debate what strategy could best stave off the British. In a remarkable exchange of papers, each made very well-reasoned arguments for his respective strategy. Vaudreuil called for continuing the existing strategy of defending New France's frontier and keeping the British as far from the Saint Lawrence valley as possible. Montcalm argued that there were not enough troops or supplies to mount such a defense; he instead advocated a hedgehog defense in which all forces were concentrated in a strategic triangle with points at Île aux Noix at Lake Champlain's north end, La Présentation on the Saint Lawrence above Montreal, and Quebec. The governor protested that Montcalm's strategy would abandon the rest of New France to the enemy and sever communications with the Great Lakes posts and Louisiana. Unable to agree, they finally decided to postpone their decision. Thus did Vaudreuil's plan win by default.[56]

Bougainville despaired over the fate of New France. Corruption, ambition, and egoism had split the colony into two warring camps: "Canadians and Frenchmen, although having the same origin, the same interest, and the same principles of religion and government, with an urgent danger facing them cannot agree among themselves; it seems that these are two bodies which cannot be amalgamated. . . . I even believe that a few Canadians pray that we do not succeed, hoping that all blame will fall on the French."[57]

One thing united New France's leading officials and officers—the realization that their colony teetered on the brink of destruction.

Each sent letters to Versailles begging for more troops and supplies, and the opening of peace negotiations.[58] In October, Vaudreuil agreed with Montcalm to send Bougainville and Doreil to Versailles to explain their plight and request aid. Versailles's ministers would get an earful.

Consequences

What did Versailles make of this increasingly uncivil war between the governor and general underlined by the Cassandra-like warnings that Canada was lost if France did not immediately sue for peace? Louis XV and his ministers, as usual, dithered. A council meeting on December 28, 1758, did note that the "estrangement" of Vaudreuil and Montcalm "had exercised an influence over all minds" and "the evil their coolness might produce." Montcalm and Vaudreuil themselves recognized the danger of their worsening relations and "became reconciled and made up as friends again, but that was in appearance only." This reconciliation was further strained by the different strategies each advocated for New France's defense in 1759. Rather than chose between the two plans, the council decided to "place their respective Memoirs under his Majesty's eyes."[59] Louis XV was just as bewildered as his ministers over what to do.

The only decision the council reached was to recall Montcalm "as his health and the debts he has contracted do not permit him to continue his service. This recall appears so much the more indispensable as the Marquis de Montcalm, on becoming Lieutenant-General of his Majesty's armies, a grade, moreover, merited by his services, would feel some objections to serve in this new capacity of the orders of the Marquis de Vaudreuil, who is only Governor Lieutenant-General; a title which does not possess, among military men, the same extent of power as that of Lieutenant-General of the armies."[60] Lévis would take Montcalm's position as head of the regular troops. Somewhat contradictorily, the council also decided that Montcalm should take over command of New France if Vaudreuil should die.

As usual, protocol trumped military necessity for Versailles in deciding who should command. New France's survival ultimately depended on the commitment of troops and supplies Versailles was willing to make, and the strategy and tactics wielded by its commanders. The conflicts between Montcalm and Vaudreuil over strategy were exacerbated by squabbles over rank, privilege, and personality. Versailles not only avoided dealing with any of these issues, but, in the end, never followed through even on its decision to recall Montcalm. Instead, the war and marine ministers continued to send letters to Montcalm and Vaudreuil, respectively, that were supportive, congratulatory of victories, understanding of difficulties, and apologetic for the inability to do more.

Privately, the ministers were just as upset as New France's leaders. Foreign minister Bernis despaired that Versailles had trapped France in a vicious circle: "No more commerce, as a result no more money and no more purchases; no more navy, and as a result no more resources to resist England. The navy has no more sailors, the army has no more soldiers, the treasury has no more cash."[61] He believed that France could fight in Europe or America, but not in both. In September, he declared, "We must end the war on the Continent so that we can at least make some semblance of fighting abroad. . . . The English have involved us in a war in Germany while we lose our colonies, our commerce, and our life."[62]

Bernis was mistaken on both counts. He pointed his finger of blame in the wrong direction. Versailles was thoroughly responsible for joining the war in Germany. But conquering Hanover was clearly in French interests since it was the best bargaining chip within the grasp of French armies. That war, however, had been miserably executed, something for which the king and ministers had no one to blame but themselves. As for America, here again Versailles was responsible for failing to maintain the navy or to provide Canada with enough troops and supplies to make the English conquest difficult if not impossible.

Versailles did, however, tiptoe toward a peace feeler that year. It was agreed that France could strengthen its ties with Spain by encouraging Madrid to mediate the war's end while pressing its own claims against England. The French leaders apparently did not see that Whitehall would reject Spain as an "objective" mediator if it was simultaneously asserting its own interests against England. Spain too increasingly saw an interest in acting as the go-between. Though the war had stalemated in both Europe and America, Madrid feared that England would eventually prevail with the power of its fleet and purse. France was a good imperial neighbor in the New World; its colonists exploited their own lands without threatening those of Spain. Should Britain conquer France's North American empire, its numerous, ambitious, and footloose colonists would swarm toward and eventually over the borders of New Spain. Madrid embraced an eighteenth-century version of the domino theory whereby if Canada fell, Louisiana would follow, thus opening the trail to Santa Fe and beyond.

By early summer, Spain had essentially aligned with France against Britain. On June 16, 1758, Ambassador Joseph Antonio d'Abreu y Bertodano voiced claims against Britain for several persistent insults it had made to Spain's empire and honor. Though the Utrecht Treaty allowed the British to cut wood on the Caribbean coast of Honduras, it did not permit them to build forts on Spanish territory. Abreu also demanded that Spanish fishermen be allowed access to the Newfoundland fisheries as interpreted under clauses of the 1713 and 1721 treaties. After debating the issue in its council, Whitehall rejected these claims. The relationship soured to a breaking point over the next two months. Then, on August 27, Queen Barbara died, plunging King Ferdinand from his melancholy into insanity. Any chance of Madrid taking a decisive foreign policy initiative disappeared.

Meanwhile, France's allies demanded that it commit more to the war. Throughout that fall, Saint Petersburg urged Versailles to formally join the Russian-Austrian alliance. The French remained coy. Letters between Elizabeth and Louis crossed in the diplomatic mail. As the French saw it, the Russian admission price remained exorbitant; Saint Petersburg still demanded huge subsidies and support in any war against the Ottoman Empire. In Russian eyes, Versailles was more interested in peace than in launching vigorous offensives. Bernis tried to allay that fear with instructions to ambassador Hôpital: "All your art must be employed so that the Russians never think that the King desires peace, but so that you leave the impression without ever openly stating it of the King's disposition for a just peace."[63] The Russians and Austrians were determined to fight until they had vanquished Frederick and condemned the French for not doing more.

The allies got a scare on September 8 when Elizabeth suffered a seizure. Though the empress recovered, she slipped into a melancholy that kept her from court for weeks at time and darkened the social whirl when she was present. Versailles dispatched renowned doctor François Poissonier to serve as her physician. He found that Elizabeth's corpulent body was steadily decaying, revealed by all manner of twitches, tremblings, pains, and bouts of lethargy.

At Versailles, Louis XV had managed to shed much of his depression of the preceding year despite or perhaps because of the turnover in the council with Belle Isle newly installed at the war ministry and Massiac at the marine ministry. The marine ministry was experiencing an especially chaotic year. In September, the council agreed that the ministry was in financial chaos and opened an investigation. On October 18, Louis named a commission to reform that ministry's finances. Massiac was fired and replaced by Nicholas René Berryer on October 31. Berryer had served as lieutenant general of the Paris police before joining the Council of Dispatches in October 1757 and the Royal Council of Finances and Council of State in 1758.[64]

Of all that year's shuffling of portfolios, none surprised and delighted the council and court more than the fall of Bernis. As usual, Pompadour was behind it as her once-powerful affection for Bernis had turned to a bitter rancor. His attempts to cut her from the policy loop had infuriated her more than his incessant defeatism. In early 1758, he recommended and the king agreed to create a policy committee of ministers that met three times a week and decided questions with formal votes. Pompadour would not sit in the committee but would retain her power to screen appointments and unofficially advise the king. Bernis explained, "Though it preserved for her an honorable function . . . it dared to take the reins of government out of her hands and restore them to the King's Council. . . . Everybody of common sense agreed . . . that it was sufficient to allow a woman, a former mistress, to keep the credit for distributing court patronage, and that it was fair and reasonable to prevent her from deciding affairs of state according to her whims."[65]

Bernis hoped to use the committee to pare royal expenses by imposing a strict annual budget ceiling of 6 million livres and by targeting for elimination a host of sinecures. All who benefited from royal extravagance, especially those who held or hoped to hold an empty office, exploded in protest against the planned cuts. The king hastily backed down from the reforms that so grossly injured his courtiers' sensitive feelings. Bernis had not merely insulted the court with notions of fiscal responsibility and sacrifice of luxury for the nation. His attempts to streamline each ministry's personnel and budgets had angered the other ministers, each of whom presided over his own miniature court and often sold positions and contracts to the highest bidder. Those ministers joined with Pompadour to pour maledictions about Bernis into the king's ear. Only Louis's aversion to confrontation and his genuine regard for Bernis kept him from being cast into political oblivion.

Bernis was not only well aware that Pompadour had turned against him but understood the reasons: "I often wounded her vanity by disagreeing with her political views. Partly through fickleness, partly through vanity, partly through jealousy of her power, she obstinately pressed for my disgrace until the King finally gave in. . . . The Marquise had none of the vices of ambitious women, but she had all their meanness, and the levity of women drunk with their own beauty and their assumed superiority of their minds. She did harm without malice, she did good by whim; her friendship was jealous like love, fickle, inconstant as love is, and never dependable."[66]

By late summer, Bernis had alienated Louis as well. His calls for peace at any cost, added to his incessant whines about overwork and ailments, increasingly strained the royal patience.[67] In August, Bernis himself finally asked to be discharged and replaced by Choiseul. Louis took the necessary step for that transfer of power to occur. On August 25, he conferred the title duc de Choiseul on comte de Stainville. But until further orders, Choiseul would remain in the all-important position of ambassador to Vienna. Bernis himself received word of an honor, not from Versailles but from Rome. The new pope, Clement XIII, named his old friend Bernis a cardinal on October 2, 1758.

By then, virtually everyone, including Bernis, wanted him to step down as foreign minister. Three scandals—the first and third genuine though trite, and the second probably untrue and equally trite—provided growing excuses to do so. In September, the news quickly spread that Bernis, an avid shooter, was caught poaching on the king's estate. The gamekeeper reported the transgression to the prince de Noailles, the ranger of the royal park, who promptly informed Pompadour, who in turn hurried to Louis's side. The crime stunned Louis. Still, he hesitated to fire Bernis. To add fuel to the flames, Pompadour gossiped that Bernis was carrying on with the king's daughter, the infante. Louis fumed but remained hesitant. Finally, Pompadour presented a letter to her from Bernis penned after the disastrous battle of Crefeld in which he suggested France needed a prime minister to sort out the worsening mess into which the nation had plunged; he suggested himself for the position. Since Cardinal Fleury's death, Louis had prided himself on being his own prime minister.

The most important excuse to relieve Bernis was his peace-at-any-price defeatism, which he did not hesitate to share with everyone, including the king. On October 9, 1758, Louis wrote Bernis, "Certainly no one wants peace more than I, but I want a solid and honorable peace; I am willing to sacrifice my interests for it, but not those of my allies." Louis ended his letter with a stunning announcement: "I permit regretfully that you turn the secretary of state over to the duc de Choiseul."[68]

Choiseul left Vienna on November 15 and reached Versailles on November 27. On December 3, Louis handed Choiseul his portfolio as secretary of state for foreign affairs. Bernis succinctly described Choiseul's challenge: "You see the destruction with which we are now menaced. Peace is the only remedy. That is your task."[69]

After Choiseul took over, Bernis had only ten days remaining to enjoy Paris. On December 13, he received a lettre de cachet from the king that stripped him of all offices and banished him to the abbey of Vic-sur-Aisne. The king hated being surrounded by people in the council and even the court who reminded him of his own failings. Like so many others, Bernis's presence deeply embarrassed Louis. The king would eventually shed himself of the embarrassment of New France just as brutally.

CHAPTER 9

Rout, 1759

Why not punish them? cries some European. Punish a Canadian?
Vaudreuil would prefer to lose a battle.

Bougainville

What is surprising is that France makes the same mistakes with
the same people over and over again.

Maurice de Saxe

Pangloss owned that he had always suffered horribly, but as he
had once asserted that everything went wonderfully well, he asserted it still, though he no longer believed it.

Voltaire, *Candide*

France's most gifted minister during the war did not receive a portfolio until the war was all but lost. By the time the king named Choiseul foreign minister, it was too late to win the war; at best, Choiseul
could win a favorable peace. Nonetheless, by March 1759, Choiseul was
directing France's war much as Pitt was directing Britain's.

What manner of man was the new foreign minister who would
guide France to the war's bitter end and beyond?[1] Born in foreign
Lorraine, Choiseul was only convinced to serve in the French rather
than Austrian army because of his friendship with Marshal Adrien

Maurice Noailles. Choiseul fought with distinction in the War of the Austrian Succession before immersing himself in the labyrinthine world of court intrigues and follies. Like so many at Versailles, Choiseul was a talented dilettante—a patron of the arts who collaborated with Jean-Philippe Rameau, amassed a huge painting collection, and hob-nobbed with the philosophes.

It was Pompadour who plucked Choiseul from that gilded obscu-rity and placed him into the highest echelons of power. Choiseul first met her through his wife around 1750. He became one of the mar-quise's favorites by diverting one of the many attempts to destroy her authority by hooking the king with another mistress. Throughout much of 1752, Louis toyed with Charlotte-Rosalie Romanet, count-ess de Choiseul-Beaupré, Choiseul's cousin by marriage. Richelieu had connived to bring Louis and Charlotte together. In his memoirs, Choiseul recorded that Charlotte had "confided to me the king's love for her and her inclination to respond to it; but she attached a con-dition to it, namely the dismissal of Mme. de Pompadour so that she should occupy her place with the same influence."[2] Acting skepti-cal, Choiseul demanded proof of the love, so Charlotte let him read Louis's letters. Choiseul chose to sacrifice his cousin, a pawn in many hands, to gain Pompadour's favor. He promptly took the incriminat-ing evidence to Pompadour, who confronted an embarrassed Louis with it. Within days, Charlotte was packed off to her château, never to be seen at court again. A half year later she died bearing a child, pre-sumably the king's.

Choiseul's intrigue may have endeared him to Pompadour, but it hardened the king against him. Louis XV would forever remain cold to him, even after Choiseul joined his council. That he would tolerate Choiseul at his elbow reveals the extent of Pompadour's power. Louis protested, then reluctantly accepted, her sponsorship of Choiseul as ambassador first to Rome in 1754, then to Vienna in 1757. By late 1757, Choiseul had become understudy to Bernis as foreign minis-ter. Bernis unburdened himself to Choiseul with extraordinary letters that explored France's defeats and dilemmas, and his own fragile state of mind. Eventually, Choiseul elbowed Bernis aside for Pompadour's affections and favors. Perhaps for this reason a cabal led by the dauphin soon arose against him. Yet, by brilliantly playing off his own strengths and his rivals' weaknesses, Choiseul managed to amass ever more power by accumulating ministry portfolios until he was essentially prime minister. He would remain the king's most powerful minister until December 24, 1770, when Louis XV exiled him to his country château. Choiseul revenged himself through his memoirs. No one has left a more blistering portrait of Louis XV: "I saw the King, a man without soul or intelligence, loving evil like children love to torture animals."[3]

Choiseul was beyond doubt the most talented of Pompadour's favorites. While he rivaled Bernis in wit and worldliness, he was utterly ruthless in advancing his interests, a political quality lacking in the cardinal. Appearances counted for little in those Pompadour tapped for power. If Bernis resembled a cherub, Choiseul reminded many of a toad—heavy, squat, bandy-legged, fat-faced, and double-chinned. Bernis, who was a better judge of character than a foreign minister, admired Choiseul for "his intelligence, his penetration, his grace and gaiety; but his main talent is to get things done: he is quick in perception, sees clearly; but his ideas lack continuity and he aims more at attracting notice to himself than at building a reputation."[4] Ambassador Hans Stanley assessed Choiseul as

a Man of lively Parts, but no Education for Business; frank enough in Talk, meaning often what He says at the time, but fickle, very indiscreet; treats all affairs, & with the Highest as Matters of Jest: He has got a Credit with the King quite independent of the Lady [Pompadour]: He treats Her often slightly: sometimes roughly: tells, Her, She is as Handsome as an Angel when She talks of Affairs; bid Her throw a Memoire, the other Day, into the Fire; did not make the Austrian Alliance . . . has expressed his Dislike thereof to His Confidents: envious of That Court's generally hated Treaty owing partly to Prussia's indiscreet Expressions about the Mistress, and Contempt of the Cardinal's verses.[5]

Choiseul had a clearheaded view of France's plight: "The only war which interests us directly is the one we must sustain against England.

That war has for its purpose the defense of our colonies and our commerce. . . . All of our efforts in Germany, even supposing them successful, can only be useful to our allies; they profit from our services and can render to us no return service of any benefit . . . we must not count on the Russians. It is necessary then to . . . draw from them all that we can for immediate operations against England . . . which will bring us peace, reestablish our trade, and repair the immense losses which our past beliefs have occasioned."[6] To that end, Choiseul drove a hard bargain with Vienna in negotiations over the subsidy renewal in May 1759; he slashed French handouts to Austria to 6 million florins.

But that was a mere drop in the swelling sea of French debt. No matter how many times he checked his figures, the new comptroller general, Étienne de Silhouette, who took over from Jean Nicolas de Boullongne on March 4, 1759, could come to only one conclusion— Versailles was broke and could no longer afford its war. The shortfall would be at least 217 million livres. New loans could not be ventured until previous subscriptions had been filled, an unlikely event. Massive taxation was France's only salvation, as far as Silhouette could see it. He proposed a property tax hike of 10 percent, a new tax on carriages, and the creation of new honors and offices for sale to fill some of the financial abyss. Even then Silhouette advised Louis to end the war no later than 1760.[7]

The king grudgingly agreed, at least on the tax hike if not the war's end. Parlementarians sneered at the proposal as they descended from their carriages and strode into the assembly. Louis ordered a lit de justice scheduled for September 20, 1759, then canceled it at the last moment. The proposed taxes would fall mostly on the rich, who would explode in rage and ridicule at the monarch's expense. It was much more politically astute to keep soaking the poor, who could least afford it but seemed so powerless.[8]

A Last-Hour Plea

With money so tight and French defeats so numerous, the time was not propitious for Louis Antoine de Bougainville's mission to get more troops and supplies for Canada. Nonetheless, throughout December and January, Montcalm's brilliant aide gamely made the rounds of ministers and other influential people at Versailles to plead his case. The most important of all was Madame Pompadour, who took him under her wing and "showed me the greatest kindness, and, as she was then the First Minister, I often worked with her over the object of my mission." But nearly everyone else to whom he turned offered the same lament—with the treasury bare, the fleet either blasted to splinters or rotting at anchor, and the army bogged down in Germany, little could be done for France's North American empire. Marine minister Berryer might have been expected to show some sympathy but did not: "This minister loved parables and told me very pertinently that one did not try to save the stables when the house was on fire."[9]

Just what argument did Bougainville make for the "stables"? Essentially, he trotted out La Galissonière's thesis that saw Canada as the front line in the defense of French colonies elsewhere. If unprofitable New France fell, the domino effect logic went, the profitable sugar islands would follow. Bougainville pleaded for Versailles to send desperately needed supplies and troops to stave off that year's expected three-pronged British attack. He then proposed a daring strategy— "landing four thousand men with arms of all sorts for a great number in Carolina. On arrival they would summon to freedom the Germans that the English treated as slaves in their colonies. . . . We would arm part of them, we would send arms and munitions to the Cherokees, Indians of this region, implacable enemies of the English."[10] The result would be a perhaps irrepressible revolt in the rear of Britain's offensives against Canada.

In the assumptions underlying this scheme, Bougainville was misinformed; the German immigrants were hardly slaves awaiting the chance for revolt, nor were the Cherokee yet Britain's enemies. Still, landing four thousand French troops anywhere in the colonies would certainly have forced the British to hurry their forces back to the invaded province. And such a landing was not infeasible. Canada's survival depended on an annual supply fleet beating the British in the race to the Saint Lawrence. That supply fleet would both sustain Canada, if it made it, and be a lure for the Royal Navy. Only after a

British fleet had anchored before Quebec should a French armada set sail for the Carolina coast. It would take weeks for word of the invasion to reach the British fleet, which would need weeks to sail to the rescue. If the British proved indomitable, the French army could then retreat overland to Fort Toulouse, which guarded Louisiana's eastern frontier.

While Berryer scoffed, Pompadour approved the plan: "It was only a question of finding the funds necessary to implement it; the King's coffers were empty. Mme. de Pompadour did everything possible to find two million, engaging herself for the sum. Her efforts were fruitless and the project failed. The Duc de Choiseul wanted me to head the expedition, although I begged off on account of my youth and small experience."[11] Quebec might well have been saved that year had enough coin been scrapped up for Bougainville's expedition.

In offering a nonexistent command to Bougainville, Choiseul may have simply been engaging in time-honored flattery. For by now, the new foreign minister had written off Canada if not all of New France. In January 1759, he gave Étienne de Silhouette two reports that involved France's abandonment of Canada and the immigration of its French subjects to Louisiana. Then, to reinforce his defeatist proposals, Choiseul engaged Silhouette to craft a report outlining France's diplomatic options for ending the war.

Within a month, Silhouette submitted five options, each subsequently conceding more to England. His first called for both sides to restore all conquests since the war began, splitting with England the Neutral Islands, of which France would take Saint Lucia and Dominica, and submitting all border disputes to arbitration by Spain, Denmark, and Holland. His second, third, and fourth involved ever-larger concessions in Acadia, with the last also allowing for a neutral region between the Wabash and Appalachians. The fifth combined the other concessions with the razing of Louisbourg and all forts on Lake Champlain. Unlike Choiseul, Silhouette still felt that Canada was worth fighting for, if not on the battlefield, at least at the diplomatic table. But, like other ministers who agreed with him, he avoided explaining just how Canada was to be saved in either case.[12]

The Cancer in Canada

In the end, Versailles decisively acted on only one issue raised by either Bougainville or Silhouette, though not for another two years. Bougainville partially succeeded in explaining the core reason for New France's problems—corruption. New France could enrich rather than drain the royal coffers if it were honestly ruled. Mustering all the reason and eloquence of the Enlightenment philosophe that he was, Bougainville explained how Intendant François Bigot's corruption machine, known as the "Great Society," was a cancer rotting New France.[13]

The ministers added Bougainville's firsthand account to the pile of reports they had received from Montcalm and his officers over the last three years. Even Canada's most fervent supporters agreed that it was an enormous drain on the Crown. Now they understood that the reason was the wholesale looting of Canada by those entrusted with its care.

By early 1759, the complaints against Bigot and his organized crime syndicate reached a critical mass. Versailles decided to mount an investigation. In a letter penned on January 19, 1759, Berryer confronted Bigot with the "abuses . . . in the employment made of the funds in the Colony. . . . I have perceived in the account called for by me of what has been done for some years back, that people are in the habit of consuming without economy, without order, and without any precaution for the King's interest." He then raised specific troubling questions: "How, for example, is it possible that the small-pox among the Indian Nations of the Upper country should have occasioned extraordinary expenses to the amount of a million? By whom has this expense been made? . . . You do not enter into any detail on this point." Berryer then identified the central scam: "The King's property is considered consumed on its arrival, and that it is afterwards resold to his Majesty at excessive rates. By this operation the King buys in France and repurchases the same effects in the Colony. I am no longer astonished that immense fortunes are seen in Canada." Finally, he turned his guns directly on Bigot: "This practice is contrary to all the laws of the Kingdom for by such operation the Intendant alone becomes . . . the fabricator of a money which has circulation in the Colony, without the King's permission, and you must be aware of all the consequences thereof."[14] But, despite the glaring evidence before it, Versailles took nearly another two years to act.

Bigot was as skilled with his pen as he was with his wit and fingers. For two more years, he managed to evade the encircling noose. In an April 15 reply to Berryer, he justified his own expenses while disclaiming responsibility for all others incurred in Canada. Bigot not only championed himself as the model of fiscal propriety but also lauded his altruism in hosting the French officers at his table and giving charity to the poor.[15] Even if he did so, he merely tossed a few coins from the horde of wealth he had scooped from Canada. He would eventually tell it to a supreme court.

Versailles's only decisive act for Canada this year was to fiddle with the line of command. On January 28, 1759, the marine minister issued a document that tapped Montcalm to replace Vaudreuil as governor general if the latter died. The rationale was to avoid a succession crisis. Montcalm would jump the line of deputy governors waiting for the top post. In itself, the policy was reasonable enough. Yet the concern is curious. Vaudreuil was in good health and, indeed, would live for another dozen years. Considerable time, energy, and thought had been expended on a purely hypothetical problem. In doing so, Versailles sidestepped the central issue, the festering command and personality conflict between Vaudreuil and Montcalm that stymied the war effort. The succession document seems to have been driven by the idea that any action was better than none at all. Once again, while Versailles fiddled, Canada literally burned.[16]

Having resolved this issue, Versailles confronted a related one— promotions. In February, His Majesty was "graciously pleased to reward the services of the Marquis de Montcalm and Chevalier de Lévis, by making the former Lieutenant-General of the armies and, the second, Major-General." Vaudreuil's ego was not neglected. Versailles awarded him the Grand Cross of the Order of Saint Louis. Unable to send Canada the supplies and troops that might save it from conquest, Louis XV did what he believed was just as important, the conferring of honors. The decree actually stated that the titles "will not fail to influence advantageously the operations of this year," presumably by inspiring the recipients to fight harder.[17]

With honors, Versailles could be generous. But when it came to supplies and troops with which to fight a war, Louis XV and his ministers were once again stingy. Along with 20,000 tons packed aboard the annual supply fleet would go only 400 replacements for Montcalm's depleted battalions.[18] War minister Belle Isle explained to Montcalm that Versailles had abandoned all hope of defending Canada on the battlefield and instead would try to win it back through diplomacy: "However trifling the space you can preserve, it is of utmost importance to possess always a foothold in Canada, for should we once wholly lose that country, it would be quite impossible to enter it again."[19]

Bougainville left Versailles at February's end and spent the next month at Bordeaux helping organize that year's twenty-three-ship supply fleet escorted by one twenty-six-gun frigate. The fleet sailed in late March. Adverse winds and ice delayed the fleet twenty-two days at the mouth of the Saint Lawrence. The fleet did not drop anchor before Quebec until May 10. There, Bougainville briefly presented Versailles's letters to Vaudreuil, then hurried to Montcalm at Montreal with the grim news that the king had committed nothing but honors and a handful of troops for New France's defense. The French officers could rejoice that Versailles had ordered Vaudreuil and Bigot to surrender to Montcalm "not only . . . on all operations but also on all areas of administration relating to the defense and preservation of the colony."[20] But that was a meager consolation given the challenges they faced. And, as it turned out, Vaudreuil clung to his former powers, issuing orders that conflicted with or complicated Montcalm's, and the general could do nothing but protest.

While Bougainville's convoy battled the Atlantic winds, Vaudreuil and Montcalm battled each other over whose strategy and ego would prevail. As he had in previous years, Vaudreuil devised an elaborate strategy. The French would conduct an active defense, with each frontier fort dispatching large raiding parties to terrorize and delay any British army marching against it. This strategy made the most of New France's meager and dwindling troops, supplies, Indian allies, and morale. So far, the plan held nothing new or controversial; it was the same strategy New France had used in all of its wars. The hitch was that Vaudreuil did "not presume the enemy will undertake coming to

Quebec."[21] Here, he could not have been more wrong. He assumed that the most powerful British blow would strike Fort Carillon. To that front's defense, he assigned not Montcalm, but Bourlamaque. It was a deliberate snub to Montcalm, whom he assigned, along with Lévis, to Quebec.

Montcalm of course replied but reserved his most powerful counterattack for Versailles rather than the governor. On April 12, 1759, the general wrote three remarkable letters in which he explored such related subjects as the nature of warfare in North America, the imbalance of power, the corruption rotting New France, and specific operations. After three years of experience with it, he had reached some sound conclusions about the nature of warfare on the new continent: "The war has changed character in Canada. The vast forces of the English . . . determines them on continuous operations in a country where the Canadians thought they were making war, and were making, so to speak, hunting excursions. Our principles of war, considering our inferiority, ought to be, to contract our defense, in order to preserve at least the body of the Colony, and retard its loss; to combine with the system of European tactics the use to be made of Indians."[22] Montcalm now had no illusions about New France's fate: "Canada will be taken this campaign, and assuredly the next, if there be not some unforeseen good luck, a powerful diversion by sea against the English Colonies, or some gross blunders on the part of the enemy."[23]

The Quebec Campaign: First Phase

Of Britain's three campaigns this year, the one against Quebec was the first into the field. To the astonishment of the French and Canadians, 21 ships of the line, 20 other warships, and 119 transports carrying 8,600 regulars commanded by General James Wolfe appeared off the Isle d'Orleans, a half dozen miles from Quebec, on June 27. In all, there were four British regulars to each French soldier or marine, though the French did have more armed men; Montcalm commanded about 2,600 regulars, 600 marines, 10,400 militiamen, 200 cavalry, and 918 Indians, or nearly 15,000 troops.[24]

Vaudreuil and his cohorts had insisted that, without skilled pilots, the British could never navigate the "traverse," a twist in the channel a dozen miles below the city. What had happened? British daring and deceit had combined with Vaudreuil's incompetence and complacency. By hoisting a French flag, the British had lured aboard pilots from the village opposite the traverse. They then thoroughly charted those waters to allow the rest of the fleet to sail up without the need for Canadian pilots.

Ironically, nearly a year and a half earlier, Montcalm had dispatched Bougainville to "inspect the northern coast from Quebec to Cape Tourmente. We have discovered on this cape an emplacement suitable for a battery of four cannon, and two mortars. They would be safe from assault, this country being almost inaccessible, and they could shoot at vessels making the passage for almost a half hour. They are forced to pass within range of this battery. It would cost little for its construction."[25] A gauntlet of powerful batteries along with others at Isle d'Orleans and Point Lévy could have rendered Quebec all but invincible to siege. They were never built. Nor was much else done to strengthen Quebec City's crumbling walls and batteries in the years before the British armada finally appeared. These failings were Vaudreuil's. He ignored or rejected repeated warnings and plans to strengthen or erect fortifications that Montcalm carried to him.

Throughout the siege, the French launched only three initiatives for Quebec's defense—two fire boat attacks bracketing an aborted night attack on the Point Lévy battery. Other than that, Vaudreuil and Montcalm simply sat back and reacted to British maneuvers and attacks for three and a half months. When the British fleet appeared, Vaudreuil ordered the five frigates and supply vessels at anchor before the city to sail sixty miles upstream to Batiscan. This flotilla's 1,200 seamen and 50 officers were then brought down to Quebec to man the city's cannons. With the supply ships and frigates safely out of the way, Vaudreuil then unleashed the weapon that he maintained would destroy any British fleet that reached Quebec, after insisting it was impossible. On the night of June 28, the French fired and unleashed seven boats dripping with tar and packed with gunpowder toward the British fleet. The British sailors scrambled into whaleboats and rowed toward those drifting volcanoes belching flames and small explosions. At an enormous risk, the sailors managed to cast grappling hooks onto the fire boats and to tow them to shallow waters where they spectacularly burned out. Neither a British ship nor even a sailor was burned. Thus did the first initiative literally fizzle out. So too would the third initiative, another fleet of fire boats launched nearly a month later on the night of July 27, which charred not a single British ship or sailor.

On June 29, Wolfe sent three thousand troops to take Beaumont on the south shore and then march on to capture Point Lévy directly opposite Quebec. There, they began to erect a battery that would eventually reduce most of Quebec to rubble. Montcalm spoke with Vaudreuil about attacking Point Lévy before the batteries were completed. Vaudreuil agreed but Montcalm got cold feet.

On July 8, Wolfe landed another three thousand troops, this time on the east bank of the Montmorency River, which flows into the Saint Lawrence eight miles downstream from Quebec. French troops and Indians skirmished as the British column sought a ford farther up the river. Each force kept to opposite sides of the river. Now Wolfe had split his already-outnumbered troops between Point Lévy, Isle d'Orleans, and Montmorency. As Montcalm worried over how to defend both the Montmorency River and the entrenchments, or Beauport line, stretching from there to Quebec, the Canadians were increasingly upset over the pending bombardment from Point Lévy.

A delegation of Quebec's leading citizens, some of them militia leaders, implored Vaudreuil to launch an expedition against the battery before it could open fire. Vaudreuil gave them permission to try. They asked for troops to support them. Montcalm had none to spare. The militia would have to row across and attack alone. Captain Jean-Daniel Dumas, who had joined the attack on Braddock five years earlier, agreed to organize and lead the expedition. The veteran frontier warrior must have shaken his head in bewilderment as he herded the armed students, merchants, peasants, and dandies into the boats around ten o'clock on the night of July 11. Montcalm thought pure folly an "attack [by] . . . a mob of militia, without discipline, on Regular troops in their entrenchments . . . and that those militia were unacquainted with the handling of arms." Although the volunteers packed into boats and rowed to the south shore, they never reached the British entrenchments at Point Lévy. Upon disembarking, those troops soon "imagined themselves surrounded by the enemy; three times did M. Dumas endeavor to rally his men, and three times did his soldiers, mistaking each other for enemies, fire on and fling one another from the top of the bank to the bottom. . . . A retreat became an absolute necessity. . . . The Indians alone, who formed the vanguard, behaved well."[26]

The British artillery at Point Lévy opened fire on Quebec that same night. The systematic destruction of Quebec had begun. On the dark night of July 18, Admiral Charles Saunders sailed the fifty-gun HMS *Sunderland*, thirty-two-gun HMS *Diana*, and twenty-gun HMS *Squirrel*; three transports; and two sloops past Quebec's guns. All passed the cannon fire safely except the HMS *Diana*, which ran aground and was later sailed to Boston for repairs. Montcalm sent Dumas with six hundred troops to shadow that squadron and march against any landings on the north shore. The British noose was steadily being drawn and tightened around Quebec.

The French nervously awaited Wolfe's main assault, which they assumed would be aimed at the Beauport line. It came on July 31. From his headquarters at the village of Beauport in the center of the French entrenchments, Montcalm could, like a spectator atop an amphitheater, watch the British attack in all its brilliant pageantry. Wolfe had tired of all the maneuvering and skirmishing on the French flanks. Instead, he opted for an Abercromby-style charge, attacking where the French were the strongest. As British warships shelled the French lines, 1,200 troops rowed ashore while another 600 waded across the ford at the mouth of the Montmorency River. As at Carillon, massed French muskets and cannon mowed down the redcoats as they surged toward the entrenchments. The mad assault cost the British 210 dead and 230 wounded while the French suffered about 60 casualties altogether.

Yet the carnage could have been far worse. Once again, Montcalm missed a chance to transform a limited victory into a decisive one. His troops stayed in their trenches as the remnants of the British attack scrambled back into their whaleboats and rowed to safety. Had Montcalm ordered a massive counterattack, he might have captured that entire brigade, one-quarter of Wolfe's army. Had that happened,

Wolfe would have had little choice but to sail for home in disgrace, and history would likely remember him as an Abercromby rather than a hero.

The Niagara and Carillon Campaigns

For the next five weeks, only British raids and looting disturbed the Quebec front, but elsewhere redcoats and provincials were marching to victory. Commanding Fort Niagara was Captain Pierre Pouchot, who not only was a first-rate officer and engineer but who also left for posterity a memoir every bit as informative as Bougainville's journal. Montcalm and Vaudreuil both esteemed Pouchot, a rare convergence in their antagonistic relationship. So too did the Indians, who called him "Sategariouaen" or "the center of good dealings." But all of Pouchot's various skills would not be enough to defeat the British siege of Fort Niagara.[27]

General John Prideaux, with Colonel William Johnson his second, commanded the expedition launched from Albany that reached Oswego on June 27. Prideaux left 1,300 provincials under Colonel Frederick Haldimand to rebuild the fortifications while he embarked 2,212 other troops in bateaux for the long row west along Lake Ontario's south shore to Fort Niagara. The two French sloops on Lake Ontario, the *Iroquoise* and *Outouaise*, each with ten twelve-pounders, were supposedly patrolling at that time but failed to detect the British advance. Those sloops could have devastated Prideaux's troops if they had caught them on the water.

While Prideaux's army was rowing west, Captain Saint Luc de La Corne and 1,191 troops arrived almost in its wake at Oswego on July 5. La Corne hoped to launch a surprise attack on Oswego. It was an audacious move. Haldimand's troops were not only fortified but more numerous. After a skirmish, La Corne recognized the impossibility of his mission and withdrew his force eastward to their base at Fort Présentation on the upper Saint Lawrence River.[28]

Prideaux's army landed near Fort Niagara on July 7. They quickly established a fortified camp from which they began zigzagging parallels toward the fort. The bombardment began on July 12. The British repulsed a French sortie against their battery. Pouchot had only two hopes left. One was that a large enough French and Indian force could be mustered to relieve the fort. The other was that he could sway the Indians accompanying the British to switch sides. Both hopes partly came true. At a series of councils with Indians of both sides, Pouchot tried to convince those with the British to sit out the fight. On July 12, those Indians, who were mostly Iroquois, announced that they would indeed move their camp to Belle Famille, a mile south of Fort Niagara, and treat with whoever won. If that were not disturbing enough to the British, on the evening of July 18, a gunner touched off a cohorn mortar just as Prideaux stepped before it. The iron ball shattered his head as if it were a pumpkin. Johnson took command of the British army.

Finally, Pouchot's pleas to various other French frontier commanders were answered. As soon as he got Pouchot's message on July 12, Captain Lignery at Fort Presque Isle immediately gathered 800 French and 500 Indians aboard a canoe fleet and led them along Lake Erie toward Fort Niagara. Johnson soon got word of their approach. Lignery gambled on defeating the British through diplomacy rather than surprise. He sent a delegation of Indians to visit the Iroquois camp at Belle Famille. There, they "held a council in the presence of Johnson . . . [and] presented five wampum belts on behalf of the nations who were to accompany Lignery. Their message was the Iroquois should withdraw, otherwise they would be attacked just like the British. The latter assured them they would not become involved in the dispute."[29]

Johnson set 150 troops to work constructing a breastwork across the road at Belle Famille. He also designated other units to march quickly there when they got word of Lignery's advance. On the morning of July 24, Lignery's troops stumbled into sight, exhausted by their eight-mile hike from the portage at Niagara Falls and little sleep the night before. Johnson immediately sent reinforcements to Belle Famille. The French and Indians assaulted the entrenchments and were repulsed. The British counterattacked. The Iroquois neutrality ended brutally as the French retreated. The Iroquois swarmed over the terrified survivors and butchered scores of them; from 250 to 344 French may have been killed or captured.[30]

Pouchot's hopes had lifted briefly when he learned of Lignery's arrival. During nineteen days of siege, he had lost one-fifth of his 618 troops, including 109 men killed or wounded, and another 37 sick. Many of the dead were among his gunners, killed or maimed by British shells or by their own overheated cannons when they burst. Then came word that Johnson's troops had repulsed Lignery's relief force and captured most of its leaders. Pouchot asked for terms. Johnson was magnanimous. The French marched out with honors of war toward captivity at New York City. Learning of Fort Niagara's capture, Lieutenant François-Marie Picoté de Belestre, left in command at Fort Presque Isle, gathered the survivors of that battle with those of his own fort and of Forts Le Boeuf and Venango and retreated to Fort Detroit. In commanding most of Lake Ontario, the British had split upper from lower Canada.[31]

Soon, the British would control most of Lake Champlain as well. By mid-July at Fort Edward, General Jeffery Amherst had massed 11,376 troops, of which 6,537 were regulars and 4,839 provincials. At Fort Carillon, Bourlamaque had only 3,000 troops and Indians. On July 20, Amherst's army began the long thirty-two-mile row up Lake George. Upon learning of Amherst's advance, Vaudreuil ordered Bourlamaque to abandon both Forts Carillon and Saint Frederic, and retreat to Fort Île aux Noix where Lake Champlain drains into the Richelieu River. Bourlamaque skillfully delayed each segment of his retreat until the last moment. At Fort Carillon, he waited until Amherst had laboriously brought up his guns to the plateau on July 23 before he slipped the last of his troops into bateaux to row north into the night. He did the same at Fort Saint Frederic sixteen miles north of Carillon. Amherst did not march his troops into Fort Saint Frederic until August 4.

And there Amherst encamped his army for another nine months. His excuse was that the four French gunboats on Lake Champlain prevented him from moving until his men could build a superior squadron. But during the same time that it took to build those boats, he could have widened the trail into a road that led along the lake's western shore and marched his army overland. When those gunboats were finally built in October, Amherst then announced that the season was too advanced and ordered his troops into winter quarters. Montreal would not witness enemy troops at its gates for nearly another year.[32]

The Plains of Abraham

Quebec almost saw the British depart from its gates. Wolfe increasingly despaired as Quebec's defenses appeared to be impregnable. By September, he had lost nearly 1,000 troops in various battles and skirmishes, while disease felled hundreds more. Though the British had passed twenty-two ships, including a fifty-gun warship and several frigates, above Quebec, 1,500 troops under Bougainville marched everywhere the British troops aboard those ships landed. British troops looted and burned their way through the villages and farms in the Saint Lawrence valley, while British gunners destroyed Quebec. But Montcalm remained defiant. The fleet commander, Admiral Saunders, increasingly pressed Wolfe that, if Quebec did not fall soon, they would have to pack up and sail away to escape the autumn storms. Wolfe and his brigade commanders were barely on speaking terms, and, to worsen matters, Wolfe was sick, perhaps as much from depression as from dysentery. In late August, he tried to interest the commanders in another go at the Beauport line. They rejected the plan for the probability of its leading to another slaughter. On September 1, the commanders implored Wolfe to send the army upriver west of Quebec; by severing Montcalm's supply lines, they would force him to march out and fight on ground chosen by the British. Wolfe agreed, but secretly planned a landing just a mile from the city's walls. Between then and September 13, Wolfe sent more ships packed with troops above Quebec and massed other troops directly across from Anse au Foulon, where he hoped to land. Montcalm responded by sending Bougainville and 3,000 troops upriver to try to keep pace with the shifting British flotilla and to block any redcoat attempt to land. This proved to be an impossible mission.

The British landing on Anse au Foulon took place around four o'clock on the morning of September 13. The troops quickly scrambled up the 150-foot path to the plain above, routed the company of French troops guarding it, and captured a nearby battery. By dawn, Wolfe had massed 4,441 troops on the Plains of Abraham spreading west of Quebec. When Montcalm learned of the enemy army's presence, he sent orders to his colonels to concentrate their battalions before the city's gates. A courier was also dispatched to Bougainville, ordering him to march against Wolfe. By ten o'clock that morning, Montcalm had gathered around 5,000 troops on the plain.[33]

Then Montcalm, normally the most prudent of commanders, committed a disastrous blunder. He ordered an attack before he had gathered all of Quebec's spare defenders or cannons, bombarded the enemy, or spotted Bougainville's column marching against the enemy's rear. Why? After the battle, Montcalm's officers claimed that the British were entrenching and bringing up their cannons and reinforcements, while Bougainville's whereabouts were unknown. Thus, they reasoned that it was better to attack while the British were still relatively weak.[34] But a glance through his spyglass would have revealed to Montcalm that Wolfe's men were not entrenching or receiving more troops and cannons. And if Montcalm did not know Bougainville's whereabouts, why did he not send couriers galloping along the open road north of the Plains of Abraham to find and urge him forward? Jealousy perhaps best explains Montcalm's rash attack. According to one anonymous officer, "Vaudreuil had, in a note requesting him to postpone the attack until he had reunited all his forces, previously advised him he was marching in person with the Montreal battalions. Nothing more was required to determine [Montcalm whose] ambition was that no person but himself should ever" enjoy acclaim for the victory."[35]

Montcalm led his troops to the attack, but the mix of militiamen recruited among the regulars unraveled the formation. By the time the battalions got within musket range of Wolfe's forces, they had had dissolved into hordes:

> Our troops, composed almost entirely of Canadians impetuously rushed on the enemy, but their ill-formed ranks soon broke either in consequence of the precipitancy with which they had been made to march, or by the inequality of the ground. The English received our first fire in good order, without giving way. They afterwards very briskly returned our fire, and the advance movement made from their centre by a detachment of about 200 men with fixed bayonets, sufficed to put to flight almost all of our army. The rout was total only

among the Regulars; the Canadians accustomed to fall back Indian fashion . . . rallied in some places, and under cover of the brushwood . . . forced divers corps to give way but were at last obliged to yield to the superiority of numbers. The Indians took scarcely any part in this affair.[36]

The battle had lasted little more than a half hour. When the smoke cleared, the British had lost 658 killed, wounded, and missing, including Wolfe, who was cut down by three musket balls. The French lost anywhere from 640 to 1,500 men; among them was Montcalm, mortally wounded when a ball slammed into him as he rode back to the city.[37]

Colonel George Townsend took command of the British army after Wolfe's death. He and his men stood their ground. They were exhausted from the lack of sleep and stress of battle. Leading two thousand troops, Bougainville had appeared on the plain's western edge around noon. Had Montcalm only waited two hours, all the while blasting Wolfe's troops with his artillery followed by an attack on three sides, he might possibly have overrun and captured the entire British force.

Vaudreuil and his officers gave up Quebec. The governor sent orders for the army to retreat toward Montreal, bypassing the British troops on the plain. Vaudreuil handed Jean Baptiste Nicholas de Ramezay, Quebec's mayor, meticulously detailed instructions on the means and ends of negotiating Quebec's surrender. The governor had obviously anticipated the event for some time and had penned his instructions long before. Ramezay was "not to wait for the enemy carrying the town by assault; therefore, as soon as he shall fail of provisions, he is to hoist the white flag." The surrender, Vaudreuil detailed, must include honors of war for Quebec's gallant defenders; the right of the people to maintain their religion, property, and person; and care given to the sick and wounded.[38] Vaudreuil then joined his retreating army.

Ramezay commanded 200 regulars, 500 marines, and 1,000 militiamen, a formidable force, behind city walls. On September 15, he called an officers' council. To them he revealed that in the three days since the battle the British on the plain had been reinforced and entrenched, and were preparing batteries. The city's food would be exhausted within a few days. The leading citizens had signed a petition asking the mayor to surrender to spare the nearly 4,000 civilians still in the city the horrors of a bombardment, assault, and sack. Despite all that, Ramezay wanted to fight to the last biscuit and bullet. But his defeatist officers prevailed. And why should they have not when Vaudreuil himself had ordered Ramezay to surrender?[39]

Unbeknownst to the defenders, help was on the way. Lévis had reached Jacques Cartier, where Vaudreuil's retreat had paused. He took command of the army and marched it back toward the city. Upon joining Bougainville at Cap Rouge, Lévis sent ahead 100 horsemen with biscuit-filled saddlebags and a message to Ramezay to hold on. The horsemen clattered into the city on September 17. But earlier that day, Ramezay had signed an agreement with the British whereby he would surrender Quebec the next morning. And, man of honor that Ramezay was, so he did. Along with Quebec, the French lost over 2,500 men, 234 cannon, 17 mortars, 4 howitzers, 694 barrels of powder, 14,800 round shot, 1,500 shells, 3,000 muskets with bayonets, and 70 tons of musket balls.[40] These troops and munitions would be sorely missed.

Townsend garrisoned Quebec with 3,000 troops under the command of Colonel James Murray, and then sailed away to London with the rest of the army crammed aboard the fleet. The next spring the French and British would race to see which supply fleet got to Quebec first. If the French were bold and swift enough, they might be able to retake the city.

Sugar and Spice

Until 1759, the Caribbean was largely a sideshow in which neither the French nor British had the strength to attack the other's colonies. The only real fighting occurred at sea as squadrons or privateers chased convoys of merchant ships. But in late 1758 Pitt decided to follow up Britain's successes elsewhere with an expedition to those waters. On November 12, 1758, a fleet of eight ships of the line under Commodore Robert Hughes and a dozen transports packed with three thousand troops led by General Peregrine Hopson set sail from England. The object was Martinique, which they reached on January 15, 1759. Fort Royal, perched on a small mountain overlooking the town, seemed impregnable. The British bombarded the fort and landed troops to probe its defenses, all to no avail. One hundred men were lost before Hopson chose to reembark his force and sail on to Guadeloupe.

The warships approached Guadeloupe's capital, Basse-Terre, and bombarded it to ashes on January 23. The French withdrew six miles into the interior. Hopson's troops landed and marched after them. Believing that the French position was impregnable, Hopson encamped his army, then as the weeks passed watched the fever steadily eat it up. By late February, diseases had killed or sickened 1,500 redcoats; on February 27, Hopson himself succumbed. Colonel John Barrington took command and holed up its remnants in Fort Louis. The French converged on Fort Louis and besieged it. This dire predicament worsened in mid-March when word arrived that Admiral Maximin de Bompart's squadron of eight ships of the line and three frigates had reached Port Royal. En route, his warships had scoured the seas of as many as 180 British merchant ships. Now they threatened the expedition against Guadeloupe.

Realizing that only bold strokes could save his command, Barrington sailed six hundred troops to raid Saint Anne and Saint François. Having diverted French troops that way, Barrington then attacked and drove off the French before withdrawing to Saint Louis. The campaign turned on April 12 when British troops landed near Arnouville and routed the French from their entrenchments on the Licorne River. The British pursued for the next several days. On April 18, the showdown came at Saint Maries, where the redcoats routed the French.

Guadeloupe was surrendered on May 1 in return for the promise that the planters would enjoy freedom of religion, their existing laws and property, and, perhaps most importantly, the same tariffs as other British colonies. In guaranteeing these rights, the British hoped to seduce other French islands into capitulating without a struggle. In the past, few French ships had reached Guadeloupe during peacetime; fewer still during war. Guadeloupe would flourish under British rule as dozens of ships annually dropped anchor there.

If the French on Guadeloupe had held out another day they might have been saved. General Alexandre Beauharnais arrived with 600 troops and 2,000 islanders offshore shortly after the ink had dried on the surrender paper. Learning of Guadeloupe's fate, Beauharnais sailed back to Martinique. Barrington sent troops to capture the nearby small but rich sugar island of Marie-Galante, which gave up on May 26. Guadeloupe cost the British 59 killed and 158 wounded in battle but 800 dead from fever. French losses are unknown.[41]

The French also suffered humiliating defeats in India this year. Until 1759, the fighting in India was indecisive. Both sides launched campaigns that accomplished little. In late January, Colonel Francis Forde advanced with an army of redcoats and sepoys against the smaller army of Admiral Conflans, who retreated before him to Masulipatam, the center of French influence in the region. Forde's army appeared before Masulipatam on March 6 and began digging siege lines. A French force captured Forde's supply depot at Rajahmundry. Other French and native forces were converging. Forde's position looked hopeless. Yet, instead of retreating, he chose to attack. On April 8, he flung his best troops against two key points in Masulipatam's defenses, carried them, and forced Conflans to surrender the city.

For the next half year, neither side mounted a major offensive. The only major fighting occurred for Wandiwash, halfway between Madras and Pondicherry. Wandiwash provided the French with both a jumping-off point and forward defense against the English. In April and July, English armies besieged Wandiwash before withdrawing. With his troops near mutiny, General Lally did not march to Wandiwash's rescue. In September, Admiral Aché's squadron appeared for the third time off Saint David. Once again, the English and French squadrons exchanged broadsides before disengaging.

Then, in October, Dutch ambitions stimulated a raid on British depots and ships in Bengal. Over the next two months, two British forces advanced up the Hugli valley, Robert Clive's by water and Forde's by land, brushing aside the small Dutch forces and capturing their trading posts and ships. By late December, Dutch Bengal was British.

The German Seesaw

The British victories in North America, the Caribbean, and India contrasted with the stalemate in Germany. With spring, the belligerents resumed their seemingly endless seesaw war. Broglie was the first to advance; he repulsed an attack by Ferdinand, Duke of Brunswick, at Bergen on April 13, then pursued him into Hesse. Meanwhile, Louis George Erasmes, marquis de Contades, split the Army of the Lower Rhine into four corps and advanced into Hesse, taking Cassel and Minden and investing Lippstadt, Munster, and Hameln. The French campaign had started out well but, as usual, ground to a halt by midsummer as the armies depleted their supplies, troops, and morale.

The strength of Ferdinand's army rose as that of the French dwindled. On August 1, Ferdinand wheeled his 41,000 troops and 170 cannons to strike Contades's 51,000 troops and 162 cannon at Minden. His troops punched through the French lines or chewed up counterattacks. Had Lord George Sackville obeyed Ferdinand's repeated orders to lead the English cavalry against the faltering enemy, they might have crushed the entire French army. Still, when the smoke cleared, the French had suffered 11,000 casualties and 43 cannons to the allies' 2,600 casualties. Ferdinand chased Contades back across Hesse, capturing thousands of French troops. On August 25, Marshal d'Estrées relieved Contades but could not reverse his army's decay. During these crucial weeks, Broglie stood his ground and ignored his colleagues' pleas for help. He finally stirred in November with a march against Ferdinand's supply depot at Cassel. Prince Louis of Brunswick-Wolfenbüttel intercepted Broglie's advance corps at Fulda, savaged it, then, in harness with Ferdinand, converged on Broglie himself. Just when it seemed that the allies would inflict on the French another devastating defeat, a message arrived from a desperate Frederick begging for reinforcements. What had happened?

Over the summer in Saxony, Frederick's brother Prince Henry launched a series of brilliant marches that destroyed Austrian supply and troop columns. This advantage disappeared at Zullichau on August 13 when General Pyotr Semyonovich Saltykov's 50,000 Russian, Croat, and Cossack troops smashed into General Karl von Wedell's

26,000-man army guarding the Polish approach to Berlin; 6,000 casualties later, Wedell retreated. Once again, the road was clear between a Russian army and Berlin.

Frederick gathered 48,000 troops and marched north. Joined by General Gideon Ernst von Laudon's 18,000 troops, Saltykov pressed his 68,000-man army on to Kunersdorf, where Frederick attacked him on August 12. It was Frederick's worst defeat—28,000 troops and 170 cannons. The Russians sustained 15,700 dead and wounded. Frederick rallied 32,000 troops for a last stand before Berlin. But, once again, the allies tossed away a golden chance to win the war.

Count Leopold von Daun and Saltykov marched in opposite directions, the Austrians to Dresden and the Russians to Glogau. Daun hoped to link up at Dresden with Friedrich Michel von Zweibrücken's Imperial army, which had captured Halle, Leipzig, and Württemberg. Outnumbered, Henry sidestepped Daun's army and raided his supply lines. Nonplused, Daun forced General Kurt von Schmettau to surrender Dresden and its 3,700 defenders. After consolidating his latest victory, Daun marched into Saxony, where on November 21 he defeated General Friedrich von Finck at Maxen and forced him to surrender all 12,000 Prussian survivors. The armies then went into winter quarters.

Peace Now?

Amidst the ever-growing heaps of carnage and debts, most leaders thought of peace, but on very different terms. The Prussians and British split on the question. After three years of war, Frederick II was ready to return to Sans Souci. On June 10, 1759, he wrote George II a letter suggesting that they organize a peace congress. The British king rejected the offer. George, his ministers, and the people sensed that 1759 would be the year of victories and the war's turning point. Peace could wait. Still Britain's leaders were split over the question of just what kind of peace they hoped eventually to win. At this point in the war, George II rather than Pitt was Whitehall's most fervent expansionist. The king insisted that he would lay aside his sword only after Versailles surrendered all of New France. Pitt "ridiculed the King's way of talking about the conditions of peace and the retaining of all our conquests."[42] On August 13, the day after his defeat at Kunersdorf, Frederick sent an even more urgent plea to Whitehall, imploring the cabinet to call jointly for a peace congress to end the war.

Most in the cabinet concurred. Pitt, however, insisted that any peace congress proposal be a sign of strength rather than weakness and thus should await news of victories in America. Just what did Pitt want? At this point, he favored just rolling back the boundary to the Great Lakes and Saint Lawrence, thus leaving a truncated Canada to France, and had not yet decided whether to keep Louisbourg and Cape Breton. Pitt's ambitions would expand with British victories.

Ironically, by now Choiseul had decided that if the British took Canada it might be wise to let them keep it in return for concessions elsewhere. After all, no country needed peace more than France, whose armies had suffered humiliating defeats on both continents, whose navy had been swept from the seas or bottled up in port, and whose empire was being ripped away, piece by piece. By now the king's council agreed that the alliance with Austria, Russia, and Sweden was a deadweight that sank any chances of victory or peace. More than anyone, Choiseul recognized this: "I think it would be possible to end the war honorably and promptly if we were not engaged, England and ourselves, in the quarrels of our allies. . . . By our treaties we are trapped in this war."[43]

By spring 1759, Choiseul had resolved to send a peace feeler to England via an unlikely go-between, King Charles IV of the Two Sicilies. On April 3, 1759, Choiseul instructed French ambassador Pierre Paul, marquis d'Ossun, to press Charles IV to join the Neapolitan fleet with that of France to sail against England. Should Charles IV rebuff that idea, Ossun would then ask the king to mediate peace between France and England. Spurning an alliance, Charles IV readily agreed to mediate.

That summer and fall, Naples's ambassador to London, Prince Albertini Sanseverino, approached Pitt several times with offers to help negotiate the war's end. These offers greatly disappointed Whitehall. The English had been egging on Charles IV to join with the kingdom of Sardinia-Piedmont in attacking Austria and splitting its Italian territories between them. Charles had spurned these offers just as firmly as he had those from Versailles. Pitt gently rebuffed Sanseverino's offers by citing his need first to get Frederick's permission, an ironic excuse given the Prussian king's own interest in peace.[44]

Leaving no diplomatic stone unturned, Choiseul even approached Denmark to mediate talks with Britain in September 1759. Through this channel, he sent word of his willingness to concede to Britain a neutral zone between the Wabash River and Appalachian Mountains and to submit Acadia's fate to the decision of a neutral power to be chosen by London. The Appalachian watershed, however, would remain the boundary between the two North American empires. But that was just the perfunctory opening move. For now, the game ended there. Whitehall rejected the Danish feeler.[45]

The question of whether now was the time to negotiate the war's end divided France's allies. The Russians had occupied not only the Duchy of Courland—a prime reason they joined the war—but also East Prussia. Saint Petersburg waved Saltykov's victories in its allies' faces to demand both captured realms. Versailles said it might be willing to accept those conquests if Russia would join its fleet with that of France and sail against England. Saint Petersburg refused. Maria Theresa and her advisors were not eager to see Russia's empire spread any farther west than was absolutely necessary to defeat Frederick; they rejected the Russian demand with the reasoning that Denmark, fearing Russia more than Prussia, might just join Frederick if Saint Petersburg scored any more victories or appeared more greedy for territory.[46]

Rolls of the Dice

Throughout 1759, rather than end, the war nearly spread as Britain's campaign against contraband threatened to push the neutral maritime powers into the enemy camp. Angry complaints from The Hague, Stockholm, Copenhagen, Lisbon, Madrid, and elsewhere soared as British privateers and warships seized more of their ships. Alarmed that relations with those states were reaching a breaking point, in May Whitehall got Parliament to pass a bill that granted privateer licenses only to owners of ships of at least one hundred tons and ten guns and that sped up the judicial process of determining a cargo's fate. After the bill took effect on June 1, 1759, complaints dropped considerably and the danger passed.[47]

Choiseul tried to capitalize on the growing animosities against Britain. His grand plan was to join the fleets and armies of France, Russia, Denmark, Sweden, Holland, and Spain in a league of armed neutrality to cut off Prussia and to war against England. He hoped such a league would either provoke a spoiling English attack or give its members the confidence to declare war. Versailles might have been able to forge such an alliance in 1756 or even 1757 when the French fleet was second only to Britain's. Now it was too late. The last thing any of these governments wished to do was to provoke a catastrophic war with Britain. France would have to continue to wage its war alone against the British fleet. If only France could inflict a sharp defeat on Britain, it might be able to rally those other beleaguered maritime powers.

Throughout 1759, rumors reached Whitehall that France was preparing to invade England. These rumors were true. War minister Belle Isle devised a plan for not one but three invasions of the British Isles. In all, he talked the king's council into an enormous gamble. By 1759, the French navy had been whittled down by battle and attrition to only 43 warships in home waters and 30 in foreign waters, compared to England's 275 ships, of which about half were in distant seas, and the rest blockading the French coast or anchored in home ports. Even worse, France's warships were scattered among its three naval bases, Brest, Rochefort, and Toulon, and were also at Dunkirk and Cap François, Haiti, in the Caribbean, while its transports were spread among those ports along with Bordeaux, Nantes, La Rochelle, Bayonne, and Morbihan. Versailles would have to coordinate the actions of those far-flung squadrons and flotillas. The Toulon and Caribbean squadrons under Jean François Bertet de La Clue-Sabran and Maximin de Bompart, respectively, would have to slip through the shadowing British fleets and somehow join the Brest fleet under Conflans. Flotillas of transports and small warships would have to reach Morbihan where one invasion army had gathered.[48]

Once the Brest fleet was gathered, a small flotilla commanded by Captain François Thurot would set out from Dunkirk to create a diversion on the Irish coast. As the British squadrons raced after him, the French would launch their two main attacks. Conflans would escort the 20,000-man army under Emmanuel Armand, duc d'Aiguillon, from Morbihan to Glasgow, while another 20,000-man army embarked at Ostend, crossed over to Malden in Essex, and force-marched to capture London. To that end, the French were building flotillas of flatboats in English Channel ports, gathering supplies, and training the troops. By midsummer, the troops and transports were ready. They awaited only a golden opportunity to sail.

As if the operation were not complex and risky enough, the French unwittingly tipped their hand to the English. On May 31, Belle Isle sent a copy of his plan to his ambassador in Stockholm. Belle Isle had hoped to entice the Swedes to join the attack on Scotland. Sweden's twenty-two ships of the line might well tip the naval balance against England in the North Sea. The Swedes demurred. Instead, a copy of the plan ended up at Whitehall in mid-June.[49]

The admiralty dealt with the threat by reinforcing and tightening the blockade. More warships joined Admiral Edward Hawke at Brest, Commodore William Boys at Dunkirk, Admiral Edward Boscawen at Toulon, a reserve squadron under Captain George Rodney at Spithead, and smaller squadrons off Rochefort and in the English Channel. On July 3, Rodney's squadron appeared off Le Havre and bombarded the port but did little damage.

Indeed, just maintaining a constant patrol powerful enough to cork each port was virtually impossible. In late June, Boscawen withdrew his squadron to Gibraltar for repairs. La Clue hurried to complete his fleet's preparations. He finally set sail on August 5. Twelve days later, frigates brought word to Boscawen of La Clue's approach. Within hours, Boscawen had rounded up his crews and headed his fleet to sea. But La Clue slipped past and surged into the Atlantic. Boscawen caught up to him thirty miles south of Cape Saint Vincent. La Clue's squadron scattered. The British warships captured one warship at sea and pursued four others into neutral Portuguese waters, where they bombarded and captured them. Determined to evade capture, La Clue ordered his flagship sailed straight to destruction on the rocky shore. Boscawen had wiped out half of La Clue's squadron. Seven warships managed to evade the pursuit and reach French ports.

Like Boscawen's earlier that summer, Hawke's squadron also verged on breaking down under the sea's constant pounding. Yet he kept his ships off Brest or had them sailing the coast day and night, month after monotonous month. In September, he tried to destroy a flotilla of transports heading north from Nantes but succeeded only in chasing it into the safety of Auray.

At Versailles, the news of La Clue's debacle only stiffened Belle Isle's will to win. He ordered Conflans to send Captain Sébastien François Bigot de Morogues with six warships to Morbihan to convoy Aiguillon's army to Scotland. Hawke's squadron sailed against Morogues as soon as he tried to leave Brest and forced him back inside. By mid-October, Versailles was desperate to unleash its squadrons and armies against the British Isles, and the blockading squadrons were as desperate to return to port for a thorough overhaul and rest. English spies intercepted yet another detailed plan from Belle Isle to the ambassador to Sweden. This time Whitehall learned that Conflans had standing orders to sail directly against Hawke and battle him while the transport fleet sailed past to its Scottish landing. The cabinet reinforced Hawke's fleet.

A gale blew off the channel on October 14 and drove blockading squadrons into the nearest friendly shelters. This was the chance the French had awaited. By the time the British squadrons returned to their stations, one of the French squadrons had disappeared from port into the open sea. Thurot did not head directly for the British Isles but instead sailed far north to shelter first at Goteborg, Sweden, then Bergen, and finally the Faroe Islands for the winter.

Another gale on November 5 forced Hawke to shelter his fleet at Plymouth and Portsmouth. By chance, Bompart arrived off the coast at the same time and was able to reach Brest. Though Bompart's ships were too battered to return immediately to sea, Conflans transferred Bompart's crews to his own. On November 14, Conflans finally sailed from Brest with twenty-one ships of the line and five frigates, but adverse winds forced his fleet to anchor just seventy miles west of Belle Isle. Frigate pickets soon brought word to Hawke, who gathered his fleet and pursued. On November 19, the two fleets spotted each other's sails. Conflans ordered his fleet to flee with the wind and seek the nearest shelter, Quiberon Bay. The next day, Hawke's fleet caught up, closed, and opened fire. When Conflans's ships sailed into Quiberon Bay itself, Hawke ordered his own ships to follow even though his captains had no charts of those shallow, rocky waters. The two fleets entangled and exchanged broadsides in that cramped bay. By the battle's end, Hawke had destroyed or captured six French ships, including Conflans's flagship, while losing two of his own. The rest of the French escaped to Rochefort or the Vilaine River.

Quiberon Bay, or Les Cardinaux, as the French called it, was the war's decisive naval battle. Throughout the war, the Brest fleet posed the greatest threat to the British Isles. No French fleet was more powerful or better positioned to reach Britain by the winds and currents. Then Hawke destroyed most of it and scattered the shards to Rochefort and other small ports along France's west coast, several hundred miles farther from Britain's shores.

Consequences

By late 1759, the war appeared to have reached a diplomatic crossroads where it could either expand or end. Ferdinand VI's tormented life ended on August 10, 1759. The king had no sons. The heir to Spain's throne fell by default on his half brother Charles, King of the Two Sicilies. He left the regent Marchese di Tanucci in charge of Naples and its new ruler, his eight-year-old son, Ferdinand IV. Charles III was only forty-three when he mounted Spain's throne on December 9, 1759. For his subsequent deeds, he would be ranked among Spain's greatest rulers.

Ministries across Europe held their breath as the new king ascended the throne. Which way, if any, would Charles III turn? Charles was no anglophile. An English insult to Charles burned long after it was inflicted. In 1742, Charles had tried to help Ferdinand VI conquer Palma. The British got wind of the expedition he was organizing.

Commodore William Martin sailed his squadron into Naples Bay and demanded that Charles desist or suffer destruction. Charles had no choice but to yield. After Charles mounted the Spanish throne in 1759, avenging that insult would be one of several reasons why he would choose to war against England.

Where Charles stood depended greatly on the view from his throne. That insult aside, Austria rather than Britain was the worst threat to the kingdom of the Two Sicilies. For centuries, the Hapsburgs and Bourbons had battled over northern Italy. Charles feared that if Austria and its allies succeeded in crushing Frederick and Prussia, Vienna would then be free to turn its guns against non-Hapsburg Italy. Thus did Naples, Spain, and France share a common interest in preserving Prussia and joining together.

The Austrian threat diminished considerably once it reached Madrid, while that from Britain loomed ever larger. French ambassador Ossun, who followed Charles from Naples to Madrid, continued to fish for a Spanish alliance. The king's advisors urged caution. His queen, Maria Amelia of Saxony, was the daughter of the king whom Frederick II had driven from his native realm into Poland. Yet she too urged her husband to remain aloof from the war. It would be another three years before Charles III stepped his kingdom off the sidelines and onto the field.

Charles III could swim against the political tide. Learning of Quebec's fall, he sent a memorial to Ambassador Abreu to be presented to Pitt. Spain's king warned Pitt that he "would not regard with indifference the disturbance by the English conquests of the balance of power in America, as established by the peace of Utrecht; he was therefore anxious to see the naval war concluded by a peace in which England would show generosity and moderation, and was himself ready to act as intermediary."[50]

Once again, Pitt politely but firmly turned down the latest mediation offer. This time, he cited the recent Anglo-Prussian call for a peace congress, something he himself thoroughly opposed. He had good reasons to be two-faced. In response to Frederick's pleas earlier that year for a peace congress, Pitt had argued that they should wait until they had racked up some decisive victories against their enemies.

In late October, word arrived that Wolfe had taken Quebec. On October 30, Pitt sent Prince Louis of Brunswick, Ferdinand's brother and the commander of Holland's army, the Anglo-Prussian peace proposal and requested that he submit it to the French, Russian, and Austrian ambassadors at The Hague. On November 25, 1759, Prince Louis presented the proposal.

Choiseul viewed the peace proposal as a godsend. Not only had Versailles received word of Quebec's loss and defeats elsewhere, but in October 1759, the marine ministry's growing mountain of financial cards collapsed. Marine minister Berryer withheld payments on all colonial debts and sharply cut his ministry's expenditures and personnel. Ironically, France could not afford to hold New France even if Britain suddenly declared peace and returned Quebec. Silhouette drew up yet another proposal for ending the war. He called for trading Canada to Britain for Georgia, to which Canadians could immigrate.[51] While the king's council mulled this rather bizarre idea, Choiseul promised Pitt that he would forge with France's allies a rapid reply to the offer. This reply would take nearly six months.

CHAPTER 10

Conquest, 1760

Political principles can only be justified in the pursuit of national interests in good faith.

Choiseul

I prefer peace to Canada. France can exist quite happily without Quebec.

Voltaire

This land will perish after having ruined France through the monstrous abuses of these privileged select.

Bougainville

We have nothing more for it than to sell our lives as dearly as we can . . . and we must die sword in hand.

Cacambo in *Candide*

If the allies had immediately agreed to the peace congress called for by England and Prussia on November 25, 1759, the momentum just might have led to serious negotiations. But for months France, Austria, and Russia squabbled over a response. As always, the fortunes of war affected the chance for peace. Each government desired peace according to how well or poorly it was fighting the war.

France was clearly losing. It was evident that Canada and much of the rest of the empire was about to be conquered. The treasury was empty. Fermier Général Jean Joseph de Laborde remarked to foreign minister Choiseul that, "It is absolutely impossible to wage war during all of 1760."[1] Comptroller General Henri Léonard Jean Baptiste Bertin advised Louis XV that yet another vingtiéme and a doubled capitation was essential to finance the war. The Paris parlement rejected the proposal. The king imposed the taxes through a lit de justice. The financial collapse bottled up the remnants of the fleet in port as effectively as the tightest British blockade; there was little coin with which to refit the few warships left at anchor. In Germany, Prince Ferdinand of Brunswick had beaten every French general who had marched against him; no one was eager to challenge him again. Canada would undoubtedly capitulate this year and Louisiana probably would the next. Indeed, Pitt seemed determined to destroy the entire French empire. Thus was Versailles eager for peace at nearly any price. Choiseul insisted, "It is absolutely necessary for our financial stability that we send our response to The Hague immediately and that we avoid giving the French public reason to believe that the King's ministry is opposed to peace."[2]

In contrast, Vienna and Saint Petersburg insisted that one last campaign would finally crush Frederick, a belief they had been acting on for years. Choiseul dismissed this belief as a delusion. He tried to convince the Austrian and Russian leaders to accept two realities. First, the war was impossible to win and easy to lose so peace now was preferable to peace later. Second, it would be easier to negotiate peace separately than together. When Choiseul pressed them to offer a favorable reply, Austria was ambivalent while Russia outright rejected the idea.

Only a huge concession could swing Russia toward peace. Versailles was prepared to make it. On February 1, 1760, Louis XV wrote Saint Petersburg in reply to its November memoir declaring its ambition to take East Prussia and destroy Frederick. In the interests of an honorable peace, Versailles now accepted Russia's war aims. In doing so, Louis XV essentially wrote off several generations of treasure and blood that France had expended for influence in eastern Europe, all in return for asserting its right to forge a separate peace with Britain! Louis reinforced his decision by removing on February 27, 1760, Jean Pierre Tercier, the last key official committed to the traditional policy. In a follow-up letter to Ambassador Hôpital, Choiseul tried to soften the king's stark abdication of French interests that affected its relations with Sweden, Poland, and Turkey by saying that Austria must accept any Russian gains in eastern Europe. He also sent Louis Charles Auguste le Tonnelier, baron de Breteuil, to Saint Petersburg unofficially to supplant the unreliable and mediocre Hôpital as his "assistant."[3]

Saint Petersburg gave the nod to talks between France and Britain. In late March, Versailles and Whitehall authorized their respective ambassadors at the Hague, Affry and Yorke to talk. They exchanged views in Affry's coach but merely agreed to disagree. In assessing the failure, Versailles concluded that perhaps it needed the weight of its allies after all.

French diplomats got to work forging an allied reply to the Anglo-Prussian peace congress proposal. In April 1760, the allies called for disentangling the two wars with two separate sets of negotiations. Spain could mediate the talks over colonial conflicts between France and Britain. Choiseul agreed to include in the Anglo-French negotiations the fate of Hanover, Hesse, and Brunswick. Meanwhile, Austrian, Russian, and Prussian diplomats would join a congress at Augsburg to negotiate the European war's end.

The proposal died, killed by France's insistence on separate negotiations. Frederick rejected the notion. Whitehall asserted that Prussia must be included in any talks between France and Britain. Versailles replied that the choice was either separate or no negotiations. France's allies sighed with relief when the answer was no; they were not genuinely interested in peace anyway. Vienna soon agreed to Russia's aggrandizement. Maria Theresa remained as determined as ever to reconquer Silesia and Glatz, and needed Russian armies to do so. Saint Petersburg's demand of territory for peace was perfectly natural. On May 21, 1760, Austria and Russia signed a secret treaty by which each accepted the other's ambitions.

Just how badly had French diplomacy blundered? It certainly seemed that Versailles had given up its interests in eastern Europe to line up its allies behind a proposed congress that never met. Yet its abandonment of eastern Europe was, if nothing else, realistic. French diplomats could do nothing to stop Russian armies from asserting control wherever they marched. Russian troops took over the Duchy of Courland and gave it to Saxony while keeping East Prussia for itself. Another concern was that Versailles, teetering at bankruptcy's brink, had no money to squander on bribes in various courts. Actually, the financial crisis and cutbacks had little effect on French interests. A bribe might elicit an eager promise from the official to help France, but an act that did so rarely followed.

A minor crisis erupted when, in the course of various talks, the Danes reacted bitterly to word that the Russians had refused to concede Holstein. In July, Copenhagen threatened to join Prussia if its demand for Holstein was not honored. Denmark was mostly bluffing, which made it easy for French diplomats to mute the bluster between Copenhagen and Saint Petersburg.[4] But the crisis reinforced the reality that France could not win a war or peace while chained to its present allies, Austria, Russia, and Sweden. The alliance merely dragged down France deeper into the German quagmire.

Temptations

France might, however, just have a chance on the battlefield and at the negotiation table if it could induce Spain into an alliance. Versailles employed every diplomatic wile at its disposal to convert Madrid into an ally, mediator, financier, or some combination of those roles. Charles III had no sooner settled on his throne when Choiseul asked him to forward a peace proposal to the British. The message was duly sent. France would accept peace in North America on the basis of Thomas Robinson's memoir of March 7, 1755—essentially the rollback of Canada's borders to the Saint Lawrence, Great Lakes, and Wabash. At this point, Choiseul insisted on the return of Cape Breton, Canada, and Guadeloupe. Acknowledging that Britain would certainly demand more after a half dozen years of war and Quebec's capture, Choiseul would then propose splitting the Neutral Islands between them, with France retaining Saint Lucia and Dominica. He toyed with the idea of demolishing Louisbourg's fortress but finally decided against it.[5]

Pitt coldly rejected the proposal. He declared that he would not agree to Spanish mediation, let alone to using the French terms as the basis for negotiation unless it was through a general peace congress. The stickler was Britain's alliance with Prussia, which forbade a separate peace. Ironically, Pitt rejected peace on that technicality rather than on Versailles's position. At this point, his war goals did not greatly exceed those of Robinson's memoir. He was willing to return Canada north of the Saint Lawrence, Great Lakes, and Wabash, along with Guadeloupe. But England's ally, Prussia, and the honor that accompanied the relationship, had to come first.[6]

All along Choiseul pressed Charles III to join in alliance against the English, or at least to give the appearance of doing so: "I care not at all that Spain enter our war, but at the same time I much desire that her preparations and her language be sufficiently impressive to get us peace."[7] With victory at sea or in North America impossible, Choiseul knew he could only win at the negotiation table. Why was he ambivalent about actually enticing Madrid into the fight? The wretched state of Spain's navy and army was notoriously well known. Such an ally could be as much a liability as an asset.

No one knew better than Charles III that Spain lacked both the means and ends to go to war. Yet he recognized that Spain and France shared a common enemy to their common interests. For now, however, prudence demanded that he stay as noncommittal as Ferdinand VI had been. In June, he instructed his ambassador to London, Joaquin, conde de Fuentes, to cordially insist that England give in to Spain's positions on Honduras logging, English depredations on Spanish shipping, and Newfoundland fisheries. On these issues Whitehall just as cordially rebuffed him.

Charles III then tried to raise the temperature on Whitehall and Versailles alike. Summoning Ambassador Ossun before him on July 4, he broached the notion of an alliance with France, exclaiming, "We are natural and necessary allies; our dominions touch on the two continents, and we have the same enemies to fear." He then casually mentioned that Madrid had always considered Louisiana part of the

Spanish empire. Finally, he dropped an even more stunning diplomatic surprise, stating, "After the peace I must arrange with France to have Louisiana on the basis of some exchange."[8]

A stunned Ossun blurted that perhaps Spain could take Saint Domingue. The king and ambassador agreed to drop the matter until Ossun received instructions from Versailles. Couriers must have exhausted their horses between the two capitals. Within two weeks, Ossun received a reply from Choiseul—rest the matter for now; the rationale for doing so would arrive later. The canny Choiseul knew that if he gave away Spain's most desired prize for joining the war, Madrid would have little incentive to put much into the actual fighting. Of course, if Madrid insisted on taking Louisiana before joining an alliance, Versailles might grudgingly have to surrender it. Yet Choiseul reckoned that the best means of pressuring Madrid to do more was to dangle Louisiana as a prize to be eventually given to Spain if it proved itself a worthy ally that otherwise Britain would snatch away. Spain's worst nightmare in the New World was to wake up with Britain alongside. Choiseul raised the old domino theory that if Quebec fell today, New Orleans would follow tomorrow, and the next day the Spaniards would find the British battering down the door to Santa Fe with an eye on Mexico City over the horizon. As importantly, Choiseul did not want to give up Louisiana except as a last throw of the dice. After all, top officials in both Versailles and Montreal seriously mulled packing up the remnants of French forces in Canada and retreating up the Great Lakes and down the Wabash and Mississippi to refuge in Louisiana, a problematic option with Louisiana in Spanish hands.[9]

By September 1760, years of British insults to Charles, first as king of the Two Sicilies, then as king of Spain, finally reached a boiling point. On September 9, Charles III had two notes delivered to Whitehall by Ambassador Fuentes. The demands were familiar, but the words were stronger. The first demand protested British logging in Honduras and Yucatan; the other asserted Spanish rights to fish around Newfoundland.

Then Charles III's wife, Queen Maria Amelia, died on September 27. Throughout their life together, the queen had restrained her husband's foreign policy with the plea that neutrality was the best policy.

Perhaps to throw off the pain of her death and the restraint of her life, Charles III signaled his readiness to issue an ultimatum if Britain did not concede to Spain's demands.

His closest advisors, however, Ricardo Wall, Julian de Arriaga, and Bernardo di Tanucci, dampened his ardor. They convinced him that Spain was simply not ready for war, and that any premature declaration would let Britain inflict punishing and humiliating blows against the realm and empire. Charles finally agreed that patience might well gain Spain Louisiana without great loss of blood or treasure. This belief would come true.[10]

Knockout Blows

In 1760, Whitehall made an all-out effort to conquer Canada and hold Hanover. Despite growing financial worries, the cabinet agreed to swell its army's ranks to 109,000 troops, 18,000 more than the previous year. When the 65,470 foreign or provincial troops on the British payroll were included, more than 174,000 soldiers marched under the Union Jack in various parts of the world. The fleet was increased to 301 ships manned by 85,000 sailors. In all, Whitehall had mustered the largest army and navy ever before seen in English history.[11]

Amidst this enormous buildup, on February 21, 1760, the long-awaited French invasion of the British Isles took place. It was not quite what war minister Belle Isle had envisioned. Having sailed down from the Faroe Islands, Captain Thurot anchored his three frigates that day off Carrickfergus in Northern Ireland and sent a thousand men ashore. The Irish militia put up a spirited defense of the town's ruined castle before capitulating. Thurot demanded food from nearby Belfast. The cowed officials complied but sent word for help. A frigate squadron prowling the sea encountered Thurot's ships on February 26 and immediately closed for battle. Within an hour and a half, all three French frigates had struck their colors; Thurot was among the dead. Thurot's quixotic raid was all that had come after over a year of planning and trying to execute a three-pronged invasion of the British Isles. The incident symbolized the impotence of French military power.

The bloody stalemate in Germany continued. While the personal-ities commanding French armies in Germany changed, the campaign plans and results stayed largely the same. In June, Claude Louis Saint Germain crossed his army over the Rhine at Dusseldorf while Victor François, duc de Broglie, marched northeast from Frankfort. As usual, the hope was to crush Ferdinand between those converging pinchers. And, as usual, Ferdinand blunted first one then the other.

With his 66,000 troops outgunned nearly two to one by the 130,000 French soldiers, Ferdinand launched several brilliant spoiling attacks. The first blow struck Broglie on July 10 at Sachsenhauscn, where the Germans routed the French advance guard. Ferdinand followed up this victory by inflicting sharp defeats on the enemy at Emsdorf on July 16 and Warburg on July 31. The French lost 8,000 men to the allies' 1,200. After each side spent the next several months replen-ishing their ranks and supplies, Ferdinand launched a finely played campaign in October that slowly maneuvered the French armies back to the Rhine and Main Rivers. Not all went according to plan. On October 16, Charles Eugène Gabriel de la Croix, marquis de Castries, fought off the attacks of Ferdinand's second-in-command, August Wilhelm, the duke of Brunswick-Bevern, at Kloster Kampen; each suf-fered 3,000 casualties, but the French retained the field. Castries pur-sued Brunswick into Westphalia, where his offensive ground to a halt for want of more men, food, and munitions. By the year's end, the French retained Hesse, but at an extravagant cost.

Meanwhile, Frederick and his generals fought desperately just to survive another year. With 35,000 troops, General Gideon von Laudon besieged Glatz in spring 1760. When Henri de la Motte, baron de Fouqué, approached with 11,000 troops, Laudon raised the siege, attacked, and destroyed him at Landshut on June 23, then resumed his siege. Glatz did not fall until July. Prince Henry marched on Laudon, who retreated into the fortress of Striegau. Henry then crossed the Oder and defeated a Russian corps that was approaching Breslau.

On July 10, Frederick besieged Dresden. When Laudon marched on Breslau, Frederick lifted his siege and marched against him. The two armies collided at Liegnitz on August 15. The Prussians repulsed Laudon's attack then charged and routed the Austrians, killing 1,400, wounding 2,200, and capturing 4,700 troops and 80 cannons. The Prussian king was almost among the dead—a spent canister ball bruised his hip. Frederick then joined Henry and marched on Schweidnitz.

In October, fearful of tangling again with Frederick, the Austrian and Russian commanders agreed to dispatch forces against Berlin itself. Marshal Franz Moritz Lacy led 15,000 troops north and General Zakhar Chernyshev led 20,000 west. Prince Eugene of Württemberg holed up his 14,000 men in Spandau Fortress. The allies entered Berlin on October 9, forced the city to hand over 1.5 million thalers, then fled at a rumor that Frederick was nearing. In fact, Frederick was marching his 44,000 troops against Daun's 50,000 near Torgau. On November 3, 1760, Frederick outflanked and attacked the Austrians.

Once again, Frederick was almost among the dead—a spent ball knocked him out. He awoke to learn that his men had held the field at an enormous cost of 13,120 casualties, while inflicting 11,260 on the Austrians. The endless carnage was finally getting to the philosopher-king, who mourned that he lived "a dog's life. All this marching and disorder which is not finished has aged me so much that you would not recognize me. The hair on the right side of my head is all gray. My teeth break and fall out; my face is as wrinkled as the folds of a skirt, my back bends like a violin bow, and my spirit is as sad and dejected as a monk of La Trappe."[12]

The decisive French defeat in India arrived in 1760, although the loss of its remaining trading posts there came the next year. Throughout much of January, the English under Colonel Eyre Coote maneuvered and skirmished around Wandiwash. General Arthur Lally marched on the English camp on January 22. At first, the French attack seemed to prevail. A valiant British stand, however, followed by a counterattack wiped out 600 of Lally's European troops and hundreds more sepoys at a cost of 63 dead and 124 wounded. Lally fled with a handful of cavalry to Pondicherry. Wandiwash was India's Plains of Abraham.

Afterward, the English merely mopped up the scattered French forces. Coote sent his troops after French towns rather than Lally, taking Arcot, Timery, Trincomalee, Permacoil, Alumparva, and Carical in a tightening land net around Pondicherry. In April, Coote besieged Pondicherry itself while Admiral George Pocock's squadron plugged the port. Yet Lally managed to hold out the rest of the year. Nature helped the defense on December 31, 1760, when a typhoon destroyed six English warships and much of the besiegers' defenses. Though Pocock sailed his squadron's remnants to Madras to refit, Coote doggedly rebuilt his siege works and held tight to Pondicherry.

Surrender

Even though it was half-expected, the news of Quebec's fall came as quite a shock. After all, aside from its capture by David Kirke in 1629, the French flag had continued to fly over Quebec throughout all the previous wars and never more proudly than when the city was threatened. Vaudreuil had shared with Versailles his belief that the treacherous stretch of river known as the Traverse and city's defenses would deter any fleet and army brought against it. The king and his council may have been skeptical, but all hoped it was true.

The death of such a loyal, skilled, and valiant general as Montcalm the previous year on the Plains of Abraham genuinely saddened Louis XV. War minister Belle Isle wrote the new commander, General Lévis, that, although the king mourned for Montcalm, he was confident that "the command could not . . . be in better hands than yours." The war minister revealed that he was dispatching "to you relief of every description in provisions, munitions of war, and recruits, whereof, despite the advantages the English possess in the occupation of . . . Quebec, which has been too hastily surrendered, you will be able to dispute the ground with them, inch by inch." He called for cooperation between Lévis and Vaudreuil. Finally, the king granted the requested crosses of Saint Louis and other awards.[13]

As usual, during the winter New France's regular officers had penned letters to Versailles detailing the colony's woes and begging for help. The artillery commander, Captain François-Marc-Antoine Le Mercier, submitted a twenty-two-point analysis to Versailles that concluded, "If the King determines to send to Canada the aid required, the recovery of Quebec is considered certain, if it arrives before the English."[14]

Mercier was half-right. If Quebec's recapture was at all possible, it depended on a French fleet beating a British fleet there. And Quebec was vulnerable. Wolfe's orders to desolate the Saint Lawrence valley came back to haunt Quebec's redcoat defenders. All winter British forage parties trudged back empty-handed from a countryside scoured of food. The supplies Townsend had left rapidly dwindled. General James Murray and his troops spent a winter in Quebec fighting disease, malnutrition, and death. French and Indian raiders repeatedly attacked the British wood-cutting parties. By early spring, of the 7,500 troops with which Murray had begun the occupation, 1,000 were in graves and 2,000 were in the hospital, leaving him little more than 4,000 fit for duty.[15]

Until the ice broke on the Saint Lawrence, Lévis could do no more than send out large raiding parties. All the draft animals that could have dragged his cannons and supply wagons to Quebec had long before been butchered for meat. Meanwhile, Lévis organized the expedition to retake Quebec, packing supplies aboard the two frigates, two sloops, and several score smaller vessels that would carry his army downriver.

Vaudreuil did his part. Desperate times called for desperate measures. The governor general issued an amnesty to all deserters who rejoined their units. In a circular letter to his militia captains, he tried to spark their dampened spirits. After detailing the large army that would soon march against Quebec, he asserted, "You approach the moment of triumph over that enemy; he cannot but succumb before the efforts of our army. . . . At length, brave Canadians . . . undertake everything, risk everything for the preservation of your religion and the salvation of your country."[16]

On April 20, Lévis embarked on the flotilla packed with 3,889 troops of 8 army and 2 marine battalions, and 3,021 militiamen to ride the snowmelt down to Quebec. Learning of Lévis's approach, Murray expelled all the Canadians from the city. In violating the surrender agreement, Murray alleviated his own supply crisis at Lévis's expense. On April 26, Lévis disembarked his army at Saint Augustin for the march overland to the British camp at Old Lorette, a half dozen miles from the city. Murray ordered the British advance guard to withdraw to Sainte-Foy.

Both commanders chose to fight for Sainte-Foy on April 27. Murray led an army of 3,886 troops, 20 cannons, and 2 howitzers onto that field by midmorning. Lévis's troops massed along the low ridge on which Sainte-Foy sat. When Murray's cannon opened fire, Lévis ordered his troops to withdraw into the woods. Murray thought Lévis was retreating and ordered his army to charge. Many of these troops bogged down in a marsh before the ridge. The French troops reemerged and opened fire. The British attack broke up, with some units advancing and the rest wavering. Canadian militiamen slipped around the British flanks and poured musket fire into them. With his army about to be crushed by a double envelopment, Murray ordered a retreat. Rather than loosen his men on the fleeing redcoats like hounds after the fox, Lévis halted and regrouped them. His troops were exhausted and bloodied, having suffered 833 casualties, of which 193 were killed and 640 wounded. But the British had lost many more—1,101 men, including 259 killed, 829 wounded, but, surprisingly, only 13 captured. Sainte-Foy ranks just after the battle before Fort Carillon as the North American war's bloodiest.[17]

Lévis marched his army across the Plains of Abraham, encamped it, then set his men to work snaking trenches forward. The 150 British cannons on Quebec's walls pounded the burrowers, killing 73 and wounding 133 during the siege.[18] On May 9, a ship was sighted sailing around Île d'Orléans. The French and British alike strained to spot what colors it flew.

The Union Jack streamed atop the first vessel of a supply convoy that would arrive within days. Quebec was saved—for Britain. When the convoy arrived on May 15, its warships immediately sailed against the half dozen French ships, capturing all but one. Lévis had no choice but to retreat. When his troops slogged off on May 17, they abandoned 34 cannons, 6 mortars, and all their wounded and sick.[19] Lévis insisted that the "arrival of a single frigate in advance of the English fleet would have decided the surrender of Quebec and secured New France this year."[20]

What had happened to France's supply convoy? Learning that the British had beaten him, Captain François Giraudais ordered his fleet to Restigouche Bay, where a British squadron eventually found and captured all his ships. The loss of the entire supply fleet was a disaster for Canada. Lévis returned to Montreal to find conditions even worse than when he left. He glumly reported, "The paper [money] that remains with us is entirely discredited; all the farmers in despair; they have sacrificed everything for the preservation of Canada; they now find themselves ruined beyond recovery. . . . We shall no longer find the same willingness among the people when we . . . reassemble them for our defense."[21]

The worthless paper money meant the army could not buy food to feed itself. Lévis implored Vaudreuil and Bigot to sell provisions to him on credit. He even resorted "to pledge myself personally to persuade the troops to give the little cash they might possess . . . and officers capable of acquitting themselves perfectly of that duty." The general's pleading with everyone from the governor to lowest private worked, at least for a while, as it "supplied us with the means to procure bread for this month."[22]

Food was not the only critical shortage. The army had only enough gunpowder for one battle. This forced field commanders to avoid even the most tempting attacks on the enemy and await an opportunity to win a decisive battle that might never come. In noting the hopelessness of their plight, Lévis could not resist an ironic observation: "The crops have a fine appearance, but if we shall be able to cut them, it remains to be seen . . . who will eat them."[23]

Pitt planned a three-pronged attack on France's remaining positions in Canada for 1760. Major General Amherst would attack from Oswego down the Saint Lawrence, Brigadier General William Haviland would move from Crown Point (Fort Saint Frederic) north down Lake Champlain, and Brigadier General Murray would head from Quebec up the Saint Lawrence. As usual, each expedition was not ready to move until midsummer. None of the British commanders encountered more than temporary checks to their advances from the French in their way. Murray simply sailed past Captain Dumas's troops that appeared on shore; Dumas had to force march his troops to stay between the British and Montreal. Captain Pouchot, having been repatriated earlier that spring, bravely defended Fort Lévy before surrendering. Colonel Bourlamaque held Île aux Noix before retreating to Montreal when the British threatened his communications. By early September, the French had retreated to Montreal. Lévis commanded only 2,200 men to face 17,000 British troops from the three surrounding armies.

Vaudreuil called an officers' council on September 6. Defense was hopeless, he told them. Food and gunpowder were nearly gone. British cannonballs would reduce Montreal's thin stone walls to rubble. The enemy grossly outnumbered the city's defenders. Montreal's leading citizens were imploring the governor to spare the city from destruction. The only choice, the governor insisted, was surrender. He then unveiled a fifty-five-clause capitulation document that he promised would guarantee the Canadians rights and the French honor if the British accepted it. Pride stiffened the will of Lévis and his officers to fight on. Amherst refused to grant honors of war to the French army. Vaudreuil was willing to concede this point but not his gallant officers, who bitterly protested the notion. Lévis argued that Amherst's terms "could not conflict more with the king's service and honor of his arms, and must be accepted only at the last extremity."[24] To this, Vaudreuil simply replied, "Whereas the interest of the Colony does not permit us to reject the conditions proposed by the English General, which are favorable to a country whose lot is confined to me, I order Chevalier de Lévis to conform himself to the said Capitulation and to make the troops lay down their arms."[25] It was a direct order. Lévis and his officers had no choice but to obey.

Amherst and Vaudreuil signed the Articles of Capitulation for the Surrender of Canada on September 8, 1760. The terms were quite lenient. All troops under the fleur-de-lis would march from their garrisons and lay down their arms, whereupon they would be shipped back across the Atlantic with the promise not to fight again for the war's duration; Canadians would be disarmed and dispersed to their homes. Canada's administrators could likewise sail for France. The British guaranteed the Canadians their property, laws, customs, and religion. His Most Christian Majesty could still appoint Canada's bishop; priests could stay in their dioceses or missions and nuns in their cloisters. The Indians would remain unmolested in their homelands. The only tenets of Vaudreuil's terms that Amherst rejected were a pardon for deserters of both sides and honors of war for the French.[26]

Vaudreuil deliberately left the boundaries of Canada and Louisiana as vague as possible as an entree for future negotiations. He almost got away with it. At some point, the British commanders became wise to the governor's ploy and General Haldimand asked him to delineate the boundaries. During the subsequent peace negotiations, what Vaudreuil said would haunt and undercut Versailles's contention that the upper Great Lakes and Ohio River valley were never part of Canada and thus should be included in French Louisiana.[27] Vaudreuil later insisted that he "drew no boundary . . . when I capitulated and only expressed myself in my conferences with the general by the simple term, Canada."[28] Haldimand recalled that Vaudreuil was quite explicit.[29] The different accounts are interesting but moot. Within three years of Vaudreuil's surrender, Britain would take not only all of Canada but all of Louisiana east of the Mississippi, except for New Orleans, and most other French colonies around the world.

Lévis was philosophical about Canada's surrender, describing it with a Gallic shrug as "by no means favorable, but how could it be otherwise comparing our force and means with the enemy? . . . On my part, I have done everything that depended on me."[30] He had kind words for the valor with which the French, Canadians, and Indians fought against overwhelming odds. In contrast, Vaudreuil trembled in anticipation of the king's wrath, as much for the corruption he had tolerated as for surrendering Canada. Before reaching Versailles, he tried to soften the reception typically by hoarding credit for Canada's triumphs while spreading blame for its defeats among its military and civilian leaders.[31]

Consequences

With Canada lost, no rational reason persisted for France to remain in the war. In October 1760, Choiseul offered a grand deal to its allies for peace: Russia could take East Prussia in return for cash compensation to Saxony; Austria would take Glatz but not Silesia; France and Russia would subsidize Sweden's war effort; and Russia would pressure Britain to conclude peace with France. Two simultaneous but separate conferences would end the war: diplomats at London would settle the world war while those at Paris would address the European war. Saint Petersburg's response would arrive at Versailles in early 1761.[32]

Meanwhile, Choiseul threw off all diplomatic restraint and urged Charles III to intervene to prevent France from ceding its North American empire to Britain. With that buffer between the Spanish and British empires dissolved, Madrid would soon suffer the same fate. Charles III replied that his navy and army could not possibly prepare for war in less than six months and more likely would need a year.[33]

The already-complex diplomacy became more so when Britons began bowing to a new king that autumn. George II had lived long enough to savor the triumph of Canada's conquest. A stroke killed him on October 25, 1760. The first command of the new king, George III, was that his friend and tutor, John Stuart, Earl of Bute, enter the cabinet as his advisor.

A dilemma trapped George III and Bute. Both wanted peace and were willing to split the difference with France to get it. The biggest block to this was William Pitt, who demanded conquest and scorned compromise. Of course, George III could simply dismiss Pitt. But the thought of Pitt's triumphant return to Parliament terrified both the king and Bute. As intimidating and obstructionist as Pitt was in the cabinet, he would be a far more dangerous enemy if he reigned again over the House of Commons. He was an extremely tough act to follow—Pitt knew how to run the war and they did not. Britain had snatched one victory after another under his leadership. Britain's mob and most of its leaders took their nation's victories and defeats quite seriously. A public inflamed with Pitt's volcanic rhetoric and expectations of endless imperial victories would scream for the head of anyone who gave them less. Any defeat would be pinned on the new rulers, to their detriment. After all, a timid Admiral Byng had been thrust before a firing squad to encourage the others. When Bute, Newcastle, and other ministers expressed to French diplomats their fear that any compromise would send them to the gallows, they were not kidding. To counter Pitt's popularity, George III and Bute had to appear as unyielding as he. But giving in to Pitt doomed any chance of peace for several years.

PART 4

The Long Denouement

CHAPTER 11

Peace or Alliance? 1761

America has been conquered in Germany.

Pitt

Mr. Pitt . . . may be a great man inasmuch as we made war like simpletons, but . . . of a surety is the worst statesman in Europe.

Choiseul to Solar

We are natural and necessary allies; our dominions touch on two continents, and we have the same enemies to fear.

Charles III

By 1761, France had lost Canada, its armies were mired in a blood-soaked quagmire in Germany, its government was bankrupt, and its navy had only 8 seventy-four-gun and 6 sixty-four-gun warships in the Atlantic. Having won most of its war aims, Britain actually began cutting back its forces. In 1761, it had 288 warships manned by 80,675 sailors and an army of 107,000 soldiers, roughly 10 percent below the previous year's record numbers.[1]

Foreign minister Choiseul's position in the king's council got stronger as France weakened. The previous year Louis had entrusted Choiseul with Touraine's governorship on July 27, 1760, and the superintendency of posts, couriers, and relays on August 28, 1760.

When Belle Isle died on January 27, 1761, Choiseul took over the war ministry as well. As if all these duties were not onerous enough, Louis ordered Berryer to hand over the marine ministry to Choiseul on October 15, 1761. He was prime minister in all but name.[2]

Wish Lists

Choiseul wielded that power to negotiate for the best possible peace. The first step was to get permission from France's allies for a separate peace. Austrian queen Maria Theresa and her chancellor, Wenzel Anton von Kaunitz-Rietberg, were ambivalent about the idea of separate negotiations. Vienna finally agreed in return for a French promise to back ceding Austria any of its conquests from Prussia and the cutoff of English aid to Frederick.

Russian empress Elizabeth and her chancellor, Mikhail Vorontsov, initially dug in their heels. Versailles offered generous concessions. In early February 1761, Saint Petersburg asked Versailles to agree that Russia would keep East Prussia until it received a large indemnity whereupon it would hand that territory to Poland in return for a favorable adjustment of the Ukrainian border; Sweden would take part of Prussian Pomerania; Austria would take Glatz and the part of Silesia it currently held; and the Russians would offer its good offices to Whitehall for peace with France. Elizabeth reinforced the official proposal with a letter to Louis XV. The Russian peace proposal disappointed Versailles. The French had hoped for a Russian war declaration against Britain. Instead, Saint Petersburg had merely promised good offices.[3]

Ironically, Frederick now agreed that separate negotiations might be a good idea after all, and was willing to be excluded from those between France and Britain. He stipulated that any treaty must include a French promise to withdraw completely from Westphalia and to send no more than 24,000 troops to Austria to fulfill its treaty duties. Whitehall and Versailles agreed to the demand. In February 1761, secret talks began at The Hague between ambassadors Yorke and d'Affray. The negotiations would soon die, undercut this time by

Austria and Russia, which feared France would abandon the alliance; they pressured Versailles to give up a separate peace if the allies sincerely tried for a joint peace. Versailles agreed.

The allies issued a joint declaration on March 26, 1761, calling on the belligerents to convene a peace congress in Augsburg. Now it remained to talk Britain and Prussia into joining the congress. In a secret side letter to Pitt, Choiseul called for separate negotiations between France and Britain to precede the congress, and for a peace based on uti possidetis—on each side keeping what it had won by May 1, 1761, in Europe; July 1, 1761, in America; and September 1 in the East Indies.[4]

The offer split Whitehall. After having mulled Canada's fate for nearly a year and a half since Quebec's fall, Pitt finally decided what he wanted. Swollen with British victories, he now proclaimed nothing less than eliminating France's empire. To George III, he declared his intention for the "total destruction of the French . . . [which] would enable us to get a peace which would secure to us all Canada, Cape Breton . . . the fisheries and particularly the exclusive fishery of Newfoundland."[5] Of the cabinet, only Richard Grenville, Earl of Temple, his brother-in-law, backed his call for total victory. The other ministers were more or less willing to make minor compromises with Versailles to end the war. Victory was not certain, they declared, pointing to the two huge French armies led by Broglie and Soubise, who would soon march against the outgunned Prince Ferdinand of Brunswick defending Hanover. Even more worrisome was the possible entrance of Spain into the war. Why not make peace now, while Britain was victorious and thus end the ever-worsening debt and body counts, along with the chance of a risky war with Spain?

The compromisers won out over the conquerors. By April 3, Whitehall had gotten Potsdam to agree to join an Augsburg peace congress, and each named diplomats. Five days later, on April 8, 1761, Pitt replied to Choiseul that Britain and France could negotiate a separate peace, but that Whitehall would accept uti possidetis only on the date when a peace treaty was signed. On April 19, Choiseul wrote that he agreed to the terms. Negotiations would occur simultaneously in each capital between special envoys and the respective foreign ministers.

That same day, Choiseul tapped François de Bussy as France's envoy to London. Upon receiving Choiseul's letter, Pitt announced on April 28 that Hans Stanley would soon leave for Paris to negotiate with Choiseul.[6]

The sixty-two-year-old Bussy seemed a good choice. Since he had entered the foreign ministry in 1726, his prominent posts included serving in Vienna from 1725 to 1733, in London from 1740 to 1743, and in Hanover from 1755 until 1761. He had risen to the rank of premier commis, or deputy minister. Alas for France, despite Bussy's public denunciations of Britain, he had been on the English payroll during his London stint. George II decided not to resume payments when he arrived in Hanover, perhaps because of Bussy's vociferous anti-English sentiments, perhaps for fear that to do so might expose an active agent. Bussy arrived in London on June 5.[7]

The first discussion involved the uti possidetis timetable. Pitt had several military operations planned and wanted time for them to succeed so he could wrack up more conquests. Choiseul was well aware of what Pitt intended but was unable to prevent it. He instructed Bussy to trade Minorca and occupied Hanover for Guadeloupe, Gorée, Senegal, Saint Lucia, Tobago, and Marie-Galante; split the Neutral Islands with France retaining Dominica and Saint Vincent; while Canada, Île Royale, and Louisbourg would be returned to France. This was a dream list. The war had tilted so victoriously toward Britain that Whitehall would be unlikely to grant more than a fraction of those demands.[8] But it was just the first card in a long game.

What Choiseul did not tell Bussy was that Louis XV's council had already written off Canada and not only expected Britain to insist on retaining it but actually hoped that it would. The king and his ministers had concluded that national interests were better served by letting New France drain Britain rather than France. New France was an economic wreck. Its population survived only because of annual food shipments and subsidies from France. A century and a half of trading had devastated the fur trade in the Saint Lawrence valley and lower Great Lakes. The still abundant furs reaped from the upper Great Lakes could just as well flow to France via New Orleans as they could via Quebec. There was a key flaw in that strategy. Louisiana was just as economically crippled as Canada; it drained 800,000 livres annually from Versailles.[9] Not everyone was eager to abandon New France. Many of those who were born or who had served there and had been repatriated urged Versailles to retake that land. Replace New France's corruption with enlightened administration and it would enrich rather than impoverish France, they argued.

Meanwhile, Whitehall debated how many spoils to take. Some remained undecided. A "Memoir on the Terms of Peace" issued on April 13, 1761, carefully analyzed the value of each French colony to France and England without drawing any firm conclusion as to which lands and waters to add to the empire and which to spurn.[10] Others were determined to seize Canada. Lord Hardwicke explained, "The King could not make Peace without retaining all Canada. . . . The reduction of all Canada was of utmost importance to the Security of our Colonies."[11] Pitt and the Board of Trade wanted more. They demanded not only Canada but Louisiana as well to free the British empire to expand westward to the Mississippi and someday beyond.

Whitehall's emphasis on taking part or all of New France provoked a backlash from those concerned with the Caribbean sugar islands. Letters from prominent merchants cascaded onto the desks of official and unofficial British leaders alike. James Douglas, Earl of Morton, a scientist and outspoken expansionist, received many of these missives. He shared some excerpts with Hardwicke, including this: "For Gods sake dont let us give up Guadeloupe as that is the only conquest that will bring Money into the Nation's pocket."[12] Still others argued that rather than chose between New France or the sugar islands, Britain should consume the entire French empire.

Bourbon Family Values

The Spanish saw virtually any expansion of the British empire in North America as a mortal peril to their own empire. Madrid much preferred having as imperial neighbors the handful of French fur traders, priests, and hardscrabble peasants, even if it meant enduring and rejecting Versailles's impertinent claims to territory that the Spaniards believed rightfully belonged to the Spanish crown. The French had no means of acting on such outrageous claims; the British did.

Canada's conquest finally spurred Charles III into action, ironically when Spain was least able to alter the war's course. On January 27, 1761, Choiseul called for a treaty of mutual commerce and defense between France and Spain. Charles III agreed to discuss the offer. Negotiations for the Pacte de Famille began in February 1761 in Paris between Choiseul and newly appointed ambassador Marquis Jerónimo Grimaldi. On March 3, Choiseul felt confident enough to suggest an offensive alliance between France and Spain. The offer set off yet another debate in Madrid. In April, Charles III authorized Grimaldi to negotiate such a pact.

Though Madrid and Versailles had agreed to unite, they differed over key details. Grimaldi presented Spain's position in April. Madrid wanted a treaty that safeguarded its empire without any duty to join the war unless attacked. The pact would be open to Portugal's membership. If Britain attacked Spain before its military was ready, Versailles would grant Minorca to Spain in compensation. Should Spain join the war, neither ally could negotiate a separate peace.[13] Beggars could not be choosers. Versailles had little choice but to accept virtually any measures that drew Spain closer. Choiseul held his nose as he conceded one point after another to Grimaldi, a diplomat for whom he had little respect. He caustically remarked that "Spain had remained at peace during the war and hoped to be victorious in the peace."[14]

By late May Choiseul submitted a counterproposal that included both a family pact that united the Bourbon kings and a treaty open to all who wished to join. Neither treaty explicitly created a military alliance; nor was either directed against Britain. The Bourbon pact required Versailles to negotiate a peace that guaranteed Spanish as well as French interests. It was difficult to find any French advantage in the formal proposals. That came in a memoir Choiseul attached to the drafts in which he asked Spain to enter the war by May 1, 1762, if an acceptable peace proved elusive.[15]

Charles III rejected not only the war's timetable but also the seemingly innocuous Bourbon pact. He feared that it would backfire, inciting instead of cowing Britain and other European states. Britain might well launch a first strike against Spain before it was ready for war. The king was still playing both sides of the diplomatic fence. His advisors, Tanucci and Wall, used the French draft not only to wring concessions from Britain on Honduras logging and Newfoundland fisheries but even to forge a possible alliance between Madrid and London. The British fumbled the chance to entice a willing Spain away from French arms. Whitehall remained split between the majority, who wanted peace as soon as possible, and Pitt, who favored conquering all, including now—thanks to the what appeared to be a pending Bourbon pact—the Spanish empire.[16]

France was also diplomatically two-faced. Choiseul wielded the possible Bourbon pact as a weapon to force the British to accept peace. On June 17 he summoned Ambassador Hans Stanley and proposed trading Minorca for Guadeloupe, Marie-Galante, and Gorée, and renounced any claims to Canada, except an unfortified Cape Breton. He also insisted on the Utrecht Treaty guarantee of French access to Newfoundland's fisheries. France would retain Louisiana, whose boundary with Canada would be drawn at the watershed between the Ohio River and Great Lakes. Having denuded Canada of easily accessible furs for a century and a half, Versailles now valued only its offshore fisheries.[17] Choiseul played his diplomatic hand for all it was worth. The trouble was that he had few good cards to play—Minorca and part or all of Hanover, Wesel, Gelderland, Hanau, Frankfort, Brunswick, and Hesse, and the threat of Spanish intervention. Meanwhile, the British kept adding to their list of conquests.

The British Bells of Victory

Despite Choiseul's hopes, the looming probability that a Bourbon pact would be consummated failed to shake Whitehall. After all, the bells of victory continued to cheer the government and public alike. If Spain joined the war, most reasoned, Britain would only reap more spoils. Though Europe would not get the news for months, the French lost India in 1761, though not permanently. After a valiant defense lasting nearly a year, Lally surrendered Pondicherry on April 5, 1761. The

British believed that they would pick the pieces off Spain's empire just as easily. They were wrong—it would actually be easier.

Indeed, the very day that Choiseul announced his swap to Stanley word reached Paris that the British had captured Belle Isle. It had been a tough nut to crack. British frigates had hovered around the island throughout the spring, at once reporting enemy positions to the invasion fleet's admiral Augustus Keppel and warning the defenders that an invasion was probable. With its rocky shores backed by cliffs and forts, Belle isle had no weak points. In mid-April, Keppel tried putting two battalions ashore. Enemy fire, adverse tides, and a sudden gale forced the remnants of those troops back to the transports. Reinforced with four fresh battalions, Keppel tried again on April 22. This time his troops captured Fort d'Arsic, overran the island, and bottled up the French in the citadel at Le Palais. On June 8, with its walls breached, the French capitulated.

Later in the year, the most recent bad news arrived from the Caribbean. On June 6, an English expedition with Captain James Douglas commanding the squadron and Lord Andrew Rollo commanding its six thousand troops anchored off Rousseau, Dominica. Following a bombardment, the troops landed and captured the town. The French surrendered the entire island the next day. The English transformed Dominica into a base for attacking nearby Martinique. They would not feel ready for that assault until early the next year.

Meanwhile, the news from Germany was as demoralizing as ever. Once again the allied army had bloodied and knocked back the French. In June, Soubise's 100,000 troops and Broglie's 60,000 advanced on Ferdinand's 93,000 in Hanover. As in previous years, Ferdinand withdrew before suddenly rushing his troops at one of the French armies. On July 15 and 16, Broglie and Ferdinand collided at Vellinghausen, where a jealous Soubise refused to join the battle. Broglie suffered the loss of 5,000 troops and 16 cannon, inflicted 1,600 casualties, and retreated. Ferdinand's troops bit at Broglie's heels while Brunswick's troops harassed Soubise.

Versailles had become fatalistic over such humiliating defeats in Germany. Belle Isle's loss, however, was seen as a catastrophe. Not only was it part of the nation rather than a distant colony, but Belle Isle would be the perfect British base for blockading the French coast. When he got the bad news, Choiseul must have feared that if Whitehall did not insist on keeping Belle Isle it would certainly demand trading it for Minorca while keeping its other conquests.

Yet the news of Belle Isle's capture did not shift the division within the mostly war-weary British cabinet. When those ministers met on June 21 to review Choiseul's draft, nearly everyone favorably received it except the uncompromising imperialists Pitt and Temple. Earl Bute and John Russell, duke of Bedford, were the most enthusiastic, willing to sign a deal with a few minor adjustments. Bedford feared American independence more than he feared New France. He actually favored letting France retain a truncated Canada, reasoning that it was just the thing to keep the Americans cowed and dependent on London; without a French threat from Canada, the Americans were likely to assert their interests increasingly against the Crown's. In this, of course, Bedford was prescient. Newcastle and Hardwicke too were pleased but argued that, if Choiseul was willing to concede all that so easily, he might be pressured to surrender even more. Hardwicke, however, worried that Britain might end up swallowing more territory than it could digest. Canada might well prove as burdensome for Britain as it had for France; it would reap little profit at enormous administrative and defense costs. Pitt grumpily dismissed Choiseul's proposal and demanded excluding the French from Cape Breton and the Newfoundland fisheries. The others objected that France's exclusion from its traditional fisheries would unite all the other European maritime powers against Britain's naked assertion of hegemony.[18]

Over the next five days, the ministers hammered out a consensus. On June 26, Pitt penned a counterproposal whereby France would cede all of Canada including Cape Breton, along with Senegal, and Gorée; the Neutral Islands would be divided; Minorca and all German conquests would be exchanged for Guadeloupe, Marie-Galante, and Belle Isle; Dunkirk's fortifications would be destroyed; and any Utrecht Treaty rights to fish in Newfoundland's waters would be surrendered with compensation.

Choiseul had expected such English demands. To Stanley he protested that French fishermen must have an abri, or unfortified island shelter, upon which to dry their fish, receive supplies, and protect themselves from storms. As for Dunkirk, Louis XV had the sovereign right to fortify that French city if he so desired. To be denied that right was a humiliating and unacceptable demand. As for the rest, Choiseul shrugged but refused to answer definitively. The talks stalled on these points with neither side willing to concede.[19]

Setting Boundaries

The negotiations forced Versailles to debate a question that it had never definitely answered for over 150 years—where did Canada end and Louisiana begin? Choiseul explained the problem and what to do about it: "The boundaries between Louisiana and Canada have never been well distinguished, and as in French books it has been claimed that the Ohio was a dependency of Canada, it is thought necessary to stipulate explicitly that the Ohio and the Wabash are to be regarded as dependencies of Louisiana; it is necessary to add that the lands between the Ohio and the mountains which border Virginia remain neutral, and that all trade and passage be prohibited to French and English alike; but that the Indians may have the freedom to cross to the one or the other people as is customary. . . . It will also be necessary to specify the boundaries of Louisiana on the side of Carolina and Georgia."[20]

Choiseul's perspective seemed reasonable enough. The king's council agreed to designate the Ohio valley from the Wabash to its sources as a cordon sanitaire between French Louisiana and British Canada. On July 15, Choiseul submitted a formal peace proposal for Bussy to submit to Whitehall. After a conciliatory introduction regretting the war, the proposal stated that it would be prepared to concede Canada with the following conditions: that the Canadians be allowed to practice their religion, sell their lands, and emigrate; that the boundary between Canada and Louisiana be fixed on the Wabash with a neutral zone extending east to the Appalachians; that French subjects be allowed to fish freely off Newfoundland as previously guaranteed by the Utrecht Treaty; and that Île Royale (Cape Breton) be restored to France in full sovereignty. Elsewhere, France demanded the return of Guadeloupe and Marie-Galante, along with Saint Lucia of the Neutral Islands, while it conceded Tobago to England and suggested that Dominica and Saint Vincent remain neutral and Gorée or some other West African slave port be returned. France asserted its sovereign right to fortify Dunkirk. France's occupation of Frankfort, Wesel, and Gelderland on behalf of Austria would continue. France would withdraw from Minorca and the other German lands. Atop all this, Choiseul tried to play his Spanish card by calling for the inclusion of Madrid's claims in the negotiations.[21]

Pitt rejected the French peace offer with a July 29 ultimatum. He categorically denied any French retention of any German lands or Spain's inclusion in the talks. He did equivocate on Dunkirk and the Caribbean Islands but asserted that Britain would retain both Senegal and Gorée. Finally, Pitt warned that the war would continue unless France surrendered to England sovereignty over Canada and its fisheries. As for Louisiana's boundaries, Pitt sidestepped the question.[22]

All along Britain's position on New France's boundaries was confused, contradictory, and hypocritical. At different times during eleven years of sporadic negotiations, different British officials had delineated the territory differently. The most persistent thread was that the Iroquois had conquered the Ohio valley then ceded it to Britain. With the 1760 conquest, Whitehall briefly insisted that the Ohio was an extension of Canada and thus British. Then the British reverted to their earlier assertion that some land beyond the Appalachians belonged neither to Canada nor Louisiana.

While the French had consistently rejected Whitehall's Iroquois-based claim, they gave the impression that they too believed the land between the Wabash and Appalachians was not strictly part of either Canada or Louisiana. With Choiseul's July 15 memorial, Versailles finally resolved the issue by asserting that, indeed, the Ohio country was a distinct area that should remain a neutral buffer between Louisiana and Canada.

Pitt rejected the neutral zone without providing a counterproposal and returned to the position that the upper Ohio was an extension of Canada. He wanted to keep his options open in order to push back Louisiana's frontier as far as possible. He had a slew of military operations being executed or planned that would ratchet up Britain's bargaining power ever higher. Why was Pitt so adamant on denying the French the right to fish in North American seas? He had become obsessed with demolishing every pillar of French power. French "fishing in troubled waters" was an unconscious metaphor for his fear of Britain's imperial neighbor and perennial enemy. Both Versailles and Whitehall thought the fisheries vital in two ways. These hardy fishermen netted wealth for France equal to all that wrung from Canada by the fur trade. More importantly, the fishing fleets provided tough, seasoned sailors for France's navy. Pitt hoped that France's strategic and economic loss would be Britain's gain.[23]

Louis XV's council debated Pitt's ultimatum. Choiseul's arguments, as usual, won out. On August 1, Choiseul insisted that "the fishery, Sire, is the real loss in Canada. . . . Canada in itself produces almost nothing. . . . Even were one to admit, what I do not admit, that Canada was the outwork of Louisiana, which also brings in nothing to France . . . I will still insist that the cod fishery in the Gulf of St. Lawrence is worth infinitely more to the kingdom of France than Canada and Louisiana." He followed up this crucial point with two related others, that the war should continue and that all efforts be made to enlist Spain as an ally.[24]

Choiseul's August 5, 1761, ultimatum differed little from his July 15 position. He repeated his insistence on retaking Guadeloupe, Marie-Galante, and Saint Lucia, along with either Gorée and Senegal or Accra and Anamabu in return for Minorca and England's German lands. Once again he insisted on France's sovereign right to fortify Dunkirk. The issue of Wesel, Gelderland, and Frankfort was irrelevant to the war between England and France, and thus was nonnegotiable. As for New France, Louis XV was prepared to give up Canada, retain Cape Breton and Louisiana, maintain French access to Newfoundland's fisheries, and insist on neutrality for the Indians in the Ohio and lower Mississippi valleys.[25]

To deepen the arguments for shedding Canada and defining Louisiana's boundary, Choiseul prepared and sent to Bussy a secret memoir on August 10. Of what value and cost was New France? It varied considerably. Canada's fur trade was annually worth 1,800,000 livres. Louisiana's more varied exports were valued at 1,200,000 livres, of which indigo accounted for 800,000 livres. Yet Versailles spent many times that amount each year in administering, defending, and supplying New France. Essentially, New France cost more than it was currently worth.[26] This report offered the best statistics yet that Canada's loss was actually a gain. The diplomatic strategy was to surrender the husk of Canada while retaining its germ. Thus France could convert defeat into victory by keeping the profitable fur trade at one end of Canada and fisheries at the other, while shedding the endless, exorbitant costs of maintaining that vast realm.

Throughout late August, Bussy met with various British ministers, each of whom rejected the French proposal with varying degrees of civility. The cabinet hammered out its formal reply on August 30. As Pitt presented it to Bussy, the Great Orator stunned the ambassador with the vehemence of his assault on the French position. He demanded that France withdraw from all German lands. He rejected any idea that France would keep Cape Breton. Britain would have total command of Canada, although its inhabitants were free to stay and practice their religion indefinitely or to leave within eighteen months. He insisted that the British empire included the entire Ohio valley all the way west to the Mississippi River by cessions of the Iroquois, who had previously conquered it.[27]

From Pitt's bluster and threats, two small concessions emerged. Britain would grant France Saint Pierre as a drying ground for fishermen in the Saint Lawrence and Newfoundland waters. Dunkirk also could be fortified. The concessions were ironic. If the cabinet had made them in June 1761, a peace might well have been speedily concluded. It took the cabinet until mid-August to agree that Choiseul's demands were indeed reasonable after all if they led to peace and staved off a French alliance with Spain. But by then it was too late. France and Spain had signed the Bourbon family pact.

Finally, Pitt thrust into the hands of a startled Bussy French documents proving that Canada included all the Great Lakes and Ohio valley and asserted, "You claim the course of the Ohio by ceding us Canada you have ceded us the whole of that river; for in an authentic memoir of M. le Duc de Mirepoix it is expressly stated that the Ohio has always been a dependency of Canada; in a printed work by M. de Silhouette the same statement is repeated; and M. le Marquis de Vaudreuil, in surrendering Canada to the English General Amherst, gave him a map of Canada and its dependencies, marked by a line that includes the whole course of the Ohio." Pitt made it quite clear that Whitehall intended nothing less than "to gain possession of all the lands and rivers as far as the Mississippi, and that the river was to be our barrier for the Continent of North America, as the Rhine was for Germany."[28]

Bussy was outgunned legally, intellectually, and rhetorically. All he could do was protest that, by trying "to push back the boundaries of Louisiana as far as the Mississippi, and gain possession of the Ohio," the British revealed their "design, not only to seize . . . Louisiana, but Mexico also . . . [and] prevent us from repairing our losses and reconstituting our navy in any degree that may give the slightest umbrage to England."[29] In other words, Whitehall sought nothing less than the emasculation of French power, and this was unacceptable.

Playing the Spanish Card

While Whitehall and Versailles debated, wrote up, and traded proposals, Spain, having suffered the English snub, diplomatically tacked back to France. Charles III agreed to reconsider Choiseul's terms and instructed Grimaldi to sign an acceptable treaty of alliance. Choiseul leapt at the opening. On July 15, he submitted to Grimaldi a draft treaty that bound France and Spain to recognize Britain as a hostile power, required Versailles to negotiate a favorable settlement of French and Spanish grievances against Britain, and required that Spain declare war no later than May 1, 1762, if Britain did not satisfy those demands. Once Spain joined the war, no separate peace was allowed and the allies would share all gains and losses. In addition, France would grant Minorca to Spain unless it was needed to regain allied losses elsewhere—a likely scenario! Spain abandoned its tenuous claims to the Neutral Islands. Other states could join the alliance.

All these tenets would immediately take effect if Britain attacked Spain before the deadline. Choiseul accompanied the treaty by once again evoking the danger to Spain's empire if the British took Canada and Louisiana. Grimaldi needed no more arguments—he was prepared to sign. Then, at the last minute, Choiseul begged for a delay while he tried one last diplomatic tumble with the English.[30]

Though the Bourbon pact was negotiated in secret, rumors, spies, and pillow talk ensured that all the powers were aware of it. Choiseul certainly hoped that word would leak to the English. He believed that the pact empowered him not militarily but diplomatically. Spain's army and navy could not help break the stalemate with Britain and Prussia in Germany or take back conquered lands in America, but they could help win an honorable peace. The pending alliance with Spain gave Choiseul the diplomatic and psychological weight necessary to demand new terms from Whitehall. Once again Choiseul played the Spanish card against Britain. He submitted the treaty draft with the war clauses deleted to Stanley so that Whitehall could ponder the consequences of its hard line on negotiations. Further pressuring Whitehall was the advance of French armies under Broglie and Soubise deep into Hanover. Versailles's bargaining position would improve considerably if those armies succeeded in defeating Ferdinand's outnumbered German and British army.[31]

But Whitehall stood firm to its demands. Even those who favored the war's immediate halt may have questioned doing so when victories were so abundant and easy. Yet even if Britain were not scoring one brilliant victory after another, Choiseul's threat of a Bourbon pact would still have enraged rather than sobered Pitt. He rejected Choiseul's latest position with decidedly uncivil but quite diplomatic vehemence.

Nor did Choiseul's double game play well in Madrid. Having been excited by Versailles and then rebuffed in signing a treaty, Charles III now played hard to get. The Spanish king raised the stakes. On July 27, he told Ambassador Ossun that he would sign only if the French gave him Louisiana! As if this were not a stumbling block enough to the alliance, on July 31, Charles III further delayed any signing until minute problems of protocol and rank between the two kingdoms were sorted out. Madrid further objected when it felt that French ambassador

Bussy had poorly represented Spanish claims to Whitehall. All along, Charles III played a canny diplomatic game that would lead Spain into a series of disastrous and humiliating military defeats.[32]

The council's patience was well-placed. On August 15, 1761, Choiseul and Grimaldi signed two treaties based on their July 15 drafts. The family pact committed Versailles and Madrid to a vague Bourbon solidarity. The Secret Convention legally bound Spain to declare war against Britain by May 1, 1762, if all outstanding Bourbon issues had not been resolved. In addition, France would return Minorca to Spain, both powers would offer Portugal a choice of alliance or war, and, finally, other maritime states would be invited to join. What explains the turnaround? Once again, heavy-handed British diplomacy had alienated the Spanish. Pitt abruptly dismissed yet another Spanish demand for concessions on Honduras logging and Newfoundland fisheries. Madrid also wanted to give the appearance of distance from France while its warships escorted the silver fleet across the Atlantic.

Once the deal was signed, Madrid stiffened its back against the British. When Ambassador George Hervey, Lord Bristol demanded to see the Franco-Spanish treaty, foreign minister Wall refused.[33] After the treasure fleet dropped anchor at Cadiz, Wall summoned Bristol and insisted that Britain concede to Spain's demands on logging, fishing, and seizures, or else—though he left the "or else" vague. Once again the English rejected the demand. Madrid stepped up its war preparations.

Charles III had very concrete and, in his mind, realistic war aims. He envisioned reconquering Gibraltar from Britain, receiving Louisiana along with Minorca as a gift from grateful ally France, and forcing Portugal into vassalage. These victories, in turn, would deter Austrian ambitions in northern Italy. Reality would shatter this dream. Spain proved to be a military and diplomatic liability rather than asset. The alliance boomeranged against Spain by giving Britain the excuse to ravage its trade and colonies. In one way, however, Spain did hurt Britain and help France but by asserting its economic rather than military power. The family pact included a clause that gave French and Spanish traders advantages in the other's market that no other nation could enjoy. The clause was so vaguely worded, however, that neither side fully capitalized on it. More importantly, Charles III agreed to a

French request to cut off Spain's trade with Britain. For the next several years, the Spanish bought French rather than British manufactured goods.[34]

Ambassador Stanley informed Choiseul on September 1 that Whitehall had conceded Saint Pierre Island in the Saint Lawrence Gulf to France as a shelter for French fishermen. Armed now with the Spanish alliance, Choiseul rejected the offer as inadequate. On September 6 and 9, Choiseul dispatched reports reasserting arguments for the French definition of Louisiana's border and the other demands of his August 10 memorial. Bussy presented it to Pitt on September 15.[35]

The hard line backfired. To varying degrees, the rest of the cabinet joined Pitt in scorning the French ultimatum. With the cabinet's support, Pitt ordered Stanley to break off relations and return to London; Stanley did so on September 20. On September 17, Pitt asked Bussy to return to France with the argument that, while France thought his terms too tough, the British public thought them too easy; continued negotiations thus would be fruitless. Britain would war mercilessly against France until it surrendered to all of Whitehall's demands, which might well increase in severity.[36]

So far the Bourbon pact had failed to meet its promise of wringing British concessions. Choiseul admitted as much in a September 6, 1761, report to Louis XV's council: his diplomatic game of playing the British and Spanish off against each other had fizzled. But what other diplomatic option did the French have for ending the war? He asked the council's patience as he continued to try using Spain to win an acceptable peace with Britain. The king and his council approved Choiseul's diplomacy. They could hardly do otherwise. France was as straitjacketed diplomatically as it was militarily.[37]

The Bourbon pact enflamed rather than intimidated the British. Whitehall knew that France and Spain had struck a deal but remained blind to its details. The alignment and perhaps secret alliance of France and Spain split the British cabinet along predictable lines. Pitt and Temple assumed the worst. Starting on September 15, Pitt daily demanded that Ambassador Bristol be recalled, the Spanish treasure fleet seized, and war declared and fought against Spain until its empire was dismembered as thoroughly as that of France. On September 21, Pitt and Temple submitted their war demand in a memorandum to George III, who refused to accept it.

To this, the other ministers unleashed a barrage of carefully reasoned objections. The showdown came at Saint James Palace on October 2. Admiralty Lord George Anson and army chief John Ligonier denounced any war with Spain that would possibly stretch the navy and army to the breaking point. Newcastle reported direly that the nation's finances would snap first; British and international financiers would not underwrite another year of war. Bute argued that war would deprive Britain of a lucrative trade with Spain and would make any favorable postwar trade agreements extremely unlikely. Hopes that the British fleet would capture this year's Spanish treasure fleet were dashed when the convoy arrived safely at Cadiz. Besides all that, the cabinet still had no firm evidence that the family pact included a military alliance. Pitt simply countered that Spain was "now carrying on the worst species of war she can for France—covers her trade, lends her money, and abets her in negotiation. This puts you actually in war with the whole House of Bourbon."[38] The other ministers remained skeptical.

Pitt bitterly resigned on October 5, declaring, "I will be responsible for nothing that I do not direct."[39] Temple followed four days later on October 9. While Charles Wyndham, Earl of Egremont, took Pitt's seal as Southern secretary, Bute took Pitt's place as de facto head of the government. In all, George III and his ministers had watched Pitt storm away with decidedly mixed feelings. All feared that Pitt would be even more aggressive and obstructionist in Parliament than he had been in the cabinet. He was. English diplomacy was cramped as long as Pitt's speeches enflamed the imperial lusts and expectations of the English people.

Having finally pried Pitt from the cabinet, Bute took great care to construct a popular peace, even if it meant going to war with Spain. He coopted some of Pitt's rhetoric in arguing that a war against Spain would pay for itself while working for last-minute diplomacy that would prevent that war from taking place. Unfortunately, the new cabinet imprisoned itself within its belligerent rhetoric. Whitehall's unyielding stand against Spain ended up precipitating an unwanted war. On October 28, Newcastle issued a stern note demanding that Spain unveil its secret treaties with France or else Britain would refuse to address Spanish grievances. Foreign minister Wall responded with a vague reply. The cabinet fumed and worried that Pitt might have been right after all. On November 19, Egremont sent an even harsher note to Madrid that essentially threatened war if Spain did not reveal the full texts of its secret treaties.

These notes deeply wounded Spanish pride. When Ambassador Bristol demanded that Wall reveal the Bourbon pact's treaty, the foreign ministry exploded in wrath. Neither Spain's fleet nor army were ready to move let alone fight, but this did not matter now. On December 10, Wall handed Bristol a scathing note that blasted English treachery and aggression. Relations were severed; ambassadors were withdrawn.[40] Bute and Newcastle now agreed that war with Spain was vital to British interests.

A shake-up within the French foreign ministry occurred amidst this aggressive posturing. On October 15, 1761, an overburdened Choiseul passed the foreign ministry to his cousin, César-Gabriel de Choiseul, comte de Choiseul-Chevigny, while he retained the Spanish department along with the marine and war ministries. After distinguished service in the War of the Austrian Succession, Choiseul-Chevigny had risen in his cousin's diplomatic shadow, taking his place as ambassador at Vienna in 1758 before receiving the foreign ministry. He would go on to head the marine ministry in 1766. Despite the formal shift in duties, Choiseul remained in control of French foreign policy, signed its most important letters and memoirs, and conducted diplomacy toward the Bourbon states of Spain, Naples, Parma, and Portugal. Choiseul-Chevigny essentially served as his chief of staff and understudy.

Consequences

The impasse between France and England seemed unbreakable for now. The chasm between their positions was unbridgeable. Diplomats were withdrawn and the war dragged on. Then, on November 17,

1761, an unlikely source emerged to act as a conduit between Britain and France. François Joseph, comte de Viry, Sardinia's ambassador to England, offered his services. Viry corresponded closely with Caspar Joseph Balli de Solar de Breille, the Sardinian ambassador to Versailles. Solar and Choiseul were very good friends. The Sardinians proposed that the English ultimatum of July 29 and French ultimatum of August 5 be made the starting points for new negotiations. Whitehall expressed its interest. Viry passed the word on to Versailles. Choiseul accepted on December 8. There followed nearly five weeks of mostly silence. Yet a diplomatic bridge had been built even if, for now, the British hesitated to cross it.[41]

Only in Germany did the French retain a slender chance to defeat the British. During the late summer and fall, mixed news dribbled in from Europe's battlefields. By August that seesaw war in western Germany tilted once again; Ferdinand's advance had stretched his supply line to the breaking point while the replenished French turned to attack. Soubise and Broglie pushed Ferdinand and Brunswick back to Hanover. On September 20, Soubise actually captured Emden, Britain's support port for its troops with Ferdinand; he then marched toward Bremen. Ferdinand split off from his nephew Brunswick to maneuver Soubise back to the Rhine, which he handily accomplished by mid-October. Broglie's advance ground to a halt for lack of will and supplies. Both sides went into winter quarters. Once again, Ferdinand had not only saved Hanover but could march off part of his army to save a desperate Frederick.

The year seemed ominously like Frederick's last. After brilliantly staving off converging armies for five blood-soaked years, Frederick's realm teetered at destruction's brink. The dire situation was apparent in the spring and steadily worsened. As the armies roused from their winter quarters, Frederick could muster only 35,000 men to Daun's 65,000 in Saxony and Laudon's 30,000 in Silesia. The exhausted armies and their leaders shadowboxed all summer without either side landing a decisive blow. Then, on September 1, the Austrians recaptured Schweidnitz, while Russian and Swedish armies besieged Stettin and Colberg, respectively. At that time Broglie seemed about to overrun all of Hanover. Colberg fell in December. The only good news for

Frederick was Sweden's announcement on December 22, 1761, that it would soon withdraw from the war, though it gave no timetable or conditions. Still, Frederick was once again strategically backed into a corner. Once the allied armies marched out of their winter cantonments, they would crush Frederick beneath their collective weight. Only a miracle could save the Prussian monarch. That miracle would come.

Meanwhile, with consummate irony, Versailles finally addressed the corruption that had festered at the heart of New France. For a half dozen years, the British had tried to capture Canada before doing so in September 1760. All along Versailles had done nothing to stop the corruption and little to prevent the British conquest. Then, on December 21, 1761, Louis decreed that all those who had engaged in the "monopolies, abuses, troubles, and double-dealings which have been committed in Canada" would be arrested and tried. Warrants were issued for fifty-five men on charges of treason and corruption, including Governor Vaudreuil and Intendant Bigot. Only twenty-two of those charged were actually captured. The trial would last through nearly two years of investigations, testimonies, and deliberations. The court's decision would be the final drama in the conquest of New France.[42]

CHAPTER 12

Last Gambles, 1762 and 1763

In politics one cannot change the facts but there is a great advantage in how one presents them.

Choiseul

In war success justifies everything.

Bernis

In 1762, the war was largely out of Versailles's hands. The French had lost Canada along with most of their colonies in the Caribbean, India, and West Africa, had buried ever more heaps of their dead in the German quagmire, and could only fume in impotent rage as the British navy vacuumed the seas of their war and merchant ships. Elsewhere, having finally talked the Spanish into joining the war the previous year, the French could merely sit back and watch what would be the cataclysmic results. And in Germany, although Frederick and Ferdinand appeared to be on the ropes, their military genius had repeatedly trounced converging allied forces, including French armies for a half dozen years. Would history repeat itself in 1762?

Yet a Frenchman could still dream big. Choiseul toyed with the scheme of combining the French and Spanish fleets for an invasion of England. By one count that armada could muster fifty-two ships of the line, including six at Brest, ten at Rochefort, eight at Ferrol, fourteen at Cadiz, four at Cartagena, and ten at Toulon. In April and

May 1762, Choiseul actually tried to talk Madrid into his plan to feint against Ireland that summer and then capture the Isle of Wight and Portsmouth in the fall.[1]

This notion was dead in the water. With the Royal Navy's mastery of the sea, the initiative was solely in Whitehall's hands. The British made the most of it. News that Spain had severed diplomatic relations reached London on December 24, 1761. After ten days of debate, Britain formally declared war against Spain on January 4, 1762. Spain returned the favor on January 11.

Bute and his colleagues devised a strategy for that year every bit as ambitious as anything Pitt could have conceived. Expeditions would reinforce Lisbon and take Martinique, Havana, and Manila. To those ends, in addition to Britain's commitments elsewhere, Whitehall won from Parliament appropriations for a 297-ship navy manned by 82,400 sailors and a 120,000-man British army, which, when the foreign contingents were included, reached 186,000 troops. The bill for all this would be a staggering 14 million pounds sterling.[2]

Whitehall engaged in a flurry of other initiatives to help win the war. Its diplomats at Constantinople urged the Porte to attack Russia to relieve pressure on Prussia. The ambassador in Copenhagen called for a Danish attack on the Russians at Colberg in return for formal Danish control of Schleswig. At Vienna, the British representative tried to incite Austrian fear at the Bourbon pact's renewal and encouraged Maria Theresa to send her armies into the Bourbon states of Italy. At Amsterdam, the Dutch were pressured to join the war against a defeated France. These ventures all failed.

A Miracle for Prussia

The toughest question was what to do about Prussia. Despite Frederick's military genius and the millions of English pounds pumped into his treasury, Prussia seemed a lost cause. Whitehall's subsidy treaty with Berlin expired in November 1761, while the allies massed to administer the coup de grace to Frederick. Perhaps the time had come to cut British losses in Germany.

Yet Frederick could be as infuriatingly audacious at diplomacy as he was at war. First, he talked the British into renewing the £670,000 subsidy, if not the formal treaty. Then, he urged Whitehall to cut a separate peace with France if it included a clause requiring Versailles to abandon its war against Prussia. Yet in the next breath he insisted that if the British did so they would have to give him 6 million crowns for breaking their treaty forbidding a separate peace! At first Bute dug in his heels on this demand, arguing that Britain had already transferred to Prussia 6 million crowns via its previous subsidies. Eventually, he would yield to Frederick's argument that British honor demanded that it fulfill its legal duty.

Then, with Frederick once again near collapse, fate intervened. On January 5, 1762, after a month of fever and seizures, Empress Elizabeth finally died. Her Frederick-worshiping, Holstein-born, Lutheran nephew took the throne as Tsar Peter III. Two days later, on January 7, 1762, he decreed that all French, including diplomats, were persona non grata. He then sent orders to General Zakhar Chernyshev to disengage his army and withdraw to Russia. On February 23, the tsar dispatched his aide, General Andrei Gudovich, to Potsdam to grant peace and restore all conquered lands to Prussia.

Frederick gratefully accepted the astonishing gift, released all Russian prisoners, and turned those Prussian forces defending against Russia south against Austria. He also sent orders to his ambassador at Constantinople to now urge the Turks to attack Austria's Hungary instead of Russia. Prussian and Russian diplomats then worked out the details of the peace. They signed an armistice on March 5 and a peace treaty on April 24, 1762. And as if that diplomatic flip-flop were not stunning enough, the tsar would make an even more stunning gyration within a few weeks.[3]

Peter III's withdrawal of Russia from the war certainly saved Frederick and perhaps even Prussia from destruction. Peter III shrugged off the cost of six years of Russian blood and treasury that had captured East Prussia. Instead, he wanted the return of Schleswig and parts of Holstein that had come under Danish suzerainty if not outright control after the Northern War (1701–1721), along with Russian puppets on the thrones of Courland and Poland. Peter III and Frederick II conspired over just how to win Russia those lands. Meanwhile, Russia's defection from the alliance threatened to destroy it. Maria Theresa despaired of warring alone against Frederick. She and her advisors began to think seriously about what, if anything, they could win at any peace negotiations.

Diplomatic Mirages and Coups

Meanwhile, the French and British negotiations had all but collapsed. After the two sides angrily broke off talks in September 1761, Choiseul hoped to revive them by approving a Sardinian go-between on December 8, 1761. But so far nothing had come of this. Growing increasingly impatient, Choiseul nearly scuttled this option on January 23, 1762, when he bluntly sent word that he expected England to offer a concrete and realistic peace proposal to his previous opening bid. Although Whitehall pointedly ignored Choiseul's brusque demand, an increasing number of ministers and the king himself sought some way to resume talks.[4]

At this point, Louis XV stepped in. If the Sardinian connection was too tenuous to promote peace between their nations, perhaps it could be used to decide the fate of one person. He wrote George III a plea that naval commander Charles, comte d'Estaing, be released from an English prison. D'Estaing was captured once, was released on a parole, which he promptly broke, and was imprisoned after being recaptured. For this, the British were certainly within their rights to toss d'Estaing behind bars. But on February 22, 1762, with George III's blessing, he was released with a conciliatory letter to Choiseul. D'Estaing had unwittingly served as a pawn to break the diplomatic impasse. With that trivial matter settled, the French and British agreed to renew discussions on the vital issue of war and peace.[5] In March a deal seemed near. Letters passed between Versailles and Whitehall via the Sardinians. In mid-March, the British accepted the French version of the Canadian boundary and included Miquelon with Saint Pierre as an abri for French fishermen in the Gulf of Saint Lawrence. British engineers would inspect Dunkirk's fortifications and determine whether they must be destroyed. The Neutral Islands would be split, with Britain taking Dominica and Tobago and France taking Saint Lucia and Saint Vincent. Gorée would revert to France.[6]

Then, on March 22, news arrived that Martinique had been captured. Martinique produced more wealth in sugar than any other island except Saint Domingue. The mountainous island was defended by 1,200 regulars, 7,000 militia, and 4,000 privateers. On January 7, 1762, a British fleet packed with 8,000 troops commanded by General Monckton appeared off the island's western tip and began disembarking. Finding their way from the beaches blocked by impassable terrain, Monckton's and his men reembarked and did not find a satisfactory landing place until January 16 at Case Navire. From there, a torturous three-mile path snaked over the mountains to Fort Royal. Monckton's troops hauled themselves, their supplies, and their cannons over the trail and emplaced batteries to command the French forts ringing the port. The bombardment began on January 24. A premature British assault left nearly 390 redcoats dead or wounded on the slopes. Three days later, Monckton ordered another attack; this one carried Morne Grenier at a loss of 100 troops. On February 3, Fort Royal was surrendered, followed by all of Martinique on February 12. Monckton dispatched small expedition to capture nearby Saint Lucia, Saint Vincent, and Grenada.[7]

Once again victory hardened most of the cabinet. The debate was rejoined over just how much more of France's empire to devour. While that debate continued, the cabinet and king did reach a consensus that now was the time to restore diplomatic relations with France. To avoid appearing weak, a proposal to do so was issued in George III's name on April 8 that made the old ultimatum the basis for negotiations for the new envoys. The announcement effectively canceled the considerable progress made through the Sardinians. Yet Choiseul promptly agreed to the exchange, reasoning that the old ultimatum assertion was just a diplomatic fig leaf and that the envoys could quickly agree to assume the more recent conciliatory positions. Now Martinique was added to that lengthening list of lands for which France demanded the unconditional return.[8]

Choiseul was to be disappointed. Whitehall debated and eventually agreed to two proposals. A report submitted by secretary for the

Southern Department Charles Wyndham, Earl of Egremont, on April 24 would give Versailles the dilemma of choosing between surrendering either Louisiana or Guadeloupe in exchange for Martinique. Britain would now retain all four Neutral Islands. As if this assertion would not rattle Versailles enough, the cabinet agreed to an even more startling demand. The cabinet reached a consensus on May 1 that the Mississippi River divide the two empires. In a conciliatory gesture, the "channel" that ran east of New Orleans through the Iberville River and Lakes Maurepas and Pontchartrain to the sea would allow that city to remain in Louisiana. These two new positions were supposed to remain in Britain's diplomatic quiver for now. However, hoping for a diplomatic breakthrough, Bute secretly revealed them to French envoy Viry on May 4. This would cause considerable confusion in the negotiations and eventual embarrassment among the English ministers over the next two months.[9]

Meanwhile, a diplomatic revolution elsewhere blossomed in May. That month Frederick's diplomacy knocked two enemies from the war and redirected the planned attacks of two distant allies. On May 5, 1762, a treaty joined Prussia and Russia as allies. On May 22, Prussia and Sweden signed a peace treaty at Hamburg. Frederick also succeeded in convincing the Turks to attack Austria rather than Russia, though the attack would not come that year. Peace and then alliance with Russia also affected Prussia's alliance with Britain. Anticipating those realignments, a financially exhausted cabinet unilaterally revoked its £670,000 subsidy to Prussia on April 30, 1762. The British argued that with Frederick's war all but won, he no longer needed a subsidy. They rebuked Frederick for conspiring with Peter III to grant Schleswig and Holstein to Russia.

It was not just Prussia that would feel the pinch of Britain's tighter purse. In May, Bute shot down Newcastle's proposal to devote £1 million each to wars in Portugal and Germany. Bute insisted instead that £1 million was sufficient to underwrite both wars. After that measure passed Parliament, Newcastle resigned on May 26, citing the cabinet's rejection of his spending proposal and earlier refusal to renew the Prussian subsidy. With Newcastle out of the way, Bute reigned supreme, taking over his portfolio as Treasury's first lord. The cabinet, however, remained split when George Grenville, Temple's brother and Pitt's brother-in-law, became secretary of state for the Northern Department. Grenville could not replace but could merely echo the views and intensity of his two relatives.

As 1762 deepened, Britain's leaders increasingly had more on their minds than war with France and Spain. The budding rapprochement among Prussia, Russia, and Sweden presented new challenges to British interests. Bute and Bedford argued for a soft peace with France as a prelude to a possible alliance to counter a potential northern alliance among Russia, Prussia, and Sweden that might seal off British merchants from markets bordering the Baltic. To entice France into such an arrangement, Whitehall was prepared to offer concessions. On May 1, Egremont informed Viry that France could have the islands of both Saint Pierre and Miquelon for its fishermen in Saint Lawrence Bay and get back the Caribbean islands of Guadeloupe, Marie-Galante, and Martinique. Belle Isle would be traded for Minorca. However, France would now have to cede all of Louisiana east of the Mississippi River including New Orleans. France would also have to evacuate Prussian Wesel and Guelders.[10]

The friendlier British faces and policies greatly relieved the French. Choiseul remarked that Versailles "sincerely regretted that we did not have My Lord Egremont to deal with last year. What misfortunes we could have avoided! and how great the difference between negotiating with My Lord Egremont and with Mr. Pitt, who may be a great man inasmuch as we have made war like simpletons, but who of a surety is the worst statesman in Europe." Other obstacles to peace, however, remained formidable. Choiseul lamented that if Louis XV "were master, the peace would be made in two weeks. But England has forced us into alliances that exact joint action. We shall lose not a minute in getting Spain to agree to our ideas." Choiseul was prepared to compromise for peace and would happily "accord the boundaries of Louisiana as England asks them; I think we can cede the Grenadines; but St. Lucia is absolutely necessary to us. Tell my opinion neither to the Comte de Choiseul nor in England, because it is no longer my affair. I concern myself solely with my dear Spain to secure a prompt ending, and that task is enough for me."[11] Choiseul refused to surrender Saint

Lucia, arguing for its strategic importance in guarding the approach to Martinique. Of course, it was for this very reason that the British were most eager to take it. He also insisted on retaining New Orleans. As for Choiseul's disclaimer about his powers, he remained in firm command of French foreign policy. And, though quite prepared to be flexible, he deemed it first appropriate to act tough.

Choiseul issued a memoir on May 29 that stunned Whitehall. He renounced France's former concessions as mere public relations ploys to evoke the sympathy and support of the other European powers. Now, he boldly asserted,

> Guadeloupe, Mariegalante, Martinique, and St. Lucia are all indispensable for the support of French commerce. The restoration of Grenada may be joined to that of Martinique as an old French possession. In compensation England will retain Dominica, St. Vincent, Tobago, and the king will cede to England the port of Mobile between Florida and the Mississippi and will agree that the Mississippi will serve as the boundary to the two states from its source as far as the Ohio River. . . . From that junction to the sea, since the chief settlement of Louisiana is on the river, the king shall be sovereign over both banks for a league's distance from the [east] bank, the line of demarcation passing between Lakes Maurepas and Pontchartrain.

Finally, he demanded either Cape Breton's full return or abri rights there.[12]

After struggling with the question for years, Choiseul finally reached a definitive answer as to what kind of empire was best for France:

> I do not think as they formerly did here that it is necessary to have many colonies; I am the sworn enemy of the American policy because I think it pernicious to France, and because I think it more essential to cultivate the wheat and vines of the Kingdom and to sustain its manufactures than to supply

foreign nations with sugar, coffee, and indigo. . . . I think that a great power should not let its money leave the kingdom in payment for these commodities that have become necessities; consequently it pertains to the perfection of the kingdom to have enough American possessions to supply its needs in that sort. But it should have more than suffices for its needs, while at the same time the possessions in question should be secure, and the commerce of the mother country should go on without fear of an unforeseen happening.[13]

Whitehall tried to kill Choiseul's assertion with silent contempt. Privately, the cabinet—even the conciliatory Bute—collectively fumed. Yet Bute was willing to concede New Orleans and Saint Lucia. Hardliners George Grenville and John Carteret, Earl of Granville, insisted that New Orleans and Saint Lucia be joined to the British empire. With the cabinet split, on June 21, Egremont could merely respond by repeating the English position of May 1. Negotiations once again ground to a halt.[14]

All along Versailles had kept its negotiations with Whitehall secret from its allies Austria and Spain. By May 1762, word had leaked to Vienna, which demanded an explanation from Versailles. On May 11, Choiseul's cousin foreign minister Choiseul-Chevigny denied the rumor. The next day, however, when Austrian ambassador Georg Adam Starhemberg presented evidence, Choiseul-Chevigny was forced not only to admit that indeed France and Britain had been secretly negotiating but also to reveal the details of their talks.[15]

A Miracle for Austria

Though increasingly isolated and desperate, Austria's armies dared not budge while the diplomatic revolution among Prussia, Russia, and Sweden unfolded. Laudon stayed around Schweidnitz and Daun in Silesia. On June 10, Peter III ordered General Chernyshev to join with Frederick against Austria. The plan was for Frederick to march from the north and Chernyshev from the east to converge on the Austrian armies blocking the roads to Vienna. Then an astonishing event occurred that led to the latest diplomatic revolution.

For nearly all of Russia's elite, the alliance with Frederick was bad enough, but Peter III went so far as to don a Prussian uniform. This outraged Russia's generals, most aristocrats, and even the new tsar's wife, who muttered treason against the German traitor corrupting the Russian throne. The hatred and fear deepened between Peter and Catherine until, on June 14, the tsar ordered her arrested and exiled to her country estate. The arrest of an officer for mouthing anti-Peter sentiments on June 27 sparked a coup. Dissident officers marched their troops to Catherine and brought her back to Saint Petersburg. Other regiments joined them until the rebels numbered 14,000 when they reached the Winter Palace. On June 28, those officers arrested Peter III and elevated Catherine as empress. On July 6, guards accidentally killed a drunken, violent Peter III at his château, or so the story goes.

Catherine promptly and literally reversed the diplomatic revolution by ordering General Chernyshev to about-face and trudge his army back to Poland. She pondered tearing up the peace treaty her husband had made with Frederick. If Russia rejoined the allies, Frederick would surely be defeated. Instead, she concluded that Russia had shed enough blood and treasury during the war. It was time to savor the spoils. The empress had General Saltykov in East Prussia make the inhabitants swear allegiance to her.

The loss of the Russian army upset Frederick's plans. Yet he did not hesitate to march on against Austrian general Gideon von Laudon, who retreated back into Moravia. Frederick then besieged Schweidnitz, Austria's last holding in Silesia. When Marshal Leopold von Daun marched to its relief, Frederick met and defeated him at Burkersdorf on July 21. Prince Henry, meanwhile, maneuvered in Saxony against an Austrian army under Johann Baptist Serbelloni and an Imperial army under Prince Christian von Stolberg. By late September, the allies had driven Henry back to Freiberg. Henry turned his 24,000 troops and pounced, inflicting 8,000 casualties on the 39,000-man allied army, while losing 3,000. In October, General Francis Guasco surrendered Schweidnitz along with his 9,000 troops. The armies then went into winter quarters. They would not emerge in the spring.

The Portuguese Card

In the war's last year, the fighting spread further. The Spanish had rebuffed all of Choiseul's attempts to organize a joint fleet and force. Madrid was concentrating its forces and attention on an invasion of Portugal. Why Portugal? Charles III believed that Portugal was to Spain as Hanover was to France. In attacking Portugal, he hoped to divert British armies and navies from attacks on Spain's empire elsewhere. And in a peace settlement he hoped to trade Portugal for any Spanish territory the British may have seized.

In all this, the king exaggerated Portugal's importance to British. It was true that trade between Portugal and Britain was vigorous and enriched both countries. Lisbon was a lair for British warships and privateers preying on French and Spanish shipping. Also true was that the 1703 Methuen Treaty required England to send 20 warships, 10,000 infantry, and 2,500 cavalry to Portugal if it were invaded. While a Spanish attack on Portugal would not immediately divert any ongoing British campaigns elsewhere in the world, it would certainly prompt Whitehall to aid Lisbon financially and militarily. But Charles III chose to war against Portugal and Britain with the belief that Lisbon was vulnerable and Havana impregnable. The opposite would prove true.

In late April, foreign minister Wall issued an ultimatum to Portugal that it sever trade with Britain and join the Bourbon pact. Lisbon angrily rejected the ultimatum. On May 3, Spanish troops marched across the frontier and took Miranda then Bragança. On May 6, John Campbell, Lord Loudoun, arrived at Lisbon to command the swelling British contingent earlier sent to stiffen Portugal's army against just such a crisis. On May 15, the Spanish marched down the Douro River toward Oporto. By early June, Loudoun joined his seven thousand troops to Wilhelm, Count Schaumburg-Lippe-Buckeburg, commanding the Portuguese army in the Douro valley. Together, they marched slowly against the Spanish and, in a series of sharp, small battles, drove them back across the border by late August. Charles III's only planned campaign had met with disaster. From then on, he would receive report after report of British attacks and captures of Spanish colonies.[16]

Distant Islands and the Heart of Europe

Since the Spanish rejected any notion of joint naval operations with France, Louis XV's surviving warships were available for action elsewhere—if they could evade the British blockade and get there. Versailles ordered Admiral Charles, comte de Blénac, to sail to Martinique's relief. He was supposed to have left Brest by November 1761, but harsh winds and the British blockade kept him bottled up until January 1762. Finding Martinique lost, he sailed on to Cap François, Saint Domingue, from which he hoped to organize an attack against Jamaica.

Two British fleets prowled the West Indies at this time. Admiral George Rodney was then stationed at the Leeward Islands. Captain Arthur Forrest anchored his squadron off Cap François but failed to intercept Blénac. Learning that Blénac had reached Saint Domingue, Rodney dispatched most of his fleet to Jamaica and sent orders to Forrest to meet him at Cap Tiburon for a joint attack on the French fleet. Rodney waited for days there before he received a note from Forrest explaining that the governor and his council forbade him from leaving them undefended.

Though exasperating to both British commanders, the delay did not matter after all; Blénac had also chosen to sit tight in a safe harbor. In June, Blénac faced a tough choice when he received a plea from Havana to rescue it from the British siege. Saint Domingue's intendant and leading citizens implored him to stay. Diseases had ravaged his crews. He lacked supplies. Finally, Blénac chose to rest at anchor. On July 28, he did emerge to chase down a passing convoy bound for Britain; his frigates captured six transports packed with five hundred troops and supplies.

Thus were the seas cleared for the British expedition against Havana. Though both Versailles and Madrid got wind of the planned attack, they dismissed its importance in the belief that Havana was impregnable. Madrid unwittingly doomed its fleet at Havana by ordering Captain General Don Juan de Prado Porto Carrero to keep his ships anchored in the harbor no matter what. Prado conveyed that order to Don Guitierre de Hevia, who commanded the twelve ships of the line and eight smaller warships at Havana, along with an order to sink three warships at the harbor's mouth. That decision at once kept out the English and trapped his own fleet from sailing to safety. Two castles guarded Havana Bay's mouth, Fort Morro on the east horn and Fort Punta on the west where the city lay. Prado massed about six thousand marines, soldiers, and militia in those forts and along the city's walls.

Admiral George Pocock's invasion fleet dropped anchor a half dozen miles east of Havana's bay on June 6. George Keppel, Earl of Albemarle, commanded the troops. Inexplicably, he chose to land his troops on the western shore and besiege Fort Morro rather than the eastern shore near the city. In doing so, for weeks the British battled not just the Spanish fort but also foul water, thin soil above coral rock, dense brush, incessant humidity, oven-like heat, and disease. Nonetheless, in mid-July British sappers completed a tunnel under Fort Morro, packed it with explosives, and lit the fuse. The explosion tore a jagged gap in the wall through which British troops swarmed and captured the fort. It was an important victory, but the bay still separated the British army from Havana. Meanwhile, General William Howe had landed troops on the bay's eastern shore and had besieged Fort Punta. The eventual bombardment breached Fort Punta's walls, which British troops carried on August 9. The following day, Albemarle summoned Pardo to surrender. Pardo finally agreed on August 15 in return for full honors of war. Spain lost not only Havana but also a treasury of 750,000 reales; twelve battleships (nine captured and three sunk), totaling one-fifth of its fleet; and over 100 merchant ships. It was England's costliest victory of the war—battle killed or wounded 560 troops while disease buried another 5,000. Those losses forced the British to postpone any attack on Louisiana until 1763. By that time the war would be over.[17]

With Versailles's last dice roll of the war, France scored first a minor victory followed by a minor defeat. On May 8, 1762, Chevalier de Ternay d'Arsic slipped through Brest's blockade with two battleships and a frigate packed with 1,500 troops commanded by Colonel Joseph Louis Bernard de Cléron, comte d'Haussonville. On June 20, the flotilla appeared before Saint John's, Newfoundland. The British surrendered that same day. It took a month for word to reach General Amherst in New York. Most of his troops were on the Havana expedition. He scraped up 1,550 troops and dispatched them from New York on August 14 under the command of his younger brother, Lieutenant Colonel William Amherst. The seven-ship convoy stopped in Louisbourg for supplies and reached Saint John's on September 12. By September 18, Amherst's troops had invested the town and forced d'Haussonville's surrender.

In this first world war, even South America became a target for conquest. Choiseul mulled an expedition against Brazil that he hoped would further strike Britain's trade and wealth. The plan was for Captain Louis Joseph Beaussier's squadron to attack Bahia and Rio de Janeiro. But the ships, troops, supplies, money, and will were just not available.[18] They were available, however, for the British. Captain Henri Pentaleon MacNamera led five hundred British and Portuguese troops in a half dozen vessels against Buenos Aires, Argentina, in November. When his frigates closed to bombard the city, Spanish gunners sank one and severely splintered the other. MacNamera ordered his ships to sail away.

But the most distant battle of that far-flung war took place at Manila. At Calcutta, Admiral Samuel Cornish and General William Draper received orders in June 1762 to mount an expedition against the Philippines. By August 1, the commanders had gathered 940 troops and enough supplies to set sail. The fifteen-ship fleet anchored off Fort Cavita guarding Manila on September 24. Draper immediately began landing his troops and supplies through the heavy surf. The Spanish were astonished at the intrusion—no one at Madrid had bothered to send word that they were at war. Two days later the redcoats captured that outlying fort and began dragging up siege guns. The bombardment of Manila's walls began on October 4; within four hours, the British gunners had silenced the Spanish cannons and breached the wall. On October 6, Draper ordered an assault, which carried the key bastion defending Manila. The Spanish not only agreed to surrender all of the Philippines but paid 4 million Spanish dollars to ransom Manila. News of Manila's fall would not reach Europe until after the peace treaty was signed.[19]

In contrast, news from the continent arrived at Versailles within days after it occurred. As usual, the news was bad. In early June when the campaign began, Charles de Rohan, prince de Soubise, and Louis Charles César Le Tellier, duc d'Estrées, jointly commanded 100,000 troops of the Army of the Main, supported by Louis Joseph de Bourbon Condé, comte de Clermont's 30,000-man Army of the Rhine. The two French armies slowly advanced against Ferdinand's 95,000 troops. By June 22, Soubise and Estrées had halted their army around Wilhelmsthal. Two days later Ferdinand sent 50,000 troops against the 70,000 troops on the French right flank commanded by General Castries. At a loss of only 700 men, Ferdinand inflicted 4,500 casualties and routed Castries. Panicked, Soubise and Estrées ordered their entire army to withdraw. Ferdinand then sent small forces to raid the French communication and supply lines. Condé finally obeyed orders to join Soubise and Estrées. Their forces combined at Freiberg on August 30. Ferdinand's second-in-command, Brunswick, attacked that same day, unaware of the huge number of troops arrayed against him. The French repulsed Brunswick but did not follow up their victory. A week later on September 7, the French army began a slow march toward Ferdinand. On September 15, Ferdinand halted his retreat at Homburg and awaited battle. The French declined to satisfy him. On September 20, French troops assaulted Amöneberg Castle. Ferdinand hurried his troops to the sound of the guns. The French paid 1,200 dead and wounded to capture Amöneberg, while the allies lost only 750 casualties. On November 1, Ferdinand won the war's last battle when he captured Cassel after a three-week siege.

Cutting Deals

As usual, it took a French defeat to jostle the stalled negotiations. News of Ferdinand's latest victory over the French on June 24 prompted a new round of diplomatic initiatives. Messages from Versailles and Whitehall crisscrossed sometime in late June. On June 28, Bute told Viry that Britain would cede Saint Lucia in return for a French alliance but would hold firm to its other demands. That same day, Louis XV submitted a draft peace treaty based on Choiseul's May 29 memoir.[20] The submission was made with little hope that the British would accept it. Instead, it was published for the benefit of Spain as well as to curry favor with European opinion. Versailles dreaded learning of Spain's reaction to France's secret peace talks. Viry summed up the trepidation when he predicted, "The Spanish will reproach us; we shall have no little trouble to appease them."[21]

In reply to the British overture, Choiseul informed Ambassador Solar on June 29 that he held fast to the May 29 memoir and June 28 peace draft. When it learned Choiseul's position, Whitehall too declared that Britain would not compromise its previous position. What Egremont did not realize was that Bute had secretly agreed to grant New Orleans to France on May 4. To both their deep embarrassment mingled with the latter's resentment, Bute was forced to admit his secret initiative to Egremont.[22]

The Spanish reaction to France's peace initiative arrived in late July. Madrid insisted on joining negotiations. In meetings with Choiseul on July 19, 20, and 21, Ambassador Grimaldi bluntly expressed Madrid's fear that France, in its zeal to end the war, had not vigorously or at all fulfilled its promise to defend Spain's Honduras logging, Newfoundland fisheries, Louisiana, and prizes of war. He also insisted that Naples's envoy to London, Prince Sanseverino, take over from the Sardinians as diplomatic go-between. Most threatening to Spanish interests were Versailles's compromises on Louisiana. Grimaldi condemned "the cession of a part of Louisiana which would give the English any foothold on the Gulf of Mexico." He further expressed his astonishment that Versailles would unilaterally make a decision of "such great consequence for the interests of Spain and of France, without taking into account the motives suggested by the union of the crowns." He declared unequivocally that "the king, my master, would never consent to make peace if that article were adopted."[23]

Choiseul deftly staved off all of Grimaldi's demands except one. Grimaldi asserted that Spain would never accept a British foothold on the Gulf of Mexico. Choiseul agreed and promised to draw Louisiana's eastern boundary a league from the Mississippi River and through Lakes Maurepas and Pontchartrain so that Britain had no outlet to the Gulf. Grimaldi countered that this still left the British on the Gulf along the entire coastline east of New Orleans. In Madrid, Charles III insisted on a boundary line that ran from Georgia's southwestern end to the Mississippi River, with Louisiana extending south from there to the Gulf while neutral Indians lived north of there to the Ohio River. Choiseul actually came to see these Spanish assertions on Louisiana as more help than hindrance: "This objection from the ambassador of Spain which is not new does not halt us; but it should make the English ministers feel the full value of the cession which we are making them."[24]

Versailles had spent years trying to seduce Madrid into an alliance. Having finally consummated that desire, Versailles increasingly longed to be free of the relationship as the alliance's constraints exceeded its benefits. Choiseul was caught between France's need for peace at almost any price and its duty to a once too reluctant and now too assertive ally. He finessed the dilemma by getting Whitehall to help him deceive Madrid. He drew up two maps, one including the Spanish demands, which he showed Grimaldi and promised to send to London, the other reflecting the line agreed to by France and England, of which the Spanish ambassador remained ignorant. The British agreed to ignore the first map accompanying Choiseul's preliminary treaty proposal and to accept the second.[25]

Choiseul played a very risky game that, if discovered by Madrid, could have blackened France's diplomatic name for decades. Sooner or later, word would undoubtedly reach Spain of France's secret peace negotiations. Why did he do it? Versailles feared that if Madrid found out, it would demand an equal seat at the peace talks or try to stop them altogether. So the French put off informing their ally. Perhaps another reason for the delay was Ambassador Grimaldi, who was universally loathed for his "indiscretion and his insufferable bluster. . . . [He] will put hindrances in a negotiation that should be ended by one conference."[26] In all, deceiving the Spanish ally seemed a gamble worth taking. Victory now was impossible. The only sensible option was to prevent France's debts, colonial losses, and casualties from soaring ever higher. Increasingly the most forbidding obstacle to peace was the need to stroke national pride.

Whitehall debated Choiseul's latest proposals on July 24. While the cabinet agreed to go along with the French deception, it split as usual on the details of Choiseul's peace proposal. Granville, Grenville, and Egremont insisted on heaping New Orleans and Saint Lucia on Britain's pile of war prizes. Bute adjourned the council and then, together with George III, worked individually with each member to give ground to allow France a face-saving way to end the war. By August 1, Bute had forged a consensus that yielded New Orleans and Saint Lucia to France, but held firm to all its previous peace conditions and issued vague statements with regard to Spanish concerns.[27]

Charles III stymied Choiseul's strategy on August 2 when he summoned the French ambassador. Ossun reported to Choiseul that the king "demands to intervene, as a contracting party, in the settlement of the boundaries of the countries ceded to the English by the French under the general designation of Canada. But this monarch . . . appears absolutely determined not to consent that these boundaries should extend as far as the sea which forms the Gulf of Mexico."[28]

To assuage Spanish fears, Choiseul dispatched envoy Jacob O'Dun to Madrid on August 7, with a reassuring letter from Louis XV to Charles III. Eventually, Versailles granted Spain a remarkable gift in compensation for all of its sacrifices. By August, Versailles had concluded that Louisiana, like Canada, was more trouble than it was worth. The council debated and approved a memoir that would use Louisiana to jolt Madrid into accepting peace: "To awaken that sentiment in the hearts of the Spaniards I proposed on my return to give the court of Madrid a serious alarm, namely the cession of Louisiana to England." When Madrid expressed its horror, the ambassador would simply offer Louisiana in return for Spain's approval of the peace treaty. Thus would Louisiana finally profit France.[29]

In August, Whitehall and Versailles finally reached an agreement. Each side would name a peace minister by September 1, and the two would meet in Calais on September 6 en route to the other's capital. Louis Jules Barbon Mancini-Mazarini, duc de Nivernais, would represent France; Whitehall dispatched John Russell, Duke of Bedford.

The French mission got off to a shaky start when Nivernais failed to reach Calais on time, delayed, it was rumored, by the challenge of finding a suitable house in London before he arrived. Nivernais was a minor writer whose efforts the French Academy recognized with a membership. He won less success as a diplomat. It was Nivernais who had cooled his heels at Potsdam in 1756 awaiting Frederick's decision over whether to cast an alliance toward England or France. Choiseul had charged Nivernais with asserting the French position on the Louisiana boundary, while presenting but not defending Spain's plan that would totally cut off British North America from the Gulf of Mexico.[30]

Bedford reached Paris on September 12. Two days later he met for four hours of talks with Choiseul-Chevigny followed on September 15 with nine hours of negotiations, first with Choiseul and then joined by Choiseul-Chevigny and Grimaldi. Choiseul was ready to concede to Britain navigation rights to the Mississippi River as long as British subjects only poled down and not up stream, while British ships were forbidden to transit the river in either direction. Perhaps to Choiseul's surprise, Bedford agreed as long as the same rule applied to the French inhabitants of Louisiana. Choiseul protested that this would sever Louisiana from France. Given Bedford's reputation for sarcasm and irony, his exact response can only be imagined. The discussion then spread to such subjects as trade, Portugal, Havana's status if captured, and Spain's list of grievances. By the meeting's end, the diplomats shared nothing but exasperation.[31]

To break the impasse, Choiseul appealed to Madrid to accept the French preliminary treaty draft that bridged the chasm between the British and Spanish positions. The absurdity of the conflict was not lost on Versailles. If the Spanish remained obstinate, Louis XV was prepared to "order the French to evacuate the whole of Louisiana than to miss a peace for a dispute over a colony with which we cannot communicate by sea, which has not and cannot have any port or roadstead that can be entered by a twelve-gun sloop, and which costs France 800,000 francs a year without returning a crown."[32] And indeed, that is what Louis eventually did.

In London, meanwhile, Nivernais's positions and personality had succeeded in irritating the British ministers forced to deal with him. Egremont called him a "headstrong silly wretch."[33] Nivernais also ruffled ambassador Viry's feathers by studiously ignoring him. Then, on September 27, presumably to make amends, Nivernais suddenly dropped the demand for the neutrality of Indian tribes in the region between the Gulf, Mississippi, Ohio, and Appalachians.[34]

Versailles frequently pointed to even tougher Spanish demands to pressure England to accept its positions. The British ministers played the same game, glancing nervously over their shoulders at the fire-breathing mob comprised of Pitt, the House of Commons, public opinion, and scores of pamphlets that swore England would conquer all. Nivernais related to Choiseul-Chevigny that during his September 16 round with Bute, the latter warned darkly of "the necessity of sign-ing promptly and the impossibility of yielding on their side on the [Louisiana] article. The English ministry regards that article as the buckler in the next parliament . . . [and] the rush of scandalous publi-cations now flooding London against the peace."[35]

Diplomatic Recalculations

Amidst these deadlocks straddling the English Channel, word arrived of Havana's fall. Nivernais was actually dining at Bute's home with sev-eral other cabinet ministers on September 29, when a courier dashed in with the electrifying news. Bute's dinner party had succeeded beyond his dreams. Nivernais sent word to Choiseul-Chevigny, who received it on October 3.[36]

Havana's fall prompted Grenville, backed by Egremont and Granville, to declare publicly that Britain should return Cuba only in return for a Spanish concession elsewhere, such as Puerto Rico and Florida. He also demanded that Parliament examine and debate the preliminary treaty draft before it was signed. Grenville's assertions threatened to destroy the negotiations and Bute's ministry. Bute man-aged to finesse Grenville's play for power by having the king postpone Parliament's opening so that it could not possibly interfere with the treaty before it was signed. The political crisis also allowed Bute to force more speedy concessions from the French and Spanish. He and his allies Fox and Bedford frequently told Nivernais that they might end up on the scaffold if they conceded too much and if an agreement were not forged and signed before Parliament opened. Though partly a negotiation tactic, these claims reflected genuine fears.[37]

Ironically, the British were not the only ones who benefited from Havana's capture. From the Spanish disaster, Choiseul gained vital diplomatic leverage with Madrid. He simultaneously called on Nivernais to urge Bute not to ratchet up England's demands and on Ossun to press Charles III to accept Versailles's preliminaries. Choiseul's instructions to Ossun along with the first word of Havana's surrender reached Madrid on October 9.[38]

The next day Ossun met with foreign minister Wall, who related the king's philosophical reaction to the bad news:

> My troops fought well; that consoles me. And I never slept more tranquilly than last night. If the English act in good faith, they will hold to the preliminaries they have offered me, in which the restitution of conquests made in America is specified; if they have acted in bad faith, I have great means to use against them; and when one has resources, and courage, one does not yield or bend easily. I am, thank God, in this case, and far from ever thinking of a separate peace from France. I charge you, Monsieur the Ambassador, to assure the King my cousin, that I may lose all, even my Indies, but I will never abandon him. Thank him, however, from me for the generous and obliging offers he has made me.[39]

Spain's troops had indeed fought valiantly. The king's call for retaliation if the English made new demands, however, was an act of bravado; Spain had no means to hurt England. By ending with a promise not to forge a separate peace, Charles III skillfully gave himself a face-saving excuse not to carry on the war. In all, it was a masterly political and psychological act. Equally so, only a remarkable and natural equanimity explains Charles III's serenity before such an unmitigated disaster.

Spain's humiliating defeats deeply troubled Louis XV. On October 9, he wrote his Spanish cousin a letter that lauded his devotion and lamented his losses. What could assuage the sufferings of His Most Catholic Majesty that had resulted from his everlasting loyalty to His Most Christian King? For years, Madrid had pointedly reminded Versailles that France had intruded on Spain's claims to much of what was called Louisiana. With a Gallic shrug, Louis tossed Louisiana into his cousin's lap as compensation for the string of Spanish disasters culminating with Havana's capture. In his letter accompanying the king's to Madrid, Choiseul presented Louisiana's cession to Spain as an extraordinary gift. After all, it was the best card left in a poor hand, and he had to play it for all that it seemed worth.[40]

Ambassador Ossun did justice to his instructions when he bore that remarkable present to Charles. The king responded with his natural magnanimity, declining such an honor as far too generous for Spain's meager contributions to the alliance. But all that was diplomatic show. Ossun insisted that Spain take Louisiana, and the king gratefully accepted the gift. The last thing Versailles would admit to Madrid was that it now saw Louisiana, like Canada, as a burden best shed as expeditiously as possible.

Only a few last jagged holes in the peace treaty puzzle wanted filling. On October 15, Choiseul received via Nivernais Whitehall's terms for peace with Spain and dutifully passed it on to Ossun. If Madrid received Louisiana from France, it was expected to grant Florida to Britain. Once again, Charles III accepted the bad news with royal grace. He had little choice. The tenets of the alliance treaty he had signed with France ceded much of his power to negotiate to Louis XV.[41]

Britain now trounced Spain at the negotiation table as thoroughly as it had on the battlefield. With Madrid's approval, Grimaldi surrendered Florida, thus giving England all the land east of the Mississippi River except for the tiny enclave of New Orleans. He also gave in on all three issues that Madrid had spent years protesting to Whitehall and for which it had ostensibly gone to war—henceforth, the British could log in Honduras at unfortified settlements, the Spanish could not fish off Newfoundland, and the fate of captured Spanish ships would rest with English judges. Madrid's hopes that the unequal trade treaties that England had forced it to sign over the decades would be revised were dashed as well. Whitehall steadfastly insisted that those treaties remain in force. Here again, Spain bowed bitterly to British power. Choiseul encouraged all of these concessions, even the trade agreement. After all, now that France had its own most-favored-nation treaty with Spain, it would enjoy all benefits accorded to Britain.

The French, however, had to make more of their own concessions. In London, Nivernais negotiated the Mississippi River boundary. With Choiseul's reluctant permission, he gave in to the British demand that the boundary be mid-channel from the river's source to the Iberville channel rather than a league from the eastern bank as the French had previously insisted. Navigation of the Mississippi was open to British and French subjects alike upstream or down; ships could sail from New Orleans duty-free. A last-minute snag arose over whether the French could fortify the mouth of the Mississippi River, a curious demand given that France had given away all land upon which to site any fort. The French eventually conceded the "right." Those changes were hammered into the treaty's final draft.

Another issue involved the disposition of German lands occupied by French troops. Earlier that year, France agreed to withdraw from the land it had taken in Hanover, Brunswick, and Hesse but insisted on holding for Austria Prussia's Rhenish provinces, Wesel, Guelders, and Cleves. Choiseul finally agreed to hand those lands back to Prussia. Vienna protested but feebly; its attention was riveted closer to home. In October, Frederick recaptured Schweidnitz, Austria's last foothold in Silesia, and then smashed an Austrian-Imperial army at Freiberg, the war's last major battle.

Consequences

Within two weeks of laborious haggling, the exhausted diplomats finally reached agreement.[42] On November 3, 1762, Choiseul-Chevigny, whom the king named the duc de Praslin to elevate his status for the occasion, Bedford, and Grimaldi signed the preliminary Treaty of Fontainebleau.[43] Resignation seemed to have been the prevailing French emotion. Choiseul explained to Ossun that "we perfectly feel here that the peace will be neither glorious nor useful for France or

Spain; but unfortunately the circumstances would not allow us to obtain better results."[44] His cousin the foreign minister remarked, "The peace was not good, but was necessary, and I believe that, given the present situation, we can not flatter ourselves with having made a better one."[45] And what did the king think? That same day, Louis wrote Charles that the task was done; all they could do now was sigh and plot revenge.[46]

The preliminary treaty still had to be ratified. That was not an issue in France or Spain, whose nearly absolute monarchs could simply sign it and the task would be done. In Britain, however, the treaty was subject to parliamentary debate before it arrived on George III's desk. As expected, when the debate opened on December 9, Pitt vehemently attacked the treaty as a travesty and insult to British sacrifices during the long war. But Pitt's extremely loud voice represented only a minority within Parliament. Liberally distributing silver, pleas, and threats as appropriate, Henry Fox mustered 319 votes for the treaty, against which Pitt could rally only 65.

On February 10, 1763, representatives of France, England, Spain, and Portugal signed the definitive Treaty of Paris, ending the war among them. Five days later, Prussia, Austria, and Saxony-Poland signed the Treaty of Hubertusberg based on the status quo ante bellum. Russia and Sweden were absent, having signed separate treaties with Prussia the previous May. The guns had finally fallen silent. The silence would not last long.

To Choiseul, the treaty's final signature was anticlimactic. A sigh of enormous relief breathes through his diary on the day his cousin and foreign minister, Praslin, did the honors on behalf of France: "This grand work is finally consummated today."[47] That night Choiseul attended a ball given by the Spanish delegation. There he drank toasts, danced, and flirted in celebration of peace if not victory.

Uncharacteristically, Louis XV uttered the war's most articulate epitaph when he conceded that the "peace we have just concluded is neither good nor glorious: no one realizes it better than me. But, given the unfortunate circumstances, it could be no better, and I can assure you that if we had continued fighting we would have had to accept a worse peace next year. . . . Let us make do with what we have and so prepare ourselves not to be overcome by real enemies."[48]

CHAPTER 13

Distant Thunder

Nothing but a name remains of those who commanded battalions and fleets; nothing results to the human race from a hundred battles gained.

Voltaire

If this is the best of all possible worlds, what then are the others?

Candide in *Candide*

With the crowd on tiptoes behind them, soldiers lined the square at the Tuileries Palace's west end on June 20, 1763. An equestrian statue atop a large monument was to be unveiled in the square's heart. The soldiers were there to honor the statue's subject and to separate the people from the aristocrats gathered in its shadow. Many among the nobles, soldiers, and mélange of Parisians beyond must have smiled at the irony of it all. A mere four months after the Treaty of Paris had ended one of the more humiliating wars in French history, all those people were there to gaze upon a statue glorifying none other than the king who had presided over that defeat, Louis XV.

The king's thoughts that day went unrecorded. Never one to worry about the crippling costs of his lifestyle and wars, Louis most likely dismissed the question of the statue's propriety when the national treasury was bankrupt, had it even entered his mind. More likely the shy monarch concentrated on retaining an icy demeanor to shield himself from all those troublesome subjects beyond his familiar nobles while imagining the delightful nymph who awaited him that night at the Parc-aux-Cerfs.

Losers and Winners

France had never before fought a more expensive war. The Seven Years' War cost Versailles 1.325 billion livres, or an average 189 million above its regular yearly expenses. But those were just the official figures. When a range of unrecorded expenses are estimated, the government may have spent as much as 4 billion livres. In 1764, Versailles was 2.324 billion livres in debt if the principal, accumulated future interest payments, and other expenses were combined. During the war, the interest payments consumed about 30 percent of the budget; after the war, they consumed 60 percent.[1]

France's taxpayers would not enjoy a peace dividend. In April 1763, Comptroller General Henri Bertin announced that, despite the war's end, the two vingtièmes and a range of other new taxes would continue until the national debt was paid down. The parlements predictably protested; Rouen's actually called for the king to convene the Estates General to resolve the crisis. In November, Louis XV promised tax relief and fired Bertin. The political crisis subsided; the fiscal crisis smoldered on.

In all, the Seven Years' War was a financial and imperial disaster for France. But it could have been much worse. The direct damage to France was limited. French troops and sailors campaigned mostly in distant lands and seas. Fighting in France was confined to British raids on the coast at Saint Malo, La Rochelle, Cherbourg, and Belle Isle. Of those targets, only Cherbourg suffered devastating burning and looting. The rest of France remained free of the pillage and rape that gutted much of Germany. Peasants tilled their fields and artisans worked their crafts undisturbed. Though perhaps as many as 100,000 Frenchmen died during that war, the nation's population actually rose slightly from 25 million in 1755 to 26.1 million in 1765. The French fleet suffered the worst losses with thirty-seven ships of the line and fifty-six frigates destroyed or captured, while its ally Spain lost twelve ships of the line and four frigates during its brief misadventure, and Britain got off rather lightly with losses of only thirteen ships of the line and nineteen frigates. It would take a generation for France to rebuild its fleet. By the late 1770s, the French navy would be ready to challenge Britain again just in time for America's War of Independence.[2]

The war likewise but lightly affected the economy. Naturally, trade plummeted to half its prewar level as Britain's fleet mopped the seas of French merchant ships. Despite this, France retained its trade surplus. From 1754 to 1763, France enjoyed an accumulated surplus of 495 million livres, a figure that excluded the wealth that smugglers and privateers brought into France and the drain of army purchases and ally subsidies elsewhere. In 1754, France exported 272 million and imported 211.5 million livres worth of goods, for a 60.3-million-livre surplus. The worst trade year was 1761 when France exported only 144.6 million and imported 109.7 million livres worth of goods, for a mere 34.9-million-livre surplus. Yet, while shippers, shipbuilders, insurers, and the populations of port cities despaired, manufacturers rejoiced over windfall profits as their foreign rivals disappeared. The excess production for most goods kept their prices stable. So France's trade surplus along with vast government procurement orders actually swelled France's growth during the war years to a 0.4 percent annual rate from the century's 0.3 percent average as the French were forced to make at home what they could not buy from abroad. In all, the war strengthened France's nascent industries and its economy.[3]

Shortages and inflation could have been much worse than they were. The merchants, however, kept their finger on the pulse of European relations, anticipated the war, and filled their warehouses when fighting first broke out in America. This helped keep their profits up and inflation low during the war's first few years. During the war, they compensated for lost overseas markets by trading overland across France and Europe with a diversified range of products. Many of the lost foreign products were nonessential items like sugar, tobacco, and indigo for which adequate substitutes could be produced in France.

French shipowners suffered the worst losses as firms from neutral countries took over their business. Yet even here could be found a silver lining. A ship captured at sea or rotting at anchor in port represented a huge investment loss. The life of a ship, however, varied anywhere from eight to sixteen years depending on the climate and vigor of its voyages. Most of the ships lost during the war would have had to be replaced sometime between 1754 and 1763 regardless. Merchants with capital and foresight began rebuilding their fleets in the early 1760s. This at once stimulated the depressed port economies and positioned those merchants for the trade explosion that followed the Treaty of Paris. In 1763, French trade was worth 348.6 million livres, with a 58.5-million-livre surplus, and in 1764 it soared to 429.1 million livres, with a 68.7-million-livre surplus, up from 269.2 million livres with a 44.9-million-livre surplus in 1762.[4] These windfall profits for the merchants and industrialists did not trickle down to the urban and rural poor. During the war, through higher prices and taxes the poor indeed got poorer. This was offset somewhat by the pay given the million men who donned a uniform. Many of those troops were underemployed and unmarried peasants or urban workers. Of course, about one-quarter of that pay was spent abroad, enriching foreign rather than French markets, cafés, and brothels.[5]

Toward the war's end, as one disaster followed another, Versailles initiated a set of military reforms that, had they been in place when the war began, might have resulted in a very different peace treaty. Eight years of mostly defeats finally forced the war ministry to examine and change some hitherto sacred practices. On December 5, 1762, the war ministry issued an ordinance that took recruiting from regimental captains, standardized numbers and uniforms for the regiments, built barracks so that local inhabitants could be spared the quartering of troops, established an artillery school near Compiègne, hiked pay for the soldiers, and limited field guns to only four sizes. These reforms were far too late to aid France in its current war. Two generations later, Napoleon and his marshals would reap their benefits.

As for the international distribution of power, the British empire was the clear winner. Britain emerged from the Seven Years' War holding the entire eastern third of North America from the Arctic to the

Gulf and the Mississippi to the Atlantic. This stunning gain did not last long, as Britain lost the empire's more prosperous half a mere generation later. Britain's territorial expansion elsewhere in the West Indies, West Africa, and, especially, the East Indies was much more durable.

More importantly, Britain's victory sealed its mastery of the seas for another century and a half. Whitehall skillfully wielded that power to erect a far-flung empire upon which the sun never set, at least until the mid-twentieth century. Along the way France, Spain, and, much later, Germany would singly or in concert challenge but fail to defeat the Royal Navy. Only in World War II would the British fleet be surpassed in power, and then by its ally, the United States. Within a generation of that war's end, nationalism would finally disintegrate the British empire.

From the Seven Years' War, France did not lose as much as Britain gained. True, Versailles's North American empire disappeared, but the crippling cost of underwriting it also dissipated. Though France was shorn of the fur trade's fluctuating profits, it still enjoyed the steady wealth that flowed from the Newfoundland and Saint Lawrence fisheries. Elsewhere, its profitable sugar islands of Martinique, Guadeloupe, Marie-Galante, and Saint Lucia and its slave port of Gorée were returned, along with Belle Isle and those portions of India it had taken up through 1749. It was not a bad peace after all.

And what about that late entry to the North American war, Spain? Like France's, Spain's peace was not as disastrous as its war. Not only were Havana and Manila returned, but Madrid received title to the Louisiana Territory, whose vague boundaries when joined to its current territory gave Spain virtually all land from the Mississippi River to the Pacific Ocean. For all that, Madrid merely paid with Florida's meager absence. Yet the Spanish lacked the enterprise and time to make much from those new lands. Within eighty years, Spain would lose that vast empire between the Mississippi and the Pacific, first by handing the Louisiana Territory back to France in 1800, then Florida to the United States in 1819, and finally by Mexican independence in 1821.

Strategic Choices and What-Ifs

Could the Seven Years' War have been fought with different strategies and results? The French and British war strategies were asymmetrical. The French sought to hold the line in North America and send massive armies against British Hanover in Europe. The British committed just enough troops to stave off the blundering French armies marching against Hanover, while committing ever more regiments to North America to the point where eventually they conquered New France by sheer weight of numbers.

Britain's command of the sea influenced but did not dictate these two strategies. Whitehall could have easily repeated the hold-the-line strategy in North America that it had followed in its previous wars there, while immersing its army once again in Europe's killing fields. Once it recognized that Britain sought to conquer New France, Versailles could have attempted to send over the several thousand more troops and mountains of supplies necessary to prevent that. Several thousand more regulars at the Plains of Abraham in 1759 might have deterred Wolfe from trying to reach those heights or might have overwhelmed him and his men if he did so. Of course, as the British blockade tightened, the chance grew that an increasing number of troop and supply ships might be captured. Was New France worth that gamble? Versailles decided otherwise.

Even so, New France's loss was not inevitable. In North America, the French and British forces began the war relatively well matched. If the American militia far outnumbered those of New France, the French marine companies outnumbered the three British "independent" regular companies in the American colonies. Yet neither then had enough to conquer the other, nor did either even dream of doing so. It was expected that the latest war would be like those previous. The French would continue their practice of launching large-scale Canadian and Indian raids on the American frontier, while the Americans might get enough British naval support to launch another campaign against Louisbourg or perhaps enough regulars to bolster a campaign against one of France's frontier forts. It was expected that the war in North America would end inconclusively as usual, dependent on what happened in Europe.

In 1755, that power balance shifted when both sides sent regular army troops to bolster their provincial forces. The intentions of the two sides, however, were opposite. Versailles had simply ordered General Dieskau to hold the line and repel any British offensive. Whitehall ordered its commander to implement a four-pronged attack that would invade and roll back the French frontier to the line claimed by Britain's negotiators.

Each year until the conquest, the number of British troops in North America increased while those of France largely stagnated. By the time three British armies converged on Montreal in September 1760, the 30,000 troops from thirty-two regiments outgunned the French more than ten to one. As the number of troops committed to North America and their victories increased, the goal shifted from rollback to outright conquest. Quebec's capture in September 1759 was the turning point. After then, William Pitt no longer thought of ceding a truncated New France back to Versailles—he wanted the entire eastern third of North America.

It was not until the French lost Quebec that all hope of staving off a British conquest vanished. Until then, the French could still muster enough troops and skilled leadership to blunt each British advance. True, the French had surrendered Louisbourg and Fort Duquesne in 1758. But those were relatively minor defeats that did not necessarily mean that New France was lost. After all, New Englanders had captured Louisbourg in 1745, but it was traded back to France in 1748 in exchange for Madras. Something like that might occur again. But once Quebec was lost, New France would follow since the British could sever all its supplies and communications.

Did the French and Canadians ultimately defeat themselves with all their animosities and corruption? In the end, the constant bickering between Vaudreuil and Montcalm, or the tensions between the soldiers and marines, or even Bigot's corruption machine that diverted so many vital supplies from the army and Indians to the black market did not lose the war. New France was lost on the battlefield.

Montcalm failed to turn all three of his limited frontier victories into decisive victories. After capturing Oswego in 1756, had he fortified it and perhaps sent a covering force to build another fort at the Great Carrying Place, he could have plugged that invasion route for years. After capturing Fort William Henry in 1757, had he marched on to Fort Edward fourteen miles away and demanded its surrender, its cowed commander would most likely have quickly agreed. Montcalm could then have marched on into a lightly defended Albany and wintered there off British provisions. Panicked by a French army at Albany, Whitehall might well have canceled its planned attack on Louisbourg and Fort Duquesne that summer of 1758 in order to concentrate forces against Montcalm. The general could then have slowly retreated back to Lake George as the British bloodied themselves against his fortified positions or stumbled into ambushes set by Canadians and Indians. Then, at Quebec in 1759, Montcalm lost three chances to destroy the British regiments that Wolfe sent against his lines. The first was the attack on the Beauport line in July when the redcoats got stranded on the mudflats. Had Montcalm ordered an attack as the British were trying to reembark, he could have bagged all of them. Another chance was lost when Wolfe abandoned the Montmorency position in August.

Finally, there was the Plains of Abraham on September 9. In that case, Montcalm inexplicably ordered a hasty attack before he had all of his own troops and cannon up and could coordinate an attack with Bougainville, who was marching his troops toward the British rear. A careful look through his spyglass at the enemy would have revealed to Montcalm that the British were not entrenching and they had only two small cannons. Had Montcalm waited the mere two hours it would have taken to mass his own guns and for Bougainville to appear, a sustained bombardment would have broken up the British regiments on the plain, after which the French infantry could have marched in with lowered bayonets.

The fighting in North America, of course, was only a portion of a world war. It was during a parliamentary debate in November 1761 that Pitt asserted his most famous declaration: "Had the armies of France not been employed in Germany, they would have been transported to America. America has been conquered in Germany."[6] Pitt was right.

Versailles's strategy of trading Minorca and Hanover for its North American claims might have worked if the French had managed to hold Hanover. French power in Germany peaked in the autumn of 1757 when Richelieu forced Cumberland to surrender his army. But Richelieu made the grievous mistake of signing a convention, which had to be ratified by the respective governments rather than a capitulation between generals. Upon learning of the humiliating convention his son had signed, George II promptly repudiated it. The war was resumed. Versailles recalled Richelieu, perhaps the best French general of a sorry lot. Afterward, France's army commanders in Germany ranged from merely mediocre to awful. After 1757, the French had to contend with a truly great general, Prince Ferdinand of Brunswick, who skillfully savaged one enemy campaign after another year after year.

Nor did the French ever try to coordinate their offensives with those of their Austrian, Russian, Imperial, and Swedish armies against Frederick. The one French foray against Frederick ended with the debacle of Rossbach in 1758. The French did not try another. But France's allies were just as inept. Nearly every year the allies pummeled Frederick to the point of collapse but failed to deliver the coup de grace. With Prussia conquered, Hanover would have soon fallen. If the British remained obstinate, Versailles could have marched its army into Holland. Eventually, Whitehall would have had to grant Versailles its demands in North America and elsewhere in order to stymie the endless nightmare of a France dominant on the Continent just beyond the English Channel.

Until recently, historians tended to exaggerate Pitt's role in leading England to victory in the Seven Years' War. Consensus shaped cabinet policies, something Pitt's force of personality and reason could influence but not command. Imagination and indomitable will were perhaps Pitt's greatest strengths; his military and diplomatic strategy changed throughout the war. Before entering the ministry, he was adamantly opposed to defending Hanover. Once in office, he accepted the cabinet and king's view that France could be defeated in Germany.

Criticism has been heaped on many of those policies that Pitt influenced, especially the raids on France's coast and his refusal to make
minor compromises in the spring of 1761 that might then have ended
the war. Even Pitt's power to appoint heads of expeditions, armies, and
fleets was limited. George Anson and John Ligonier handled opera-
tional details for the navy and army, respectively.

How valid are those criticisms? The British raids on the French
coast indeed accomplished little and cost much. True, the 1758 attacks
on St. Malo and Cherbourg did succeed in destroying small fleets of
privateers and other wealth, while the capture of Belle Isle in 1762
did provide Britain a fine bargaining chip for Minorca's return. Other
raids suffered varying degrees of defeat. The 1757 raid on Rochefort
fizzled with no landing. The second raid on Saint Malo in 1758 turned
into a British bloodbath. Regardless, each raid cost Whitehall vast
sums of money, troops, transports, supplies, and warships that could
have given Prince Ferdinand enough to win even more decisive victories against the French in western Germany. No raid succeeded in
diverting significant amounts of French troops from Germany back to
France. French coastal troops were numerous enough to counter any
British incursion. The French problem was not the number of troops
per se, but the difficulty in massing and getting them to the redcoats
before they reembarked.[7]

In many ways Versailles bungled as badly at the diplomatic table as
it did on the battlefield. In 1756, the realignment of powers that historians would dub a "diplomatic revolution" occurred. Ancient enemies
France and Austria joined hands with Russia and Sweden against more
recent enemies Britain and Prussia, now allies. The diplomatic revolution occurred when statesmen recognized and acted upon shifts in
Europe's imbalance of powers and interests that had been taking place
for some time. More than anyone, Austrian chancellor Kaunitz was
the catalyst for this realignment of power. He had worked for it since
1750 when he was appointed ambassador to France. His efforts took
six years to triumph and were by no means inevitable. Had Frederick
stuck with France rather than embraced England, Kaunitz's efforts
would have been in vain; the Seven Years' War's alliances would have
repeated those of the previous war.

The alliance with Austria, Russia, and Sweden may well have weakened rather than strengthened France. Versailles's war aims could not have been more different from those of its allies. While the French hoped to retain their North American empire, their allies strove to enlarge their respective European empires by stealing land from Prussia and Poland. One diplomatic historian described the alliance as "a trap in which France blithely ensnared itself, and from which France struggled to escape through years of growing weakness and paralyzing frustration."[8]

It did not have to come to that. If used wisely, the alliance could have greatly benefited France. With Russian and Austrian troops battling Frederick, French armies could conquer Hanover, the single most valuable bargaining chip available in its global struggle with England. Yet Versailles would never realize that alliance's potential. The reasons had mostly to do with bad strategy and bad generals. Throughout the war, the allies failed to coordinate their respective campaigns, thus giving Frederick and Ferdinand ample chances to defeat them separately. Compounding that failure of grand strategy were the jealousies and inept generalship that prevented the French commanders from working closely and intelligently together either to turn limited into decisive victories or to stave off crushing defeats. All along, Versailles poured huge annual subsidies into Austria to keep its armies in the field. In addition, Versailles abdicated its influence in eastern Europe to Russia, thus alienating the relations with Sweden, Poland, and Turkey it had spent a generation nurturing. In retrospect, maintaining the alliance with Prussia would have served French interests much better than its historic realignment.

Despite all these dilemmas, the allies most likely would have crushed Prussia in 1762, had Empress Elizabeth not died and the throne been taken by her Frederick-worshiping nephew, Peter III. Had the empress lived but a half year longer, first Prussia then Hanover would most likely have been overrun. How then would the peace treaties have been negotiated?

If Elizabeth died too soon for French interests, Spain's Ferdinand VI died too late. From 1754 until 1762, Spain was the war's diplomatic wild card. Each year that Madrid sat on the sidelines watching the war diminished its ability to help France as its fleet was swept from the seas or bottled up in port. But what if Charles III had mounted the throne in 1756 or 1757 when France was victorious rather than in 1760 after years of humiliating defeats capped by Canada's loss? A Bourbon pact in 1756 combining the fleets of France, Spain, and possibly the Two Sicilies would not have overwhelmed England's navy, but certainly would have stretched it to its limit.

How then would Whitehall have deployed its fleet? Tough choices would have had to be made. Britain simply did not have enough ships and sailors to simultaneously convoy troops and supplies to the American colonies, blockade the ports of France and Spain, launch large-scale raids on France's coast, gobble up one Caribbean sugar island after another, fight sea battles, send troops and supplies to save Portugal from invasion, and attack Louisbourg and finally Quebec. Even as late as the new year of 1760, Spain might have made a difference had Madrid dispatched one of its fleets in the race to reach Quebec that spring. But by 1761, Spain had little chance of contributing anything to the war other than more conquests for Britain

France's loss of its North American empire had many causes—Versailles's failure to send over enough troops and supplies to blunt British campaigns, Montcalm's failure to follow up his victories, Richelieu's failure to force a capitulation rather than a convention upon Cumberland, the failure of the allies to find better generals and coordinate their offensives against their enemies, and the failure of Ferdinand to die sooner or Elizabeth, later.

What role did the love between Louis and Pompadour play in all this? As the king's alter ego and prime minister, the mistress provoked jealousies and intrigues, which at crucial moments caused gridlock in council or campaign. Pompadour's insistence on promoting such mediocrities as Soubise, Contades, and Clermont to command armies in Germany time after time snatched defeat from likely victory. However, she can be commended for her choices of Bernis and Choiseul as foreign ministers. So did the eighteenth century's greatest power couple lose the war for France? Quite possibly yes. In the myriad of forces shaping that global war's outcome, the relationship between Louis and Pompadour may well have tipped the balance from victory to defeat.

The Rot Within

Behind these reasons for defeat lurked a failed political system, both in France and New France. The philosophe Paul Heinrich Dietrich von Holbach had the French monarchy in mind when he condemned "unjust sovereigns, enervated by luxury, corrupted by flattery, depraved by licentiousness, made wicked by impurity, devoid of talents, without morals . . . and incapable of exerting an energy for the benefit of the states they govern. They are consequently but little occupied with the welfare of their people, and indifferent to their duties, of which, indeed, they are often ignorant. . . . Stimulated by the desire . . . to feed their insatiable ambitions, they engage in useless, depopulating wars, and never occupy their minds with those objects which are the most important to the happiness of their nation."[9]

Which brings us to New France. Like every French officer who served there, shortly after arriving in 1755, François Charles de Bourlamaque soon understood why that colony was such a debilitating drain on French wealth. Upon returning to France after the 1760 conquest, he wrote a memoir for Louis XV's council to counter those who argued that Canada's loss would leave France stronger rather than weaker: "Were an opinion to be formed respecting this Colony from the expenses which it has occasioned during the war, and the profits derived from it since its establishment, its possession would appear disadvantageous to France. But in seeking for the causes of those expenses and the sources of those profits, it will be easy to convince oneself that the errors of administration have produced the one and dried the other." He cited the myriad of woes afflicting Canada, then proposed measures for their alleviation. He concluded that Canada, if properly administered and settled, could enrich rather than impoverish France. It was a brilliant analysis. But like all the others making the same argument, it was ignored.[10]

As has been seen, Versailles did not get around to trying to clean Canada's Augean stables of corruption until December 1761, over a year after that colony had been irretrievably lost. While Versailles was busy persecuting Bigot and his mob, it might have turned the investigators loose on the corruption eating away at France much closer to home. Still, the persecution was a small step in the right direction.

The corruption show trial lasted almost exactly two years, from the time the arrest warrants were issued on December 21, 1761, until the sentences were pronounced on December 10, 1763. At first, the defendants had united in declaring their innocence. Over time, one by one, they turned against each other. Bigot finally cracked when the prosecutor demanded that he be publicly beheaded. In the plea bargain, Bigot agreed to tell all for a lesser sentence. When the court issued its final judgment, of the twenty-two suspects brought to trial, ten were condemned to death, three received an admonition, two were dismissed for lack of evidence, and six were acquitted. Of the thirty-seven who had evaded arrest, seven were sentenced to varying terms and the rest were acquitted. Bigot got off with a 1.5-million-franc fine, a pittance compared to the estimated 20 million livres he had wrung from Canada. Vaudreuil was among those acquitted.

Whether the trial brought closure to the surviving Canadians and French who had fought so hard and suffered so greatly to save New France will never be known. Only one thing was certain—New France was lost forever.

Consequences

And as for that statue of Louis XV, the mob tore it down in 1792. The Revolutionaries renamed the square the Place de la Révolution and erected there a guillotine that decapitated over 1,200 "enemies of the people." The statue's only surviving fragment can be seen in the Musée Carnavalet. On a small monument rests Louis XV's black iron right hand with fingers curled slightly upward. It is an expressive hand whose gesture is open to varying interpretations. Does it convey majestic disdain, bewilderment, or merely resignation?

Notes

Abbreviations

AMAE	Archives du Ministère des Affaires Étrangerès, Paris
AN	Archives Nationales, Paris
AN Marine	Archives Nationales Marine, Paris
BL, Add. MSS	Additional Manuscripts, British Library, London
BN, SM NAF	Salle des Manuscrits, Nouvelles Acquisitions Françaises, Bibliothèque Nationale, Paris
CL, Mildmay Papers	William Mildmay Papers, Clements Library, University of Michigan
CL, Shelburne MSS	Shelburne Collection Manuscripts, Clements Library, University of Michigan
CP Angl.	Correspondance Politique, Angleterre
CP Esp.	Correspondance Politique, Espagne
CP Russie	Correspondance Politique, Russie
Mem. et Doc.	Mémoires et Documents
NYCD	*Documents Relative to the Colonial History of the State of New York*
Suppl.	supplement

Introduction

Epigraph 1. Quoted in Walpole, *Memories of the Reign of George the Second*, 1:xxxv.

Epigraph 2. Casanova, *History of My Life*, 3:4.

1. Voltaire, *Candide*, 64.

2. I have explored the French and English struggle for North America through three volumes: Nester, *The Great Frontier War* ; *The First Global War*, and *"Haughty Conquerors."*

For an in-depth exploration of a crucial front during the year of the war's turning point, see Nester, *The Epic Battles for Ticonderoga*. There some good books on dimensions of the global struggle. For the British point of view in North America, see Anderson, *Crucible of War*. For the war in Europe, see Szabo, *Seven Years War in Europe*. For the global war, see Baugh, *Global Seven Years War*. For the imperial rivalries for North America from the Treaty of Utrecht to the Treaty of Paris, see Mapp, *Elusive West and the Contest for Empire*. Other good single-volume books on the subject include Leckie, *"A Few Acres of Snow,*" Borneman, *French and Indian War*, Fowler, *Empires at War*, and Sheppard, *Empires Collide*.

3. Kennett, *French Armies*, ix.

4. Only one other scholarly book in English explores the French and Indian War from France's perspective, but not as widely or deeply as mine: Brecher, *Losing a Continent*.

The best books in French were written more than a century ago: Waddington, *La Guerre de Sept Ans*. Waddington's works remain classics flawed by his untimely death before he could finish and by the absence of a century of scholarship since they were first published.

Several limited studies in French appeared in the late nineteenth and early twentieth century and are still valuable: Waddington, *Louis XV et le Reversement*; Broglie, *Le Secret du Roi*; Bourguet, *Le Duc de Choiseul et l'Alliance Espagnole*; Lacour-Gayet, *La Marine Militaire*; Bourguet, *Études sur la Politique Étrangère*; Renaut, *Le Pacte de Famille et l'Amérique*.

Over the last four decades, Michel Antoine has explored virtually all sides of Louis XV's reign. See Antoine, "Les Conseils des finances sous le règne de Louis XV"; *Le Conseil du Roi sous le Règne de Louis XV*; "L'Entourage des ministres aux XVIIe et XVIIIe siècles"; *Le Gouvernement et l'Administration sous Louis XV*; and *Louis XV*. Though none of the works directly analyze French policy making during the Seven Years' War, they all give varying degrees of insight into that subject. Antoine's *Louis XV*'s section on the Seven Years' War is 120 pages of first-rate analysis.

As insightful and almost as prolific, though less focused on Louis XV, has been Roland Mousnier: Mousnier and Labrousse, *Le XVIIIe Siecle, l'Epoque des Lumières*; Mousnier, *Institutions de la France sous la Monarchie Absolue*, vols. 1 and 2; and Mousnier, "La Fonction publique."

Other first-rate analyses of French policy making include Samoyault, *Les Bureaux du Secrétariat*; Egret, *Louis XV et l'Opposition Parlementaire*; Perrault, *Le Secret du Roi*; Vergé-Franceschi, *La Marine Française*.

Though not as scholarly, broad, or deep as Antoine's biography, Chiappe's *Louis XV* is also a good read. Alas, both biographies suffer from the French habit of dispensing with footnotes. The best biography of Pompadour to appear to date is Danielle Gallet, *Madame de Pompadour du le Pouvoir Féminin* (Paris: Fayard 1985); unfortunately, the sequel was never penned to Butler, *Choiseul.*

My book has tapped greatly into the published memoirs and collections of letters from participants: Bernis, *Mémoires*; Louis XV and Noailles, *Correspondance de Louis XV et du Marechal de Noailles*; Luynes, *Mémoires du Duc de Luynes sur la Cour de Louis XV*; Mopinot de la Chapotte, *Sous Louis le Bien-Aimé*; Argenson, *Journal*; d'Angerville, *Vie Privée de Louis XV*; Dufort, *Mémoires sur les Règnes de Louis XV et Louis XVI*; Du Hausset, *Mémoires de Madame du Hausset*; and Choiseul, *Mémoires.* Two brilliant French accounts of the war in Canada by participants exist in translation: Bougainville, *Adventure in the Wilderness* (hereafter cited as Bougainville, *Journals*); and Pouchot, *Memoirs.*

Many excellent works in English have explored different aspects of French policy making: Beik, *Judgment of the Old Regime*; Bosher, "French Government's Motives"; Bosher, "Financing the French Navy"; Kaplan, *Bread, Politics, and Political Economy*; Kennett, *French Armies*; Pritchard, *Louis XV's Navy*; Riley, *Seven Years' War*; Rogister, *Louis XV and the Parlement*; Van Kley, *Damiens Affair*; and Woodbridge, *Revolt.*

Some excellent diplomatic histories have appeared. Two early ones were Pease, *Boundary Disputes*; and Savelle, *Diplomatic History of the Canadian Boundary.* Both were first-rate studies that made extensive use of primary sources. Still to be read for profit are the much earlier Grant, "Canada Versus Guadeloupe"; and Reid, "Pitt's Decision to Keep Canada," 21–32.

More recent important foreign policy studies include Carter, *Dutch Republic*; Kaplan, *Russia and the Outbreak of the Seven Years' War*; Middleton, *Bells of Victory*; Oliva, *Misalliance*; Rashed, *Peace of Paris*; Schweizer, *England, Prussia, and the Seven Years' War*; and Calloway, *Scratch of a Pen.*

Several fine studies have explored Canadian politics during the Seven Years' War: Fregault, *Canada: The War of the Conquest*; Fregault, *François Bigot*; Fregault, *Le Grand Marquis*; Michalon, "Vaudreuil et Montcalm"; Robitaille, *Montcalm et ses Historiens*; Roy, *Bigot et sa Bande.*

1. The "Absolute" Monarchy

Epigraph 1. Quoted in Antoine, *Louis XV*, 29.

Epigraph 2. Quoted in Guizot, *History of France*, 159.

1. By far the most scholarly and comprehensive biography is Antoine, *Louis XV*; a more recent, but not nearly as good, biography is Chiappe, *Louis XV*; other biographies include d'Angerville, *Vie Privée de Louis XV*; Barbier, *Journal*; Perkins, *France Under Louis XV*; Carre, *Le Règne de Louis XV*; Dufort, *Mémoires sur les Règnes de Louis XV et Louis XVI*; Gaxotte, *Le Siècle de Louis XV*; Gooch, *Louis XV: The Monarchy in Decline*; and Bernier, *Louis the Beloved.*

2. Quoted in Antoine, *Louis XV*, 29.

3. Argenson, *Journal* ("*Journal*" refers to the English translation unless otherwise noted by "untranslated version"), 1:313. Argenson's journal provides by far

the most comprehensive and insightful of the handful penned by insiders during the war. Like any journal, it must be handled with care. Argenson's vivid, perceptive views undoubtedly exaggerated the attributes of his friends and the flaws of his foes.

4. Ibid., 2:345.

5. Ibid., 2:171 ("more attached to persons" and "dull, inhuman ministers"), 62 ("tortured with remorse").

6. Ibid., 2:330.

7. For excellent insights into the king's character and his relationship with Pompadour by her closest attendant, see Du Hausset, *Mémoires de Madame du Hausset.*

8. Ibid., 1:117–18.

9. Historians have long debated Pompadour's influence on policy. Her contemporaries certainly believed that she was the unofficial prime minister. In addition to the Marquis d'Argenson, see Du Hausset, *Mémoires de Madame du Hausset*; Bernis, *Mémoires*; and Choiseul, *Mémoires*. For more a recent view, see Pompadour's best biography, Gallet, *Madame Pompadour ou le Pouvoir Féminin*, as well as Lever, *Madame de Pompadour*; and Mitford, *Madame de Pompadour*. For views that Pompadour's role has been exaggerated, see Nolhac, *Madame de Pompadour et la Politique*; Bernier, *Louis the Beloved*, 141; Nicolle, *Madame de Pompadour*, 166; and Antoine, *Louis XV*, 498–99.

10. Quoted in Bernier, *Louis the Beloved*, 135–36.

11. Walpole, *Memoirs of George II*, 1:145. Walpole was Britain's equivalent of Argenson as an insider who not only brilliantly observed the politics within Whitehall but also, through friends and spies, was informed about politics at Versailles. And, as with Argenson's accounts, one must read Walpole's memories as brilliant but inevitably prejudiced and distorted.

12. Argenson, *Journal*, 1:357–58.

13. Durant and Durant, *Age of Voltaire*, 279–85.

14. Argenson, *Journal*, 3:334.

15. Choiseul, *Mémoires*, 110.

16. Argenson, *Journal*, untranslated version, 6:472–73.

17. Argenson, *Journal*, 1:357–58 ("thinks he rules"); 2:128 ("She determines").

18. Butler, *Choiseul*, 1067.

19. Du Hausset, *Mémoires de Madame du Hausset*, 53–54.

20. Argenson, *Journal*, 2:216. Antoine asserts that she was no longer his mistress as early as 1750 (Antoine, *Louis XV*, 500).

21. Argenson, *Journal*, 2:215.

22. Barbier, *Chronique*, 3:533.

23. Argenson, *Journal*, 1:322.

24. Ibid., 2:3.

25. Ibid., 2:342–43.

26. Alas for historians, the Council of State kept no minutes. The Conseil d'Etat was also called the "conseil d'en haut," "grand conseil," "conseil secret," "conseil du Roi," "Conseil prive," "conseil de cabinet," and "conseil d'en haut." For an interesting discussion, see Rashed, *Peace of Paris*, 32, 230–33. See also Antoine, *Le Conseil du Roi*; Antoine, "Le Conseil des dépêches sous le règne," 158–208; Antoine, *Le Gouvernement de l'Administration sous Louis XV*; and Marion, *Dictionnaire des Institutions de la France*.

27. Some of most prominent studies of the old regime's bureaucracy include Church, *Revolution and Red Tape*; Antoine, "L'entourage des ministres"; and Mousnier, "La fonction publique."

28. Pritchard, *Louis XV's Navy*, 4.

29. Casanova, *Memoirs*, 4:840.

30. Argenson, *Journal*, untranslated version, 4:62.

31. Antoine and Ozanum, "Le Secret du Roi"; Perrault, *Le Secret du Roi*.

32. Gruder, *Royal Provincial Intendants*; Bordes, *L'Administration Provinciale*.

33. Durant and Durant, *Age of Voltaire*, 253–58.

34. Kalm, *Travels*, 449.

35. Woodbridge, *Revolt*, 10.

36. Durant and Durant, *Age of Voltaire*, 157.

37. For an outstanding discussion of parlement, king, church, and related issues, see Kley, *Damiens Affair*.

38. Kley, *Damiens Affair*, 100; Riley, *Seven Years' War*, 143; Glasson, *Le Parlement de Paris*; Hardy, *Judicial Politics in the Old Regime*; Shennan, *Parlement of Paris*; Egret, *Louis XV et l'Opposition Parlementaire*; Kreiser, *Miracles, Convulsions, and Ecclesiastical Politics*; Autrand, *Naissance d'un Grand Corps de l'État*; Rogister, *Louis XV and the Parlement*.

39. Durant and Durant, *Age of Voltaire*, 251–52; Ford, *Robe and Sword*.

40. Argenson, *Journal*, 1:337.

41. Ibid., 2:122.

42. Durant and Durant, *Rousseau and Revolution*, 84.

43. Argenson, *Journal*, 2:282–83.

44. Kennett, *French Armies*, 88.

45. For the best discussion, see Riley, *Seven Years' War*, chap. 2.

46. Riley, *Seven Years' War*, 64; Matthews, *Royal General*; Durand, *Finance et Mécénat*; For Casanova's contribution to French finances, see Casanova, *Memoirs*, 4:889–93, 924–30.

47. Behrens, "Nobles, Privileges, and Taxes," 451–75; Behrens, "A Revision Defended," 451–75; Cavanaugh, "Nobles, Privileges, and Taxes in France," 681–92; Mathias and O'Brien, "Taxation in Britain and France," 601–50.

48. Argenson, *Journal*, 2:5.

49. Riley, *Seven Years' War*, 177, 180.

50. Kennett, *French Armies*, 89, 97; Riley, *Seven Years' War*, 85–86 and chap. 5.

51. Kennett, *French Armies*, 97.

52. The War of the Austrian Succession between Prussia and Austria began in 1740 and was joined by France and Britain in 1744.

53. Riley, *Seven Years' War*, 87. See also Mathon de la Cour, *Collection de comptes-rendus, pièces authentiques.*

54. Riley, *Seven Years' War*, 26.

55. Ibid., 14–16, 35, 84, 87. Crouzet, "Angleterre et France," 261; Riley and McCusker, "Money Supply, Economic Growth," 274–93; Kaplan, *Bread, Politics, and Political Economy*; Labrousse, "Les ruptures périodiques de la prospérité."

56. Riley, *Seven Years War*, 34, 107; Crouzet, "Angleterre et France," 261; Léon, *Aires et Structures du Commerce Français*; McCusker, *Money Exchange in Europe and America.*

57. Durant and Durant, *Age of Voltaire*, 259–61, 289, 292.

58. Dupaquier, *La Population Françaises*, 34–35, 37; Durant and Durant, *Age of Voltaire*, 259–61; Bourde, *Agronomie et Agronomes en France*; Hufton, *Poor of Eighteenth-Century France.*

59. Argenson, *Journal*, 2:145.

60. Ibid., 199.

61. Quoted in Durant and Durant, *Age of Voltaire*, 302. See also Durant and Durant, *Rousseau and Revolution*, 118–31.

62. Durant and Durant, *Age of Voltaire*, 294.

63. Durant and Durant, *Age of Rousseau*, 76.

2. War, Wealth, and the Great Powers

Epigraph 1. Quoted in White, *Marshal of France*, 206.

Epigraph 2. Voltaire, *Candide*, 52–53.

1. Hutchinson, *Before Adam Smith*; Cole, *Colbert and a Century of French Mercantilism.*

2. Childs, *Armies and Warfare in Europe*; Corvisier, *Armies and Societies in Europe.* Weigley, *Age of Battles*; Nosworthy, *Anatomy of Victory*; Chandler, *Art of Warfare*; Frederick II, *Frederick the Great on the Art of War*; Smith, *Armies of the Seven Years' War.*

3. Corvisier, *L'Armee Françoise*; Kennett, *French Armies*; Pajol, *Les Guerres sous Louis XV.*

4. Samoyault, *Les Bureaux du Secrétariat.*

5. Quoted in Kennett, *French Armies*, 20.

6. Ibid., 57, 65, 66.

7. Ibid., 57.

8. Ibid., 67.

9. Quoted in ibid., 24.

10. Fortescue, *History of the British Army*, 2:602.

11. Louis Dupré d'Aulnay, "Traité général des subsistances militaires" (1744); Puysegur "Art de la Guerre" (1749); François de Chennevieres, "Détails militaires

dont la connaissance et nécessaire a tous les officiers et principalement aux commissaires des guerres," 6 vols. (1750); Comte Turpin de Crisse, "Essai sur l'Art de Guerre" (1754); Chevalier d'Arc's "Noblesse Militaire" (1756), Nicoloas d'Hericourt, "Eléments de l'Art Militaire," 5 vols. (1756); Maurice de Saxe, "Rêveries" (1756); Louis de Boussanelle, "Observations Militaire" (1761). Also widely read among French officers were Frederick II's *Principles Generaux de la Guerre* (1746) and *Testament Politique* (1752).

12. Kennett, *French Armies*, 77.

13. Corvisier, *L'Armee Françoise*, 1:55, 57, 65, 155, 259–74.

14. Kennett, *French Armies*, chap. 9.

15. Ibid., 116, 136.

16. Ibid., 85.

17. Pritchard, *Louis XV's Navy*, viii.

18. Vergé-Franceschi, *La Marine Française*, 140; Pritchard, *Louis XV's Navy*, 126–27, 131, 136.

19. In addition to Vergé-Franceschi and Pritchard, see Lacour-Gayet, *La Marine Militaire*; Chevalier, *Histoire de la Marine Française*; Bamford, *Forests and French Sea Power*; Legoherel, *Les Trésoriers Généraux*.

20. Pritchard, *Louis XV's Navy*, chaps. 3–4.

21. See the masterly analysis of the different accounts in Pritchard, *Louis XV's Navy*, 215–22. Vergé-Franceschi, *La Marine Française*, 115, gives different figures: 17,746,000 livres in 1754; 31,326,000 in 1755; 40,006,000 in 1756; 39,006,000 in 1757; 42,370,000 in 1758; 56,903,000 in 1759; 23,713,000 in 1760; 30,200,000 in 1761; 24,500,000 in 1762; and 20,064,000 in 1763. See also Bosher, "Financing the French Navy," 115–33.

22. Le Goff and Meyer, "Les Constructions Navales," 173–85.

23. Pritchard, *Louis XV's Navy*, 89–125.

24. Bamford, *Forests and French Sea Power*; Pritchard, *Louis XV's Navy*, 143–59.

25. Vergé-Franceschi, *La Marine Française*, 103–13; Pritchard, *Louis XV's Navy*, 59.

26. Pritchard, *Louis XV's Navy*, 81–84.

27. Ibid., 55.

28. Richard Pares, "American versus Continental Warfare," 429–65; Richard Pares, *Colonial Blockade*.

29. Fortescue, *History of the British Army*, 2:267; Corbett, *England in the Seven Years' War*; Baugh, *British Naval Administration*; Rodger, *Wooden World*.

30. Deane and Cole, *British Economic Growth*, 78. For a lower and probably more accurate rate, see Harley, "British Industrialization before 1841," 267–89. See also Crouzet, "Angleterre et France"; Mathias and O'Brien, "Taxation in Britain and France," 601–50; and McCloskey, "Mismeasurement of the Incidence of Taxation," 209–10.

31. Lindsay, *Old Regime*.

32. Quoted in Durant and Durant, *Age of Voltaire*, 247.

33. Clark, *Dynamics of Change*; Browning, *Duke of Newcastle*.

34. Quoted in Durant and Durant, *Rousseau and Revolution*, 697. See also Trench, *George II*.

35. Walpole, *Memoirs of George II*, 1:116–18. For a critical account of Walpole and his memories, see Croker, "Walpole's Memoirs," 178–215.

36. Middleton, *Bells of Victory*, 31.

37. Eldon, *England's Subsidy Policy*; Horn, *Great Britain and Europe*; Browning, "Duke of Newcastle and the Imperial Election Plan," 28–47; Clayton, "The Duke of Newcastle," 571–603.

38. Sherrard, *Lord Chatham*, 96–97; Namier, *England in the Age of American Revolution*; Namier, *Structure of Politics*; Williams, *Life of William Pitt*; Long, *Mr. Pitt and America's Birthright*; Ayling, *The Elder Pitt*; Brown, *William Pitt, Earl of Chatham*; Peters, *Pitt and Popularity*; Black, *Pitt the Elder*.

39. Marriott and Robertson, *Evolution of Prussia*.

40. Horn, *Frederick the Great*; Asprey, *Frederick the Great*.

41. Quoted in Green, *The Hanoverians*, 68.

42. Crankshaw, *Maria Theresa*; McGill, *Maria Theresa*.

43. McGill, "Roots of Policy."

44. Quoted in Butler, *Choiseul*, 978.

45. Quoted in ibid.

46. Durant and Durant, *Age of Voltaire*, 431–32.

47. Bain, *Daughter of Peter the Great*.

48. Oliva, *Misalliance*, 122–34; Kaplan, *Russia and the Outbreak of the Seven Years' War*.

49. Durant and Durant, *Rousseau and Revolution*.

50. Parry, "Rivalries in America," 514–28.

51. Carter, *Dutch Republic*; Carter, "Dutch as Neutrals," 818–34; Boxer, *Dutch Seaborne Empire*.

52. For an interesting account of all this, see Murphy, *Charles Gravier*, 53–135.

53. Cabinet Memorandum of December 15, 1753, in O'Callaghan and Fernow, *Documents Relative to the Colonial History of the State of New York* (hereafter cited as *NYCD*), 10:259–60.

54. Choiseul to Ossun, December 24, 1759, quoted in François Rousseau, *Règne de Charles III d'Espagne, 1759–1788*, 2 vols. (Paris: Plon-Nouritt 1907), 1:39.

3. The French Empire

Epigraph 1. Voltaire, *Candide*, 23.

Epigraph 2. Voltaire, *Candide*, 48.

Epigraph 3. Bougainville, *Journals*, 56.

Epigraph 4. Quoted in Durant and Durant, *Rousseau and Revolution*, 19.

1. Choiseul Memoir on Canada Boundary to Bussy, August 10, 1761, AMAE, CP Angl. 444:150.

2. Gipson, *Zones of International Friction*, 26.

3. Duchêne, *La Politique Coloniale de la France*; Roquebrune, "La direction de la Nouvelle-France"; Charlevoix, *Histoire de Description Generale de la Nouvelle France*; Eccles, *France in America*; Hamelin, *Economie et Société en Nouvelle-France*; Douville and Casanova, *La Vie Quotidienne en Nouvelle-France*; Eccles, *Canada under Louis XIV*; Stanley, *New France*; Cox, *Native People, Native Lands*; Lanctôt, *History of Canada*; Greer, *People of New France*; Moogk, *La Nouvelle France*; Havard, *Histoire de l'Amérique Française*.

4. La Galissonière Memoir, December 1750, *NYCD*, 10:223.

5. Capitation List of 1754, *NYCD*, 10:271–75; Menard, "Growth and Welfare," 475; McCusker and Menard, *Economy of British America*, 112, 172, 203; Wells, *Population of the British Colonies*. Although 70,000 people in New France is the standard figure, a more comprehensive survey found 82,000 people in 1759. However, that number undoubtedly included the French soldiers and sailors in the province. Montcalm to Belle Isle, April 12, 1759, *NYCD*, 10:962; Population of British North America, August 1755, in *NYCD*, 6:993; Cassedy, *Demography in Early America*.

6. Kalm, *Travels*, 411.

7. Kalm, *Travels*, 404; Bosher, *Canada Merchants*.

8. Innis, *Cod Fisheries*, 119–43; Williams, *Life of William Pitt*, 2:84; Rashed, *Peace of Paris*, 102–103; Balcom, *Cod Fishery of Isle Royale*.

9. Choiseul's Memoir on New France, August 10, 1761, AMAE, CP Angl. 444:150.

10. Innis, *Fur Trade in Canada*; Phillips, *Fur Trade*; Ray, *Indians in the Fur Trade*; Lawson, *Fur*; Ray and Freeman, *"Give Us Good Measure"*; Martin, *Keepers of the Game*; Krech, *Indians, Animals, and the Fur Trade*; Eccles, "Belated Review," 341–41; Eccles, "Fur Trade," 341–62.

11. Choiseul's Memoir on New France, August 10, 1761, AMAE, CP Angl. 444:150; Miller Surrey, *Commerce of Louisiana*; Usner, *Indians, Settlers*.

12. Lanctôt, *History of Canada*, 123.

13. Ibid., 126.

14. Kalm, *Travels*, 396.

15. Fregault, *François Bigot*; Roy, *Bigot et sa Bande*.

16. Bougainville, *Journals*, 201.

17. Compiled from Kalm, *Travels*, 431, 447.

18. Ibid., 558.

19. Pouchot, *Memoirs*, 321–22.

20. Officer's letter, August 22, 1756, *NYCD*, 10:454.

21. Kalm, *Travels*, 526.

22. Montcalm to Argenson, April 24, 1755, *NYCD*, 10:550.

23. Ibid.

24. Pouchot, *Memoirs*, 321.

25. Journal of Quebec, 1759, *NYCD*, 10:1044.

26. Montcalm to Paulmy, April 18, 1758, *NYCD*, 10:699.

27. Kalm, *Travels*, 381–82.

28. Bougainville, *Journals*, 6–7.

29. Chartrand, *Canadian Military Heritage*, 2:9–14, 16–19. See also Chartrand, *Canadian Military Heritage*, vol. 1; Steele, *Guerrillas and Grenadiers*; Eccles, "French Forces," 3:xv–xxii; Stanley, *Canada's Soldiers*; and Hamilton, *French Army in America*.

30. Pouchot, *Memoirs*, 76; See also, Andre Corvisier, "La société militaire française au temps de la Nouvelle France," *Histoire Sociale/Social History* 10, no. 20 (1977).

31. Montcalm to Argenson, August 28, 1756, *NYCD*, 10:463.

32. Pouchot, *Memoirs*, 77.

33. Montreuil to [recipient unknown], June 12, 1756, *NYCD*, 10:419.

34. For an excellent account of Rogers and the nature of North American wilderness warfare, see Ross, *War on the Run*.

35. Pouchot, *Memoirs*, 78.

36. For excellent studies of relations between white and Indians during this and related eras, see Jennings, *Ambiguous Iroquois Empire*; Jennings, *Empire of Fortune*; White, *Middle Ground*; Richter, *Ordeal of the Longhouse*; MacLeod, *Canadian Iroquois and the Seven Years' War*; and Havard, *Great Peace of Montreal*.

37. Pouchot, *Memoirs*, 282.

38. Ibid., 57.

39. Onondaga and Mohawk chiefs to Beauharnais, July 26, 1745, *NYCD*, 10:23. For an excellent book on Iroquois diplomacy, see Aquila, *Iroquois Restoration*.

40. Bougainville, *Journals*, 134.

41. Pouchot, *Memoirs*, 461–62.

42. Bougainville, *Journals*, 45.

43. Pouchot, *Memoirs*, 460.

44. Bougainville, *Journals*, 37.

45. Ibid., 54.

46. Pouchot, *Memoirs*, 476–77.

47. Bougainville, *Journals*, 114.

48. Ibid., 41.

49. Ibid., 191.

50. Pares, *War and Trade*, 375; Innis, *Cod Fisheries*, 120.

51. Montcalm to Le Normand, April 12, 1759, *NYCD*, 10:962–65.

52. Bougainville, *Journals*, 252–53. For an excellent account of fortress building and siege warfare, see "Memoir on the Defense of the Fort of Carillon," 196–226.

53. Quoted in Pease, *Boundary Disputes*, 347.

4. The Clash of Empires through 1754

Epigraph 1. Quoted in Observations on the English Counterproject, February [March?] 13, 1755, AMAE, CP Angl. 438:139.

Epigraph 2. Voltaire, *Candide*, 43–44.

Epigraph 3. Argenson, *Journal*, 2:319.

1. For a brilliant analysis of Champlain and early French colonization, see Fischer, *Champlain's Dream.*

2. Mims, *Colbert's West India Policy;* Pares, *Yankees and Creoles;* Andrews, *Trade, Plunder, and Settlement;* Rediker, *Between the Devil and the Deep Blue Sea.*

3. Giraud, *History of French Louisiana;* Miller Surrey, *Commerce of Louisiana.*

4. The Treaties of Utrecht (1713), http://heraldica.org/topics/france/utrecht.htm#utrecht_france.

5. Board of Trade Report, 1721, *NYCD,* 5:624. For other Board of Trade reports, see *NYCD,* 5:602, 619–20; 9:959–85, 996–1007, 1014–18.

6. Alvord, *Mississippi Valley in British Politics;* Volwiler, *George Croghan and the Westward Movement.*

7. Crane, *Southern Frontier;* Lanning, *Diplomatic History of Georgia.*

8. Report of M. Boishébert on Indians Affairs, November 1747, *NYCD,* 10:83–84.

9. Higonnet, "Origins of the Seven Years' War."

10. Quoted in Raymond to La Jonquiere, May 22, 1750, AN, Colonies C11A 95:397.

11. Quoted in Abstract of Despatches from Canada to November 7, 1749, *NYCD,* 10:199–201.

12. Abstract of Despatches, November 1749, *NYCD,* 10:205.

13. Quoted in ibid., 202.

14. Quoted in McLennan, *Louisbourg,* 190.

15. Abstract of Despatches from Vaudreuil, Louisiana Governor, September 18, 1750, *NYCD,* 10:219.

16. Céleron to Hamilton, August 6, 1749, *NYCD,* 6:532–33.

17. Quoted in Kent, *French Invasion,* 9–10.

18. La Jonquière to Minister, November 12, 1749, AN, Colonies C11A 93:58, 61; La Jonquière to Minister, August 24, September 20, 1750, AN, Colonies C11A 95:211, 237.

19. Council between the Cayuga and de la Jonquière, May 15, 1750, *NYCD,* 10:205–206.

20. Ibid.

21. La Galissonière Memoir, December 1750, *NYCD,* 10:222–23.

22. La Galissonière Memoir, 1751, AMAE, Mem. et Doc. Amer. 24:110.

23. Minute on French Policy, approved by the king, September 23, 1751, AN, Colonies C11A 97:258.

24. Cabinet memorandum on the Ohio valley, September 23, 1751, *NYCD,* 10:239–40.

25. Instructions to Duquesne, April 1752, *NYCD,* 10:243–44.

26. Halifax on French Encroachments, August 15, 1753, BL, Add. MSS 33, 029:96; Pease, *Boundary Disputes,* 42–44.

27. Cabinet Minute, August 21, 1753, BL, Add. MSS 32,995:26; Pease, *Boundary Disputes,* 45.

28. Quotes from Kent, *French Invasion*, 48. For the entire expedition, see pages 46–51.

29. Quoted in Conference Minutes, New York, June 16, 1753, *NYCD*, 6:788.

30. Dinwiddie to M. de St. Pierre, October 31, 1753, *NYCD*, 10:258.

31. St. Pierre to Dinwiddie, December 15, 1753, *NYCD*, 10:259; Washington, *Diaries*, 144–52; West, *War for Empire*.

32. See Savelle, *Diplomatic History of the Canadian Boundary*, chap. 2; Pease, *Boundary Disputes*; Savelle, "Diplomatic Preliminaries," 1–43; Pease and Jenison, *Illinois on the Eve*; and Gipson, *Zones of International Friction*.

33. William Mildmay and William Shirley, *The Memorials of the English and French Commissionaires Concerning the Limits of Nova Scotia or Acadia* (London: s.n., 1755). "Mémoire de la Cour de France pour les Instructions à donner aux commissaires pour la règlement des Limites en Amérique en Amériques et des Prises faites en mer," "Réponse au Mémoires intitule Project des Instructions pour les Commissaires qui doivent s'assembler a Paris," and "Mémoire d'Observations sur le Projet d'Instructions pour le Com. Anglais," all in CL, Mildmay Papers, "Memorials"; CL, Mildmay Papers, "Letters from Paris."

34. Walpole, *Memoirs of George II*, 1:136.

35. Mirepoix to foreign minister, January 28, 1752; December 15, 1752; and January 18 and 25, 1753, all in AMAE, CP Angl. 434:223; 435:236; 435:283, 298. Mirepoix to St. Contest, February 20/March 2, 1752; and St. Contest to Mirepoix, March 2/13 1752, both in AMAE, CP Angl. 434:187, 214. Mirepoix to minister, October 12, 1753; minister to Mirepoix, October 29, 1753; Mirepoix to minister, November 9, 1753; and Mirepoix to minister, December 10, 1753, all in AMAE, CP Angl. 436:335, 358, 388, 422.

36. Choiseul, *Mémoires*, 112.

37. Bernis, *Mémoires*, 101–102.

38. Argenson, *Journal*, 2:70.

39. Ibid., 1:131.

40. Quoted in Gaxotte, *Le Siècle de Louis XV*, 244; See also Christelow, "French Interest," 515–37; and A. Soulange-Bodin, *La Diplomatie de Louis XV et le Pacte de Famille* (Paris: Perrin, 1894).

41. Duras to Rouillé, 1754, AMAE, CP Esp. 510:165–75, 387.

42. Louis to Ferdinand, 1754, AMAE, CP Esp. 516:83.

43. Extract of Villiers Journal in Varin Letter to Bigot, July 24, 1754, *NYCD*, 10:261.

44. Quoted in Washington, *Diaries*, 170.

45. Varin to Bigot, July 24, 1754, *NYCD*, 10:260–61.

46. Duquesne to Machault, September 31, 1754, *NYCD*, 10:266.

47. Secret Iroquois Council at Montreal, September 23, 1754, *NYCD*, 10:267–69.

48. Duquesne to Machault, October 28, 1754, *NYCD*, 10:264–65.

49. Machault to Duquesne, November 6, 1754, *NYCD*, 10:270.

50. Albemarle to Robinson, November 27, 1754, BL, Add. MSS 33,027:283; Albemarle to Robinson, December 18, 1754, BL, Add. MSS 33,027:287; Pease, *Boundary Disputes*, 56–59.

51. Instructions to Mirepoix, December 30, 1754. See also Private Memoir for Mirepoix,
    December 31, 1754, both in AMAE, CP Angl. 437:433.

5. Escalation, 1755

Epigraph 1. Bernis to Choiseul, December [n.d.], 1757, quoted in Cheke, *Cardinal de Bernis*, 157.

Epigraph 2. Quoted in Walpole, *Memoirs of George II*, 2:52.

Epigraph 3. Bougainville, *Journals*, 191.

1. Rouillé Instructions to Mirepoix, December 30 and 31, 1754, AMAE, CP Angl. 437:431, 433; Pease, *Boundary Disputes*, xli–lvi. For a discussion of the secret channel between the king and ambassador, see Waddington, *Louis XV et le Renversement*, 162.

2. Mirepoix to Rouillé, January 16, 1755, AMAE, CP Angl. 438:15. See also Mirepoix to Robinson, January 16, 1755; Robinson's Memoir, January 22, 1755; Reply to Robinson's Memoir, February 6, 1755; and Rouillé to Mirepoix, February 3, 1755, all in AMAE, CP Angl. 438:31, 38, 94, 81.

3. Mirepoix to Rouillé, January 16, 1755, AMAE, CP Angl. 428:15.

4. British Memorial, January 22, 1755, AMAE, CP Angl. 438:38; Mirepoix to Rouillé, January 23 and 30, 1755, AMAE, CP Angl. 438:40, 54.

5. Rouillé to Mirepoix, February 19, 1755, AMAE, CP Angl. 438:175.

6. Rouillé to Mirepoix, February 3, 1755, AMAE, CP Angl. 438:81.

7. Mirepoix to Rouillé, February 19, 1755, AMAE, CP Angl. 438:154.

8. French Project for a Preliminary Convention, February 19, 1755, AMAE, CP Angl. 438:154.

9. Rouillé to Mirepoix, February 19, 1755, AMAE, CP Angl. 438:163, 175.

10. Cabinet Minute, February 20, 1755, BL, Add. MSS 32,996:34; Mirepoix to Rouillé, February 28, AMAE, CP Angl. 438:232.

11. For the foreign minister's unfolding perspectives on the negotiations, see Rouillé to Mirepoix, February 28, 1755; March 5 and 17, 1755, all in AMAE, CP Angl. 438:232, 247, 280, 285.

12. Rouillé to Mirepoix, March 17, 1755, AMAE, CP Angl. 438:280.

13. Mirepoix to Rouillé, March 22, 1755, AMAE, CP Angl. 438:297.

14. Mirepoix to Rouillé, March 24, 1755, AMAE, CP Angl. 438:307.

15. Mirepoix to Rouillé, April 6, 1755, AMAE, CP Angl. 438:362.

16. Robinson to Newcastle, April 5, 1755, BL, Add. MSS 32,854:55.

17. Cabinet Minute, April 10, 1755, BL, Add. MSS 32,996:73.

18. For the unfolding perspectives and negotiations during this time, see Mirepoix to Rouillé, March 22 and 24, 1755; April 6, 21, and 25, 1755; May 1, 5, 10,

and 15, 1755, all in AMAE, CP Angl. 438:297, 307, 362, 418, 439:4, 24, 30, 65, 76; Rouillé to Mirepoix, March 27, 1755; April 13 and 24, 1755; English Note, April 25, 1755, all in AMAE, CP Angl. 438:332, 392, 397, 426; 439:14, 20; 438:440.

19. French Memoir to the English Ministry, May 9, 1755, AMAE, CP Angl. 439:38; English Answer, June 7, 1755, AMAE, CP Angl. 439:172. Mirepoix to Rouillé, June 7 and 18, 1755; July 3 and 10, 1755, all in AMAE, CP Angl. 439:166, 191, 223, 233.

20. Rouillé to Mirepoix, May 24, 1755; June 29, 1755, both in AMAE, CP Angl. 439:96, 209.

21. Bernis, *Mémoires*, 134.

22. Machault to Duquesne, February 17, 1755, *NYCD*, 10:275. For other Versailles instructions to officials of New France and other French colonies, see Machault to Varin, February 17, 1755, *NYCD*, 10:279–80; and Manchault to Bompart, governor of the Windward Island, February 17, 1755, *NYCD*, 10:280–81.

23. Drucour and Prevost to Duquesne, February 27, 1755, *NYCD*, 10:281–84.

24. Fregault, *Le Grand Marquis*; Private Instructions to Vaudreuil, April 1, 1755, *NYCD*, 10:290–94; Instructions to Vaudreuil, April 1, 1755, *NYCD*, 10:295–96.

25. Instructions for Dieskau, March 1, 1755, *NYCD*, 10:286–98; Commission for Dieskau, March 1, 1755, *NYCD*, 10:285.

26. Argenson, *Journal*, 2:312.

27. Vaudreuil journal excerpts, May 3 to June 26, 1755, *NYCD*, 10:297–99; Salvert to Machault, July 6, 1755, *NYCD*, 10:302–303. For an exact account of the French ships, guns, and troops, and the voyage, see Pouchot, *Memoirs*, 67–72.

28. Quoted in Walpole, *Memoirs of George II*, 2:52.

29. Argenson, *Journal*, 2:319–20.

30. Ibid. For a succinct account of Machault's tenure as marine minister and especially this crisis, see Vergé-Franceschi, *La Marine Française*, 120–23.

31. Rouillé to Mirepoix, July 18, 1755, AMAE, CP Angl. 439:255.

32. Duquesne to Vaudreuil, July 6, 1755, *NYCD*, 10:300–302.

33. Vaudreuil to Machault, July 10, 1755, *NYCD*, 10:305. See also Vaudreuil to Machault, July 24, 1755, *NYCD*, 10:306–308.

34. Duquesne to Machault, July 15, 1755, *NYCD*, 10:306.

35. Pouchot, *Memoirs*, 73.

36. Chartrand, *French Soldier*, 32–35.

37. Pouchot, *Memoirs*, 76.

38. Walpole, *Memoirs of George II*, 2:53. See also McCardell, *Ill-Starred General*.

39. Quoted in Franklin, *Benjamin Franklin*, 173–74.

40. Quoted in French Battle Account, August 8, 1755, in Cumberland, *Military Affairs*, 129.

41. Duquesne to Minister of Marine, June 25, 1755, in Stevens and Kent, *Wilderness Chronicles*, 64–65.

42. For an excellent reconstruction of the battle that succeeds in making sense of the often contradictory accounts, see Kopperman, *Braddock at the Monongahela*.

The book includes copies of the battle's twenty-two firsthand accounts, many of which are also in Cumberland, *Military Affairs*, 98–129.

43. Quoted in Gipson, *Great War for the Empire: Years of Defeat*, 233; Webster, *Journals of Beauséjour*; Fiedmont, *Siege of Beauséjour*.

44. Fiedmont, *Siege of Beauséjour*, 31.

45. Argenson, *Journal*, 2:349; Lanctôt, *History of Canada*, 99. For an excellent overview of Acadian history, see Sauvageau, *Acadie: La Guerre de Cent Ans*.

46. Memoir to Dieskau from Vaudreuil, August 15, 1755, *NYCD*, 10:327–31. See also Vaudreuil to Dieskau, September 25, 1755, *NYCD*, 10:328; Vaudreuil to Machault, September 15, 1755, *NYCD*,10:325–26; Dieskau to Doreil, August 16, 1755, *NYCD*, 10:311–12; Osgood, *American Colonies in the Eighteenth Century*, 4:367.

47. Vaudreuil to Machault, September 25, 1755, *NYCD*, 10:319.

48. Dieskau to Commissary Doreil, August 16, 1755, *NYCD*, 10:311–12.

49. Dieskau to Vaudreuil, September 15, 1755, *NYCD*, 10:318.

50. English Prisoner Answers, August 29 and 30, 1755, *NYCD*, 10:333–34.

51. Dieskau to Argenson, September 14, 1755, *NYCD*, 10:317.

52. Wraxall, Return of Casualties, September 11, 1755, *NYCD*, 6:1006–1007; Wraxall to Delancey, September 10, 1755, *NYCD*, 6:1003–1004; Doreil to Argenson, October 20, 1755, *NYCD*, 10:360–61; Gunner to his cousin, September 10, 1755, *NYCD*, 6:1005; Thomas Pownall to Board of Trade, September 20, 1755, NYCD, 6:1008–1009; Journal of Army Operations, July 22 to September 30, 1755, *NYCD*, 10:337–40; Dialogue between Saxe and Dieskau in Elysian Fields, *NYCD*, 10:340–45; Johnson, *William Johnson Papers*, 9:234–38; Montreuil to Argenson, August 16, 1755, *NYCD*, 10:313; Journal of Army Operations, July 22 to September 30, 1755, *NYCD*, 10:337–40; Montreuil's Account of Lake George Battle, September 1755, *NYCD*, 10:335–37; Montreuil to Argenson, October 10, 1755, *NYCD*, 10:353–54; Montreuil to Argenson, October 14, 1755, *NYCD*, 10:355–56; Doreil to Argenson, October 25, 1755, *NYCD*, 10:360–61.

53. Dieskau to Vaudreuil, September 15, 1755, *NYCD*, 10:318.

54. Vaudreuil to Machault, September 15, 1755, *NYCD*, 10:324, 327.

55. Pouchot, *Memoirs*, 93.

56. Vaudreuil to Machault, October 30, 1755, *NYCD*, 10:374–75.

57. See Breard to Machault, August 13, 1755, *NYCD*, 10:309–10; Malartic to Argenson, October 6, 1755, *NYCD*, 10:347–52; Vaudreuil to Machault, October 18, 1755, *NYCD*, 10:358–59; Lotbinière to Argenson, October 24, 1755, *NYCD*, 10:365–68; Abstract of Vaudreuil's Despatches, December 1755, *NYCD*, 10:380–81; and Account of the year in Canada, December 1755, *NYCD*, 10:381–84.

58. Doreil to Argenson, October 28, 1755, *NYCD*, 10:370. For full account, see pages 368–74.

59. Vaudreuil to Machault, October 31, 1755, *NYCD*, 10:378. See also Vaudreuil and Seneca Council, October 1, 1755, *NYCD*, 10:345–47; Vaudreuil to Five Nations, October 22, 1755, *NYCD*, 10:361–64; and Vaudreuil to Machault, October 30, 1755, *NYCD*, 10:376.

60. Antoine, *Louis XV*, 672; Walpole, *Memoirs of George II*, 2:53, 56.

61. Machault to Vaudreuil, September 5, 1755, *NYCD*, 10:314.

62. For the best surviving accounts of French policy, see "Projet de Conduit dans la Situation Présente des Affaires relativement a l'Angleterre," March 23, 1755, AMAE, Mem. et Doc. Angl. 41:1–12; La Galissonière to Rouillé, March 7, April 30, 1755, AMAE, CP Angl. 438:259, 455, 457; Rouillé to La Galissonière and Silhouette, April 29, 1755, AMAE, CP Angl. 438:454; and "Note sur le Droite de la France au Territoire de la Belle Riviere," AN, Colonies C11E 7:2.

63. Machault to Bompart, February 17, 1755, AN, Colonies B 101; Bompart to Machault, August 1, 1756, AN Marine, B4 73.

64. Walpole, *Memoirs of George II*, 2:48.

65. Bernis, *Mémoires*, 146.

66. Durant and Durant, *Rousseau and Revolution*, 40–41.

67. For an excellent background to these negotiations and his own role in it, see Bernis, *Mémoires*, 137–57. See also Bernis, *Mémoires et Lettres de François-Joachim de Pierre, Cardinal de Bernis*, ed. Frédéric Masson, 2 vols. (Paris: Plon, 1882); and Frederic Masson, *Le Cardinal de Bernis* (Paris: Plon, 1884). For a fine biography on Bernis, see Cheke, *Cardinal de Bernis*.

68. Argenson, *Journal*, 2:158.

69. Casanova, *Memoirs*, 3:602, 646, 650.

70. Bernis, *Mémoires*, 144–45.

71. Ibid., 131.

72. Argenson, *Journal*, 2:316–17.

73. Bernis, *Mémoires*, 135.

74. Argenson, *Journal*, 2:330.

75. Ibid., 2:333–34.

76. Ibid., 2:329.

77. Ibid., 2:322. For other descriptions, see ibid., 325, 339.

78. Ibid., 2:330–31.

79. Ibid., 2:331.

80. Louis XV to George II, December 21, 1755, *NYCD*, 10:379.

81. Observations on the English Counterproject, February [March?] 13, 1755, AMAE, CP Angl. 438:139.

6. World War, 1756

Epigraph 1. Bernis, *Mémoires*, 163.

Epigraph 2. Argenson, *Journal*, 2:336.

1. For some classic studies of the diplomatic revolution, see Waddington, *Louis XV et le Renversement*; Broglie, *L'Alliance Autrichienne*; and Duclos, *Mémoires Secrets*. For a good summary, see Higonnet, "Origins of the Seven Years' War."

2. Argenson, *Journal*, untranslated version, 9:172–73.

3. For an intriguing but unproven conspiracy theory that Conti was in league

with Protestants to assassinate and overthrow Louis XV, see Woodbridge, *Revolt.*

4. British Ministry to Louis XV, January 1756, *NYCD*, 10:391.

5. Pease, *Boundary Disputes*, cxlix–cl.

6. Rouillé to Douglas, February 9, 1756, BN, SM NAF 22009:37–39; Rouillé to Vorontsov, February 9, 1756, BN, SM NAF 22009:41.

7. Casanova, *Memoirs*, 3:667.

8. Quoted in Corbett, *England in the Seven Years' War*, 1:86. For the full accounts, see pages 84–87.

9. Corbett, *England in the Seven Years' War*, 1:88–95, 96–97.

10. Ibid., 1:99; Lacour-Gayet, *La Marine Militaire*, 226, 235, 261.

11. E. Guillon, *Port Mahon, la France à Minorque sous Louis XV* (Paris: Presses Universitaires de France,1983).

12. Voltaire, *Candide*, 61.

13. Argenson, *Journal*, 2:362.

14. Bernis, *Mémoires*, 163. For an argument that Minorca was more a strategic liability than asset for England, see Corbett, *England in the Seven Years' War*, 1:135.

15. Carter, *Dutch Republic.*

16. Pares, *War and Trade*, chap. 8.

17. Argenson to Vaudreuil, February 29, 1756, *NYCD*, 10:392.

18. Argenson to Doreil, February 29, 1756, *NYCD*, 10:393–94.

19. Montcalm Commission, March 1, 1756, *NYCD*, 10:395.

20. Martin, *Le Marquis de Montcalm*; Bonnechose, *Montcalm et le Canada Français*; Guénin, *Montcalm*; Casgrain, *Montcalm et Lévis*; Eccles, "Montcalm," 3:458–69.

21. Vaudreuil to Argenson, June 8, 1756, *NYCD*, 10:411–12.

22. Montcalm to Machault, June 12, 1756, *NYCD*, 10:418.

23. Ibid.

24. Montcalm to Argenson, June 19, 1756, *NYCD*, 10:422; Michalon, "Vaudreuil et Montcalm, les hommes, leurs relations."

25. Montreuil to [recipient unknown], June 12, 1756, *NYCD*, 10:419.

26. Montcalm to Argenson, November 1, 1756, *NYCD*, 10:492.

27. Montcalm to Argenson, July 20, 1756, *NYCD*, 10:433.

28. Montcalm to Argenson, November 1, 1756, *NYCD*, 10:491.

29. Montcalm to Moras, July 11, 1757, *NYCD*, 10:577.

30. Bougainville, *Journals.*

31. M. d Léry, Capture of Fort Bull, 1756, *NYCD*, 10:403–405; Thorpe, "Chaussegros de Léry, Gaspard-Joseph," 4:145–47; Hagerty, *Massacre at Fort Bull.*

32. Montcalm to Argenson, July 24, 1756, *NYCD*, 10:434; "Journal of Occurrences in Canada," *NYCD*, 10:402.

33. Montcalm to Argenson, May 21, 1756, *NYCD*, 10:400.

34. Montcalm to Argenson, July 20, 1756, *NYCD*, 10:432–33.

35. Pouchot, *Memoirs*, 99–105; 1756 Campaign, August 28, 1756, *NYCD*, 10:466–70; Officer's Letter, August 22, 1756, *NYCD*, 10:453–56; Montcalm's Journal of Siege of Oswego, August 1756, *NYCD*, 10:57–61; Montcalm to Argenson, August 28, 1756, *NYCD*, 10:461–65; Desandrouins to [recipient unknown], August 28, 1756, *NYCD*, 10:465–66; Vaudreuil to Argenson, August 20, 1756, *NYCD*, 10:471–74; Lotbinière to Minister, November 2, 1756, *NYCD*, 10:493–96.

36. Montcalm Journal of the Siege of Oswego, August 11 to 21, 1756, *NYCD*, 10:443; see also pages 440–43. Articles of Capitulation, August 14, 1756, *NYCD*, 10:444. See also Montcalm to Argenson, June 17, June 19 and July 20, 1756, *NYCD*, 10:420–21; 421–22; 432–35.

37. Bougainville, *Journals*, 180.

38. Conference between Vaudreuil and the Five Nations, August 20, 1756, *NYCD*, 10:447–448. For the entire report, see pages 445–53.

39. Abstract of Occurrences in Canada, 1755, 1756, *NYCD*, 10:397–99; Journal of Occurrences in Canada from October 1755 to June 1756, *NYCD*, 10:401–406. Abstract of Despatches received from Canada, June 4, 1756, *NYCD*, 10:407–10; Montcalm to Argenson, June 12, 1756, *NYCD*, 10:413–17; Abstract of Despatches from Canada, 1756, *NYCD*, 10:428; Vaudreuil to Machault, August 8 and 13, 1756, *NYCD*, 10:435–38, 438–39; Abstract of Despatches, August 30, 1756, *NYCD*, 10:475–87; Abstract of Despatches received from Canada, January 15, 1757, *NYCD*, 10:518–23.

40. Montcalm to Argenson, November 1, 1756, *NYCD*, 10:492.

41. Vaudreuil to Machault, November 6, 1756, *NYCD*, 10:496–97.

42. Ibid., 496.

43. Quoted in Durant and Durant, *Rousseau and Revolution*, 44.

44. Asprey, *Frederick the Great.*

45. Douglas to Rouillé, September 25, 1756, AMAE, CP Russie 51:23–27.

46. Douglas to Tercier, October 2, 1756, AMAE, CP Russie 51:40; Douglas to Rouillé, October 9, 1756, Russian Circular to the Polish Nobility, November 14, 1756, BN, SM NAF 22011:4, 82–86.

47. Rouillé to Douglas, no. 24, November 20, 1756, BN, SM NAF 22010:216; Rouillé to Douglas, no. 7, January 20, 1757, AMAE, CP Russie 52:63–66.

48. Broglie to Douglas, November 9, 1756, AMAE, CP Russie suppl. 9:6–7; Rouillé to Douglas, no. 4, October 11, 1756, AMAE, CP Russie suppl. 8:412.

49. Hôpital to Rouillé, December 23, 1756, AMAE, CP Russie 54:407.

50. Argenson, *Journal*, untranslated version, 9:370.

51. Argenson, *Journal*, untranslated version, 6:341.

7. Killing Fields, 1757

Epigraph 1. Bougainville, *Journals*, 142.
Epigraph 2. Quoted in Argenson, *Journal*, 2:369–70.
Epigraph 3. Bernis, *Mémoires*, 241.

1. Croÿ, *Journal Inédit*, 1, 364. For the best account of the incident, see Kley, *Damiens Affair*. For some intriguing but ultimately unproven conspiracy theories, see Woodbridge, *Revolt*.

2. Argenson, *Journal*, 2:369–70. For the best overview of the politics surrounding the attack on the king, struggle with parlement, firing of Argenson and Machault, and entrance into the war, see Bernis, *Mémoires*, 191–227. For another vivid account, see Walpole, *Memoirs of George II*, 2:196–98.

3. Quoted in Argenson, *Journal*, 2:370.

4. Quoted in Antoine, *Louis XV*, 714.

5. Kley, *Damiens Affair*, chap. 5.

6. Casanova, *Memoirs*, 3:784.

7. Montcalm to Paulmy, July 11, 1757, *NYCD*, 10:575.

8. Argenson, *Journal*, 2:367.

9. Bernis, *Mémoires*, 226.

10. Ibid., 230.

11. Schweizer, *England, Russia, and the Seven Years' War*, 63.

12. Louis XV to Tercier, November 9, 1756, reprinted in Louis XV, *Correspondance*, 1:212–13; Broglie to Louis XV, December 21, 1756, Broglie, *Correspondance*, 1:1.

13. Most secret declaration, Saint Petersburg, January 11, 1757, AMAE, CP Russie suppl. 9:79–81; Oliva, *Misalliance*.

14. Austro-Russian treaty of January 22, 1757 (February 2 under the new calendar), reprinted in F. F. Martens, *Recueil des Traités et Conventions Conclus par la Russie avec les Puissances Étrangères* (Paris: Bibliobazaar, 2010), 9:352.

15. Rouillé to Douglas, February 16, 1757, AMAE, CP Russie 52:134.

16. Louis XV to Elizabeth, January 24, 1757, Elizabeth to Louis XV, March 14, 1757, AMAE, CP Russie 52:215. See also Douglas to Rouillé, no. 23, April 26, 1757, AMAE, CP Russie 52:357.

17. Rouillé to Douglas, January 21 and April 2, 1757, AMAE, CP Russie 52:67, 288.

18. Louis to Tercier, February 13, April 9, and July 20, 1757, reprinted in Louis XV, *Correspondance*, 1:217–18, 220–21, 222.

19. Oliva, *Misalliance*, 128–29.

20. Quoted in Walpole, *Memoirs of George II*, 2:187.

21. For celebratory accounts of British victories, see Corbett, *England in the Seven Years' War*; and Williams, *Life of William Pitt*. For critical accounts, see Ayling, *The Elder Pitt*; and Middleton, *Bells of Victory*.

22. Durant and Durant, *Rousseau and Revolution*, 47–48.

23. Bernis, *Mémoires*, 241.

24. Quoted in Pares, *War and Trade*, 562.

25. Alfred Bourguet, *Le Duc de Choiseul et l'Alliance Espagnole* (Paris: Plon, 1906).

26. Bernis to Hôpital, July 30, 1757, AMAE, CP Russie 53:234; Hôpital to Bernis, August 22 and September 16, 1757, AMAE, CP Russie 53:314–21; 54:42. For an in-depth discussion of the controversy, see Rambaud, *Russes et Prussiens.*

27. Quoted in Woodbridge, *Revolt,* 130.

28. Walpole, *Memoirs of George II,* 2:154.

29. Woodbridge, *Revolt,* chap. 5.

30. Ministerial Minute on the Military Force in Canada, January 15, 1757, *NCYD,* 10:523–26. For fleet statistics, see Middleton, *Bells of Victory,* 24.

31. Bougainville, *Journals,* 108.

32. Quoted in Lanctôt, *History of Canada,* 150.

33. Belle Isle to Moras, February 13, 1757, *NYCD,* 10:526–27.

34. Paulmy to Vaudreuil, March 20, 1757, *NYCD,* 10:535; Paulmy to Montcalm, March 20, 1757, *NYCD,* 10:536.

35. Montcalm to Moras, July 11, 1757, *NYCD,* 10:576.

36. Ibid., 578.

37. Paulmy to Montcalm, April 10, 1757, *NYCD,* 10:538.

38. Attack on Fort William Henry, February 1757, *NYCD,* 10:545. See also Vaudreuil to Keeper of the Seals, April 22, 1757, *NYCD,* 10:542–43.

39. Montcalm to Argenson, April 24, 1757, *NYCD,* 10:549.

40. Bougainville, *Journals,* 98.

41. Vaudreuil to Machault, April 19, 1757, *NYCD,* 10:539–41; Account of Five Nations' Council, April 24, 1757, *NYCD,* 10:555–63.

42. Montcalm to Paulmy, July 11, 1757, *NYCD,* 10:573–76.

43. Vaudreuil's Orders to Montcalm, July 7, 1757, *NYCD,* 10:661–63; Vaudreuil to Moras, July 12, 1757, *NYCD,* 10:584–86.

44. Intelligence from Cape Breton, June 28, 1757, *NYCD,* 10:572–73; McLennan, *Louisbourg;* Fortier, *Fortress of Louisbourg.*

45. Holburne to Pitt, September 29, 1757; Holburne to Pitt, September 30, 1757; Holburne to Pitt, October 13, 1757; Holburne to Pitt, October 15, 1757; Holburne to Pitt, October 20, 1757, all in Pitt, *Correspondence,* 114–15, 115–16, 116–17, 117–19, 120–21.

46. Moras to La Motte, 1757, quoted in McLennan, *Louisbourg,* 300.

47. Montcalm to Paulmy, July 11, 1757, *NYCD,* 10:573–75; Pouchot, *Memoirs,* 116–21.

48. Montcalm to Paulmy, July 11, 1757, *NYCD,* 10:574–75.

49. Quoted in Bougainville, *Journals,* 115. See also Vaudreuil to Moras, July 12, 1757, *NYCD,* 10:580–84; Vaudreuil to Moras, July 13, 1757, *NYCD,* 10:586–88; Vaudreuil to Moras, July 13, 1757, *NYCD,* 10:588–90; and Ministerial Minute on Iroquois Policy, July 31, 1757, *NYCD,* 10:595–96.

50. Bougainville, *Journals,* 150–53; Bougainville to Paulmy, August 19, 1757, *NYCD,* 10:606–607.

51. Bougainville, *Journals,* 119.

52. Both quotes from Montcalm to Vaudreuil, July 27, 1757, *NYCD*, 10:591. See also Doreil to Paulmy, July 31, 1757, *NYCD*, 10:593–94.

53. Bougainville, *Journals*, 142–43.

54. For two excellent accounts of the siege and aftermath, see Steele, *Betrayals*; and Hughes, *Siege of Fort William Henry*.

55. Montcalm Journal, August 3, *NYCD*, 10:601.

56. Bougainville, *Journals*, 158–59.

57. Montcalm Journal, August 5, 1757, *NYCD*, 10:603.

58. Bougainville to Paulmy, August 19, 1757, *NYCD*, 10:614–15.

59. Montcalm Journal, August 9, 1757, *NYCD*, 10:604–605.

60. Montcalm to Paulmy, August 15, 1757, *NYCD*, 10:597–98. For other accounts of the campaign and atrocities, see Doreil to Paulmy, August 14, 1757, *NYCD*, 10:596–97; Montcalm Journal of Expedition Against Fort William Henry, July 12 to August 16, 1757, *NYCD*, 10:598–605; Bougainville to Paulmy, August 19, 1757, *NYCD*, 10:605–18; Order of March on Fort William Henry, July 30, 1757, *NYCD*, 10:620–25; Return of Army, August 3, 1757, *NYCD*, 10:625–26; and Campaign of 1757, July 30 to September 4, 1757, *NYCD*, 10:627–30.

61. Montcalm to Lord Loudoun, August 14, 1757, *NYCD*, 10:619.

62. Vaudreuil to Montcalm, August 7, 1757, *NYCD*, 10:660.

63. Vaudreuil to Moras, September [n.d.], 1757, *NYCD*, 10:631–34.

64. Vaudreuil to Moras, August 18, 1757, *NYCD*, 10:665, 663–66.

65. Ministerial Minute on the neglect of Montcalm to attack Fort Edward, November 1, 1757, *NYCD*, 10:659–60.

66. Montcalm to Paulmy, September 18, 1757, *NYCD*, 10:636.

67. Document Attached to Montcalm's dispatch to Paulmy, September 18, 1757, *NYCD*, 10:640.

68. Montcalm to Paulmy, September 18, 1757, *NYCD*, 10:640. On this point, see also Montcalm's Memorandum to Moras, November 4, 1757, *NYCD*, 10:672. For an account of how expensive it was to provision New France, see Bigot to Moras, November 3, 1757, *NYCD*, 10:666–67.

69. Doreil to Paulmy, October 25, 1757, *NYCD*, 10:652.

70. Bougainville, *Journals*, 182–83.

71. Montcalm to Paulmy, September 18, 1757, *NYCD*, 10:639.

72. Ibid., 638.

73. Corbett, *England in the Seven Years' War*, 1:361.

74. Havrincourt to Douglas, June 7, 1757; Russian Ministry to Hôpital, July 16, 1757, both in AMAE, CP Russie 51:309–314, 53:410–11; Bain, *Gustavus III*; Anderson, *Europe in the Eighteenth Century*, 184.

75. Waddington, *La Guerre*, 1:584–90.

76. Aubeterre to minister, July 6, 1757, AMAE, CP Esp. 522:3, Aubeterre to minister, October 31 and December 19, 1757, AMAE, CP Esp. 522:381, 486; minister to Aubeterre, November 15, 1757, AMAE, CP Esp. 522:408.

77. Walpole, *Memoirs of George II*, 2:272.

78. Quoted in Woodbridge, *Revolt*, 135.

79. Durant and Durant, *Age of Voltaire*, 496.

80. Bernis to Choiseul, December [n.d.], 1757, quoted in Cheke, *Cardinal de Bernis*, 157.

81. Bernis to Hôpital, December 31, 1757, AMAE, CP Russie 54:436.

8. Turning Point, 1758

Epigraph 1. Bernis to Hôpital, September 15, 1758, AMAE, CP Russie 57:279.

Epigraph 2. Bougainville, *Journals*, 253.

Epigraph 3. Clermont to Louis XV, quoted in Cheke, *Cardinal de Bernis*, 158.

Epigraph 4. Voltaire, *Candide*, 5.

1. Bernis to Stainville, January 14, 1758, in Bernis, *Mémoires*, 2:165. Bernis to Hôpital, January 25, 1758, AMAE, CP Russie 55:90. Stainville is the same person as "Choiseul," to which his name changed on August 25, 1758.

2. Louis XV to Elizabeth, March 13, 1758, AMAE, CP Russie 55:246; Oliva, *Misalliance*, 89–90.

3. Bernis to Stainville, May 13, 1758, in Bernis, *Mémoires*, 2:226–27.

4. Alluded to in Bernis to Stainville, May 24, 1758, in Bernis, *Mémoires*, 2:230–35.

5. Bernis to Stainville, August 1, 1758, in Bernis, *Mémoires*, 2:255.

6. Choiseul Memoir on Holstein, December 15, 1758, AMAE, CP Russie 58:351–56. Choiseul to Hôpital, May 22, 1758, AMAE, CP Russie 60:159–61; June 11 and 24, 1758, AMAE, CP Russie 60:212–13, 234; and July 24, 1758, AMAE, CP Russie 60:316. Bernstorff to Choiseul, July 28, 1758, AMAE, CP Russie 60:336–37.

7. Schweizer, *England, Prussia, and the Seven Years' War*, 63.

8. Gipson, *Great War for the Empire: Culmination*, 3, 287.

9. Pares, *War and Trade*, 390–91.

10. Bernis to Choiseul, August 20, 1758, in Bernis, *Mémoires*, 2:239.

11. Kennett, *French Armies*, xiv.

12. For insights into Belle Isle, see Dussauge, *Études sur la Guerre de Sept Ans*, 87; Argenson, *Journal*, 1:363–64. For background on the brief tenures of Moras and Massiac, see Vergé-Franceschi, *La Marine Française*, 123–30.

13. Quoted in Cheke, *Cardinal de Bernis*, 158.

14. Middleton, *Bells of Victory*, 78.

15. La Motte Rouge, *Saint Cast le Guildo*, 17; English estimates of the dead varied from six hundred to seven hundred, less than half the French estimate; however, both agree that four hundred troops were captured. See Corbett, *England in the Seven Years' War*, 1:301–302; and Fortescue, *History of the British Army*, 2:349–51.

16. Doreil to Belle Isle, April 30, 1758, *NYCD*, 10:702.

17. Montcalm to Moras, February 19, 1758, *NYCD*, 10:686.

18. Doreil to Belle Isle, April 30, 1758, *NYCD*, 10:702.

19. Montcalm to Paulmy, April 18, 1758, *NYCD*, 10:699.

20. Montcalm to Moras, February 19, 1758, *NYCD*, 10:686.

21. Militia of Canada, 1758, January 1758 [n.d.], *NYCD*, 10:680–82.

22. Ibid.

23. Montcalm to Moras, February 19, 1758, *NYCD*, 10:688. Lévis to Paulmy, February 20, 1758, *NYCD*, 10:688–90; Doreil to Belle Isle, April 30, 1758, *NYCD*, 10:701–704.

24. Montcalm to Paulmy, April 10, 1758, *NYCD*, 10:692–93.

25. Bougainville, *Journals*, 204.

26. Vaudreuil to Moras, February 18, 1758, *NYCD*, 10:683–84; Montcalm to Paulmy, February 23, 1758, *NYCD*, 10:690–91; Montcalm to Paulmy, April 10, 1758, *NYCD*, 10:692–94; Pouchot to Belle Isle, April 14, 1758, *NYCD*, 10:694–95; Pouchot's Observations on the Frontier, April 14, 1758, *NYCD*, 10:695; Vaudreuil to Moras, April 21, 1758, *NYCD*, 10:700–701; Daine to Belle Isle, May 19, 1758, *NYCD*, 10:704–706.

27. Bougainville, *Journals*, 206–207.

28. Doreil to Belle Isle, June 16, 1758, *NYCD*, 10:717–18.

29. Quoted in Operations during the winter of 1757–58, April 18, 1758, *NYCD*, 10:697. See also Doreil to Belle Isle, April 30, 1758, *NYCD*, 10:703; and Pouchot, *Memoirs*, 130–31. For an excellent account not only of Robert Rogers but on the nature of frontier warfare, see Ross, *War on the Run*.

30. Pouchot, *Memoirs*, 134–36.

31. Bougainville, *Journals*, 221.

32. For firsthand accounts of the 1758 campaign, see "Extracts from Captain Moneypenny's Orderly Book," 56–67; "Montcalm's Order of Battle," 67–69; "Battle of Carillon," 69–78; "Josiah Goodrich Orderbook," 39–61; "Life of David Perry," 4–8; "Journal of Captain Samuel Cobb," 12–31; "Montcalm at Carillon," 4–11; "List of French Killed and Wounded, July 8, 1758," 12; "Attack and Repulse at Ticonderoga," 15–18; Pell, "Strategy of Montcalm"; "Moneypenny Orderly Book, June 30 to August 7," 434–61; Furcron and Boyle, "Building of Fort Carillon," 13–67; "Moneypenny Orderly Book, March 23 to June 29, 1758," 328–57.

33. Vaudreuil Campaign Instructions to Montcalm, June 23, 1758, *NYCD*, 10:787. For full letter, see pages 786–88.

34. Bougainville, *Journals*, 215.

35. For an in-depth analysis of the Fort Carillon campaign in the context of all other key events in the region and beyond, see Nester, *Epic Battles for Ticonderoga*.

36. Malartic Journal at Carillon, June 30 to July 10, 1758, *NYCD*, 10:721–25; d'Huges to Belles Isle, June 1, 1758, *NYCD*, 10:706–10; Sautai, *Montcalm at the Battle of Carillon*.

37. Bougainville, *Journals*, 222.

38. Abercromby to Pitt, July 12, 1758, *NYCD*, 10:725.

39. Pouchot, *Memoirs*, 145.

40. "List of French Killed and Wounded, July 8, 1758," 12; "British Casualty List at Carillon," 76–78; Abercromby to Pitt, July 12, 1758, *NYCD*, 10:727.

41. Bougainville, *Journals*, 236.

42. Montcalm to Massiac, July 28, 1758, *NYCD*, 10:761–62.

43. Montcalm to Belle Isle, July 12, 1758, *NYCD*, 10:732–33.

44. Vaudreuil to Montcalm, July 12, 1758, *NYCD*, 10:757.

45. Montcalm to Vaudreuil, July 18, 1758, *NYCD*, 10:759–60; Vaudreuil to Montcalm, July 17, 1758, *NYCD*, 10:760; Montcalm to Vaudreuil, July 21, 1758, *NYCD*, 10:803–805; Montcalm to Vaudreuil, August 2, 1758, *NYCD*, 10:778.

46. Montcalm to Belle Isle as dictated to Doreil, July 28, 1758, *NYCD*, 10:754.

47. Vaudreuil to Massiac, August 4, 1758, *NYCD*, 10:779–83.

48. Doreil to Belle Isle, July 31, 1759, *NYCD*, 10:770.

49. Downey, *Louisbourg*; Fry, *"Appearance of Strength"*; McLennan, *Louisbourg*, 263.

50. Drucour to Massiac, September 23, 1758, *NYCD*, 10:833–34; Pouchot, *Memoirs*, 155–57.

51. McLennan, *Louisbourg*, 288.

52. Pouchot, *Memoirs*, 154; Vaudreuil to Massiac, September 2, 1758, *NYCD*, 10:822–24; Montcalm to Belle Isle, September 9, 1758, *NYCD*, 10:831–32; Mulligan, "Colonel Charles Clinton's Journal," 292–315. Godfrey, *Pursuit of Profit*, 106–10, 123–25; Preston and LaMontagne, *Royal Fort Frontenac*; Frederick A. Rahmer, *Dash to Frontenac: An Account of Lt. Col. John Bradstreet's Expedition to and Capture of Fort Frontenac* (Rome, N.Y.: Frederick A. Rahmer, 1973).

53. Pouchot, *Memoirs*, 136.

54. Ibid., 154.

55. Daine to Belle Isle, November 3, 1758, *NYCD*, 10:884–85; Bougainville to Crémille, November 8, 1758, *NYCD*, 10:887–89; Montcalm to Belle Isle, November 15, 1758, *NYCD*, 10:900–901; Montcalm to Crémille, November 21, 1758, *NYCD*, 10:901–902; Account of Grant's Defeat, October 5, 1758, *NYCD*, 10:902–903; General Forbes to Governor Denny, November 26, 1758, *NYCD*, 10:905–906; Pouchot, *Memoirs*, 157–62.

56. Vaudreuil to Massiac, November 1, 1758, *NYCD*, 10:866–68; Vaudreuil Plan, *NYCD*, 10:868–70; Montcalm Plan, *NYCD*, 10:870–72; Vaudreuil's Observations on Montcalm's Plan, *NYCD*, 10:872–73; Montcalm's Observations on Vaudreuil's Plan, *NYCD*, 10:873; Vaudreuil's Response, *NYCD*, 10:873–74; Montcalm's Reflections on Defense of Canada, *NYCD*, 10:874–77.

57. Bougainville, *Journals*, 314.

58. Doreil to Belle Isle, August 31, 1758, *NYCD*, 10:820; Doreil to Massiac, August 31, 1758, *NYCD*, 10:828–29; Malartic Journal of Occurrences in Canada, 1757, 1758, *NYCD*, 10:835–55; Montcalm to Crémille, October 21, 1758, *NYCD*, 10:855–57; Montcalm to Belle Isle, October 27, 1758, *NYCD*, 10:860–62; Situation in Canada, Lotbinière to Belle Isle, May 1758, *NYCD*, 10:889–97; French Campaigns in North America, 1754–58, *NYCD*, 10:912–22.

59. Ministerial Minute on Dispatches from Canada, December 28, 1758, *NYCD*, 10:906–907.

60. Belle Isle to Vaudreuil, September 23, 1758, *NYCD*, 10:832. See also Belle Isle to Montcalm, September 23, 1758, *NYCD*, 10:832–33; Abstract of Despatches received at the War Department Complaining of Vaudreuil, October 26, 1758, *NYCD*, 10:857–59.

61. Bernis to Choiseul, August 26, 1758, AMAE, Mem. et Doc. France 571:189.

62. Bernis to Hôpital, September 15, 1758, AMAE, CP Russie 57:279.

63. Bernis to Hôpital, May 11, 1758, AMAE, Russie 56:161. See also Bernis to Hôpital, April 25, June 22, August 1, October 8, 1758, AMAE, Russie 56:126, 56:339, 57:82–83, 58:54; Louis XV to Elizabeth October 24, 1758, AMAE, Russie 58:127–32; and Elizabeth to Louis XV, October 28, 1758, AMAE, Russie 58:157.

64. Vergé-Franceschi, *La Marine Française*, 128–30.

65. Quoted in ibid.

66. Bernis, *Mémoires*, 286–87.

67. Bernis to Stainville, June 24, 1758, in Bernis, *Mémoires*, 2:233.

68. Louis to Bernis, October 9, 1758, in Bernis, *Mémoires*, 2:299–300.

69. Bernis to Choiseul, August 20, 1758, AMAE, Mem. et Doc. France 571:189.

9. Rout, 1759

Epigraph 1. Bougainville, *Journals*, 259.

Epigraph 2. Quoted in White, *Marshal of France*, 222.

Epigraph 3. Voltaire, *Candide*, 85.

1. Bourget, *Études sur la Politique*; Ramsey, *Anglo-French Relations*; Butler, *Choiseul*; Brierre, *Le Duc de Choiseul*.

2. Choiseul, *Mémoires*, 96, 86–105.

3. Choiseul, *Mémoires*, 192.

4. Bernis, *Mémoires*, 249.

5. Quoted in Pease, *Boundary Disputes*, lxvii.

6. Choiseul Memoir to Hôpital, January 19, 1759, AMAE, CP Russie 59:119–23.

7. Guillaumat-Vallet, *Le Contrôleur-Général Silhouette*.

8. Riley, *Seven Years' War*, 151–59.

9. Bougainville, *Journals*, 322–23.

10. Ibid., 323.

11. Ibid., 323–24.

12. Choiseul to Silhouette, January 27, 1759, AMAE, CP Angl. 442:33; Silhouette to Choiseul, February 8, 1759, *NYCD*, 10:940; Silhouette to Berryer, February 8, 1759, *NYCD*, 10:940–43.

13. Bougainville, *Journals*, 284–85.

14. Berryer to Bigot, January 19, 1759, *NYCD*, 10:937–39.

15. Ibid.

16. Minute on Governor-General if Vaudreuil died, January 28, 1759, *NYCD*, 10:939–40.

17. Minute Respecting Promotions, February 1759, *NYCD*, 10:940.

18. Ministerial Minute on Supplies to Canada, March 9, 1759, *NYCD*, 10:944–45.

19. Belle Isle to Montcalm, February 19, 1759, *NYCD*, 10:943–44.

20. Marine Ministry to Vaudreuil and Bigot, February 3, 1759, *NYCD*, 10:941.

21. Vaudreuil's Plan of Operations, 1759, *NYCD*, 10:954, 952–56.

22. Montcalm to Crémille, April 12, 1759, *NYCD*, 10:959.

23. Montcalm to Belle Isle, April 12, 1759, *NYCD*, 10:960–61. For more of Montcalm's views on corruption, see Montcalm to Normand, April 12, 1759, *NYCD*, 10:962–66.

24. Journal at Quebec, 1759, *NYCD*, 10:1017.

25. Bougainville, *Journals*, 186. For the Quebec campaign, see also Montcalm to Belle Isle, May 8, 1759, *NYCD*, 10:970–71; Montcalm to Belle Isle, May 23, 1759, *NYCD*, 10:971; Montcalm to Belle Isle, May 24, 1759, *NYCD*, 10:971–72; Montcalm Journal of Siege of Quebec, 1759, *NYCD*, 10:993–1001; Canada Campaign from June 1 to September 15, 1759, *NYCD*, 10:1001–1003; and An Impartial Opinion on the Military Operations in Canada, 1759, Bishop de Pontbriand, *NYCD*, 10:1059–62. The best secondary account of the siege is Stacey, *Quebec, 1759*, 139–42.

26. Montcalm Journal at Quebec, 1759, *NCYD*, 10:1023.

27. Pouchot, *Memoirs*, 221–35; Pouchot's Journal of Siege of Niagara, 1759, *NYCD*, 10:976–92. For the best secondary account, see Dunnigan, *Siege—1759*.

28. Pouchot, *Memoirs*, 235.

29. Ibid., 216.

30. Ibid., 232.

31. Ibid., 224–30.

32. Bourlamaque to Belle Isle, November 1, 1759, *NYCD*, 10:1054–57.

33. Estimates for the number of British and French troops on the Plains of Abraham vary considerably. For a discussion of the various estimates, see Stacey, *Quebec, 1759*, 139–42.

34. Montreuil to Belle Isle, September 22, 1759, *NYCD*, 10:1013–14; Bigot to Belle Isle, October 25, 1759, *NYCD*, 10:1051–52.

35. Quoted in Journal at Quebec, *NYCD*, 10:1039.

36. Ibid.

37. Stacey, *Quebec, 1759*, 152.

38. Vaudreuil's surrender instructions to Ramezay, September 13, 1759, *NYCD*, 10:1004–1007.

39. Minute of the Council of War for Quebec's Surrender, September 15, 1759, *NYCD*, 10:1007; Vaudreuil to Berryer, September 21, 1759, *NYCD*, 10:1010–13; Daine to Belle Isle, October 9, 1759, *NYCD*, 10:1014–16.

40. Bernier to Belle Isle, September 19, 1759, *NYCD*, 10:1007; Daine to Belle Isle, October 9, 1759, *NYCD*, 10:1015.

41. Corbett, *England in the Seven Years' War*, 1:394; Fortescue, *History of the British Army*, 2:355–63.

42. Newcastle to Hardwicke, October 31, 1759, quoted in Nish, *French Canadians*, 25.

43. Choiseul to Hôpital, July 8, 1759, AMAE, CP Russie 60:275.

44. Choiseul to Auterre, April 23, 1759, AMAE, CP Esp. 524:449; May 22, 1759, AMAE, CP Esp. 525:28; and August 14, 1759, AMAE, CP Esp. 525:190. Aubeterre to Choiseul, May 7, 1759, AMAE, CP Esp. 525:4; Ossun to Choiseul, November 24, 1759, quoted in Waddington, *La Guerre*, 3:434.

45. Choiseul to Bernstorff, September 23, 1759; Bernstorff to Choiseul, November 23, 1759, in Bernstorff and Choiseul, *Correspondance*, 73, 96.

46. Memoir from Russian Ministry, November 6, 1759, AMAE, CP Russie 61:232–48; Hôpital to Choiseul, November 10, 1759, AMAE, CP Russie 61:274; Choiseul to Choiseul-Praslin, December 25, 1759, AMAE, CP Russie 61:409–10.

47. Corbett, *England in the Seven Years' War*, 2:8.

48. Waddington, *La Guerre*, 3:374–79; Lacour-Gayet, *La Marine Militaire*, 342–56; Corbett, *England in the Seven Years War*, 1–71; Middleton, *Bells of Victory*, 108–109.

49. Choiseul to Hôpital, January 9, 1759, AMAE, CP Russie 59:51–55; February 12, 1759, AMAE, CP Russie 59:210; March 24, 1759, AMAE, CP Russie 59:275; and April 10 and 22, 1759, AMAE, CP Russie 60:22–23, 56–57. Oliva, *Misalliance*, 139–42.

50. Quoted in Rashed, *Peace of Paris*, 47.

51. Silhouette to Choiseul, December 30, 1759, AMAE, CP Angl. 41:395.

10. Conquest, 1760

Epigraph 1. Choiseul, *Mémoires*, 143.

Epigraph 2. Quoted in White, *Marshal of France*, 205.

Epigraph 3. Bougainville, *Journals*, 258.

Epigraph 4. Voltaire, *Candide*, 36.

1. Quoted in Durand, "Memoire de Jean-Joseph de la Borde," 155.

2. Choiseul to Hôpital, February 15, 1760, AMAE, CP Russie 64:94; Note from Russian Ministry, December 12, 1759, AMAE, CP Russie 61:353–58.

3. Louis XV Response to Russian Memoir of November 6, 1759, February 1, 1760, Choiseul to Hôpital, March 1, April 3, 1760, Hôpital to Choiseul, April 2, 1760; AMAE, CP Russie 64:122–30, 239, 160, 227–35.

4. Bernstorff and Choiseul, *Correspondance*; Breteuil to Choiseul, December 7, 1760, AMAE, CP Russie 63:373.

5. Choiseul to Ossun, January 6, 1760, AMAE, CP Esp. 527:11; French proposals for Peace, January 9, 1760, AMAE, CP Angl. 442:275.

6. Ossun to Choiseul, January 21, 1760, AMAE, CP Esp. 527:91; Ossun to Choiseul, February 4 and 22, 1760, AMAE, CP Esp. 527:140, 268; Choiseul to Ossun, February 19, 1760, AMAE, CP Esp. 527:232.

7. Quoted in Waddington, *La Guerre*, 3:264.

8. Ossun to Choiseul, July 4, 1760, AMAE, CP Esp. 529:22.

9. Choiseul to Ossun, July 15 and August 19, 1760, AMAE, CP Esp. 529:73, 180; Ossun to Choiseul, October 13, 1760, AMAE, CP Esp. 530:50.

10. Ossun to Choiseul, October 30 and December 8, 1760, AMAE, CP Esp. 530:138, 292.

11. Middleton, *Bells of Victory*, 150.

12. Quoted in Asprey, *Frederick the Great*, 554.

13. Belle Isle to Lévis, February 9, 1760, *NYCD*, 10:1068–69.

14. Memoir of Chev. Le Mercier on Canada, January 7, 1860, *NYCD*, 10:1068. See also Memoir of M. Masse de Maurice on Canada's defense, January 3, 1760, *NYCD*, 10:1063–65.

15. Knox, *Siege of Quebec*, 227.

16. Vaudreuil to militia captains, April 16, 1760, *NYCD*, 10:1073. See also Vaudreuil's Instructions to Lévis, April 16, 1760, *NYCD*, 10:1069–71; and Vaudreuil's amnesty to deserters, April 16, 1760, *NYCD*, 10:1074–75. The war's bloodiest battle was Abercromby's attack on Montcalm's entrenchments before Fort Carillon in 1758.

17. Pouchot, *Memoirs*, 254–56; "List of Officers Killed and Wounded," *NYCD*, 10:1084–86.

18. Lévis *Collection des Manuscrits*, 1:269.

19. Knox, *Siege of Quebec*, 261.

20. Lévis to Belle Isle, June 30, 1760, *NYCD*, 10:1100.

21. Ibid., 1101.

22. Lévis to Belle Isle, August 7, 1760, *NYCD*, 10:1103.

23. Lévis to Belle Isle, July 14, 1760, *NYCD*, 10:1101–1102.

24. Protest of Lévis against the surrender, September 8, 1760, *NYCD*, 10:1106.

25. Vaudreuil to Lévis, September 8, 1760, *NYCD*, 10:1106.

26. Articles of Capitulation for Canada's Surrender, September 8, 1760, *NYCD*, 10:1107–20.

27. Pease, *Boundary Disputes*, lxxx–lxxxi.

28. Vaudreuil to Choiseul, October 30, 1761, AMAE, Mem. et Doc. Amer. 21:96.

29. Haldimand to Amherst, December 10, 1762, BL, Add. MSS 21,661:257; Pease, *Boundary Disputes*, 402–408.

30. Lévis to [recipient unknown], November 27, 1760, *NYCD*, 10:1126.

31. Vaudreuil to Berryer, December 10, 1760, *NYCD*, 10:1128–29; Vaudreuil to Berryer, November 28, 1760, *NYCD*, 10:1128

32. Choiseul to Breteuil, October 24, 1760, AMAE, CP Russie 63:248; Breteuil to Choiseul, November 26 and 27, 1760, AMAE, CP Russie 63:324, 353.

33. Choiseul to Ossun, November 14, 1760, AMAE, CP Esp. 530:192; Choiseul to Ossun, December 16 and 23, 1760, AMAE, CP Esp. 530:340, 360; Choiseul

to Ossun, January 27, 1761, AMAE, CP Esp. 531:96; Ossun to Choiseul, November 28, 1760, AMAE, CP Esp. 530:244; Ossun to Choiseul, December 22, 1760, AMAE, CP Esp. 530:345.

11. Peace or Alliance? 1761

Epigraph 1. Quoted in Long, *Mr. Pitt and America's Birthright,* 401.

Epigraph 2. Choiseul to Solar, May 12, 1762, CL, Shelburne MSS 9:307.

Epigraph 3. Ossun to Choiseul, July 4, 1760, AMAE, CP Esp. 529:22.

1. Pritchard, *Louis XV's Navy,* 131; Middleton, *Bells of Victory,* 175.

2. Rashed, *Peace of Paris*; Pease, *Boundary Disputes*; Vergé-Franceschi, *La Marine Française,* 135–41.

3. Breteuil to Choiseul, January 30, February 6, 1761, Notes on Russian Conference of February 1 and 4, 1761, AMAE, CP Russie 66:60, 127, 132–160; Choiseul to Choiseul-Chevigny, February 22, 1761, AMAE, CP Russie 66:252.

4. Choiseul to Pitt, March 26, 1761, AMAE, CP Angl. 433:53–54.

5. Newcastle quoting Pitt in Nish, *French Canadians,* 27.

6. Pitt to Choiseul, April 8, 1761, AMAE, CP Angl. 433:71; Choiseul to Pitt, April 19, 1761, AMAE, CP Angl. 433:72.

7. Pease, *Boundary Disputes,* xcv–xcvi.

8. Choiseul Instructions to Bussy, May 23, 1761, AMAE, CP Angl. 443:119.

9. "Memoire sur les limites a donner a la Louisiana du cote des Colonies Angloises et du cote du Canada, en cas de cession de ce dernier pays," August 10, 1761, AMAE, CP Angl. 444:150 et seq.; Choiseul to Ossun, September 20, 1762, AMAE, CP Esp. 537:160.

10. Memoir on the Terms of Peace, April 13, 1761, BL, Add. MSS 33,030; Pease, *Boundary Disputes,* 291.

11. Hardwicke to Newcastle, March 17, 1761, BL, Add. MSS 32,920:2701; Pease, *Boundary Disputes,* 289.

12. Morton to Hardwicke, June 15, 1761, BL, Add. MSS 32,924:104; Pease, *Boundary Disputes,* 301–302.

13. Choiseul, January 27, 1761, AMAE, CP Esp. 531:95–97; Ossun to Choiseul, February 9 and 14, 1761, AMAE, CP Esp. 531:188, 232; Choiseul to Ossun, February 17 and 24, 1761, AMAE, CP Esp. 531:266, 295; Choiseul to Ossun, March 3, 1761, AMAE, CP Esp. 531:325.

14. Choiseul to Ossun, April 21, May 2, June 29, 1761, AMAE, CP Esp. 532:68, 235, 383.

15. Draft Treaty to Ossun, June 2, 1761, AMAE, CP Esp. 532:316.

16. Ossun to Choiseul, May 25, 1761, AMAE, CP Esp. 532:265.

17. Bussy to Choiseul, June 11 and 14, 1761, AMAE, CP Esp. 443:164, 195; Waddington, *La Guerre,* 4:599.

18. Pease, *Boundary Disputes,* ci–cii, cxiii–cxxiv.

19. Choiseul to Ossun, June 30, 1761, AMAE, CP Esp. 532:488.

20. Ibid.

21. French Proposals of July 15, 1761, AMAE, CP Angl. 444:8.

22. Pitt's Ultimatum, July 29, 1761, AMAE, CP Angl. 444:87.

23. Williams, *Life of William Pitt*, 2:84; Innis, *Cod Fisheries*, 119; Rashed, *Peace of Paris*, 102–108.

24. Choiseul's Speech to the Council, August 1, 1761, quoted in Pease, *Boundary Disputes*, 336–41.

25. Ultimatum of France, August 5, 1761, AMAE, CP Angl. 444:118.

26. Memoir on Canada Boundary to Bussy, August 10, 1761, AMAE, CP Angl. 444:150; Draft Proposals for Louisiana Boundary, August 18, 1761, AMAE, Etats-Unis suppl. 6:117, 118.

27. British Answer to French Ultimatum, August 30, 1761, AMAE, CP Angl. 444:233.

28. Bussy to Choiseul, August 30, 18, and 25, 1761, AMAE, CP Angl. 444:216, 164, 202.

29. Ibid.

30. French-Spanish Convention, July 15, 1761, AMAE, CP Esp. 533:102.

31. Choiseul to Bussy, July 15, 1761, AMAE, CP Angl. 533:51; Bussy to Choiseul, July 21 and 26, 1761, AMAE, CP Angl. 533:32, 59.

32. Ossun to Choiseul, July 27 and 31, 1761, AMAE, CP Esp. 533:145, 179; Ossun to Choiseul, August 3 and 10, 1761, AMAE, CP Esp. 533:223, 231; Choiseul to Ossun, July 31 and August 1, 1761, AMAE, CP Esp. 533:173, 210.

33. Bussy to Choiseul, July 31, 1761, AMAE, CP Angl. 444:100; Choiseul to Bussy, August 5 and 10, 1761, AMAE, CP Angl. 444:118, 145.

34. Pares, *War and Trade*, 574–75.

35. Choiseul Memoir, September 6 and 9, 1761, AMAE, CP Angl. 444:255, 266; Bussy to Choiseul, September 19, 1761, AMAE, CP Angl. 444:311.

36. Bussy to Choiseul, September 9 and 19, 1761, AMAE, CP Angl. 444:264, 266.

37. Choiseul report to Council, September 6, 1761, AMAE, CP Angl. 444:255; Choiseul to Bussy, September 9, 1761, AMAE, CP Angl. 444:264; Waddington, *La Guerre*, 4:591–93.

38. Quoted in Pares, *War and Trade*, 584.

39. Quoted in Corbett, *England in the Seven Years' War*, 2:206.

40. Ossun to Choiseul, December 10, 1761, AMAE, CP Esp. 534:269.

41. Viry to Solar, December 13 and 15, 1761; Solar to Viry, December 13, 1761; Choiseul to Solar, December 8, 1761, all in Viry-Solar Correspondence, CL, Shelburne MSS 9:13–16, 18–25, 39, 46–49.

42. Bosher, "French Government's Motives," 59–78; Roy, *Bigot et sa Bande*; Fregault, *Canada: The War of Conquest*.

12. Last Gambles, 1762 and 1763

Epigraph 1. Choiseul, *Mémoires*, 122.

Epigraph 2. Bernis, *Mémoires*, 183.

1. Choiseul to Ossun, April 5, 1762; May 4 and 29, 1762, AMAE, CP Esp. 536–39. See also Corbett, *England in the Seven Years' War*, 2:303–17.

2. Middleton, *Bells of Victory*, 204, 206.

3. Scott, "Frederick II," 153–75.

4. Viry to Solar, January 5 and 12, 1762; Solar to Viry, January 5, 1762, February 1, 1762, and February 23, 1762, all in Viry-Solar Correspondence, CL, Shelburne MSS 9:13–16, 18–25, 36–37, 46–49, 50–58.

5. Egremont to Choiseul, February 22, 1762, CL, Shelburne MSS 9:69–71.

6. Viry to Solar, February 9, 1762, CL, Shelburne MSS 9:41–42; Viry to Solar, March 12 and 23, 1762, CL, Shelburne MSS 9:81–82, 85–86; Solar to Viry, February 11, 1762, CL, Shelburne MSS 9:63–65; Solar to Viry, April 1, 1762, CL, Shelburne MSS 9:83–84.

7. Fortescue, *History of the British Army*, 2:548–50.

8. Viry to Solar, March 16 and 27 (two letters), 1762, CL, Shelburne MSS 9:82, 88–95, 96–99; George III diplomatic declaration, April 8, 1762, CL, Shelburne MSS 9:105–107; Choiseul to Solar, April 15, 1762, CL, Shelburne MSS 9:118–27.

9. Viry to Solar, May 4, 1762, CL, Shelburne MSS 9:154–58.

10. Egremont to Viry, May 1 and 20, 1762, CL, Shelburne MSS 9:169, 231–32; Viry to Solar, May 22, 1762, CL, Shelburne MSS 9:239–45; Choiseul to Solar, May 23 and 25, 1762, CL, Shelburne MSS 9:249–57, 258–61.

11. Choiseul to Solar, May 12, 1762, CL, Shelburne MSS 9:307.

12. Choiseul Memoir, May 29, 1762, CL, Shelburne MSS 9:261–79.

13. Choiseul to Solar, May 28, 1762, CL, Shelburne MSS 9:284.

14. Viry to Solar, June 4, 11, 15, and 28, 1762; Solar to Viry, June 24 and 27, 1762; Choiseul to Solar, May 25, 26, and 28, 1762, CL, Shelburne MSS 10:1–12, 175–76, 25–28, 29–30, 9:258–61, 282–84, 284.

15. Waddington, *La Guerre*, 5:287.

16. Fortescue, *History of the British Army*, 2:554–56.

17. Corbett, *England in the Seven Years' War*, 2:282; Fortescue, *History of the British Army*, 2:550–53.

18. Plan de campagne par mer pour l'annee 1762, Plan to attack Bahia and Rio de Janeiro, October 19, 1762, AN Marine, B4 104, 105.

19. Fortescue, *History of the British Army*, 2:553–555.

20. Viry to Solar, June 28, 1762; French peace treaty draft, June 28, 1762, both in CL, Shelburne MSS 10:29–30, 108.

21. Viry to Solar, July 12, 1762, CL, Shelburne MSS 10:302.

22. Choiseul to Solar, June 29, 1762, CL, Shelburne MSS 10:132–38; Solar to Viry, July 4 and 5 (two letters), 1762, CL, Shelburne MSS 10:204–10, 216–24,

216–24; Viry to Solar, July 6 and 12, 1762, CL, Shelburne MSS 10:236–40, 302–20. See Pease, *Boundary Disputes*, ccxxxi–clvi.

23. Grimaldi quotes from Grimaldi to Choiseul, July 20, 1762, AMAE, CP Esp. 536:521. See also Viry to Solar, June 28, 1762, CL, Shelburne MSS 10:176–79; and Solar to Viry, July 20 and 21, 1762, CL, Shelburne MSS 10:326–33, 330–36.

24. Choiseul to Solar, July 21, 1762, CL, Shelburne MSS 10:356–61. See also Grimaldi to Choiseul, July 20, 1720; Choiseul to Grimaldi, July 21, 1762; Ossun to Choiseul, August 2, 1762, AMAE, CP Esp. 536:521, 522, 497, 537:4.

25. Choiseul to Solar, July 21, 1762, CL, Shelburne MSS 10:361–65; Solar to Viry, July 20 and 21 (two letters), 1762, CL, Shelburne MSS 10:326–30, 423–28, 428–33.

26. Solar to Viry, September 5, 1762, CL, Shelburne MSS 11:303.

27. Egremont to Choiseul-Chevigny, July 31, 1762, CL, Shelburne MSS 11:8–16; Egremont to Viry, July 31, 1762, CL, Shelburne MSS 11:32–52; Viry to Solar, August 1, 1762, CL, Shelburne MSS 11:52–69; Choiseul to Solar, August 1, 1762, CL, Shelburne MSS 11:85–87; Solar to Choiseul, August 4, 1762, CL, Shelburne MSS 11:88–92.

28. Ossun to Choiseul, August 2, 1762, AMAE, CP Esp. 537:4.

29. Solar to Viry, August 12 (three letters), 1762, CL, Shelburne MSS 11:99–103, 114–33, 136–43. Quote from Memoir on Louisiana, August 1762, AMAE, CP Angl. 446:306.

30. Choiseul to Solar, August 12, 1762, CL, Shelburne MSS 11:103–13; Solar to Viry, August 26, 1762, CL, Shelburne MSS 11:254–55; September 12, 1762 (two letters), CL, Shelburne MSS 11:258–65, 361–66; Viry to Solar, September 1, 1762, CL, Shelburne MSS 11:309–10; Choiseul Instructions to Nivernais, September 2, 1762, AMAE, CP Angl. 447:13.

31. Nivernais to Choiseul-Chevigny, September 16 and 18, 1762, AMAE, CP Angl. 447:83, 79; Choiseul-Chevigny to Nivernais, September 19 and 20, 1762, AMAE, CP Angl. 447:92, 100.

32. Choiseul to Ossun, September 20, 1762, AMAE, CP Esp. 537:184.

33. Quoted in Pease, *Boundary Disputes*, clv.

34. Nivernais to Choiseul-Chevigny, September 16, 1762, AMAE, CP Angl. 447:83.

35. Nivernais to Choiseul-Chevigny, September 29, 1762, AMAE, CP Angl. 447:182.

36. Nivernais to Choiseul-Chevigny, September 15, 1762, AMAE, CP Angl. 447:179.

37. Ibid.

38. Choiseul-Chevigny to Nivernais, October 3, 1762, AMAE, CP Angl. 447:221; Nivernais to Choiseul-Chevigny, October 11, 1762, AMAE, CP Angl. 447:278; Ossun to Choiseul, September 29, 1762, Choiseul to Ossun, October 2 and 20, 1762, AMAE, CP Esp. 537:201, 208, 256, 279.

39. Ossun to Choiseul, October 10, 1762, AMAE, CP Esp. 537:227.

40. Louis XV to Charles III, October 10, 1762, AMAE, CP Esp. 537:246; Choiseul to Ossun, October 9, 1762; November 28, 1762, AMAE, CP Esp. 537:215, 223, 355.

41. Ossun to Choiseul, October 22, 1762, AMAE, CP Esp. 537:266; Ossun to Choiseul, November 12 and 15, 1762, AMAE, CP Esp. 537:315, 326.

42. For an excellent overview of the geopolitical context, specific negotiations, and results, see Calloway, *Scratch of a Pen.*

43. Nivernais to Choiseul, October 12, 24 (two letters), 25, and 29, 1762; Choiseul-Chevigny to Nivernais, October 31, 1762, December 26, all in AMAE, CP Angl. 447:288, 351, 355, 361, 377, 425; Nivernais to Choiseul-Chevigny, December 30, 1762, AMAE, CP Angl. 448:443; Nivernais to Choiseul-Chevigny, January 5, 10, 12, and 14, 1763, AMAE, CP Angl. 449:39, 76, 91, 99; French treaty drafts to Whitehall, AMAE, CP Angl. 448:124, 181.

44. Choiseul to Ossun, November 3, 1762, AMAE, CP Esp. 537:290.

45. Choiseul-Chevigny to Nivernais, November 3, 1762, AMAE, CP Angl. 448:11.

46. Louis XV to Charles III, November 3, 1762, AMAE, CP Esp. 537:292.

47. Choiseul diary, February 10, 1763, in Bibliothèque Mazarine, 2388:43.

48. Louis to Broglie, February 26, 1763, Louis XV, *Correspondance*, 1:112.

13. Distant Thunder

Epigraph 1. Quoted in Bingham, *Wit and Wisdom*, 72.

Epigraph 2. Voltaire, *Candide*, 13.

1. Riley, *Seven Years' War*, 138–39, 183, 231.

2. Dupaquier, *La Population Française*, 34–35; Choiseul diary, January 16, 1763, in Bibliothèque Mazarine, 2388:19–20; Vergé-Franceschi, *La Marine Française*, 140.

3. Riley, *Seven Years' War*, 14–16, 107, 110.

4. Ibid., 110; Le Goff and Meyer, "Les Constructions navales."

5. Imbert and Legoherel, *Histoire Economique*; Labrousse, *Crise de l'Economie Françoise*; Taylor, "Noncapitalist Wealth"; Gisey, "Rules of Inheritance," 271–89.

6. Quoted in Walpole, *Memoirs of George III*, 1:76.

7. Middleton, *Bells of Victory*, 84–85.

8. Oliva, *Misalliance*, 154.

9. Quoted in Durant and Durant, *Age of Voltaire*, 708.

10. Bourlamaque, Memoir on Canada, August 1763, *NYCD*, 10:1139–55.

Bibliography

Manuscript Collections

ENGLAND
British Library Additional Manuscripts

FRANCE
Archives du Ministère des Affaires Étrangères: correspondance politique avec
Angleterre, Espagne, Russie; dossiers personnels; mémoire et documents;
correspondance consulaire
Archives Nationales: Colonies, series B, C11a, and C11e; affaires étrangère;
ministère de la marine; correspondance consulaire
Bibliothèque Nationale: Salle des Manuscrits, Nouvelles Acquisitions Françaises;
Manuscrit françaises; Nouvelles à la main; Département des manuscrits

UNITED STATES
William L. Clement Library, University of Michigan, Ann Arbor, Michigan: Viry-
Solar Correspondence; Shelburne Collection, vols. 9, 10, 11; William
Mildmay Papers

Books and Articles

Abarca, Ramon. "Classical Diplomacy and Bourbon 'Revanche' Strategy, 1763–
1770." *Review of Politics* 32 (1970): 313–37.

Aiton, Arthur Scott. "The Diplomacy of the Louisiana Cession by France to Spain." *American Historical Review* 36, no. 4 (1930:) 701–20.

Albion, Robert G. *Forests and Sea Power: The Timber Problem of the Royal Navy, 1652–1862.* Cambridge, Mass.: Harvard University Press, 1926.

Alvord, Clarence Walworth. *The Mississippi Valley in British Politics: A Study of the Trade, Land Speculation, and Experiments in Imperialism Culminating in the American Revolution.* 2 vols. 1916. Reprint, New York: Russell and Russell, 1959.

Anderson, Fred. *Crucible of War: The Seven Years' War and the Fate of Empire in British North America, 1754–1766.* New York: Vintage, 2000.

Anderson, M. S. *Europe in the Eighteenth Century.* New York: Holt, Rinehart and Winston, 1961.

André, Louis. *Michel Le Tellier et L'organization de L'armée Monarchique.* Paris: Felix Alcan, 1906.

Andrews, Kenneth R. *Trade, Plunder, and Settlement: Maritime Enterprise and the Genesis of the British Empire, 1480–1630.* Cambridge: Cambridge University Press, 1984.

d'Angerville, Mouffle. *Vie Privée de Louis XV, ou Principaux Événements, Particularités et Anecdotes de on Regne.* 4 vols. London: J. P. Lyton, 1781.

Antoine, Michel. "Le Conseil des dépêches sous le règne de Louis XV." *Bibliothèque de l'Ecole des Chartres* 3, no. 3 (1953): 158–208.

———. *Le Conseil du Roi sous le Règne de Louis XV.* Paris: Droz, 1970.

———. "Les Conseils des finances sous le règne de Louis XV." *Revue d'Histoire Moderne et Contemporaine* 5, no. 3 (1958): 161–200.

———. "L'Entourage des ministres aux XVIIe et XVIIIe siècles." In *Origines et Histoires des Cabinets des Ministres en France.* Edited by Michael Antoine et al. Geneva: Libraire Droz, 1975.

———. *Le Gouvernment et l'administration sous Louis XV: Dictionnaire Bibliographie.* Paris: CNRS, 1978.

———. *Louis XV.* Paris: Libraire Artheme Fayard, 1989.

Antoine, Michel, and D. Ozanam. "Le Secret du Roi." In *Annuaire-Bulletin de la Société de l'Histoire de France, 1954–55.* Paris: Société de l'Histoire, 1954.

Aquila, Richard. *The Iroquois Restoration: Iroquois Diplomacy on the Colonial Frontier, 1701–1754.* Detroit: Wayne State University Press, 1983.

Argenson, René-Louis de Voyer, marquis d'. *Journal et Mémoires du Marquis d'Argenson.* Edited by E. J. Rathéry. 9 vols. Paris: Renouard, 1759–1767.

———. *Journal and Memoirs of the Marquis d'Argenson.* Translated by Katharine Prescott Wormeley. 2 vols. Boston: Hardy, Pratt, 1901.

Arredondo, Antonio de. *Arredondo's Historical Proof of Spain's Title to Georgia: A Contribution to the History of One of Spain's Borderlands.* Edited by Herbert E. Bolton. Berkeley: University of California Press, 1925.

Asprey, Robert B. *Frederick the Great: The Magnificent Enigma.* New York: Ticknor and Fields, 1986.

Atkins, Thomas B., ed. *Selections from the Public Documents of the Province of Nova Scotia.* Halifax, NS: Charles Annand, 1869.

"Attack and Repulse at Ticonderoga, July 1758." *Bulletin of the Fort Ticonderoga Museum* 7, no. 1 (January 1945): 15–18.

Autrand, Françoise. *Naissance d'un Grand Corps de l'État: Les Gens du Parlement de Paris, 1345–1454.* Paris: Fayard, 1981.

Ayling, Stanley. *The Elder Pitt, Earl of Chatham.* London: Collins, 1976.

Back, Francis, and Rene Chartrand. "Canadian Militia, 1750–1760." *Military Collector and Historian* 34, no. 1 (Spring 1984): 18–21.

———. "French Engineers, New France, 1750–1763." *Military Collector and Historian* 38, no. 1 (Spring 1986): 26–27.

Bailey, Alfred Goldworthy. *The Conflict of European and Eastern Algonkian Cultures, 1504–1700.* Toronto: University of Toronto Press, 1969.

Bain, R. Nisbet. *The Daughter of Peter the Great: A History of Russian Diplomacy and of the Russian Court under the Empress Elizabeth Petrovna, 1741–1762.* New York: E. P. Dutton, 1900.

———. *Gustavus III and His Contemporaries, 1746–1792.* 2 vols. London: Constable, 1894.

———. *Peter III, Emperor of Russia.* New York: E. P. Dutton, 1902.

Balcom, B. A. *The Cod Fishery of Isle Royale, 1713–58.* Quebec: Canadian Government Publication Centre, 1984.

Bamford, P. W. *Forests and French Sea Power, 1660–1789.* Toronto: University of Toronto Press, 1956.

Barbier, Edmond-Jean-François. *Chronique de la Régence et du Règne de Louis XV (1718–1763).* 8 vols. Paris: Société de l'histoire de France, Didot-Frère, 1857.

———. *Journal Historique et Anecdotique du Règne de Louis XV.* 8 vols. Paris: Didot-Frère, 1857.

"The Battle of Carillon." *Bulletin of the Fort Ticonderoga Museum* 2, no. 8 (July 1930): 69–78.

Baugh, Daniel A. *British Naval Administration in the Age of Walpole.* Princeton, N.J.: Princeton University Press, 1965.

———. *The Global Seven Years War, 1754–1763: Britain and France in a Great Power Contest.* Harlow, UK: Longman, 2011.

Baxter, Douglas Clark. "Pension Expectations of the French Military Commis." In *Adapting to Conditions: War and Society in the Eighteenth Century,* edited by Maarten Ultee, 177–234. Tuscaloosa: University of Alabama Press, 1986.

———. "Premier Commis in the War Department in the Latter Part of the Reign of Louis XIV." *Proceedings of the Western Society For French History* 8 (1981): 81–89.

Baxter, S. B., ed. *England's Rise to Greatness.* Berkeley: University of California Press, 1983.

Beattie, Judith, and Bernard Pothier. "The Battle of the Restigouche." In *Canadian Historic Series, Occasional Papers in Archaeology and History, no. 16.* Ottawa: Department of Indian and Northern Affairs, 1977.

Behrens, Betty. "Nobles, Privileges, and Taxes in France at the End of the Ancien Regime." *Economic History Review*, 2nd ser., 15, no. 3 (1963): 451–75.

———. "A Revision Defended: Nobles, Privileges, and Taxes in France." *French Historical Studies* 9, no. 3 (Spring 1976): 521–27.

Behrens, C. B. A. *Society, Government, and the Enlightenment: The Experiences of Eighteenth-Century France and Prussia.* New York: Harper and Row, 1985.

Beik, Paul H. *A Judgment of the Old Regime: Being a Survey by the Parlement of Provence of the French Economic and Fiscal Policies at the Close of the Seven Years' War.* New York: AMS Press, 1967.

Bernier, Olivier. *Louis the Beloved: The Life of Louis XV.* Garden City, N.Y.: Doubleday, 1984.

Bernis, Cardinal de. *Mémoires.* Paris: Mercure de France, 1986.

Bernstorff, Johann Hartwig, Graf von, and Étienne-François, duc de Choiseul. *Correspondance entre le Comte Johan Hartvig Ernst Bernstorff et le Duc de Choiseul, 1758–1766.* Paris: Gyldendal, 1871.

Bingham, Colin, ed. *Wit and Wisdom: A Public Affairs Miscellany.* Melbourne: Melbourne University Press, 1982.

Black, Jeremy. "British Foreign Policy in the Eighteenth Century: A Survey." *Journal of British Studies* 26 (1987): 26–53.

———. *Pitt the Elder.* New York: Cambridge University Press, 1992.

Bonnechose, Charles de. *Montcalm et le Canada Français.* Paris: Bibliobazar, 2008.

Bordes, M. *L'administration Provinciale et Municipale en France au XVIIIE Siècle.* Paris: Société d'Edition d'Enseignement Supérieur, 1972.

Borneman, Walter. *The French and Indian War: Deciding the Fate of North America.* New York: HarperCollins, 2006.

Bory, Gabriel de. *Mémoires sur l'Administration de la Marine et Colonies.* Paris: P. D. Pierres, 1789–90.

Bosher, J. F. *The Canada Merchants, 1713–1763.* Oxford: Oxford University Press, 1987.

———. "Financing the French Navy in the Seven Years' War: Beaujon, Goosens et Campagnie in 1759." *Business History* 28, no. 3 (July 1986): 115–33.

———. *French Finances, 1770–1795: From Business to Bureaucracy.* Cambridge: Cambridge University Press, 1970.

———. "The French Government's Motives in the 'Affair du Canada,' 1761–63." *English Historical Review* 96, no. 378 (January 1981): 59–72.

Bougainville, Louis Antoine de. *Adventure in the Wilderness: The American Journals of Louis Antoine de Bougainville, 1756–1760.* Translated and edited by Edward Hamilton. Norman: University of Oklahoma Press, 1964.

Bourde, André J. *Agronomie et Agronomes en France au XVIIIe Siècle.* 3 vols. Paris: Severn, 1967.

Bourguet, Alfred. *Le Duc de Choiseul et l'Alliance Espagnole.* Paris: Plon, 1906.

———. "Le Duc de Choiseul et l'Alliance Espagnole, âpres le Pacte de Famille." *Revue Historique* 94 (1907): 1–27.

———. "Le Duc de Choiseul et l'Angleterre, la Mission de Monsieur de Bussy a Londres." *Revue Historique* 71 (1899): 1–32.

———. "Le Duc de Choiseul et l'Angleterre, Les Pourparlers de la Haye." *Revue d'Histoire Diplomatique* 17 (1903): 456–68, 541–56.

———. *Études sur la Politique Étrangère du Duc de Choiseul.* Paris: Plon, 1907.

Boxer, C. R. *The Dutch Seaborne Empire.* London: Penguin, 1991.

Brasseaux, Carl A. *The Founding of New Acadia: The Beginnings of Acadian Life in Louisiana, 1765–1803.* Baton Rouge: Louisiana State University Press, 1987.

Brecher, Frank W. *Losing a Continent: France's North American Policy, 1753–1763.* Westport, Conn.: Greenwood Press, 1998.

Brierre, Annie. *Le Duc de Choiseul: La France sous Louis XV.* Paris: Albatros, 1986.

"British Casualty List at Carillon." *Bulletin of the Fort Ticonderoga Museum* 2, no. 8 (July 1930): 76–78.

Broglie, Albert, duc de. *L'alliance Autrichienne.* Paris: Lévy, 1895.

———. *Correspondance Secrète du Comte de Broglie Avec Louis XV (1756–1784).* Edited by D. Ozanam and M. Antoine. 2 vols. Paris: Société de l'histoire de France, 1956–61.

———. *Frederic II et Louis XV.* 2 vols. Paris: Lévy, 1883.

———. *La Paix D'aix-La-Chapelle: 1748.* Paris: Lévy, 1895.

———. *Le Secret Du Roi, 1752–1774: Louis XV et Ses Agents Diplomatiques.* 2 vols. Paris: Cassell, 1878.

Brown, George, David M. Hayne, Francess G. Halpenny, and Ramsay Cook, eds. *Dictionary of Canadian Biography.* Toronto: University of Toronto Press, 1966–.

Brown, Peter Douglas. *William Pitt, Earl of Chatham: The Great Commoner.* London: Allen and Unwin, 1978.

Browning, R. *The Duke of Newcastle.* New Haven, Conn.: Yale University Press, 1975.

———. "The Duke of Newcastle and the Imperial Election Plan, 1749–1754." *Journal of British Studies* 7, no. 1 (1976): 28–47.

Brumwell, Stephen. *White Devil: A True Story of War, Savagery, and Vengeance in Colonial America.* New York: Da Capo, 2004.

Buffington, Arthur H. "The Canada Expedition of 1746: Its Relation to British Politics." *American Historical Review* 45 (1940): 552–80.

Buot de l'Epine, Anne. "Les Bureaux de la Guerre à la fin de l'Ancien Régime." *Revue d'Histoire de Droit Français et Étranger* 54 (1976): 533–58.

Burt, Alfred LeRoy. *The Old Province of Quebec.* Toronto: Ryerson Press, 1933.

Butler, Rohan. *Choiseul.* Vol. 1, *Father and Son, 1719–1754.* Oxford: Clarendon Press, 1980.

Calloway, Colin G. *The Scratch of a Pen: 1765 and the Transformation of North America.* New York: Oxford University Press, 2006.

Cardy, Michael. "The Memoirs of Pierre Pouchot: A Soldier's View of a Doomed Campaign." *War, Literature, and the Arts* 4 (Spring 1992): 1–23.

Carre, Henri. *Le Regne de Louis XV, 1715–1774.* Paris: Hachette, 1907.

Carter, Alice Clare. "The Dutch as Neutrals in the Seven Years' War." *International and Comparative Law Quarterly* 12, no. 3 (July 1963): 818–34.

———. *The Dutch Republic in Europe in the Seven Years War.* Coral Gables, Fla.: University of Miami Press, 1971.

Casanova, Giacomo. *The History of My Life.* 6 vols. New York: Harcourt, Brace, and World, 1967.

———. *The Memoirs of Jacques Casanova de Seingalt.* Edited by Frederick A. Blossom. Translated by Arthur Machen. 8 vols. New York: Regency House, 1938.

Casgrain, H. R., ed. *Extraits des Archives des Ministères de la Marine et de la Guerre à Paris.* Quebec: Demers and Frère, 1890.

———. *Montcalm et Lévis.* 2 vols. Quebec: Hachette, 2013.

Cassedy, James H. *Demography in Early America: Beginnings of the Statistical Mind, 1600–1800.* Cambridge, Mass.: Harvard University Press, 1969.

Catherine II. *Correspondence of Catherine the Great When Grand Duchess.* Translated by Earl of Ilchester. London: Thornton Butterworth, 1928.

———. *Memoirs of Catherine the Great.* Translated by Moura Budberg. Edited by Dominique Maroger. New York: Collier, 1961.

Cavanaugh, G. J. "Nobles, Privileges, and Taxes in France: A Revision Revised." *French Historical Studies* 8, no. 4 (Fall 1974): 681–92.

Chandler, David. *The Art of Warfare in the Age of Marlborough.* New York: Sarpedon, 1994.

Charlevoix, Pierre-François-Xavier de. *Histoire de Description Generale de la Nouvelle France, avec le Journal Historique d'un Voyage Fait par Ordre du Roi dans l'Amérique Septentrionnale.* 6 vols. Paris: Hachette, 1744.

Chartier, Roger. *The Cultural Origins of the French Revolution.* Translated by Lydia G. Cochrane. Durham, N.C.: Duke University Press, 1991.

Chartrand, Rene. *Canadian Military Heritage.* Vol. 1, *1000–1754.* Montreal: Art Global, 1993.

———. *Canadian Military Heritage.* Vol. 2, *1755–1871.* Montreal: Art Global, 1993.

———. "Les Drapeaux en Nouvelle-France." *Conservation Canada* 1, no. 1 (1974): 24–26.

———. *The French Soldier in Colonial America.* Ottawa: Museum Restoration Service, 1984.

———. "The Troops of French Louisiana, 1699–1769." *Military Collector and Historian* 25, no. 2 (Summer 1973): 58–65.

Chaussegros de Léry, Gaspard-Joseph. *Inventaire des Papiers de Léry.* Edited by Pierre-George Roy. 3 vols. Quebec: Archives de la Province de Québec, 1939–40.

Chaussinand-Nogaret, Guy. *The French Nobility in the Eighteenth Century: From Feudalism to Enlightenment.* Translated by William Doyle. Cambridge: Cambridge University Press, 1985.

Cheke, Marcus. *The Cardinal de Bernis.* London: Cassell, 1958.

Chevalier, Louis Édouard. *Histoire de la Marine Française depuis les Débuts de la Monarchie Jusqu'au Traité de Paix de 1763.* Paris: Hachette, 1902.

Chiappe, Jean-François. *Louis XV.* Paris: Perin, 1996.

Childs, John. *Armies and Warfare in Europe, 1648–1789.* New York: Holmes and Meier, 1975.

Choiseul, Étienne-François, duc de. *Choiseul à Rome, 1754–1757: Lettres et Mémoires Inédits.* Edited by Maurice Boutry. Paris: Lévy, 1895.

———. *Mémoires du Duc de Choiseul, 1719–1785.* Paris: Mercure de France, 1987.

Christelow, Allan. "Economic Background of the Anglo-Spanish War of 1762." *Journal of Modern History* 18 (1946): 22–36.

———. "French Interest in the Spanish Empire During the Ministry of the Duc de Choiseul, 1759–1771." *Hispanic American Historical Review* 21 (1941): 515–537.

———. "Great Britain and the Trades from Cadiz and Lisbon to Spanish America and Brazil, 1759–1783." *Hispanic American Historical Review* 27 (1947): 2–29.

Church, Clive H. *Revolution and Red Tape: The French Ministerial Bureaucracy, 1770–1850.* Oxford: Clarendon Press, 1981.

Clark, Andrew Hill. *Acadia: The Geography of Early Nova Scotia.* Madison: University of Wisconsin Press, 1968.

Clark, J. C. D. *The Dynamics of Change: The Crisis of the 1750s and the English Party System.* New Haven, Conn.: Yale University Press, 1982.

Clark, John G. *La Rochelle and the Atlantic Economy during the Eighteenth Century.* Baltimore: Johns Hopkins Press, 1981.

Clayton, T. R. "The Duke of Newcastle and the Origins of the Seven Years' War." *Historical Journal* 23, no. 2 (1981): 571–603.

Cole, Charles W. *Colbert and a Century of French Mercantilism.* 2 vols. Hamden, Conn.: Archon, 1939.

Cole, W. A. "Trends in Eighteenth Century Smuggling." *Economic History Review,* 2nd ser., 10 (1957–58): 394–410.

Conn, Stetson. *Gibraltar in British Diplomacy in the Eighteenth Century.* New Haven: Yale University Press, 1942.

Conrad, Glenn R. *The Cajuns: Essays on Their History and Culture.* Lafayette: Southwestern Louisiana University Press, 1978.

Cooke, Jacob Ernest, ed. *Encyclopedia of the North American Colonies.* 3 vols. New York: Scribner's, 1993.

Coolidge, Guy Omeron. *The French Occupation of the Champlain Valley from 1609 to 1759.* 1838. Reprint, Harrison, N.Y.: Harbor Hill Books, 1979.

Corbett, Julian S. *England in the Seven Years' War: A Study in Combined Strategy.* 2 vols. London: Longmans, Green, 1907.

Corvisier, André. *L'Armée Française de la Fin du XVIIe Siècle au Ministère du Choiseul.* 2 vols. Paris: Presses Universitaires de France, 1964.

————. *Armies and Societies in Europe, 1494–1789.* Translated by Abigail T. Siddall. Bloomington: University of Indiana Press, 1979.

————. "Clientèles et fidélités dans l'armée française aux XVIIe et XVIIIe siecles." In *Hommage à Roland Mousnier, Clientèles et Fidélités en Europe à L'époque Moderne,* edited by Yves Durand, 217–18. Paris: Presses Universitaires de France, 1981.

————. "La société militaire française au temps de la Nouvelle France." *Histoire Sociale/Social History* 10, no. 20 (1977): 219–27.

Courville, Louis de. *See* Webster, John Clarence.

Cox, Bruce A., ed. *Native People, Native Lands: Canadian Indians, Inuits and Metis.* Ottawa: Carleton University Press, 1988.

Crane, V. W. *The Southern Frontier, 1670–1732.* Durham, N.C.: Duke University Press, 1928.

Crankshaw, Edward. *Maria Theresa.* New York: Viking, 1969.

Crouzet, François. "Angleterre et France au XVIIIe Siècle: Essai d'analyse comparée de deux croissances économiques." *Annales E.S.C.* 21, no. 2 (March–April 1966): 254–91.

Crow, Thomas E. *Painters and Public Life in Eighteenth-Century Paris.* New Haven, Conn.: Yale University Press, 1985.

Croÿ, Emmanuel de. *Journal Inédit.* Paris: Ulan Press, 2012.

Cumberland, William August, Duke of. *Military Affairs in North America, 1748–1765: Selected Documents from the Cumberland Papers in Windsor Castle.* Edited by Stanley Pargellis. New York: Archon, 1969.

Dagnaud, G. *L'administration Centrale de la Marine Sous l'Ancien Régime.* Paris: Revue Maritime, 1912.

Dahlinger, Charles W. "The Marquis Duquesne, Sieur de Mennevilles, Founder of the City of Pittsburgh." *Western Pennsylvania Historical Magazine* 15 (1932): 2–23.

Day, Gordon M. *The Identity of the Saint Francis Indians.* Ottawa: National Museums of Canada, 1981.

Deanne, Phyllis, and W. A. Cole. *British Economic Growth, 1688–1959.* Cambridge: Cambridge University Press, 1969.

D'Eon, Chevalier de. *Mémoires de la Chevalier d'Eon.* Edited by Frederic Gaillhardet. 2 vols. Paris: Treuttel, 1866.

Devonshire, William Cavendish, Duke of. *The Devonshire Diary: William Cavendish, Fourth Duke of Devonshire, Memorandum on State of Affairs, 1759–1762.* Edited by P. D. Brown and K. W. Schweizer. London: Offices of the Royal Historical Society, 1982.

Dickinson, John A. "La guerre iroquoise et la mortalité en Nouvelle France, 1608–1666." *Revue d'Histoire de l'Amérique Française* 36, no. 1 (1982): 31–54.

Dippel, H. "Prussia's English Policy after the Seven Years' War." *Central European History* 4 (1971): 195–214.

Dorn, Walter L. *Competition for Empire, 1740–1763.* New York: Harper, 1940.

———. "Frederick the Great and Lord Bute." *Journal of Modern History* 1 (1929): 529–60.

Douville, R., and J. D. Casanova. *La Vie Quotidienne en Nouvelle-France: Le Canada de Champlain à Montcalm.* Paris: Famot, 1979.

Downey, Fairfax. *Louisbourg: Key to a Continent.* Englewood Cliffs, N.J.: Prentice-Hall, 1965.

Doyle, Wiliam. *Origins of the French Revolution.* Oxford: Oxford University Press, 1990.

———. *The Oxford History of the French Revolution.* Oxford: Oxford University Press, 1990.

Dûchene, Albert. *La Politique Coloniale de la France: Le Ministère des Colonies depuis Richelieu.* Paris: Payot, 1928.

Duclos, C. P. *Mèmoires Secrets sur les Règnes de Louis XIV et de Louis XV.* 2 vols. Lausanne: Mourer, 1791.

Duffy, Christopher. *The Army of Frederick the Great.* New York: David and Charles, 1974.

———. *The Fortress in the Age of Vauban and Frederick the Great, 1660–1789.* London: Routledge and Kegan Paul, 1985.

Dufort de Cheverny, Jean Nicolas. *Mémoires sur les Règnes de Louis XV et Louis XVI et sur la Révolution par J. N. Dufort de Cheverny.* Edited by R. De Crèvecœur. 2 vols. Paris: Plon, 1909.

Du Hausset, Nicole. *Mémoires de Madame du Hausset sur Louis XV et Madame de Pompadour.* Paris: Mercure de France, 1985.

Dull, Jonathan R. *The French Navy and the Seven Years' War.* Lincoln: University of Nebraska Press, 2005.

Dunnigan, Brian Leigh. *Siege—1759: The Campaign against Niagara.* Youngstown, N.Y.: Old Fort Niagara Association, 1986.

Dupaquier, Jacques. *La Population Françaises aux XVIIe ET XVIIIe Siècles.* Paris: Presses Universitaires de France, 1970.

Durand, Yves. *Les Fermiers-Généraux Au Xviie Siècle.* Paris: Presses Universitaires de France, 1971.

———. *Finance et Mécénat: Les Fermiers Généraux au XVIIIe Siècle.* Paris: Hachette, 1976.

———, ed. "Memoire de Jean-Joseph de la Borde, fermier général et banquier de la court." In *Annuaire-Bulletin de la Société de l'Histoire de France, 1968–69.* Paris: Société de l'Histoire, 1971.

Durant, Will, and Ariel Durant. *The Age of Voltaire: A History of Civilization in Western Europe from 1715 to 1756.* New York: Simon and Schuster, 1965.

———. *Rousseau and Revolution, A History of Civilization in France, England, and Germany from 1756, and in the Remainder of Europe from 1715 to 1789.* New York: Simon and Schuster, 1967.

Dussauge, André. *Études sur la Guerre de Sept Ans: Le Ministère de Belle-Isle.* Paris: Fournier, 1914.

Duverger de Saint-Blin, Paul François. *Mémoire pour le Sieur Duverger de Saint-Blin, Lieutenant d'infanterie dans les Troupes Étant Ci-Devant en Canada.* Paris: Moreau, 1763.

Eccles, W. J. "A Belated Review of Harold Adams Innis, *The Fur Trade in Canada.*" *Canadian Historical Review* 60, no. 4 (1979): 419–41.

———. *Canada under Louis XIV, 1663–1710.* Oxford: Oxford University Press, 1979.

———. *The Canadian Frontier, 1534–1760.* New York: Holt, Rinehart and Winston, 1969.

———. *France in America.* New York: Harper and Row, 1972.

———. "The French Forces in North America during the Seven Years' War." In *Dictionary of Canadian Biography.* Vol. 3. University of Toronto, 1974.

———. "The Fur Trade and Eighteenth-Century Imperialism." *William and Mary Quarterly,* 3rd ser., 40, no. 3 (July 1983): 341–62.

———. "The History of New France According to Francis Parkman." *William and Mary Quarterly,* 3rd ser., 18 (1961): 163–75.

———. "Montcalm, Louis-Joseph de, Marquis de Montcalm." In *Dictionary of Canadian Biography.* Vol. 3. University of Toronto, 1974.

Edmunds, David. "Pickawillany: French Military Power versus British Economics." *Western Pennsylvania Historical Magazine* 58 (1975): 169–84.

Egret, Jean. *Louis XV et l'opposition Parlementaire.* Paris: A. Colin, 1970.

Eldon, C. W. *England's Subsidy Policy towards the Continent during the Seven Years' War, 1756–1763.* Philadelphia: Lippincott, 1938.

"Extracts from Captain Moneypenny's Orderly Book, June 30 to July 7, 1758." *Bulletin of the Fort Ticonderoga Museum* 2, no. 8 (July 1930): 56–67.

Fabre, Jules. *Stanislas Auguste Poniatowski et l'Europe des Lumières.* Paris: Lévy, 1952.

Fagniez, Gustave. "Les antécédents de l'alliance Franco-Russe, 1741–1762." *Revue Hebdomadaire* (August 1916) : 316–38.

Fauteux, Aegidius. *Le Chevaliers de Saint-Louis en Canada.* Montreal: Les Edition Dix, 1940.

———. "Officiers de Montcalm." *Revue d'Histoire de l'Amérique Française* 3, no. 3 (December 1949): 367–82.

———. "Quelques officiers de Montcalm." *Revue d'Histoire de l'Amérique Française* 5, no. 3 (December 1951): 404–15.

Favier, George. *Politiques de Tous les Cabinets de l'Europe Pendant les Règnes de Louis XV et de Louis XVI.* 2 vols. Paris: Chez Buisson, 1793.

Fiedmont, Jacau de. *The Siege of Beauséjour in 1755: A Journal of the Attack on Beauséjour.* Translated by Alice Webster. Edited by John Clarence Webster. St. John, NB: New Brunswick Museum, 1936.

Filion, M. *Maurepas, Ministre de Louis XV, 1715–1749.* Montreal: Lemeac, 1967.

Fischer, David Hackett. *Champlain's Dream: The European Founding of North America.* New York: Simon and Schuster, 2008.

Flammermont, Jules F. *Les Correspondances des Agents Diplomatiques Etrangères en France avant la Révolution.* Paris: Imprimerie Nationale, 1896.

Flassan, Gaëtan de Raxis de. *Histoire Général et Raisonnée de la Diplomatie Française depuis la Fondation de la Monarchie Jusqu'à la Fin du Règne de Louis XVI, avec des Tables Chronologiques de Tous les Traités Conclus par la France.* 7 vols. Paris: Treuttel et Wurtz, 1811.

Ford, F. L. *Robe and Sword: The Regrouping of the French Aristocracy after Louis XIV.* New York: Harper, 1965.

Fortescue, J. W. *A History of the British Army.* 20 vols. London: Macmillan, 1910.

Fortier, John. *Fortress of Louisbourg.* Toronto: Oxford University Press, 1979.

Fowler, William. *Empires at War: The French and Indian War and the Struggle for North America, 1754–1763.* New York: Walker, 2005.

Franklin, Benjamin. *A Benjamin Franklin Reader.* Edited by Nathan G. Goodman. New York: Crowell, 1945.

Frederick II. *Correspondance de Frederick II, Roi de Prusse, avec le Comte Algarotti.* Berlin: Gropius, 1837.

———. *Frederick the Great on the Art of War.* Translated and edited by Jay Luvaas. New York: Da Capo Press, 1999.

Fregault, Guy. *Canada: The War of the Conquest.* Translated by Margaret M. Cameron. Toronto: Oxford University Press, 1969.

———. *François Bigot, Administrateur Française.* 2 vols. Ottawa: Institut d'histoire de l'Amérique Française, 1948.

———. *Le Grand Marquis: Pierre de Rigaud de Vaudreuil et la Louisiane.* Montreal: Fides, 1952.

Fry, Bruce W. *"An Appearance of Strength": The Fortifications of Louisbourg.* 2 vols. Ottawa: Parks Canada, 1984.

Funck-Bretano, Frantz. *The Old Regime in France.* New York: Howard Fertig, 1970.

Furcron. Thomas B., and Elizabeth Ann Boyle. "The Building of Fort Carillon, 1755–1758." *Bulletin of the Fort Ticonderoga Museum* 10 (1955): 13–67.

Gaboury, Jean-Pierre. *Le Nationalisme de Lionel Groulx: Aspects Idéologiques.* Ottawa: Éditions de l'université d'Ottawa, 1970.

Gallet, Danielle. *Madame de Pompadour du le Pouvoir Féminin.* Paris: Fayard 1985.

Gaxotte, Pierre. *Le Siècle de Louis XV. [Louis the Fifteenth and His Times].* Translated by J. L. May. London: Jonathan Cape, 1934.

Geffroy, Michel. *Recueil des Instructions Données aux Ambassadeurs de France, depuis les Traités de Westphalie.* Paris: Imprimerie Nationale, 1884.

Gelinas, Cyrille. *The Role of Fort Chambly in the Development of New France, 1665–1760.* Ottawa: Parks Canada, 1983.

Giesey, Ralph E. "Rules of Inheritance and Strategies of Mobility in Prerevolutionary France." *American Historical Review* 82, no. 2 (April 1977): 271–89.

Gilbert, Felix. "The New Diplomacy of the Eighteenth Century." *World Politics* 4 (1951–52): 1–38.

Gipson, Henry Lawrence. *A Bibliographical Guide to the History of the British Empire, 1748–1776.* New York: Knopf, 1968.

————. "British Diplomacy in the Light of Anglo-Spanish New World Issues, 1750–1757." *American Historical Review* 51, no. 4 (July 1946): 627–48.

————. *The British Empire before the American Revolution.* 15 vols. New York: Knopf, 1939–70.

————. *The British Empire before the American Revolution.* Vol. 5, *Zones of International Friction: The Great Lakes Frontier, Canada, and the West Indies, India, 1748–1754.* New York: Knopf, 1942.

————. *The British Empire before the American Revolution.* Vol. 6, *The Great War for the Empire: The Years of Defeat, 1754–1757.* New York: Knopf, 1946.

————. *The British Empire before the American Revolution.* Vol. 7, *The Great War for the Empire: The Victorious Years, 1758–1760.* New York: Knopf, 1949.

————. *The British Empire before the American Revolution.* Vol. 8, *The Great War for the Empire: The Culmination, 1760–1763.* New York: Knopf, 1954.

————. "A French Project for Victory Short of a Declaration of War, 1755." *Canadian Historical Review* 26 (1945): 351–68.

Giraud, Marcel. *A History of French Louisiana.* Vol. 1, *The Reign of Louis XIV, 1698–1715.* Baton Rouge: University of Louisiana Press, 1974.

Gisey, Ralph E. "Rules of Inheritance and Strategies of Mobility in Pre-revolutionary France." *American Historical Review* 82, no. 2 (April 1977): 271–89.

Glasson, E. *Le Parlement de Paris, son Rôle Politique depuis le Règne de Charles VII jusqu'au la Révolution.* 2 vols. Paris: Hachette, 1901.

Godfrey, William. *Pursuit of Profit and Preferment in Colonial North America: John Bradstreet's Quest.* Waterloo, Ontario: Wilfred Laurier University Press, 1982.

Gooch, G. P. *Louis XV: The Monarchy in Decline.* London: Longmans, Green, 1956.

Goodman, Dena. "Enlightenment Salons: The Convergence of Female and Philosophic Ambitions." *Eighteenth-Century Studies* 22 (Spring 1989): 329–50.

Graham, Gerald S. "The Naval Defense of British North America, 1739–1763." *Royal Historical Society Transactions,* 4th ser., 30 (1948): 95–110.

Grant, William L. "Canada versus Guadeloupe, an Episode of the Seven Years' War." *American History Review* 17, no. 4 (July 1912): 735–43.

Graves, Donald E. *French Military Terminology, 1670–1815.* Saint John, NB: New Brunswick Museum, 1979.

Green, V. H. H. *The Hanoverians, 1714–1815.* London: Arnold, 1956.

Greer, Allan. *The People of New France.* Toronto: University of Toronto Press, 1997.

Grenier, Fernand, ed. *Papiers Contrecœur et Autres Documents Concernant le Conflit Anglo-Français sur l'Ohio de 1755 à 1756.* Quebec: Les Presses Universitaires Laval, 1952.

Gruder, V. R. *The Royal Provincial Intendants: A Governing Elite in Eighteenth-Century France.* Ithaca: Cornell University Press, 1968.

Guénin, Eugène. *Montcalm.* Paris: Hardpress, 2013.

Guillaumat-Vallet, Maurice. *Le Contrôleur-Général Silhouette et ses Réformes en Matières Financière.* Paris: Plon, 1914.

Guillon, E. *Port Mahon, la France à Minorque sous Louis XV.* Paris: Presses Universitaires de France,1983.

Guizot, François M. *The History of France from the Earliest Times to the Year 1789.* New York: Peter Fenelon Collier, 1908.

Hackman, W. K. "William Pitt and the Generals: Three Case Studies in the Seven Years' War." *Albion, Proceedings of the Conference on British Studies* 3, no. 3 (1971): 128–37.

Hagerty, Gilbert. *Massacre at Fort Bull: The de Léry Expedition against Oneida Carry, 1756.* Providence, R.I.: Mowbray, 1971.

Hamelin, J. *Economie et Société en Nouvelle-France.* Quebec: Presses de l'Université Laval, 1960.

Hamer, Philip M. "Anglo-French Rivalry in the Cherokee Country, 1754–1757." *North Carolina Historical Review* 2 (July 1925): 303–22.

———, ed. *A Guide to Archives and Manuscripts in the United States.* New Haven: Yale University Press, 1961.

Hamilton, Edward Pierce. "Colonial Warfare in North America." *Massachusetts Historical Society Proceedings* 80 (1968): 3–15.

———. *The French and Indian Wars: The Story of Battles and Forts in the Wilderness.* Garden City, N.Y.: Doubleday 1962.

———. *The French Army in America.* Ottawa: Museum Restoration Service, 1967.

Hammang, Francis H. *The Marquis de Vaudreuil: New France at the Beginning of the Eighteenth Century.* Louvain, Belgium: Universite de Louvain, 1938.

Hanley, Sarah. *The "Lit de Justice" of the Kings of France: Constitutional Ideology in Legend, Ritual, and Discourse.* Princeton, N.J.: Princeton University Press, 1983.

Hardy, James D. *Judicial Politics in the Old Regime: The Parlement of Paris during the Regency.* Baton Rouge: Louisiana State University Press, 1967.

Harley, C. Knick. "British Industrialization before 1841: Evidence of Slower Growth during the Industrial Revolution." *Journal of Economic History* 42, no. 2 (June 1982): 267–89.

Hatton, Ragnhild. *George I: Elector and King.* Cambridge: Harvard University Press, 1978.

Havard, Gilles. *The Great Peace of Montreal of 1701: French-Native Diplomacy in the Seventeenth Century.* Montreal: McGill University Press, 2001.

———. *Histoire de l'Amérique Française.* Paris: Flammion, 2008.

Higginbotham, Don. "The Early American Way of War: Reconnaissance and Appraisal." *William and Mary Quarterly,* 3d ser., 44, no. 2 (April 1987): 230–73.

Higham, Robin, ed. *A Guide to Sources of British Military History.* Berkeley: University of California Press, 1971.

Higonnet, Patrice Louis-Rene. "The Origins of the Seven Years' War." *Journal of Military History* 40, no. 1 (March 1968): 57–90.

Hirsch, Adam J. "The Collision of Military Cultures in Seventeenth Century New England." *Journal of American History* 74 (1987–88): 1187–1212.

Horn, D. B. "The Cabinet Controversy on Subsidies in Time of Peace, 1749–1750." *English Historical Review* 45 (1930): 463–66.

———. *Frederick the Great and the Rise of Prussia.* London: English Universities Press, 1967.

———. *Great Britain and Europe in the Eighteenth Century.* New York: Oxford University Press, 1967.

———. "The Origins of the Proposed Election of a King of the Romans, 1748–1750." *English Historical Review* 42 (1927): 361–70.

Houlding, J. A. *Fit for Service: The Training of the British Army, 1715–1795.* Oxford: Oxford University Press, 1981.

———. *French Arms Drill of the 18th Century.* Bloomfield, Ontario: Museum Restoration Service, 1988.

Hufton, Olwen H. *The Poor of Eighteenth-Century France, 1750–1789.* Oxford: Oxford University Press, 1974.

Hughes, Ben. *The Siege of Fort William Henry: A Year on the Northeastern Frontier.* Yardley, Pa.: Westholme, 2011.

Hunt, William. "Pitt's Retirement from Office, 5 October 1761." *English Historical Review* 21 (1906) : 119–32.

Hunter, William A. *Forts on the Pennsylvania Frontier, 1753–1758.* Harrisburg: Pa.: Historical and Museum Commission, 1960.

Hutchinson, Terence. *Before Adam Smith: The Emergence of Political Economy.* Oxford: Oxford University Press, 1988.

Imbert, Jean, and Henri Legoherel. *Histoire Economique des Origines à 1789.* Paris: Presses Universitaires de France, 1974.

Innis, Harold. "Cape Breton and the French Regime." *Transactions of the Royal Society of Canada.* 2 (1935): 51–87.

———. *The Cod Fisheries: The History of an International Economy.* New Haven, Conn.: Yale University Press, 1940.

———. *The Fur Trade in Canada: An Introduction to Canadian Economic History.* New Haven, Conn.: Yale University Press, 1930.

Irvine, Dallas D. "The Newfoundland Fisheries: A French Objective in War of American Independence." *Canadian Historical Review* 13 (1932): 268–84.

Jackson, Richard A. "Peers of France and Princes of the Blood." *French Historical Studies* 7 (Spring 1971): 27–46.

Jacobs, Wilber R. *Wilderness Politics and Indian Gifts: Anglo-French Rivalry along the Ohio and Northwest Frontiers, 1748–1763.* Stanford, Calif.: Stanford University Press, 1950.

Jaenen, Cornelius J. *The French Relationship with the Native Peoples of New France and Acadia.* Ottawa: Research Branch, Indian and Northern Affairs Canada, 1984.

———. "The Role of Presents in French-Amerindian Trade." *Explorations in Canadian Economic History: Essays in Honour of Irene M. Spry.* Ottawa: University of Ottawa Press, 1985.

Jennings, Francis. *The Ambiguous Iroquois Empire: The Covenant Chain Confederation of Indian Tribes with English Colonies from Its Beginnings to the Lancaster Treaty of 1744.* New York: Norton, 1988.

————. *Empire of Fortune: Crowns, Colonies, and Tribes in the Seven Years' War in America.* New York: Norton, 1988.

————. *The Invasion of America: Indians, Colonialism, and the Cant of Conquest.* Chapel Hill: University of North Carolina Press, 1975.

Johnson, Hubert C. *Frederick the Great and His Officials.* New Haven, Conn.: Yale University Press, 1975.

Johnson, William. *The Papers of Sir William Johnson.* Edited by James Sullivan and Alexander C. Flick. 14 vols. Albany: State University of New York, 1921–1965.

Johnston, A. J. B. *Endgame, 1758: The Promise, the Glory, and the Despair of Louisborg's Last Decade.* Lincoln: University of Nebraska Press, 2007.

"Josiah Goodrich Orderbook." *Bulletin of the Fort Ticonderoga Museum* 14, no. 1 (Summer 1981): 39–61.

"Journal of Captain Samuel Cobb, May 21, 1758–October 29, 1758." *Bulletin of the Fort Ticonderoga Museum* 1, no. 3 (January 1928): 12–31.

Kalm, Peter. *Peter Kalm's Travels in North America.* Edited by Adolph B. Benson. New York: Dover, 1987.

Kaplan, H. *Russia and the Outbreak of the Seven Years' War.* Berkeley: University of California Press, 1968.

Kaplan, Steven. *Bread, Politics, and Political Economy in the Reign of Louis XV.* 2 vols. The Hague: Nijhoff, 1976.

Kellogg, Louise P., ed. "La Chapelle's Remarkable Retreat through the Mississippi Valley, 1760–61." *Mississippi Valley Historical Review* 27 (June 1935): 63–81.

Kelly, George A. "From Lese-Majeste to Lese-Nation: Treason in Eighteenth Century France." *Journal of the History of Ideas* 42 (1981): 269–86.

————. "The Machine of the Duc d'Orleans and the New Politics." *Journal of Modern History* 51 (December 1979): 667–84.

Kennedy, J. H. *Jesuit and Savage in New France.* 1950. Reprint, Hamden, Conn.: Archon, 1971.

Kennett, Lee. *The French Armies in the Seven Years' War: A Study in Military Organization and Administration.* Durham, N.C.: Duke University Press, 1967.

Kent, Donald H. *The French Invasion of Western Pennsylvania, 1753.* Harrisburg: Pennsylvania Historical and Museum Commission, 1954.

Kirchner, Walter. "Relations économique entre la France et la Russie au XVIIIe Siècle." *Revue d'Histoire Economique et Sociale* 39, no. 2 (1961): 158–97.

Knox, John. *The Siege of Quebec and the Campaigns of North America, 1757–1760, by Captain John Knox.* Edited by Brian Connell. Mississauga, Ontario: Pendragon House, 1980.

Kopperman, Paul E. *Braddock at the Monongahela.* Pittsburgh: University of Pennsylvania Press, 1977.

Kreiser, B. Robert. *Miracles, Convulsions, and Ecclesiastical Politics in Early Eighteenth-Century Paris.* Princeton, N.J.: Princeton University Press, 1978.

Krech, Shepard, ed. *Indians, Animals, and the Fur Trade: A Critique of "Keepers of the Game."* Athens: University of Georgia Press, 1981.

Kunstler, Charles. *La Vie Quotidienne sous Louis XV.* Paris: Hachette, 1953.

Labrousse, C.-E. *Crise de l'Economie Françoise la Fin de l'Ancien Régime et au Début de la Révolution.* Paris: Plon, 1944.

Labrousse, Ernest. "Les ruptures périodiques de la prospérité: Les crises économique du XVIIIe siècle." In *Histoire Economique et Sociale de la France.* Edited by Fernaud Braudel and Ernest Labrousse. Paris: Perin, 1970.

Lacour-Gayet, G. *La Marine Militaire de la France sous la Règne de Louis XV.* Paris: Libraire Ancienne, 1910.

La Motte Rouge, Daniel de. *Saint Cast le Guildo.* Quimper: L'Imprimerie Bargain, 1973.

Lanctôt, Gustave. *A History of Canada.* Vol. 3, *From the Treaty of Utrecht to the Treaty of Paris, 1713-1763.* Translated by Josephine Hambleton and Margaret M. Cameron Cambridge, Mass.: Harvard University Press, 1965.

Lanning, John Tate. *The Diplomatic History of Georgia: A Study of the Epoch of Jenkins' Ear.* Chapel Hill: University of North Carolina Press, 1936.

Lawson, Murray G. *Fur: A Study in English Mercantilism, 1700–1775.* Toronto: University of Toronto Press, 1975.

Leckie, Robert. *"A Few Acres of Snow": The Saga of the French and Indian Wars.* New York: Wiley, 1999.

Le Goff, T. J. A., and Jean Meyer. "Les constructions navales en France pendant la seconde moitié du XVIIIe siècle." *Annales E.S.C.* 26, no. 1 (January–February 1971): 173–85.

Legoherel, H. *Les Trésoriers Généraux de la Marine, 1517–1788.* Paris: Editions Cujas, 1965.

Leliepvre, Eugene, and Rene Chartrand. "Bearn Regiment, New France, 1755–1757." *Military Collector and Historian* 39, no. 3 (Fall 1987): 126–27.

———. "Corps of Cavalry, Canada, 1759–1760." *Military Collector and Historian* 28, no. 3 (Fall 1976): 131–32.

Le Loutre, Jean Louis. *The Career of the Abbé Le Loutre in Nova Scotia with a Translation of His Autobiography.* Edited by John Clarence Webster. Shediac, NB: Privately printed, 1933.

Léon, Pierre. *Aires et Structures du Commerce Français au XVIIIe Siècle.* Paris: Centre d'Histoire économique et sociale de la région lyonnaise, 1975.

Lever, Evelyne. *Madame de Pompadour: A Life.* New York: St. Martin's Griffin, 2003.

Lévis, François Gaston, duc de. *Collection des Manuscrits du Maréchal de Lévis.* Edited by H. R. Casgrain. 12 vols. Montreal: Public Archives of Canada, 1889–95.

"Life of David Perry." *Bulletin of the Fort Ticonderoga Museum* 14, no. 1 (Summer 1981): 4–8.

Lincoln, Charles Henry, ed. *Manuscript Records of the French and Indian War in the Library of the Society*. Transactions and Collections of the American Antiquarian Society 11. Worcester, Mass.: American Antiquarian Society, 1909.

Lindsay, J. O., vol. ed. *The New Cambridge Modern History*. Vol. 7, *The Old Regime, 1713–1763*. Cambridge: Cambridge University Press, 1957.

"List of French Killed and Wounded, July 8, 1758." *Bulletin of the Fort Ticonderoga Museum* 1, no. 3 (January 1928): 12.

Lodge, Sir Richard. "The Continental Policy of Great Britain, 1740–1760." *History* 16 (1931–32): 298–304.

————. *Great Britain and Prussia in the 18th Century*. New York: Oxford University Press, 1971.

Long, John C. *Mr. Pitt and America's Birthright: A Biography of William Pitt, the Earl of Chatham, 1708–1778*. New York: Frederick A. Stokes, 1940.

Louis XV. *Correspondance Secrète Inédite de Louis XV, sur la Politique Etrangère, avec le Comte de Broglie, Tercier, etc*. Edited by Edgard Boutaric. 2 vols. Paris: Plon, 1866.

Louis XV and Noailles, Adrien Maurice, duc de. *Correspondance de Louis XV et du Marechal de Noailles*. Edited by C. Rousset. 2 vols. Paris: P. Dupont, 1865.

Lounsbury, Ralph Greenlee. *The British Fishery at Newfoundland, 1634–1763*. New Haven: Yale University Press, 1934.

Lunn, Jean Elizabeth. "Agriculture and War in Canada, 1740–1760." *Canadian Historical Review* 16 (June 1935): 123–36.

Luynes, Charles-Philipe d'Albert, duc de. *Mémoires du Duc de Luynes sur la Cour de Louis XV, 1735–1758*. Edited by L. E. Dussieux and E. Soulié. 17 vols. Paris: Firmin-Didot, 1860–65.

MacLeod, D. Peter. *The Canadian Iroquois and the Seven Years' War*. Toronto: Dundern Press, 1996.

Mapp, Paul. *The Elusive West and the Contest for Empire, 1713–1763*. Chapel Hill: University of North Carolina Press, 2011.

Marion, M. *Dictionnaire des Institutions de la France au XVIIe et XVIIIe Siècles*. Paris: A. Picard, 1972.

Marlartic, Le Comte de Maures. *Journal ses Campagnes au Canada de 1755 à 1760*. Edited by Paul Gaffarel. Paris: Plon, 1890.

Marmontel, J. F. *Memoires*. 6 vols. Paris: Firman, 1804–1805.

Marriott, J. A., and C. Robinson. *The Evolution of Prussia: The Making of an Empire*. Oxford: Oxford University Press, 1937.

Martin, Calvin. *Keepers of the Game: Indian-Animal Relationships and the Fur Trade*. Berkeley: University of California Press, 1978.

Martin, Felix. *Le Marquis de Montcalm et les Dernières Années de la Colonie Française au Canada, 1756–1760*. Paris: Ulan Press, 2012.

Mathias, Peter, and Patrick O'Brien. "Taxation in Britain and France, 1715–1810: A Comparison of the Social and Economic Incidence of Taxes Collected for the Central Governments." *Journal of European Economic History* 5, no. 3 (Winter 1976): 601–50.

Mathon de la Cour, Charles Joseph. *Collection de Comptes-rendus, Pièces Authentiques, États et Tableaux Concernant les Financiers les Finances de la France Depuis 1758 Jusqu'au 1787.* Paris: Cuchet, 1788.

Matthews, George T. *The Royal General Farms in Eighteenth-Century France.* New York: Columbia University Press, 1958.

McCardell, Lee. *Ill-Starred General: Braddock of the Coldstream Guards.* 1958. Reprint, Pittsburgh: University of Pennsylvania Press, 1986.

McCloskey, Donald N. "A Mismeasurement of the Incidence of Taxation in Britain and France, 1715–1810," *Journal of European Economic History* 7, no. 1 (Spring 1978): 209–10.

McCusker, John J. *Money and Exchange in Europe and America, 1660–1775.* Chapel Hill: University of North Carolina Press, 1978.

McCusker, John J., and Russell R. Menard. *The Economy of British America, 1607–1789.* Chapel Hill: University of North Carolina Press, 1991.

McGill, William. *Maria Theresa.* New York: Twayne, 1972.

McGill, W. J. "The Roots of Policy: Kaunitz in Vienna and Versailles." *Journal of Modern History* 43, no. 2 (1971): 228–44.

McLachlan, Jean O. "The Seven Years' Peace and the West Indian Policy of Carvajal and Wall." *English Historical Review* 53 (1938): 457–77.

———. *Trade and Peace with Old Spain, 1667–1750.* Cambridge: Cambridge University Press, 1940.

McLennan, J. S. *Louisbourg from Its Foundation to Its Fall, 1713–1758.* 1918. Reprint, Halifax, NS: Book Room, 1994.

McNeill, John Robert. *Atlantic Empires of France and Spain: Louisbourg and Havana, 1700–1763.* Chapel Hill: University of North Carolina Press, 1985.

Mémoire Historiques Concernant l'ordre Royale de Militaire de Saint-Louis et l'Institution du Mérite Militaire. Paris: Imprimerie Royale, 1785.

Mémoire Historique sur la Négociation de la France et de l'Angleterre; Depuis le 26 Mars 1761 Jusqu'a 20 Septembre de la Même Année. Paris: Imprimerie Royale, 1761.

Mémoires des Commissaires du Roi et de Ceux de Sa Majesté Britannique. 6 vols. Paris: Imprimerie Royale, 1756.

Mémoires des Commissaires du Roi et de Ceux de Sa Majesté Britannique, sur les Possessions et les Droit Respectifs des Deux Couronnes en Amérique; Avec les Actes Publics et Pieces Justificatives. 6 vols. Paris: Imprimerie Royale, 1755–57.

"Memoir on the Defense of the Fort of Carillon." *Bulletin of the Fort Ticonderoga Museum* 8, no 3 (1972): 196–226.

Menard, Russell R. "Growth and Welfare." In *Encyclopedia of the North American Colonies,* edited by Jacob Ernest Cooke, 467–82. New York: Scribner's, 1993.

Michalon, Roger. "Vaudreuil et Montcalm, les hommes, leurs relations, influence de ces relations sur la conduite de la guerre, 1756–1759." In *Conflits des Sociétés au Canada Français pendant la Guerre de Sept Ans et leurs Influence sur les Operations.* Edited by Jean Delmas. Vincennes, Fr.: Service historique, Armée de terre, 1978.

Middleton, Richard. *The Bells of Victory: The Pitt-Newcastle Ministry and the Conduct of the Seven Years' War, 1757–1762.* Cambridge: Cambridge University Press, 1985.

Mildmay, William, and William Shirley. *The Memorials of the English and French Commissionaires Concerning the Limits of Nova Scotia or Acadia.* London: s.n., 1755.

Miller Surrey, N. M. *The Commerce of Louisiana during the French Régime, 1699–1763.* New York: Columbia University Press, 1916.

Mims, Stewart. *Colbert's West India Policy.* New Haven, Conn.: Yale University Press, 1912.

Mitford, Nancy. *Madame de Pompadour.* New York: Random House, 1953.

"Moneypenny Orderly Book, March 23 to June 29, 1758." *Bulletin of the Fort Ticonderoga Museum* 12, no. 5 (December 1969): 328–57.

"Moneypenny Orderly Book, June 30 to August 7, 1758." *Bulletin of the Fort Ticonderoga Museum* 12, no. 6 (October 1970): 434–61.

"Montcalm at Carillon." *Bulletin of the Fort Ticonderoga Museum* 1, no. 3 (January 1928): 4–11.

Montcalm-Gozon, Louis Joseph de. "Montcalm's Correspondance." In *Report of the Public Archives of Canada for the Year 1929*, edited by Simon Fraser, 31–108. Ottawa, Public Archives, 1930.

"Montcalm's Order of Battle." *Bulletin of the Fort Ticonderoga Museum* 2, no. 8 (July 1930): 67–69.

Moogk, Peter. *La Nouvelle France: The Making of French Canada, a Cultural History.* East Lansing: Michigan State University Press, 2000.

Mopinot de la Chapotte, Antoine-Rigobert. *Sous Louis le Bien-Aimé: Correspondance Amoureuse et Militaire d'un Officier Pendant la Guerre de Sept-Ans (1757–1765).* Edited by J. Lemoine. Paris: Lévy, 1905.

Moreau, Jacob Nicolas. *Mémoire Contenant le Précis des Faits avec Leur Piéces Justificatives.* Paris: L'Imprimerie Royale, 1756. Translated as *The Conduct of the Late Ministry or, a Memorial Containing a Summary of the Facts with Their Vouchers, in Answer to the Observations, Sent by the English Ministry, to the Courts of Europe.* London: Bizet, 1757.

Mousnier, Roland. "La Fonction publique en France du début du seizième siècle a la fin du dix-huitième siècle. Des officiers aux commissaires puis aux commis, puis aux fonctionnaires." *Revue Historique* 530 (April–June 1979): 321–35.

———. *Institutions de la France sous la Monarchie Absolue.* Vol. 1, *Société et État.* Paris: Presses Universitaires de France, 1974.

————. *Institutions de la France sous la Monarchie Absolue*. Vol 2, *Les Organes de l'état et la Société*. Paris: Presses Universitaires de France, 1980.

Mousnier, Roland, and Ernest Labrousse. *Le XVIIIe Siècle, l'Époque des Lumières, 1715–1815*. Paris: Presses Universitaires de France, 1959.

Mulligan, Robert E., ed. "Colonel Charles Clinton's Journal of His Campaign in New York July to October, 1758." *Bulletin of the Fort Ticonderoga Museum* 15, no. 4 (December 1992): 292–315.

Muret, Pierre. "L'Histoire diplomatique du milieu du XVIIIe siècle d'âpres les travaux de Sir Richard Lodge." *Revue d'Histoire Modern* 6–7 (1931–32): 77–83.

Murphy, Orville T. *Charles Gravier, Comte de Vergennes: French Diplomacy in the Age of Revolution, 1719–1787*. Albany: State University of New York, 1982.

Namier, Lewis. *England in the Age of American Revolution*. London: Macmillan, 1961.

————. *The Structure of Politics at the Accession of George III*. London: Macmillan, 1963.

Nester, William R. *The Epic Battles for Ticonderoga, 1758*. Albany: State University of New York Press, 2008.

————. *The First Global War: Britain, France, and the Fate of North America, 1755–1775*. Westport, Conn.: Praeger, 2000.

————. *The Great Frontier War: Britain, France, and the Imperial Struggle for North America, 1607–1755*. Westport, Conn.: Praeger, 2000.

————. *"Haughty Conquerors": Amherst and the Great Indian Uprising of 1763*. Westport, Conn.: Praeger, 2000.

Nicolle, Jean. *Madame de Pompadour, et la Société de son Temps*. Paris: Editions Albatros, 1980.

Nish, Cameron, ed. *The French Canadians, 1759–1766: Conquered? Half-Conquered? Liberated?* Montreal: Copp Clark, 1966.

Nolhac, Pierre de. *Madame de Pompadour et la Politique d'apres des Documents Nouveaux*. Paris: L. Conard, 1928.

Nosworthy, Brent. *The Anatomy of Victory: Battle Tactics, 1689–1763*. New York: Hippocrene, 1992.

Observations sur le Mémoire de la France Envoyées dans les Cours de Réquisition de l'Europe, par le Ministère Britannique, pour Justifier la Réponse Faite à la Réquisition de S.M.T.C. du 21 Decembre 1755. Bound with Moreau's memoir. Paris: Imprimerie Royale, 1756.

O'Callaghan, E. B., ed. *The Documentary History of the State of New York*. 4 vols. Albany, N.Y.: Weed, Parsons, 1849–1851.

O'Callaghan, E. B., and Berthold Fernow, eds. *Documents Relative to the Colonial History of the State of New York*. 15 vols. Albany, N.Y.: Weed, Parsons, 1856–87.

Oliva, L. Jay. *Misalliance: A Study of French Policy in Russia during the Seven Years' War*. New York: New York University Press, 1964.

Osgood, Herbert L. *The American Colonies in the Eighteenth Century*. 4 vols. Gloucester, Mass.: Peter Smith, 1958.

Ozanam, D. *Claude Baudard de Saint-James: Trésorier Général de la Marine et Brasseur d'affaires (1738–1787)*. Geneva: Droz, 1969.

Pajol, Charles-Pierre-Victor. *Les Guerres sous Louis XV*. 7 vols. Paris: Adamant Media, 2001.

Pares, Richard. "American versus Continental Warfare, 1739–1763." *English Historical Review* 51, no. 203 (1963): 429–65.

———. *Colonial Blockade and Neutral Rights, 1739–1763*. Oxford: Oxford University Press, 1938.

———. *War and Trade in the West Indies, 1739–1763*. London: Frank Cass, 1963.

———. *Yankees and Creoles: The Trade between North America and the West Indies before the American Revolution*. London: Longmans, Green, 1956.

Parkman, Francis. *Montcalm and Wolfe: The French and Indian War*. New York: Da Capo Press, 1995.

Parry, H. "Rivalries in America." In *The Old Regime, 1713–1763*, edited by J. O. Lindsay, 514–28. Cambridge: Cambridge University Press, 1957.

Parry, Peter. "America," in "Colonial Development and International Rivalries Outside Europe." In *The New Cambridge Modern History*. Vol. 3. Edited by R. B. Wernham. Cambridge: Cambridge University Press, 1968.

Pease, Theodore Calvin, ed. *Anglo-French Boundary Disputes in the West, 1749–1763*. Collections of the Illinois State Historical Library 27, French ser. 2. Springfield: Trustees of the Illinois State Historical Library, 1936.

———. "The Mississippi Boundary of 1763: A Reappraisal of Responsibility." *American Historical Review* 40 (January 1935): 278–86.

Pease, Theodore Calvin, and Ernestine Jenison, eds. *Illinois on the Eve of the Seven Years' War, 1747–1755*. Collections of the Illinois State Historical Library 29, French ser. 2. Springfield: Trustees of the Illinois State Historical Library, 1940.

Pell, Robert. "The Strategy of Montcalm, 1758." *Bulletin of the Fort Ticonderoga Museum* 9, no. 3 (Summer 1953).

Perkins, James Break. *France under Louis XV*. 2 vols. New York: Houghton Mifflin, 1897.

Perrault, Gilles. *Le Secret du Roi*. Paris: Librairie Générale Française, 1992.

Peters, Marie. *Pitt and Popularity: The Patriot Minister and London Opinion during the Seven Years' War*. Oxford: Clarendon Press, 1980.

Phelps, Dawson A. "The Vaudreuil Expedition, 1752." *William and Mary Quarterly*, ser. 3, 15 (October 1958): 483–93.

Phillips, Paul Chrisler. *The Fur Trade*. Vol. 1. Norman: University of Oklahoma Press, 1961.

Pitman, Frank Wesley. *The Development of the British West Indies, 1700–1763*. New Haven: Yale University Press, 1917.

Pitt, William. *The Correspondence of William Pitt, When Secretary of State, with the Colonial Governors and Military and Naval Commissioners in North America*. Edited by Gertrude S. Kimball. 2 vols. New York: Macmillan, 1906.

Pouchot, Pierre. *Memoirs on the Late War in North America between France and England.* Translated by Michael Cardy. Edited by Brian Leigh Dunnigan. Youngstown: Old Fort Niagara Association, 1994.

Preston, Richard A., and Leopold LaMontagne. *Royal Fort Frontenac.* Toronto: Champlain Society, 1958.

Pritchard, James S. *Louis XV's Navy, 1748–1762: A Study of Organization and Administration.* Kingston, Ontario: McGill-Queen's University Press, 1987.

————. "Some Aspects of the Thought of F. X. Garneau." *Canadian Historical Review* 51 (1970): 276–91.

Proulx, Gilles. "Le Dernier Effort de la France au Canada—secours ou fraude?" *Revue d'Histoire de l'Amérique Française* 36 (1982): 413–26.

————. *The Garrison of Quebec from 1748 to 1759.* Ottawa: National Historic Sites Park Service, 1991.

Rahmer, Frederick A. *Dash to Frontenac: An Account of Lt. Col. John Bradstreet's Expedition to and Capture of Fort Frontenac.* Rome, N.Y.: Frederick A. Rahmer, 1973.

Rambaud, Alfred. *Russes et Prussiens: Guerre de Sept Ans.* Paris: Firmin-Didot, 1895.

Ramsey, John F. *Anglo-French Relations, 1763–1770: A Study of Choiseul's Foreign Policy.* University of California Publications in History 17. Berkeley: University of California Press, 1939.

Rashed, Zenab Esmat. *The Peace of Paris, 1763.* Liverpool: Liverpool University Press, 1951.

Ray, Arthur J. *Indians in the Fur Trade: Their Role as Trappers, Hunters, and Middlemen in the Lands Southwest of Hudson Bay, 1660–1870.* Toronto: University of Toronto Press, 1974.

Ray, Arthur J., and Donald Freeman. *"Give Us Good Measure": An Economic Analysis of Relations between the Indians and the Hudson's Bay Company before 1763.* Toronto: University of Toronto Press, 1978.

Recueil des Instructions Données Aux Ambassadeurs et Ministres de France depuis les Traites de Westphalie Jusqu'à la Révolution Française. 28 vols. Paris: La commission des Archives Diplomatique au Ministre des Affaires Etrangères, 1884–1960.

Rediker, Marcus. *Between the Devil and the Deep Blue Sea: Merchant Seamen, Pirates, and the Anglo-American Maritime World, 1700–1750.* Cambridge: Cambridge University Press, 1987.

Reid, Marjorie. "Pitt's Decision to Keep Canada in 1761." *Report for the Annual Meeting of the Canadian Historical Association* 5, no. 1 (1926): 21–32.

Renaut, Francis Paul. *Le Pacte de Famille et l'Amérique: La Politique Coloniale Franco-Espagnole de 1760 à 1792.* Paris: Plon, 1922.

Richter, Daniel K. "Iroquois versus Iroquois: Jesuit Missions and Christianity in Village Politics, 1642–1686." *Ethnohistory* 32, no. 1 (1985): 116.

————. *The Ordeal of the Longhouse: The Peoples of the Iroquois League in the era of European Colonization.* Chapel Hill: University of North Carolina Press, 1992.

Richter, Daniel K., and James H. Merrell, eds. *Beyond the Covenant Chain: The Iroqouis and Their Neighbors in Indian North America.* Syracuse, N.Y.: Syracuse University Press, 1987.

Riley, James C. *The Seven Years' War and the Old Regime in France: The Economic and Financial Toll.* Princeton, N.J.: Princeton University Press, 1986.

Riley, James C., and John J. McCusker. "Money Supply, Economic Growth, and the Quantity Theory of Money: France 1650–1788." *Explorations in Economic History* 20, no. 3 (1983): 274–93

Ritter, Gerhard. *Frederick the Great: A Historical Profile.* Berkeley: University of California Press, 1970.

Robinson, Percy J. *Toronto during the French Regime.* Toronto: Ryerson Press, 1933.

Robitaille, Georges. *Montcalm et Ses Historiens, Étude Critique.* Montreal: Levis, 1936.

Rodger, N. A. M. *The Wooden World: An Anatomy of the Georgian Navy.* New York: Norton, 1986.

Rogister, John. *Louis XV and the Parlement of Paris, 1737–1755,* New York: Cambridge University Press, 1995.

Roquebrune, R. La Roque de. "La direction de la Nouvelle-France par le ministère de la marine." *Revue d'Histoire de l'Amérique Française* 6, no. 4 (March 1953): 470–88.

Ross, John F. *War on the Run: The Epic Story of Robert Rogers and the Conquest of America's First Frontier.* New York: Random House, 2009.

Rousseau, François. *Règne de Charles III d'Espagne, 1759–1788.* 2 vols. Paris: Plon-Nouritt 1907.

Roy, Pierre-George. *Bigot et sa Bande et L'Affaires du Canada.* Quebec: Levis, 1950.

———. "Les Commandants du Fort Niagara." *Le Bulletin des Recherches Historiques* 54, no. 5 (May 1948): 131–40; no. 6 (June 1948): 163–77; no. 7 (July 1948): 195–99.

———. "Les Commandants du Saint Fréderic." *Le Bulletin des Recherches Historiques* 51, no. 3 (September 1945): 317–32.

———. *Homes et Chose du Fort Saint-Frederic.* Montreal: Les Editions Dix, 1946.

Rule, John. "The Commis of the Department of Foreign Affairs Under the Administration of Colbert de Croissey and Colbert de Torcy, 1680–1715." *Proceedings of the Western Society For French History* 8 (1981): 69–80.

Saint-Amand, Imbert de. *The Court of Louis XV.* New York: Scribner's, 1915.

Samoyault, Jean-Pierre. *Les Bureaux du Secrétariat d'etat des Affaires Étrangères sous Louis XV.* Paris: Pedrone, 1971.

Sautai, Maurice. *Montcalm at the Battle of Carillon (Ticonderoga) (July 8th, 1758).* Ticonderoga, N.Y.: Fort Ticonderoga Museum, 1941.

Sauvageau, Robert. *Acadie: La Guerre de Cent Ans, Français d'Amérique aux Maritime et en Louisiane, 1670–1769.* Paris: Berger-Levrault, 1987.

Savelle, Max. *The Diplomatic History of the Canadian Boundary, 1749–1763.* New Haven, Conn.: Yale University Press, 1940.

———. "Diplomatic Preliminaries of the Seven Years' War in America." *Canadian Historical Review* 20 (1939): 1–43.

———. *Seeds of Liberty: The Genesis of the American Mind.* New York: Knopf, 1948.

Schoenfeld, Max. *Fort de la Presqu'ile.* Erie, Pa.: Erie County Historical Society, 1989.

Schutz, John A. "Cold War Diplomacy and the Seven Years' War." *World Affairs Quarterly* 26 (1958): 323–37.

Schweizer, Karl W. *England, Prussia and the Seven Years' War: Studies in Alliance Policies and Diplomacy.* Queenston, Ontario: Edwin Mellen Press, 1989.

Scott, Elizabeth. *French Subsistence at Fort Michilimackinac, 1715–1781.* Mackinac Island, Mich.: Mackinac Island State Park Commission, 1985.

Scott, H. "Frederick II, the Ottoman Empire, and the Origins of the Russo-Prussian Alliance of April 1764." *European Studies Review* 7 (1977): 153–75.

Severance, Frank H. *An Old Frontier of France: The Niagara Region and Adjacent Lakes under French Control.* 2 vols. New York: Dodd, Mead, 1917.

Shennan, J. H. *The Parlement of Paris.* London: Sutton, 1968.

Shepherd, James T., and Gary M. Walton. *Shipping, Maritime Trade, and the Economic Development of Colonial North America.* Cambridge: Cambridge University Press, 1972.

Sheppard, Ruth. *Empires Collide: The French and Indian War, 1754–63.* Oxford: Osprey, 2006.

Sherrard, O. A. *Lord Chatham: Pitt and the Seven Years' War.* London: Bodley Head, 1955.

Shortt, A., ed. *Documents Relating to Canadian Currency, Exchange, and Finance during the French Period.* 2 vols. Ottawa: King's Printer, 1925.

Simmons, R. C., and P. D. G. Thomas, eds. *Proceedings and Debates of the British Parliaments Respecting North America.* Millwoood, N.Y.: Kraus International, 1982.

Smith, Digby. *Armies of the Seven Years' War: Commanders, Equipment, Uniforms, and Strategies of the "First World War."* London: Spellmount, 2012.

Soulange-Bodin, A. *La Diplomatie de Louis XV et le Pacte de Famille.* Paris: Perrin, 1894.

Stacey, C. P. *Quebec, 1759: The Siege and the Battle.* Toronto: Macmillan, 1959.

Stanley, George F. G. *Canada's Soldiers: The Military History of an Unmilitary People.* Toronto: Macmillan, 1959.

———. *New France: The Last Phase, 1744–1760.* Toronto: McClelland and Stuart, 1968.

Steele, Ian K. *Betrayals: Fort William Henry and the "Massacre."* New York: Oxford University Press, 1990.

———. *Guerrillas and Grenadiers: The Struggle for Canada, 1698–1760.* Toronto: Ryerson, 1969.

———. "Thin Red Lines: Governors of England's Empire Before 1681." *Review in American History* 8, no. 3 (1980): 318–22.

———. *Warpaths: Invasions of North America.* New York: Oxford University Press, 1994.

Stevens, Sylvester K., and Donald H. Kent, eds. *Wilderness Chronicles of Northwestern Pennsylvania.* Harrisburg: Pennsylvania Historical Commission, 1941.

Stotz, Charles Morse. *Outposts of the War for Empire: The French and English in Western Pennsylvania: Their Armies, Their Forts, Their People, 1749–1764,* Pittsburgh: Historical Society of Western Pennsylvania, 1985.

Summers, Jack L., and Rene Chartrand. *Military Uniforms in Canada, 1665–1970.* Ottawa: Canadian War Museum, 1981.

Sutherland, L. S. "The East India Company and the Peace of Paris." *English Historical Review* 62 (1947): 179–90.

Szabo, Franz. *The Seven Years War in Europe, 1756–1763.* Harlow, UK: Pearson, 2008.

Tanner, Helen Hornbeck. *Atlas of Great Lakes Indian History.* Norman: University of Oklahoma Press, 1987.

Taylor, George V. "Noncapitalist Wealth and the Origins of the French Revolution." *American Historical Review* 72, no. 2 (April 1967): 469–96.

Temperly, H. W. V. "The Peace of Paris." In *The Cambridge History of the British Empire.* Vol. 1, *The Old Empire from the Beginnings to 1783,* edited by J. Holland Rose, A. P. Newton, and E. A. Benians, 485–506. New York: Macmillan, 1929.

Thomas, Daniel H. "Fort Toulouse: The French Outpost at the Alibamos on the Coosa." *Alabama Historical Quarterly* 22 (Fall 1960): 135–230.

Thomas, John. *See* Webster, John Clarence.

Thorpe, F. J. "Chaussegros de Léry, Gaspard-Joseph." In *Dictionary of Canadian Biography.* Vol. 4. University of Toronto Press, 1982.

Thwaites, Reuben Gold, ed. *The Jesuit Relations and Allied Documents: Travels and Explorations of the Jesuit Missionaries in New France, 1610–1791.* 73 vols. 1896–1901. Reprint, New York: Pageant, 1959.

Trench, Charles. *George II.* London: Allen Lane, 1975.

Trigger, Bruce G. "Early Native North American Responses to European Contact: Romantic versus Rationalistic Interpretations." *Journal of American History* 77 (1990–91): 1195–1215.

Turner, F. J. "The Diplomatic Contest for the Mississippi Valley." *Atlantic Monthly* 93 (1904): 676–91, 807–17.

Ultree, Maarten, ed. *Adapting to Conditions: War and Society in the Eighteenth Century.* Tuscaloosa: University of Alabama, 1986.

Usner, David H. *Indians, Settlers, and Slaves in a Frontier Exchange Economy: The Lower Mississippi Valley Before 1793.* Chapel Hill: University of North Carolina Press, 1992.

Vandal, Albert. *Louis XV et Elizabeth de Russie.* Paris: Plon, 1882.

Van Kley, Dale K. *The Damiens Affair and the Unraveling of the Ancien Régime, 1750–1770.* Princeton: Princeton University Press, 1984.

Vauban, Sebastian Le Prestre de. *A Manual of Siegecraft and Fortification*. Ann Arbor: University of Michigan Press, 1968.

Vergé-Franceschi, Michel. *La Marine Française au XVIIIe Siècle*. Paris: Société d'Edition d'Enseignement Supérieur, 1996.

Vitzhum, Richard C. "The Historian as Editor: Francis Parkman's Reconstruction of Sources in Montcalm and Wolfe." *Journal of American History* 53 (1966–67): 471–86.

Voltaire. *Candide*. New York: Dover, 1991.

Volwiler, Albert T. *George Croghan and the Westward Movement, 1741–1782*. Cleveland: Arthur H. Clark, 1926.

Waddington, Richard. *La Guerre de Sept Ans: Histoire Diplomatique et Militaire*. 5 vols. Paris: Firmin-Didot, 1899–1914.

———. *Louis XV et le Reversement des Alliance*. Paris: Firmin-Didot, 1896.

Walpole, Horace. *Memoirs of King George II*. Edited by John Brooke. 3 vols. New Haven, Conn.: Yale University Press, 1985.

———. *Memories of the Last Ten Years of the Reign of George the Second*. 3 vols. New York: Nabu Press, 2011.

Washington, George. *The Diaries of George Washington, 1748–65*. Edited by Donald Jackson. Vol. 1. Charlottesville: University of Virginia Press, 1976.

Webster, John Clarence, ed. *Journals of Beauséjour: Diary of John Thomas, Journal of Louis de Courville*. Sackville, NB: Tribune Press, 1937.

Weigley, Russell F. *The Age of Battles: The Quest for Decisive Warfare from Breitenfeld to Waterloo*. Bloomington: University of Indiana Press, 1991.

Wells, Robert V. *The Population of the British Colonies in America before 1776: A Survey of Census Data*. Princeton, N.J.: Princeton University Press, 1975.

West, Martin, ed. *War For Empire in Western Pennsylvania*. Ligonier, Pa.: Fort Ligonier Association, 1993.

White, Jon Manchip. *Marshal of France: The Life and Times of Maurice, Compte de Saxe, 1696–1750*. Chicago: Rand McNally, 1962.

White, Richard. *The Middle Ground: Indians, Empires, and Republics in the Great Lakes Region*. New York: Cambridge University Press, 1994.

Whitworth, R. *Field Marshall Lord Ligonier, A Story of the British Army*. Oxford: Oxford University Press, 1958.

Williams, Basil. *The Life of William Pitt, Earl of Chatham*. 2 vols. 1913. Reprint, New York: Octagon Books, 1966.

Wilson, A. N. *French Foreign Policy during the Administration of Cardinal Fleury, 1726–1743: A Study on Diplomacy and Commercial Development*, Cambridge, Mass.: Harvard University Press, 1936.

Winzerling, Oscar William. *Acadian Odyssey*. Baton Rouge: Louisiana State University Press, 1955.

Wolkonskii, G. "La France et la menace d'expansion russe 1756–63." *Revue d'histoire Diplomatique* 70 (1956): 193–99.

Wood, George Authur. "Céleron de Blainville and French Expansion in the Ohio Valley." *Mississippi Valley Historical Review* 9 (March 1923): 302–19.

Wood, William, ed. *The Logs of the Conquest of Canada.* Publications of the Champlain Society 4. Toronto: Champlain Society, 1909.

Woodbridge, John D. *Revolt in Prerevolutionary France: The Prince de Conti's Conspiracy against Louis XV, 1755–1757.* Baltimore: Johns Hopkins University Press, 1995.

Woods, Patricia D. "The French and the Natchez Indians in Louisiana, 1700–1731." *Louisiana History* 19 (1978): 421–38.

———. *French-Indian Relations on the Southern Frontier, 1699–1762.* Ann Arbor: University of Michigan Press, 1980.

Wright, James Leitch, Jr. *Anglo-Spanish Rivalry in North America.* Athens: University of Georgia Press, 1971.

Yorke, Philip C. *The Life and Correspondence of Philip Yorke, Lord of Hardwicke.* 3 vols. Cambridge: Cambridge University Press, 1913.

Zeller, Gaston. "Le Principe d'équilibre dans la politique internationale avant 1789." *Revue Historique* 215 (1956): 25–37.

Zoltvany, Yves F. *The Government of New France: Royal, Clerical, or Class Rule?* Scarbourgh, Ontario: Prentice-Hall, 1971.

———. *Philippe de Rigaud de Vaudreuil, Governor of New France, 1703–1725.* Toronto: McClelland and Stewart, 1974.

Index